iv

vi

The
SOUTH AMERICAN
HANDBOOK
1924

INCLUDING

CENTRAL AMERICA, MEXICO, & CUBA

———————

Founded on " The Anglo-South American Handbook,"
by the late W. H. KOEBEL

———————

PUBLISHED BY

SOUTH AMERICAN PUBLICATIONS LTD.

ATLANTIC HOUSE, MOORGATE, LONDON, E.C.2

Printed in Great Britain

PREFACE.

THE preface to the SOUTH AMERICAN HANDBOOK in its new form necessarily opens upon a note of regret at the death of Mr. W. H. Koebel, its founder and first editor, an able writer and a much esteemed man, widely known through two hemispheres as an authority upon the South American countries and their international relations. This untoward event, following swiftly upon an attack of pneumonia, has complicated the task of issuing the new volume.

It is hoped and believed that the re-arrangement of the matter hitherto provided in the "Anglo-South American Handbook" will be accepted as an improvement. An attempt has been made to render the work more truly a handbook. The changes in form have been suggested by a desire to make it a book for the pocket and the travelling bag, and those re-arrangements are calculated to bring first to the eye the information that the traveller most urgently requires. Without ceasing to be a desk book, serviceable for reference, the Handbook assumes more of the character of a guide-

book and, in a modest degree, an encyclopædia of South American and Central American, Mexican and Cuban life and affairs. Accompanied as these improvements are by a heavy reduction in price, it is confidently believed that the effect will be largely to increase the extensive circulation attained by past issues.

All practicable care has been exerted to ensure the accuracy of the information conveyed but certain of the matters treated are susceptible of change and it would be too much to hope that none of the statements is beyond challenge.

Corrections of errors whether of omission or commission will be gratefully received, and in this matter the Editor is largely in the hands of his readers. The chances of error have been greatly minimised by the large amount of assistance that the compilers have received, and sincere thanks are tendered for the ungrudging assistance of the numerous contributors to the present volume. Their help in the work is gratifying from all points of view, and especially as proving our belief in the need for, and the value of, such a book as this. Their labour in correcting existing data and furnishing fresh details of information has indeed been considerable but in the end the exertion tends to reduce the troubles of those from whom enlightenment is naturally sought. In answering the queries addressed to them from the compilers of the Handbook these authorities are answering in anticipation inquiries arising from an indefinitely large numbers of sources. They have the satisfaction also of spreading broadcast information upon countries of which disproportionately little is known.

Had Latin America been better served with compact and easily accessible information it is improbable that the present series of annuals would have come into being, and the absence of any other work of a similar kind gives the present volume a special title to interest. The Handbook appeals in particular to those who are contemplating journeying to the southern

portions of the American continent and the information respecting hotels, steamers, railways routes, scenes and objects of interest is primarily for them.

The uncommercial traveller has his interest in the economic life of the countries, and the commercial traveller is interested in many other affairs than his immediate business. In recognition of these facts a proportion of the space is devoted to descriptions of economic products in terms not too technical for the untrained. A chapter is given to Sport and another to Beasts and Birds, while for the benefit of the inexperienced travellers there is a chapter upon South American Travel at large.

The political and historical sides receive short consideration in the form of summaries. Here and there the costumes and customs of the people are touched upon, and although the Handbook in its present edition is less comprehensive than it promises to become in future years a varied set of requirements are catered for.

Acknowledgments are due in particular to the London ministers and officials of the several Republics .

> H.E. the Argentine Minister and Staff of the Legation; the Argentine Consul-General and Staff of the Consulate-General.

> H.E. the Bolivian Minister and Staff of the Legation; the Bolivian Consul-General and Staff of the Consulate-General.

> H.E. the Brazilian Ambassador and Staff of the Embassy, the Brazilian Consul-General and Staff of the Consulate-General.

> H.E. the Chilean Minister and Staff of the Legation; the Chilean Consul-General and Staff of the Consulate-General.

H.E. the Colombian Minister and the Staff of the Legation; the Consul-General, and Señor Dr José Medina,
Director in London of the Bureau of Information of
the Republic of Colombia.

The Costa Rican Consul-General and Staff of the Consulate.

H.E. the Cuban Minister and the Staff of the Legation;
the Consul for Cuba in London.

The Ecuadorean Consul-General and Staff of the Consulate-General.

H.E. the Guatemalan Minister; the Guatemalan Consul-
General in Liverpool and the Consul in London.

The Honduranean Consul-General and Staff of the
Consulate-General.

The Consul-General for Mexico.

The Nicaraguan Chargé d'Affaires; and the Consul in
London.

The Panamanian Consul in London.

The Paraguayan Consul-General in London.

The Peruvian Chargé d'Affaires and Staff of the Legation,
the Peruvian Consul-General in London.

The Salvadorean Consul-General in London.

H.E. the Uruguayan Minister and Staff of the Legation,
and the Consul-General.

H.E. the Venezuelan Minister and Staff of the Legation,
and the Consul in London.

Special thanks are to be accorded to the officials of the
Foreign Office, the Colonial Office, and to the Comptroller-
General of the Department of Overseas Trade, the Comp-
troller of the Industrial Department of the Board of Trade and
the Chief Passport Officer. The Controller of His Majesty's
Stationery Office has courteously permitted extracts to be
taken from numerous official British Reports, and from the
"Board of Trade Journal."

Invaluable assistance has been rendered by the staff and
agents of the Royal Mail Steam Packet Co. and the Pacific
Steam Navigation Co., to whom the HANDBOOK is indebted
for a multitude of suggestions and corrections, whether of fact

or in matters of perspective. Among the several railway officials to whom acknowledgment is rendered must be mentioned in particular Mr E. J Bray, of the National Railways of Mexico. A gratifying amount of interest has been shown in the work by the officials of other shipping companies, banks, railways, and industrial companies.

Informative particulars have been taken from "The South American Journal" (London), "The Review of the River Plate" (Buenos Aires), "The West Coast Leader" (Lima), among other periodicals. The publications of the Pan-American Union and the United States Government have been drawn upon as well as those of the Governments of the countries of Latin America. Quotations have been taken from a variety of books to which reference is made elsewhere.

It has been a privilege to direct an increasing number of inquirers to sources from which fuller or more explicit information upon particular points can be gained, and inquiries of that kind receive the most careful attention.

J A. HUNTER.

CONTENTS.

CONTENTS.

Publishers note: a very few pages containing adverts are missing from our rare copy of the 1924 edition. We have replaced them with similar adverts which were published in the South American Handbook 1925, 1926 or 1928 editions.

EIGHTY - FIVE Y E A R S' EXPERIENCE

ALMOST a century—from the paddle-boat to the great 1924 liner. *That means experience.* Growth from a tonnage in 1839 of under 30,000 to a tonnage, with associated companies, of over 2,000,000 in 1924. *That means success.* It means success that comes of long experience united with progressive methods. Both are part of "Royal Mail" tradition—good may yet be better, first class must be made super-first class—always for the benefit of the passenger.

THE ROYAL MAIL STEAM PACKET COMPANY

LONDON : Atlantic House, Moorgate, E.C.2 and America House, Cockspur Street, S.W.1

LIVERPOOL · BIRMINGHAM · MANCHESTER
GLASGOW · SOUTHAMPTON or Local Agent

NOBEL INDUSTRIES LTD.

Nobel Industries Ltd. is a group of over thirty-three manufacturing concerns which produce various allied commodities, the most important of which are commercial explosives.

Nobel Industries Ltd. was formed in 1918 with an authorized capital of £18,000,000. The manufacturing sources at its disposal are comprised in over a hundred factories in England and Scotland and abroad. The Ardeer Explosives Factory, the largest in the world, alone covers an area of 1,200 acres. It is served by efficient representatives throughout the world.

The Companies comprising Nobel Industries Ltd., which are equipped for the manufacture of Explosives and Munitions, have for many years been contractors to the British and other Governments. For a number of years they have supplied a large proportion of the requirements of the British Navy and Army, and during the Great War they successfully met enormous demands for all classes of munitions. Not only did they render incalculable assistance in the manufacture of all propellants and shell explosives, but in particular through Nobel's Explosives Company, Ltd., of Glasgow, they also built, equipped, trained and provided the technical staff and managed some of the extensive explosive factories set up by the British Government.

Since then all the interests of Nobel Companies have been considerably extended, and to-day Nobel's play an important part in reconstruction work, and many of the factories supply materials indispensable to the production of commodities necessary in daily life.

The manufacture of different types of explosives for blasting and mining work, cordite, nitrocellulose powders, and black and smokeless sporting powders is carried on at the Nobel Factory at Ardeer in Scotland, which turns out the most reliable and efficient explosives and accessories on the market to-day.

Safety fuse, electric fuse, cordeau detonant and detonators are made at specially equipped factories, some in Scotland and some in England, but all operating under the Nobel method of centralization.

At the Eley and Kynoch factories of Nobel Industries the production of rifle, revolver, and automatic-pistol ammunition and shot-gun cartridges is carried on under the most up-to-date conditions.

The manufacture of industrial collodions supplies the leather and allied trades with such products as enamels for split leather, dopes for leather manufacturing, finishes for grain leather and cement for all adhesive purposes, while the engineering trade is supplied with a long-felt want, in plastic wood, a mouldable material which hardens upon exposure into a substance similar to wood.

At the works of Kynoch Ltd. non-ferrous metals are produced for the hardware trades in various forms of brass and copper and alloys of copper in wire, sheet, strip and extruded rods, small castings and forgings.

The British Pluviusin Co., Ltd., manufactures at Manchester leather cloth (P-V Brand) which is obtainable in many grades, colours and finishes. It is used for upholstering furniture, railway carriages and motor cars and in the manufacture of trunks, attaché cases, etc. For hot climates P-V is in many ways superior to leather, for it is waterproof, unaffected by sudden climatic changes, and insects dislike it.

Carbon-free metals and alloys, including ferro-tungsten, chromium and manganese, are made at the works of the Continuous Reaction Co., Ltd.

Lamps, gas burners, and incandescent mantles for paraffin, petrol, and vapour lamps, etc., are marketed by Lighting Trades Ltd., incorporating Curtis's & Harvey, Ltd. (makers of the "Ironclad" Mantle), the Volker Company (makers of the "Volker" Mantle), and the Ramie Company (makers of the "Zeimar" Mantle)

The famous "Sunbeam" bicycles and motor bicycles are embraced in the Nobel organization by its ownership of John Marston, Ltd.

Among the many other products manufactured by the Companies operating under Nobel Industries Ltd., are the Amac Carburettors, fertilizers, yarns, nails, gold and aluminium bronze powders (Golden Dawn Brand), Edison All-steel accumulators, sulphuric acid, nitric acid, nitrate of lead, electric welding and complete plant, electrodes, welding compounds, electric motors, generators, and accessories. Further details of the products of Nobel Industries Ltd. are obtainable on application to the Head Office, Nobel House, Buckingham Gate, London, S.W 1

INDEX

A

U

V

INDEX TO ADVERTISERS

(Alphabetical)

INDEX TO ADVERTISERS

(Trade Classification)

1

THE SOUTH AMERICAN CONTINENT

THE SOUTH AMERICAN CONTINENT.

Columbus, the first of European navigators to touch South America, reached the Orinoco River in 1498, and in the succeeding ten years the coast was explored by others as far as the River Plate. Balboa discovered the Pacific at the Gulf of Panamá in 1513, and in 1520 Magalhães passed into the Pacific through the Magellan Strait, on which his name has been conferred.

Europeans—chiefly Spanish and Portuguese—began to settle in South America soon after the date of the discovery of the continent, and their settlements, beginning as colonies of Spain and Portugal, have developed into Republics, excepting always the three Guianas —British, Dutch, and French. The great attraction to the adventurers was the silver of the Andes and in especial the riches of Potosí (Bolivia). Gold was found in Minas Geraes (Brazil) in 1693, and the district long remained the chief source of gold products. Diamonds were discovered in the gold-bearing districts of Brazil circa 1729, and, until the opening of the Kimberley fields, Brazil was the largest producer of diamonds.

Around these discoveries has grown up the wealth of romance always associated with the Spanish Main, the Gold Road, and the buccaneers.

COUNTRIES AND THEIR SIZES.

The area of the South American Continent is some 6,800,000 square miles. Boundaries of countries are not in all cases defined beyond dispute, but the comparative sizes of the several republics and colonies can be judged from the following table :—

	Square Miles.			Square Miles.
Argentina	1,153,000	Ecuador		276,000
Bolivia	515,156	French Guiana		34,000
Brazil	3,291,416	Paraguay		110,000
British Guiana	90,000	Peru		532,000
Chile	307,774	Uruguay		72,210
Colombia	440,846	Venezuela		398,594
Dutch Guiana	46,000			

The areas of the countries of Central America are given :—

	Square Miles.			Square Miles.
British Honduras	8,598	Nicaragua		49,200
Costa Rica	23,000	Panamá		32,300
Guatemala	42,546	Salvador		7,225
Honduras	45,000			

The ex-Director General of the Pan-American Union, Mr John Barrett enters into comparisons of the future of the South American Republics as compared with North America and Europe. He calculates that South America covers an area of nearly 7,500,000 square miles, or only one million less than all North America from Panamá to the Arctic Sea, and more than twice the area of the United States, including Alaska. The area of North America unsuited by barrenness and cold for human habitation is much larger than that of South America unsuited by barrenness and heat.

IN THE SCALE OF COMPARISON.

All Europe could be placed inside the area occupied by South America, together with all of the United States, including Alaska. The continent is able to produce every product of the soil found in Europe and the United States, as well as important food products that cannot grow in Europe or the United States. Had the supply of food stuffs and raw products, agricultural, mineral, and metal from South America been cut off during the world war, the allies, including the United States, would have been almost as much hampered as was Germany by her isolation.

Brazil is bigger than the United States by nearly 300,000 square miles. Brazil's territory of 3,300,000 square miles could contain the United States proper and still have room to engulf all of Italy and Spain.

Argentina has an area, largely in the South Temperate Zone, of 1,131,000 square miles, and a magnificent capital city, with a population of nearly 1,800,000.

Either Bolivia or Peru, with an approximate area each of 600,000 square miles, could hold California, Oregon, and Washington twice over If Chile, with an extent of 300,000 square miles, on the Pacific Seas, were placed upon the Pacific shore of the United States she would almost cover these same States.

POPULATIONS BY COUNTRIES.

South America remains sparsely populated, and when a comparison was made in 1905 the population (then 38,500,000) represented about 5 persons to the square mile, as against 104 persons to the square mile in Europe. Large tracts of country carry probably no more inhabitants than they did 400 years ago, and the chief increase that has taken place occurs in certain well-defined regions, as in Argentina and the River Plate area and around the larger cities of Brazil.

Striking variations occur in the estimates of population and it is probable that the increase within recent years is exaggerated. Taking such data as are available, it would appear that the population of South America has increased to some 66,000,000. Certain of the particulars are to be accepted under reserve. There follows a summary relating to South America (inclusive of the Falkland Isles) :—

Argentina	.	9,500,000	Falkland Islands	.	2,300
Bolivia		3,000,000	French Guiana	..	49,000
Brazil	.	30,635,600	Paraguay . *	.	800,000
British Guiana	.	306,000	Peru .	..	6,000,000
Chile .	.	4,050,000	Uruguay		1,500,000
Colombia	.	5,855,500	Venezuela ..		2,800,000
Dutch Guiana	.	100,000			
Ecuador	.. .	2,000,000			66,598,400

The equivalent figures for Central America, are :—

British Honduras	.	44,000	Panamá	..	434,800
Costa Rica	.	468,400	Salvador		1,501,000
Guatemala	.	1,600,500		
Honduras		637,100		
Nicaragua	.	750,000		5,435,800

To these are added those of other countries included within the scope of the present book :—

Mexico	.	16,000,000	Porto Rico	.	1,297,800
Cuba	.	2,898,900			
					20,196,700

Estimates published by the Pan-American Union give the following particulars of the population, and trade of the Republics of the two Americas :—

Total population of the 21 American republics, including the United States, approximates 200,000,000, of which in the United States · 110,000,000, Latin America 90,000,000.

Total **area** of the American republics, approximately 12,000,000 square miles, Latin America 9,000,000 square miles, The United States (without Alaska, etc.) 3,000,000 square miles.

Total **foreign commerce,** exports and imports, of Latin America : $3,730,000,000, Share of the United States in Latin American trade $1,525,800,000.

This latter total is divided as follows :—

Imports from the United States $833,800,000, Exports to the United States . $692,000,000.

RIVER SYSTEMS.

The Amazon and its tributaries form the largest river system in the world. The navigable length from Pará on the east to Huallaga (Peru) on the west is 3,000 miles, and there are hundreds of navigable side channels parallel with the main stream. The river spreads over a plain so wide in many places that the appearance is rather that of a sea than a river

The Orinoco, rising in the highlands between Venezuela and Brazil, flows west and north before turning eastward to the Atlantic. Dense forests cover the banks of its lower course, and the water is navigable during certain seasons for 1,000 miles. The Amazon, Orinoco, and La Plata rivers together drain some 3,686,400 square miles. The River Plate estuary, forming one of the greatest trading harbours of the world, is formed by the confluence of the rivers Paraná, Uruguay, and Paraguay

The São Francisco, rising in the highlands of Minus Geraes, flows entirely through hilly and mountainous country, and is navigable for 140 miles below the falls of Paulo Affonso and for some distance above the falls.

The Magdalena, 2,000 miles long, is navigable up to Honda.

MOUNTAIN CHAINS.

The Andes mountain chain, of some 4,400 miles long, has an average height of 13,000 ft., and a width at some points of 100 miles. There are two principal and approximately parallel chains with a depression between. The eastern chain is generally called Los Andes, and the western La Cordillera, but the eastern chain is known in Colombia, Peru, and Bolivia as the Cordillera Real do Los Andes. In Chile and Argentina the western chain is known as the Cordillera do Los Andes, a contrariety which would be more confusing did the eastern chain not end in mid-Argentina, leaving only one ridge extending to the extremity of the continent.

The snow-line is highest in parts of Peru (about 16,500 ft.), the general range is 14,000 to 15,000 ft., descending in Patagonia and in Tierra del Fuego lying at about 4,900 ft. Generally the snow-line is lower on the east side than the west.

MOUNTAIN PEAKS ANDES AND CORDILLERA.

	feet.	
Aconcagua	23,080	Argentina.
Mercedario	22,315	
Tupungato	21,550	
Illampu (Sorata)	21,500	Bolivia.
Illimani ..	21,030	
Chimborazo	20,545	Ecuador.
Juncal	20,180	Chile.
Cotopaxi .	19,613	Ecuador
Antisana	19,335	
Cayambe	19,186	
Tolima	18,300	Colombia.
Misti	17,934	Peru.
Maipo	17,670	Argentina.
Sierra de Santa Marta	16,640	Colombia.
Pichincha	15,918	Ecuador

Cotopaxi, Tunguragua, Maipo, and Sangai are said to be the highest volcanic peaks in the world.

The Guiana Highlands, on the Borders of Brazil, Venezuela, and Courand, while not of the same grandeur as the mountains of the Andes, are of great magnitude and of an impressive wildness of scenery. They form the source of the great Orinoco River

PEAKS OF THE GUIANA HIGHLANDS

	Feet.			Feet.
Roraima ..	8,740	Ouida ..		8,500
Maraguaca ..	8,230	Turagua		6,000

VOLCANOES.

The range of the Andes is studded with volcanoes, mostly extinct, and the chain includes the loftiest volcanic eminences in the world. The volcanoes of Ecuador, including Cotopaxi, are regarded as the finest from the spectacular standpoint.

Central America has many active volcanoes, some of them of fairly recent origin. Izaleo in Salvador came into existence in 1770. Guatemala has many cones, including the Volcan de Fuego and the Volcan de Agua, that of Santa Maria, and the Cerro Quemado, or Volcano of Quezaltenango. The Santa Maria, which burst into activity in 1902, is 120 miles from Guatemala City.

The **Mexican** plateau has a band of volcanoes across the country from Colima to Tuxtla (Vera Cruz). Orizaba, (or Cithattepetl) is 18,200 ft., and the Cofre de Perote (Nauchampapetl), 13,400 ft.; Popocatepetl, or " Smoking Mountain," is 17,880 ft., and no longer active. The volcano of Jorullo, near Tolvea, some 4,330 ft. above sea level, came into existence in 1735.

Travel in South America.

Mr Barrett, ex-Director-General of the Pan-American Union, remarks that the traveller who visits South America expecting to find hotels, railways, street cars, taxicabs, restaurants, amusements, conditions of living of the same quality, comfort, and character as in the principal cities of the United States and Europe may be disappointed. If he will undertake the trip appreciating that he cannot expect to find South America on an equality with the long established and best conditions in the United States and Europe, he will avert disappointment.

The traveller is advised above all things to avoid patronising native people and criticising their conditions of living, entertainment, hospitality, and administration. An attitude of sympathetic appreciation of these countries and peoples, of the progress they have made, of the civilization they possess, their resources and potentialities, and of what they have achieved culturally, as well as commercially, brings blessings upon both visitors and hosts.

STANDARDS OF COMFORT

Not many hotels in South America are as good in service, comfort, cleanliness, and food as the average high-class hotel in the large cities of the United States and Eastern Europe, but they are better than most expect, in view of the fact that only in the last few years has travel to South America developed to proportions demanding the best hotels. Rio has put forth a big effort to make up for its past deficiencies. Buenos Aires has the best hotels in South America, and Montevideo, Santiago, and Lima are also making progress in this direction. Upon the west coast the steamships often prove the best hotels, but these afford the traveller little opportunity for special study of the countries and peoples visited. Any lack of comfort is too slight to offset the advantages.

Meals :—Morning coffee, with bread and butter, is usually served in one's room, and brought to the door By special request milk may be had in place of hot water (for the coffee) Fruit can commonly be obtained by ordering it. Eggs are not usually served, and an extra charge is made for them. Heavy breakfasts are unknown in Latin America.

Almuerzo, a rather heavy luncheon, is served from 11 to 1 or 2 o'clock, taking the place of breakfast. It usually includes a salad, a " dulce " or sweet, and cheese.

Comida, or dinner, is served in the evening, generally from 6 to 9. The general habit of the people is to dine rather late.

The visitor who follows the regular routes is not inconvenienced more by heat and cold than in North America. The traveller, should carry about the same kind of wardrobe that would be taken to Palm Beach or Coronado in the winter, or to the Jersey Coast in summer, with a small reserve of heavier clothes for wear at the higher altitudes. Men do well to take formal clothes for functions, such as high hat and frock coat. Women can suit themselves in heavy and light wraps, but they will find use for attractive and styled dresses.

Mr Barrett says the question is often asked whether one is much handicapped by not knowing Spanish and Portuguese— Spanish for all countries except Brazil, where Portuguese is the tongue. He adds that every person going to South America to build up a business, sell or buy goods, or make extended studies, should be able to speak fairly well the language of the countries in which he will spend most of his time. Want of knowledge of the language is a real shortcoming.

On the other hand it should be understood that one with no knowledge of Spanish or Portuguese can travel all through South America and thoroughly enjoy and profit by his trip. He will be surprised at the number of persons he meets who speak English. As far as steamships, hotels, and railways are concerned, he will have little difficulty in the matter of language.

OVERLAND JOURNEYS.

Roads are generally classified either as "carreteras" or "caminos de herradura." The carretera is preferable to the camino de herradura, and is generally suitable for ox-carts, mules, or in rare cases for motor-cars. Carreteras exist in various degrees of perfection, ranging up to macadam. During the rainy season they are often impassable. The camino de herradura is a bridle path or trail, usually very narrow, and serviceable for mules, burros, alpacas, llamas, or native horses. These tracks are used by pack trains, but are unsuitable for ox-carts. The caminos de herradura run so close to the mountain side that trunks are often damaged, special sizes of trunks are needed for mule back.

CHOOSING PACK ANIMALS.

In all the Latin American Republics, it is necessary to a greater or lesser degree to use mules, donkeys, burros, and horses for certain journeys. The traveller should be careful in his arrangements. The horses or mules should be inspected. Choice is not always possible, but experienced travellers find that by insistence they are often able to obtain "bestias" of more endurance than others from the same owner. The staying power of the animals is important in the mountains where an accident may cause serious delay. The cost of a pack train depends on the length of trip and other conditions.

When a pack train is engaged an attendant is usually furnished, and his pay is included in the charge for the animals. The traveller is expected to pay the keep of the attendant and to feed him en route. On long trips the feed for the animals is also paid by the traveller

Experienced travellers do not take it amiss if the muleteers desire to take small loans. These sums are regular perquisites and should be granted cheerfully without expectation of repayment. The "peons," "mozos," or "cholos," who look after the animals are mainly patient and good-natured, and more can be had from them by considerate treatment than from harshness.

In hiring mules it is well to examine the back of each animal, particularly if a long trip is contemplated. It is better to hire extra mules, horses, donkeys or burros, than to overload, where roads are fairly good, it is cheaper to obtain ox-carts, which may be sent on ahead with the baggage. A team of oxen and cart on a fairly good road cover about 3 kilometres an hour

The capacity of a good horse is 25 to 45 miles per day over fairly good roads.

Wayside sleeping accommodation is indifferent in the less frequented parts of the country.

The **tambos** are small primitive inns found in villages through which a traveller passes in making trips by "carretera" or "camino de herradura." They present sometimes the only means of obtaining shelter overnight. The food is often limited and poor. A traveller expecting to stop at a tambo should carry his own hammock, bed linen, and mosquito netting. Tinned food may advisably be carried as an emergency ration.

The **Mesones** are taverns of an inferior kind, affording lodging for the traveller and quarters for his animals. They should be avoided if possible.

The **Fondas** are similar to the "mesones," but still poorer and still more to be shunned.

Hygiene and Health.

Hints for the Tropics :—While vessels are in dock in tropical ports it is advisable to keep the cabin doors and windows closed. Some heat is preferable to the mosquito as sickness often follows bites.

Travellers in the tropical parts of Latin America need to take special precautions against damage by moisture to their baggage. In the rainy season, and in particular from March to August, boots are apt to become covered with white mould. When leaving clothing in hotel wardrobes it is not uncustomary to hang an electric bulb inside the cupboard and its gentle heat helps to counteract damp.

Upon steamer trips on tropical rivers a folding mosquito canopy is an essential, and preferably one going into small compass. Gloves to protect the hands against mosquitoes while on deck, high shoes to protect the ankles, and a gauze canopy for the face and neck should be carried. The conditions on certain river steamers make it desirable to carry changes of bed-linen and an air pillow Some travellers recommend an air mattress in taking long trips in the less advanced quarters of the tropics.

Change of Temperature :—In many tropical places there is a marked difference in temperature between the interior of cathedrals and the outer air In the higher altitudes, colds may be contracted by entering these buildings. The danger of pulmonary disease being greater because of the rarity of the atmosphere, a light overcoat should be carried. Precaution should be taken against sudden changes of temperature.

In making sudden ascents to the higher altitudes, travellers sometimes suffer from " sorocha," or mountain sickness. Those with weak hearts are cautioned against a too rapid change. Travellers who wish to avoid the sickness usually divide the trip from the lowlands to the uplands of Peru or Bolivia into two stages, stopping en route at Arequipa or elsewhere.

Health and Hygiene :—The reiterated warnings of experienced travellers against the misuse of alcohol is well-founded, and particularly when travelling in high altitudes. No hard and fast rules regarding food can be laid down, but the wise traveller is temperate in all his habits. The drinking of unboiled water is unwise, except in places where the purity of the supply is unquestioned. The insanitary conditions in many of the small places make the utmost caution imperative. In the absence of evidence as to the purity of local water, the traveller should confine himself to well-known brands of mineral waters. The use of locally bottled mineral waters is inadvisable. Uncooked vegetables and salads are to be regarded with suspicion in places without modern sanitation.

It is well to include in one's baggage aperient medicines and quinine pills. To ward off mosquitoes, oil of citronella, sparingly applied to the exposed parts of the skin, is very effective.

Adequate supplies of toilet soap, tooth paste, skin lotion, should be taken. Motor goggles for use in sandy districts, and coloured spectacles as a protection against sun-glare are items more necessary in certain parts of the continent than others.

Vaccination :—Access to some countries, for instance Brazil, is barred failing satisfactory evidence of successful vaccination. The prospective traveller should thus be vaccinated before departure. Under any conditions the precaution is wise, and the traveller feels a greater security against possible infection from smallpox, particularly in out-of-the-way quarters. The advisability of inoculation against other diseases may fitly be discussed with one's medical adviser

Yellow Fever :—It was proved in 1900 by the late Major Walter Reed and other medical officers of the U.S. Army, that yellow fever was spread only by the mosquitoes and by a particular sex or kind of mosquito—the Stegomyia. This is the female domestic mosquito whose eggs are laid in water contained in such vessels as tanks, pails and basins. Yellow fever has been conquered and almost expelled from Central and South America by the simple, albeit arduous, process of depriving the insect of its breeding places and by screening dwelling houses against such insects as matured.

The triumph over this devastating disease may be traced through the work done in Havana during the Spanish-American war, and through that done in the Panamá Canal zone. The labours of Dr. Oswaldo Cruz in Rio de Janeiro and of Dr. Licéaga in Vera Cruz are gratefully recalled by scientific sanitarians. South American scientists had the advantage of Government backing, notably in Ecuador, Peru, and Brazil. In 1916 General Gorgas visited Central and South America, and recommended systematic efforts in well-known endemic centres, such as Guayaquil in Ecuador, Merida in Yucatan, and an area in North Brazil. He advised investigation of suspected foci in Venezuela and on the West Coast of Africa. Measures were promptly adopted. Dr. Hideyo Noguchi, of the Rockfeller Institute for Medical Research, made investigations in Guayaquil and Merida, discovered the yellow fever germ and prepared a vaccine and a serum which have given encouraging results. In November 1918 a campaign was begun in Guayaquil, and since June 1919 no case has been reported there. General Gorgas organized national yellow fever commissions in the chief countries. A serious outbreak in northern Peru was promptly controlled.

As the consequence of both the recognized and the unrecognized efforts of those who have fought this foe of the human species, a position has been reached enabling Dr George E. Vincent, President of the Rockfeller Foundation to write (1922) :

"To one familiar in the history of yellow fever the fact that for a whole year Central America, the West Indies, and all but one country of South America were free from the scourge which for nearly two centuries ravaged these regions is strikingly significant. It is hard to realize that the latest phase of the fight on yellow fever began only five years ago."

Quarantine Regulations :—As a rule delay is not to be feared. Port sanitation has improved greatly, and only in exceptional instances do Latin-American ports declare quarantine against each other When travellers are detained the expense usually falls upon their own pockets.

CLOTHES AND CLIMATE.

On Overland Journeys :—A strong waterproof bag, in which to pack one's outfit, is especially desirable in long cross-country journeys upon mule or horseback.

In mountaineering, it is incumbent upon the traveller to take his own saddle and blankets. A good and comfortable saddle is particularly necessary, and care should be exercised in adjusting the straps, which are often subject to severe strains. One or two umbrellas of a quality to withstand heavy rain and hard usage can profitably be included. A good automatic electric lamp is always welcome. Warm steamer rugs and more than one thermos flask ought to be carried. Warm steamer rugs make good substitutes for blankets. Flannel shirts for hard journeys may be used with advantage.

Suitable Apparel :—Women are advised to travel with a sufficient assortment of blouses, light and dark. A cape should be taken, and silk and wool sweaters or knitted coats are desirable. Dark skirts are necessary, and strong parasols. For formal occasions such toilettes are suitable as would be worn for similar gatherings at home. In the tropics white garments are especially necessary

Travellers do well to take with them a good stock of collars, underwear and socks. These articles can always be bought on arrival, but the prices are materially higher than at home.

One reason for taking a good supply of linen is the wear and tear on such articles by laundering. In the more remote places primitive methods of washing are used, with detrimental effects upon one's apparel.

Discussing **clothing** for Latin-America from a trade point of view, the United States Commerce Reports say that most of the better dressed men in Argentina, Chile, Paraguay, Uruguay, southern Brazil, Peru, Bolivia, and Ecuador prefer custom-tailored suits made of British cloth. American ready-made "beach" cloth and cool-cloth suits have been introduced in Peru, and are popular for summer

Considerable quantities of ready-made suits are sent into Chile by parcel post. Well-to-do South Americans dress well and demand good material. They want the suit well made, and gladly pay a higher price for style, fit, and smartness. In general, their coats fit a little closer at the waist than do American, and the trousers are more in the British style, with a high waistband. The colours worn are similar to the quieter patterns common in the United Kingdom.

Except in southern Chile and south Argentina thin suits are worn in summer and heavy in winter. The Punta Arenas district offers the best market for woollen suits in Chile. In Paraguay and some of the other countries tailors purchase British cloth from Buenos Aires on which an import duty is paid on entering Argentina and another duty in Paraguay, so that the locally-tailored suit has little, if any, advantage in cost over the ready-made. It is believed a good ready-made overcoat would sell in Chile, Peru, Paraguay, Bolivia, Ecuador, and interior towns in Argentina. They might sell in Buenos Aires and southern Brazil, but in any of the South American centres the same troubles would be met with as in marketing ready-made suits.

Care of Baggage.

Instructions to Passengers :—Steamship companies make regulations with a view to the greatest expedition and security. The following notices are important :—

Only Baggage packed in trunks and hand-packages can be transferred and accepted as " Baggage," and must consist only of the personal effects of passengers. Any article not coming within this description must be shipped as merchandise, and freight according to tariff paid thereon.

Packages containing jewellery, plate, or other valuables, must be specially declared and registered before being taken on board, and freight paid thereon according to tariff.

Labelling of Baggage :—All baggage should be securely fastened, painted with the owner's name, port of destination, and bear adhesive labels stating whether wanted on the voyage or not.

Passengers are recommended also to use the Alphabetical Labels which the various companies furnish, as these assist rapid sorting both on board and in the Custom House.

All old labels should be removed, as retention often leads to misdelivery

Labels, " CABIN," " BAGGAGE ROOM," " NOT WANTED ON VOYAGE," and labels showing the port of destination, are supplied by the shipping companies.

When breaking the voyage en route, labels for the first port of landing should be pasted on the baggage.

Goods of a Dangerous Nature must not be carried. Any passenger who carries, or attempts to carry, cartridges, gunpowder or goods of a dangerous nature, for example, lucifer matches, chemicals, cinematograph films, or articles of an inflammable or damaging kind, is liable not only to a penalty of £100 (Stat. 57 & 58 Vic., c. 60), but also for all damages resulting from carrying such articles, and if such should be discovered in the possession of passengers during the voyage, the articles may be thrown overboard.

Cartridges cannot be carried under any circumstances to Argentina, Chile or Ecuador, or to Peruvian ports unless consigned to the Peruvian Government.

Firearms are not allowed to be introduced into Guatemala.

Insurance :—Baggage is conveyed entirely at passengers' own risk, unless insured.

Size of Trunks :—Cabin baggage, to go under the berths, should not be more than 16 inches high, 24 inches wide, and 36 inches long

Cycles and Perambulators are only accepted if packed in crates at the passenger's entire risk, they are **not** included in the baggage allowance. In taking motor-cars or motor-cycles, everything of an inflammable nature must be taken out before shipment.

Deck Chairs can be hired on board the steamers.

Valuables :—Passengers are warned to look after small baggage in their Cabins, especially while in port when strangers are on board. Valuables may be deposited in care of the ship's purser

Letters of Credit for limited amounts can be obtained at the Head Offices of some of the various Shipping Companies not later than two days before sailing.

Locking Baggage :—It may not be superfluous to mention the desirability of locking trunks and bags securely In especial, personal baggage should not be delivered into the hands of shore touts without being carefully locked in advance.

Fruit :—Passengers are warned that such articles as fruit or other merchandise cannot be accepted as " Passengers' Baggage," Tariff Freight Rates have to be paid and a Bill of Lading or Parcel Receipt issued.

The traveller will find it advisable to bargain with the **Cargadores,** or porters, for carrying baggage to the piers, and with the boatmen who lighter it from pier to steamer This is especially important in the small towns, and should be done in advance of departure, when a good deal of money can be saved.

The **Fleteros** are the boatmen owning or working small landing boats in the ports. At Callao, the "fletero," like the "cargador" in other places, has a brass licence badge. The traveller can ascertain the correct charge from the purser and should not permit himself to be overcharged for the carriage of his baggage to the shore.

GLOSSARY
ENGLISH AND SPANISH TERMS

AN ANGLO-SPANISH GLOSSARY.

DAYS OF THE WEEK.

Sunday.—Domingo.
Monday.—Lúnes.
Tuesday.—Mártes.
Wednesday.—Miércoles.

Thursday.—Juéves.
Friday.—Viérnes.
Saturday.—Sábado.

MONTHS OF THE YEAR.

January.—Enero.
February.—Febrero.
March.—Marzo.
April.—Abril.
May.—Máyo.
June.—Júnio.

July.—Júlio.
August.—Agosto.
September.—Setiémbre.
October.—Octúbre.
November.—Noviémbre.
December.—Diciémbre.

TIMES AND SEASONS.

The afternoon.—La tarde.
Christmas Eve.—La nochebuena.
The day.—El dia.
Day after to-morrow.—Pasado mañana.
Days of the week.—Los dias de la semana.
Easter.—La Pascua.
A fortnight.—Una quincena.
Half-an-hour.—Media hora.
Holidays.—Las vacaciones.
Last month.—El mes pasado.
Lent.—La cuaresma.
Mid-day.—El mediodia.
Midnight.—La media noche.
Minute.—El minuto.
Month.—El mes.

Morning.—La mañana.
Next day.—El dia proxómo.
New Year's Eve.—La vispera de año nuevo.
A second.—Un segundo.
To-day.—Hoy
To-morrow.—mañana.
To-night.—Esta noche.
Week.—La semana.
Whitsuntide.—El Pentecostés.
Year.—El año.
Yesterday.—Ayer.
Spring.—La primavera.
Summer.—El verano.
Autumn.—El otoño.
Winter.—El invierno.

TRAVELLING.

Arrival.—La llegada.
Berth.—La litera.
Bill.—La cuenta.
Boat.—El bote.
Boarding house.—La casa de huespedes.
"Boots" (hotel).—El limpiabotas.
Cab.—El coche.
Cabin.—El camarote.
Coffee-room.—El café.
Custom House.—La aduana.
Deck.—La cubierta.
Departure.—La salida.
Embark, to.—Embarcar
Fare, the.—El pasaje.
Guide.—El conductor.
Hall-porter.—El portero.
Land, to.—Desembarcar.
Landlord.—El fondista.
Lavatory.—El lavatorio.
Lifebelt.—La cintura.
Lift.—El elevador.
Lodgings.—Los cuartos amueblados.
Lost property office.—La oficina de equipage perdido.

Luggage.—El equipage.
Luggage label.—La etiqueta.
Motor-bus.—El omnibus motor
Motor-car.—El automovil.
Newspapers, English.—Periodicos, Ingleses.
Porter.—El mozo.
Railway.—El ferrocarril.
Railway station.—La estación.
Receipt.—El recibo.
Rug (travelling).—La manta.
Sleeping car.—El coche dormitorio.
Smoking room.—El salón de fumar
Station master.—El jefe.
Steward.—El camarero.
Stewardess.—La camarera.
Ticket.—El billete.
Time-table.—El horario.
Tip.—La propina.
Train.—El tren.
Traveller.—El viajero.
Waiter.—El mozo.
Waiting room.—La sala de descanso.

GLOSSARY

FOOD AND DRINK.

Bacon.—El tocino.
Beef.—La carne de vaca.
Beer.—La cerveza.
Bottle.—La botella.
Bread.—El pan.
Breakfast.—El desayuno.
Butter.—La manteca.
Cake.—La torta.
Champagne.—Vino de Champaña.
Cheese.—El queso.
Chocolate.—El chocolate.
Cigar.—El cigarro.
Cigarette.—El cigarrillo.
Claret.—Vino tinto.
Cocoa.—El coco.
Coffee (black).—El café solo.
Coffee (with milk).—El café con leche.
Cream.—La crema.
To dine.—Comer.
Dinner.—Comida.
Drink.—La bebida.
Dry.—Seco.
Egg.—El huevo.
Fowl.—El ave.
Fried.—Frito (a).
Fruit.—La fruta.
Hunger.—El hambre.

Knife.—El cuchillo.
Lamb.—El cordero.
Marmalade.—La marmelada.
Meat.—La carne.
Milk.—La leche.
Mineral water.—El agua mineral.
Mustard.—La mostaza.
Mutton.—El carnero.
Omelet.—La tortilla.
Pear.—La pera.
Pepper.—La pimienta.
Pipe.—La pipa.
Plate.—El plato.
Pork.—El cerdo.
Ripe.—Maduro.
Salt.—La sal.
Siphon.—El sifón.
Smoking.—Fumando.
Soup.—La sopa.
Spoon.—La cuchara.
Sugar.—El azúcar.
Thank you.—Gracias.
Veal.—La ternera.
Vegetables.—Los legumbres.
Water.—El agua.
Wine.—El vino.

WEARING APPAREL.

Boots.—Las botas.
Braces.—Los tirantes.
Brush.—El cepillo.
Clothes brush.—El cepillo de ropa.
Coat.—La casaca.
Collars.—Los cuellas.
Cuffs.—Los Punos.
Curling tongs.—El encrespador.
Dress.—El vestido.
Evening dress.—El traje de etiqueta.
Fur.—La piel.
Gloves.—Los guantes.
Hairpins.—Las horquillas.
Handkerchief.—El pañuelo.
Hat.—El sombrero.
Jewellery.—La pedreria.
Necktie.—La corbata.
Nightgown.—Bata de dormir.
Parasol.—El quitasol.

Pocketbook.—La cartera.
Powder.—El polvo.
Purse.—La bolsa.
Razor.—La navaja.
Ring.—El anillo.
Rouge.—Colorete.
Shoes.—Los zapatos.
Skirt.—La falda.
Slippers.—Las chinelas.
Soap.—El jabón.
Socks.—Los calcetines.
Sponge.—La esponja.
Stockings.—Las medias.
Stud.—El boton de camisa.
Towels.—Las toallas.
Trousers.—Los pantalones.
Umbrella.—El paraguas.
Waistcoat.—El chaleco.
Watch.—El reloj.

TOPOGRAPHY.

Cliff.—El peñasco.
Climate.—El clima.
Coast.—La costa.
Bay.—La bahia.
Beach.—La playa.
Hill.—La colina.
House.—La casa.
Island.—La isla.

Lake.—El lago.
River.—El rio.
Sea.—El mar.
Street.—La calle.
Town.—La ciudad.
Village.—La aldea.
Water.—El agua.

COMMERCIAL.

To close the Account.—Cerrar la cuenta.
Current Account.—La cuenta corriente.
Joint Account.—La cuenta mitad.
On Account.—Por cuenta de.
Accountant.—El contador.
Acknowledge receipt.—Acusar recibo.
To pay in advance.—Pagar adelantado.
Advertise.—Anunciar.
Balance.—Saldo.
Bank.—El banco.
Bill of exchange.—La letra de cambio.
Bill of lading.—El conocimiento de embarque.
Brokerage.—El corretaje.
Business.—El negocio.
Buyer.—El comprador.
Cargo.—La carga.
Carriage paid.—Porte pagado.
Cash.—La caja.
Cash account.—La cuenta de caja.
Cheque.—El cheque.
Clerk.—El dependiente.
Contract.—El contrato.
Cost.—El coste.
Credit balance.—El saldo a favor

Custom house.—La aduana.
Customs duty.—Los derechos.
Debit and credit.—Débito y crédito.
To deliver.—Entregar
Discount.—Descuento.
Dollar.—Peso.
Enclosed herewith.—Adjunta (con esta).
Endorse.—Endoso.
Forwarding.—El envio.
How much money.—¿ Cuánto dinero ?
Insurance.—El seguro.
Invoice.—La factúra.
Manager.—El gérente.
Negotiable.—Capaz de ser negociodo.
Price.—El precio.
Quotation.—La cotización.
Receipt.—El recibo.
Reduction.—La rebaja.
Registered letter.—La carta certificada.
Remittance.—La remesa.
Reply by telegram.—La contestación por telegrama.
Shipping charges.—Los derechos de navegación.
Trade.—El comercio.

CARDINAL NUMBERS.

1.—Uno (m) una (f).
2.—Dos.
3.—Tres.
4.—Cuatro.
5.—Cinco.
6.—Seis.
7.—Siete.
8.—Ocho.
9.—Nueve.
10.—Diez.
11.—Once.
12.—Doce.
13.—Trece.
14.—Catorce.
15.—Quince.
16.—Dieciseis.
17.—Diecisiete.
18.—Dieciocho.
19.—Diecinueve.
20.—Veinte.
21.—Veintiuno (a).
22.—Veintidos.
23.—Veintitres.
24.—Veinticuatro.
25.—Veinticinco.
26.—Veintiseis.
27.—Veintisiete.
28.—Veintiocho.
29.—Veintinueve.
30.—Treinta.

31.—Treintiuno (na).
32.—Treintidos,* etc.
40.—Cuarenta.
50.—Cincuenta.
60.—Sesenta.
70.—Setenta.
80.—Ochenta.
90.—Noventa.
100.—Cien, ciento.
101.—Ciento uno (una f).
200.—Doscientos (m). Doscientas (f).
300.—Trescientos (tas)
400.—Cuatrocientos (tas)
500.—Quinientos (tas)
600.—Seiscientos.
700.—Setecientos (tas)
800.—Ochocientos.
900.—Novecientos.
1,000.—Mil.
1,001.—Mil uno (una f).
1,100.—Mil ciento.
1,101.—Mil ciento uno.
1,200.—Mil doscientos (tas)
2,000.—Dos mil.
100,000.—Cien mil.
200,000.—Doscientos mil.
1,000,000.—Un millón.
2,000,000.—Dos millones.

* The compound numbers (17 to 99, except the even tens) can also be spelt diez y seis, veinte y dos, cuarenta y cinco, etc.

ORDINAL NUMBERS.

1st.—Primero.
2nd.—Segundo.
3rd.—Tercero.
4th.—Cuarto.
5th.—Quinto.
6th.—Sexto.
7th.—Séptimo.

8th.—Octavo.
9th.—Noveno, nono.
10th.—Décimo.
11th.—Un décimo *or* décimo primero.
12th.—Duodécimo *or* décimo segundo.
20th.—Vigésimo.
21st.—Vigésimo primero, etc.

HOURS OF THE DAY.

One o'clock.—La una; **Two o'clock.**—Las dos, **Five o'clock.**—Las cinco, etc. La, las, are used because Hora (hour), which is understood, is feminine. **Quarter** is translated cuarto, and **half,** media.

A quarter-past-four.—Las cuatro y cuarto.

Half-past-four.—Las cuatro y media.

A quarter to five.—Las cinco menos cuarto.

Twelve minutes past six.—Las seis y doce.

Twenty minutes to seven.—Las siete menos veinte.

THE COURSE OF EXCHANGE.

From The South American Journal.

Quotations in pence, except for Chilean money, which is shown in pesos to the £.

Buenos Aires.		Montevideo.		Rio de Janeiro.		Valparaiso.		Silver.	
Par. 47.62d.		51 1/8 d.		16d.		13.33ps.=£1		—	
Year 1918	51 3/4	59 5/8		12 3/4		16.27		43 5/8	
,, 1919	53 5/8	58 1/4		14 5/8		22.64		56 7/8	
,, 1920	59 5/8	60 1/4		14 3/4		19.83		61 1/4	
,, 1921	45 1/2	43 1/4		8 1/2		33.11		36 1/4	
,, 1922	44 5/8	43 1/4		7 1/2		37.13		34 1/4	
	1922	1923	1922	1923	1922	1923	1922	1923	1922	1923
JAN.	43 3/4	43 7/8	41 1/2	43 7/8	7 1/4	5 7/8	43.17	35.66	35	32
FEB.	45 5/8	43 5/8	44 3/8	42 5/8	7 7/8	6	42.42	38.70	33 1/2	30 7/8
MAR.	45 1/4	43	44 1/4	43 7/8	7 7/8	5 3/4	39.06	36.64	33 5/8	32 5/16
APL.	43 13/16	42 7/8	43	43 1/4	7 1/2	5 1/2	39.52	37.47	34 5/8	32 1/16
MAY	44 7/16	42 5/8	43 5/8	42 1/4	7 9/16	5 7/16	37.95	35.45	36	32 13/16
JUNE	44 5/8	41 1/2	44	42 1/4	7 1/2	5 1/2	35.44	34.25	37 1/2	31 5/8
JULY	44 1/8	40 5/8	44 1/2	41 5/8	7 1/2	5 7/16	34.15	36.05	35 3/4	30 15/16
AUG.	44 5/8	39	43 1/2	38 3/4	7 1/4	5 1/4	32.02	36.82	35	30 15/16

BRITISH CAPITAL IN SOUTH AMERICA.

British capital has for a considerable number of years taken a foremost part in the development of the South American continent, and in particular of Argentina and Brazil. Estimates of the amount of British capital invested in the Republics vary within limits, but the amounts contained in the following table may be taken as authoritative :—

Argentina	.			£395,000,000
Brazil	.	.	.	255,000,000
Chile		.		80,000,000
Uruguay	..			46,00,0000
Peru			.	29,000,000
Colombia		..	..	10,500,000
Venezuela		..		8,500,000
Paraguay	.	.	.	3,500,000
Ecuador	..	..	.	3,000,000
Bolivia	..	..	..	..	400,000
				£830,900,000

ON THE WAY TO
SOUTH AMERICA

ON THE WAY TO SOUTH AMERICA.

The ports of call between England and South America vary according to the individual arrangements of the steamship lines. There follow items of interest concerning the ports more usually visited, with particulars in some instances of the attractions in the vicinity, although visits to the places named will not invariably be practicable to through passengers.

CHERBOURG

The French naval port and arsenal is one of the European ports of call for steamers bound for South America. It faces the Isle of Wight. Its docks and defences were designed initially by the great Napoleon, and have been much increased.

The time spent in port is commonly too short to admit of a visit to the city, which displays comparatively little activity. Wood and coals are imported, and dairy produce, vegetables and stone exported. There are two large engineering works and quarries in the neighbourhood. The industrial energies of the bulk of the population are absorbed in the arsenal and dockyards.

Landing :—By tender.

Conveyances :—Motor-cars, 2.00 frs. per kilometre (near quay). Electric tram (cost in city), 0.25 c. Tram to Urville, 1.45 frs.

Hotels :—Casino (about 45 frs. per diem.), Anglo-American (40 frs.), De l'Etoile (25 frs.), De France (25 frs.), Moderne (25 frs.), Messent (de la Plage) (20 frs.).

Shopping Centres :—Quai de Caligny, Rue du Bassin, Rue Gambetta, Rue de la Fontaine.

LA ROCHELLE-PALLICE.

Is touched by certain of the steamship services to South America. Outward mail boats stay long enough in port to give passengers an opportunity of visiting the interesting and historic city of La Rochelle, four miles distant. Trains and tramcars run between La Rochelle-Pallice and La Rochelle. The principal sights are the cathedral in the Place d'Armes—built 1780, in the Grecian style ; the Hotel de Ville (Gothic) , the "Mail," a popular promenade, with Casino, etc. The houses and shops in this old city are quaint— many side walks are covered by arches, which recall Chester and other old-world English towns.

Trains leave La Rochelle at short intervals for Niort. Saintes, Bordeaux, Nantes, Pau, Biarritz, Bayonne, and Central and Southern France.

There is every facility at La Rochelle-Pallice for the rapid and safe handling of motor-cars. The point is a convenient one for passengers for the South of France and the Touraine.

Garage :—Hotel de France and Hotel du Commerce, and also at M. Armand Roux's, La Rochelle, the Representative of the Royal Automobile Club.

Landing :—Usually from steamer to wharf.

Conveyances :—Trams, cabs and motor-cars.

Hotels :—Hotel de France, Hotel du Commence, "Touring et de la Plage," provided with motor garages.

Post Office :—Place de l'Hôtel de Ville.

Shopping Centres :—Rue du Palais, R. du Temple, R. des Merciers.

Bordeaux is distant four hours by train from La Rochelle. Rochefort is less than one hour away, and between these points is Fouras, sixteen miles a pretty watering place with a park and casino Marsilf, five miles out, has the ruins of a Gothic church rebuilt 1608, with a curious belfry, and many interesting old houses.

Saint-Soulle, seven miles away, contains relics of the Middle Ages, amongst others, La Gremenaudière, where Richelieu stayed during the siege of 1628, and Le Treuil au Secret, where, in the fourteenth century, Du Guesclin negotiated the surrender of La Rochelle by the English.

San Sebastian (Spain) :—Reached by railway from La Rochelle-Pallice in about ten hours, is much patronised by the Spanish Royal Family Throughout the year fêtes are held, and an increasing number of people annually visit this charming spot, which is about fifty minutes' rail journey from the French frontier The bathing is excellent, there are a splendid casino, high-class hotels, and a bull-ring. Mount Ulia, connected by aerial railway, is a delightful pleasure centre.

Hotels :—Londres, Palais, Continental, Ezcurra, Albeniz, Biarritz, Central.

CORUÑA.

The town is for ever associated in English memory with the name of Sir John Moore, who, after being chased from the interior by the great Napoleon, turned upon Soult and administered a check in January 1809, which enabled the British forces to escape to the ships. His grave lies in the Garden of St. Carlos on the outskirts of the town.

The city contains two quarters, and the upper town on the mountain side is surrounded by ancient battlements. The lower town or Pescaderia is of less interest. The finest streets are the Calle Réal, the Cantones and Calle Linares-Rivas.

The principal church is Santa Maria del Campo, in the Plaza de Santa Maria. It is a small Gothic erection with three naves, a Norman porch and a pyramidal tower The church of San Jorge (Plaza de Santo Jorge) contains two famous paintings, "Annunciation" and "Purgatory," by Pierre Vanderlaken. A fine fifteenth century bas-relief in the side tower of the Capucine convent (Calle de Pinaderas) calls for notice.

The port is a fine one and the entrepôt for Galicia. Excellent bathing is obtainable. The environs afford charming motor drives, and there are many good trout streams.

Coruña is the capital of Galicia, and the terminus of the Great Northern Railway from Madrid.

Landing :—Shore boat, 1s. 6d. return.

Conveyances :—Electric trams and motor-cars.

Hotels :—Ferro Carrilana, in Calle Réal, Europa, in Calle San Andres; Francia, in Calle Juana de Vega; Palace Hotel, in Cantones.

Shopping Centres :—Calle Réal, Calle San Andres, Avenida de Rubiné.

Arteijo :—Outings from Coruña include a motor ride to Arteijo, distant seven miles, cost 3.25 to 4.00 pesetas. The spa life is gay and in the season the youth of Coruña flock for the excellent promenades and balls.

Carballo, another spa, twenty miles from Coruña on the same road, has also a hot spring. Approximate cost of journey, 5 to 7.50 pesetas.

Corcubion, sixty miles from the city on the same road, is reached by motor at a cost of from 16.00 to 25.50 pesetas. It is a pretty little fishing village with a lace (camariñas) industry.

Sada :—By a good half-hourly tramway service, costs 1 20 pesetas. One of the most attractive trips.

Ferrol :—Reached from Coruña by railway at a cost from 7.55 pesetas, is divided into three quarters   old Ferrol, new Ferrol, and Esteiro. It owes its importance to the security of its harbour from attacks by outside foes, an advantage first realized when the relics of the "Great Armada" found refuge there. Essentially a naval and military town, it has a good school of arts and crafts, casino and library. Of the many fine promenades the best is the Alameda, to the south of the new town.

Hotels :—Varela and Suizo, both in Calle Réal.

Shopping Centres :—Calle Réal and Calle Magdalena.

Santiago de Compostella can be reached from Coruña by a motor drive of forty miles; fare, 12 pesetas, starting at 8 a.m., 9 a.m., mid-day and 2 p.m.

VIGO.

Vigo Bay is one of the finest in the world and ranks as the fifth best bay, and is large enough to hold the whole of the world's navies at once. Cabo Estay on the south and Sobrido Point on the north guard an opening nine miles in width. The rocky and picturesque Islas Cies form as complete a natural breakwater against westerly gales as could have been designed by man.

The city lies nine miles up the bay on the southern shore, and presents a remarkably clean and well-kept appearance. The city spreads tier by tier up a steep hill from an avenue of plane trees at the base to the citadel crowning the height.

Principal Buildings :—The church (Plazuela de Inglesia) is built in the Doric Greek order. The Theatre Tamberlick in the Calle de Eduardo Inglesias, the School of Art and Theatre "Rosalia de Castro" in Policarpo Sang, and Bank of Vigo in Calle Colón. There is also a branch of the Anglo-South American Bank with English staff, Calle de Principe 45.

The Citadel at the top of the hill, built by Philippe IV, forms one of three forts that guard the town. En route to this Citadel lie the prison and the barracks.

There are 25 kilometres of electric tramways serving the neighbourhood. Excellent sea-fishing may be had at Redondela, up harbour from Vigo City, and there are many good trout streams in the neighbourhood.

Landing :—By shore boat, ptas. 2.00 per person, baggage extra. Hotels send motor launches.

Conveyances :—Carriages, ptas. 4 to 6 per hour; open motor-cars, ptas. 1.25 per kilo., closed motor-cars, ptas. 1.50 per kilo.

Hotels :—Continental, Moderno, Universal, Europa. Inclusive charges from ptas. 25 to 30 per day

There are many mineral water springs around Vigo for the treatment of liver, rheumatism, and chest diseases.

Shopping Centres :—Calle del Principe and Puerta del Sol.

Excursions :—By motor launches to the Island of San-Simon, Puente de San Payo, and other picturesque spots up the river. Steamers leave hourly for Cangas and Moaña, fishing villages on the north of the bay, from where are pleasant walks to hamlets in the interior.

OPORTO.

Cathedral Hill and Victory Hill look down upon the River Douro, the entrance to the port wine district—the only place from which real port can come. The wine comes by river from the grape-growing country to the lodges in Oporto, from whence export is made. On these two hills (Da Sé and Da Victoria) and in the neighbouring valleys lies the second metropolis of Portugal. The vista, best appreciated from the top of the cathedral or the Clerigos Tower, is magnificent.

The cathedral is of ancient foundation. Tradition attributes one of the churches (San Martinho de Cedofeita) to King Théodomir, who is said to have built it in A.D. 559 to contain certain specially sacred relics. Many of the dwellings date from the sixteenth century The streets of the old town are narrow and tortuous, and there are some fine modern boulevards. Good examples of the latter are the Calçada dos Clerigos, the streets of 31 de Janeiro and Santa Catharina, and the Rua das Flores (the "Regent Street" of Oporto). The last-named shows beautiful examples of the local gold and silver filigree work.

There are many public squares, the principal being the Praça da Liberdade, with a fine bronze statue of Dom Pedro IV All over the city are fountains and well laid-out promenades. The Sunday promenade in the Crystal Palace gardens is especially fashionable.

The cathedral (Sé) has a fine interior, including a solid silver altar and re-table. The church of São Francisco, close to the Bolsa (Exchange), is a mass of delightful carving of the fifteenth and sixteenth centuries. The Clerigos church has the highest spire in Portugal (246 ft.), which dominates the city from every point. The post office lies in Praça da Batalha, east of the Central Railway Station.

A remarkable bridge—the Ponte de Dom Luis Primeiro—is a quarter of a mile to the south of the Praça da Liberdade. It crosses the Douro in a single span of 560 ft. at a height of 120 ft. The engineer of this bridge, as of one higher up the gorge, was the great Eiffel, designer also of the celebrated Paris tower From the monastery between these bridges the great Duke of Wellington launched his attack upon the French General Soult, driving him out from Oporto.

Conveyances :—There is a good service of electric trams. The Central Railway Station, São Bento, in the middle of the town, is the terminus for long-distance traffic. The Campanha Station, a mile and a half distant on the east side, and Boa Vista Station, in the north-western district, serve minor lines.

Landing :—Launches and rowing boats.

Hotels :—Grand Hôtel do Porto and Palace in Rua Santa Catharina, Hôtel de Paris in Rua Da Fabrica.

Shopping Centres :—Rua das Flores, Praça da Libredade, Rua 31 de Janeiro.

Leixões is the seaport for Oporto, and has been secured from storms by two great jetties seen on either side as the steamer enters the harbour. A railway and an electric tram connect it with the city, five miles distant.

The authorized boat charges for embarking and landing are Per passenger (rowing boat), 80 centivos., per passenger (motor launch), Esc. 1 20 cts., minimum charge per boat, Esc. 3.20 cts. Charges are doubled when storm cone is hoisted.

LISBON

The south-western coast of Portugal is low-lying and insignificant-looking from the sea. At length a gap is seen, and the vessel steams up the estuary of the Tagus. The scenery changes, and there comes into view the Rome of the Iberian Peninsula, Lisbon, standing out in all the majesty of her seven hills. The city rises in picturesque terraces from the sea-level, and affords a most striking spectacle from the estuary

Mail steamers to South America from Southampton and Liverpool steam up the river and land passengers by tender at the Posto de Desinfeccão Passengers like to visit the famous "Black Horse Square" (Praça do Comercio), so named from the bronze equestrian statue of José I, in the centre. Almost all the edifices in this square are Government buildings. On the east is the Bolsa (Exchange) and the Custom House, and on the west the Post Office. It was at the north-west corner at the opening of the Rua do Arsenal, that King Carlos and the Crown Prince were assassinated in 1908. Lisbon possesses other fine squares, including the Praça do Municipio, with a curious marble pillar; the Praça Rocio (Rolling Motion Square), Camoëns Square, with its monument to the illustrious poet, and the grand new promenade "Avenida da Liberdade."

The public gardens in all parts of the city are wonderful for the uxuriance of their vegetation.

The Cathedral or Basilica of St. Vincent preserves in part its original Gothic architecture, and in part the French style of Louis XIV, introduced when the edifice was restored after the earthquake. It contains the bones of St. Vincent, the patron saint of Lisbon. In blue and white tiles round the walls are depicted the legends of the Sacred Ravens.

The San Roque Church, now a museum, has, despite a mean exterior, rare marvels within. The crowning glory is the Chapel of St. John the Baptist, to the right of the High Altar Permission for a visit can be obtained from the custodian. It is a perfect casket of jewelled stones. The altar is amethyst, lapis-lazuli, and silver, and pictures executed in wonderful mosaics line the walls. Other sacred buildings worth visiting are São Vicente de Fora (on rising ground east of the cathedral), the Estrella Church (dominating the west of the city), and Nossa Senhora da Conceição Velha (Rua da Alfandega, off the east side of Black Horse Square)

Other points of interest include the Museum at the Palacio da Imperatriz at the Janellas Verdes, containing art treasures and ancient royal carriages. The Palacio das Cortes (Parliament House) in Largo de São Bento on the west side of the city Museu Nacional das Bellas Artes, open Sundays and Thursdays, 11 a.m. to 4 p.m.; other days, mid-day to 2 p.m., by application. Museu Archeologico do Carmo (antiques, etc.), open daily 10 a.m. to 4 p.m., charge 1 Escudo. Academia das Sciencias (Rua do Arco de Jesus), open week days, 10 a.m. to 3 p.m. Botanical Gardens (north-west of Rolling Motion Square), said to be the finest in Europe. Bull-ring (in Praça do Campo Pequeño) bull fights in summer. National Library, north-west of Black Horse Square, with many rare MSS. and books. The waterworks of Lisbon are remarkable. The water is laid from a source fifteen miles outside the city, and conducted by an aqueduct (built 1713–1732), which traverses the valley of Alcantara on thirty-five arches, some of which attain a height of 200 ft., with a span of 114 ft.

Theatres :—San Carlos (Italian opera), Theatro Nacional (National drama), Theatro Apollo (light opera), and numerous smaller theatres and concert halls.

Hotels :—Avenida Palace, de l'Europe, Rua Alecrim (near Railway Station), Hôtel Metropole (in Rocio) and Hôtel Borges (in Rua Garrett).

Landing :—By Companies' tender to Posto de Desinfecção (Disinfection Station). Passengers are conveyed from or to the steamer free of charge, except transit passengers, who are conveyed by special tender to and from the Caes do Sodré, price 5s. return.

Conveyances :—Electric trams, motor-cars, and hackney carriages.   Inclined railways connect the upper and lower towns.

Railway Stations :—(1) Estação Rocio (Central Station), the principal terminus for inland routes.

(2) Estação de Barreiro, on the south side of the Tagus. A steam ferry connects it with "Black Horse Square."

(3) Estação Caes dos Soldados, on the East quay
(4) Estação Caes do Sodré, on the West quay
(Nos. 3 and 4 are minor stations for local lines.)
Shopping Centres :—Rua do Commercio, Rua Aurea, and Rua Garrett.

Within a short distance from Lisbon is **Belem,** reached by electric tram or rail from Caes do Sodré Station. Close by the mouth of the Tagus, it contains the Tower of St. Vincent, the first building seen by passengers arriving by steamer Here also are the Church and Convent of St. Mary, generally known as the Jeronymos. The church was built in 1500 to commemorate the discovery of the Cape of Good Hope by Vasco da Gama. The famous museum contains a collection of historical coaches.

Cintra is reached by rail in about an hour from Rocio Station It is one of the beauty spots of the world, and enjoys a world-wide fame. Mountain peaks, rich groves, parks of camelias, myrtles and geraniums, make an earthly paradise. The time of year to see Cintra in perfection is March-April. The Palace is a fine example of Byzantine architecture.

Places of interest in the neighbourhood include Montserrat, Cork Convent, Praia das Maçãs and the old Moorish castle ; also Colloares, famous for its vineyards

Hotels :—Netto and Nunes.

Estoril (Mont' Estoril) :—About thirty-five minutes by rail express train from Caes do Sodré Station, lies on the Bay of Cascaes, sheltered by the pine-clad hills of Cintra, and is a delightful winter resort. The mean temperatures from October-March, are 61° to 55° Fah. The Portuguese Riviera is free from mistral, and there is no sudden change of temperature at sunset. Frost and snow are unknown. The hotels are good and the charges moderate. Excellent boating, fishing, and bathing are obtainable, and lovely walks abound.

Hotels:—Miramar, D'Itali.

Mafra :—The town lies six miles from the station. A public conveyance plies between the two, fare, Esc. 8 $oo. A combination of a convent church and palace is remarkable for its peal of 365 bells.

Queluz, reached in half an hour from Rocio Station, contains a royal palace and garden, a miniature Versailles built by King John V in 1735.

Cacilhas and Almada :—Reached by steamer from Caes do Sodré landing place. The heights of Almada command a splendid panorama of Lisbon and the Tagus.

MADEIRA.

The island is notable for a sunny climate that is yet not oppressively hot, and for an abundance of moisture without any heavy rainfall. There are hills 6,000 ft. high, on which flourish pines and the vegetation of temperate zones. The valleys between glow with the lustre of the tropics. Geraniums luxuriate in the hedges.

31

Funchal, the capital, lies at the foot of a vast amphitheatre of hills. The scene as the steamer enters is fascinating in the extreme. The town is lit by electricity and picturesquely laid out. The streets are paved with smooth round cobbles, and sledges are much used for transit. The bathing is remarkably fine and good facilities are available. Wicker-work, embroidery, lace, and jewellery are offered for sale from boats, and can be purchased also ashore.

The public buildings are not devoid of merit, but it is the peculiarities of costume and domestic architecture which will most interest the passer-by The highly-polished cobble stones of the streets are trying, and those who wish to explore the town should wear boots with soft soles, preferably india-rubber Whatever the season of the year, the market-place is well supplied with tropical and other fruits, and each passer-by, from the hammock-bearers in their white linen clothes to the peasant in his strange and often grotesque head-gear, excites attention. The public gardens are prettily laid out, and, if it is not too late in the day, the fish as well as the fruit market should be visited. The fame of Madeira as a health resort is of such ancient date that little need be said on the subject.

Landing :—By launch, each way, 2s.

Conveyances :—In the town (bullock sledges or "Carros"), per hour, 2s. 6d., motor-cars, according to journey, train to Monte, 5s.; train to Terreiro da Luta, 7s. 6d., rowing boats can be hired at 1s. 6d. per hour per head.

Shopping Centres :—The principal shops cluster round the top of the Entrada da Cidade, the avenue leading from the centre of the town to the quay.

Hotels :—Reid's Palace, Bungalow, Cliff (from 21s.), Javes' Bella Vista (from 14s.); Savoy, Atlantic, New English (from 15s.); Golden Gate (from 12s.), Monte Palace (from 15s.)

Restaurants :—Terreiro da Lucta, Golden Gate, Benthami Monaed.

ST VINCENT.

The Cape Verde Islands lie 350 miles west of Cape Verde, on the African coast. Of all islands in the Atlantic they least deserve the name of "green." They are volcanic. Porto Grande, in St. Vincent, is an important coaling station and cable companies' centre. Most of the cable staffs are English, and delight to have a (coco-nut matting) cricket match with the passengers of passing vessels. There is an eighteen-hole golf course along the shore, easily accessible to passengers, and golfers are welcome. Shoes with heavy nails are prohibited on these links.

Landing :—By tender.

Hotel :—Central.

MARITIME DISTANCES.

```
Southampton.
  84 | Cherbourg.
 592 |  508 | Coruña.
 693 |  606 |  126 | Vigo.
 793 |  681 |  180 |   75 | Leixões.
 936 |  860 |  359 |  243 |  179 | Lisbon.
1478 | 1402 |  901 |  785 |      |  542 | Madeira.
2505 | 2429 | 1915 | 1799 | 1735 | 1569 | 1051 | S. Vincent.
4121 | 4037 | 3531 | 3415 |      | 3185.| 2667 | 1616 | Pernambuco.
4511 | 4427 | 3921 | 3805 |      | 3575 | 3057 | 2006 |  390 | Bahia.
5253 | 5169 | 4663 | 4547 | 4405 | 4317 | 3799 | 2670*| 1132 |  742 | Rio de Janeiro.
5461 | 5377 | 4871 | 4755 | 4613 | 4525 | 4077 | 2956 | 1340 |  950 |  208 | Santos.
6347 | 6263 | 5757 | 5641 | 5499 | 5411 | 4893 | 3842 | 2226 | 1836 | 1035*|  886 | Monte Video.
6471 | 6387 | 5881 | 5765 | 5623 | 5535 | 5013 | 3966 | 2350 | 1960 | 1159 | 1010 |  124 | Buenos Aires.
```

* Direct.

The distance from port to port is to be read at a glance in the table above thus Southampton to Pernambuco = 4,121 nautical miles, Lisbon to Buenos Aires = 5,535 miles.

ZONE STANDARD TIME.

Standard times, fast or slow of Greenwich mean time by an integral number of hours, have been adopted as follows :—

Azores, Cape Verde Islands .	2 hours slow
Eastern Brazilian Zone	3 ,, ,,
Central Brazil, Argentina, Uruguay, French Guiana	4 ,, ,,
Venezuela	$4\frac{1}{2}$, ,,
Peru, Panamá, Western Brazil	5 ,, ,,
Honduras	6 ,, ,,

ARGENTINA

Branches of the

ANGLO-SOUTH AMERICAN BANK,

Head Office: Limited

62, OLD BROAD STREET, LONDON, E.C.2

Northern District Office—69, Market Street, Bradford.
Lancashire Branch—39, Mosley Street, Manchester.

ARGENTINA—

Bahia Blanca	*Puerto Deseado*	*San Rafael*
Buenos Aires	*Rio Gallegos*	*Santa Cruz*
Comodoro Rivadavia	*Rosario*	*Trelew*
Mendoza	*San Julian*	

CHILE—

Antofagasta	*Coquimbo*	*Santiago*
Concepcion	*Iquique*	*Talcahuano*
Copiapo	*Punta Arenas*	*Valparaiso*

URUGUAY	MEXICO—	FRANCE—
Montevideo	*Mexico City*	*Paris*

PERU—	SPAIN—	
Lima	*Barcelona*	*Seville*
U.S.A.—	*Bilbao*	*Valencia*
New York (Agency)	*Madrid*	*Vigo*

Branches of the

British Bank of South America,

Head Office: Limited

4, MOORGATE, LONDON, E.C.2

Manchester Office—2, Norfolk Street.

BRAZIL—

Bahia	*Rio de Janeiro*	*Santos*
Pernambuco	*Rio Grande do Sul*	*São Paulo*
Porto Alegre		

URUGUAY—	ARGENTINA—
Montevideo & Mercedes	*Buenos Aires : Rosario : Pergamino*

Branches of the

Commercial Bank of Spanish America,

Head Office: Limited

9, BISHOPSGATE, LONDON, E.C.2

Manchester Office—42, Whitworth Street.

COLOMBIA—

Barranquilla	*Cartagena*	*Santa Marta*
Bogota	*Medellin*	

ECUADOR—	GUATEMALA—	NICARAGUA—
Guayaquil	*Guatemala*	*Managua*

PERU—	SALVADOR—
Iquitos	*San Salvador*

VENEZUELA—	U.S.A.—
Caracas & Puerto Cabello	*New York & San Francisco.*

See pages ii, 170.

ARGENTINA.

Buenos Aires, distant 6,500 miles from Southampton and 109 from Montevideo, stands at the head of a great ocean route and is served by vessels of all nationalities, trading to and from all countries. The capital of Argentina, the largest city south of the Equator and the largest Spanish-speaking city in the world, it is one of the world's handsomest and wealthiest cities. The population is 1,750,000. The lay-out of the city is on the American plan, in squares like a chessboard, and the topography is easily mastered. The main thoroughfares are modelled on Paris, and the water and drainage system on London.

Landing :—Alongside Custom House wharf in Darsena Norte (North Basin)

Currency :—Argentine paper (moneda nacional).

Points of Interest :—Avenida de Mayo, the central thoroughfare, Government House, Plaza de Mayo, Cathedral, Plaza de Mayo (tomb of San Martin), British Clock Tower, commemorating Centenary of Independence, Colón Theatre (Grand Opera season, June to August), Congress Hall, Plaza Congreso, New Law Courts, Plaza Lavalle, Cementerio del Norte (at Recoleta), Palermo Park (Zoological and Botanical Gardens), Racecourse, at Palermo (Races Sundays and Holidays), Wool Market (the largest in the world), Parque Lezama (Museum containing historical trophies)

Railways :—Central Argentine, Buenos Aires and Pacific, Buenos Aires Great Southern, Buenos Aires Western, Buenos Aires Central, Córdoba Central, and Entre Rios railways.

TERMINALS :—

Retiro Central Argentine, Pacific & Central Córdoba Railways.
Chacarita N E. Argentine, Entre Rios & Central Buenos Aires Railways.
Once . B. A. Western Railway
Plaza Constitucion Southern Railway
Puente Alsina · Midland, Western & Southern Railways.
Vélez Sanfield F F C. C. de la Province de B. A.

Hotels.

NAME OF HOTEL.	CABLES.	BEDS.	TARIFF PER PERSON PER DAY		REMARKS.
PLAZA, Florida and Charcas.	"Plazotel"	350	$25--50	With pension	
			$12–15	Without „	
SAVOY, Callao and Cangallo.	"Savoy"	300	$18–35	With „	High Class.
			$10–25	Without „	
PALACE, 25 de Mayo 215.	"Palacotel"	130	$18–25	With „	
			$10–15	Without „	
MAJESTIC, Avda. de Mayo 1317	"Majestic"	190	$15–25	With „	French.
PHOENIX, San Martin 780.	"Oyloyd"	160	$12–25	With „	English family

NAME OF HOTEL.	CABLES.	BEDS.	TARIFF PER PERSON PER DAY		REMARKS.
PARIS, Avda. de Mayo and Salta.	—	160	$12–20	With pension	
CECIL, Avda. de Mayo 1201.		180	$15–20	With ,,	
GRAND, Florida 25.	"Granhotel"	150	$15–30 With ,, $ 8–20 Without ,.		Commercial.
AVENIDA PALACE, Victoria 442.	"Avenipal"	150	$12–16 With ,, $ 7–10 Without ,,		
LONDRES, Victoria 386.	—	200	$10	Without ,,	
CAVIEZEL, Avda. de Mayo 815.	—	65	$ 5–15	Without ,,	} Portuguese and Brazilian.
CAVIEZEL'S NEW, Avda. de Mayo 915		80	$10–15	With ,,	
APOLO, San Martin 365.	—	80	$10–15	With ,,	
GRAN HOTEL ESPAÑA, Avda. de Mayo 916.	—	360	$ 4–10	Without ,,	Spanish.
GRAN HOTEL FRASCATI, Avda. de Mayo 1086.	—	100	$10–15	With ,,	Italian.
GARDEN, Callao 950	—	60	$12–20	—	Superior Boarding House.
L'UNIVERSELLE, Reconquista 325.	—	50	$ 6–10	With pension	
DEUX MONDES, San Martin 391.	—	35	$ 7–12	With ,,	

Restaurants :—Sportsman, Plaza Grill Room; Paris Hotel, Petit Salon, Savoy Grill Room, Conte, Cangallo 960.

Excursions:—To Tigre, the local Henley, by Central Argentine Railway electric service. Here are many boating clubs :(the Marina, Tigre, Buenos Aires, the Argentine, and the headquarters of the Yachting Club. Gala days, March 25 and November 11, when International Regattas take place.

To Mar del Plata, the Brighton of Argentina, by B.A. Great Southern Railway. Quequen and Necochea are growing seaside resorts on B.A. Great Southern Railway.

To Rosario de Santa Fé, by Central Argentine Railway. The second city of Argentina.

To Sierras de Córdoba, by Central Argentine and Central Córdoba Railways. A favourite hill resort.

To Mendoza at foot of the Andes by B.A. Pacific Railway

To Falls of Iguazú.

To Paraguay by river steamer or train.

To La Plata, Great Southern Railway

Golf:—Numerous courses in the suburbs.

Local Steamship Services :—

To Montevideo daily, by Argentine Steam Navigation Co. steamers. To Asunción (twice weekly), Rosario and Sante Fé weekly (Mihanovich) by River Paraná.

British Shops :—British Pharmacy, Florida, 716, Brown & Co., Outfitters, Cangallo, 684, Burberrys, Ltd., Avenida del Mayo, 1268, English Pharmacy, Reconquista, 416, Diego Gibson, Chemist, Defensa, 168, and Florida, 159, Robert Grant, Bookseller, Cangallo, 342, A. N Guy, Jeweller, Cangallo, 540, Hamptons, Ltd., Sarmiento, 643, Harrod's Stores, Florida, 877, Lacey and Sons, Outfitters, Maipú, 95; Lamson Paragon Supply Co., Stationers, Corrientes,

ARGENTINA.

462, George McHardy, Outfitters, Maipú, 250, C. Mackern, News-agent, Reconquista, 449, Maples, Ltd., Suipacha, 658, Mappin and Webb, Ltd., Florida, 36, Mitchell's English Bookstall, Cangallo, 567, Sumner, Permain & Co., Wine Merchants, Avenida Leandro N Alem, 102, Waring and Gillows, Ltd., Avenida Alvear, 1572.

Markets :—The principal is Calle Cangallo, corner of Calle Carlos Pellegrini.

Conveyances :—Electric cars serve all parts of the city and certain places 20 to 25 miles out. From the Plaza Mayo to the Western suburbs there is an underground electric railway   Taxi-cabs.

Suburbs of Buenos Aires.

Tigre on the Central Argentine Railway, about 18 miles from Buenos Aires. There is a good road for automobiles. It is a centre for yachting and rowing. Hotel Tigre, 200 beds. $20/38 per day.

Hurlingham, on the Pacific Railway, about half an hour's journey of 17 miles. Has a fine club, the principal sports are polo, cricket, golf, and tennis. Almost all the residents are British.

Belgrano, about 10 minutes by train and 25 by tram. A suburb of modern houses, and a favourite resort of British residents. There are cricket and tennis clubs, an English high school, and church.

Flores, about 10 minutes by train from Plaza Once, the terminus of the Western Railway, and 25 from Plaza Victoria by tram.

San Isidro, on the Central Argentine Railway and the left bank of the river Paraná.

Temperley, a junction on the Great Southern Railway, about 20 miles from Plaza Constitución. Fine country houses and many British residents.

Lomas, also on the Great Southern Railway Club and golf links, English school for boys and girls, and church.

Quilmes, population 43,000, on the Great Southern Railway. Many British residents, and English college and church. Two miles inland from the River Plate. A noted brewing centre.

Rosario, the chief city of the province of Santa Fé, stands on the river Paraná, population 250,000. It ranks next to Buenos Aires and has on a slightly smaller scale all the activities of the Federal capital; it is growing rapidly, and each decade brings a growth in the network of railways connecting it with every part of the Republic. It is the natural port of N W Argentina. There is a British Chamber of Commerce at Entre Rios, 679.

Hotels :—Savoy, Calle San Martin; Italia, Calle Maipú.

Restaurants :—Rotisserie Cifre, Rotisserie Italia, and Rotisserie Savoy

Markets :—Mercado Central, Calle San Martin; also Mercados Norte, Sud, Este and Oeste. Best time, 6-8 a.m.

ARGENTINA.

Points of Interest :—Parque Independencia (New Rose Garden), Boulevard Oroño, Parish Church (Roman Catholic) in Calle 25 de Mayo, S. Bartholomew's Church (English), Calle Paraguay; Racecourse, Law Courts, Alberdi (by boat), Saladillo (salt water springs). Golf Club, Station, Parada Links, F.C.C.A.

Conveyances :—Electric cars. Cabs.

Garages :—Several in the centre of the city   Hire according to h.p.

Railways :—Rosario is 4½ hours from Buenos Aires on the Central Argentine Railway, and is served also by the Province of Santa Fé Railway (narrow gauge), and the Rosario and Puerto Belgrano Railway   Express trains to Córdoba, Tucumán, and Santa Fé, morning. Daily express to Buenos Aires.

Córdoba, the capital city of the province of the same name, is famous for the scenery of its mountain districts.   The city is called by the Argentines " La Ciudad Docta," or learned city, on account of its university (founded 1613)   Córdoba is picturesquely situated in the valley of the river Primero and has a famous observatory, the " Greenwich " of Argentina. Population 160,000.

Conveyances :—Cabs, and electric trams.

Hotels :—Plaza (140 beds, $15-30), Plaza San Martin.

Points of Interest :—The churches.

Excursions :—To Alta Córdoba by electric car and then to Chalet Crisol and Parque Sarmiento, a park on the outskirts of the city where is a Zoological Garden. Rail or motor-car to the following places in the Sierras de Córdoba, famous as health and pleasure resorts, within a few hours' journey of the city   To Alta Gracia (one hour) (Sierras hotel, from $11 a day). To La Falda (Eden Hotel, from $10 a day). To La Cumbre (Hotel Lumsdaine, from $10 a day). To Capilla del Monte (Hotel Britanico, from $10 a day). To Capilla del Monte (Hotel Victoria, from $10 a day). New branch lines opened by the Central Córdoba to the hills. To Ascochinga, in the heart of the Sierras, for shooting, fishing, etc., with good hotel accommodation. Particulars of Córdoba hill resorts can be obtained from the Publicity Department of the Central Argentine Railway, Bme. Mitre 299, Buenos Aires.

La Plata, the capital of the province of Buenos Aires, dates from 1882. It contains wide streets and imposing public buildings. Otherwise known by the names of " model city," the " enchanted city," and similar titles, because, like the fabled buildings of the fairy tales, it was built in a night, La Plata remains a monument of the days when the tide of capital reached its flood mark.   Population 150,000.

Points of Interest:—Natural History Museum (with the finest collection of extinct animals in the world) , well-laid-out Zoological Gardens ; fine racecourse (under B.A. Jockey Club rules) and Observatory   The Museum, Zoological Gardens, and Observatory are all in the public park. The Town Hall and Cathedral are in the Plaza Morena.

Hotels:—" Sportsman " and " El Argentino."

Conveyances:—Electric trams, motor cars and cabs.

Railways:—Great Southern to Buenos Aires.

Bahia Blanca is a port in the province of Buenos Aires, south of the capital, at the mouth of the Naposta river   Population about 80,000. The city is the great grain-shipping port for the south of the Argentine Republic.

Landing :—From steamer to wharf.

Conveyances :—Electric cars, motor-cars and coach.

Hotels :—Sud Americano, Avenida Colón, 122 (corner of Calle Brown). Rate per day, from $8 m/n.

Restaurant :—Universal, Calle O'Higgins, 138.
Post Office :—Calle Zellerayan, 101
Market :—Near Pacific Railway Station.
Excursions :—To Sierra de la Ventana, 2½ hours' rail.
Points of Interest :—Military Port. Arsenal (with largest dry dock in Southern Hemisphere). Town Hall. Municipal Palace.

Served by the Buenos Aires Great Southern and Buenos Aires and Pacific Railways.

Tucumán, capital of the province, is the busiest and most populous town in the north of Argentina, with a population of about 100,000. Chief centre of the sugar industry It has a cathedral and Jesuits' College, and here the first congress of the Republic was held in 1816. On the Central Argentine Railway, 25 hours from Buenos Aires.

HOTELS :—Savoy, Artigas, Frascati.

Mendoza, capital of the province, 620 miles from Buenos Aires on the Transcontinental railway to Valparaiso. Important wine, grape, and fruit centre. Has a national college, and a school of agriculture, centre of a cattle-raising district. Population about 64,000. Suffered severely from earthquake in 1861 About 26 hours from Buenos Aires on the Buenos Aires and Pacific Railway.

HOTELS :—Rivierre, Sierra, Grand.

Santa Fé, capital of the province, on the Paraná, 295 miles from Buenos Aires. Population about 80,000. Seat of a Jesuit College. Two large docks for ocean-going steamers. Principal exports, cereals, and quebracho. On the Central Argentine, Central Norte Argentino, and Provincial Government Railways.

HOTELS :—España, Italiano, Globo, Internacional.

Paraná :—Port on the right bank of the Paraná. Important cereal centre. Railway connection with Buenos Aires. Population, 76,800.

HOTELS :—España, Central, Cransac.

Mercedes, an important agricultural and pastoral centre; 98 kilometres from Buenos Aires on the Buenos Aires Western Railway 15,000 inhabitants.

HOTELS :—Mercédes, Nogues, Iris.

Salta :—Provincial capital. Notable for leather and goatskins. Population, 37,600. On the Central Norte Argentino Railway, 925 miles from Buenos Aires.

HOTELS :—Nacional, Colón, Casino.

Mar del Plata, about 8 hours from Buenos Aires on Great Southern Railway, is the Brighton of Argentina, and has good hotels and golf links.

HOTELS :—Bristol (400 beds, $25.50), Grand (100 beds, $15 30), Victoria (100 beds, $15.30), Royal (120 beds, $15,30)

Alta Gracia :—Some 570 metres above sea-level in the pure and bracing air of the Sierras de Córdoba, the town is reached by the Central Argentine Railway from Buenos Aires in 15 hours. Sleeping accommodation is provided on the train.

HOTEL :—Sierras (200 suites), good 9-hole golf course, tennis, croquet and shooting.

Puente del Inca :—A famous natural bridge of rock, crosses the Mendoza river   Hotel under the management of the South American Hotels Co.   Near the thermal baths of Cacheuta.   Served by the Buenos Aires and Pacific Railway

PHYSICAL CHARACTERISTICS.

The greater part of Argentina lies in the temperate zone and is divisible into three regions   the Andine, the Pampean, and the Patagonian.

The Andine occupies the eastern slope of the Cordillera of the Andes, of which several branches penetrate into the country, notably the Sierra del Aconquija, the Sierras of Córdoba and of San Luis.

The Pampa, or plain land, affords pasture for immense herds of cattle, and produces great crops of cereals.   Upon it exist great agricultural colonies.   In the northern territory, between the Salado and the Pilcomayo rivers, are forests containing timber for cabinet work and rougher purposes.

Rivers :—The more important parts of the basins both of the Paraná and the River Plate belong to Argentina.   The Paraná and Paraguay rivers are navigable for steamers everywhere within the republic.   The Salado, Pilcomayo and Bermejo, tributaries of the Paraná, are shallow and difficult of navigation.   The chief rivers of the south, the Colorado, Negro, Chubut, Chico, and Santa Cruz, flow directly into the Atlantic.

Small lakes are scattered over the pampas, and large and beautiful lakes exist farther south, at the base of the Andes, including Nahuel Huapi, Viedma, and Argentino.

River communication between Buenos Aires and the northern provinces, as well as the Republics of Paraguay and Uruguay, is afforded by the rivers Plata, Paraná, Uruguay, and Paraguay.

There is an efficient service between Buenos Aires and Asunción, and transit by water between the capital and Rosario.

With the extreme southern territories communication is only possible by sea. There are regular sailings between the ports situated in the Chubut, Santa Cruz, and Tierra del Fuego territories, and those of Buenos Aires and Bahia Blanca.

Patagonia, the most southerly part of the Argentine Republic, consists of vast plains or plateaux stretching from the Cordilleras to the Atlantic. Fresh water is scarce, but brackish lakes or pools are found. Towards the Straits of Magellan the country is wooded.

The **climate** is considered one of the most favourable for European immigration in the Latin-American continent. There are broadly three climatic zones the Littoral, the Mediterranean, and the Andine. The mean temperature in the first is 66° Fahr ; in the second 105° is frequently attained in very hot summers, with low temperatures registered in the winter—the mean being about 61° In the Andine region the climate varies greatly, and fluctuations of 36° within twenty-four hours are not uncommon.

Rain is frequent, especially in the N and E., and tends to make the temperature milder Endemic complaints are much rarer than in Europe.

Fauna and Flora :—The chief source of wealth lies in cattle, sheep, horses, mules, goats, and hogs. Among wild animals the puma, jaguar, armadillo, guanaco, vicuña, tapers, ant-eaters, and various sorts of deer are found. There is an abundance of bird life, ranging from condors, ostriches, flamingoes, and penguins down to partridges, parrots, pigeons, and cardinal birds. Land and fresh-water tortoises are fairly common. The iguana, viper, and rattlesnake haunt various parts of the republic.

AN ARGENTINE CALENDAR.

1515. Rio de la Plata entered by Juan Diaz de Solis, who lands on the Uruguayan coast and is murdered by Charrúa Indians.
1520. Mouth of the Rio de la Plata explored by Magellan.
1526. First settlement on banks of river founded by Sebastian Cabot; subsequently destroyed by Indians.
1530. Portuguese expedition under Martin Affonso de Sousa explores Rio de la Plata.
1536. First city of Buenos Aires founded by Pedro de Mendoza. Owing to Indian hostility settlement subsequently abandoned, and the Spaniards proceed upstream to Asunción in Paraguay
1573. City of Santa Fé founded by Juan de Garay
1580. Buenos Aires founded for the second time by Juan de Garay
1591. Hernandarias becomes the first colonial Governor of the Rio de la Plata (Paraguay and Argentina).
1595. Negroes first introduced into Rio de la Plata.
1600. Buenos Aires is permitted to export some of its produce to Brazil.
1610. First arrival of Jesuit missionaries.
1618. Province of Rio de la Plata officially instituted with separate Governor.
1665. Royal Audience established in Buenos Aires, but abolished in 1672.
1726. War between Brazil and Buenos Aires.
1735. Jesuits expelled from Rio de la Plata.
1750. Treaty between Brazil and Buenos Aires.
1762. War between Brazil and Buenos Aires.
1776. Establishment of the Vice-Royalty of Buenos Aires, with jurisdiction extending over the present Republics of Bolivia (part), Uruguay, Paraguay, and the Argentine Confederation. Shelter huts constructed in the Andes to facilitate journeys to Chile. War between Buenos Aires and Brazil.

ARGENTINA.

1777   Treaty between Buenos Aires and Brazil.
1794.   Irish colony of meat curers established in La Plata. First merino sheep introduced.
1801.   Foundation of the first River Plate newspaper.
1806.   First British expedition to the River Plate, commanded by General Beresford. Buenos Aires captured, but after an occupation of forty-five days, recaptured by Spanish and Argentine troops under a French officer, Liniers. Liniers proclaimed Viceroy
1807.   Montevideo captured by Brig.-General Auchmuty General Whitelocke leads an expedition against Buenos Aires, which results in failure. The British forces evacuate the Rio de la Plata.
1809.   Cisneros replaced Liniers as Viceroy
1810.   Independence of Argentina declared on May 25 Resignation of the Spanish Viceroy Cisneros. Cornelio Saavedra elected President of the Primera Junta, the other members being Juan José Castelli, Manuel Belgrano, Miguel Azcuénaga, Juan Larrea, Domingo Mathieu, and Manuel Alberdi.
1811.   First naval battle fought between Spanish and Argentine vessels.
1812.   San Martin lands in the Rio de la Plata. General Belgrano gains a victory over the Spaniards near Tucumán.
1813.   San Martin clears the Paraná of the Spanish forces.
1814.   Belgrano and Rivadavia proceed on a mission to Europe. Admiral Brown gains a victory over the Spanish fleet off Montevideo. Argentina divided into seven provinces Buenos Aires, Entre Rios, Corrientes, Córdoba, Cuyo, Tucumán, and Salta.
1815.   Alvear made President.
1816.   Formal Declaration of Independence made at Tucumán.
1817.   San Martin leads the army of liberation across the Andes to Chile.
1822.   San Martin leaves Argentina for Europe.
1824.   First South Down sheep introduced into Argentina.
1825.   Foundation of the Scottish Colony at Monte Grande. National Congress organized by Bernadino Rivadavia. Federated Constitution decreed for Argentina. First Treaty of Peace signed between Argentina and Great Britain.
1826.   Bernadino Rivadavia made President. Argentina negotiates in London a loan for £1,000,000. Naval action between Argentina and Brazil off Buenos Aires.
1827   Alvear defeats the Brazilians at Ituzaingo.
1828.   Struggle between Rosas and Lavalle.
1829.   Juan Manuel de Rosas defeats the Unitarians at Puente Marquez and is created Dictator of the Republic.
1838.   Buenos Aires blockaded by the French Fleet.
1841.   Death of General Lavalle.
1843.   Admiral Brown blockades Montevideo.
1844.   Introduction of wire fencing. First South Down ram imported.
1845.   Combined British and French squadrons ascend the River Plate. Blockade of Buenos Aires by these forces until 1847
1849.   Rosas declares war on Brazil.
1850.   Death of San Martin at Boulogne. Royal Mail Steam Packet Co. begins its mail service.
1851.   Rosas defeated near Buenos Aires by Urquiza. Rosas and his daughter escorted to Southampton in a British warship. Urquiza becomes Dictator of Argentina.
1853.   Modern Federal Constitution drawn up. Urquiza elected President of Buenos Aires.
1857   Construction of Western Railway begun.
1861.   General Bartolomé Mitre defeats Urquiza. Bartolomé Mitre elected President.
1863.   Construction of Central Argentine Railway begun.
1864.   Construction of Buenos Aires Great Southern Railway begun.
1865.   Outbreak of war with Paraguay Establishment of the Welsh colony at Chubut.
1866.   Sociedad Rural Argentina founded.
1870.   Conclusion of the Paraguayan War Establishment of the Henley Agricultural Colony
1871.   Sarmiento elected President. Yellow fever attacks Buenos Aires.
1874.   Dr. Nicolas Avellaneda elected President.
1878-9.   General Julio Roca finally subdues the warlike Indian tribes and opens up much new territory
1880.   General Roca elected President of the Republic.

ARGENTINA.

1883. Process of freezing mutton begun in Argentina.
1886. Dr Juárez Celman elected President.
1890. After a revolution Pellegrini comes into office.
1892. Dr Luis Saenz Peña elected President.
1895. Vice-President Uriburu made President.
1898. General Roca re-elected President.
1901. Beginning of a frontier dispute with Chile.
1902. On conclusion of the Holdich Boundary Delimitation treaty signed with Chile.
1905. Manuel Quintana made President.
1906. Quintana dies and is succeeded by Dr Alcorta. Death of General Mitre and Pellegrini.
1910. Dr. Roque Saenz Peña made President.
1916. Dr. Roque Saenz Peña dies and is succeeded by the Vice-President La Plaza. Hipólito Irigoyen elected President.
1922. Dr Marcelo T de Alvéar elected President.

GOVERNMENT

The form of Government is modelled on that of the United States, or the " representative, republican, federal " system. The Central Government deals with such matters as affect the State as a whole, but the governors of the provinces have extensive powers, and are elected for terms of three or four years. The National Territories (those portions of the country which are not yet ranked as provinces) are administered by officials nominated directly by the President. The municipal government of the capital is exercised by a Mayor appointed by the President with the approval of the Senate, and a deliberative council elected by the taxpayers. The Argentine political constitution is exceptionally liberal.

PAST PRESIDENTS
(since 1861).

General Bartolomé Mitre	1862
Dr Domingo Faustino Sarmiento	1868
Dr. Nicolás Avellaneda	1874
General Julio A. Roca	1880
Dr. Miguel Juárez Celman (resigned)	1886
Dr Carlos Pellegrini	1890
Dr. Luis Saenz Peña (resigned)	1892
Dr. José E. Uriburu	1895
General Julio A. Roca (second term)	1898
Dr Manuel Quintana (died in office)	1904
Dr José Figueroa Alcorta	1906
Dr. Roque Saenz Peña (died in office)	1910
Dr Victorino de la Plaza	1916
Dr. Hipólito Irigoyen	1916

PRESIDENTS.

President	Dr. Marcelo T de Alvear (1922–28).
President of Senate	Dr. Elpidio González.
President of the Chamber of Deputies	A. Goyeneche.

MINISTRY

Interior	Dr. José Nicolas Matienzo.
Foreign Affairs	Dr Angel Gallardo.
War	Dr Coronel Agustin P Justo.
Navy	Almirante Manuel Domecq García.
Justice and Public Instruction	Dr. Celestino J Marcó.
Finance	Dr. Rafael Herrera Vegas.
Agriculture	Dr. Tomás A. Le Breton.
Public Works	Dr. Eufrasio S. Loza.

45

Federal **Courts** deal with cases of national importance. They consist of the Supreme Courts, having five judges at Buenos Aires, five Appeal Courts, one with five judges at Buenos Aires and others with three judges each at La Plata, Paraná, Córdoba, and Rosario (Santa Fé), and courts of first instance in each of the provinces and territories.

CURRENCY

Public accounts are kept in paper **currency**—the paper dollar, under conversion law, being reckoned approximately at 1s. 9d. The chief contributory items of the revenue are export and import duties, tobacco, stamped paper, posts and telegraphs.

Argentine currency is governed by the Conversion Law (No. 3871 of 1899), which provides that paper money shall be converted into gold at the rate of 44 centavos gold for every 100 centavos paper, thus fixing the value of $227·27 m/n for each $100 gold. Paper currency is issued by the Caja de Conversion against delivery of gold at the above-mentioned rate. In normal times it delivers gold against notes, but under emergency legislation of 1914 the delivery of gold against paper money was temporarily suspended. The gold peso is distinguished by the sign $ o/s, oro sellado (coined gold), and the paper peso by $ m/n, moneda nacional (national money), the abbreviations usually following the figures, e.g., $500 o/s, $500 m/n. The only money in circulation is the paper money

£1 sterling = $5·04 Argentine gold.

Silver coins = 5, 10, 20, and 50 cents and 1 peso, also nickel coins of 5, 10, 20 and 50 cents.

The par rate of exchange for the gold dollar is 47·62 pence. The Argentine gold dollar is intrinsically worth $0·9649 U.S.

WEIGHTS AND MEASURES.

The legal system is the metric, but the Spanish system is also used and in some places the old Argentine system :

WEIGHTS.

1 Grano	=	0·769273 grain (avoirdupois).
1 Adarme (36 granos)	=	27·693832 grains.
1 Onza (16 adarmes)	=	1·012803 ounces.
1 Libra (16 onzas)	=	1·012803 pounds.
1 Arroba (25 libras)	=	25·320080 pounds.
1 Quintal (4 arrobas)	=	3·617153 quarters.
1 Tonelada (20 quintals)	=	0·904288 ton.
1 Kilo	=	2·205 lbs.
1 Metric Ton	= {	1,000 kilos. 2,204 6 lb. ·984 ton.

Weights for Gold and Silver

1 Grano	=	0·769273 grain troy
1 Quilate (4 granos)	=	3·077092 grains troy
1 Onza (144 quilates)	= {	18·462555 dwts. troy 0·923128 ounce troy
1 Marco (8 onzas)	=	7·385022 ounces troy

ARGENTINA.

Weights in Use for Hides and Sheepskins.

A pesada of dry hides (35 libras)   = 35·448105 pounds.
A pesada of salted hides (60 libras)   = 60·76818 pounds.
A pesada of washed sheepskins (30 libras) = 30·38409 pounds.

LINEAL MEASURES.

1 Pulgada	= 0·947086 in.
1 Pie (12 pulgadas)	= 0·947086 ft.
1 Vara (3 pies)	= $\begin{cases} 0·947086 \text{ yd.} \\ 2·841258 \text{ ft.} \end{cases}$
1 Metre	= 39·371 met. in.
1 Kilometre	= $\begin{cases} 1,000 \text{ metres.} \\ 0·62 \text{ mile.} \end{cases}$

1 Legua (Spanish) (league) = 6,000 varas = 3·228703 miles.
1 Legua (Argentine) (league) = 3·106912 miles.
The square legua (square league) varies in some provinces and in the National Territories.
In Buenos Aires Province, 1 square league = 1,600 squares = 6,672 acres.
National lands. 1 square league = 1,600 squares = 6,177·85 acres.

CAPACITY (DRY).

1 Cuartilla	= 7·549188 gallons (0·9436485 bushel)
1 Fanega (4 cuartillas)	= 30·196752 ,, (3·774594 bushels)

CAPACITY (LIQUID).

1 Cuarta	= 1·04552 pints (0·52276 quart).
1 Frasco	= 4·18208 pints (2·09104 quarts).
1 Galón	= 6·691328 pints (3·345664 quarts).
1 Barril	= 66·91328 quarts (16·72832 gallons).
1 Pipa	= 401·47968 quarts (100·36992 gallons).
1 Litre	= 1·76 pints.
1 Hectolitre	= 22 gallons.

POPULATION OF PROVINCES AND TERRITORIES.

The population at the Census of 1914 was 7,885,237   The estimated population on December 31, 1920, was 9,500,000.

(Post-census estimate of December 31, 1918.)

Federal District :—Federal Capital (Buenos Aires) and Island of Martin Garcia 1,750,000.

Provinces.	Population.	Capital.
Buenos Aires	2,235,756	La Plata.
Santa Fé	967,189	Santa Fé.
Entre Rios	452,796	Paraná.
Corrientes	362,115	Corrientes.
Córdoba	776,155	Córdoba.
San Luis	126,585	San Luis.
Santiago del Estero	288,956	Santiago del Estero.
Tucumán	354,425	Tucumán.
Mendoza	302,113	Mendoza.
San Juan	130,066	San Juan.
La Rioja	83,882	La Rioja.
Catamarca	108,128	Catamarca.
Salta	150,768	Salta.
Jujuy	78,909	Jujuy
Territories.		
Chaco	49,593	Resistencia.
Chubut	26,762	Rawson.
Formosa	20,945	Formosa.
La Pampa	115,320	Santa Rosa.
Los Andes	2,588	San Antonio de Los Cobres.
Misiones	58,869	Posadas.
Neuquen	31,304	Neuquen.
Rio Negro	45,695	Viedma.
Santa Cruz	11,101	Gallegos.
Tierra del Fuego	2,537	Ushuaia.

AGRICULTURAL WEALTH.

Cereals :—The principal crops are wheat, linseed, maize, oats, and alfalfa. Barley, vines, potatoes, and sugar-cane are also cultivated, in 1922, there were under cultivation wheat, 6,507,800 hectares, linseed, 1,638,610 hectares, 1923 maize, 3,177,155 hectares, oats, 1,059,350 hectares, barley, 242,850 hectares, rye, 86,955 hectares. It is estimated that in 1921 there were under cultivation wheat, 6,076,100 hectares, linseed, 1,409,850 hectares, maize, 3,200,000 hectares, oats, 835,000 hectares.

Exports.

Year	Wheat. Tons.	Maize. Tons.	Linseed. Tons.	Oats. Tons.
1917	935,828	893,939	141,308	271,713
1918	2,996,408	664,683	391,382	542,097
1919	3,286,260	2,485,465	855,455	333,243
1920	5,029,958	4,387,736	1,014,840	410,539
1921	1,703,330	2,829,174	1,351,002	394,437
1922	3,753,793	2,849,933	933,343	282,252

The United Kingdom is the largest customer for Argentine cereals.

It was only in 1912 that **dairying** began to be developed on a sound basis. A great impetus was given by the war, when production and export reached record figures, owing to the purchase by the British Government of the entire output available for export. Total shipments of butter for 1922 estimated in cases, 782,643. The Latin races prefer oil to butter for cooking operations, and use relatively a small quantity of butter as a direct food.

The **wine**-growing industry is centred in the provinces of Mendoza and San Juan, where the vineyards are cultivated by the aid of irrigation, and also in La Rioja, Catamarca, Salta and Neuquen. Seasons of over-production and speculation in vineland values have caused periodical crises, but the industry is now on a sounder basis.

The best **timber** is found in the sub-tropical forest region, which comprises the plains of Santiago del Estero and the Chaco, the lowlands of Tucumán, Salta, and Jujuy, Northern Corrientes, and Misiones. The forests furnish some thirty varieties of wood. The tree with the greatest commercial value is the red quebracho, yielding tannin extract.

The province of Tucumán is the chief centre of the **sugar** industry, but it is also cultivated in the provinces of Jujuy, Salta, and Santa Fé. The average consumption of sugar in Argentina is 200,000 tons.

Tobacco is both grown and manufactured in Argentina. Planters have introduced a coarse grade Kentucky tobacco in the province of Buenos Aires. It is almost exclusively used for the coarse Italian type of cigars known as " toscanos " smoked by the labouring classes.

Number of establishments (1914), 234.

Value of production, $M/N.35,604,030.

Forty per cent. of the material of cigars and cigarettes is of national production.

Wool on the Buenos Aires market is quoted in paper dollars and per 10 kilos. Sheep's wool is dealt in mainly in the following eight qualities :—

Fine Cross Bred : good to superior, inferior to medium; Medium Cross Bred : good to superior, inferior to medium, Coarse Cross Bred : good to superior, inferior to medium, Rambouillet good to superior, inferior to medium.

Lamb's wool in the following four qualities :—

Fine Cross Bred good to superior; Medium Cross Bred · good to superior; Coarse Cross Bred good to superior, Fine Rambouillet good to superior.

Sheepskins in Buenos Aires are quoted in paper dollars per kilo, and in the following chief kinds :—

Unshorn Skins good to superior, inferior to medium, Shorn Skins and Quarter Woolled , Lambs.

The principal wool-producing provinces are Buenos Aires, Entre Rios, Santa Cruz, Rio Negro, Corrientes, La Pampas, Chubut, Córdoba, Neuquen, Tierra del Fuego, Santiago de Estero, San Luis.

Reliable figures are not available, but it is generally agreed in farming circles that the sheep stock has been considerably reduced during the past three years. The slump in wool and mutton values came earlier than in beef and cattle products.

For many years past Argentine exports of **hides** have averaged some 5,000,000 annually, of which over 3,000,000 are wet salted hides from the meat-freezing establishments and the remainder dry hides. The United States is the principal market. The number of dry hides exported during the first seven months of 1922 were 1,593,670 and of salt hides 2,168,675, showing a great increase on the corresponding amounts for the previous year

ARGENTINE INDUSTRIES.

Industry in Argentina has been directed of late years towards turning agricultural wealth to the greatest possible profit. Meat freezing, flour milling, sugar and wine production have been followed by dairying, brewing, lumbering, and the manufacture of tanning extract. Industries which have benefited by war conditions include the manufacture of wool cloths, stockings, footwear, harness and saddlery, boots, bags, hats, buttons, perfumery, jewellery, toys, enamelled goods, glassware, electrical appliances, soap, candles, vegetable oils, chemical products, firebricks, chocolate, sweets, cements, furniture, beer, tobacco, iron and steel manufactures, vehicles and household utensils. The manufacture of paper is increasing, and pulp is being made in the country

The Argentine tanning and leather industry has become an important one, and further series of industries which have been

started in the manufacture of edible oils, production and preparation of rice, fruit canning and preserving, malt, fishing, leather
industry, cotton and wool weaving, cordage and rope making,
agricultural machinery, candle making, manufacture of powder
and explosives, distillation of wood.

Meat refrigeration is still the foremost Argentina industry,
depending on the United Kingdom as a consuming market, and
based originally on the provision of British and United States
capital. In the year ended 31 August, 1922, approximately
1,750,000 head of cattle and 3,200,000 head of sheep and lambs
were disposed of for export. These numbers included cattle slaughtered for canning and meat extract, and a relatively small number
of cattle and sheep exported on the hoof. The total exports of
refrigerated meat during the twelve months ended 31 August,
compared with those of the two preceding years, were as follows :—

Year.	Beef—Quarters.		
	Chilled.	Frozen.	Total.
1921–22	3,248,706	2,417,100	5,665,806
1920–21	1,406,934	4,853,481	6,260,415
1919–20	306,192	6,186,640	6,492,832

Year.	Mutton—Carcases.		
	Sheep.	Lambs.	Total.
1921–22	2,034,414	1,059,083	3,093,497
1920–21	1,890,782	962,681	2,853,463
1919–20	1,448,326	366,263	1,814,589

Recent changes in the meat business and the inclusion of Dutch
capital have led to probabilities of working up a Continental trade
in frozen meat. There is evident an increasing interest on the part
of Continental butchers in the possibilities of Argentine meat,
and no trade which promises to relieve the stock of second grade
cattle is negligible.

The saladeros are the slaughtering yards preparing meat for
canning, drying and the manufacture of meat extract. The
freezing works at which meat is chilled and frozen for export are
known as frigorificos. Both are supplied with cattle by the
estancieros, who breed cattle upon the estancias or farms.

Flour Milling has risen to the front rank of Argentine industries,
and has an annual production second only to the meat-packing
industry.

Year.	Production. Tons.	Exportation. Tons.
1917	938,747 .	112,465
1918 .	1,081,269	. 176,445
1919 .	1,071,863	328,107
1920	930,569	172,971
1921	—	46,566
1922	—	92,103

MINERAL WEALTH OF ARGENTINA.

Oil is found in several parts of the Republic from Comodoro Rivadavia in the South to the province of Jujuy in the extreme North.

Considerable development has taken place in Comodoro Rivadavia, where oil was first discovered in 1908.

The Argentine Government has undertaken prospecting operations in the Plaza Huincul Oilfield in the territory of Neuquen, and has completed several productive wells. The quality is very high grade, containing over 60 per cent. of light products, comparing more than favourably with the oil found at Comodoro Rivadavia, which is essentially a fuel oil, containing less than 10 per cent. of light products.

Several wells have been drilled in the Cacheuta district in the province of Mendoza, the first oil wells drilled in the Argentine Republic were sunk in this area in 1886. The oil obtained in this district contains a large proportion of paraffin wax.

The most important gold deposits are found in the territory of Los Andes, and parts of Jujuy, Salta, and Catamarca. Auriferous seams and quartz deposits exist in the provinces of San Juan, Mendoza, Córdoba, San Luis, and the territory of Neuquen. In many of these mines considerable workings have been carried out, but in no case have they been carried to success, owing partly to the deficient economic conditions of the region, partly to financial difficulties.

The zone of Puna de Atacama (comprising Los Andes and parts of Jujuy, Salta, and Catamarca) is an important silver-bearing region. Next comes the district of Famatina, in La Rioja, the mines of Guandacol in the same province, and several others in San Juan, Mendoza, Córdoba and Neuquen. Lead and zinc are found mingled with the silver-bearing minerals. The mines have been worked only superficially, chiefly owing to lack of good pumping apparatus.

In the North of Argentina the best-known deposits of copper lie in the district of San Antonio de los Cobres in the Puna de Atacama and in the province of Salta. Important deposits exist in the Capillitas district of Catamarca and in Famatina.

Wolfram and Tin are found in the provinces of San Luis, Catamarca, and La Rioja. New and important discoveries have been made in the sierras of Córdoba, Belén, Jujuy, and San Juan.

Other Minerals :—Vanadium mines form part of the Andine mineral system. Manganese has been found in abundance in Córdoba, Santiago del Estero, and Tucumán, with iron ore in conjunction. Sulphur has been worked to some extent, with asbestos, mica and talc.

Salt deposits are numerous. Great salt beds occupy the lower half of the extensive undrained basins of the central provinces and the best known are the " Salinas Grandes " in the Puna de Atacama. Other important sources are near the coast, such as Salinas Chicas, near Bahia Blanca. Borate fields are worked in the Puna region and elsewhere. Building stone, the ornamental stone known as Brazil onyx, marble and clay are worked in many places.

COMMERCIAL INFORMATION

Bankruptcy Law :—Bankruptcy applies where a person belongs to two or more companies, one of which is declared bankrupt.

A declaration of bankruptcy abroad cannot be invoked against creditors in the Republic.

Should the bankruptcy also be declared by the Tribunals in the Republic, the creditors abroad will not be taken into account except where there is a balance after the creditors in the Republic have been paid.

Should the bankrupt be a Company or Association which develops railways, water supply, lighting, irrigation canals, navigation, and other enterprises of national, provincial, or municipal interest it must continue to function.

It may, however, stop any part of the work which may be under construction, provided that said stoppage does not interfere with the regular working of the part already at work.

Proceedings in bankruptcy can only be started by a merchant, by one or more creditors, or by the Public Ministry in a case where a merchant has taken flight or is in hiding without leaving a representative to control his affairs and meet his obligations.

Bankruptcy can be declared after the death of a merchant if death occurred during suspension of payments. The petition must be filed within six months from death.

A person no longer a merchant can be declared bankrupt if stoppage of payments is due to obligations incurred before he gave up business. The petition must be filed within 12 months from his giving up business.

Declaration of bankruptcy of a Company (Sociedad Colectiva) or a Limited Company constitutes a state of bankruptcy for all the partners in it.

One partner being bankrupt does not constitute a Company bankrupt. His interest in the Company belongs to creditors in the Company or Association before his private creditors.

The **import tariff** in Argentina is in the main a valuation tariff. Values are assigned to goods belonging to particular classes and duties are levied upon these bases. Upon certain selected articles the duty is specific and levied upon the weight of the material. The Customs Law of 1923 adding 60 per cent to the rates in the valuation tariff and 25 per cent to the specific duties. requires that all tariffs and charges be calculated upon a gold basis. The net effect is to increase the import duties by an average of 40 per cent. and to make the tariff protective in a higher degree.

A proposal to exempt from import duty goods landed at Patagonian ports south of the 42nd parallel and latitude (i.e., south of Bahia Blanca) has been defeated.

POSTAL COMMUNICATION

Postage Rates :—Inland For each 20 grammes or fraction, 5 cents.

For countries not in Postal Union, for every 20 grammes, 24 cents.

For Bolivia, Chile, Colombia, Paraguay, Peru and Uruguay (the Postal Union of South America) Letters, 20 grammes or fraction, 10 cents, for every succeeding 20 grammes, 5 cents.

Telegraph rates Ordinary, first ten words (including name and address), 50 cents, each additional word, 3 cents, maximum limit, 100 words. Telegrams in foreign languages, double tariff English, French, Spanish, Italian, German, Latin, Portuguese only accepted. Code telegrams four times ordinary tariff

There are 12 **wireless** stations. All ships with crews of fifty or over touching at Argentine ports have to be equipped with wireless.

ARGENTINE COMMERCIAL INSTITUTIONS IN BUENOS AIRES.

Camara Oficial Española de Comercio, Industria, Navigación, y Bellas Artes en la República Argentina, Chacabuco, 869.

Camara Sindical de Comercio de Buenos Aires, Bartolomé Mitre, 544.

Centro de Importadores, Moreno, 452. Founded 1907 to further the development of the import trade.

Centro de Navigación Transatlantico, Bolsa de Comercio, Escritorio, 409. Founded 1900.

Chamber of Commerce of the United States of America in the Argentine Republic (Camara de Comercio en los Estados Unidos de America en la Republica Argentina), Bartolomé Mitre, 455.

Liga de Defensa Comercial, Bartolomé Mitre, 836, Buenos Aires. (Legal matters trade marks, patents, arbitrations, collections, etc.)

Sociedad Rural Argentina, Sarmiento, 834, Buenos Aires (with provincial branch towns). Holding annual stock shows and publishing information for stock-breeders.

Unión Industrial Argentina, Cangallo, 2461, Buenos Aires. Owners of industrial establishments, etc.

BRITISH INSTITUTIONS IN BUENOS AIRES.

Commercial :—The British Chamber of Commerce in the Argentine Republic, Inc. (Camara de Comercio Britanica en la República Argentina), Reconquista, 46, Buenos Aires. Address of London Representative 14, Queen Anne's Gate, Westminster, S.W.1

Philanthropic, etc. :—The British and American Benevolent Society (Sociedad Britanica y Norte-Americana de Beneficencia), 25 de Mayo, 159, Buenos Aires.

The British Society in the Argentine Republic (Sociedad Britanica en la República Argentina), Lavalle 349, Buenos Aires.

Buenos Aires Sailors' Home and Mission (Victoria Sailors' Home). Missionary and Manager, Mr. P J Wyatt, Independencia 20, Buenos Aires.

ARGENTINA.

The Salvation Army   Headquarters for South America : Calle Alsina 319 (Postal address, Casilla de Correo, 442), Buenos Aires.
Young Men's Christian Association. Paseo Colón, 161, Buenos Aires.
Other Institutions :—The British Institute, the British Hospital, and St. George's Hall. British Schools : St. George's College, Quilmes (Headmaster, Rev. G. H. Knight-Clarke); Laidlaw's English High School, Florida (Rector, J Laidlaw).
British and Foreign Bible Society   Secretary, W C. K. Torre, Tucumán, 854, Buenos Aires. London   146, Queen Victoria Street, E.C.4.

Clothing :—In Buenos Aires and the large towns of the South European town clothing is de rigueur   In the Northern provinces a costume suitable to the sub-tropics is desirable. When travelling by train in summer, it is necessary to take precautions against dust. Special coats are sold for this purpose in Buenos Aires.

PRESS.

The principal publications are : Buenos Aires, morning dailies : "La Nación' (special edition sent by aeroplane to Uruguay), "La Prensa," "La Argentina."
British : "The Standard," "The Herald."
Evening dailies   "La Razón," "La Epoca," "La Tarde," "El Diario," "La Tribuna," "La Ultima Hora."
Illustrated weeklies   "Caras y Caretas," "Fray Mocho, P.B.T.," "El Hogar," "El Mundo Argentino," "El Jockey "
British weeklies : "Review of the River Plate," "Journal of the River Plate."
About 125 organs of the Press are published in Buenos Aires alone.
Provincial Publications : Rosario, "La Capital" (daily), "La Critica" (evening daily).
Mendoza : "Los Andes" (daily).
Bahia Blanca : "Bahia Blanca " (daily).
Tucumán : "El Orden" (daily).

Interest in **aviation** has greatly increased in Argentina, arising out of the commercial missions from the United Kingdom, the United States, and Italy, and of official missions from France and Italy. The Aero Club of Argentina at Buenos Aires has has compiled regulations concerning aviation which are voluntarily accepted until superseded by legislation. In commercial aviation, the River Plate Aviation Company, founded in 1919 under British control, has carried large numbers of passengers.

PUBLIC HOLIDAYS.

January 1. New Year's Day.
January 6. Epiphany
February 2. The Purification.
March 25. Feast of the Incarnation.
May 25. Independence Day
June 29. Saints Peter and Paul.
July 9. Proclamation of Independence.
August 15. Assumption of Our Lady
August 30. Santa Rosa de Lima.
September 8. Birth of Our Lady.
October 12. Discovery of America.
November 1. All Saints' Day
December 8. Immaculate Conception.
December 25. Christmas Day.
Monday, Tuesday, and Wednesday of Carnival Week (week before Lent).
Corpus Christi, Thursday, Friday, and Saturday in Holy Week.
Buenos Aires alone, November 11; Saint Martin's Day (patron saint).
Each town celebrates the feast of its patron saint.

ARGENTINA.

BRITISH LEGATION IN ARGENTINA.

RESIDENCE.	RANK.	NAME.
Buenos Aires	Envoy Extraordinary and Minister Plenipotentiary	Sir B. F Alston, K.C.M.G., C.B.
	Second Secretary	J H. Leche, O.B.E.
	Commercial Secretary (first grade)	H. O. Chalkley, C.B.E.
	Translator	Chas. F A. Bristow.
	Archivist	E. Lamb.

BRITISH CONSULATES IN ARGENTINA.

The letter (M) denotes that the Consular Officer holds a Marriage Warrant. Members of the Diplomatic Service do not require Warrants.

RESIDENCE.	RANK.	NAME.	CONSULAR DISTRICTS.
Buenos Aires	(M) Consul-General	H. W Wilson, O.B.E.	
	(M) Vice-Consul	L. P Cross	
	Vice-Consul	Robert John Knox	
San Julian	Vice-Consul	R. Paterson	Argentine Republic with the exception of the provinces of Santa Fé, Córdoba, Corrientes, and Entre Rios.
Santa Cruz	Vice-Consul	L. A. Harris	
Comodoro Revadavia	Vice-Consul	M. M. Venter	
Bahia Blanca	Pro-Consul	G. H. Walsh	
		H. McRobbie	
Gallegos	Vice-Consul	Duncan M. Aitchison	
La Plata	Vice-Consul	S. H. Puleston	
	Pro-Consul	Wilfrid Puleston	
Mendoza	Vice-Consul	A. G. B. Taylor	
Port Madryn	Vice-Consul	H. C. H. James	Territories of Chubut and Santa Cruz.
Tucumán	Vice-Consul	Major Lloyd, D.S.O.	Provinces of Santa Fé, Córdoba, Corrientes and Entre Rios.
Rosario	(M) Consul	H. W W Bird	
Paraná	Vice-Consul	William Y. Mackinnon.	
Santa Fé	Vice-Consul	Robert H. Smiles	
Villa Constitución	Vice-Consul	F W Darch	

ARGENTINE LEGATION AND CONSULATES IN GREAT BRITAIN.

RESIDENCE.	DESIGNATION	NAME.
London (Aldford House, 26 Park Lane, W.1.)	Envoy Extraordinary and Minister Plenipotentiary	Doctor José Evaristo Uriburu.
	Counsellor	Paulino Llambi Campbell (absent).
	Counsellor	Luis H. Dominguez.
	Secretary	Carlos Miguens.
	Naval Attaché	Commander Leon L. Scasso.
	Financial Secretary	Carlos M. Dominguez.
London (7 Gower St., W.C.2.)	General Consul	Doctor Sergio Garcia Uriburu.
Liverpool	Consul	Juan Carlos Godoy
Cardiff	Consul	Estevan de Loqui.
Newport, Mon.	Consul	Arturo Parker.
Newcastle-on-Tyne	Consul	F. Datto Tessitore.
Glasgow	Consul	José Diaz Herrera.
Southampton	Consul	Carlos P Cadiz.
Swansea	Vice-Consul	Sidney Burgess.
Hull	In charge of Consulate	B. Dixon.
Belfast	Vice-Consul	Henry Tighe Rea.
Aberdeen	Vice-Consul	A. T. Cruickshanks.
Middlesbrough	Vice-Consul	J W. Brown.
Birmingham	Vice-Consul	J B. Hale.
Bristol	Vice-Consul	Maurice C. Houlder.

PASSENGERS' LUGGAGE.

Article 201 of the Regulations of Customs reads :—

" By Baggage shall be understood the clothes and articles of personal use belonging to passengers, and the clothes, furniture, and tools of immigrants, provided that the quantity thereof does not lead to the belief that they are going to be used for trading purposes."

The Buenos Aires Custom House will not permit to be landed as Baggage any package containing furniture, carriages, pianos, or anything of a similar nature measuring more than one cubic metre. Any such Baggage, exceeding such measurement or not, in accordance with Article 201 of the Customs Law, will have to be included in the General Manifest (as freight) and dealt with as ordinary cargo.

Baggage at Buenos Aires :—The Custom House Authorities at Buenos Aires insist on presentation of Baggage Declarations by all first and second class passengers landing at that port. A special form has been prepared in accordance with these requirements, and this must be filled in, in duplicate, one copy to be kept by the passenger for presentation in the Custom House and the other retained by the ship, to be handed to the Customs' Officials on arrival.

Passengers making tours round South America via the Andes are required to attend the clearance of their baggage at the frontier station Los Andes, during customs inspection, in order to obviate delay

---

Guidance for Commercial Travellers.

Commercial travellers are not required to register but they are required to pay heavy licences (known in Spanish as ''patentes'') Licences costing $500 to $5,000 paper pesos are payable to the Federal Government for permission to work in Buenos Aires, and there are provincial licences costing varying amounts for every province visited.

Until 1917 the Federal licence cost $500 but in that year the scale $500 to $5,000 was adopted. No basis is fixed for the graduation of the licence, and in practice the fee of $500 has invariably been charged. The Argentine Government has stated that the minimum of $500 will be applied in general, and increased proportionately for categories found to be of relatively greater commercial importance. The duration of the licence is for one calendar year, or what may remain of the calendar year when the licence is taken out, with the exception that on the occasion of a first visit a traveller need only pay for the remaining months in the year in which he arrives. The Federal licence is obtainable from the Administracion General de Contribucion Territorial de Patentes y Sellos, Calle San Martier, 561, Buenos Aires.

The penalty for contravention is immediate arrest, with detention for one month unless the licence fee and a fine of double the amount of the fee are paid. For a second offence detention may last two months.

Provincial licence fees may vary annually They were for 1921 :—

Jujuy :—200 pesos in respect of the representation of one firm and 100 pesos in respect of each additional firm represented.

Salta :—The tariff varies according to the class of goods offered for Textiles it is $800, for Haberdashery and Hardware, $500; for Hats, Boots, Groceries, or Perfumery, $400; for Spirits, Stationery, Lace, $300, Furniture, Drugs, China and Glass, $200, Biscuits, Confectionery, or Wallpaper, $100. Travellers selling general merchandise for one firm, pay a fee of $1,000.

Tucumán :—$600 for the first six months, $300 pesos for the second six months.

Córdoba :—$400 for the first six months, $200 pesos for the second six months.

Santa Fé :—$400 per annum.

San Juan :—$500 for the first four months, $400 for the second four months, $300 for the third four months.

Mendoza :—$500 for the first four months, $400 for the second four months, $300 for the third four months.

Corrientes :—$700 per annum plus an additional tax of 10 per cent., making a total of $770 per annum.

Santiago del Estero :—$300 for the first six months, $150 for the second six months.

La Rioja :—$200 for the first six months, $100 for the second six months.

Buenos Aires (province of) :—Firms established in the province, $300 per annum ; firms established outside the province, $600 per annum.

Catamarca :—$300 per annum.

San Luis :—$400 per annum. $200 per annum for applicants established within 10 squares of the Office of Rents.

Entre Rios :—$600 for the first six months, $300 for the second six months.

National Territories :—$100 per annum.

No special documents are required by commercial travellers arriving from abroad, nor are there any formalities to be observed. A Decree of 1916 provides that the luggage and samples of commercial travellers shall not be cleared through the Customs until the required licence has been obtained. This provision is not enforced in practice.

The heavy charges for licences have naturally led to evasion. One method of avoiding the expense of the Federal licence in Buenos Aires, is to work solely in the name of a resident agent or importing house. It is rarely necessary or profitable for foreign travellers to visit the provinces, except perhaps Santa Fé (for Rosario, Mendoza, and Tucumán) In these cases expense is avoided by arranging with local houses sending travellers to those provinces for orders to be booked in their name or that of some Buenos Aires importer Some travellers visit the provincial capitals and either take or refrain from taking out a licence according to the prospects of doing business.

ARGENTINA.

There is no provision in Argentina for the duty-free admission of samples of commercial value. Such samples, may however, be brought in under bond for a period of six months. Should any part of the samples be sold, import duty is payable upon that part. In the samples brought in at Buenos Aires, and taken overland to Chile, the traveller can deliver his samples to the railway company to be carried under bond to Chile.

Once import duty has been paid on samples, no re-fund is made on re-export.

Merchandise which may be introduced as samples under these regulations is defined as follows :—

" Single pieces of articles which usually arrive in sets and only one or two pieces of each class , or articles of different kind, class or quality, not exceeding one or two pieces or each kind or quality, and being such as usually arrive in larger quantities and of one species and quality in each package."

Provision is made for the admission free of import duty of samples without commercial value. They are defined as :—

" Small fragments or portions of material, which obviously cannot be offered for sale and measure not more than 10 centimetres in length . or pieces and objects rendered useless, which from their special nature and condition cannot be considered as an article of commerce."

When the import duty on a collection of samples brought by a commercial traveller is an inconsiderable sum it is often simpler to pay and be free from further trouble. It is customary to let a forwarding or customhouse agent attend to the formalities of clearance of samples through the customs.

THE TRANSANDINE JOURNEY.

BUENOS AIRES TO VALPARAISO.

The Southern Pacific Railway transports the traveller to Chile across the Andes. The " Rapido Internacional " leaves the Retiro Station at 8.30 a.m., crossing the illimitable Pampas, a great green and brown plain. The monotony is broken here and there by clusters of trees surrounding the farm buildings of estancias. Cattle-raising and wheat-growing are seen everywhere. Droves of cattle driven by swarthy gauchos, brightly coloured birds rising from little lakes, and probably a driving rain of locusts looking like a snow-storm in the sunshine, meet the eye. At the stations are seen ranch-owners or estancieros, in rich ponchos and high boots with wonderful silver spurs; half-breed Indians and gauchos with long knives through their belts.

The night is spent in a comfortable berth, and after an excellent dinner in the restaurant car this is pleasurable indeed. Early the next morning Mendoza is neared, bringing into sight what looks like a long line of crumpled cones of aluminium rising from the plain. These are the foothills of the Andes; a barrier through which engineers have bored a hole, ten thousand feet above the level of the sea, through which runs the Transandine Railway, South America's first transcontinental railway, eight hundred and eighty-eight miles long.

Breakfast is served at **Mendoza** and the through passenger has not time to see more of the place than can be viewed from the railway, although the town and neighbourhood repay a visit. Mendoza streets are lined with trees as are its Plazas, and these trees thrive by irrigation. As the rainfall is practically nil, they are dependent for water upon the melted snow brought down by the river Mendoza. Despite that fact the country for miles around is a huge vineyard, 2,470 feet above the level of the sea.

The extensive Park of the West bears comparison with the Palermo Park in Buenos Aires in its lakes, woods, and flowers. Mendoza makes annually 2,500,000 barrels of wine.

Through passengers to Chile exchange into narrow-gauge to traverse the mountains and the Cumbre tunnel to Los Andes, where another change is made to the broad-gauge Chilean State Railway leading to Valparaiso and Santiago. The journey from Atlantic to Pacific occupies 36 hours.

Thirty-five minutes after arrival at Mendoza the narrow-gauge train resumes its journey along the beautiful Mendoza valley laden with green leaves and purple fruit. Twelve miles away are the foothills of the Andes, where the limit of irrigation is defined by the appearance of scrub and stunted trees upon the slopes.

The engine begins to labour up the gradients. A curve reveals a crevice out of which the river Mendoza debouches on to the plain. In the foothills, past Cacheuta, where are mineral baths, the line curves right and left, following the river, crossing lattice-work bridges and rushing through short tunnels. The railway follows an old trail over which primitive people passed for centuries before the coming of the Spaniard who named it "Camino de los Andes."

The old road over the Cumbre Pass, two thousand six hundred and thirty feet above the line, has fallen into disuse. Travellers do not see the bronze "Christus" statue on the summit of the Cumbre marking the boundary between two nations and pointing to their eternal peace. Argentina and Chile have carven on the base of the statue these words :—

> " Sooner shall these mountains crumble into
> dust than the people of Argentina and Chile
> break the peace which they have sworn to
> maintain at the feet of Christ the Redeemer "

Across the Andes :—Well in the heart of the mountains, the river Mendoza is still in close attendance. At Cacheuta, where the mineral springs are said to be very efficacious against rheumatism, there is good accommodation in the hotel. The train, ever mounting, draws its load past a number of typical Transandine railway stations. Beyond Uspallata is a vast, open, undulating plain, wild and bare, with dried bushes and cactus as the only vegetation. On the edge of the plain, behind, on either side and in front, are mountains, grey, gaunt, and barren. Upon the other side of the plain the valley narrows until Rio Blanco or White River is reached, and their mountain torrents rush into the river, churning the waters. The point is six or seven thousand feet above the level of the sea. Along the Paramillo de las Vacas are seen heaps of detritus marking the lower slopes of the Andine valleys. There is no vegetation to affect the process of denudation or to cover its results.

Up the Tupungato valley is seen the noble snow-clad cone which gives its name to the valley. One of the giants of the Andes, it rises 22,451 feet above the sea. It comes into sight at forty miles' distance. Then are passed a fine mass of pinnacled rocks, "Los Penitentes," on the top of a huge ridge. It is impossible to appreciate their proportions from the valley below, but it can be believed that their summit affords one of the grandest views imaginable. Out of the steep slopes, under the Penitents, smaller pinnacled rocks shoot up. The high rocks give the impression of a Cathedral, and the smaller sharp rocks on the slopes might almost be monks marching up to the Cathedral. On the other side of the ridge is a glorious view of the monarch of the Andes—Aconcagua, spotlessly white, sharply cut against an azure sky.

Puente del Inca is the best centre from which to make excursions into the Andine valleys or to attempt the ascent of Aconcagua— the loftiest mountain in the Western Hemisphere and one of the highest mountains in the world, rising to over 23,300 feet.

There is a good Hotel at Puente del Inca with every convenience and excellent service.

The bridge spanning the river Cuevas some 65 feet above the water, has a span of 70 feet, and a width of 90 feet.

Leaving Puente del Inca, the train climbs the Paramillo de los Horcones, passing over the high-level bridge that spans the Horcones river. The Paramillo is the moraine of an ancient glacier, on the flanks of Aconcagua. After a comparatively level stretch of valley, the train climbs by rack rail through the narrow gorge of the " Paramillo de las Cuevas," which before the boring of the tunnel through the Cumbre was the terminus of the Argentine Transandine Railway The altitude is now 10,400 feet, 109 miles from Mendoza.

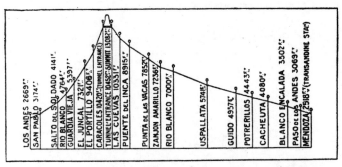

THE CLIMB AND THE DESCENT; WAYSIDE STATIONS AND THEIR ALTITUDES.

From the posting-house here it was customary to take coaches or mules. Now the tunnel serves and leads into Chile. The tunnel is 90 yards short of two miles long, and its length is 27 yards short of its height above sea level. This is the highest point to which the railway attains.

From the tunnel on the Chilean side at Caracoles, the descent, at first winding and of a slight gradient, suddenly becomes very steep. Between Caracoles and Portillo lies perhaps the grandest rock scenery in the world. No word-picture gives any conception of the prodigious grandeur of the snow-clad, towering, sharp-pointed peaks, standing in relief against the blue of the sky, nor do photographs give more than a poor impression of them. At intervals on the downward course are passed small, squat refuge-huts. The river Aconcagua is now at hand. Bare rock gives place to verdure, increasing as we descend. Golden-yellow blossom blazes out. Flowers of many hues mingle with the cactus. The mountain barrier causes the clouds from the Pacific Ocean to discharge upon this side, and hence at once the verdure of the Pacific slope and the absence of rainfall upon the other side of the mountains.

Santa Rosa de los Andes, commonly called Los Andes—the terminus of the Chilean Transandine Railway, is beautifully situated, and its roads are lined with poplar trees. The line traverses the Salto by short tunnels and follows the south bank of the river The valley widens out and cultivation extends until, on reaching Los Andes, is reached the head of a wide and cultivated valley reaching to the sea. After dinner a change is made to the broad-gauge Chilean State Railway, whose turn it is to take up the route to Santiago and Valparaiso. It is a four hours' run to the latter, and three and a half hours to the former The junction for Santiago s Llai-Llai. Presently, the end of the journey is in sight. On the right is deep blue water—the first glimpse of the Southern Pacific, then comes Viña del Mar—the Brighton of Chile—and a few minutes more brings Valparaiso.

FARMING LANDS AND FARMING LIFE IN ARGENTINA.

A valuable report upon farming conditions in South America was prepared by the special agents of the U.S. Tariff Board, 1913, and to this readers are referred for fuller information than is given in the following abstract. The investigation being made in relation principally to wool, the report deals more fully with sheep and cattle and arable operations, although the incidental references to these departments of work are informing.

Second only in importance to Australasia in the production of sheep and wool, South America presents conditions differing materially from those prevailing upon the other continents.

THE FAR SOUTH.

The island of Tierra del Fuego, one-half of which is Chilean, is reckoned one of the best sheep countries in the world. On this island and on the adjacent mainland, in Chilean territory, exists one of the greatest sheep ranches in the world, and one of the best managed, producing good wool and excellent mutton.

The island has a rich, black soil, often inclined to be peaty, usually abundant rainfall, not enough snow to do harm, and is covered with good, close-set, nutritious forage plants, white clover, redtop, and many similar grasses. The types of sheep seen are Romney, Lincoln, Corriedales (New Zealand), a cross between Lincoln and merino. Very good but rather coarse wools come from the region along the Straits of Magellan. Wild dogs and a few foxes are the sole enemies. Owing to violent winds and cold summers little or no agriculture is practised.

North of the island is the Argentine territory of Santa Cruz. This vast region is not yet fully stocked with sheep. Its south and west are well grassed, its north and east are semi-desert, yet this region is capable of carrying about 1,200 sheep to the league of about 6,250 acres. At Rio Gallegos one sees fine, fat muttons, and again at the Coyle, with fewer fat sheep as one goes northward. The sheep of the region were originally Rambouillets from the Rio Negro, or Lincolns from the Falkland Islands. Many Romney rams are used, and also Lincolns. The wools of Santa Cruz are clean and strong, but somewhat coarse nature, except from northern coast lands.

IN PATAGONIA.

Eastern Chubut is practically a desert, covered thinly with shrubs, with a small amount of nutritious grass under and between the shrubs. It is almost too poor to pay to fence and stock, yet this is being done on a considerable scale. The wools of Chubut, while very good, are often heavy with sand, owing to the nature of the soil and the furious winds that often prevail throughout all the Patagonian region.

The immense territory of Rio Negro is not heavily stocked with sheep, but along the rivers and in the west along the mountains are estancias. The sheep are mainly of Rambouillet blood.

All of Patagonia has been the bed, and later the beach, of the sea. The soil is very thin and rests on coarse gravel or shingle. From a little way below Bahia Blanca the shingle beds stretch nearly to the coast of Punta Arenas. Alluvial valleys of small extent and occasional mountains rise above the shingle, but 99 per cent of the land well toward the mountains is of this character The rainfall is light and irregular

THE RICHER SOILS.

The best types of soils are found in the province of Buenos Aires, and the most regular rainfall. The area of the province is about half that of France, nearly all of it fertile soil. It is mostly alluvial and was doubtless laid by the great rivers before the land was lifted above the sea. It is singularly free from watercourses. In many parts of the province one could drive a plough for ten or twenty miles without encountering either tree, stone, marsh, or watercourse. The rainfall is so nicely proportioned to the capacity of the soil that there is little to run off. There is not enough rain to fully saturate the earth, and drought is a bugbear of Buenos Aires, as it is of other parts of Argentina. In the west there is alfalfa, grazed by cattle, not sheep. In the south the Basque sheep farmers sow oats for sheep grazing. The summer droughts make it hard to grow cultivated grasses. Alfalfa is a success everywhere, but it thrives best in the west, where the soil is underlaid with a sandy subsoil.

Lands are constantly being subdivided into farms or " chacras " and sold to farmers or the so-called " chacereos." These farms are devoted mainly to potatoes, wheat, oats, flaxseed, or to peaches and other fruits near the cities. Estancieros often lease lands to the chacereos, usually for wheat growing. This withdraws the land from stock growing for from three to five years, when it is sown to alfalfa and returned to stock again, while the colonist moves on to develop another piece of land from the wild camp to wheat, and later, to alfalfa.

The province of Buenos Aires, probably the greatest expanse of rich soil in the world, is greatly hampered by drought and periodical visitations of locusts.

Entre Rios has very rich soil. Undulating rather than flat, it is thinly covered with rather small trees. It is a good sheep country, a land where perennial grasses are not much seen and those hard and coarse. The nutritious grasses are mostly annuals, and annual clovers abound.

Corrientes, north of Entre Rios, has a hotter climate and a low surface, with much marsh land and subtropical forests and palms. It is a great cattle country, with many herds of the unimproved native stock, with wide horns and huge bony frames. They go to the saladeros, or salting works, at about five or six years of age.

Beyond the River Paraná lies the Chaco, an immense region of timber and open glades, with a little agriculture, but little live stock. It grows good cotton, oranges, and tropical products. Southward, from Santa Fé, are areas of maize lands.

PASTORAL LIFE.

Probably in all the world there is no region where the shepherd's life is easier than in Argentina. Since the wild dogs have been killed off there have been practically no wild animals to trouble, except in the mountains a few pumas or mountain lions. Except along the base of the Andes the climate is so mild that no winter feeding is needed. In the north, if there is rain, grasses remain green almost the year round. Disease is rare, except in the marshy regions, or during cycles of unusual rainfall.

The great defect in Argentina is the uncertain weather. Rains may come at any time of the year, or not at all. Sometimes a region will be without much rain for two or three years. The rainfall is, in normal years, just sufficient for the grasses and crops, and in exceedingly rare seasons excessive. One year in seven, more or less, it is withheld. In 1830 nearly all the cattle, horses, and sheep of Argentina perished. No doubt the losses were more severe than they could be to-day, for the animals probably perished of thirst more than hunger

Coupled with drought is the uncertainty of temperature. The heat is intense during the summer, but south of Buenos Aires there is hardly a month when frost is unknown, and this depends upon the direction of the wind.

The locusts are erratic in their coming. There are series of years with no locusts, then the insects come swarming from the north and devour every green and living thing. Once they have come they may return yearly for four to six years and then no more seen for a term of years. They are supposed to breed in northern forests and the southern camps.

FARMING METHODS.

The farming of Argentine soils is done on the extensive, rather than the intensive system. The colonists are for the greater part Italians who take large tracts of land, sometimes as much as 400 or more acres, and till them as best they can. Ploughing is done with American riding ploughs as a rule, and all the family assist, the women and even the children driving the animals. Sowing is done with machinery, as is also the harvesting. The yields of wheat are low, compared with the fertility of the soil, and when a good yield is

obtained the colonists are usually unable to cope with the harvest
The tenants are given the naked land, furnishing their own houses
of adobe walls and iron roofs. They commonly have no trees or
flowers about them, and often no garden. After about four or five
years of such culture the land is taken over by the landlord and sown
with alfalfa. The tenant takes a piece of virgin camp and repeats
his operation.

The greatness of Argentina comes from three causes :—Marvellous soil and alluvial deposits over an enormous area. The
great ease of tillage in a land where the earth is seldom too wet
to plough, and free from stone, watercourse, marsh, hill, or gully
for thousands of square miles. The work of the Italian immigrants, industrious, patient and frugal, accustomed to poverty,
and content to live in huts, unsheltered in summer and un-
warmed in winter

The most successful estancias are managed by English, New
Zealand, or American managers.

A Typical Estancia :—It may be interesting to obtain a general
idea of the nature of an Argentine camp. The name " camp," in
universal use, means the estancia, or ranch, and in general it means
the pastoral regions as distinct from the farms or " colonias."
A fair idea of the country and its ways is obtained from the train,
as it usually runs through the pasture land. The land is astonishingly
level and would be monotonous to one not keenly interested in
farming. The fields are fenced into very large potreros, or pastures, of, say, from 100 to 5,000 acres each. Cattle, sheep, and
horses usually graze in the same pastures.

The fences are wire and well built at great cost, for all wood has
to be brought from the northern forests. The posts are mostly of
quebracho, as hard and heavy as stone and as durable. The wires
pass through the posts and are kept perfectly taut. The wires
are run through the upright sticks or stays that space them the proper
distance apart, since the posts are very far one from the other There
may be one barbed wire, no more. The gates are wide and strong,
and seldom drag on the ground.

Alighting from the train, one sees a village of houses in Spanish
style, usually with unpaved streets. Driving out of the village one
finds, if it has been a wet time, heavy roads, unimproved by man ;
if a dry·time, there are clouds of dust. The roads are wide and
commonly treeless, though now and then one passes an estancia
where trees have been planted with care. The chinaberry tree
is the favourite tree, since it is not devoured by locusts. Next comes
the Eucalyptus globulus.

It is astonishing to drive mile after mile and see no brook or
river, and to learn that one can drive a hundred miles in some parts
without encountering one permanent watercourse. Nor will
there be ponds or pools, save in times of unusual rain, when shallow
pools will be seen. Windmill pumps stand in the fields, and from

them radiate long lines of galvanized iron troughs for the sheep and cattle.

There may be few buildings on the estancia aside from the rather large dwelling of the manager, an office for the bookkeeper, a coach house and harness house and a shearing shed. There may be sheds for sheltering and feeding rams and choice ewes but these provisions are limited. There are modest houses for the peons, or labourers, and in each large pasture there is commonly a hut or small house for the peons whose work is to look after the fences and animals in that pasture.

THE SHEPHERD'S YEAR.

Lambs are born in May, June, and in the winter month July, or in the spring, say, in August. Early lambs thrive best.

Shearing comes in October, November, and December   Machines are in common use. Often the wool is baled on the estancia and sent direct to Europe. More commonly it is sent to the great wool market of Buenos Aires, where it is assorted and sold for export.

Dipping goes on more or less the year round. Usually four dippings per year are given.

In ordinary times there is little work to be done with the sheep. The fences are built so well that animals do not break out or in. There is the least possible repair work to be done. Once an estancia is well equipped with fences, gates, corrals, and dip, the maintenance cost is low.

The shepherds manage the sheep from horseback, and are usually native Argentines of mixed Spanish and Indian blood. They prove fairly faithful and efficient when well selected and well supervised.

BOLIVIA

BOLIVIA.

There is no seaboard, and access to Bolivia is made normally through the ports of Mollendo, Antofagasta, or Arica.

The **trade routes** from the Pacific coast are :—

(1) From Mollendo (Peru) to Puno on Lake Titicaca by rail, thence by lake steamer to Guaqui (Bolivia), thence to La Paz by rail , 48 hours (525 miles)

(2) From Antofagasta (Chile) to La Paz by rail, passing through Uyuni and Oruro, 48 hours (719 miles)

(3) From Arica (Chile) to La Paz , about 16 to 18 hours. The State railways afford a short route from the coast to the capital. The distance is 449 kilometres, as against 846 kilometres from Mollendo and 1,155 from Antofagasta. The greatest elevation attained is 4,256 metres at Jeneral Lagos. The line crosses the Bolivian frontier at Charaña, where there is a Custom House. At Viacha are rail connections with Antofagasta, Mollendo, and Oruro.

Those from the Atlantic coast are :—

(1) From Buenos Aires to La Quiaca by rail, thence to Atocha by coach, connecting with the Antofagasta Railway

(2) From Pará by the Amazon and Madeira Rivers to San Antonio, thence by rail to Villa Bella in North-East Bolivia, thence by river and mule-back to La Paz.

There are **customs houses** at La Paz, Puerto Suarez, La Quiaca, Tupiza, Villazon, Tarija, Yacuiba, Villa Bella, Cobija, Guaqui, Uyuni, Abuná, Guayaramerin, and Oruro.

La Paz is the highest capital in the world, it lies in a natural basin, 1,500 ft. deep, at an elevation of 12,700 ft. above sea-level.

It is a city of about 108,000 inhabitants. Of the 3,000 foreign residents, about 100 are British, with a similar number of United States citizens. The climate is cold (maximum 77° F) and the air rarefied.

There is little level ground in La Paz, and the streets generally conform their direction to the topography The gradients are often steep, and some of the streets extend well up the wall of the "alto." Most of the streets are paved with rough cobblestones, though some are not paved at all. The thoroughfares best suited for motor traffic are the Prado and the Avenida Montes. The Prado, otherwise known as the Avenida 16 de Octubre, is a wide avenue, lined with eucalyptus trees. It connects the business part of the city with the residential quarter of Sopocachi, and is bordered by attractive residences.

C*

The Plaza Murillo, the centre of the city's life, is a small park set with trees and flower beds. Facing it are the National Palace, the Congress Building, the unfinished cathedral, and the leading hotel and club of La Paz. From the north-west corner of the plaza start Calles Comercio and Socabaya, two of the most important business streets of the city. Other business streets are Calle Diez de Medina and Calle Recreo.

On first arriving at La Paz the visitor will probably experience some slight discomfort from the rarefied air, due to the altitude of the town. Moderate exercise is advisable for a short time, when the scantiness of breath is wont to disappear As regards clothing, precautions should be taken against both heat and cold.

Situated about fifty miles east of Lake Titicaca, it is connected by rail with most of the other cities and with the Pacific ports of Mollendo (525 miles) and Antofagasta (719 miles) The copper mines of Corocoro (78 miles distant) are linked by rail with the Arica-La Paz line.

Electric trams run throughout the city, and electricity is used for lighting and heating. There is an electric railway from the centre of the city to Alto, the heights above La Paz. A golf course exists there.

Hotels :—Hotel Paris, Central, Mrs. Murray's Boarding House.

Restaurant :—"Paris" on Plaza Murillo.

Conveyances :—Electric trams, autos, and carriages.

Materials and Curios :—May be bought at Julio Cordero, Calle Ayacucho.

Points of Interest :—Plaza, Cathedrals, Museum, Colegio "Don Busco," Market, etc. The many-coloured garments worn by the Indians make a visit to the Market especially interesting.

Excursions :—(1) An afternoon drive down the valley presents charming features. The setting sun tints Illimani and the surrounding mountains with glorious hues, against which stand out sharply the pinnacles of the crags and rocks.

(2) By electric railway to Alto La Paz, thence to Guaqui (on Lake Titicaca) for Mollendo.

Sucre is legally the capital of the Republic, and the Supreme Court of Justice holds its sessions there, but La Paz (318 miles) is really the seat of government. Sucre has 30,000 inhabitants, and is situated at an altitude of 9,600 ft. It has an agreeable, dry climate, and an average temperature of 56° F There are a cathedral, university, theatres, and many fine buildings. It is not yet connected by rail, but there is an automobile service for passengers and goods to Potosí (about 150 miles distant), whence to the rail connection with the principal centres.

Hotels :—España, Hispaño-Americano, Uyuni, Colón, etc.

Oruro has a population of 25,000, mostly Indians, but with a considerable foreign element, and is a mining centre for silver, tin, copper, wolfram, and antimony. It is connected by rail with Antofagasta (560 miles), and is the junction for railways running north, south, and east. It was the first city in Bolivia to establish a tramway service and the second to install electric light. Situated at an altitude of 12,110 ft., the mean yearly temperature is about 50° F There is a School of Mines.

Hotels :—Quintanal, Unión, Terminus, Metropol, Comercio, Francia, etc.

Cochabamba (originally Oropeza) has a population of 35,000, and is an important agricultural centre. It is the second city of the Republic, and has fine buildings, including the Government Palace, the Law Courts, the Town Hall, the Cathedral, and University. There are hospitals and an American Institute. It is connected by rail with Oruro (125 miles) There is a mule service from Oruro. The altitude is about 8,340 ft., and there is a mild and healthy climate, average temperature 66° F in the shade.

Hotels :—Sucre, Americano, Unión, Continental, Central, etc.

Potosí, situated at a height of 14,350 ft., in one of the richest silver-mining departments, has a population of 30,000. Cobalt has been discovered there. It is connected by rail with Antofagasta. There are numerous buildings of historical interest, principal amongst which are the Mint, the Government and Municipal Palaces, and the churches. The climate is cold, the temperature rarely rising above 59° F., but descending as low as 9° F below zero.

Hotels :—Internacional, Esplendid, Central, Paris.

Santa Cruz de la Sierra, 1,450 ft. above sea-level, has a population of 20,000, and is an important agricultural centre, producing sugar, rice, and coffee. Petroleum deposits in the district remain unworked for lack of capital and transport. It is 585 miles east of La Paz, and 425 miles by road from Puerto Suarez. As the nearest railway is at Cochabamba (300 miles), transport has to be effected by pack mules or bullock wagons. Yacuiba, on the Argentine frontier, is 370 miles distant.

Hotels :—Comercio, Continental.

Tarija lies 85 miles east of Tupiza and 180 miles south of Sucre. Population, 10,000. It has an excellent climate, the average temperature being about 64° F It is a cattle and tobacco centre, and wine is also produced. A large trade is done in foreign imports, which arrive via Buenos Aires, Rosario de Santa Fé, and La Quiaca (Argentina) (85 miles) by rail, and thence by road. With the completion of the railway from the latter town to Tupiza (66 miles), a branch line will probably be constructed to Tarija. The chief buildings include the Palace of Justice, a theatre, an ancient convent, and the public schools. •

Hotels :—Gran, Nacional, Social.

Tupiza is about 140 miles south-east of Potosí and is connected by rail with La Paz. It is a centre of the silver, tin, lead, and bismuth mining industries With a population of some 5,000, it stands at an altitude of 9,800 ft. and possesses a temperate climate.

Trinidad, on the Mamoré River, with a population of 6,000, is a centre of the cacao and coffee industries.

Sorata, with a population of 2,000, is a rubber centre and is connected with the Pacific direct by Lake Titicaca (rail to Mollendo)

PHYSICAL FEATURES.

Bolivia has an estimated **area** of 515,156 square miles, and is bounded north and east by Brazil, south by Paraguay and Argentina, and west by Chile and Peru. The lofty plateau of Bolivia, covering 6,500 square miles, with an average range of 12,000 ft. and a breadth of 150 miles, runs between the Andes and the Cordillera Real, and falls naturally into two divisions. The northern part is the most inhabited, and includes the great lake Titicaca, with an area of 3,200 square miles and a depth of 120 fathoms. Lake Titicaca is connected by the Rio Desaguadero (160 miles long) with the salt lake and swamps of Poopo. The southern portion of the plateau is mainly desert. The mountains of the Eastern Range trend, in the north, to the Amazon watershed, and on the east fall in steep precipices towards the plains. They constitute one of the world's greatest ranges, and the snow-clad peaks of Illampu, Illimani, and Chacacomani exceed 21,000 ft. To the extreme south are the fertile Chaco and open plains of Manzo.

The Republic possesses three **river systems,** those of the Amazon, La Plata, and the central plateau. The principal rivers of the first are the Beni and Rio Grande which unite to form the Mamoré, which, in turn, with the Madre de Dios forms the Madeira. The Rio Grande is the chief Bolivian tributary of the Mamoré, its course of 700 miles is partly navigable by flat-bottomed steamers. Of the Plata system, entering the Paraguay River, the only Bolivian stream of importance is the Pilcomayo, which, traversing the Sierra region, receives sundry tributaries. Several small rivers discharge into Lakes Titicaca and Poopo, the former having an area of over 3,000 square miles, and situated at 12,500 ft., is the highest navigable sheet of water in the world.

The rivers are open to vessels of all nations. Of the total network there are about 12,000 miles navigable, affording excellent means of transportation and communication. The Paraguay is navigable for 1,100 miles by steamers of 8 ft. to 10 ft. draught, the Itenes for 1,000 miles, and the Beni for 1,000 miles (6 ft. draught only) Other rivers navigable by light-draught craft are the Pilcomayo, Mamoré, Madre de Dios, Itonama, Sara, Orton, Baures, Inambari, Pirai, Chapare, Abuna, Yacuma, and Desaguadero.

A regular line of steamers is maintained on Lake Titicaca, and the principal Bolivian ports on that inland sea are Guaqui, Puerto

Pérez, Huata, Ancoraimes, Carabuco, and Escoma. There is direct
transit from Puno on the Peruvian bank to Guaqui, the Bolivian
frontier and Customs post. Titicaca is connected with Lake
Aullagas by the river Desaguadero.

Although situated entirely within the torrid zone the **climate**
varies greatly. The western portion is high and mountainous, and
in the eastern are low plains or jungles. The temperature of the
western districts is high by daytime and low at night. The plains
are tropical, and the temperature is high and somewhat oppressive.
The summer temperature of the plateau is from 50° to 60° F., and
in winter (May, June, and July) it falls to zero in the shade. Little
rain falls in any part from April to December, and to the west of
the Cordillera the rainfall at all seasons is meagre.

PEOPLE OF BOLIVIA.

Subjoined are the most recent estimates of the **population** of the
several departments and chief cities :—

Department.	Population.	Capital.	Population.
La Paz	734,000	La Paz	107,250
Chuquisaca	319,300	Sucre	30,000
Cochabamba	512,600	Cochabamba	35,000
Potosí	515,500	Potosí	30,000
Santa Cruz	327,400	Santa Cruz de la Sierra	20,000
Tarija	160,180	Tarija	10,000
Oruro	137,330	Oruro	25,000
El Beni	50,260	Trinidad	6,000
North-western territory	49,760	Riberalta	1,500
Gran Chaco territory	13,230	Villa Montes	—
National Eastern territory	—	Puerto Suarez	—

The approximate total is 3,000,000. The last census classed
50 per cent. as Indian and 26 per cent. as mestizos, 80 per cent. of
the population live at an altitude of over 10,000 ft. The Bolivians
are remarkable for longevity, and a recent census revealed the
existence of 1,261 centenarians.

The mestizos, or mixed breeds, locally known as **cholos,** are a
mixture of the Spaniard and the Indian, and share to a certain
extent the qualities of both. The cholo generally lacks initiative
and persistence, and only too often a strict regard for responsibility

The cholo occupies an important place in both industrial and
political life. He furnishes nearly all the skilled labour and some
of the unskilled. The major-domos, or superintendents, of the large
landed estates are usually cholos, and many are themselves independent proprietors. Nearly all the small shopkeepers are "cholos"
or "cholas." The women of this class are uncommonly shrewd and
independent. The class of household servants is also largely recruited from them. There are different castes or gradations of the
general class, depending on the degree of their prosperity, the social
standing of their occupation, or the proportion of white blood in
their veins. The high and the low class are generally distinguishable
apart by their dress, the former wearing the high, polished white
hat, bright-coloured "manta" or shawl (often silk), and high but-

toned boots so familiar a sight in La Paz. The garb of the low-class chola shades off, like her complexion, until it approximates that of her Indian cousin. All classes wear several heavy skirts, made of bright-coloured baize, or bayeta, one over the other, often to a very considerable thickness.

The **language** of the educated classes is Spanish, that of the natives Quechua and Aymará.

The State recognizes and supports the Roman Catholic religion, but all beliefs are tolerated. There is an Archbishopric and three Bishoprics, those of La Paz, Cochabamba, and Santa Cruz. There are various missions with schools in which the Indians are taught trades.

A BOLIVIAN CALENDAR.

1054–1533. The Empire of the Incas.
1107. Death of Manco-Capac, founder of the Inca Empire, in the fifty-third year of his reign.
1525–28. Francisco Pizarro and Diego de Almagro explore the coast.
1531. Pizarro and Almagro begin their conquest of what was later known as Peru and Bolivia.
1533. Execution of the Inca Atahualpa.
1535. Bolivia invaded by Pizarro.
1536. Quesada's expedition against the Chibchas.
1543. Arrival of first Viceroy
1545. Discovery of the silver mines of Potosí.
1546. Rebellion of Gonzalo Pizarro.
1573. City of Cochabamba founded.
1718. Establishment of the Vice-Royalty of Santa Fé de Bogotá.
1721. The Presidency of Quito made part of the Vice-Royalty of New Granada.
1736. Visit of the famous French Scientist, Condamine.
1776. Establishment of the Vice-Royalty of Buenos Aires, with jurisdiction over the present Republics of Bolivia (part), Uruguay, Paraguay, and the Argentine Confederation.
1780. Indian rising under Tupac-Amaru.
1809. First revolt against Spanish rule in Charcas.
1810. Defeat of the Spaniards at Suipacha.
1813. Patriot forces defeated at Villapugio and Ayuma.
1816. Invasion by the Spaniards under the Viceroy Laserna.
1822. Patriot forces destroyed by Spaniards in the neighbourhood of La Paz. Santa Cruz becomes the leader of the Bolivians.
1823. Santa Cruz defeated by Spaniards.
1824. Signal patriot victory at Ayacucho.
1825. Bolivár proclaims the Republic of Bolivia.
1825. Sucre made first President of Bolivia.
1828. After strife with Peru, General Santa Cruz becomes President.
1835. Santa Cruz intervenes in Peru and establishes the Peru-Bolivian Confederation.
1839. Peru-Bolivian Confederation defeated by Chile.
1843. General Ballivián abolishes the Constitution.
1847. Unsuccessful invasion of Peru by General Ballivián.
1858. A flock of llamas, alpacas, and vicuñas introduced from Bolivia into Australia
1865. Melgarejo becomes Dictator.
1871. Melgarejo overthrown by General Morales.
1876. Morales defeated by Hilario Daza.
1879. Daza deposed.
1879. Outbreak of war with Chile.
1880. New Constitution proclaimed by General Narciso Campero.
1884. Treaty signed with Chile. Señor Pacheco becomes President.
1892. Treaty signed between Chile and Bolivia.
1899. General José Manuel Pando becomes President.
1900. Construction begun of the railway from Lake Titicaca to La Paz.

1902. Guaqui-La Paz Railway opened.
1904. Señor Montes elected President.
1917. Bolivia breaks off diplomatic relations with Germany; José Gutierrez Guerra elected President.
1919. Bolivia joins the League of Nations.
1921. Bautista Saavedra appointed President.

COINAGE AND MEASURES.

Although there is no Bolivian gold coin, the standard of **currency** is upon a gold basis, and English and Peruvian sovereigns and half-sovereigns circulate as legal tender up to any amount. For purposes of inland transactions the exchange is fixed by law at 12 bols. 50 c. to the pound sterling. The boliviano (silver) is the unit, containing 100 centavos, equal to about 1s. 8d. normally Other silver coins are the 50-, 20-, and 10-centavo pieces, and there are nickel coins of 10 and 5 centavos. Convertible banknotes are issued for values 1, 5, 500, and 1,000 bolivianos respectively

The **metric** system is established by law, but the following old Spanish measures are largely employed :—

Lineal.—1 vara = 3 pies = 36 pulgadas = 33 43 in.
Surface.—1 square vara = 0·859 sq yd.
Capacity.—Dry 1 arroba = 6·70 gallons. Liquid 1 galon = 0·74 gallon.
Weight.—1 libra = 16 onzas = 1·0147 lb., 1 arroba = 25 libras = 25·36 lb., 1 quintal = 100 libras = 101·47 lb.

GOVERNMENT

The **constitution** of Bolivia, dating from 1880, guarantees freedom of religion, of speech, and of the Press. The executive power is vested in the President and two Vice-Presidents, who are elected by popular vote for a term of four years. The President is ineligible for an immediately following second term of office. He nominates the Ministers of State—six in number—who hold the portfolios for Foreign Affairs and Worship, Finance, Interior and Justice, Industry and Public Works, War and Colonization, and Education and Agriculture.

The Legislature is composed of Congress, consisting of the Senate, with sixteen Senators, and the Chamber of Deputies, of whom there are seventy-five. Senators are elected by popular vote for a term of six years, one-third retiring every two years. Deputies are elected for four years, one-half retiring every two years. Congress meets at La Paz on 6 August each year, to receive the Presidential Message and the Budget proposals.

For administration the Republic is divided into eight departments and three territories, subdivided into provinces, cantons, and sub-cantons. The ruling officials are prefects, sub-prefects, corregidores, and alcaldes.

Municipalities are autonomous and control their own revenue and expenditure. The municipal council is elected by popular vote, one-half of the members retiring annually.

All male citizens over twenty-one years of age, officially registered, who can read and write and have a fixed income, may vote.

The Judiciary consists of a **Supreme Court,** sitting at Sucre, with seven judges, who are appointed by Congress for a term of ten years, a District Court in each Department, and provincial and local courts.

PAST PRESIDENTS.

General Sucre	1825	General H. Daza	1876
Marshal Santa Cruz	1828	General N Campero	1880
General Velasco	1839	Señor Pacheco	1884
General Ballivián	1841	A. Arce	1889
General Belzu	1848	Dr M. Baptista	1982
General J Córdova	1856	Dr S. F Alonso	1896
Dr J M. Linares	1857	General Pando	1899
General J M. de Acha	1861	Dr I. Montes	1904
General M. Melgarejo	1865	Dr. E. Villazon	1909
Col. A. Morales	1871	Dr. I. Montes	1914
Colonel Adolfo Ballivián	1872	José Gutierrez Guerra	
Dr T Frias	1874	(deposed 1920)	1917

PRESIDENT.
Bautista Saavedra.

MINISTRY.

Foreign Affairs	Roman Paz.
Interior	Francisco Traizós.
Justice	Carlos Zalles.
Public Instruction and Agriculture	Felix A. del Granado.
War and Colonization	Juan Manuel Sainz.
Industry	Adolfo Flores.

WATER TRANSPORT

The principal obstacles to **navigation** in the Amazonian headwaters consist of bars and "palisadas," or snags, reports an agent of the United States Government. During high water these streams eat away their banks, with the result that large trees fall into the river and impede craft. Light-draft boats are needed to clear the channels thus obstructed. The course of some of the rivers is broken by dangerous "cachuelas," or rapids. The Madeira-Mamoré Railway was built to avoid the rapids in these two rivers, and before the construction of this line numbers of boatmen were drowned and quantities of rubber were lost from "batelones" capsized in attempts to shoot the rapids. Often the cargo was unloaded and portages made, causing loss of time. One of the most famous rapids is the Cachuela Esperanza in the Beni, a short distance above Villa Bella. The Cachuela Forteleza, in the Upper Abuna, is another bad pass. At the Cachuela Esperanza the Beni is about 900 yd. wide, and in a distance of about 300 yd. the river has a fall of nearly 20 ft.

The navigability of these rivers depends largely on the season of the year. Streams that can be used by steamers of relatively large draft during the rainy season may only be passable for rowing boats during the height of the dry season. This is particularly true of the Acre, by which steamers from Manaos can reach Cobija for several months of the year, but is only open for "batelones" during much of the dry season. The difference in the amount of water between the two seasons is illustrated by conditions at Concepción on the Beni, where the level of the river varies from 8 ft. in August to 25 ft. in February At Carmen on the Madre de Dios the level of water varies from 7 ft. in August to a maximum of 30 ft. in February, and at Porvenir, on the Tahuamanu, the difference is between 3 ft. and 21 ft.

Several types of boats are used on these rivers, known as "balsas," "batelones," "callapos," "chalupas," "monterias," and others. The "balsa" is a kind of raft, made of light wood known as "palo de balsa." It is about 25 ft. long and 5 ft. wide, with a capacity of about 800 lb. of cargo, exclusive of the rowers. "Balsas" are most commonly found on the Mapiri and the Upper Beni. The "callapo" is made by lashing two or three "balsas" together, carries up to a ton and a half. The "chalupa" is a dugout canoe used by the Guarayos and Caripunas Indians. The "batelones" are the craft most used for transporting rubber These boats are sometimes 40 ft. or 50 ft. long by 10 ft. wide, with a capacity of several tons.

Most of the launches on these rivers are of 10 to 50 tons burden. There are some fifteen steamers of this class in service on the Mamoré and its affluents. The tonnage of these boats varies from 10 to 120, but the majority are 25 tons. Most of the launches are operated by rubber companies, which use them for general freight and passenger business as common carriers. The launches burn wood fuel and travel leisurely, stopping wherever there is cargo to take on or disembark. The more important launch owners are Suarez Hermanos (Madre de Dios, Orton, Beni, and Mamoré Rivers); Braillard & Co. (Beni, Mamoré), Alfredo W Barber & Co. (Beni, Mamoré, Itenez), Zeller, Villinger & Co. (Mamoré, Itenez), Madeira-Mamoré Railway Co. (Mamoré), Societe Picollet (Abuna), Komarez and Bruckner (Itenez), Sociedad Comercial Matto Grosso y Bolivia (Itenex); and C. M. Barbery (Mamoré) The Bolivian Government operates a small fleet of launches in trading over portions of the rivers.

NATURAL RESOURCES.

Bolivia ranks third after the United States and Mexico as the richest mineral-producing country of the whole American continent. **Tin** accounts for 85 per cent. of her total exports, and Bolivia is the second tin-producing country in the world, following the Malay Straits Settlements. The deposits are numerous along the Bolivian range of the Andes, but more especially in the spurs westward from the inland range. About 40,000 tons are produced annually.

The principal mining centre is Oruro, the products being tin, copper, and silver Of copper Bolivia has an annual output of about 30,000 tons. There are numerous wolfram ore mines, and antimony, lead, silver, and gold are exported. The silver mines of Potosí are historic. Of bismuth, found almost exclusively in Bolivia, the total output is shipped to England.

Considerable oil deposits are believed to exist in La Paz, while large oilfields are stated to be in Chuquisaca. Cochabamba and the North-West Territory afford indications of deposits.

Rubber ranks next in importance to tin. The fact that Bolivian rubber is classed as either Pará or Mollendo on the foreign market does an injustice. Amazonian rubber is known to the trade only by the ultimate port of shipment, which is generally either Pará, Brazil, or Mollendo, Peru. The rubber from the lower reaches of the rivers is exported through Pará, and that from the Beni headwaters through the Pacific port of Mollendo.

On the arrival of a consignment of rubber at Manaos or Pará, a " bolacha," or sample ball, is cut through several layers with a knife for the purpose of classifying the lot. There are eight classes, according to this preliminary inspection, though the rubber is generally shipped as of two classes. The eight classes are . Fina, fina flaca, entrefina, entre-fina-flaca, sernamby en rama, sernamby virgen, sernamby de caucho, and caucho. These are exported to the foreign market as " fine " or " ordinary " The rubber known as fine hard Pará is the prime product of the latex of the hevea. Sernamby is second-quality rubber, and contains impurities which mar its value, it is sometimes made of the residue after the preparation of the fine Pará. If rain has fallen in the cups while the latex is being collected, the product will be classified as sernamby Caucho is the product of the caucho tree and is altogether a lower grade.

Other products are wheat, beans, manioc, barley, rice, cotton, rubber, cocoa, nutmeg, and Peruvian bark, and the supplies of coca are also valuable.

The headwaters of the affluents of the Beni are the principal source of the Bolivian supply of **quinine** bark. The product is placed on the market under different names, such as " cassarilla," " calisaya," " cinchona," and " quina." Bark stripped from the trunk of the tree is known as " quina tabla," and that stripped from the branches " quina canuto," or " quill." The bark is well dried and exported in bundles of approximately 50 pounds.

COCA IN BOLIVIA.

The cultivation of **coca** is the principal basis of the agricultural industry of the Yungas, and the most lucrative business of that region. There are no large plantations. Coca is grown on terraces, an acre or two in size, built up on the hillsides. The terraces are about 10 inches wide, protected by a rampart of earth of about the same width and 6 inches high. The ramparts are faced on the outside with stones or a rough cement. The use of terraces prevents the heavy rains from washing the plantation down the mountain side, and helps to hold the moisture about the roots of the plants. The plants are set at intervals from 6 to 10 inches. The unit of measurement for lands devoted to coca is the cato, or approximately one-fourth of a hectare. Coca lands fetch from 300 to 500 bolivianos per cato.

The plant is a shrub usually 2 or 3 ft. in height, although, if allowed to mature, it reaches 4 or 5 ft. It is cut to the ground before attaining that height, as the quality of the leaves deteriorates with the height of the plant. The young shoots are grown under a cover of dried banana leaves and transplanted to the terraces. The plant begins bearing at two years and continues for about twenty years. The leaf, in which lies the commercial value of the plant, is oval and light green, about 1½ inches long and ¾ inch wide.

Three or four crops are picked from the same plants during the year Each cato planted to coca will produce from seven to fourteen " cestos " of leaves annually, and the " cesto " is equivalent to about 25 pounds. Two " cestos " make a " tambor," which thus contains about 50 pounds of leaves. Coca is packed for shipment in units of 1 " tambor " Of the coca production of the Department of La Paz, the Province of Nor Yungas produces about 37 per cent., Sur Yungas about 58 per cent., and Inquisivi the rest.

After the leaves are picked, they are dried in the sun on a slate floor and pressed into bales (one " tambor," or 50 pounds) The dimensions of the bales are about 20 by 14 by 12 inches, and they are wrapped with dried banana leaves and canvas to protect them against the weather and rough handling. The coca is carried into La Paz by mules.

The production of coca in the Department of La Paz is about 3,700 tons annually The production of the Department of Cochabamba is smaller

The greater part of Bolivian coca goes to Argentina or Chile and competes with that from Peru. Peruvian leaf is reckoned inferior in quality to Bolivian.

Coca is known abroad chiefly as the basis of the anæsthetic cocaine, none of which is manufactured in Bolivia, although some is made in Peru. Most of the Bolivian crop is consumed within the country, where it is chewed by the natives of the plateau for the sake of its narcotic effects. The natives mix it with the ashes of the quinua plant, which serves as a condiment. Its use enables the Indian to go without food and to work for long stretches without rest. Its prolonged use deadens the nerves and has been a potent factor in the degeneration of the Indians of the plateau. The coca habit is widespread in some parts of northern Argentina and certain districts of northern Chile.

The chief obstacles to the working of **timber** in the forestal regions of Bolivia are the lack of transportation and the character of the tropical forest. No railways tap the timber country Many of the native hardwoods are too heavy to be carried in rafts. The forests of the Amazonian region are so dense and so tangled that it is difficult to penetrate them, and lumbering operations are attended with great difficulties. A Franciscan mission in the Province of Belasco sent 125 specimens of woods to the Panamá-Pacific Exposition in 1915, and 82 specimens were sent from one estate in the Chapare region of the Department of Cochabamba.

Among the most common woods of eastern Bolivia are cedro (or Spanish cedar), jacaranda, lapacho, laurel, quebracho blanco, urundey, palo santo, palo blanco, mahogany, walnut, ebony, incienso, and the giant carob. Some of these are valuable cabinet woods. Among trees with a high tannin content is the curupay These woods are generally known by Indian names, and the same tree has different names in as many parts of the country. Some of the native woods, such as the tajibo negro, or " iron tree," are of extraordinary hardness, and others extremely light, like the palo de balsa, is used for making canoes.

Sawmills are small and few in number, and axes, adzes, and cross-cut saws are the principal tools used.

FURS AND HAIR.

The principal **fur-bearing** animals in Bolivia are the vicuña, chinchilla, and fox. The vicuña, a wild member of the family to which the llama and alpaca belong, is found among the mountains throughout the plateau country, though in diminishing numbers. It is much smaller than either the llama or alpaca and has a fine, silky wool of a tawny colour It is hunted by the Indians, who either weave its wool into a very attractive poncho or use its skin for the manufacture of " colchas " or rugs. Uyuni is the largest market for this and other classes of furs.

The chinchilla is found in the more remote parts of the Cordillera Occidental, from the Atacama country in the south up to the Province of Pacajes. Most of them, however, live in the region of Mount Tatasabaya, in the Province of Carangas, where a large area of ground is covered with large rocks, among the which the chinchillas make their homes. In spite of a law prohibiting their taking, they are fast disappearing, being trapped by Indians and clandestinely exported. There have been projects to domesticate them on chinchilla farms.

The animal known as the " chinchillon " is a member of the same family, as is the vizcacha, though their fur is inferior to chinchilla. The chinchillon is smaller than the chinchilla, but the texture of its fur is similar to the touch and has the same bluish-grey colour, though shorter than the fur of the chinchilla.

The red fox is found in many parts of Bolivia, and numbers of the skins are sold in La Paz.

BOLIVIA.

Llamas in Bolivia are estimated to number half a million. They serve as pack animals and are sheared at irregular intervals of two to five years, and they yield per head about five pounds of wool.

Alpaca :—There are probably about 200,000 alpacas in Bolivia, though no effort has been made to take a census. The animal belongs to the same family as the llama and the vicuña, but its legs are shorter than those of the llama. The alpaca flourishes in the region about Lake Titicaca and the Province of Carangas in the Department of Oruro. The centres of the alpaca wool trade are Charana and Puerto Acosta. The former town is on the Arica-La Paz Railway. Puerto Acosta is on Lake Titicaca. Most of the herds belong to Indians, who give them little attention, but understand the peculiarities of the animal and are able to domesticate it. A more careful study of alpaca raising has been made in the Arequipa district of Peru than in Bolivia.

It is customary to shear the herds every two years, though many are sheared at much longer intervals—even of five years. About ten pounds of wool are obtained per animal. The most common colours are the various shades of brown. Blacks are common, and white animals are much rarer Rugs are made from alpaca skins, and sell as bed coverings for 100 to 200 bolivianos, dependent on size and colour The alpaca is sometimes crossed with the llama, and the wool of the hybrid is sold as alpaca.

LEGATION AND CONSULATES IN GREAT BRITAIN

RESIDENCE.	DESIGNATION.	NAME.
London (pro. tem., 20 Copthall Avenue, E.C.2.)	Envoy Extraordinary, and Minister Plenipotentiary	Alberto Gutiérrez.
	First Secretary	H. Mamerto Urriolagoitia.
London (20 Copthall Avenue, E.C.2.)	Consul-General	H. Mamerto Urriolagoitia.
	Vice-Consul	Gerald Bryans Wolfe.
Liverpool . (18 James Street.)	Consul-General	Arturo Aramayo del Rio.
	Vice-Consul	J Lionel Barber.
Aberdeen ..	Consul	James H. Edwards.
Birmingham	Consul	George Brison.
Cardiff .	Consul	Alfred Bovey
Dover	Consul ..	W Rutley Mowll.
Dublin .	Consul	J. Weir Johnston.
Edinburgh and Leith	Consul	John Sharp.
Glasgow .	Consul	V Sanchez Peña.
	Vice-Consul	Peter Hamilton.
Hull .	Consul .	Norman Oughtred.
Manchester	Consul	Emeterio Cano de la V.
Newport (Mon.)	Consul	E. L. Melville Heard.
Newcastle	Consul	E. Cameron.
Sheffield .	Consul	Amador M. Berisa.
Southampton	Consul	Roderick M. Stewart.

BRITISH LEGATION AND CONSULATES IN BOLIVIA.

The letter (M) denotes that the Consular Officer holds a Marriage Warrant.
Members of the Diplomatic Service do not require Warrants.

RESIDENCE.	RANK.	NAME.	CONSULAR DISTRICT.
La Paz	Envoy Extraordinary, Minister Plenipotentiary, and Consul-General.	William E. O'Reilly	Republic of Bolivia.
Cochabamba	Vice-Consul	D. G. Rydings	—
	Vice-Consul	Quinius D. Pictor	—
Concepción de Velasco.	Vice-Consul	C. G. McEwen	—
Oruro ..	Consul	William Gray, M.B.E.	—
Potosí	Vice-Consul	John Davidson	—
Santa Cruz	Vice-Consul	H. E. Bloomfield	—
Sucre	(M) Consul	Ernest F Moore .	Departments of Chuquisaca and Tarija.

The principal **newspapers** are published at La Paz and circulate throughout the country :—" El Diario," " El Norte," " La Razón," " El Tiempo," and " La Verdad." Other leading papers are . at Sucre, " La Capital," " La Industria," " La Prensa " (weekly), at Cochabamba, " El Ferrocarril," " El Republicano," " La Tarde ", at Oruro, " La Nación," " La Patria," " La Prensa," " El Industrial ", at Potosí, " El Potosí", at Santa Cruz, " El Pais ", at Tarija, " El Boletin Antoniano," " El Guadalquivar "

Outward **mails** are sent via Buenos Aires and Quiaca via United States, and by Pacific Steam Navigation Line via Panamá.

Postage, 3d. first ounce, $1\frac{1}{2}$d. each ounce after

Homeward mails at frequent intervals.

There are 61,858 kilometres of **telegraph** lines under State control, and 1,740 in private ownership. The Marconi Company have **wireless** stations at La Paz, Riberalta, Yacuiba, Cobija and other places.

PUBLIC HOLIDAYS.

May 25.—Sucre Municipal Holiday
June 24.—National Feast.
July 15, 16, and 17.—La Paz Municipal Holidays.
August 5, 6, and 7.—National Festival.
The usual Roman Catholic Church Festivals are observed.

Guidance for Commercial Travellers.

The tax payable by commercial travellers in Bolivia is a municipal one, and varies in the 85 different Municipalities. The duration of the licence varies in the different districts. Travellers are generally classified for licence purposes according to the importance of the business represented.

The following table gives particulars for the capitals of Departments. The arrangements in the smaller places are similar, but the rates are generally lower

Town.	Fee in bolivianos, according to class.	Period.
La Paz ..	250.	Annual.
Cochabamba	500, 300, 200, 100.	3 months.
Oruro . ..	300, 200, 100, 50.	3 months.
Potosí .	500, 400, 300, 200, 100.	Per visit.
Santa Cruz	600, 400, 200.	Per visit.
Sucre	400, 300, 200.	Annual.
Tarija .	300, 200, 100.	Annual.
Trinidad	300,200.	Annual.

JOURNEY FROM THE COAST.

Mollendo—La Paz by Southern Railway.

Mollendo, the principal port of entry for Bolivia, is a picturesque little city upon the cliffs, and as viewed from the sea is striking by reason of the bright colours of the roofs and buildings. The reds and greens make the city stand out in relief against the drab of the foothills and the white of the cliffs.

The roughness of the sea at Mollendo and the difficulty of landing have been exaggerated. The passenger is hoisted from the launch, in a chair and set down on the pier The fleteros, boatmen and hoist operators are expert, and safely transport baggage and passengers under all conditions. Hotel touts, baggage carriers, and launch agents beset the passenger until he is at last established at some hotel. The charge demanded may be exorbitant, but a reasonable sum is generally accepted in the end. A day or two's stop can profitably be made in Mollendo.

For nearly fourteen miles the line to Arequipa runs on a sandy beach, with the brown and grey foot-hills on the left. The noise of the train does not drown the sound of the breakers against the rocky cliffs, and in between the cliffs are long stretches of sand which would delight a lover of bathing.

ON THE FOOT-HILLS.

As the sea is left behind, a steady climb begins, winding in, out and around the foot-hills. The Tambo Valley comes into view on the right, and miles of fields with alfalfa, sugar cane, and cotton contrast with the barren slopes on the left. Eden could have been no more beautiful than Tambo Valley, and Sahara is not more devoid of vegetation than the foot-hills of the Andes on this coast. At every station there is a little oasis, irrigated by water from the railway tanks, and these places are veritable tropical gardens, bearing vivid testimony to the fertility of the soil and climatic conditions which, given water, would enable these millions of acres of hill-side and plateau to supply cotton, sugar, grain, and fruit. Cotton plants are to be seen in several of these gardens, twelve or more feet high, with blossoms and mature bolls on the same bush throughout the year Cotton, corn, figs, cane, and roses grow side by side in luxuriance.

The sand dunes near La Joya, on the broad level plateau about half-way between Mollendo and Arequipa, are unique in formation and appearance. The main formation of the plateau is a coarse, brownish lava sand which appears too heavy to be blown. Scattered irregularly, are curious crescent-shaped dunes of a light grey ash colour All crescent-shaped and of varying sizes, they are from 30 to 100 ft. across and from 6 to 15 ft. high, with the points of the crescent on the leeward side. The dunes creep across the desert in a northerly course at the even rate of 40 to 60 ft. per year blown by the wind. The sand is slowly blown up the convex side and it drifts down into the hollow side of the crescent. This slow movement marks the years with almost the same accuracy that an hour glass marks the hours. One has to look back but half a mile to see the spot where the dune was fifty years ago, and by looking five miles back one sees where it was when the Indian·runners were crossing the plain, bearing messages to and from the Inca at Cuzco.

Clinging to the steep mountain sides, and following across the plains, parallel to the railway, is the eight-inch water line which supplies the locomotives and stations along the way and finally the city of Mollendo with water from near Arequipa. Laying this water line a distance of 107 miles, from an altitude of more than 7,000 ft. to sea level, was an engineering feat in itself.

SIGHT OF THE ANDES.

The view of Mount Misti brings a vivid realisation of the real grandeur of the Andes. On these rainless slopes is preserved all the original colourings of the mineral laden peaks, whose soft shades make the mountain sides velvety with a blending of shades most restful to the eye. The deep narrow valley of the Rio Chile comes into view, carpeted with rich green. Perpendicular sides of rich yellow wall the green valley in a frame of gold. The glistening silver of glacier peaks makes the whole a picture which lingers in the memory The Rio Chile flows by Arequipa and on into the fertile Camana valley

The glistening lights of Arequipa bring the first lap of the railway journey nearly to an end. No other half-day's railway ride in the world is more enjoyable to the lover of ocean, valley, and mountain scenery than this 107-mile trip from Mollendo to Arequipa.

A day or two may be very pleasantly spent here in Arequipa, famous for its eternal sunshine. In the background are three snow-capped mountains, Misti (18,967 ft.), Chachani (19,970 ft.), and Pichu-Pichu (17,800 ft.) A visit to the Harvard University's Observatory should not be missed.

At **Jesus,** thirty minutes by motor from Arequipa, are situated baths famous for their medicinal waters.

Tingo is easily reached from Arequipa by tram line and is worth a visit to see its parks and up-to-date baths.

At **Yura,** about half a mile from the station, are baths famous for their mineral waters, and good hotel accommodation.

Not all the wealth and culture of Peru are to be found in Lima City The fact is fully realized at first sight of Arequipa, the metropolis of Southern Peru, the wholesale distributing centre for that great expanse of mountain, pampa, and montaña which was once the heart of the Inca Empire.

Arequipa, as viewed from the train in the evening in the winter months, is a panorama of glittering electric lights, giving a very cheerful and pleasing impression. On alighting from the train and passing through the station, which is one of the most modern in Peru, one is astonished at the line-up of waiting automobiles and the clanging of tramcar bells. A ten-minute ride for 10 centavos by street-car or 50 centavos by auto brings the traveller to the Plaza de Armas, the centre of the city

The sunshine, with which Arequipa is blest, is always moderated by cool breezes from the coast, and the 7,500 ft. altitude gives a most exhilarating tang to the air without the difficulties experienced in higher altitudes. The view is a grand panorama of mountain and valley El Misti is the most admired and most noted of all the peaks of the Andes. At its base, a few hundred feet above the level of the city, is the University Observatory already mentioned.

The atmospheric conditions at the base of Misti have greatly assisted scientific knowledge of the stars.

TOWARDS CUZCO.

The early morning scene from the train as it winds its way up the valley from Arequipa towards Cuzco is one of enchanting interest. In the foreground are irrigated fields of alfalfa, wheat, and other grains. El Misti towers 18,000 ft. above the sea and almost two miles higher than the city To the right, Pichu-Pichu, only a thousand feet lower, and to the left, most magnificent of all, is the glacier-capped monarch, Chachani, with its top nearly 20,000 ft. in the sky With but one tunnel, few bridges, and no switchbacks the ascent is made by almost even gradients, and the divide is crossed at Crucero Alto, the highest point upon the Southern Railway, 14,688 ft. above, and 210 miles from the sea.

The train stops for twenty-five minutes at meal stations, and the mountain air whets the appetite. The meals are excellent and seem to improve with every stop. Passing over the summit, the heart quickens its pace and one becomes aware of the unusual strain upon the lungs. A few are victims of soroche at this altitude , headache, nausea, and ringing of the ears , symptoms of no more consequence than sea-sickness. Soroche is usually the penalty of constipation.

The first mountain lakes are to be seen soon after crossing the summit, and the mountain sides and canyons are covered with flocks of sheep, llamas, alpacas, and occasionally vicuñas. The two largest lakes seen from the train are Lagunillas and Saracocha. These two are very pretty and both come into sight at the same time from opposite sides of the train, which winds along their edges for nearly an hour Wild duck and other fowl offer good sport. As the descent continues streams become more plentiful. Signs of cultivation appear, and the scene changes in a few hours from desolate mountain peaks to fertile pampa, carrying a fairly populous agricultural community.

This is a land of probably the most industrious women-folk in the world. Tending the flocks, cultivating the fields or harvesting the crops, the Indian women are always in evidence, generally with baby on back and one or more trudging by her side ; dressed in the quaint, brightly coloured costumes, whenever the hands are not engaged in other work, they are busily spinning or knitting or weaving coarse woollen garments. Curios, woollen blankets, hand spun and hand woven, hand-knitted woollen socks, hoods, and ponchos in bright colours tempt the traveller to part with the few centavos or soles asked for these goods. A pair of baby stockings may be had for 10 centavos, very pretty children's hoods and caps for 40 centavos, and children's coats and sweaters for 80 centavos. Furs in great variety are offered at from a few soles for collar pieces, up to several pounds for beautiful alpaca and vicuña rugs.

The trains arrive at Juliaca in the evening, where passengers for Cuzco spend the night.

Passengers for Lake Titicaca and La Paz, do not stop at Juliaca, but continue on the same train to Puno, a distance of 30 miles, where they arrive at 6.45 p.m. and make connection with lake steamers.

ON FROM JULIACA.

In the first hundred miles north from Juliaca through Cuzco, the train ascends until it again reaches above 14,000 ft., this time on the ridge from which the water flows one way back into Lake Titicaca, and the other way down into the Amazon and so to the Atlantic. This hundred miles has been cultivated in every available spot, and is well watered by mountain streams from the glaciers. The cultivation is primitive. Flocks of sheep, llamas, and alpacas are met with, always attended by the Indian woman herdess. Scattered herds of cattle, a few horses and pigs indicate the diversity of agriculture. At Chuquibambilla is a Government experimental farm, where experienced Scotch breeders, using pure bred imported animals, demonstrate the possibility of producing four times the average wool clip. Visitors interested in stock raising are welcomed at the farm.

After the summit is passed at La Raya, the descent is rapid. The passenger watches the engine wind round the short curves as it follows the course of the widening stream down the narrow canyon. There are thrills as the shriek of the whistle and the grinding of the brakes tell that the driver is trying to stop the train before it runs over some Indian driving his pack mule, or some herder attempting to cross the track with his flocks. The line is not fenced or guarded, but the diligence of herders and the watchfulness of the drivers prevent accidents.

The valley widens, fields become greener, habitations look more "livable," towns are more frequent, and cultivation more general reaching higher up the steep slope. Piles of stones, occupying in many fields a larger area than remains to cultivate, bear testi-

mony to the patience and industry of the Indians who for generations have cultivated these slopes. At Aguas Calientes are springs
of boiling water, and for some distance the stream beside the track
is steaming 'hot. It is soon cooled by the rivulets of ice water
from the snow-capped peaks above. At Marangani the traveller
is astonished to see a large, modern, woollen mill where fleeces
are carded, spun, and woven by modern machinery.

Inca ruins come into view from the train windows, bringing
evidences of ancient civilization. Every little pueblo has its church,
every prominent hill-top is mounted with a cross, open out-door
shrines are scattered here and there, and every hut and habitation
is adorned with a small cross. The descendants of the race which
once worshipped the Sun and obeyed the mandates of the
" Children of the Sun " now profess the religion of the conquerors.

At Cuzco, there is a choice of a ride in a tramcar, a mule ride,
or a motor ride to the hotels in the centre of the city

THE INCA CAPITAL.

Cuzco, the scene of the rise and fall of the ancient Inca Empire,
has for nearly three centuries been a centre of interest for students
of civilization, writers of history, archæologists, and searchers
after treasure and adventure. An inland city in a remote and
inaccessible valley far up in the Andes, it was built in such a
manner that the attacks of conquerers, revolutionaries, invaders
and treasure hunters have failed to destroy the handiwork of a
civilization that flourished for centuries before Columbus discovered America. Probably few cities in the world have clung
so persistently to their ancient customs as Cuzco.

Cuzco is unique. The narrow street and cobble-stone pavements
remain unimproved. Wagons and carts are almost unknown.
Goods of all kinds are transported about the city on the backs of
men, mules, and llamas. The burden which barefooted Indians are
able to carry on their backs up and down these steep, rough
streets is almost incredible, and the price at which they do it is as
astonishingly low. Sacks of grain, bundles of corrugated iron,
trunks, cases of merchandise, sacks of cement, kegs of nails, and
cases of beer are among the things carried. It is said that some
Indians carry 400 lb. each trip.

Ice, although not badly needed in the cool air of this altitude,
may be had in most of the better restaurants and bars. The
Indian supplies the need with ice from the glacier.

The Fortress of Sachsahuaman, immediately in rear of the city
and about 700 ft. above the town, is in plain view from almost any
point in the city A forty-minute walk brings the sightseer to
the first of the ancient fortifications. From this point, the city
itself, with its bright red roofs, gaily painted walls, with trees and
shrubbery make an enchanting picture. Just beyond, the broad
fertile valley is cut into irregular fields, marked by grey stone
walls which dwindle in the distance to mere lines across the valley.

To the left is a narrow and rocky canyon, the natural bed of a stream of water, nearly all of which is diverted for irrigation and for the open-ditch sewer system which disposes of part of the city debris. Across this canyon are the remains of a stone aqueduct, in culvert form, three rows of arches high. This aqueduct was, centuries ago, one of the principal sources of water supply for the city In the Incaic days, when Cuzco had more than 200,000 population, the water was so well conserved and distributed in stone aqueducts and ditches that there was ample to supply all the needs of the city, irrigation included. To-day, with only about one-eighth the population, the supply is scarcely adequate.

INCA ARCHITECTURE.

The Fortress ranks among the wonders of the world. The hilltop had three series of stone walls, built of large blocks of flinty like stone, some of them 25 ft. high and more than 12 ft. thick, accurately cut and fitting to a nicety. How many thousands of hands and hundreds of years were required in its construction ? By what power were these enormous stones brought and placed in position ? It is uncertain whether the work is Incaic or pre-Incaic.

In front of the main wall of the fortress is a broad level space, which was perhaps once the parade ground for the armies of the monarch. On the opposite side of this space a series of seats has been carved in the solid rock ledge, known as the " Inca's Throne." Immediately behind this is the sliding-rock or Rodadero, said to be a natural glacier formation, of perfectly rounded, slippery groves at an easy slope fifty or more feet in length where one may slide to the ground below This is exciting, and without danger except to the clothing It is a favourite spot for children. At the other end of the " parade-ground," is another large rock, about thirty feet high and fifty in diameter in which a winding flight of stairs some two feet wide is perfectly carved from base to top. The top and side of this rock are carved with comfortable seats and chairs. One of the seats, larger than the rest, with a smaller one on either side, is known as the " Devil's Seat." Why, nobody knows. Near by is the " Inca's Bath " chiselled out of solid rock and surrounded by finely carved lounging seats, surprisingly comfortable, considering the hardness of the rock out of which they are formed. In and about these rocks are openings, credited with being the mouths of tunnels, into one of which one may crawl for one hundred feet to the exit opposite. Within are several chambers, and tradition has it that some one or more of these tunnels originally connected with the " Temple of the Sun " and other structures in the city Several such tunnels have been opened up beneath buildings in the city. In recent years several of these tunnels have been explored, and probably for long to come their mystery and romance will continue to tempt examination.

North of Cuzco, within a few miles are the remains of an Inca Palace, another fortress, the ancient reservoir of the Incas, and many caves, stone carvings, and interesting ruins. Within a day's horse ride are so many ruins and relics that it would take weeks to examine. There is a temptation to spend hours pondering over the downfall of an Empire which was able to accomplish such wonders.

RELICS OF THE PAST

Cuzco has more cathedrals, churches, monasteries, nunneries, and edifices of a religious type than any city of its size in the new world, nearly all constructed during the Colonial period out of material from the Inca structures. The stone-work of that period is commonplace, as compared with the remains of the Inca's structures. The several periods of construction can be readily identified by the architecture and workmanship, and the oldest is decidedly the best.

By what miracle the main stone work of the Temple of the Sun was preserved from the wreckers, no one knows.

Almost in the heart of the city, a short distance from the main plaza, it stands as a monument to the skill of its builders. The mechanical and architectural perfection of this piece of circular stone work is probably without equal in the world. A skilled cabinet maker could not exceed the delicate fineness of the joints between these perfectly cut stones. Centuries of earthquakes have not disturbed them except for a crack which ruptured the slabs of granite diagonally, with scarcely any injury to the inter-secting joints.

Almost every street in Cuzco has the remains of Incaic or pre-Incaic walls, arches and doorways. The city itself was surrounded by a wall, enough of which remains to show its course from end to end. Many streets are lined by walls of perfect stone work, now serving as foundations for rude adobe structures. This ancient stone work has one distinguishing feature. Every wall has a perfect line of inclination, toward the centre, from bottom to top. In the language of the stone-mason, they are all " battered " walls, and every corner rounded, in this fact probably lies the secret of their permanence. On these walls, over arches and around doorways may frequently be seen carvings of animals, serpents, and characters without present-day significance.

It is said that one of the first printing presses operated on the Western Hemisphere was set up in Cuzco. One of the oldest Universities in Latin America is the University of Cuzco, established 1692, on the site of the Palace of one of the Inca rulers. Francisco Pizarro is said to have entered Cuzco in 1553, some time before Lima was founded, and during the early Spanish Colonial period Cuzco was a city of greater importance than Lima, and has ever since been loth to yield the mantle of authority to the capital.

BOLIVIA.

Some twenty-five miles down the valley near Calca is the English Mission Farm. The farm employs more than 300 Indians. Everything needed by the Mission is produced there, except sugar and salt.

There is probably no place on the Western Continent where a month or two can be more profitably spent in sightseeing than in the vicinity of Cuzco. Most travellers who visit Cuzco once, return, and those who are unable to do so, express regret.

Detailed information on almost any subject relative to the Department of Cuzco may be obtained by addressing either the President of the University of Cuzco, or the Secretary of the Peruvian Corporation, at Lima. Books which may be profitably read before a visit to Cuzco, are: "Travels and Explorations in the Lands of the Incas" by Squier, "Across South America" by Bingham, "Along the Andes and down the Amazon" by Mozans; "The Incas of Peru ' by Markham, "Staircase Farms of the Ancients" by Cook, "Impressions and Observations of a Trip around South America" by James Bryce, and "South of Panamá" by E. A. Ross.

LAKE TITICACA.

It is curious after travelling for several days on the Southern Railway in the high altitudes of the Andes, to alight on the shores of Lake Titicaca and see at the pier a vessel which has the appearance and almost the size of an ocean liner

Baggage and passports are examined by the Bolivian officials before travellers board. The ship sails as soon after the arrival of the train as the passengers and baggage can be transferred and the formalities complied with, which on the direct steamers is about sundown. The state-rooms are roomy and fully as comfortable and well equipped as the average sea-going passenger ship. The " Inca " was built at Hull in 1905. She is 128 ft. long and has a 46 ft. beam, with quarters for 86 first class passengers, and is rated for 1,000 tons of cargo. The engineers and mechanics who piloted her up over the railway, piece-meal, and reassembled and made her sea-worthy on Lake Titicaca, accomplished a remarkable feat. Still more remarkable must have been the voyage of the " Yapura," the oldest of the Titicaca fleet, which has been navigating the lake since 1861 She came all the way from the sea on mule-back and Indian-back.

Lake Titicaca is not only the highest, but one of the most beautiful bodies of navigable fresh water in the world. On the maps of the old school geographies, the lake is a mere dot, and the impression is likely to remain until one crosses it, that altitude alone is its most distinguishing feature. A larger scale map, however, reveals the fact that is nearly one-third the size of Lake Ontario, and is among the largest bodies of fresh water. Situated as the central point of a vast basin, on the Western side of the main Cordillera of the Andes, where that water might reasonably be expected to flow into the Pacific, the overflow from Titicaca is drained by the river Desaguadero into Lake Poópo, which has no visible outlet. It is generally agreed that evaporation eventually returns the water from this vast water-shed to the heavens.

The fish in Titicaca are of but one kind, and it is believed that sea level varieties cannot be propagated at this altitude. All efforts to stock the lake with other than the native habitant have been in vain. The fish are small, a specimen more than eight inches long being very rare, and look like a cross between the chub and trout. They are plentiful, and the tables of the entire country from Cuzco to La Paz are supplied with their Friday meal from the lake.

Before sunrise, just as the first silver rays begin to light up the snow-capped range east of the Lake, is the correct time to rise on board the " Inca." Nearly seventy-five miles of perpetual snow is then in sight, looking deceptively near and but little above the level of the waters. It is almost incredible that some of the peaks are more than 22,000 ft. high, or nearly two miles above the lake. The freaks of vision are nowhere greater than at sunrise on Titicaca. Everything looks near There are no colour combinations which the slowly rising sun does not bring out, as its first rays strike the silvery heights, the browns and greys and greens of mountain side and valley, and the deep blue of the lake. One can understand how the Incas came to make the sun their god.

The port of Guaqui, on the shores of Bolivia, is at the southern end of the lake.

GUAQUI TO LA PAZ.

The Guaqui and La Paz Railway was built by the Bolivian Government, and although entirely within that republic, is controlled and operated by the Peruvian Corporation in connection with the Southern Railway of Peru and the Navigation of Lake Titicaca. It is the connecting link between La Paz and the fertile regions of Southern Peru whence come sugar and many other imports, and it is the outlet for many Bolivian products which are shipped to Peru. Bolivian exports and imports to and from the United States and Europe largely go through Mollendo and over the Southern Railway

The Bolivian highlands to the south and east of Lake Titicaca have many remains and ruins of a civilization without doubt pre-Incaic, and absolutely pre-historic. The most important of these are on the plains of Tiahuanaco, thirteen miles from Guaqui. Many are in sight from the railway and there are enough within easy walking distance of the stations to require several hours for even a cursory examination. Ruins of immense walls with doorways and archways still intact , human figures and animals carved from solid rock , doorways and archways covered with carved images, figures and designs. One such archway, near the railway station, is used by the boys of the pueblo as a target for rifle practice. There are no known quarries of similar rock within many miles and it is beyond belief that such immense stones were ever moved long distances and placed in position by mere man power

It is said that in building the Guaqui and La Paz Railway, hundreds of carloads of these ruins were broken up and used in the grading and in construction of culverts, foundations, and buildings.

From Guaqui to Alto the railway follows the broad plateau at an almost even gradient, rising only about 1,000 ft. in the 55 miles. The first evidence that a city is near is the well-kept golf course near the railway at Alto. Here the steam locomotive is exchanged for a powerful electric motor, and it is only after the precipitous descent is begun that La Paz comes into view, nearly 1,200 ft. straight below Alto has every appearance of being the " jumping-off place " and it looks as if nothing short of an aeroplane could possibly negotiate the descent in safety, but by a series of circles and loops, traversing a distance of only five miles, the train is brought to the station at the edge of the city

CITY OF LA PAZ.

La Paz is said to have steeper hills, better shops, more boot-blacks and a greater range of altitude than almost any other South American city It is the terminal of three railways, and a fourth is under construction : one to the south to Antofagasta , one to the west to Arica ; one to the north to Lake Titicaca and Mollendo, and that under construction to the east, tapping the immense fruit and agricultural belt of the lower montaña. Trains already run upon this line.

In the Plaza de Armas are the Government Palace, the Congressional Buildings, the Hotel Paris, and a Cathedral which has been under construction for nearly two hundred years. It is being built after an old Colonial design and promises to be a very imposing structure.

The altitude of the main portion of the city is about 12,000 ft. Motors can be hired at very moderate prices, and the city is served by an excellent tramway service. The trams make it possible to ascend nearly 1,400 ft. above the city to the golf course and descend nearly 1,000 ft. below the city, through the residential quarter The difference in climatic conditions within this range of nearly half a mile in altitude is remarkable. Upon the golf course it may be snowing, while below in the parks and gardens in the canyon the sun shines and flowers bloom almost continually Not so very far below oranges and other tropical fruits flourish perpetually

The public market in La Paz is a great attraction for strangers and tourists, and in many respects unique. The stalls are practically all occupied by Indian women and children in picturesque native costumes, and articles of food and apparel are displayed for sale to residents of the place at ridiculously low prices, and to tourists and strangers at very high prices. The stranger is able to purchase at bottom prices if familiar with local values. The most interesting articles to visitors are the hand woven woollen goods ; blankets, ponchos, rugs, shawls and apparel of all kinds, mostly in gay colours and costing from twenty centavos to twenty bolivianos. Many shops sell fur goods. Alpaca and vicuña rugs are beautiful and cheap enough to be irresistible. Few visit La Paz without spending money on fur goods.

La Paz presents a prosperous and busy aspect. It is not only the political, but the commercial centre of Bolivia. It is the whole-sale distributing centre for a territory, rich in minerals, agriculture, fruits, cocoa, rubber, and live stock. Seemingly small wholesale agencies transact a surprisingly large business, and retail shops, well stocked with merchandise from every quarter, present a metropolitan appearance.

To the north and east of La Paz are fascinating mountain scenes. Nearly seventy-five miles of peaks covered with perpetual snow are in view. The steep walls of the canyon within which the city is built are picturesque in colouring and formation. The erosion of centuries has gashed the mountain sides into grotesque shapes. The tourist who fails to visit La Paz misses one of the wonder-sights of the world. A visit to La Paz makes a fitting climax to the journey from Mollendo over the Southern Railway, up and up, around and through and across the Andes.

BRAZIL

Brazil

BRAZIL.

Rio de Janeiro, the capital of Brazil, is the second largest city in South America, with a population of 1,500,000. The climate is specially favourable in winter. It has a beautiful bay extending northward about fifteen miles, and two to seven miles in width, flanked by mountains and dotted with islands. The Sugar Loaf Mountain, 1,200 ft. high, stands on the western side of the entrance to the bay The steamer passes the slopes and granite peak of Corcovado. Behind the city rises the Tijuca range of hills, dominated by Tijuca itself. Over the bay, some thirty miles distant, rise the fantastic shapes of the Organ Mountains, including the five picturesque peaks known as the Dedos de Deus.

The city is worthy of its setting. The promenade facing the sea is of white marble, and five miles long. Many of the buildings are palatial, the city squares are of great beauty, with bronze statuary, fountains, and luxurious verdure. The main artery is the Avenida Rio Branco, containing the chief public buildings. On the Rua Primeiro de Março are the Exchange, the Post Office, and the Banco do Commercio. One of the principal streets, Rua Ouvidor, beginning at the quay, near Praça 15 de Novembro, and ending at São Francisco Square, is the " Regent Street " of the city and the best tailors, dressmakers, jewellers, bric-à-brac dealers are found there.

Landing :—Alongside quays at end of Av Rio Branco.

Hotels :—Internacional, in the hills, half-hour from city, 100 beds, 15$000-25$000 per day, Central Sea front, 80 beds, 16$000-25$000 per day, Avenida, Avenida Central, 150 beds, 14$000-20$000 per day; Rio Palace, five minutes from city, 60 beds, 6$000-8$000 per day, Palace, Avenida Central, 200 beds, 25$000-30$000 per day, Estrangeiros, ten minutes from city, 120 beds, 16$000-20$000 per day, Metropole, ten minutes from city, 50 beds, 12$000-15$000 per day, Splendid, Sea front, 40 beds, 10$000-15$000 per day, Albion, ten minutes from city, 30 beds, 12$000-15$000 per day (English)

Restaurants :—" Rotisserie Americano," Rua Gonçalves Dias ; " Franciscana," Avenida Rio Branco , also the " Assyrio," Avenida Rio Branco.

Clubs :—Central, Country, Jockey, Naval, Club dos Diarios, Club dos Politicos.

Tea Rooms :—Alvear, Colombo.

Points of Interest :—Avenida Rio Branco, the main street of Rio contains the Government Buildings, Municipal Theatre, School of Art, and Supreme Court of Law Rua Ouvidor, shopping centre.

Avenida Beira Mar, the promenade. Parque de Bôa Vista, with the National Museum; trams marked "S. Januario," "Alegria," "Cajú" or "Jockey Club," single fare, 200 reis. Ipanema, Copacabana, and Leme, facing the sea, single fare by tram, 400 reis. Botanical Gardens, open daily 6.30 a.m. to 6 p.m., tram marked "Gavea" from Avenida Rio Branco, single fare, 400 reis. Nictheroy, residential suburb opposite Rio. Ferry-boats every twenty minutes from Praça 15 de Novembro.

Markets :—"Mercado Novo," close to Praça 15 de Novembro, "Flower Market," Rua 7 Setembro. Visit early morning.

Rail :—(1) Central Brazilian Railway to São Paulo, Santos, the South and the interior (2) Leopoldina Railway to Victoria and the North. (3) Rio de Oruro. (4) Corcovado.

Excursions :—CORCOVADO, by tram marked "Aguas Ferreas," from Av. Rio Branco to Cosme Velho Station, thence by rack railway, or by "Sylvestre" tram from Largo da Carioca and rack. Trains leave Cosme Velho for the summit. A superb view is had from the summit of the Corcovado (over 2,000 ft. high).

PÃO DE ASSUCAR, by tram marked "P Vermelha," from Av R. Branco, thence to the summit by aerial railway in two stages, P Vermelha to Morro da Urca (500 ft. high) · M. da Urca to Pão de Assucar (1,100 ft) Complete journey, 4$000.

TIJUCA, by tram marked "Alto da Bôa Vista," from Praça 15 de Novembro. Fare, 700 reis each way, thence by horse or foot. The best way is by motor from the city in a car sufficiently powerful to negotiate the gradients. The view from the peak of Tijuca (over 3,000 ft.) gives a good idea of the tropical vegetation of the interior.

PETROPOLIS (2,600 ft. above sea-level) is the summer hill resort. Take tram marked "S. Januario," "Cajú," "S. Luiz Durão," or "Praia Formoza," to Leopoldina Railway Station, whence trains leave for Petropolis, the fastest making the journey in one and three-quarter hours. For the first hour the line is fairly level, from Raiz da Serra a rack locomotive hauls the train for thirty minutes. The view from the carriage is particularly fine. Petropolis is a pretty town, and interesting rides can be made in the neighbourhood. Frequent trains.

Petropolis is the " Simla of Rio " and beautifully situated in mountainous country, by train from Rio about 1¾ hours. The residential town of foreign diplomats, an important cotton manufacturing centre. Population 30,000. Electric tramway service.

HOTELS. Rio de Janeiro, Majestic, Palace, Europa, Bragança.

Nictheroy :—Residential suburb of Rio de Janeiro opposite to it on the Bay. Population of 88,000. Electric tramways and a ferry connect it with the city.

São Paulo, the second of Brazilian cities, has a population of 750,000. Standing at an elevation of nearly 3,000 ft., its temperature is moderate and its air bracing. The shape of the town is an irregular polygon and the centre embraces the districts of Rua Direita, Quinze de Novembro, São Bento and Praça Antonio Prado. This is the hub of the city, and is continually extending into the new districts, where fine buildings, most of them in the Italian style of architecture, are growing up.

São Paulo bears the impress of energy The streets are lit by gas, and the main thoroughfares by electric light ; the water supply is excellent; the electric tramway service is one of the best in Brazil. The new municipal theatre is scarcely excelled anywhere. The city is 10 hours by rail from Rio de Janeiro, and 2 hours from Santos, with which it is connected by mountain railway.

Hotels:—Esplanada, Terminus Regina; also Palace, La Paz, Grande, Suisso, Victoria.

Tea Rooms :—Mappin Stores, Rua Direita.

Restaurants :—Harrison & Morris, Rua José Bonifacio 29, Anglo-American, Travessa do Grande Hotel 10.

Markets :—25 de Março, in the Rua 25 de Março, is open daily, and among the others that which is held on Saturdays at the Largo do Arouche is especially worth visiting.

Amusements : — Racecourse, football, tennis, bowls, rowing, sailing, motoring, cinemas, theatres, music-halls.

Points of Interest :—Steam tram or motor to Cantareira Waterworks, Jardin da Luz, Luz Railway Station, Avenida Paulista, Municipal Theatre, and Sant' Anna by electric tram. Alto da Serra, by motor " Butantan " (snake farm), by motor

Excursions :—Electric trams (short circular lines) Avenida, Hygienopolis, Campos Elyseos, Avenida Angelica, Santa Cecilia, Avenida Grande and Paraizo. Out of town (one hour to one and a-half hours return) by electric tram Bosque da Saude, Parque Jabaquara, Lapa, Penha, Santo Amaro, Jardim da Acclimacao Pinheiros and Sant' Anna.

Museum:—Ypiranga.

Rail :—São Paulo Railway to Santos and interior; Central Brazilian Railway to Rio de Janeiro , Sorocabana by Southern Brazil-Uruguay

Santos had formerly an ill-name, but to-day its health is excellent. The population is 112,000. Santos is *par excellence* the coffee port of the world. The wharves on the river front are always alive with shipping.

The buildings stand upon a large plain, between the mountain and the sea. The old quarter, from the docks to Rua Quinze de Novembro, has narrow winding thoroughfares. The new quarter **extends** southwards, and embraces a large area reclaimed from the sea by the Empreza das Docas , it is dominated by the hill on which stands the church of Nossa Senhora de Mont-Serrat.

Landing :—Steamer to wharf

Hotels : — Guaruja Hotel, Guaruja Bay, facing Atlantic. (Cable " Guaruja Hotel "), 250 beds, 20$000-100$000 per day High class. Casino, etc., Parque Hotel, Gonzaga, on sea front of Santos Bay (Cable " Parque "), 150 beds, 20$000-80$000 per day. High class, Palace Hotel, Praia Jose Memino, (Cable " Palace Hotel "), 150 beds, 15$000-60$000 per day, Casino, etc., Rotisserie Sportsman, centre of city (Cable " Rotisserie "), 60 beds 16$000-30$000 per day, Deodoro Hotel, near sea front (Cable " Deodoro Hotel "), 21 beds, 10$000-15$000 per day; Bristol Hotel, in the town, 50 beds, 10$000-20$000 per day, Washington Hotel, in the town, 60 beds, 10$000-20$000 per day; (Portuguese), International, Santos Bay (Cable " International "), 80 beds, 12$000-25$000 per day (Commercial).

Conveyances :—Electric trams, cabs and motor cars.

Rail :—São Paulo Railway to São Paulo.

Excursions :—To Guaruja, crossing river by ferryboat and continuing by light railway. Journey about forty minutes. Guaruja on a sandy bay facing the open Atlantic is a popular health resort. A new Grand Hotel is being opened. The place is the fashionable seaside resort of Brazil, and one of the finest in the world.

Pernambuco, the most important city in Northern Brazil, consists of three portions connected by bridges . (1) Recife (the Reef), lying on a peninsula, and the port is often known by this name, (2) São Antonio, on an island between the peninsula and the mainland; (3) Bôa Vista on the mainland. The three divisions are connected by stone and iron bridges, and the city is known as the " American Venice, transported floating o'er the waves." The streets are narrow, and the houses tall, the object being to obtain the maximum amount of shade. The city is undergoing a metamorphosis. Wide avenidas are being made with buildings worthy of one of the largest cities. Electric cars connect the business quarter with the suburbs. The population is about 260,000, the proportion of coloured folk is large.

The port is 1,120 nautical miles from Rio de Janeiro, 120 from Maceió, 382 from Bahia, which is reached in about 28 hours' steaming.

Landing :—By motor launch.

Hotels :—Palace, Beribe (Cable " Palacehotel "), 17 beds, 14$000-35$000 per day, Recife Hotel, Rua 15 de Novembro (Cable " Recifotel "), 65 beds, 14$000-20$000 per day, Parque Hotel, Rua do Hospico (Cable " Parque "), 36 beds, 12$000-18$000 per day; Hotel Luzitano, P. Independencia, 38 beds, 8$000-12$000 per day, Hotel Modelo, P Espirito Santo, 20 beds, 8$000-12$000 per day, Bôavista, P Marciel Pinheiro, 60 beds, 8$000-10$000 per day; Universo, Rua D de Caxias, 27 beds, 7$000-12$000 per day, Portuense, Ave. M. de Barros, 25 beds, 7$000-12$000 per day, Avenida.

Boarding Houses :—Landy, Rua Benifica, 60 beds, 13$000-22$000 per day; Francaise, Ave H. Portuguez, 24 beds, 14$000-22$000 per day, Estancia, Rua V de Goyanna, 12 beds, 10$000 per day, Saguillon, Rua B. de S. Borja, 10 beds, 14$000 per day.

Restaurants :—Hotel do Parque, Recife Hotel, and Hotel Commercial.

Shopping Centres :—Rua Nova (New Street) in Recife, S. José Market, and Rua Duque de Caxias.

Local Steamers :—Services to Maceió, Bahia, Penedo, Aracaju, Victoria, Rio de Janeiro, Santos, Paranagua, San Francisco, Rio Grande do Sul, Peletas, Port Alegre, Cabedello, Natal, Macau, Mossoro, and River Plate.

Points of Interest :—Churches of Nossa Senhora da Penha, in Recife, and Bôa Vista in the suburb of that name. Republica Square in São Antonio.

Excursions :—To Olinda, a seaside resort, by electric car every twenty minutes. This town contains several old Dutch churches and other relics of the 17th century Dutch occupation.

Rail :—Recife is the headquarters of the Great Western of Brazil Railway, which joins the city with Parahyba, Natal, and Maceió, and with the inland town of Pesqueria.

Pará (or Belem), at the mouth of the Amazon, is one of the chief ports for river traffic, and is reached from Pernambuco by local steamer The population is 280,000. The streets are ill-paved, but the city is picturesque. The squares are fine and the buildings, plastered and coloured in vivid hues, contrast with the brilliant foliage and bright sky For further description see pp. 134–136.

Landing :—Usually alongside.

Hotels :—Grand, Praça da Republica, 140 beds, 12$000-17$000 per day, Cafe da Paz, Praça da Republica, 100 beds, 9$000-12$000 per day, Rotisserie Suisse, Praça da Republica, 15 beds, 10$000 per day, Central Hotel, Rua de Sant' Anna, 40 beds, 8$000-12$000 per day, Hotel America, Rua Cons. J Alfredo, 40 beds, 7$000-10$000 per day

Steamship Service :—Regular communication with New York, Liverpool, Antwerp, Rio de Janeiro and New Orleans.

Three small river steamers maintain a monthly service between Pará and the upper reaches of the Rio Hura. The two principal ports are Foz de Jura and Foz de Taruaca.

Porto Alegre, like the other two ports of the district, Rio Grande and Pelotas, is on the Lagôa dos Patos, a large fresh-water lake. Porto Alegre is the capital. The Lagôa dos Patos is entered over a bar at the opening to the sea, and twenty-four hours' steaming carries the vessel to the city

The panorama of Porto Alegre is delightful, reminding one both of Bahia and Montevideo. Most of the houses are on a promontory of fair height, dominated by the new Presidential Palace and by the two high white towers of the old church of Nossa Senhora das Dores.

A up-to-date port is in the course of construction, and eventually the work will allow ocean-going steamers of fair size to come up to Porto Alegre. The population of the town is 160,000.

Conveyances :—Electric cars, cabs, taxi-cabs and motor-buses.

Points of Interest :—Racecourse, football grounds, tennis clubs, several picture palaces and theatres, rowing, sailing and motoring. The scenery is pretty and the roads are fair

Excursions :—Tristeza, Belem Novo, Belem Velho, Itapuam, Cidreira, and others by water or road.

Hotels :—Grande, Metropole, Lagache, Bianchi.

Rail :—To Rio de Janeiro, Montevideo and Buenos Aires. The journey takes five days to Rio, three to Buenos Aires and two to Montevideo. There are trains three times weekly to Rio, four times a week to the Argentine and Montevideo.

Communications :—Small coasting passenger steamers to and from Rio de Janeiro twice a week, a small steamer on the Lagôa dos Patos leaves Porto Alegre about once a week for Rio Grande.

Maceió lies between Pernambuco and Bahia, and has a population of about 75,000. It is a cotton and sugar port with a lighthouse built on an eminence in the middle of the town, quite half a mile from the sea. The seaport is called Jaraguá.

Landing :—By shore boat.

Conveyances :—Electric trams and motor cars.

Hotels :—Bella Vista, Grande Ponto, Nova Cintra, Petropolis.

Market :—Praça Tavares Basto.

Excursions :—S. Francisco River (via Penedo) to visit magnificent Paulo Affonso Falls; or by train to Quebrangulo or Garanhuus, and thence by motor To Alagôas, the old capital of the State, across the lakes.

Rail :—Great Western of Brazil to Pernambuco.

Bahia :—Bahia de São Salvador de todos os Santos (Bay of the Holy Saviour of All Saints)—to give it its full title—is one of the greatest coastal cities in Brazil, and it has a population of 350,000. Founded in 1510, it was till 1763 the capital of Brazil. The buildings of the old town include many interesting churches, and the harbour is magnificent. It is a great cocoa and tobacco centre, and the cigars and cigarettes of Bahia are renowned. From Bahia are also exported piassava, rubber, coffee, and many other kinds of produce. A great part of the city has been remodelled, and a fine Avenida extends from the Upper City to the Barra and thence along the cliffs near to the little fishing town of Rio Vermelho.

Landing :—By launch, the charge varies with the number of passengers taken. By boat, Rs. 5$ooo per trip.

Conveyances :—Motor cars, Rs. 15$ooo per hour.

Hotels :—Mme. Schleier, Rua Corredor da Victoria 80 (English House). Pensao Ingléza, Rua Corredor da Victoria 72. Pensao Harbord, Barra, Hotel Meridonal, Grand Hotel. The average terms for any of the above are Rs. 10$ooo to 12$Qoo per day

Excursions :—To Upper City by lift. Tram to Rio Vermelho or to Barra. The former goes inland, and the latter runs along the shore to the Lighthouse. There are two routes to each.

Rio Grande do Sul, near the entrance of the Lagôa dos Patos, is the third city of the Brazilian State of the same name, 50,000 population. It is well laid out. Most of the houses (except in Rua Marechal Floriano) have but one story It is reached from Rio de Janeiro by rail and local steamers.

Landing :—Alongside wharf.

Hotels :—Paris, Brazil, both in Rua Marechal Floriano.

Conveyances :—Electric cars, cabs and motor cars.

Market :—Praça General Telles. Best time, 7 a.m.

Points of Interest :—Various praças, racecourse, football grounds, park, new port works, etc.

Excursions :—To Villa Sequeira, a seaside resort, about forty minutes by train, good bathing.

Rail :—To Pelotas, Bage, and Rio de Janeiro.

Matto Grosso, in the State of the same name, has about 5,000 inhabitants, a Government military station. There is trade in rubber, medicinal herbs, etc.

Victoria, capital of Espirito Santo State, and 680 miles from São Paulo, has a population of 12,000, and is a port with a large distributing business with the interior.

Curityba, capital of Paraná State, is the principal centre for the herva-matte milling industry, with a population of 70,000, and is easily reached from São Paulo by rail.

Florianopolis (Desterro), capital of Santa Catharina State, and its principal port, has a population of 40,000.

HOTELS : Macedo, Metropol, Taranto.

Bello Horizonte, capital of the State of Minas Geraes, is an agricultural and mining centre, with a population of about 50,000. It is 376 miles from Rio de Janeiro and reached from that point by a 15 hours' rail journey

HOTELS . Anaieda, Internacional, Globo, Grande.

Ceará (Fortaleza), a port, capital of the State of the same name, with a population of 80,000, has an open roadstead, and ships drawing up to 25 ft. discharge into lighters. It is 360 miles from Maranhâo, and reached from Parnahyba and Natal by steamer Large trade with Pernambuco.

Maranhão, a port, in Maranhão State, has a population of 60,000. Cargoes are loaded or discharged by lighters. It is 250 miles from Ceará and has a large trade, with good railway connections.

HOTELS : Central, Champoredryo.

Natal, capital of the State of Rio Grande do Norte, has 30,000 inhabitants, and is a flourishing sugar and cotton export port.

HOTELS . Internacional, Avenida, Tyrol.

Parahyba, capital of the State, on the Parahyba river, with 35,000 inhabitants, is used for coasting traffic. Ocean-going steamers load and unload at Cabedello, 12 miles down the river, where there is a railway wharf.

HOTELS : Central, Europa, Do Norte.

PHYSICAL FEATURES.

The fourth largest country in the world, Brazil is the largest of the South American Republics, and touches the boundaries of all except Ecuador and Chile. It has an area of 3,291,416 square miles, which is three-sevenths of the whole of the South American sub-continent. Its sea board is 4,060 miles. It extends 2,629 miles from Cape Orange to the River Chuy, and 2,600 miles from Olinda westwards to the Peruvian boundary The two vast river-basins of the Amazon and La Plata comprise about three-fifths of the total area of Brazil. Both are heavily wooded, and the Amazon basin is annually in flood over a wide extent. The huge plateau forming the country's main physical feature is a tableland from 1,000 to 3,000 ft. above sea level, and traversed by two great mountain-chains. The coast range (Serra do Mar) culminates in the Organ Mountains near Rio de Janeiro at an elevation of 7,323 ft., while the inland range attains a height of 9,823 ft. (probably the highest in Brazil) at the Itatiaya peak. There is also the Central or Goyana mountain system, consisting of an eastern range, 4,206 ft. at its highest, and a western range which forms the parting of the Paraná and Tocantins-Araguaya river-basins, and has a peak of 4,500 ft. near the city of Goyaz. This enormous region consists principally of chapadões, or large tablelands, and deep river-valleys. Much the vastest of these chapadões is the Amazonian, which comprises the greater part of the States of Matto Grosso and Goyaz, most of southern Pará, and considerable portions of West Maranhão.

The **Amazon** river-system covers and drains the whole north-west of Brazil. In the extreme north-east there is a smaller area, outside the Amazon sphere, whose rivers—the Araguary, Amapá, Calçoene, Cassiporé, and Oyapok—flow east to the Atlantic. Of the rivers of the great plateau, the Parnahyba has a course of 900 miles, and is the boundary between the States of Piauhy and Maranhão. The largest river of the east coast is the São Francisco, a stream belonging essentially to the inland tableland region. Similarly, the Parahyba do Sul is the greatest of the Atlantic coast rivers south of the São Francisco, it flows from east to west through the fertile State of Rio de Janeiro, and has a total course of 658 miles, about 150 of which are navigable.

There are no large coastal rivers south of Cape Frio, but the rivers of the other great system—the Rio de la Plata—are important. The tributaries of the Paraguay and of the Paraná respectively drain the south-west of Matto west of Minas Geraes. The Paraná is much broken by falls and rapids, though between its two great waterfalls is an open channel nearly 300 miles long. A similar remark applies to the River Uruguay whose tributaries are also impeded by rapids.

Although its rivers are numerous and magnificent, Brazil has comparatively few **lakes**. The most important, are the Lagôa do Norte (a salt lake), on which stands the city of Maceió, the Lagôa do Sul, a few miles south, and, on the coast of Rio Grande do Sul, Lagôa dos Patos (124 miles long by 37 broad) and Lagôa Mirim (108 miles long by 15 miles broad)

The country is fortunate in its bays and harbours. The two most important are those of Rio de Janeiro, and Todos os Santos, where stands the city of Bahia. Both ports accommodate vessels of the heaviest draught. Espirito Santo is the harbour for the city of Victoria. Santos, São Francisco, and Paranaguá have excellent ports. Pernambuco, the inner harbour of which is accessible to vessels of medium draught, stands at the confluence of the small rivers Capibaribe and Beberibe. Maranhão and Santa Catharina likewise have fine bays.

The principal waterways are the Amazon river, on which are situated the chief river ports of the Republic, and the Paraná river, which passes through Argentine and Paraguayan territory, and affords a means of communication between these countries, Bolivia and Brazil.

There are 30,070 miles of navigable rivers in Brazil, over 17,130 miles of which there is a regular service of vessels.

The **climate** of Southern Brazil, including Rio de Janeiro, is sub-tropical. Light clothing is essential, though overcoats are frequently necessary in high-standing towns, such as São Paulo and Petropolis. With the stamping out of yellow fever the climate may now be considered healthy throughout these regions.

Northern Brazil is tropical and inclined to be enervating, although a more bracing climate prevails on the table lands. Precautions should be taken against malaria.

POPULATION

(Based on census of 1920.)

States.	Population.	States.	Population.
Alagôas	978,748	Paraná	685,711
Amazonas	363,166	Pernambuco	2,154,835
Bahia	3,334,465	Piauhy	609,003
Ceará	1,319,228	Rio de Janeiro	1,559,371
Federal District (Rio de Janeiro)	1,157,873	Rio Grande do Norte	537,135
		Rio Grande do Sul	2,182,713
Espirito Santo	457,328	Santa Catharina	668,743
Goyaz	511,919	Sao Paulo	4,592,188
Maranhão	874,337	Sergipe	477,064
Matto Grosso	246,612	Acre Territory	92,379
Minas Geraes	5,888,174		
Pará	983,507	Total	30,635,605
Parahyba	961,106		

Equivalent to 3·61 head per square kilometre and showing an increase of nearly 77 per cent. upon the 1900 total.

Immigration :—The best immigrant for Brazil continues to be the Italian. The Japanese continue to send immigrants to São Paulo. The Ministry of Agriculture maintains a commissariat in Germany to deal with emigration to Brazil and with general propaganda abroad, and various German societies exist to send emigrants to Brazil.

The Brazilian Government encourages the formation of groups of colonists, and there are nearly 9,000 such groups. A census of this colonist-population on 31st December, 1921, showed :—8,029 families, consisting of 44,459 persons, of which 23,566 men and 20,893 women, viz., 18,708 Brazilians and 25,751 foreigners.

The value of the agricultural production of these groups is over Rs.20,000,000$ annually, and their cattle production was valued at nearly Rs.10,000,000$ in 1921.

GOVERNMENT

Constitution :—Brazil was an Empire from September 7, 1822. A Republic was declared on November 15, 1889, a provisional Government being established and a Constituent Assembly convoked. This latter promulgated the Federal Constitution of the Republic of the United States of Brazil on February 24, 1891, former provinces being converted into Federal States.

The constitution is based on that of the United States of North America. The Federal States are empowered to legislate on all matters not pertaining exclusively to the Federal Government, and each has its own Government and administration, revenue and budget. To the Federal Government belongs the right of civil and commercial legislation throughout the Republic and criminal legislation in the Federal District. Judicial organization is on the same basis, and judicial power is vested in the Federal Judiciary authorities.

Legislative power is exercised by the Senate and the Chamber of Deputies. The Senate is composed of three senators from each State, who are elected for a term of nine years, one-third of the members retiring every three years. A Senator must be at least thirty-five years old and have been a Brazilian citizen for more than six years. The same rule applies to the Deputies, of whom there is one for every 70,000 inhabitants, and not less than four for each State.

Executive power is vested in the President, who is elected by direct vote for a term of four years, and is ineligible for an immediately following second term. The Vice-President is elected with the President and acts as his deputy in cases of necessity, and is also President of the Senate. The Ministers have no seat in Congress, and are responsible for their acts only to the President.

The elections are on the basis of universal suffrage for all citizens over twenty-one, if registered according to the law, with the exception of beggars, illiterates, soldiers, and members of monastic orders.

The constitution guarantees to Brazilians and foreigners residing in the country inviolability of rights respecting the liberty and safety of the individual and his property Foreigners enjoy all civil rights, but are ineligible for certain professions, such as stockbrokers, auctioneers, and lawyers.

Brazil is a member of the Berne International Convention for the Protection of Industrial Property Rights in literary property are guaranteed to foreigners whose countries have adopted reciprocity

Civil legislation is based chiefly on old Portuguese laws, but civil and commercial codes have been drawn up which meet present-day requirements and progress.

In cases of internal disturbance or foreign aggression a state of siege can be declared by Congress or, if it is not in session, by the President of the Republic.

The constitution recognizes **naturalization** in the following instances :—

Foreigners who were in Brazil on November 15, 1889, when the Republic was proclaimed, and did not declare within six months thereafter their wish to retain the nationality of their birth.

Foreigners who possess real estate in Brazil and are married to Brazilians or have Brazilian sons, so long as they reside in Brazil and do not state their intention of not becoming Brazilian citizens.

Foreigners who become naturalized by any other procedure,

PAST PRESIDENTS.

Marshal Deodora da Fonseca (proclaimed the Republic) ..	1889
Marshal Floriano Peixoto .	1891
Dr Prudente José de Moraes e Barros . .	1894
Dr Manoel Ferraz de Campos Salles .	1898
Dr Francisco de Paula Rodrigues Alves .	1902
Dr Affonso Augusto Moreira Penna (died during tenure of office)	1906
Dr Nilo Peçanha (former Vice-President)	1909
Marshal Hermes da Fonseca	1910
Dr Wenceslao Braz .	1914
Dr Epitacio Pessoa . . .	1919

Dr Rodrigues Alves was re-elected and should have taken office on November 15, 1918, but he died shortly before, and for some time prior to the general elections in 1919 Dr Delphim Moreira, the Vice-President, officiated.

PRESIDENT AND VICE-PRESIDENT

President of the Republic	Arthur Bernardes.
Vice-President . .	Estacio Coimbra.

MINISTRY

Foreign Affairs . . .	Félix Pacheco.
Justice and Interior	João Luis Alves.
War . . .	Gral Setembrino de Carvalho.
Marine	Admiral Alexandrino de Alencar
Finance .	Sampaio Vidal.
Transport and Public Works	Francisco Sá.
Agriculture	Miguel Calmón.

A BRAZILIAN CALENDAR.

1499. Part of the coast explored by Vicente Pinzon.
1500. Coast near Bahia discovered by Pedro Alvarez Cabral.
1501. Americo Vespucci commands an expedition to Brazil.
1503. First settlement established at Bahia. Duarte Coelho founds first settlement at Caravellos.
1510. First visit of a French fleet to the Bay of Todos os Santos.
1530. Brazilian coast visited by William Hawkins. Affonso de Sousa made Admiral of the coast.
1532. Coastal regions of Brazil divided into captaincies.
1542. Bahia visited by Thomas Pudsey of Southampton.
1549. Thomé de Sousa lands at Bahia as Captain-General. First Jesuits arrive in Brazil.
1555. The French establish themselves at Rio de Janeiro.
1560. Defeat of the French at Rio de Janeiro.
1564–1572. Vice-Royalty of Mem da Sa.
1567. French finally expelled from Rio de Janeiro by the Portuguese.
1572. Brazil divided into two Governments with capitals at Bahia and Rio de Janeiro.
1577. General Government re-established. First English commercial relations opened up with Santos by John Whithall.
1580. Brazil, with Portugal, becomes subject to Spain.
1591. Santos raided by Cavendish.
1594. The French found establishments in Maranhão. Pernambuco raided by James Lancaster.

BRAZIL.

1614. The French expelled from Maranhão.
1617. First news sheet founded.
1624. City of Bahia captured by the Dutch.
1625. Bahia recaptured by the Portuguese.
1629. Dutch West India Company formed for the conquest of Northern Brazil.
1630. Pernambuco captured by the Dutch.
1637. Arrival in Recife of the Count of Nassau.
1654. Dutch finally driven from Pernambuco.
1662. Holland signs a treaty surrendering her claims in Brazil.
1680. Disputes with Spain concerning left bank of the La Plata River.
1681. First discovery of gold.
1684. Insurrection in Northern Brazil.
1710. French squadron under Duguay-Trouin unsuccessfully attacks Rio de Janeiro.
1711. The French Admiral, Duguay-Trouin, bombards Rio.
1724. Discovery of diamond fields.
1726. War between Brazil and Buenos Aires.
1750. Treaty between Brazil and Buenos Aires.
1762. War between Brazil and Buenos Aires.
1763. Seat of Government transferred from Bahia to Rio de Janeiro.
1776. War between Brazil and Buenos Aires.
1777. Treaty between Brazil and Buenos Aires.
1789. Conspiracy in Minas Geraes to overthrow Portuguese rule defeated.
1808. Arrival of the Portuguese Court, escorted by a British naval force, in Brazil.
1809. The Brazilian, Lucas Alves de Alvarenga, commands a relief expedition to China to clear the coast of pirates.
1815. Brazil elevated to the rank of a kingdom.
1816. The Prince Regent reigns as Dom João VI.
1817. The Portuguese capture Montevideo, which becomes temporarily Brazilian territory.
1820. The opening of the Rio de Janeiro Exchange.
1821. Dom João VI departs for Lisbon, leaving the Regency of the Kingdom of Brazil to his son Dom Pedro.
1822. Dom Pedro proclaims at São Paulo the independence of Brazil, and is declared Emperor. Portugal declares war on Brazil. Brazil becomes an Empire.
1823. Lord Cochrane arrives in Brazil to take command of the Brazilian fleet in its operations against the Portuguese.
1825. Independence of Brazil acknowledged by Portugal. Imperial Academy of Fine Arts inaugurated.
1826. Naval action between Brazil and Argentina off Buenos Aires. Dom Pedro abdicates the throne of Portugal in favour of his daughter, Dona Maria.
1827. The Brazilians defeated by Alvear at Ituzaingo. Faculties of the Law of Pernambuco and of São Paulo founded.
1828. Treaty between Brazil and Buenos Aires.
1831. Dom Pedro abdicates the Brazilian throne in favour of his son, aged five, who reigns as Dom Pedro II. Feijo appointed Regent.
1838. Imperial forces beat the rebels in the North, but they, in turn, suffer in the South.
1840. The majority of the Emperor proclaimed.
1845. Civil War in the province of Rio Grande do Sul ends.
1849. Rosas proclaims war against Brazil.
1850. The Royal Mail Steam Packet Company begins its service.
1853. First railway travelling accomplished near Rio.
1858. First section of Central Railway of Brazil inaugurated.
1865. War breaks out between the allied States of Brazil, Argentina and Uruguay, and the Republic of Paraguay
1867. Duke of Edinburgh visits Rio de Janeiro.
1868. Paraguayans defeated at Villeta.
1870. Treaty of Peace with Paraguay
1871. Slave Emancipation Bill.
1873. Treaty with Argentina.
1874. First South American cable laid between Pernambuco and Lisbon.
1888. Slavery abolished.
1889. Republic proclaimed. Dom Pedro II. sails for Europe. General Deodoro da Fonseca elected first President.
1890. Republic recognized by Great Britain and the United States.

1891. The Constituent Assembly promulgates the Federal Constitution of the United States of Brazil, former provinces being converted into Federal States.
1893. Outbreak of Civil War.
1897. Treaty of Arbitration between France and Brazil.
1906. Second Pan-American Congress held at Rio de Janeiro.
1909. Permanent Arbitration Treaty with Great Britain.
1917. Brazil declares war on Germany.
1919. Brazil joins League of Nations.

Local Administration :—Each Federal State is governed by a President who exercises the executive power, and by a Provincial Assembly which legislates on all matters affecting provincial administration and provides for State expenses and needs by levying taxes. It also legislates on civil and criminal affairs affecting its own territory

Mines and waste lands belong to the State in which they are situated, the Federal Government claiming only lands indispensable for national defence, fortifications, and Federal railways.

Each State is divided into municipal districts, administered by their respective municipal governments. There are 20 Federal States and one territory, the latter is under Federal control and is divided into prefeituras.

One of the principal sources of revenue of the Federal States, apart from local taxation, is the export tax on produce and minerals.

The **language** is Portuguese. Italian and German are much spoken in the Southern States, as many Italians and about 500,000 Germans have settled in these districts. Over 600 German schools exist in Brazil.

Failing Portuguese, correspondence should be conducted in French or English.

There is no State **religion**, but the Roman Catholics, with a Cardinal Archbishop, and Bishops in all the larger cities, predominate. The separation of Church and State was carried out by the Republic. All religions may be practised, whether privately or publicly

Courts of Law :—The Supreme Federal Court sitting at Rio de Janeiro is composed of fifteen judges, nominated by the President subject to the approval of the Senate, and of as many judges of lower courts as Congress may appoint. The appointments are for life.

There are Divisional Courts throughout the various States, in each of which there is a Federal Judge, and municipal magistrates and justices of the peace who are elected for a term of four years. The Civil Courts are closed from February 1 to March 31 The Criminal Court is open all the year

Capital punishment is abolished, except under military law Criminal irresponsibility is recognized up to nine years of age, and power of discernment is presumed from that age until 14, when full criminal responsibility applies. There is no divorce.

Extradition is permitted of both natives and foreigners, but in the case of the former is only granted when the country requesting it gives an assurance of reciprocity   It is not conceded for political offences, military excesses, offences against religion or the press; crimes entailing under Brazilian law imprisonment for less than 12 months, when the offence was committed outside the period of statutory exemption of the petitioning country; or where the offender would have to answer before a special court in his own country

BRAZILIAN MONEY,

The **currency** is in notes, silver, nickel and bronze.   The decimal unit is one real (plural, réis)   The actual unit is 1,000 réis (milréis) or 1 $000.   For convenience, the last three cyphers may be omitted in dealing with large figures.   The term " one thousand milréis " is not used.   This amount (1,000$000) is called one " conto de réis," and amounts of more than 1,000$ are reckoned and spoken of as so many " contos de réis."

Brazilian " exchange " is the rate of exchange on London in pence per milréis (1$000)   It is usual to calculate the rate of exchange on New York, Paris, and other financial centres in terms of the value in milréis of the foreign unit (dollars, francs, lire, etc.).

Exchange in recent years has been :—

Year.	London.		New York.	Paris.
	Pence per milréis.	Milréis per £1.	Milréis per dollar.	Milréis per franc.
	d.			
1915	12	19$345	4$053	$737
1916	11	20$131	4$257	$723
1917	12	18$870	3$998	$694
1918	12	18$663	$947	$703
1919	14	16$860	3$816	$555
1920	14	16$528	4$758	$335
1921	8 9/32	28$981	7$776	$558

Cost of Living :—The aberrations of the rate of the exchange do not solely account for a rise in the cost of living which has given ground for lively complaints.   In one of its monthly reports the London and River Plate Bank observes that a practical cessation of building operations for some years, and a consequent shortage of housing accommodation in Rio and other cities of Brazil, have been a source of considerable over-crowding and have given landlords power to extort exorbitant rentals.   The Government have passed the " Tenants' Act," but this, although giving some measure of protection to actual tenants, does not preclude landlords from exacting onerous terms from incoming tenants.   Empty houses have been virtually offered to the highest bidder, with the result that rents have been raised by 50 per cent. to 100 per cent, and even more. As an unavoidable result a large number of foreigners in Rio are obliged to reside in hotels and boarding-houses, and this has caused increases of tariffs.

The peculiar system of taxation in Brazil, with taxes and duties on almost every article of ordinary utility, causes the prices of articles to pass through a mill of vicious increment, so that when reaching the public they become preposterous. Imports still form a large section of the commodities of ordinary life. Even in the "open markets" in Rio de Janeiro, the prices demanded almost approximate those charged in the shop.

NATURAL RESOURCES.

The **agricultural** products of the several States are as follows :—

AMAZONAS.—Cocoa, guaraná.

PARÁ.—Rubber, tobacco, cocoa.

MARANHÃO.—Cotton, manioc, nuts.

PIAUHY.—Sugar, manioc, rice, earnaúba wax, coco-nut (babassú)

RIO GRANDE DO NORTE AND CEARÁ.—Cotton, manioc, Indian corn.

PARAHYBA.—Coffee, sugar, coco-nut, Indian corn, manioc.

PERNAMBUCO.—Sugar, cotton, coffee.

ALAGÔAS.—Coco-nut, cotton.

SERGIPE.—Sugar, cotton.

BAHIA.—Cacáo (cocoa), coco-nut, coffee, tobacco, Indian corn, oranges.

ESPIRITO SANTO.—Coffee, cocoa, sugar

RIO DE JANEIRO.—Sugar

SÃO PAULO.—Coffee, cotton, vines, rice.

PARANÃ.—Coffee, potatoes, herva-matte, wheat, Indian corn.

SANTA CATHARINA.—Wheat, rice, potatoes, tobacco, beans, oranges, vines, Indian corn.

RIO GRANDE DO SUL.—Wheat, rice, alfalfa, vines, potatoes, onions, tobacco.

MINAS GERAES.—Coffee, vines, oranges, rice, potatoes, tobacco, Indian corn, beans, sugar.

MATTO GROSSO.—Indian corn, sugar

GOYAZ.—Tobacco.

From the census of agriculture, based on figures collected in September 1920, it appears that there are 648,153 rural establishments in Brazil, of which nearly half (317,785) consist of farms and small holdings of less than 40 hectares (roughly 100 acres), the average is 270 hectares. In the States of Amazonas, Matto Grosso, and Goyaz, and the Acre Territory, the estates are much larger, and in the Federal District the average is 25 hectares.

The total value of the area, which extends to 175 million hectares, is calculated at ten and a half million contos of réis, inclusive of buildings, machinery, etc., of which a little over ten per cent. is the property of foreigners, among whom Italians and Portuguese predominate.

The **live-stock** includes :—Cattle, 34,271,324, Horses, 5,253,699, Asses and Mules, 1,865,259, Sheep, 7,933,437; Goats, 5,086,655, Swine, 16,168,549. The total value in 1920 was computed to be a little over six million contos of réis.

The value of the agricultural products during the year 1919-1920 amounted to over four million contos of réis, of which, coffee represented one quarter, maize, cotton, rice, and sugar following in the order named.

Coffee :—Brazil is far ahead of any other country in the production of coffee, the quantity is about 800,000 tons per annum. The importance of the coffee crop to the economic life of Brazil may be gauged in part by the statistics of coffee production. The market is regulated, and the control rests in the Federal, not the State Government. The Government is dependent for 70 per cent. of its remittances on coffee bills, and if the supply of these bills falls short of requirements by reason of the low gold price of coffee the Government is hard pressed to find the remittances needed for the service of foreign loans. Large stocks of coffee used to be carried in Hamburg, Antwerp, Havre, Marseilles, and Trieste, but no stocks of any importance are carried in those ports to-day Brazil, therefore, was forced to step in and, with the help of London credits, carry stocks herself in order to carry over surplus supplies from the fat years, and thus equalise distribution. London bankers advance money as readily against warrants issued by well-accredited public warehouse companies in Brazil as against warrants issued elsewhere.

The exports of coffee have been :—

	Sacks per annum.	Value per sack.
1909–13	12,642,130	44 $860
1913–18	11,881,860	41 $110
1919–22 ..	12,382,300	93 $090

The average price per sack in 1920, was 74 $70, and in 1922, was 118 $690.

Tobacco :—The cultivation of tobacco in Brazil was introduced with the early Portuguese colonization. Tobacco was for about three hundred years one of the most important products, and reached its zenith in the latter half of the nineteenth century, since when it has declined, owing chiefly to :—(1) decrease in the consumption of twine tobacco abroad and in Brazil, (2) increase in export taxes imposed by the States, and (3) falling off in the demand, due to protective tariffs in foreign markets. Added to these may be cited the rise in wages—especially since abolition of slavery in 1889—the financial crisis resulting from the war, and the loss of free entrance previously enjoyed to the Plate Republics.

The diminished consumption may be explained by the demand by consumers for leaf, in preference to twine tobacco. The leaf is lighter and fresher, and cultivation gives good results in the State of Rio Grande do Sul as well as in Bahia.

It is evident that American, Cuban, Turkish and Egyptian tobaccos are partly securing local markets, as well as Brazil's former foreign markets.

There are about 126,000 hectares under tobacco cultivation, the principal sorts concerned being Bahia, Rio Grande do Sul, and Minas Geraes. In certain districts a leaf is now being produced which closely resembles Virginian.

The average annual exports have been :—

					Tons.
1909–13	..	.	.	.	27,303
1914–18	.				26,027
1919–22	..	..	..	..	37,677

Cotton :—Brazilian cotton is similar generally to American, but harsher and dirtier. Though it is classed under different names (according to the ports of shipment), there is a general resemblance between the several varieties. The better-known growths are . Pernambuco, Parahyba, Maceió, Ceará, Maranham, and Mossoro. Of these, " Pernam " is the best. A fairly large quantity of Brazilian cotton is used in England. Brazil possesses a large area of suitable cotton-growing land, and with better methods of picking and handling, and more transport facilities, the country should greatly increase its cotton crop.

Cotton-growing in Brazil has attracted capital from other less remunerative enterprises, for instance rubber, " because it ensures better results, and can compensate for the heavy losses which might attend the cultivation of rubber " The system of cultivation is still backward, but the Ministry of Agriculture has been endeavouring to introduce better methods of cultivation, and has an experimental station for the intensive cultivation of cotton in the State of Maranhão.

The Commercial Association of São Paulo gives the export of Brazilian cotton during the decades of the century 1821-1920 :—

1821–1830	.	.	122,173 tons.
1831–1840		.	113,844 ,,
1841–1850	.	..	111,111 ,,
1851–1860	.	..	141,248 ,,
1861–1870	.	.	288,939 ,,
1871–1880		.	282,436 ,,
1881–1890	.	.	227,778 ,,
1891–1900	.	.	159,002 ,,
1901–1910	.	..	193,881 ,,
1911–1920	.	..	150,962 ,,

During the past half-century liberal development has taken place in cotton spinning and weaving in Brazil. The production during recent years has been well over one hundred tons. The export during 1921 was 19,607 tons and in 1922, 30,146 tons.

Cotton was exported during 1919-22 at an average quantity per annum of 22,600 tons, a large part of the production remaining in the country of origin to supply Brazilian spinning mills.

Rubber :—Before the development of the rubber plantations in the East, Brazil was by far the chief source of rubber, and trees taken from Brazil to the rubber producing countries still afford the main supply A general depression which has hampered the rubber industry in the Amazon district during the last few years was occasioned by the enormous fall in values as compared with the pre-war period. Producers have been constrained to turn their attention to more profitable crops. The following gives the average annual exports. :—

Years.		Tons.
1909-13	.. .	38,528
1914-18		31,370
1919-22	. .	23,600

Rice became an article of export just before the war, and a rapid development took place during the hostilities. Latterly the shipments of rice have diminished considerably It seems that more careful attention to cultivation and treatment, and to the standards of types is desirable to encourage a more general popularity of Brazilian rice in Europe. Large tracts of land are eminently suitable as rice fields. The following gives the annual average exports :—

Years.	Tons.
1909-14	38
1914-18	. 14,365
1919-22	64,365

Sugar :—The average annual production of sugar in Brazil since 1906 has been computed (1923) at 314,000 tons, and almost half of it coming from the State of Pernambuco. There are 215 steam mills in the country for dealing with sugar-cane, of capacities varying from 20 tons to 300 tons and upwards per 12 hours.

The average annual exports have been :—

Years.				Tons.
1909-13	..	..	.	35,027
1914-18	..	.	.	79,855
1919-22	..		.	150,693

Wheat :—It is estimated that the annual consumption of wheat in Brazil amounts approximately to 700,000 tons, and that the production is less than one-quarter of this quantity In view of the possibility of growing wheat in Brazil, for which large tracts in the Southern States are suitable, the Ministry of Agriculture is exercising great care in promoting its cultivation. An experimental growing station has been set up at Ponta Grossa.

Brazil imported in 1922 wheat worth £5,052,000, and wheat flour valued £2,050,000.

Timber :—With a view to assisting the timber industry, and particularly that in Brazilian pine, the Government has been authorized to open a credit not exceeding Rs. 15,000 000$, for the purpose of granting loans to national companies up to 50 per cent. of their effective capital. Such loans bear interest at the rate of 5 per cent. per annum, during periods not exceeding five years.

Mahogany cedar, and teak, from the forests, are floated down the Amazon from the interior in large rafts upon which families live for weeks in grass huts.

The difficulty of transport impedes the development of what is sure to become a large source of wealth. Average annual exports have been :—

Years.		Tons.
1914-18	.	70,173
1919-22	.	113,575

Jute :—The possibility of the cultivation of jute has been discussed. Brazil requires annually some 25,000 tons of raw jute and jute yarns for its local industries, and attention has been directed to the possibility of cultivating jute in Brazil itself. Opinion seems to be that, technically, jute could be grown in sufficient quantities and in excellent quality

Cacao is produced upon a scale which makes Brazil the second largest grower in the world. Average annual exports have been :—

Years.		Tons.
1909-13		31,646
1914-18		45,392
1919-22	.	51,291

Herva Matté, better known under its Spanish name, or as Paraguayan tea, is grown in, and exported from Brazil. Average annual exports :—

Years.		Tons.
1909-13		61,587
1914-18	..	70,139
1919-22	.. .. ..	83,783

Vegetable Oil, Nuts, etc. :—Brazil nuts, cotton seed, and kapok seed all yield valuable oil. Kapok, best known for its fibre, yields an oil which resembles that obtained from cotton seed, used for soap-making. Of the numerous varieties of oil seeds and kernels obtained wild in the forests, the babassu is already being used in considerable quantities for the manufacture of margarine, soap, and candles. It commands almost the same price as copra. The supply available in the Amazon Valley can be called unlimited.

The average annual exports have been :—

Years.				Tons.
1909-13	.	.	.	50,988
1914-18	.	.	..	33,336
1919-22	.	..	.	77,241

Turpentine :—A relatively new product is derived from the "Turpentine Tree," which when "tapped," or pierced, yields Amazon oil, closely resembling French turpentine in its physical characteristics. The spirit is obtained in an almost pure state by boring one hole high in the trunk to form an air inlet and another to act as an outlet for the liquid. There is little doubt that in future there will be a considerable demand for anamoim oil or Amazonian tree-turpentine.

Fruit :—Fruit growing, apart from bananas and Brazil nuts, is undeveloped. The United States and the United Kingdom take practically the entire nut export. The export of fresh table fruit upon a larger scale is contemplated from Santos, Bahia, and Pernambuco. Assuredly a great trade is possible, given energy and organization.

Meat :—Of late the annual slaughter of cattle in the State of Rio Grande do Sul has amounted to approximately a million head. These included 615,384 in 1922 for jerked beef, against 506,046 in 1921, 31,789 and 134,407 respectively for frozen beef, and 364,335 and 337,934 for local consumption. The chief killing season is in the first half of the year.

The export of Brazilian meat was not undertaken until the war encouraged the enterprise. Considerable set-backs have occurred, but the more careful attention now given, both to the quality and preparation of shipments, gives hope that meat will become an article of increasing value.

The average annual exports of conserved meat have been :—

Years.					Tons.
1913-17	..	.	..	..	1,939
1918-22	..	.	..	..	9,260

Chilled meat :—

Years.				Tons.
1914-18	.		.	33,827
1919-22	.	..	.	52,984

Hides :—

Years.					Tons.
1909-13	..	.	.	..	34,601
1914-18	.	..	.	.	36,847
1919-22	.			.	38,621

Fisheries :—Both sea and river fishing are in a backward state Large quantities of dried and preserved fish are imported, notwithstanding the great possibilities of the home industry Surrey trout in large numbers have been put down in Minas Geraes streams, affording promise both of sport and of a welcome addition to the food supply.

MINERAL RICHES.

A new geological map of Brazil at present in preparation will add greatly to the right appreciation of the mineral wealth of the Republic. Recent borings for coal (in Amazonas, Paraná, Santa Catharina and Rio Grande do Sul), and petroleum (Alagôas, Bahia, São Paulo and Paraná) have been made. Surveys of waterfalls are being made in the Rivers São Francisco, Parahyba, Rio Grande, Parahybuna and Paraná.

Mining is distributed as follows :—

Iron, manganese, gold, precious and semi-precious stones.	State of Minas Geraes.
Coal	States of Santa Catharina and Rio Grande do Sul.
Clay for earthenware	
Sand for glass, for which a large number of factories exist.	State of São Paulo.
Lignite	
Manganese, precious and semi-precious stones.	State of Bahia.
Precious and semi-precious stones, crystals, gold.	States of Matto Grosso and Goyaz.

Aluminium, in the form of bauxite, is found in Minas Geraes and has been discovered at Campinas (State of São Paulo).

Chromite, in the State of Bahia. A deposit at Sta. Luzia was worked during the war A large deposit is reported near Campo Affonso.

Copper :—Deposits exist in Bahia, Rio Grande do Sul and Parahyba.

Lead :—The best deposits are in Santa Catharina.

Iron :—The largest deposits are in Minas Geraes. The Usina Esperança produced 9,990 tons of pig-iron, and the Usina Miguel Burnier a daily average of 125 tons in 1921 An installation at Ribeirão Preto is new and important.

The State Government of Minas Geraes grants favours to concerns undertaking to manufacture iron and steel in any State of the Federal Union. The main concession is the reduction of the State export taxes from 3$000 to 200 réis per ton on ore destined for manufacturing purposes in Brazil.

Manganese :—The largest deposits are in Minas Geraes and Matto Grosso. The deposits in Bahia have stopped working, and those in Matto Grosso have never been exploited, chiefly owing to lack of transport facilities. The ore goes almost entirely to the United States.

Average annual exports :—

Years.				Tons.
1909-13	.	.	..	. 189,167
1914-18	..	..	.	.. 380,334
1919-22	..	..	..	.. 318,964

Nickel is found in various places in Minas Geraes.

Gold :—The only mines belong to two British companies in Minas Geraes, viz., the St. John del Rey Mining Company at Morro Velho, and the Ouro Preto Gold Mining Company at Passagem.

Non-Metals :—The principal deposits exploited are . Granite, clays for the ceramic industry, mica, lime, and abrasive substances. Graphite, ochres, saltpetre, pyrites, mineral fertilizers, and asbestos are found.

Coal :—The principal mine is that of São Jeronymo which yielded 215,000 tons in 1921 The economic destiny of Brazil is linked to coal-mining and the organization of iron industries. Both are still in their infancy, coal production does not exceed 30,000 tons per month.

PRECIOUS STONES.

Gems, more or less precious, are found in Brazil in great variety Among the kinds are colourless tourmaline or achroite (Minas Geraes) and amethysts (especially in Rio Grande do Sul) Anatase or Brookite occurs in the diamond-bearing gravels and in the Ribeira do Iguapé, São Paulo. Andalusites are found in Minas Nevaes in several colours but rarely in perfect crystals. Beryls blue and green and pale gold occur in Minas Geraes and are trafficked in on Marambaia island (River Mercury), Cachalong, a variety of opal is found at Rio do Peixe, Santa Catharina, chrysoberyl and cymophane (true cat's-eye) in Minas Novos and in quartz veins in several streams. Citrine, known as false topaz or smoky quartz, occurs in good crystals in the Serra do Crystals.

Diamonds have been obtained from Brazil for 200 years. Diamantina, 800 kilometres N W. of Rio de Janeiro and 250 miles from the coast, reached by Central Railway, is the chief field. Grão Mogul, in .Northern Minas Geraes, and the Rivers Paranápanema, Paraná, and Verde in Southern Minas Geraes, Matto Grosso, Goyaz, Salobro and Chapada Diamantina (both Bahia) are other sources. Great diamonds have been found, including one of 255 carats for which the Gaekwar of Baroda paid £80,000. The subject is treated at some length in ''Brazil, Past, Present, and Future,'' by Mr J C. Oakenfull (John Bale, Sons & Danielsson, Ltd., 15s., 1919)

Emeralds have been occasionally discovered. Garnets occur in quartz and gneiss in many parts of Brazil. Iolite or water sapphire is obtained from the river beds of N.E. Minas. Jade has been seen in large blocks at Amargosa, Bahia. Jasper, together with agates, cornelians, and sards, is common in the river beds of Rio Grande do Sul. Precious opal has been obtained at Agua Saija. **Pearl** fishing is not organized, but pearls are recovered from the lagoons of the Araguaya and its tributaries. Rubies, although scarce, are not unknown. **Sapphires** are found with diamonds in the River Coxim and its tributaries (Matto Grosso). Topaz has been obtained for a century past from Pescaria, an island near Rio de Janeiro. There are said to be deposits near Ouro Preto. Tourmalines are most found in N.E. Minas.

INDUSTRIES OF SÃO PAULO.

Since the beginning of this century, the manufacturing industries of the State of São Paulo, under the protection of a heavy customs tariff, and the utilization of electric power, have made extra-ordinary progress. The hat, boot, textile, and beer factories, and those engaged in the manufacture of alimentary products, have been able to satisfy local demands, and have exported to other parts of Brazil.

The quantities of principal articles produced were :—

Year.			Cotton Textiles. Metres.	Boots and Shoes.	Hats.
1900	.	.	33,540,000	1,600,000	1,606,000
1905			36,646,000	1,980,000	1,400,000
1910			75,833,470	3,608,287	1,372,567
1915		.	121,589,728	4,865,021	2,477,253
1921	.	.	197,184,698	7,293,386	2,098,167

Year.			Jute Fabrics. Metres.	Matches. Boxes.	Beer. Litres.
1900	..	..	14,200,000	28,300,000	8,000,000
1905	.	.	17,850,000	32,850,000	14,200,000
1910			19,087,755	61,637,180	18,973,519
1915			33,462,805	133,345,047	27,959,360
1921			25,366,800	95,228,400	32,800,631

The value of the principal articles manufactured in 1921 is given below :—

Textiles	.	.		358,540:542 $867
Made-up goods	.	..		8,411:737 $000
Hats	.			26,106:154 $000
Boots and Shoes			.	75,073:335 $000
Beverages	.	.		46,914:473 $350
Pharmaceutical Specialities	..		.	53,138:529 $664
Perfumery	.	.		4,673:771 $762
Tobacco				10,692:933 $000
Candles	.	.		1,274:038 $000
Matches	.	.		4,785:280 $000
Playing Cards	..	.		516:388 $000
Earthenware and Glass	.	.		5,647:803 $700
Hardware	..	..	.	6,361:596 $500
Furniture	.	.		16,977:705 $000
Conserves	..	..	..	5,290:107 $000
Articles for adornment	.	..	..	129:412 $500
Various	..	..	..	180,034:200 $000

804,378:007 $343

Ten mills are engaged in the manufacture of woollen goods, and 1,256 hands are given employment. The production, valued at 6,712 contos, is principally cashmeres, flannels, and rugs. Ten mills, representing a capital of 5,138 contos, produce silk fabrics and ribbons, valued at 2,750 contos. The boot and shoe industry is important. In 1921 there were 42 factories employing electric power, 47 employing between six and twelve workmen, and 2,263 workshops with less than six hands each. In the hat-making industry there are 25 factories, and 200 smaller workshops. There are 96 establishments of first importance, and 506 of secondary importance, engaged in the manufacture of beer and other alcoholic beverages. The beers, liqueurs and similar beverages made in the State are well-known throughout Brazil. There are 17 glass-making factories, giving employment to 3,052 hands.

In the manufacture of earthenware there are six factories, two of which are engaged in turning out enamelware. The paper mills, numbering six, represent an investment of 15,600 contos. 11,800 tons of newsprint, wrapping and other paper, and 3,000 tons of cardboard are annually produced.

Matches are made in six factories.

Tanneries, to the total of 78, have more than 11,681 contos invested in them. About 250,000 hides are tanned annually, the tannin being obtained from national plants and trees.

There are other industries in metal manufactures, the production of agricultural machinery, furniture, rope, and string. There are 2,715 industrial establishments of more or less importance, representing an invested capital of 646,689 . 430$000, and giving work to 82,221 operatives.

Brazilian Industries:—During the ten years ended 1921, Brazilian manufactures almost doubled in value, the totals being . 1911, Rs. 914,611 620$, 1921, Rs. 1.808,816 964$. In the latter year woven goods headed the list with 824 thousand contos, followed by beverages with 300 thousand, preserves, bootware, and tobacco, each with over 100 thousand, pharmaceutical specialities and hats.

TRADE AND COMMERCE.

Laws and Foreign Companies :—Companies sending a representative to Brazil need to provide him with a power of attorney. A representative cannot carry on business in the name of a company, but only in his own name, and he has to pay tax to both the Federal and local governments. Should a representative die, the business automatically ceases and the company must appoint another representative. The Company's property cannot be disposed of except by the Courts, until the arrival of the new representative. Foreign companies are advised to apply to the Brazilian Government for domestication or to form a Brazilian company A domesticated company requires only one legal representative. Brazilian companies require at least seven shareholders, a board of directors, advisory committee, and substitutes who must act in Brazil. A domesticated company is under diplomatic protection and exempt from the Federal dividend tax of 5 per cent.

In order to domesticate a company, a copy of its charter should be lodged, with a copy of the by-laws, list of subscribers and number of shares held by each, a power of attorney for the representative, and a resolution of the directors authorizing operations in Brazil and stating the amount of capital set aside for that purpose. All documents must be certified by the Brazilian Consulate. Certain fees are payable.

Commercial Terms :—From 90 to 120 days sight is generally accepted by local Importers. Terms are often expressed as so many days from the actual date of the Bill of Lading (usually 120 to 180) For immediate payment the term is at sight or at 30 days.

Bills drawn on customers in Brazil should specifically stipulate whether they are to be collected at the 90 days' sight rate, or at sight rate. No clause being inserted, the bill is, by law, payable at the sight rate. It has been for many years the general practice in Brazil to state that the bill is payable at the 90 days' sight rate. The voyage to Brazil by cargo vessel occupies about 30 days. It is possible that another 30 may transpire before the bill is actually accepted. It takes a further 30 days for proceeds of the bill to be returned to Great Britain. Upon its arrival there the term of the draft has to expire, so that in the case of an ordinary bill drawn on Brazil at 90 days' sight rate, the drawee should calculate approximately nine months' interest on the sum involved.

Importers greatly object to paying bills with the clause " and all collection charges."

Should a merchant be unable to wait for his money, he should present the bills to one of the four British Banks operating in Brazil, which will generally be prepared to make an advance of probably 70% or 80%, or to negotiate the bills outright.

Trade Marks :—As Brazil was not a party to the Berne Convention, the registration of an international trade mark in Switzerland provides no protection in Brazil. It is strongly advisable to register marks in Brazil. The period which elapses between the deposit of the necessary documents and the publication in the "Diario Official" is generally six to eight weeks.

Prohibited Imports :—Any articles with false indication of origin; all alcoholic beverages containing more than a trace of absinthe or any other noxious ingredients. Brandy, whisky, rum, gin, or other alcoholic beverages containing more than 5 grammes of toxic impurities (grease, ethers, etc.). Arms and ammunition (when so decreed).

Consular Invoices :—Shippers should bear in mind the necessity of complying very accurately with the regulations governing the drawing up of Consular invoices. The slightest error entails heavy fines. In some recent cases it has been possible to secure the remission of fines, but success cannot be guaranteed. Consular fees upon invoices and bills of lading are charged by the Brazilian Consulate General, Liverpool, at rates of exchange based upon the closing rate of the previous month.

A **Free Zone** has been established on the Ilha do Governador, on the Bay of Rio de Janeiro. Brazilian and foreign goods can be stored awaiting clearance, re-shipment, or export, free from any but local charges for services rendered. Explosives, arms, and munitions are prohibited.

The **British Capital** invested in Brazil, according to "Wileman's Brazilian Review," includes £270,000,000, as follows :—

Industrial, Commercial and Loan Capital ..	£254,113,766
Five British Banks	2,970,000
Fourteen Insurance Companies, 10,000 contos, at 15d. exchange, equivalent to .	667,000
	£257,750,766

To this should be added the capital of private companies not quoted on the London Stock Exchange, and capital employed in Brazilian enterprises, estimated at not less than £10,000,000.

British Chambers of Commerce :—British Chamber of Commerce in Brazil (Inc.) 51/53, Avenida Rio Branco, RIO DE JANEIRO. Caixa do Correio 56 (Telegraphic address, "Chambrit, Rio de Janeiro") Established 1916. Affiliated with the Association of British Chambers of Commerce, 1917 Secretary : George Marr

Representative in London . F. W. Perkins, c/o Messrs. Norton, Megaw & Co., Ltd., 36 Lime Street, London, E.C.3

BAHIA Branch c/o British Consulate.

PERNAMBUCO Branch : P.O. Box 46.

PARÁ Branch · P.O. Box 47.

British Chamber of Commerce of São Paulo and Southern Brazil Rua 15 de Novembro, 20 SÃO PAULO. Caixa Postal 1621 (Telegraphic address, " Britchamb, São Paulo.") Established 1916. Affiliated with the Association of British Chambers of Commerce, 1918. Secretary : Gilbert A. Last. This Chamber issues a valuable monthly " Journal."

London Representative Association of British Chambers of Commerce, 14 Queen Anne's Gate, Westminster, London, S.W 1.

SANTOS Branch · Rua Santo Antonio, Santos, 25.

PORTO ALEGRE Branch : Rua dos Andradas 215.

POSTAL COMMUNICATION.

Outward **mails** are dispatched at frequent intervals by the Royal Mail, Pacific Steam Navigation, Lamport and Holt, etc., Lines, and at uncertain intervals by French packet. Outward mails to Pará and Manáos are also despatched by the Booth Line.

Postage 3d. first ounce and 1½d. each ounce after

Homeward mails are dispatched at frequent intervals.

POSTAL RATES.

	Inland. Reis.	Abroad. Reis.
Letters, per 15 grammes	200	400
Letter cards	150	200
Post cards	100	200
Samples, per 50 grammes or fraction thereof	100	120
Manuscripts, per 50 grammes or fraction thereof	100	200
Printed matter, per 50 grammes or fraction thereof	40	80
Newspapers, Magazines, etc., per 100 grammes	10	—
„ „ per 50 grammes ..	—	50

Telegrams :—Throughout the Republic, 200 reis per word, in addition to the fixed charge of 1 milreis per message. Press and Parliamentary telegrams, 20 reis per word.

Wireless :—There are many wireless stations along the coast and frontiers. The Government has granted permission to the Agencia Americana to install and operate high-power wireless telegraphy stations, and to establish a system of wireless telephony

Telephones exist in most of the principal towns of the Republic. The total length of lines is about 570,000 miles.

PUBLIC HOLIDAYS.

January 1 : New Year.
February 24 : Proclamation of the Republican Constitution.
April 21 : Execution of Tiradentes.
May 3 : Discovery of Brazil.
May 13 : Abolition of Slavery.
July 14 : Confraternity of People.
September 7 : Independence of Brazil.
October 12 : Discovery of America.
November 15 : Proclamation of the Republic of the United States of Brazil.
Besides the usual Church holidays, there are local holidays in each of the States.

Athletic Pursuits :—The disposition to encourage athletic pursuits is shown by the exemption from dues and other Customs taxes granted on all sports goods imported direct by athletic football and rowing clubs which are members of leagues or federations recognized by the Brazilian Sports Federation, in accordance with the following list :—

Football :—Leather boots, stockings, knickers, shirts, knee caps, caps, coats, handkerchiefs, metal and cloth badges, balls and their respective bladders, leather laces, goal nets, iron and wire fences for enclosing the fields.

Gymnastics :—Gymnastic apparatus and accessories, gymnasium mattings, mattresses and accessories, skates and accessories, leather balls, mechanical apparatus worked by hand or by electricity, iron or wooden boxes in which to deposit and keep uniforms, exercise clothing and sports materials, foils, swords, sabres, face shields, chest shields, padding for fencing, balls, rackets, and nets for ping-pong.

Nautical Sports :—Shirts, knickers, caps, metal and cloth badges, rowing, sailing and petrol boats and their accessories.

Lawn Tennis :—Balls, rackets, nets, and accessories.

Duties and other Customs taxes paid for rowing and sailing boats imported during 1921 shall be returned, also Customs "bonds" which were signed by authorization of the Minister of Finance shall be cancelled.

Aviation :—Apart from the machines in use in the Army and Navy there are five schools in São Paulo. In ·June 1922 a successful aeroplane flight was made between Portugal and Brazil. Negotiations· have been opened for regular airship services between Portugal, Africa, and South America, as well as between Hamburg and Pernambuco.

Press :—RIO DE JANEIRO "Rio Jornal," "O Dia," "A Noticia," "A Tribuna," "O Jornal," "O Combate," "Correio da Manhâ," "Jornal do Brasil," "Jornal do Commercio," "Gazeta de Noticias," "O Imparcial," "A Noite," "O Paiz," "A Rua." SÃO PAULO. "Correio Paulistano," "Diario Popular," "O Estado de São Paulo," "A Gazeta," "A Platea." BAHIA· "Diario de Noticias," "O Jornal de Noticias," "A Tarde." PERNAMBUCO "Jornal do Recife," "A Provincia," "Jornal do Commercio," "Diario de Pernambuco," "Provincia," "Jornal Pequéno." SANTOS "O Diario de Santos," "A Tarde," "A Tribuna." PARÁ "A Folha do Norte," "O Imparcial." MANÁOS· "O Jornal dio Commercio." PORTO ALEGRE "O Correio do Povo," "A Federação." RIO GRANDE DO SUL. "Echo do Sul."

BRAZILIAN EMBASSY AND CONSULATES IN GREAT BRITAIN

RESIDENCE.	DESIGNATION.	NAME.
London . .. .. (19 Upper Brook Street, W.1.)	Ambassador Extraordinary and Plenipotentiary.	Domicio da Gama.
	Councillor .	Carlos Martins (absent).
	First Secretary .	L. A. Gurgal do Amaral.
	Second Secretary	A. Camillo de Oliveira.
	Second Secretary .	Heitor Lyra.
	Attaché .	Fenelon Alcoforado.
	Naval Attaché	Captain de Corvette Americo de Araujo Pimentel.
	Commercial Attaché	Julio Barboza Carneiro.
London (Coventry House, South Place, E.C.2.)	Consul-General .	Augusto Sarmento Pereira Brandão.
Belfast .	Vice-Consul	John McCaldin Loewenthal.
	Commercial Agent	James Stanfield.
Birmingham	Vice-Consul	Ernest Martineau.
	Commercial Agent	Wilfrid Martineau.
Bradford	Vice-Consul	Henry Hunter Duncan.
	Commercial Agent	Joseph Hudley Sutcliffie.
Bristol .	Vice-Consul	Benjamin Alfredo Baker.
	Commercial Agent	Francis Henry Cecil Barnard.
Cardiff	Consul	Domingos de Oliveira Alves.
	Vice-Consul ..	Narciso José Nogueira Braga.
Cork .	Vice-Consul .	James William Scott.
	Commercial Agent	James Charles Rohan.

BRAZIL.

RESIDENCE.	DESIGNATION.	NAME.
Cowes	Vice-Consul	Thomas William Burnell Faulkner.
	Commercial Agent	William Thomas Mahy
Dover	Consul	Francis William Prescott.
	Vice-Consul	Percy Crundall.
Dublin	Vice-Consul	Henry Charles Neilson, Jr.
	Commercial Agent	Henry Charles Neilson.
Dundee	Vice-Consul	David Stuart Nicoll, J.P
	Commercial Agent	Robert Kinnison.
Falmouth	Vice-Consul	Jorge Henrique Fox.
	Commercial Agent	Cuthbert Lloyd Fox.
Glasgow	Consul	Joaquim Eulalio do Nascimento Silva.
	Vice-Consul	Alvaro Gastão de Aragão e Mell.
Guernsey	Vice-Consul	William Henry Smith.
	Commercial Agent	Gervase F Peck.
Hull	Vice-Consul	Edward Percy Hutchinson.
	Commercial Agent	Robert James Watkin.
Jersey	Vice-Consul	Sydney George Crill.
	Commercial Agent	Snowden Benest.
Leeds	Vice-Consul	Alfred Edwards Evans.
	Commercial Agent	William Smith.
Leith	Vice-Consul	James Chalmers.
	Commercial Agent	Oswald A. Chalmers.
Liverpool	Consul-General	Dario Freire.
	Consul-Assistant	James Philip Mee.
Manchester	Consul	George William Chester.
	Vice-Consul	João Godoy de Oliveira Rocha.
Milford Haven	Vice-Consul	G. S. Kelway
	Commercial Agent	H. F. Thomas.
Newcastle	Vice-Consul	R. K. V White.
	Commercial Agent	
Newport (Mon.)	Vice-Consul	Bonn Henry Jones.
	Commercial Agent	Alan Treverton Jones.
Plymouth	Vice-Consul	Walter Henry Jago.
Portsmouth	Vice-Consul	Arthur Richard Holbrook.
Sheffield	Vice-Consul	Percy J. Meneer.
	Commercial Agent	Thomas Porter Lockwood.
Southampton	Vice-Consul	John de Grouchy
Swansea	Consul	Galileu de Brago Mello.
	Commercial Agent	D. H. Morgan.

BRITISH EMBASSY AND CONSULATES IN BRAZIL.

The letter (L) denotes that the Consular Officer has authority to register lex loci marriages; the letter (M) that he holds a Marriage Warrant. Members of the Diplomatic Service do not require Warrants.

RESIDENCE.	RANK.	NAME.	CONSULAR DISTRICT.
Rio de Janeiro	Ambassador Extraordinary and Plenipotentiary.	Sir John Anthony Tilley, K.C.M.G., C.B.	—
	Counsellor (First Grade).	W. A. Stewart	—
	Third Secretary	Henry Dobinson	
	Commercial Secretary (First Grade).	E. Hambloch	
Rio de Janeiro	(M) Consul-General	E. E. N MacDonell, C.M.G.	

BRAZIL.

RESIDENCE.	RANK.	NAME.	CONSULAR DISTRICT.
Rio de Janeiro	Vice-Consuls	{ S. H. Gudgeon { R. Ross	States of Rio de Janeiro, including the Federal
Bello Horizonte.	Vice-Consul	D. Elysio Britto	District, Espirito
Corumba	Vice-Consul (temp.)	Francisco M. Wanderley	Santo, Goyaz, Minas Geraes,
Morro Velho	Vice-Consul	Dr. John Spear	and Matto
Victoria .	Vice-Consul	—	Grosso.
Bahia . .	(M) Consul Vice-Consul	F J Patron Reginald de C. Steel	States of Bahia and Sergipe.
Aracaju .	Vice-Consul	Thales Ferraz	
Ilheos .	Vice-Consul	Lt.-Col. F R. Hull..	
Pará ...	(M) Consul .	George B. Michell, O.B.E.	
	Vice-Consul	D. S. Michell	States of Grand Pará, Amazonas, and Maranhão.
Manáos	(L) Vice-Consul	A. MacFarlane (acting)	
Maranhão	(M) Vice-Consul Pro-Consul	H. B. Harrison —	
Porto Velho	(L) Vice-Consul	Wm. J Knox-Little	
Pernambuco	(M) Consul Pro-Consul	A. E. R. Browne M. J da Costa Carvalho	
Ceará	Vice-Consul	William Studart	States of Pernambuco, Alagôas,
Maceió	Vice-Consul Pro-Consul	Kenneth C. Macray —	Paraiba, Rio
Parahyba	Vice-Consul Pro-Consul	John H. Scott Robert V Kerr	Grande do Norte, Ceará, and Piauhy
Parnahyba	Vice-Consul	C. E. Clissold .	
Rio Grande do Norte (Natal)	Vice-Consul Pro-Consul	} Robert Vance	
Porte Alegre	(M) Consul	Dr. Thomas C. Dillon, O.B.E.	
Rio Grande	(M) Vice-Consul	Edward J Wigg (acting)	State of Rio Grande do Sul.
Uruguayana	Vice-Consul	Arthur F L. Thompson	
São Paulo	(M) Consul Vice-Consul	Arthur Abbott J R. McCarthy (acting)	
Curityba	Vice-Consul Pro-Consul	Cyril Lynch . H. C. Withers	States of São Paulo, Paraná, and Santa Catharina.
S. Catharina (Florianopolis)	Vice-Consul	J Williamson (acting)	
Santos .	Vice-Consul Pro-Consul	E. R. Seccombe A. Thomson	
São Francisco	Vice-Consul	Roland O. N Addison	

Guidance for Commercial Travellers.

No registration or licence is required from British Commercial travellers, and no taxes are levied. The local firms for which, or through which, they may work is liable to industrial or professional Taxes. No formalities are required from a Commercial traveller in order to enable him to operate, and he is not required in his capacity as commercial traveller to carry any official documents, although it is advisable to carry a passport.

Samples of little or no marketable value are free of import duty on a proper petition being made, and after due verification by the Inspectorate. The following are considered samples of little or no value   Fragments or part of any product or merchandise in such quantity as only is absolutely necessary to afford a proper appreciation of its nature, species, or quality, and the duties on which would not exceed one milreis per package.   Complete objects, but such as are already rendered useless and unfitted for the purpose for which they are intended, are also considered as of no value , no merchandise may, however, at the time of its examination or verification, be rendered useless with the object of freeing it from the import taxes.

Samples of value are treated as ordinary imports, and are subject to the same Customs formalities and duties.

The clause as to samples   " The duties are not refunded in the case of re-export and no deposit is allowed," is revoked by the following

Commercial travellers' samples intended for re-exportation are admitted subject to the deposit of the amount of duty payable or to the furnishing of adequate guarantees.   Such samples must be re-exported within the limit of time guaranteed, otherwise the appropriate duties are collected.   In order to obtain refund of the duty deposited on samples, the commercial traveller should obtain a certificate to the effect that he is a bona fide commercial traveller or representative and therefore entitled to this concession. This certificate should be authenticated by a Brazilian Consul.

Such samples must be accompanied by a Consular certificate issued in the country from which the samples are imported, and all the samples contained in each package must be properly specified in a detailed note.   A 5 per cent. registration charge is, however, made.

Catalogues, prospectuses, posters, and show cards of any kind are, if containing prints (estampas), subject to half the duties if their sole purpose is to advertise industrial products , articles suitable for advertisements (such as small knives, pencil holders, cigar holders, etc.) pay the duties fixed by the Tariff with a reduction of 50 per cent. provided they are not offered for sale, and that their use as advertisements is indicated by a legend engraved on the articles.

Free re-exportation to the port of origin is permitted if the goods have not left the Customs House, and no duties have, therefore, been paid.   The general practice is for travellers to dispose of their samples before leaving the country

Samples on which duties have been paid may be shipped to other ports in Brazil, though care should generally be taken that they are carried by Brazilian coasting vessels. Samples in transit may be shipped to other ports in Brazil on the signature of a bond guaranteeing the payment of the respective duties, it being necessary to obtain a certificate from the Custom House in which the goods are finally dispatched in order to be freed from responsibility under the bond. At some ports a deposit of duties is demanded, and refunded on production of a certificate that they have been paid at the port of destination.

In general no rebates are granted to commercial travellers on the railways, though the Central of Brazil Railway has lately adopted the kilometre book system, which should mainly benefit commercial travellers. Besides effecting a great reduction in the price of tickets, it allows travellers to break their journey The Leopoldina Railway grants a 20 per cent. reduction on travellers' samples and fares.

UP THE AMAZON RIVER.

Ocean liners of 7,000 tons regularly negotiate the Amazon for a distance of 1,000 miles up to Manáos, well in the heart of the continent. Travelling by the Booth Line steamer from Liverpool the passenger penetrates the Equatorial forests of Brazil without change of cabin. The experience is unique. Days are spent in quaint cities reminiscent of old Brazil. Curious natives are passed near the palm-thatch dwellings of their jungle homes. Hours speed by on a tropical river through forests of vivid colouring alive with brightly-plumed birds and gorgeous butterflies. Twilit forest, open campos, little-known mountains, and palm-fringed beaches cross the vision until the Ultima Thule of civilization is reached—the El Dorado of the conquistadores, the hospitable jungle-town of Manáos.

Salinas brings into view the first glimpse of the New World and of the waters of the Amazon, which has changed the colour of the sea from deep blue to pale yellow-green. To starboard is Marajo Island, and opposite a dense, green wall of the equatorial forest, with its distances veiled in mist. Between the ship and the shore native catamarans, with blue sails, may usually be seen.

This is the Pará River, one of the mouths of the Amazon, nearly 200 miles broad, with many forest-clad islands. Small settlements of white bungalows and palm-thatch native huts become frequent. Chapeo Virado is passed, then Mosqeiro, both riverside resorts of the people of Pará, where the ship comes to a momentary rest.

In **Pará City,** the traveller has the option of staying ashore, or of sleeping on board. The hotel is comfortable and modern. Pará reminds the experienced traveller of the East. There are beggars showing their deformities, naked children with mops of dark hair, white towers and tall waving palms.

One of the first places to visit is the Bosque, a public garden, —an area of jungle left untouched to serve as a public park. This can be reached by motor-car or tram. Paths have been cut into the jungle, disclosing beautiful, curious, and weird sights. The frail assai mingles with the bamboo and great buttressed giants. In the middle of the Bosque is a large pond where dwells an old manatee or cow-fish, which enjoys being fed on the leaves which grow out of reach of his curious snout. This mammal is found upon many Amazonian waterways. Near by is a cave of bats, where in semi-darkness hundreds of bats, some of the vampire variety, fly restlessly within inches of the visitor's head.

Passing from the cave into sunlight one traverses the central mango avenue of modern Pará and enters the old town, where are the market and quayside, with river craft and natives, from

Approximate times of high and lowest water on the Amazonian Rivers.

River.	Highest.	Lowest.	Difference between Highest and Lowest.	General Character of the River.
MAIN STREAM. Marañón. Solimes. Amazonas.	June and July A smaller rise occurs in October to December, 15 ft.	October, after great flood; February, after second flood.	At Iquitos 30 to 40 ft. In Brazilian territory 40 to 60 ft.	The level of the Amazon is not much raised by the influx of its tributaries, the floods of which do not always coincide with the time when it receives the waters of the melted Andean snow from March to June.
TAPAJÓS .	End June	End October	Up river 20 to 25 ft. At junction with Amazon same as that river.	In flood time some of the reaches of this river are 10 miles wide and more than 30 miles in length. The bed is covered with white sand, and in the background are thickly wooded, red, rocky cliffs. The current is slow in navigated parts, the waters being held back by the stream of the Amazon itself.
MADEIRA .	End April to May	October	Up river 30 to 40 ft. At junction same as Amazon.	The highway to Bolivia, and the greatest tributary river, being the one on which the rubber industry of Amazonas was first developed. The rocky bottom obliges careful navigation.
JURUÁ	February	September	Up river 30 to 35 ft. At junction same as Amazon.	The Juruá is very tortuous.
NEGRO	June	End January	Up river 30 to 45 ft. At junction same as Amazon.	The scenery differentiates from that of the Amazon rivers, its course being through hilly districts. There are numerous islands, rocks, and rapids.
PURÚS .	April	October	Up river 30 to 40 ft. At junction	Exceptionally tortuous, and is mostly narrower than the tributaries of the Amazon.
TOCANTIUS	April to May	September and October.	Affected by tides as far as Baião.	Very broad for the first 120 miles from its mouth, the water being bright and clear. The scenery is attractive and the climate healthy. Islands and side channels abound as far as Baião, beyond which navigation is impossible on account of rapids.

At Pará the rise and fall of the tide is 10-11 ft.

At Manáos the difference between highest and lowest river is 50-60 ft.

The ocean tides are said to be felt about as far up as Obidos, 533 miles from Pará.

The main stream of the Amazon when in flood imposes itself on all confluents, thrusting them back and obliging them to store their waters in the vast marginal lakes and lagoons until it is ready to receive them.

the dark-skinned and sometimes fair-haired caboclo to the coffee-coloured Amazonian Indian and the coal-black Barbadian negress. The black population of Pará form a considerable proportion of the congregation of the English Church. The English Chaplain to the whole Amazon Region, the Rev. A. Miles Moss, is a naturalist. His cure extends to Porto Velho, on the Madeira River, nearly 2,000 miles distant.

SIGHTS AND SOUVENIRS.

In the Pará market examples of native work can be purchased cheaply, such as decorated calabashes, snake and onça skins, alligator skulls and teeth, curious pottery, woodwork, pipes, and baskets ; together with tropical fruit, tobacco, and Amazonian fish. Near by are the shopping centres in the Rua S. Antonio and João Alfredo. Another place worth a visit is the Zoological Gardens, containing egrets, macaws, parakeets, and other birds of beautiful plumage. Cages of the fauna of the forest, from the baby coati to the giant onça, or South American leopard, are placed among the palms. Back in the old town, the fort, built where the Portuguese explorers first landed, is the Palace of the Governor of the State, with inlaid floors and furniture in Amazonian woods, a Cathedral and churches, all worth a visit. The streets contain curiosities. Laid out to dry on the pavement, are small balls of crude rubber, cocoa beans, brazil nuts, and other forest products.

The Grand Hotel is modern, with a menu card in English. Two nights can be spent ashore in comfort.

A few hours up the broad river the region of the thousand islands is entered. The passage between this maze of islets is known as " The Narrows." The ship winds through lanes of yellow flood with equatorial forest within 20 or 30 yards on both sides. In the Furo Grande the vessel rounds a hairpin bend touching the trees, bow and stern. For over a hundred miles these lanes of water lead through the jungle. Natives in their dugout canoes cease paddling to gaze at the huge vessel. Families of naked children stand on platforms raised above the flood on poles.

When the sun suddenly goes down, troops of monkeys hold conversation before retiring. The moon silhouettes the line of palms—ghostly in their loveliness—and often the indigo vault is ablaze with lightning These soundless electric storms, illuminating the dark jungles and streaks of river and agarapé, although harmless, are awe-inspiring.

After the Narrows, the first point of special interest is formed by the curious flat-topped mountains, on one of which stands the little adobe and stucco town of Monte Alegre, an oasis in the desert of forest. Santarem, a few hours up-stream, and on the opposite bank, stands at the confluence of the Tapajós River with the Amazon. The yellow Amazonian water is mottled with greenish patches from the Tapajós. By day gorgeous butterflies flit about the decks, and birds of brilliant plumage, disturbed from their siesta, cross the river, or fly along the banks. At night, immense moths are attracted by the tiers of lighted decks.

Obidos is passed during the night There the river is comparatively narrow, and for many miles little is seen except the wall of the great Amazon Forest. The river shines like molten gold in the rays of the noonday sun, changing to silver, when the tropical moon rises in the wake of the ship.

A line of white and pink bungalows on a green bank, upon a clearing, denotes the little town of Itacoatiara, the entrepôt for wild rubber, brazil nuts, and other produce, from the great Madeira River, which runs northward for over 1,000 miles to its junction with the Amazon.

About nine miles from Manáos the steamer leaves the main stream and enters the Rio Negro, with blue-black water, which forms dark patches and whirlpools in the yellow Amazonian flood.

Up the many igarapés, or creeks, the giant water-lily, the Victoria Regia, abounds. Motor launches can be chartered in Manáos for visits to the fields of these beautiful floating flowers. On the west bank of the Rio Negro shoals of alligators can be seen about sunrise and sunset, whisking their tails or floating with the tide.

Manáos, from the river, forms a wonderful picture of white and red in a setting of emerald green. It is a clean and hospitable town.

TROPICAL RECREATION

Days in the forest, at Campos Salles, Flores, and S. Raymundo, and evenings in the cafés, clubs, and bungalows, pass the time even too quickly. The chief excursion, when the height of the river permits, is to the Taramá Falls. Motor launches are hired, lunch is taken aboard, and the way lies up the sunlit Rio Negro, and into a small tributary. Native canoes are entered, and guides lead the way through miles of flooded forest to dry land. A narrow path has been opened through the jungle, and for 30 minutes the traveller threads his way behind native guides into the heart of the forest. In a gorgeous pit of tropical growth, a stream of water falls, into a natural pond in the twilit Guiana forest. There is something fascinating in being thus in the heart of an equatorial jungle, with giant trees almost blotting out the sunlight. It is a glimpse of the real thing, which can be obtained and enjoyed by old or young, man and woman.

Manáos market is a most interesting place for the curio hunter.

Approximate distances up-stream on the Amazon River (English Statute Miles) :—

Pará			80	—	Santarem	.	100	610
Narrows (entrance)			145	225	Obidos	.	80	690
Narrows (exit)		..	105	330	Parintins	..	100	790
Gurupa	..	..	45	375	Itacoatiara		150	940
Oteiras	..	.	90	465	Manáos		120	1,060
Prainha	..		45	510				

Liverpool to Manáos, 5,898 miles.

THE BRAZILIAN ABORIGINES.

To the traveller in Brazil there is certain to come a desire to know the life of the aborigine; his history, and his mode of life. A letter of Pero Vaz, dated A.D 1500, of which there are facsimile copies in the National Library in Rio (the original is in Lisbon), is the first ethnographical account of Brazil's Indians.

Pero Vaz liked the Indians. "I find the Indians very likeable," he wrote, "with long, intensely black hair, dark, reddish complexions, good faces and good noses—well shaped." Of the rich and wonderful land which Alvares Cabral had discovered Caminha wrote "This land, Sire, is all beach and meadow and very beautiful. It is so fertile that, should we wish to cutivate it, it would produce everything."

From documents and manuscripts in the National Library of Rio, Mr F H. Dodge obtained for the "New World Review" interesting facts about the life, character, and appearance of the aborigine of Brazil in Colonial times.

A classification of the native Brazilians was made by Dr Osorio Duque Estrada. They composed, he says, "four nations—the Tupis, Tapuias, Carahibas and Nu-Aruac. Of these only the first two lived on the coast and were therefore the only tribes known to the discoverers of Brazil."

Gabriel Soares says. "These savages (the Tapuias) do not know how to swim, they will, however, go leagues up the river hunting for a ford in order to reach the other side   . They eat human flesh for food and pleasure," continues Soares, "not merely for vengeance and hate like the Tupis," but this statement is not corroborated by other travellers in early days.

Cardim states that the Indians who lived on the seashore were the Tupis, that they received the Portuguese with friendliness; and had only one language, with slight variations in different localities.

THE TUPI INDIANS.

The Tupis appeared later, and were the conquerers of the Tapuias whom they gradually drove west. They gave the Tapuias their name, which is the Tupi word for barbarian. Two facts made the Tupis stronger than their enemies: they were homogeneous and united, and were expert in hunting and war, navigation and swimming. The fact that the Tupis could swim kept them ahead of their competitors in the race for supremacy The Tupis were a gregarious people, living in villages composed of large community dwellings called ócas. Half a dozen ócas made a village. Each óca, roofed with straw or palm leaves, had two or three tiny doors opening on a round inner court, the court covered with a sloping roof of palm leaves, higher than the roof of the "house" proper Surrounding the óca was a slender picket fence on which were hung the bodies of enemies killed in war, and which had only one gate. In each óca lived several families, sometimes as many as thirty or forty. A communal fire was kept burning in the centre of the court. There were no inner divisions, hammocks composed the chief articles of furniture. When the wooden posts became rotted and the neighbourhood bare of provisions, the inhabitants migrated to some new place.

The Tupis cultivated corn and mandioca, but they were not vegetarians. They ate meat and even, it is said, ate their prisoners of war Their cannibalism was nothing but a ritual. Life after death was included in their beliefs. Valiant warriors would go away to inhabit the " blue mountains where the sun never ceases to shine," and where they would " banquet gloriously in company with their ancestors."

THE TAPUIAS.

The Tupis were thrown into closer contact with the early colonizers than the Tapuias. They were friendly, as Vaz Caminha said. "These people are good, simple folk," he wrote, " and can be moulded to any form we choose. And since the Lord has given them good bodies and intelligent faces—the bodies and faces of good men—I think He did it for some purpose."

" Very heterogeneous," Cardim calls the Tapuia group, and says " the various tribes fought each other and had many different and difficult languages." Without houses or villages, the Tapuias lived isolated. They were nomads, moving about more than the Tupis, wandering over plains and mountains, sleeping on leaves and, when it rained, taking refuge under trees. They had an aversion from work, a fact offering circumstantial evidence that the Tupis and not the Tapuias were the ancestors of the energetic Brazilian mestiço. They lived on wild fruit and roots, animals and birds, which they ate raw or cooked.

Both groups went almost or entirely naked. Both wore head-dresses of red or yellow feathers, both wore at the waist, on some occasions, a belt or scarf of feathers. Both painted their faces and feet with the red ink of the urucú and their bodies with the black of the geniparo. The juice of the green fruit of the geniparo is clear but it dyes the skin deep brown. Both groups pierced their ears, lips, and nose, and sometimes their cheeks. A round bone, wood, or green stone disc, sometimes two inches in diameter, was wedged into the nostril, the lobe of the ear, or one of the lips. The men wore heavy necklaces of the bones or teeth of their late enemies, the women wore bead necklaces and bracelets.

To the men fell the cares of war and the chase, fishing, and planting; to the women the gathering of the harvest, the preparation of food and alcoholic drinks and poisons. Domestic utensils consisted chiefly of a basket, a hollowed stone for grinding flour and a wine jar

TRIBAL CUSTOMS.

Polygamy was practised by any man able to support more than one family There was no elaborate wedding ceremony, the husband gave a present to the father of the bride or worked for him as Jacob did for Rachel's. Marriage normally took place between fifteen and twenty-five, but was not limited to these ages. A man was compelled to marry his widowed sister-in-law Divorce was recognized and was not the sole prerogative of the men. Government, when it existed, was purely patriarchal. Children were generally given the names of trees, fish, birds, or animals.

The bow and arrow, lasso, wooden lance, and stone hatchet were used by the men of both groups. A few tribes were reported as possessing shields made from alligator hides. Musical instruments included bells, horns, drums, pipes, and reeds. Songs, of a profane nature, were popular

Religion ranged from worship of the Sun, " mother of the living," and the Moon, " mother of plants," and Rudá, the god of love, their chief deities, to the lowest fetichism. The Aymorés were the greatest idolaters of all. Much power was accorded the chiefs and medicine men, particularly when one person practised both professions.

Accounts of the prescriptions made by the doctor appear unexpectedly modern. He prescribed dancing to cure many maladies, and when the patient was too weak to execute the dance the doctor did it for him. Herbs were the chief remedies. For serpent bites was the external application of fire, a treatment not without efficacy.

BRITISH GUIANA

BRITISH GUIANA.

The Colony of British Guiana, the only British Possession upon the South American continent, lies between the first and ninth degrees of north latitude and the fifty-seventh and sixty-first degrees of west longitude. The seaboard, of roughly 270 miles, extends from near the mouth of the Orinoco River on the west to the Corentyne River on the east. The Colony is bounded on the north by the Atlantic Ocean, on the south and south-west by Brazil, on the east by the Dutch Colony of Surinam, and on the west by Venezuela, and is divided into the three counties of Essequebo, Demerara and Berbice. The area is approximately 90,000 square miles, of which only about 275 along the coast and up the rivers are cultivated.

Georgetown (until 1812 called Stabroek) is the capital, and upon the right bank of the Demerara River, near the mouth. It is the seat of the Government. The population in 1919 was estimated at 53,580. The mean temperature is 79° Fahr

Places of Interest include the Botanical Gardens, Museum, Anglican Cathedral, Promenade, Sea Wall, as well as the Stabroek, Cummingsburg, and Bourda markets, three places which should be visited in the early morning or on Saturday afternoon.

Hotels :—Park (40 beds), $4-5, Tower (40 beds), $4, Victoria (21 beds), $2.50-5, Demerara Ice House (18 beds), $2.50-3.

Cable Office :—Corner of Robb and Hinck Streets.

Conveyances :—Georgetown Stables, High Street, King Street Stables, Croal Street Stables.

Motor Cars :—Moderate prices. Bookers' Garage, The Gaiety Garage, de Nobroga's Garage, Georgetown Stables.

Car Services :—Electric trams run at fifteen-minute intervals during the day, fare 3d. any distance.

Motor 'Bus :—From New Amsterdam along the Corentyne Coast and back, daily

Local Steamers :—Sprostons, Ltd. , Colonial Transport Service.

Ferries :—Government Steamers across the Demerara River between Georgetown and Vreed-en-Hoop every hour Fares, first class 4d., second class 2d.

Inland Communications :—Sprostons' steamer, launch, and railway services (offices in Lombard Street, Georgetown), provide the only public means of access to the interior, and trips of from one to five days' duration can be made at moderate fares.

Curios for Collectors :—The East Indian depots in Water Street, Georgetown, afford a fine assortment of the beaten brass-work commonly known as Benares ware. There, may be bought gold and silver coolie jewellery, and knick-knacks. In Georgetown, the pawnbrokers' shops provide a good hunting ground for collectors.

Among the available souvenirs are parrots, stuffed alligators, fragrant kus-kus grass, guava jelly, cassava cakes, and aboriginal Indian curios, such as bead aprons, bows and arrows, blow pipes, basket work, and bright-plumed head-dresses, purchasable in Stabroek Market, Georgetown. Indian curios can be obtained from pedlars, who buy a stock in the Bush, and hawk their articles about Georgetown. These itinerant salesmen visit the hotels and boarding houses. The most interesting method of collection is to go into the Bush amongst the Aborigines.

Trains :—(1) Leave Georgetown at 8 a.m. daily (except on Sundays), due at Rosignol (for Berbice) at 10.55 a.m., leave Rosignol at 7 a.m., due at Georgetown at 9.56 a.m.

(2) Leave Georgetown at 7.15 a.m. and 2 p.m. for Mahaica, returning to Georgetown at 10.34 a.m. and 5.28 p.m.

(3) West Coast Railway from Vreed-en-Hoop to Parika connecting with Colonial Government steamers for Supenaam, Adventure, Loguan, and Bartica.

New Amsterdam, the capital of Berbice, the most westerly district of British Guiana, is on the right bank of the Berbice River, near its mouth. It is about sixty-three miles south-east of Georgetown, from which it is reached by steamer (6½ hours), by rail to Rosignol (3 hours), then by ferry-boat or by road and ferry The population in 1919 was estimated to be 8,470. Outside the town is the racecourse.

SIGHTS AND SCENERY

The Kaieteur Falls, in the heart of tropical British Guiana, rank with the Niagara, Victoria, and Iguazu Falls for majesty and beauty, and are nearly five times the height of Niagara. These falls, with a sheer drop of 741 ft. pour their water over a channel nearly 300 ft. in width.

Tourist traffic is increasing. More tourists are journeying to the great **Kaieteur Waterfall,** which is the highest known Fall in the world. The trip is well worth the moderate cost, and quicker transport will bring larger numbers to see it. Transit is by Sprostons' steamer from Georgetown to Wismar, thence by train to Rockstone, where a launch is got for Tumatumari Cataract. Thence there is a launch for Potaro landing, whence by foot to Kangaruma. A boat from that point for the Amatuk Cataract is followed by boat to Waratuk Cataract and thence to Tukait, from which the climb is made to the top of the Kaieteur Falls.

Rockstone, upon the Upper Essequebo River above the rapids that exacted a heavy toll in life and treasure before the railway from Wismar was built, has a comfortable hotel. A steamer leaves Georgetown for Wismar (65 miles up the Demerara River) at 8 a.m. every Saturday, Tuesday, and Thursday, and a train connects with Rockstone, returning every Monday, Wednesday, and Friday

HOTEL :—Rockstone.

The **Tumatumari Falls** form the first barrier to the approach to the famous Kaieteur Waterfall. A comfortable house-boat is towed for the comfort and convenience of ladies. On a hill overlooking Tumatumari Falls is a rest house, with every convenience. A personal attendant is usually sent to look after visitors on the journey and at Tumatumari.

The Kaieteur Ravine.—Sir Everard im Thurn, formerly Government Agent of the North-west District, thus describes the Kaieteur Fall

"It was at Amatuk, that is, on first entering the Kaieteur ravine, that we reached the most beautiful scenery of that beautiful river If the whole valley of the Potaro is fairyland, then the Kaieteur ravine is the penetralia of fairyland. Here, owing to the moisture-collecting nature of the sandstone rock, the green of the plants would seem yet greener and more varied. Under the thick shades were countless streamlets trickling over little ledges of rock among pigmy forests of filmy ferns and mosses. The small feather-like tufts of these ferns each formed of half transparent fronds of a dark, cool-looking green colour, were exquisite. Larger ferns, with a crowd of ariods, orchids, and other plants, covered the rocks between these streams in new and marvellous luxuriance. Two curious forms of leafless white-stalked parasitic gentians (voyria), one yellow the other white, were especially noticeable. On either side rose the tall granite cliffs, which form the sides of the ravine, the sandstone rock, of which they are part, extends in an unbroken piece from this to Roriama. The appearance of their perpendicular tree-crowned walls, broken here and there by gaps, recalls the pictures of that mountain. Far up on the faces of the cliffs were ledges, on which grew a few green plants. Some idea of the size of these cliffs may be drawn from the fact that the field glasses showed these plants to be tall forest trees. After two hours' climb through the forest we came out on the Savannah from which the Kaieteur falls.

"Crossing the Savannah we soon reached the Kaieteur cliffs. 750 ft. below, encircled in black boulders, lay a great pool, into which the columns of white water thundered from by my side. Behind the Fall, through the thinnest parts of the veil of foam and mist, a great black cavern made the white of the water look yet more white."

Sir Everard im Thurn upon his second visit made at the end of a heavy rainy season, wrote ·

"Crossing the Savannah, and coming to the edge of the cliff over which the Potaro falls, we once more lay down, bodies along the top of the cliff, heads over its edge. It was a very different scene from the last time. Then it was beautiful and terrible; but now it was something which it is useless to try and describe. Then a narrow river, not a third of its present width, fell over a cliff in a column of white water, and was brought into startling prominence by the darkness of the great cave behind, and this column of water before it reached the small black pool below had narrowed to a point. Now, an indescribable, almost inconceivable, vast curtain of water—I can find no other phrase— some 400 ft. in width, rolled over the top of the cliff, retaining its full width until it crashed into the boiling water of the pool which filled the whole space below, and at the surface of this pool itself only the outer edge was visible, for the greater part was beaten and hurled up in a great high mass of surf and foam and spray.

Mount Roraima :—Sir Everard im Thurn was the first to ascend Roraima, the remarkable mountain in the Pakaraima range on the western border of the colony, upon which the boundaries of Guiana, Venezuela, and Brazil meet. Few care to face the exertion which an expedition to this mountain involves. Sir Everard im Thurn wrote

"The first impression was one of inability to grasp such surroundings, the next, that one was entering on some strange country of nightmares, for which an appropriate and wildly fantastic landscape had been formed—some dreadful and stormy day, when in their mid-career, the broken and chaotic clouds had been stiffened in a single instant into stone. For all around were rocks and pinnacles of rocks of seemingly impossible fantastic forms standing in apparently impossibly fantastic ways—nay, placed one on or next to the other in positions seeming to defy every law of gravity—rocks in groups, rocks standing singly, rocks in terraces, rocks as columns, rocks as walls and rocks as pyramids, rocks ridiculous at every point with countless apparent caricatures of umbrellas, tortoises, churches, cannons, and of innumerable other most incongruous and unexpected objects. And between the rocks were level spaces, never of great extent, of pure yellow sand, with streamlets and little waterfalls and pools and shallow lakelets of pure water, and in some places there were little marshes filled with low, scanty and bristling vegetation. And here and there, alike on level space and jutting from some crevice in the rock, were small shrubs in form like miniature trees, but all apparently of one species. Not a tree was there, no animal life was visible, nor, it even seemed, so intensely quiet and undisturbed did the place look, ever had been there. Look where one would, on every side, it was the same, and climb what high rock one liked, in every direction, as far as one's eye could see was this same wildly extraordinary scenery"

Costumes of the Country :—The population includes English, Portuguese, East Indians, Chinese, Africans, mixed races and aboriginal Indians. As the immigrant races keep usually to their national dress, many varieties of picturesque costume are to be seen.

The East Indians, or coolies, form the bulk of the agricultural labouring population, and work on the sugar estates, cocoa and coffee plantations, and rice fields. Some are found scattered in the bush, where they convert forest tracks into profitable market gardens. The Indians, as a whole, are of fine physique, and good looking. The men wear cream loin-cloths, white, magenta or saffron shirts, white or coloured turbans, or a bespangled velvet cap, and silver bangles. The women wear short cotton skirts and embroidered boleros, coloured handkerchiefs round their heads and gold and silver ornaments. Most of the children wear a single garment, a short shirt.

The springtime festivals of the Indian population are worth seeing. The Pagwa involves anointing with a magenta-coloured dye. The Tadja—a Mussulman celebration—is held in February on the sugar estates, and is an occasion of great merry-making.

CLIMATIC CONDITIONS.

The **climate,** although hot, is not unhealthy The mean temperature throughout the year is 80·5° F., the mean maximum being about 85° F., and the mean minimum 75° F The heat is greatly tempered by cooling breezes from the sea and is felt most from July to October There are two wet seasons, from June to the end of August, and during December, January, and February The annual rainfall averages about 93 in. in Georgetown. The rainfall in 1921 was 106·73 in.

The estimated **population** in 1918 was 305,991, made up as follows Aborigines, 6,541, East Indians, 130,638, Chinese, 2,788, Portuguese, 9,489, Europeans other than Portuguese, 3,762, Blacks, mixed, etc., 152,773.

The immigrant population (East Indians) was 133,801

Anti-malaria and anti-mosquito measures are enforced. Quinine has been for some years sold at all post offices to the general public at cost price, and distributed by the sugar estates free to their labourers.

PAST AND PRESENT

The Colony was first partially settled between 1616 and 1621 by the Dutch West India Company, who erected a fort and depot at Fort Kyk-over-al (County of Essequebo) In 1624 a settlement was founded on the Berbice River by Van Peere, a Flushing merchant. The first English attempt at settlement was made by Captain Leigh on the O'apock River (now French Guiana) in 1604. The effort, though followed up by Robert Harcourt in 1613 and 1627, failed to establish a permanent settlement. Lord Willoughby, famous in the early history of Barbados, founded a settlement in Surinam in 1663, which was captured by the Dutch in 1667, and ceded to them at the Peace of Breda in exchange for New York. The Dutch retained their hold on the three colonies with more or less firmness, now yielding to England, now to France or Portugal, till 1796, when, during the war of the French Revolution, they were captured by a British fleet sailing from Barbados. The territory was restored to the Dutch in 1802, but in the following year was retaken by Great Britain, and finally ceded to that Power in 1814.

SETTLERS' OPPORTUNITY

The Government of British Guiana has the ambition to attract more settlers, and a new economic survey is in progress to supply fuller information of the natural wealth of the country

Investigations are being made on the Rupununi hinterland with special reference to :—

(a) Climate and temperature.

(b) Suitability of the soil for the growing of cereals such as wheat, barley, corn, etc., vegetables, fruits for commercial purposes, gums, oils.

(c) Suitability for cattle rearing, domestic animals, ostrich farming, etc., and the best methods to be adopted in developing such industries.

(d) Timber resources for export purposes.

(e) Geological indications of metals and minerals, and the inducements that should be offered to prospectors.

(f) Necessity or otherwise for a survey of the hinterland.

(g) Necessity or otherwise for a hinterland railway with branch lines tapping the timber, balata, gold, and diamond fields, also to report on the prospect of such a railway being a commercial success or otherwise, in the event of a railway scheme being reported upon favourably, to indicate the best methods to be employed in building the line or lines so that no financial burden is incurred by the colony

(h) To suggest the best means to be adopted to attract permanent settlers and explorers to the colony, either by grants of land or concessions or both.

River Transport :—The three rivers, Demerara, Essequebo, and Berbice, are navigable for small steamers for 66, 58, and 130 miles respectively. Beyond these distances are cataracts and waterfalls. There are roads on the coast-lands and on the lower reaches of the rivers adjoining the plantations, but these do not extend inland and communication beyond their limits is by water Steamers ply to Christianburg (65½ miles) from Georgetown, on the Demerara River, to Bartica (56 miles) from Georgetown, on the Essequebo River, and to Paradise (100 miles) from New Amsterdam, on the Berbice River

Rail Communication :—There are three lines of single-track **railway,** of which two have been acquired by the Government, and one owned and operated by Sprostons, Limited. One Government line runs from Georgetown along the east coast of Demerara for 60½ miles to Rosignol, diagonally opposite to New Amsterdam. The other runs along the west coast of Demerara for 18½ miles, starting at Vreed-en-Hoop on the left bank of the Demerara River and ending at Parika, opposite the Island of Leguan, in the estuary of the Essequebo River

Messrs. Sprostons' line runs from Wismar on the left bank of the Demerara River to Rockstone on the right bank of the Essequebo River, a distance of 18¾ miles, and forms a means of reaching the Potaro gold-diggings. In connection with this railway a tri-weekly service of river craft is run on the Demerara and Essequebo Rivers.

The Colony offers a wide field for the **investment** of outside capital. The opening up of the country by adequate means of communication and the development of the natural resources call for large expenditure. The established industries, timber, gold, diamonds and bauxite, could be materially extended. The raising of cattle on the savannah lands of the Rupununi District is an industry also capable of considerable expansion. A railway from Georgetown would make Georgetown an important entrepôt.

Agricultural Produce :—Sugar is a main crop and has averaged 104,000 tons per annum over a decade. Rice is planted on some 56,000 acres, cocoa is grown on a small scale, and rubber is planted on about 3,000 acres. It has been proved that the Para rubber tree grows well on suitable lands in the Colony, where it has suffered from the Para rubber leaf disease. The tappings of five-year to ten-year-old trees not affected and the yields of dry rubber per tree compare favourably with those obtained in the Straits Settlements, Malaya, and Ceylon, and the quality of the product is excellent.

The area under coffee is some 5,000 acres.

Coco-nuts are planted on 26,000 acres, and nuts, copra, and coco-nut oil are exported. A very wide area is suitable for coco-nuts, and the crops promise to increase.

The cultivation of limes occupies about 1,100 acres. A small Government factory for the preparation of concentrated lime-juice exists at Onderneeming, Essequebo.

There are large areas suitable for the raising of cattle. The number in the Colony was 122,886 in 1921. Horses were returned at 1,762, sheep at 20,602, goats at 11,642, swine at 12,312, and donkeys at 6,581

Sugar, rum, molascuit, rice, hides, balata gums, citrate of lime, essential oil of limes, and coco-nut oil are the principal exports.

There remains room for considerable development in **sea-fishing,** curing with the aid of ice, and smoking. In early times smoked or barbecued paku was obtained from the north-west District. Salt cod, herrings, and mackerel are imported. Freshwater fish is obtainable in the markets, but not to the extent desired. The angler enjoys good sport with tarpon, cuffum, and others which make better eating. The river fishing in the interior is exceptionally good.

Fish glue or isinglass from the gilbaker is exported.

Crabs and prawns add to the food supply of the country districts.

Several sugar firms have been investigating the possibilities of producing **motor spirit** from waste molasses, and formulæ for the manufacture of alcohol motor fuel mixtures have been secured. These show that a high-grade motor fuel can be manufactured from sugar-cane molasses on a commercial scale. The Government is assisting the enterprise by temporarily exempting the industry from taxation. No large quantities of **rum** are being produced and the low class molasses has been thrown away Moreover, if mechanical tillage is to be employed to a greater extent, there must be a cheap and readily available source of fuel for tractors, pumping engines, etc.

Diamonds are obtained, and 102,600 carats were exported in 1921, comprising 507,200 stones valued at £329,800.

Gold is found by surface washing, and about 700 claims are in existence.

A contour survey has been commenced above the Great Falls on the Demerara River, with a view to ascertaining the possibility of damming the falls and creating a reservoir for hydro-electric works.

Currency :—Bank accounts are kept in dollars and cents. Sterling and U.S. coinage are both current and both legal tenders. There is a local paper currency in one dollar and two dollar notes.

The Colonial Bank and Royal Bank of Canada have establishments at Georgetown, with branches at New Amsterdam and Berbice. The Colonial Bank has branches at Mahaica and Mahaicony on the east coast, Demerara, and at Suddie, Essequebo. The Royal Bank of Canada has a branch at Rose Hall, Berbice. Both banks carry on Savings Bank business.

Postal Rates :—Local Letters—

First oz.	1d.
Over 1 oz., not exceeding 2 oz.	1½d.
Over 2 oz., not exceeding 4 oz.	2d.
Over 4 oz. and up to 2 lb., for each additional 2 oz.	½d.

Foreign Letters—

To the British Empire and United States—	
First oz.	2d.
Each additional oz.	1½d.
Foreign countries—	
First oz.	3d.
Each additional oz.	1½d.
Post Cards—	
Single	1½d.
Reply	3d.

There is regular fortnightly and monthly communication with the United Kingdom, Canada, the United States of America and the West Indies, by vessels of the Harrison Direct Line, the Royal

Mail Steam Packet Company, the Trinidad Line, the Royal Nether-lands West Indian Mail Company, and the Compagnie Générale Transatlantique.

Telegrams :—

For 12 words or less	.	9d.
Every additional 6 words or part	. .	3d.

Import Duties :—The tariff is subject to revision from time to time. The general ad valorem rates under the British Preferential and General Tariffs have respectively been 16 and 33 per cent. during 1922.

IMPORTS AND EXPORTS.

The imports for 1921 (including transit trade) amounted to £3,487,608, £1,691,878 less than in 1920.

The goods imported are classified as :—

	1920. £		1921. £
1. Food, Drink and Tobacco	1,388,075	.	967,712
2. Raw materials and articles mainly un-manufactured	514,970		314,620
3. Articles wholly or mainly manufactured	2,797,711		1,946,293
4. Miscellaneous and unclassified	18,074	.	10,846
5. Bullion and Specie	3,859	.	33,497

Exports :—The total of the exports for 1921 was £3,424,491 classified thus :—

	1920. £		1921. £
1. Food, Drink and Tobacco	5,021,893	.	2,579,533
2. Raw materials and articles mainly un-manufactured	413,050	.	605,454
3. Articles wholly or mainly manufactured	205,268		146,669
4. Miscellaneous and unclassified	3,914	.	451
5. Bullion and Specie	42,096		92,384

Two **newspapers** are published at Georgetown, "The Daily Chronicle" founded 1834, and "The Daily Argosy," founded 1842.

The Georgetown Chamber of Commerce issues a monthly "Commercial Review "

Foreign Consuls :—

Belgium		F. van der Heyde (Chargé d'Affaires—resides at Caracas).
Brazil		Albert Gracie.
Denmark		P Cressall, junr.
France		P A. Serre, Vice-Consul (resides in Trinidad); C. Paila (Consular Agent).
Italy		C. F Wheating (Vice-Consul).
Netherlands	.	C. Paila (Acting); Jules Pairaudeau (Vice-Consul).
Norway		Joseph Kidd, Jorgen Brumelhorst (Consul-General at Havana).
Portugal	.	C. A. A. Cotello; Jorge Camacho (Vice-Consul).
Spain		C. Paila (Acting Honorary Vice-Consul).
Sweden		Jules Pairaudeau.
United States		W. Davis; W G. Harvey (Vice-Consul).
Venezuela	.	A. Pardo.

Lloyd's Agents and Sub-agents :—

Agency and District.	Agents and Sub-agents and Telegraphic Addresses.
BERBICE . From the Frontier of Dutch Guiana to the Abary Creek.	S. Davson & Co., Ltd. "Davson"
DEMERARA From the Abary Creek to the Frontier of Venezuela.	Booker Bros., McConnell & Co., Ltd., Georgetown. "Booker"

Guidance for Commercial Travellers.

Commercial travellers must register or take out a licence at a cost of $48. Any commercial traveller entering the Colony must within 24 hours of commencing business register his name at the office of the General Commissary and take out the licence indicated.

Trade licences cost from $8 to $250 per annum, according to the annual rental value of premises occupied.

Commercial travellers not holding a trade licence cannot dispose of their samples themselves, but it is customary in lieu of the payment of duty to facilitate the dispatch of business by accepting a guarantee for reshipment of the samples from a well-known member of the mercantile community In such cases a traveller may dispose of his samples through the medium of his guarantor

Commercial travellers are required to produce to the authorities any certificates or powers of attorney from the firms they represent.

Commercial travellers may obtain a permit for the importation into the Colony of any articles which the Comptroller of Customs is satisfied are bona fide samples, by either of the following methods .

(1) By depositing with the Receiver-General the amount of duty payable.

(2) By depositing at the Customs House a written guarantee for the payment of the import duty on any samples not accounted for on the departure of the traveller from the Colony.

Articles liable to duty serving as patterns or samples introduced into the Colony by commercial travellers are to be admitted free of duty subject to the following conditions requisite to ensure their being re-exported, or placed in bond :—

(A) An application in writing to be made to the Comptroller requesting the samples to be declared on deposit. The application is to state that " the goods are not intended for sale, and are to be returned for shipment."

(B) The proper examining Officer of Customs will thereupon ascertain the amount of duty chargeable on the samples. The amount must either be deposited with the Comptroller of Customs for subsequent withdrawal on his certificate, or ample security must be given for it. A written guarantee in prescribed form has been approved to meet cases in which the duty has not been deposited. One surety must in every case sign the guarantee in addition to the principal giving the guarantee.

(c) A certificate is to be prepared by the Officer examining the samples on importation and such certificate is to show :—

(1) A list of the patterns or samples imported specifying the nature of the goods, and also such marks as may be necessary for the purpose of identification.

(2) A statement of the duty chargeable on the patterns or samples, and also, whether the amount was deposited in samples, and also as to whether the amount was deposited in money or whether security was given for it.

All patterns or samples imported under the provisions of these regulations are to be re-exported or placed in bond within six months from the date of first delivery as shown on the certificate. Due notice of re-exportation must be given by the commercial traveller to the Surveyor to allow the necessary arrangements for examination of the patterns or samples to be made. If before the expiration of the appointed time the patterns or samples are presented to the proper Customs Officer for the purpose of re-exportation or of being placed on bond, the officer is to satisfy himself by examination whether the articles which are brought to him are the same as those detailed on the certificate at the time of importation. If so satisfied the officer will certify the re-exportation or deposit in bond and submit the certificate to the chief clerk, who will take the necessary steps to refund the duty which has been deposited, or for the discharge of the guarantee.

Dutiable goods imported as samples may be admitted as samples without payment of duty provided that the Comptroller of Customs or Sub-Comptroller is satisfied that such goods are bona fide samples imported in the ordinary course of commercial business, and that the duty payable upon any one sample shall not exceed two dollars, and that the duty payable on the aggregate, imported at any one time shall not exceed five dollars.

Resident agents of British firms are not liable to any taxes or fees as such.

ABORIGINES OF BRITISH GUIANA.

The Aborigines of British Guiana are scattered in small groups or families all over the colony In the census of 1921 the Aboriginal population was returned at 9,700. The " Buck " Indians are of small stature. Their smooth and almost hairless skin varies in colour from a dark coppery-brown to a light reddish-yellow hue. The face is broad, the hair black and lank, the eyes dark and usually narrow, and the neck short. The whole countenance resembles the Japanese type. The chest is deep, broad, and muscular, the legs and arms are well-shaped but somewhat thick, the hands and feet, especially those of the women, are remarkably small.

THE BUCK INDIANS

The character of the Buck Indian in his natural state is a moral one. He is peaceful and amiable, and readily responds to fair and just treatment. He is not " civilised," but he certainly does not deserve to be considered a savage.

Buck Indians are usually willing to act as boat-hands, carriers or guides. They cheerfully assist the traveller within the limits of their tribal district, but seldom care to go beyond these somewhat vague boundaries. If much dissatisfied they quietly disappear, abandoning their wages and leaving the traveller stranded—a serious state of things in the far interior Amongst themselves family feuds or vendettas are not unknown, and sometimes lead to mysterious murders which are ascribed by them to the " Kanaimas " or Evil Spirits.

This belief in spirits may be said to constitute their religion, and the Buck, cannily arguing that he has nothing to fear from the good spirits, seeks to propitiate or drive away the evil spirits through the influence of the Peai or Medicine man. They indulge periodically in drinking bouts, generally combined with dancing, when both sexes imbibe large quantities of paiwari and cassiri—their native drinks—until they become quite intoxicated. Paiwari is fermented cassava and cassiri fermented sweet potatoes. The method of preparation involves a preliminary mastication of the ingredients by the women—a fact which the intending traveller will do well to forget, for on occasion the drinking of the " cup of courtesy " is compulsory

COSTUME.

The native costume consists of a long strip of cloth or " lap " for the men and a tiny apron called a " queyu," made of seeds or beads, for the women. The men do not consider themselves decently dressed unless they have their tribal mark painted on their faces. On festive occasions they adorn themselves with feather crowns of various colours. Along the coast-lands and in the more settled parts of the colony nearly all the Indians have adopted European clothes, and when so clad they have an uncomfortable, slovenly and somewhat ludicrous appearance. They appear to best advantage in native costumes amidst their natural surroundings.

THE PRINCIPAL TRIBES.

The Aborigines of the colony are divided into four distinct tribes speaking entirely different languages :—

(1) The Warraus, or Swamp Indians, are found on the low-lying coast-lands and around the mission stations near the coast. They are timid, dirty, and skilled in the making of " dug-outs " or corials.

(2) The Arrawaks live on the slightly elevated lands lying between the lower reaches of the rivers. They are cleanly and more civilised than the other tribes. Nearly all of them can speak English, and some of them Spanish. They wear European clothes and are excellent boathands and expert wood-cutters. They have a great aversion to the other tribes, particularly to the Caribs.

(3) The Carib tribe includes the true Caribs, the Arecunas, the Akawois, and the Macusis. The few remaining true Caribs are scattered over the country, mostly on the upper Barima, Barama, and Cuyuni Rivers. Their fighting propensities are historical, and they are held in great fear by the other tribes.

The Akawois are born traders and are distributed chiefly over the forest-clad country round the Upper Mazaruni basin. They are good-humoured and easily amused at trifles.

The Macusis, a small tribe, are confined to the Savannah country between the lower Rupununi and the Ireng and Takutu rivers. Of all the Indian tribes they present the handsomest appearance and have the most pleasing manners. They are the chief makers of the famous " wourali " poison, experts in the use of the blow-pipe, keen huntsmen, and generally of a sporting disposition.

(4) The Wapisiana tribe inhabit the Savannah country around the upper reaches of the Rupununi and the Takutu Rivers. They are the great traders of the southernmost parts of the colony and the canoe makers of the interior They have a somewhat taciturn nature and much decision of character

Some isolated tribes are to be found in the little explored portions of the colony to the extreme south and east. Little is known of them and they cannot therefore be classified, but one, the Wai-Wois, located around the head waters of the Essequibo river, are famous for their trained hunting dogs and their ornamental feather work.

The Indian dwellings may be divided into two types :—

(1) The forest type or Benab, rectangular with open sides and sloping roof, thatched with palm leaves and almost touching the ground.

(2) The savannah house, round or oval, with a high conical roof thatched with palm leaves and resting on a low wall built of wattle and plastered with kneaded clay

A constant feature of Indian houses is the hammock, which civilization owes to the Guiana Indian. At night the Buck lights a fire beneath his hammock to prevent the chill of the night air

PROTECTION OF INDIANS.

The care of the Aboriginal Indians throughout the colony is vested in the Commissioner of Lands and Mines as Chief Protector of Indians under the Aboriginal Indians Protection Ordinance No. 28 of 1910. All district officers of that department are sub-protectors of Indians under the Ordinance. Every person desiring to employ Aboriginal Indians must obtain a permit to do so from a sub-protector and sign a memorandum of agreement as to wages and conditions of service.

The areas set apart as Reserves for the Aboriginal natives of the colony are ten in number, as follows :—

No.					
1	Moruka Reserve containing	305	square miles.	
2	Wakapau ,,	,,	18	,,	,,
3	Upper Pomeroon	,,	262	,,	,,
4	Ituribisi Creek	,,	65	,,	,
5	Vlissengen	,,	15	,,	,,
6	Muritaro	,,	·25	,,	,,
7	Wikki Creek	,,	95	,,	,,
8	Orealla	,,	54	,,	,,
9	Epira	,,	52	,,	,,
10	Rupununi	,,	442	,	,,

The Moruka Reservation :—This Reservation was first so declared by Proclamation dated September 13, 1904, under the Aboriginal Indians Protection Ordinance, 1902, and it was subsequently enlarged by proclamation dated May 6, 1908, and as now constituted contains an area of about 305 square miles. The population number about 1,000 souls, chiefly Spanish Arawak Indians and their half-breed descendants. That portion of the Reserve adjoining the Moruka River for the most part consists of low peat savannahs, which in the wet season form a series of inland lakes from which rise the numerous islands of clay and sand that form the dwelling places of the greater portion of the inhabitants. Between these Savannahs and the sea coast is " terra incognita," whilst inland of these open lands the forest-covered " mainland " rises a couple of hundred feet and extends throughout the remainder of the reservation. The inhabitants engage principally in the cultivation of cassava and other ground provisions, fishing, woodcutting, etc., but a large proportion of the adult male population work as farm labourers in the adjoining districts (Pomeroon and North West District) returning in time to cut down the forest and clear new fields for the women to cultivate.

Situated within this Reservation are the missións at Santa Rosa and Warramuri. The former is a mission supported by the Roman Catholic Church and has a resident priest in charge and a small Convent of Mercy where the nuns conduct a school of some 150 children. There is a small branch of this mission at Assakata Creek. The Anglican Mission at Warramuri has no resident minister, but is served by periodical visits of the resident missionary stationed at Cabacaburi on the Pomeroon River   There is a school at Warramuri in charge of a negro schoolmistress with an attendance of about 100 children. Both the Roman Catholic and Anglican mission schools receive a small Government grant-in-aid.

Wakapau Reservation :—By Proclamation under the Aboriginal Indians Protection Ordinance, 1902, dated September 13, 1904, the Wakapau Reservation, which is situated on the Wakapau River, a tributary on the left bank of the Pomeroon River, was so declared as from October 1, 1904, and is officially described as " consisting of all the savannah land on both banks of that portion of the Waka- pau Creek extending upwards from its junction with the Hanna- bassia Giah Creek." The Reservation contains an approximate area of 18 sq miles. With the exception of a small sand elevation, on which stands the Anglican mission of St. Cuthbert's, the Reserva- tion comprises a wide expanse of wind-swept grass covering a boggy flat which in wet weather forms practically an inland lake. On the forest-covered sand hills bordering this low-lying area live the 300- 400 Aborigines, including their half-breed descendants for whose protection the Reservation has been made. As in the case of the Moruka Reserve the Indians work as labourers on the farms by the Pomeroon River, returning at intervals to clear the forest and plant their fields. At St. Cuthbert's mission some forty children attend the school, which is presided over by a coloured schoolmistress under the supervision of a voluntary Lay Reader, who in turn is responsible to the missionary resident at Macca-Siema, who pays periodical visits.

Upper Pomeroon Reservation :—This Reservation, as first declared by Proclamation dated September 13, 1904, was of larger extent, but was reduced to its present dimensions of 262 sq miles by a later Proclamation of March 7, 1921, the area of 1,000 sq. miles originally reserved having been regarded as unnecessarily large for the number of Indians in the locality. The number of Indians inhabiting the Reserve is estimated at 250 souls, practically all of whom live within a five-mile radius of the mission station at Cabacaburi situated on the right bank of the Pomeroon River in the north-east corner of the Reserve. The area embraced by the Reserve is forest-covered and hilly, and contains extensive forests of bullet trees which the Indians are permitted to bleed for balatá gum. In addition to bleeding balatá, the Indians on this Reserve cut timber for sale to the farmers on the lower Pomeroon River, cut spars, firewood, and offer palm leaves for sale at Anna Regina, and take emplóyment as labourers on the farms.

The Ituribisi Creek Reservation was declared a Reservation by Proclamation dated September 13, 1904. The area is 65 sq miles. The greater portion of the land to the north of Ituribisi River is " muri " or scrub lands with more or less narrow belts of forest bordering the streams, the southern portion of the Reserve is chiefly forested hilly country; while the eastern part comprises Ikuraka Lake and the grass-covered peat flats adjoining the Ikuraka Creek and Ituribisi River which are submerged in the rainy season.

There are only two small settlements of Indians on the Reserve—on the Ikuraka Lake and Mashabo Creek on the south bank of Ituribisi respectively The population numbers about forty-five Indians who, in addition to cutting spars and firewood for sale at Riverstown and other estates on the Essequibo River, occasionally seek employment outside the Reservation. They attend services at Airy Hall Church on the Essequibo River, and their children attend school at Dufferyn mission near to that place.

Muritaro Reservation :—This Reservation on the Demerara River was declared as such by Proclamation dated September 13, 1904, and is only a clearing in the forest one-quarter of a square mile in extent. It is used solely for mission purposes, there being an Anglican Church and school house on the Reservation, the former being visited periodically by the missionary who resides at Wismar The children live at the mission from Monday to Friday of each week, returning to their homes for the week-end.

The Wikki Creek Reservation :—Situated on the east bank of the Berbice River at the steamer terminus, this area was first declared a Reservation by Proclamation dated September 13, 1904, extending only to the Parwe Creek on the Berbice River It was subsequently enlarged by Proclamation dated May 30, 1908, the southern limits being extended to the lower boundary of Plantation Klien Polgeest on Berbice River The area of the Reserve is 95 sq miles, and it consists of forested country with some balatá trees. The population is about 120. The Indians are permitted to bleed balatá trees, and in addition to this cut timber and fuel, wood and hire themselves out to the grant-holders and others in the river

There is a mission church and schools at Calcuni on the Reservation, supported by the Congregational denomination, and these are in charge of a catechist, and the missionary visits the Reservation periodically One of the Indians has been appointed as captain and rural constable.

The Vlissengen Reservation :—Situated on the west bank of the Berbice River, this Reservation was declared by Proclamation dated September 13, 1904. It is only 1½ sq mile in extent, and consists of flat forest-covered land on which live only half a dozen Indians.

The Orealla Reservation :—Situated on the Courantyne River this area, comprising 54 sq miles, was declared a Reservation by Proclamation dated September 13, 1904. A small portion of the Reserve along the river's bank is flat land on which a number of the Indians live, and where the Anglican Church and school are located. Immediately aback of this flat the land rises abruptly to about 80 ft. level, and on the eastern edge of these hills other Indians have their houses. The remaining area of the Reserve consists of a flat elevated savannah and undulating forest country   The Indians comprise Arawaks, Warrows, and Carribs, and are estimated to number about 300 souls. They are employed by balatá companies for work in tapping balatá trees in that and other districts, and they also cut timber for sale at Warleigh Saw Mill or at the two sugar estates situate at the mouth of the river   There is a catechist and schoolmistress in charge of the mission church and school, which latter receives a Government grant-in-aid.   The missionary priest at Skeldon visits the Reserve periodically   One of the Indians has been appointed captain and rural constable.

Epira Reservation:—Epira, on the left bank of the Courantyne River was declared a Reservation under Proclamation dated September 13, 1904.   The area, 52 sq miles, consists of elevated forest land. The Indian population is only about sixty-eight souls, one of the men has been appointed captain and rural constable.   There is a school on the Reserve.   The Indians go to Orealla, which is only fourteen miles distant overland, during the visit of the missionary to that place.   The men, like those of the Orealla Reservation, are employed by the companies in bleeding balatá.

Rupununi District Reservation :—Situate between the Takutu and Totowau Rivers, and containing 442 sq miles, of which, 124 sq miles are savannah land and 318 sq miles forest land.   This area has not been officially declared a Reservation, but has been set aside as a potential asylum for the Indians inhabiting the country south of the Kanaku Mountains, estimated to number about 1,000 souls, who at present live scattered about along the edge of the forest-covered country south of the Kanaku Mountain ranges and between the Takutu and Kwitaro Rivers, which encloses the savannah country leased to the Rupununi Company for cattle ranching.

THE ABORIGINAL RESERVATION FUND.

A scheme was inaugurated by the late Frank Fowler, F.G.S., when Commissioner of Lands and Mines and Protector of Indians, whereby the Indians residing in the Reservations in which balatá trees grow were allowed to bleed balatá and forward the dried gum to Georgetown to be sold by tender.   From the proceeds of these sales the Indian bleeders were paid at a rate per lb. considerably in excess of what was paid to the ordinary individual.   The balance (after deduction of royalty) was placed to a fund termed the " Aboriginal

Indian Reservation Fund," held in trust jointly by the Protector of Indians and the Colonial Treasurer for the benefit of the Indians. From this fund depots were erected in Georgetown and New Amsterdam for the accommodation of Indians coming to the town, and relief in the way of food and medical comforts has been provided to the Indians on the Reservations in times of sickness and famine through failure of their crops.

All Aboriginal Indians have the right to travel, hunt, and fish over the unlicensed Crown lands of the colony and its rivers, and may dwell on and cultivate such lands. They are permitted to cut and sell timber from the unlicensed Crown lands, but must first obtain a permit, issued free of charge by sub-protectors and " Authorities " created for the purpose. These " Authorities " are generally missionaries or other suitable persons residing amongst the Indians. Sales of timber so cut are conducted by the Department of Lands and Mines on behalf of the Indians wherever practicable so as to ensure that they are fairly dealt with.

BRITISH   HONDURAS

BRITISH HONDURAS.

Belize, the capital, is distant some 5,700 miles from London, and transit occupies usually 17 days. The town is approached from the sea by a narrow tortuous channel between reefs which afford a natural shelter for vessels in the harbour   Steamers have to lie off from the shore one to four miles, according to their draught. Green islands fringe the coast and coco-palms wave over high roofs and broad verandas.   Sea breezes cool the air of the coastal belt and high tides lave the mangrove swamps and purify them.   The climate is on the whole healthy, and during the trade winds Belize is pleasant.   The district is malarial, for it is swampy, without natural drainage, and dependent on rain-water for the water supply The screening of water vats, barrels, and other containers is not thoroughly effective, and for a permanent solution an adequate pipe water supply and the raising of the low-lying parts of the town is required.   Population, 13,500.

Hotels : International, Union.

Although the climate has a reputation as an unhealthy one, it compares not unfavourably with that of other tropical countries with small European populations.   Europeans leading a normal life and taking common precautions find the climate pleasant and healthy

Other ports are Corozal, where boats drawing 4 ft. of water can approach the port.   At Stann Creek there is a railway pier alongside which vessels drawing up to 14 ft. can lie.   At Punta Gorda, the chief town in the Toledo District, deep water is found some miles from the shore.

Belize and Stann Creek are visited by the United Fruit Company's steamers.

Local Communications are frequent between the towns and villages along the coast by sailing and motor boats, and by the latter on the rivers.   There is a short railway from the coast inland, near the Stann Creek Town, about 25 miles in length which taps the banana plantations.

External communication is provided weekly with New Orleans or Mobile by the steamers of the United Fruit Company   The Canadian Government Merchant Marine run a steamer via Jamaica every fortnight, and the Harrison Line a monthly steamer from Liverpool and an occasional steamer to carry mahogany to London.

Communication by sailing vessels with the neighbouring republics is frequent.

Roads :—In the Corozal District a good road runs across the Louisville swamp, and this is the main road from the town to the Rio Hondo. The total length of metalled roads outside Belize is about 30 miles. The difficulty of obtaining material makes road-building expensive.

HISTORICAL.

It is probable that Columbus discovered the coast about 1502, when on his way from Cuba to find a passage to the Indies. It is probable that the great Córtez passed through the western part of the Colony on his expedition to Honduras in 1524. But long before the Christian era—possibly 5,000 years ago—the inhabitants of this part of the world were sufficiently civilized to have an exact system of chronology   It is even suggested that the civilization of Central America is older than that of Babylon or Assyria.

The Colony became known to Englishmen about 1638, probably through a shipwrecked crew   It is probable that people from Jamaica visited the Colony, and, finding logwood abundant and easily accessible, established themselves. They must have come in contact with the Spaniards and Indians of Yucatan and the Peten district of Guatemala. There are records of many conflicts between them. Long after the Thirty Years' War had ended in Europe, conflicts occurred between the subjects of the Kings of England and Spain in this Colony. The Spaniards made frequent attempts to expel Englishmen who came with slaves from Jamaica. The Governor of Massachusetts sent H.M.S. " King George " to help the settlers against their enemies in 1667   In 1671 the settlement was reported by the Governor of Jamaica as having " increased His Majesty's Customs and the natural commerce more than any of His Majesty's Colonies." This was no doubt due to the great value of logwood and mahogany.

In 1717 the Board of Trade asserted the absolute right of Great Britain to cut logwood. In the next year the Spaniards endeavoured to conquer the settlement, and got as far as " Spanish Lookout " on the Belize River, which they fortified. In 1754 another attempt was defeated " principally by slaves " at a place called Labouring Creek. In 1779 St. George's Caye was attacked and a great many settlers were carried off to Merida and thence to Havana. A battle at St. George's Caye, 1798, was the last of these disturbances. Troubles with the Indians in Yucatan persisted from 1849-1872.

PHYSICAL CHARACTERISTICS,

The mainland is low and swampy near the coast, but rises inland. The northern half of the Colony is generally flat, but in the south hilly and mountainous, rising in the Cockscomb range to a height of 3,700 ft. The country is well watered, and its many rivers provide the chief means of communication. The soil is rich and productive.

British Honduras lies on the Atlantic side of the mainland of Central America within 18° 29′ 5″ to 15° 53′ 55″ North latitude and 89° 9′ 22″ to 88° 10′ West longitude. It is bounded by Yucatan on the north and west and Guatemala on the west and south. Its greatest length is about 174 miles and width about 68 miles. The total area is 8,598 square miles. The Colony is larger than Wales and slightly smaller than Palestine. It is divided into six Districts, Belize, Corozal, Orange Walk, Stann Creek, Cayo and Toledo. There are numerous islands or cayes off the mainland, area about 212 square miles. Some are inhabited by fishermen, and on others coco-nuts are grown, but many are uninhabited swamps.

The Colony is outside the track of hurricanes, and earthquakes are unknown.

The population was estimated at 43,586 in 1919, inclusive of 400 Europeans, and 200 white Americans, and about 2,000 of European descent.

The characteristic **soils** of the Colony are the Cahoon ridge (vegetable alluvium along the river valleys), the Pine ridge (sandy tracts covered with pine, scrub, and wiry grass), and Broken ridge (intermediate between these two) Besides these there are swamp, savanna, and mountain.

The chief rivers are in the north, and run north-easterly, the Belize reaching the sea on the east and the Hondo and the New River on the north.

NATURAL RESOURCES.

The chief **industry** is wood-cutting (mahogany, cedar and logwood) Fruit (bananas, plantains and coco-nuts) is cultivated for export to the United States, and sapodilla gum (i.e. chicle), sponges, and tortoiseshell are collected.

The area of the forests in which mahogany is found is estimated at 2½ million acres. Yearly exports average 25,000 tons.

There are several sugar mills and stills, but sugar is manufactured entirely for home consumption as it does not pay to export.

Alternating with stretches of sandy plain and yielding pine-trees, are large areas of very rich land, on which, in addition to mahogany and many beautiful hardwoods of which little or no use is made, the cahoon and other palms are the most noticeable. The Colony has not been exploited by the economic botanist, or these rich oil-bearing nuts and vanilla would have been turned to account. There is a wide field for the colonist with enough capital and common sense.

The quality of the **mahogany** is the finest known. The local cedar, botanically related to mahogany, is employed principally in boat-building.

The output of mahogany is small in relation to the extent of the forests in which it is found. The yearly exports average only 25,000 tons. The mahogany tree occurs very sparsely in the forests, the proportion rarely exceeding one tree per acre, and this makes logging difficult and expensive. The high cost of putting the timber on the market has operated to restrict the expansion of the industry On the other hand, the difficulties of extraction have acted as a check on the depletion of the mahogany by felling.

Expert investigations suggest that silvicultural treatment can at least double the rate of growth of the existing mahogany stock, and increase the proportion crop from one to at least forty trees per acre. It should be possible to grow mahogany to market-able size in twenty to forty years.

There are numerous hardwoods and deciduous softwoods, of excellent qualities, technical and ornamental.

Sapodilla is a hard, elastic, and extremely durable timber, of good promise as a material for golf-club shafts. Honduras walnut is an exceptionally beautiful furniture wood; there is a limited trade in rosewood. These forests should afford some of the finest railway sleeper woods in the world. An output of a couple of million tons per annum should be practicable. Among softwoods, the feather-weight balsa wood is notable. Other woods, such as yemeri, a timber analogous to American poplar, may replace coniferous softwoods. Very soft timbers, like qualm wood, have importance as a source of pulp and for match manufacture.

About one-third of the area of the colony bears Cuban pine, yielding an excellent timber of the type of pitch pine, and which may become important as a source of turpentine and rosin.

AGRICULTURAL METHODS.

Banana Cultivation :—A report by the Attorney-General (1923), says that except on the rich "vegas" or "riven bottoms," where small areas of fine alluvial soil exist in this Colony, the cultivation of banana without systematic pruning, and a careful, and in some poor sections ploughing and forking, cannot give satisfactory results. The methods hitherto in vogue in the Stann Creek Valley are condemned as primitive and wasteful. A majority of planters plant more areas at one time than can be properly kept under control. In some sections the bits planted are of so inferior a quality, that after being cleaned a couple of times they are abandoned as unproductive. In other sections, open spaces where suckers could be grown to great advantage, and produce additional bunches, no proper attention is paid to "supplying."

Opportunities of sport in the interior are good for those whose love of the chase rises superior to the small annoyances of tropical forests. In the neighbourhood of towns, villages, and mahogany camps little game is found, but sport is good away from the haunts of men. Of large animals the jaguar, puma, tiger cat, and tapir are the most popular objects of chase in the thick forest. Of smaller and edible animals and birds, the antelope, armadillo, gibonet, the wild turkey, with his cousins the curassow and the quam, provide a sufficient variety of food. The wild turkey (*Meleagris ocellatus*) is valued for his plumage. Deer are plentiful in the pine forests, and in the rivers and lagoons the hunter may, with head-light and harpoon, indulge in the exciting but not dangerous sport of spearing alligators from a canoe. In the sea and lower reaches of the rivers are an abundance of fish, including large tarpon.

There are a polo club, a golf club, and two lawn tennis clubs.

The sea around the cayes teems with excellent eating fish, the best known being snapper, grooper, king-fish, Spanish mackerel, and barracouta. Turtle, both logger-head and hawk's bill, are captured for the sake of the shell, a fair amount of which is exported. Green turtle are fairly plentiful and are in great request as food.

ADMINISTRATION

Standard Time is six hours slow of Greenwich Mean Time. From 1st November to 15th March the clock has been advanced forty-five minutes as a measure of " daylight saving."

The standard **currency** is the U.S. gold dollar The British sovereign and half-sovereign are legal tender for $4.86 and $2.43 respectively There is a subsidiary silver currency of 50 cents, 25 cents, 10 and 5 cents, nickel 5 cent pieces, and bronze 1 cent pieces coined specially for the Colony There is a paper currency of tens, fives, twos and one dollar issued by the Government. United States notes circulate freely

The postal **telegraph** system is a Government one. There are 500 miles of line with thirty offices. Communication is commendably good. The charge for telegrams is 25 cents for fifteen words and 1 cent for each additional word.

A **wireless** station in Belize communicates with the United Fruit Company's ships. Direct communication with Jamaica is to be established.

There is a **telephone** exchange in Belize with about two hundred and fifty subscribers.

The value of the Colony's **trade** in 1921 was $6,388,591, of which $3,343,132 was the value of imports and $3,045,459 of exports. The United States of America supplied 56 per cent. of the imports and took 76 per cent. of the exports, the Empire, 21 per cent. of imports and 17 per cent. of exports.

Guidance for Commercial Travellers.

Commercial travellers are required to take out a licence in Belize ; the fee is 50 dollars gold (£10 8s. 4d.). Licences remain in force up to and including the 31st December following, but if a licence is granted after the 1st December of any year, it remains in force for one calendar month.

Samples of no commercial value are not liable to duty. The duty on samples of value may be either deposited or guaranteed, and the goods re-exported from any port within the permission of the Customs authorities, no time limit being fixed.

CHILE

THE SOUTH AMERICAN BANKS

The
ANGLO-SOUTH AMERICAN BANK,
Limited.

Capital and Reserves
exceed - £13,000,000

Head Office :
62 OLD BROAD STREET, LONDON, E.C. 2

Affiliated Institutions :
The British Bank of South America,
Limited,
and
The Commercial Bank of Spanish America,
Limited.

Branches in the principal Cities of :—

Argentina	Guatemala
Chile	Nicaragua
Uruguay	Salvador
Peru	Venezuela
Mexico	The U.S.A.
Brazil	France
Colombia	and Spain.
Ecuador	

(See also pages ii and 36.)

CHILE.

Valparaiso, the chief seaport and the second of Chilean cities, is accessible by rail from Buenos Aires (*see* Transandine Railway, p. 61) It is the normal point of landing for voyagers by sea, and distant from England some 9,000 miles via Panamá, or 11,000 via Magellan Strait. The population is some 200,000, and the bay is one of the most beautiful in the world.

The town has arisen anew from the ashes of the fire which followed the earthquake of 27 August, 1906, when three thousand persons were killed, many more injured and a hundred thousand rendered homeless. It is a long narrow city consisting chiefly of three streets parallel with the sea. The best portion of the town skirts the bay, and there are all the best hotels, shops, and business streets.

English people are much in evidence, as is the English language. English names have been given to some of the streets. The Chileans call themselves the Britons of South America. The naval cadets in the naval schools at Valparaiso not only look English but speak English. The street scenes are picturesque, and there may continually be seen porters and carters in bare feet, the latter with spurs on the left foot, gaily-coloured ponchos, horsemen with broad-brimmed straw hats, ponchos, leather gaiters with silver fastenings, and lasso attached to the saddle, ladies in native black " mantos ", strings of carts with postilion-riders, trains of heavily-laden mules, and now and again in the middle of the road a lumbering railway train, drawn by an engine which might have come from a museum of antiquities.

Valparaiso, although not attaining to the size or grandeur of Santiago, has greater natural advantages. " The Vale of Paradise " sits upon the shores of the Pacific. From the edge of the blue waters, on its circular shore, the buildings rise tier above tier up the hills, and behind them are higher hills and valleys. A city, a port, a bathing and a pleasure resort, all in one, it is a city of surprises, with lifts to take one up the cliff.

Valparaiso prices are reckoned cheap as compared with Buenos Aires. The evidence of wealth is less marked, but the purchasing power of money is nearly doubled. There are other differences between the countries. The Chilean and the Argentine are different persons. The latter takes life more seriously, and the former is happy-go-lucky, jovial, and often of fine physique. There are fine avenues and historical monuments, Government buildings, two libraries, and a museum. There is also an English club. Valparaiso is the seat of administration of the Naval Head-quarters, the Customs, and the chief shipping companies. Many industries are carried on, including engineering, shipbuilding and foundries.

Hotels :—Astur, Candell St. (Cable "Astur," Auto. 3091), 250 beds, $15–50 per day; Royal, Esmeralda St. (Auto. 4684), 170 beds, $20–40 per day; Colón, Esmeralda St. (Tel. 1791), 60 beds, $12–15 per day; Paris, Blanco St. (Auto. 4644), 90 beds, $15–18 per day; Palace, Blanco St. (Auto. 4654), 300 beds, $12–15 per day, Lebelle, Brazil Avenue, 414–6 (Cable "Lebelle," Auto. 4731), 30 beds, $14–20 per day (French management), Liguria, Pedro Montt Avenue (Cable "Liguria," Auto. 4778), 80 beds, $12–15 per day, Rolfs, Serrano St. (Auto. 4681), 50 beds, $10–15 per day (German management). Prices in Chilean currency, "American plan."

Restaurants :—Trocadero, Prat St. (Table d'Hôte, $6), Lucien, Serrano St. corner (à la carte); Martini, Av Pedro Montt ($5); Jockey Club, Av Pedro Montt (à la carte), Bunout, Cochrane (near Port Station), ($5), English cuisine.

Tea Rooms :—Suiza, Rio Janeiro, Ramis Clar, Ideal, Colón, The English.

NEAR VALPARAISO are the following resorts :—

Viña Del Mar, a holiday centre with good racing facilities.
Hotels :—Grand, Alvarez St. (Tel. 66 and 296 Vina, and National 10), 130 beds, $20–35 per day, $450 per month, with a higher tariff January to March, France, Alvarez St. (Tel. Ingles, 215 National, 26 Vina), 150 beds, $15–30 per day, $250–350 per month.

Concon, at the northern point of Valparaiso Bay, by motor ¾-hour from Viña del Mar
Hotel :—Gran Hotel (Tel. Ingles 6 National 5 Concon.), 140 beds, $13–16 per day

Limache, 50 minutes express from Valparaiso.
Hotel :—Bellavista (Tel. 26 Limache), 100 beds, $10–18 per day (French management).

Zapallar, on the coast 4 hours by train from Valparaiso or Santiago.
Hotels :—Gran Hotel (Tel. Zapallar), 180 beds, Papudo Hotel (Tel. Catapilco 5), 200 beds.

Santiago, the capital, distant 116 miles from Valparaiso, is the third largest city in South America and one of the most beautifully-situated capitals. In a wide plain, 1,706 feet above the sea, it is backed by the Andes. The city covers about eight square miles, and is crossed from east to west by the Mapocho River, which passes through an artificial stone channel, 130 feet wide, spanned by five iron bridges. The population is some 686,000. The streets are well paved and lighted, and electric tramcars run in all directions. A wide and beautiful avenue—the Alameda de las Delicias—runs through the heart of the city for two miles and in it are to be found the majority of the fine handsome private residences. It forms a magnificent drive and promenade. Trees have been planted, adding to the beauty of the avenue.

Probably the principal object is the Santa Lucia Hill, rising a sheer 400 feet, affording magnificent views over the city. It is almost in the centre of the city and ornamented with gardens, balustrades, and balconies. The view gives possibly the best idea of what Santiago is, although that from the Cerro Cristobal at the other end of the town is almost equally good. Manners are different in Chile, and on the fashionable promenades youths stare at ladies as they pass, and make audible remarks on their appearance. This is not rude according to the Chilean canons, but rather correct conduct. The evening " Paseo " or promenade is perhaps the most characteristic custom of Chilean towns. Everybody goes, young and old, rich and poor, to the park, plaza, or alameda. The masses keep apart from the better-dressed people, and no jealousy or ill-feeling is apparent.

Hotels :—Mundial, Moneda Esq. Bandera (Cable "Luksic"), 80 beds, $15–50 per day, Ritz, Huerfanos 976 (Cable "Ritz"), 49 beds, $15–40 per day; Savoy, Agustinas 1025 (Cable "Kehle"), 70 beds, $12–80 per day, Oddo, Ahumada 327 (Cable "Hotel Oddo"), 80 beds, $10–25 per day, Oddo Anexo, Huerfanos (Cable "Anexo"), 50 beds, $10–14 per day, Grand, Huerfanos 1164 (Cable "Kehle"), 80 beds, $15–30 per day, Casa Residencial, Ahumada 351 (Cable "Monot"), 40 beds, $18–35 per day, Imperial Meuble, Moneda 977 (Cable "Imperial"), 35 beds, $12–20 per day, De la Marne, Agustinas 978 (Cable "Hotel Marne"), 25 beds, $11–12.50 per day, Milan, Ahumada 319 (Cable "Hotel Milan"), 45 beds, $12–20 per day; France, Puente 530 (Cable "Hotel France"), 70 beds, $15–20 per day; Plaza, Plaza de Armas (Cable "Hotel Plaza"), 140 beds, $10–20 per day; Espanol, Merced 777 (Cable "Hotel Espanol"), 75 beds, $12–18 per day

Restaurants :—Santiago, Huerfanos 1024; Savoy, Agustinas 1025; Picart, Agustinas 943, Mundial, Moneda corner Bandera; Playa, Monjitas 826, Rotisserie Parisienne, Moneda 943 (Table d'Hôte), Gath & Chaves Tea Rooms. Huerfanos & Estado, the best place for tea.

Points of Interest :—Santa Lucia Hill, Parque Cousiño (tramcar), The Alameda, (the chief avenue) Casa Moneda, and the President's Palace (Calle Moneda), Public buildings, Cathedral, Law Courts (Plaza de Armas), Congress Palaces (Calles Bandera and Compania), Art buildings, Parque Forestal, Railway station, Mapocho, Quinta Normal (Quinta tramcar), Military Museum (Parque car), Cavalry School (Macul car), Plaza Italia National Library

Racecourses :—Club Hipico, racing every Sunday afternoon, Hippodrome Chile, racing every Sunday morning.

Tennis :—Santiago Tennis Club, Parque Cousino, International Tennis Club.

Golf :—Los Leones Golf Club (car from Plaza Italia).

Outings :—Apoquindo and Tobalaba (round trip from centre, about 1½ hours by motor). San José de Maipu and Penalolen (return journey about 3 hours by motor). El Volcan, 1,407 metres above sea level; train 8.30 a.m., arriving back in Santiago 6.30 p.m. through mountains and gorgeous scenery

Conveyances :—Electric trams fares—10 cts. City, 20 cts. Suburbs.
Victorias : $1 per journey. Two or more persons, $1.50 per journey $2 per hour for one or more persons.
Taxi : $1.50 per journey, every additional person, 50 cts. $7.20 per hour for one or more persons within the city limits. Visitors going outside the city are advised to arrange the charge beforehand.

Cable Offices :—West Coast Cable Co., Calle Huerfanos 944; All America Cable Co., Calle Huerfanos 1041.

Theatres :—Municipal, Comedia, Santiago.

Cinemas :—Union Central, Alhambra, Splendid, Imperio.

Department Stores :—Gath & Chaves, Corner Estado & Huerfanos; Struther & McRostie, Corner Estado & Huerfanos; McRostie & Co., Calle Ahumada; Casa Francesca, Corner Estado & Huerfanos, Casa Escocesa, Calle Ahumada, McKenzie & Co., Calle Huerfanos.

Booksellers :—Hardy & Co., Corner Huerfanos & Ahumada; Hume & Walker, Calle Ahumada.

Grocers :—Weir & Co., Calle Estado.

British Legation :—Calle Huerfanos, near Santa Lucia Hill.

U.S. Embassy :—Parque Forestal.

British Consulate :—Corner San Antonio & Moneda.

Rail :—By Chilean State Railway to Valparaiso (express), 3 hours 30 minutes, Talca (express), 4 hours 40 minutes; Talcahuano (express), 10 hours 50 minutes, Valdivia (express), 22 hours 45 minutes.
Bookings by Transandine Railway Office at Expreso Villalonga, Agustinas 840.

Antofagasta, capital of the province of that name, is a mineral-shipping port 234 miles south of Iquique. It serves Bolivia as an export outlet, and there is a Bolivian Custom House there. It is 640 miles from Valparaiso, with which town, and with Iquique farther north, it is connected by rail and steamer Santiago (964 miles) is also linked by rail. It has a population of over 70,000, and is the best-paved town in the Republic, with asphalt roadways and stone footpaths. There are fine public gardens. The water supply is drawn from the great reservoir, 10,000 feet above sea-level, at San Pedro, 193 miles away The British colony numbers over 400. The town is the entrepôt for one of the most important mining centres in South America. It is the terminus of the Antofagasta and Bolivia Railway, serving the Bolivian and Chilean mining districts. From Antofagasta, through the barren desert of the Central Pampa nitrate fields, the railway climbs to the picturesque little town of Calama (altitude, 7,400 feet.) From this point are the mining establishments of the Chile Exploration Company, working the largest copper mines in the world. The scenery is grand, and the railway, which finally attains 13,000 feet, winds amidst mountains and lakes to its terminus, the Bolivian town of Oruro. From Oruro the Bolivian Railway Company runs to La Paz, close by to that great inland sea Lake Titicaca.

Landing :—Shore boat.

Conveyances :—Motor 'buses.

Hotels :—Londres, Belmont, and Buenos Aires.

Railways :—Antofagasta and Bolivia Railway to Oruro and La Paz. A sleeping and dining car train leaves Antofagasta every Saturday The journey to Oruro occupies about 36 hours and to La Paz, 2 days. The gauge is only 2 ft. 6 in., but the train is exceptionally comfortable. North-bound passengers wishing to visit Bolivia should leave the steamer at Antofagasta and take train for La Paz, resuming by steamer at Mollendo.

Climate :—Never too hot in summer, moderately warm in winter.

Ancud, is a port on Chiloé Island, with a population of 4,000, and is about 760 miles from Santiago, an agricultural and timber centre with a good trade with Puerto Montt.

Hotels :—Central, Royal.

Arica, the most northerly Chilean port, in Tacna province, with a population of 9,000, is the terminus of the line to La Paz, in Bolivia (273) miles) It can be reached by rail from Tacna (39 miles)

The town is built at the foot of the Morro headland and fringed by sand-hills. The Andes are clearly in view from the anchorage. The Morro was the scene of a great battle in 1879 between Chilean and Peruvian forces.

Landing :—Shore boat.

Hotels :—Vergara and Palace.

Rail :—To Tacna daily To Alto de La Paz every Monday at 4 p.m., dining and sleeping cars, arriving La Paz following day at 2.20 p.m.

Concepción, at the mouth of the Bio-Bio river, the most important city in southern Chile, has a population of some 65,000. It is connected by rail with Santiago (354 miles) and with Talcahuano, its port, about 9 miles distant. The cathedral is interesting
Hotels :—Wachter, France, Medici.

NEAR CONCEPCIÓN are the following :—
Penco, a favourite summer resort is 6 miles by rail from Concepción.
Hotel :—Balneario.

Tome, distant 18 miles from Concepción, a pretty town, is popular as a seaside resort.
Hotel : De France.

Corral, the outport of Valdivia City, is at the mouth of the river There is a steamboat service daily to Valdivia, 1½ hours. Was the scene of a great victory by the Chileans under Admiral Cochrane, in the War of Independence of 1818.

Coquimbo, with about 15,000 inhabitants, is one of the principal ports of the Republic, and it exports copper It is 9 miles from La Serena, and connected with Santiago (357 miles) and with Valparaiso (198 miles) by rail and steamer
It has one of the best harbours on the coast. It is in a mixed agricultural and mining district known favourably for a palatable local wine. The harbour has a mole and pier
Hotels :—Rosariov de Cordovez, Luksic and Sparsic, José Tomas Molinas.

Constitución, a port of call, south of Valparaiso, on the Maule river, 115 miles north-east of Concepción. Has hitherto been classed among the second-rate harbours, though it serves a large and wealthy district producing grain, lumber, etc. When the new improvement works, at a cost of nearly 14,000,000 gold pesos (1 gold peso 1s. 6d.), are carried out Constitución should vie with Valparaiso.

Copiapó, capital of the province of Atacama, has a population of 12,000 and is the principal Chilean mining centre. It is connected by rail with the port of Caldera, about 50 miles distant, and with Santiago, Valparaiso, Iquique, and Antofagasta.
Hotels :—Atacama, Ingles.

Chillán, 323 miles from Santiago, with which town and with Valdivia, Valparaiso, Talca, and Concepción it is connected by rail, has a population of 40,000, and is an important agricultural centre. Mineral springs and baths in the district.

Chuquicamato, 162 miles from Antofagasta city, has a population approaching 15,000, and is a very important mining town.

Curicó, an inland agricultural town, with about 18,000 inhabitants, is 122 miles south of Santiago on the railway

Coronel, the chief coaling port of the Republic, has a population of 13,000, and is 17 miles from Concepción.

Landing :—Shore boat.
Hotel :—Hotel de la Bolsa.
Rail :—To Concepción daily; journey, 70 minutes. To Lota daily, 20 minutes.

Calbuco, minor post in the south of Chile, with very little movement. It is 594 miles south of Valparaiso and 21 miles from Puerto Montt

Chañaral, a port in Atacama, has 3,000 inhabitants, and is a rich mining and copper-smelting centre.

Cruz Grande, on the gulf of that name, 32 miles north of Coquimbo, and 130 miles from Valparaiso, has good anchorage of 8 to 20 fathoms, with cranes and loading plant, and is an iron-ore shipping port.

Huasco, a port for mining products, 30 miles from Vallenar, has 3,000 inhabitants.

Iquique, in the province of Tarapacá, is the principal port of northern Chile, and a great centre for nitrate and iodine. It has a population of 70,000, is well built, and has electric light and tramways. It was partially destroyed by earthquakes in 1868 and 1875. There is an English colony, and an English Club. It is reached by steamer from Valparaiso (784 miles), Arica (74 miles), and Antofagasta (225 miles) Climate, rainless.

Landing :—Shore boat.
Conveyances :—Trams, coaches, and motors.
Hotels :—Europa, España, Châlet Suisse.
Market :—In Calle Vivar; best time, 7 a.m.
Railway :—By nitrate railways to Pisagua daily, except Sunday Time, 8 hours. The Nitrate Oficinas are worth a visit. Time, 2 to 3 days.

Junín, in Tarapacá province, a nitrate port 10 miles south of Pisagua, with only a small collection of warehouses and workmen's dwellings. Its whole importance derives from the export of nitrate.

Los Andes, in Aconcagua, has a population of 10,000, and is the terminus of the Transandine Railway, giving railway connection with Argentina.

Hotel :—Sudamericano.

Lebu, at the mouth of the river of that name, is the capital of Arauco province, and has a population of 5,000.

Los Angeles, capital of the province of Bio-Bio, has a population of 20,000.

Lota, on the Bay of Arauco, south of Coronel (5 miles) and Concepción (21 miles), is a coal-mining centre with 12,500 inhabitants.

In the neighbourhood are the famous Cousino Park and Château, one of the sights of Chile. The management and organization of the Cousino mines are of extraordinary interest, economically and politically

Landing :—Shore boat.
Rail :—To Coronel (20 minutes), and Concepción (1½-hours) daily
Hotels :—Gran Maury, Del Comercio.

Linares, capital of the province of that name, has 13,000 inhabitants, and is 31 miles from Talca.

Hotels :—Panimavida, Lazari.

La Serena, capital of Coquimbo province, on the coast about 9 miles north of Coquimbo, is a mining and industrial centre, with some 18,000 inhabitants.

Hotels :—Santiago, Gran.

Mejillones, on the coast, 57 miles north of Antofagasta, with 4,000 inhabitants, principally exports minerals, and is connected by rail with Bolivia.

Hotels :—Colón, Francia.

Pisagua, the northern terminus of the Nitrate Railway Company, is a port in Tarapacá province, exporting iodine and nitrate. The town has about 4,000 inhabitants, and is reached by coast steamer and rail from Iquique (39 miles). It is a coaling station of the Pacific Steam Navigation Company

Puerto Montt, the capital of Llanquihué province and 12 miles from Lake Llanquihué, is a well-kept town of about 7,000 inhabitants, and the terminus of the Central Railway It is 670 miles from Santiago.

Hotels :—Hein, Miramar, Central.

Punta Arenas, in Magallanes Territory, the most southerly Chilean town and about 1,300 miles from Santiago, is on the Straits of Magellan. It is the most important commercial port between Buenos Aires and Valparaiso. From the former it is distant 1,355 miles and from the latter 1,445 miles by sea. There are 34,000 inhabitants. It is a great cattle, sheep, and wool centre. The town is in wireless connection with Valparaiso and has a land wire to Buenos Aires. "Sandy Point," to give it its English name, was founded in 1843 as a convict station. The population of about 34,000 has well-built, permanent houses in place of the original wooden shanties with corrugated iron roofs. Coal mines and sheep rearing are the source of the local prosperity and the port has a good frozen meat trade.

Landing :—By launch.
Hotels :—Royal, and Cosmos.
Excursions :—By steamer to the glaciers. There is a motor-car service to Patagonian ports and for inland tours during the season.

Rancagua, capital of O'Higgins province, with a population of 15,000, is on the Central Railway about 165 miles from Valparaiso.

Hotels :—Peralta, Americano.

San Felipe, in Aconcagua province, is an agricultural centre with 13,000 inhabitants, and connected by rail with Valparaiso, Santiago, and Argentina.

San Fernando, capital of the province of Colchagua, has 10,000 inhabitants, and is 83 miles from Santiago and 197 miles from Valparaiso on the Chilean Railway

Tacna, capital of the province of that name, is 1,800 feet above sea-level, it has 11,000 inhabitants, and is a mining centre.

Hotels :—Raiteri, Americano.

Taltal, a port in the province of Antofagasta and 110 miles south of that city, has a population of 15,000, and is a nitrate centre.

Hotels :—Central, Cosmopolita.

Talca, on the Claro river, population of 60,000, trades principally in cereals and wines. It is connected by rail with Santiago (155 miles), Concepción (52 miles), and Constitución.

Hotels :—Internacional, National.

Talcahuano, the port of Concepción is connected with that city by electric tram and rail. A leading grain and export centre and a naval station, dry docks accommodating vessels of 30,000 tons. The population is 38,000. It is about 11 hours (363 miles) by rail from Santiago, and 240 miles by steamer from Valparaiso.

Hotels :—France, Royal.

Temuco, capital of Cautin province, an inland town about 108 miles from Valdivia, has 30,000 inhabitants, and is in the centre of a magnificent wheat and orchard zone. It is the chief point to which the Araucanian Indians bring their manufactures for sale. The South American Missionary Society maintains two schools for boys and girls.

Hotels :—Central, Temuco, De France.

Tocopilla, in Antofagasta province, with a population of 6,000, is chiefly concerned with shipping nitrate, iodine, and copper-ore.

Hotels :—America, Cosmopolita.

Valdivia, on the river Calle-Calle, 12 miles from its mouth, is 440 miles from Valparaiso by sea, and about 23 hours by rail from Santiago, has the best shipbuilding yards in the Republic, turning out 3,000-ton vessels. It has a population of 27,000, and shoe factories, tanneries, flour-mills, and breweries. The city is accessible to craft of 800 tons. The Pacific Steam Navigation Company's boats call at Corral, and discharge into lighters for Valdivia.

Hotels :—Colón, Yungay ($12—$15), etc.

PHYSICAL FEATURES.

Situated between the Andes and the Pacific, **Chile** has an area of 307,774 square miles, and is bounded north by Peru, east by Bolivia and Argentina, and south and west by the Pacific. It may be said to consist of three regions : the deserts of the north, the arable lands of the centre, and the forest country of the south. Between the ocean and the Andes lies a fertile plain some 620 miles long and 60 broad, sometimes styled " The Vale of Chile."

The agricultural portions are estimated at about 40,000 square miles, or nearly an eighth of the whole area. The rest of the country is mountainous, the Western Andes running east and the Cordillera Maritima westward.

The Chilean lateral range includes the great peaks of the Cerro Doña Ines (16,706 feet) and the Cerro Bolson (16,017 feet) The system is volcanic, and the culminating point of the Chilean Andes, Aconcagua, attains 23,097 feet. In Central Chile the Uspallata Pass, between Santiago and Mendoza in Argentina, rises 12,780 feet above the sea. The famous " Vale of Quillota" between Santiago and Valparaiso is extremely fertile.

The coast has a remarkably large number of islands and islets, three separate groups being known as the Chiloé, Guaytecas, and Chonos archipelagos. The Diego Ramirez group is 63 miles west of Cape Horn. The greater part of Tierra del Fuego also belongs to Chile.

The principal **rivers** have their sources in the Andes, flow west to the Pacific, and possess only short navigable channels. The rivers of the desert region (of which the longest is the Loa (1,250 miles) are lost in the sand before reaching the coast. The agricultural provinces are well watered by the Bio-Bio (220 miles), Maipó, Itata, and other streams. The southern areas of Chiloé and Magallanes have the Pudeto, Palena, Yelcho, and others, and in this region are a large number of glaciers on the slopes of the Cordilleras and other eminences.

Most of the **lakes** are in the south. The largest are Lake Llanquihué (300 square miles) and Lake Ranco (200 square miles), and most of them drain westwards towards the Pacific through short and partially navigable rivers. In the far south occur the big fresh-water Laguna Blanca and the salt lakes, Otway Water and Skyring Water

The **climate** is temperate, the northern deserts are not altogether rainless, and it is not too hot. The south has a good rainfall, and the temperature is cool and even. The average rainfall is at La Serena, 6¾ inches, Santiago, 16, Talca, 22, Concepción, 53, Puerto Montt, 104 · and Valdivia, 112 inches. The average temperature in Santiago is 56° F The highest temperature in the north is 91° F., and the lowest in the south 17° F Snow does not fall north of 36° S., except at altitudes of 200 to 300 metres.

Ordinary European **clothing** is worn, except in the districts to the north of Coquimbo. The hot season is from November to May

POPULATION

The population of about 4¼ millions is by no means concentrated in the large cities, but well distributed over the cultivated areas The Republic is divided into 23 Provinces and one Territory

Provinces.	Sq. Miles.	Population.	Capital.
Aconcagua	5,487	132,000	San Felipe.
Antofagasta	46,611	220,000	Antofagasta.
Arauco	2,458	75,000	Lebú.
Atacama	30,729	64,000	Copiapó.
Bio-Bio	5,246	107,000	Los Angeles.
Cautin	5,832	164,000	Temuco.
Chiloé	8,593	100,000	Ancud.
Colchagua	3,856	164,000	San Fernando.
Concepción	3,252	272,000	Concepción.
Coquimbo	13,461	191,000	La Serena.
Curicó	2,978	116,000	Curicó.
Linares	3,942	120,000	Linares.
Llanquihué	45,515	151,000	Puerto Montt
Malleco	2,973	136,000	Angol.
Maule	2,475	110,000	Cauquenes.
Nuble	3,407	198,000	Chillán.
O'Higgins	2,342	125,000	Rancagua.
Santiago	5,665	628,000	Santiago.
Tacna	9,251	39,000	Tacna.
Talca	3,840	131,000	Talca.
Tarapacá	18,131	135,000	Iquique.
Valdivia	8,649	187,000	Valdivia.
Valparaiso	1,953	348,000	Valparaiso.
Magallanes Territory	71,127	65,000	Punta Arenas.

In 1920 the foreign population included :—

	Population.		Population.
Spaniards	24,775	French	6,924
Bolivians	15,957	British	6,899
Peruvians	12,052	Turks	5,419
Italians	11,535	Austrians	3,950
Germans	8,551	North Americans	1,896
Argentines	7,047		

A CHILEAN CALENDAR.

1535. Diego Almagro sets out from Peru to explore Chile.
1536. Pedro de Valdivia begins to colonize Chile.
1541. City of Santiago founded. Beginning of war with Araucanians.
1550. City of Concepción founded.
1551. City of Imperial founded. Valdivia defeats the Araucanians.
1552. City of Valdivia founded.
1553. Death of Valdivia at the hands of the Araucanians.
1565. Pedro de Villagran is succeeded by Rodrigo de Quiroga.
1579. Drake raids the coast.
1587. Coast raided by Sir Thomas Cavendish.
1593. Jesuits first arrive from Peru.
1602. Araucanians capture most of the important southern cities.
1609. Royal Audience established.
1638. Coast harassed by Dutch squadron.
1640. Treaty of Quillan concluded with the Araucanians.
1643. Coast harassed by Dutch squadron.
1647. University of Santiago founded.
1655. Renewed hostilities with the Araucanians.
1657 Garcia Hurtado de Mendoza made Governor of Chile.

1665. Treaty concluded with Araucanian Indians.
1707–17. Coast blockaded by French squadrons.
1722. Araucanian war breaks out again.
1751 Santiago and Concepción damaged by earthquake.
1773. Peace concluded with Araucanians.
1776. Province of Cuyo, hitherto Chilean, handed over to the new Vice-Royalty of La Plata.
1778. Cadiz commercial monopoly suppressed as regards Chile and all South America.
1792. Ambrose O'Higgins made Captain-General.
1810. Chile declares war on Spain.
1812. Schools for poor children founded. First girls' school founded.
1813. Province of Concepción invaded by Spanish army commanded by Colonel Pareja. First naval engagement between the Spaniards and patriot forces.
1814. Spaniards defeat Chileans at Rancagua.
1817. Patriot forces, led by San Martin, defeat the Spaniards at Chacabuco.
1818. Arrival of Lord Cochrane to command the Chilean fleet. Bernardo O'Higgins becomes Director-General of Chile.
1819. First Chilean fleet puts to sea. The Chilean victory at the battle of Maipu, which frees all but the south of the country from the Spaniards.
1820. First shipment of nitrate to England.
1823. Bernardo O'Higgins forced to resign.
1826. Spaniards finally driven from the Archipelago of Chiloé. Peace with Spain concluded.
1829. Civil war between the parties of General Prieto and General Francisco de Lastra.
1830. Civil war between the parties of Prieto and General Freire.
1832. Freire banished to Peru.
1833. New Constitution defines the limites of the Chilean State.
1836. After an unsuccessful attempt at revolution General Freire taken prisoner and permanently banished. He retires to Australia. War declared between Chile and the Peru-Bolivian Confederation.
1839. Final victory of the Chileans.
1840. First arrival of Pacific Steam Navigation Co.'s steamers.
1841. President Bulnes elected.
1851. President Manuel Montt elected.
1852. First line railway opened between Caldera and Copiapó.
1859. Rising of the Araucanian Indians.
1861. President José Joaquin Perez elected.
1866. Spaniards bombard Valparaiso.
1868. Treaty of peace with Spain.
1871. President Errazuriz Zañartu elected.
1876. President Anibal Pinto elected.
1879. War with Peru and Bolivia, known as the Nitrate War.
1881. President Santa Maria elected.
1883. Conclusion of Nitrate War.
1886. Balmaceda elected President.
1891. Civil war between the Balmacedists and the party headed by Montt, Silva and Barros Luco. Balmaceda, defeated, commits suicide. Admiral Montt elected President.
1892. Treaty signed with Bolivia.
1896. General Errázuriz elected President.
1901. Germán Riesco elected President. Beginning of a frontier dispute with Argentina.
1902. On the conclusion of the Holdich Boundary Delimitation, treaty signed with Argentina.
1906. Severe earthquakes at Valparaiso and Santiago.
1910. Transandine tunnel on the Chilean side officially opened.
1919. Chile joins the League of Nations.

GOVERNMENT

Constitution :—Executive power is vested in the President, who is elected (by delegates chosen by the people) for a term of five years, and is ineligible for a second term immediately ensuing.

He nominates his Ministers, the appointments being subject to the approval of Congress. There are six Ministries Finance, Foreign Affairs, Interior; War and Marine, Education and Justice, Agriculture, Public Works and Railways. Every order of the President has to be countersigned by the Minister of the Department affected.

The Council of State consists of the President and five members nominated by him, the Ministry, and six members elected by Congress. In the event of the Presidency being vacated, the Minister of the Interior acts *pro tem.*, and orders a new Presidential election within ten days.

The National Congress consists of the Senate and the Chamber of Deputies, the former composed of 32 and the latter of 94 members. Senators (who must not be less than 33 years old) are elected for the provinces, for a term of six years, in the proportion of one Senator for every three Deputies, one half their number retiring every three years. Deputies are elected for every 30,000 inhabitants, or for groups not falling below 15,000, for a term of three years.

The ordinary Session of Congress is from June to September, but Extraordinary Sessions may be convoked. During the recess a Permanent Committee, composed of seven Senators and seven Deputies, acts for Congress.

The suffrage is exercised by all literate male citizens over 21 years of age who are not domestic servants.

PAST PRESIDENTS.

Bernardo O'Higgins	1818
(Ten different Presidents)	1823
General Prieto	1831
General M. Bulnes	1841
M. Montt	1851
J J Pérez	1861
F Errázuriz	1871
A Pinto	1876
D Santa Maria	1881
José Manuel Balmaceda	1886
C. Vicuña (elected but did not take office)	1891
Admiral J Montt	1891
F Errázuriz (son of F Errázuriz)	1896
G. Riesco	1901
Pedro Montt (died in office)	1906
E. Fernandez (died in office)	1910
Emiliano Figueroa	1910
Ramón Barros Luco	1910
Juan Luis Sanfuentes	1915

PRESIDENT
Arturo Alessandri.

CHILE.

MINISTRY

Interior	Don Cornelio Soavedra.
Foreign Affairs	Don Luis Izquierdo.
Justice	Don Luis Sales Romo.
Finance	Don Victor Celis M.
War	Don Jorge a Guerra.
Public Works	Don Vicente Adrian.

The Roman Catholic **religion** is maintained by the State, but the Constitution guarantees liberty and protection to all other religious beliefs.

The **metric** system is obligatory, all other measures being excluded by law

The unit of **currency** is the gold peso, nominally worth 1s. 6d. In the paper currency, which is in general use, the peso has a fluctuating value. The silver and other coins in use represent fractions of the 100 centavos of which the peso is made up. There are 50-, 40-, 20-, 10-, 5-, 2½-, 2-, 1-, and ½-centavo pieces.

CHILEAN LEGATION IN GREAT BRITAIN

RESIDENCE.	DESIGNATION	NAME.
London (22 Grosvenor Square, W.1.)	Envoy Extraordinary and Minister Plenipotentiary	Agustin Edwards.
	First Secretary	Manuel Salinas.
34 Pont Street, S.W.1.	First Secretary	Santiago de Ossa.
	Financial Adviser	Luis Waddington.
	Juridical Adviser	Alejandro Alvarez.
	First Secretary	Jorge Silva.
	Second Secretary	Luis Renard.
	Naval and Air Attaché	Comm. Edgardo von Schroeders.
	Military Attaché	Major Juan Negrete
	Air Attaché	Julio F A. Bittencourt.
	Attaché	Santiago Monk.
	Attaché	Agustin R. Edwards.
	Commercial Attaché	Jorge Buchanan.

CHILEAN CONSULATE, UNITED KINGDOM.

RESIDENCE.	DESIGNATION.	NAME.
Liverpool (325 Tower Buildings, Water Street.)	Consul-General for the United Kingdom.	Alberto Phillips.
London	Consul	Vicente Echeverria.
Glasgow	Consul	Tomás de la Barra.
Cardiff	Consul	Alberto Porter.
Belfast	Consul	Alejandro Bulloch.
Queenstown and Cork	Consul	James W Scott.
Nottingham	Consul	Alejandro Seeling.
Birmingham	Consul	Ernest Lord.
Port Talbot	Consul	Abelardo Aldana.
Newcastle-on-Tyne	Consul	Clodomiro R. Lopez.
Dublin	Consul	William P Kelly
Sheffield	Consul	Percy Albert Reuss.
Southampton	Consul	Ramón Araya Novoa.
Dover	Consul	Eduardo Prescott.
Newport	Consul	J W Beinon.
Plymouth	Consul	Walter H Jago.
Hull	Consul	Joaquin Soler

CHILE.

NATURAL RESOURCES.

The chief **agricultural** zone is in the central provinces, from a little north of Valparaiso to Valdivia in the south. The latest statistics give the following areas as under cultivation :—

685,798 hectares	Cereals and crops.
491,326 hectares	Sown pasture.
124,224 hectares	Fruit and timber.

The principal crops are wheat, barley, alfalfa, maize, oats, hemp, flax, and all European vegetables and fruits, including apples, of which 700,000 trees exist. The beginning has been established of what should become an important export of fruit, principally to the United States. Wild strawberries flourish in the south, and bee-farming is conducted on a large scale. The wheat provinces are Coquimbo, Concepción, Aconcagua, Valparaiso, Santiago, O'Higgins, Curicó, Talca, Bio-Bio, Malleco, and Cautin.

The areas under cereals are stated as:—Wheat 484,093, Barley 50,930, Oats. 26,076, Maize: 25,065 hectares.

Vineyards are numerous in the south, and the Chilean wines are reputed the best in South America. In 1919 there were 65,884 hectares under cultivation, and the yield of wine was 1,182,928 hectolitres. Among the finest brands are Tocornal, Subercasseaux, Urmeneta, and Concha y Toro. Measures have been prepared to restrict the area under vines.

The western slopes of the Andes from the Beagle Channel to Valdivia are covered with splendid **forests,** and there are in Chile more than 5,000,000 acres of timber adapted for furniture manufacture, building, etc. Forests provide valuable barks; medicinal herbs are found in the mountains. Steps are being taken for the utilization of suitable timber for paper pulp.

The acreage of **cattle-raising** lands is about 90,000,000. In 1918 it was estimated that there were in the Republic 391,718 horses, 36,489 donkeys, 51,411 mules, 2,163,141 head of cattle, and 4,500,190 sheep.

The pelts of the vicuña, alpaca, and guanaco are valuable, and quantities of chinchilla skins are exported.

The island of Juan Fernandez is an important fishing centre, and magnificent lobster and crayfish abound. The pejerry fish is found off the Chilean coast. There is a whaling station at Corral.

MINERAL WEALTH.

Chile is the only country in the world producing nitrate in a natural state, and the fields constitute a source of enormous wealth.

Nitrate is chiefly found in the desert tracts of Tarapacá and Antofagasta, ceded to Chile after her victory over Peru and Bolivia in 1883. It is to the almost rainless character of these lands that the existence of the great beds of caliche is due. There are about 170 oficinas, the productive capacity considerably exceeds three million tons per annum, employing 45,000 men. The ownership of these oficinas, calculated as a matter of productive capacity and nationality, is approximately Chilean 74½% ; British 23%, United States 2½%

The proportion of nitrate produced in the several districts varies considerably, for while the Antofagasta district sometimes produces practically the same as Tarapacá, during the last nitrate year the percentage was roughly : Tarapacá, 42%, Antofagasta, 28%, Aguas Blancas, 6% ; Tocopilla, 12%, Taltal, 12%

The statistics for the past seven nitrate years are as under :—

	Production. Tons of 1,000 Kilos.	Exports. Tons of 1,000 Kilos.
July 1916—June 1917	2,907,630	2,863,478
„ 1917— „ 1918	2,979,580	2,912,967
„ 1918— „ 1919	2,332,564	1,794,326
„ 1919— „ 1920	1,957,271	2,206,964
„ 1920— „ 1921	2,174,099	2,051,512
„ 1921— „ 1922	890,964	613,637
„ 1922— „ 1923	1,499,621	2,101,034

Chile is one of the few South American countries possessing **coal**, and the industry has been developed further than in any other Coal is found principally at Lota, Coronel, Lebu, Penco, Curanilahue, Colico, Santa Ana, Dichato, and Talcahuano. The output in 1915 was about 1,170,000 tons. The annual Chilean consumption can be put at about 2,500,000 tons.

Borax is of great importance, and Chile supplies half of the world's consumption from the Ascotán deposits, those at Chilcaya being held in reserve. About 43,350 tons were produced in 1913.

Common salt is found abundantly, but only the domestic market is supplied. The Punta de Lobos deposit is stated to be capable of supplying the world's demands for years.

More than half the world's consumption of **iodine** is produced in Chile.

Chile commenced to produce **copper** in 1601, and during the ensuing century produced a total amount of 4,550 tons, in the 18th century this amount was increased to 62,000 tons, and again rose to 1,800,000 tons in the 19th century For 22 years of the present century over 1,200,000 tons have been produced. In 1876 the amount produced by Chile was 38·14 per cent. of the world's production, this percentage fell to 3·62 per cent. in 1906, but is again on the increase, and stands at 15 to 20 per cent.

The principal copper enterprises are the Braden Copper Company near Sewell, in O'Higgins province; the Chile Copper Company at Chuquicamata, works at Naitagua and Catemu, and at Potrerillos, El Salado, Las Condes, etc. The mines and foundries employ about 23,000 men.

The principal **gold** centres are Coquimbo, Valdivia, Magallanes, and Concepción. Gold was produced to the value of $2,178,764 in 1918.

Silver was produced in 1918 to the value of $3,752,883.

Sulphur was produced in 1918 to the value of $3,129,120 gold pesos.

Iron is found in the provinces of Coquimbo, Valdivia, Cautin, Santiago, Aconcagua, Valparaiso, and Atacama. Iron production temporarily increased during the European war to about three million tons.

Molybdenum occurs near Valparaiso and in Tacna province, and at Vallenar, Santiago, and Coquimbo. The main deposits are at Campanani, near Arica.

Other minerals found in Chile include lead, aluminium, plumbago, manganese, bismuth, cobalt, saltpetre, potassic salts, mercury, mica, zinc, and clay

Local Industries :—Chile is becoming an industrial country Patriotic feeling, Government legislation, and frequently the cheaper cost of national production, are all helping.

Chile will become, as time goes on, less and less a buyer of manufactured goods. Her needs will be limited more to machinery and raw materials. The principal industries to-day in Chile are the manufacture of matches, glassware, boots and leather goods, cement, iron and brass bedsteads and mattresses, furniture, soap, and candles, tobacco, cigars and cigarettes, spirits, alcoholic liquors and mineral water, condensed milk, wire nails, hats and ready-made clothing.

Textiles, in which Great Britain leads, form the largest import, followed by iron and steel manufactures and hardware.

There are about 3,000 manufacturing establishments throughout the Republic, employing over 70,000 persons.

There is a **British Chamber of Commerce** in the Republic of Chile (Incorporated), Valparaiso, Calle Cochrane, 741 (Casilla 329), with branches at Antofagasta, Concepción, Iquique, Santiago, and Talcahuano, and correspondents at Chañaral, Punta Arenas, and Valdivia.

The Chilean Press :—One of the principal papers, "El Mercurio," is published at Santiago and Valparaiso, and also at Antofagasta. The evening edition, "Las Ultimas Noticias," appears at Santiago. Other daily papers—Santiago "La Nación," "El Diario Ilustrado," "La Opinión", Antofagasta "El Industrial," "La Nación", Iquique · "El Nacional," "El Tarapacá, Coquimbo "El Longitudinal," ; Arica "El Ferrocarril" ; Tacna "La Provincia," ; Taltal "La Razón" , La Serena "El Chileno," "El Coquimbo ", Concepción · "El Sur "

Outward **mails** are dispatched (i) via Buenos Aires and the Andes; (ii) by Pacific Steam Navigation Line, via Panamá, at intervals, and (iii) via United States. Correspondence for Punta Arenas, unless specially addressed, is dispatched via Buenos Aires. During the winter in South America (April to September) correspondence is forwarded via New York and Panamá, or by direct ship. Only specially superscribed correspondence is forwarded via Buenos Aires and the Andes.

Postage, 3d. first ounce, 1½d. each ounce after

Homeward mails are dispatched at frequent intervals.

CHILE.

Ordinary **telegrams** (Spanish), 6 centavos (paper) per word; urgent telegrams (Spanish), 18 centavos. Telegrams in code or foreign languages are charged higher rates.

About 18,000 miles of telegraphs, with 367 offices, are owned by the State. Other telegraph lines amount to 4,500 miles.

The telephones are in the hands of private companies.

There is a chain of **wireless** stations at Arica, Antofagasta, Coquimbo, Valparaiso, Talcahuano, Valdivia, Puerto Montt, Punta Arenas, and Juan Fernandez. Wireless stations have been constructed also at Castro, Huafo Island, Rio Aysen, Cape Praper, Puerto Bories, Evanglistas Island, Faro Felix, Punta Arenas, and Mocha Island.

BRITISH LEGATION AND CONSULATES IN CHILE.

The letter (M) denotes that the Consular Officer holds a Marriage Warrant. Members of the Diplomatic Service do not require Warrants.

RESIDENCE.	RANK.	NAME.	CONSULAR DISTRICT.
Santiago	Envoy Extraordinary and Minister Plenipotentiary	A. C. Grant Duff.	
	Second Secretary .	C. H. Bateman, M.C.	—
Santiago	Vice-Consul	Thomas C. Sargent	
Antofagasta .	(M) Consul	Henry W W Bird	
	Vice-Consul	James K. M. Clarke	
Iquique	Vice-Consul	J C. Hardie	
	Vice-Consul (acting)	T. G. Patrickson .	Provinces of Antofagasta, Atacama, Tacna, and Tarapacá.
Arica	Vice-Consul	B. S. Fry .	
Caleta Buena	Vice-Consul	T W Pye	
Junín	Vice-Consul	D. S. Henderson	
Pisagua	Vice-Consul	John B. Howden	
Caldera	Vice-Consul	D. J MacKenzie	
Caleta Coloso	Vice-Consul	Alfred E. Danks .	
Chañaral	Consular Agent	William Sheriff	
Copiapó	Consular Agent	G. R. Pearson	
Mejillones	Vice-Consul .	Laurence J M. Hawke.	Provinces of Antofagasta and Atacama.
Taltal	Vice-Consul	H. J Turpie .	
Tocopilla .	Vice-Consul .	Charles Wesley Nicholls.	
Tacna ..	Vice-Consul	C. M. Elliott	Provinces of Tacna and Tarapacá.
Valparaiso	(M) Consul-General	James M. MacLeod, C.M.G.	
	Vice-Consul	F G. Coultas	
	Pro-Consul	H. T Mundy .	
Coquimbo	Consular Agent	A. V Gondio	
Concepción, Lota and Coronel.	Consul	Edward Cooper	Republic of Chile, with the exception of the Provinces of Tacna, Tarapacá, Antofagasta, and Atacama.
Los Andes	Consular Agent	Louis Murray	
Puerto Montt	Consular Agent	A. E. Trim	
Punta Arenas	(M) Vice-Consul	T B. Wildman	
Talca .	Consular Agent .	Charles A. Stringfellow.	
Talcahuano	Vice-Consul	Henry James Coke	
Temuco	Consular Agent	John Patillo	
	Consular Agent (acting).	A. H. B. Perkins	
Valdivia and Corral.		Donald R. Macmillan	

Public Holidays :—New Year, Good Friday, Holy Saturday, The Ascension, May 21, Battle of Iquique, Corpus Christi; June 29, SS. Peter and Paul, The Assumption, September 18, National Independence Day, September 19, Army and Navy Victories; All Saints' Day, December 8, Immaculate Conception, Christmas Day, and the day of a Presidential election.

IMPORTS AND EXPORTS.

	Exports.	Imports.	Total.	Balance.
	£	£	£	£
1922	25,394,026	17,788,618	43,182,644	7,605,408
1921	32,281,485	28,597,687	61,879,172	4,683,798
1920	58,416,392	34,130,920	92,547,312	24,285,472
1919	22,609,356	30,324,314	52,933,670	*7,714,958
1918	57,271,688	32,705,554	89,977,242	24,566,134
1917	53,421,677	26,630,777	80,052,454	26,790,900
1916	38,518,855	16,689,062	55,207,917	21,829,793
1915	24,560,937	11,490,867	36,051,804	13,070,070
1914	22,074,105	20,031,752	42,305,857	1,842,353
1913	29,342,789	24,713,835	54,056,624	4,628,954
1912	28,742,095	25,084,107	53,826,202	3,657,988

* Adverse.

Guidance for Commercial Travellers.

The Superintendent of Customs in Chile was authorised by a decree of 1898, to permit the dispatch to private warehouses of the samples with which the agents of commercial houses are travelling, provided that they are not whole pieces of stuff or complete sets of objects which would divest them of their character as samples. In virtue of this exemption, travelling salesmen may introduce their samples of foreign merchandise into any port of the Republic without paying in ready money the ordinary import duties, and are allowed a term of six months in which to pay the duties if the samples which they bring are designed for consumption in the country. If they re-ship the samples to a foreign country, the I.O.U (pagaré) which they have signed for the value of the duties is cancelled without charge.

If samples carried by commercial travellers consist of objects which can be put to industrial use or sold, import duty is leviable on them according to class. Refund of duty, with a reduction of 25 per cent., can be obtained provided that the samples are re-exported within one year

Samples of no commercial value and no industrial use are free of duty

Commercial travellers must register in the first town called at, if they intend to remain in the country ten days or longer. Licences are required for each separate Department and are obtainable at the Municipal Offices of the chief town thereof.

The following fees are payable half yearly and travellers intending to stay six months or less, pay one half of the amounts posted.

CHILE.

FEES.

$1,000 in Santiago, Valparaiso, Viña del Mar, Concepcion or Talcahuano.

$800 in each of the 65 Departments having between 20,000 and 100,000 inhabitants.

$700 in each of the 11 Departments having between 10,000 and 20,000 inhabitants.

$600 in each of the 4 Departments having between 5,000 and 10,000 inhabitants.

CHILEAN PATAGONIA.

The Magallan Territory, together with various archipelagos, forms the most southerly part of the South American continent, the apex of an inverted triangle Taking an imaginary line from this apex and extending it northwards towards the base of the triangle it gives Argentine Patagonia on the East and Chilean Patagonia or Magallan Territory, as it is known politically, on the West.

The Territorio de Magallanes comprises 260,000 square kilometres or seven times the size of Belgium. The Island of Tierra del Fuego alone has an area of 48,000 square kilometres 28,000 of which belong to Chile, and the remainder to the Argentine Republic, the dividing line being a perpendicular North and South between longitudes 68 and 69. The territory stretches from the Taitao Peninsula at 47° South Latitude and includes all the archipelagos which follow to the South down to Cape Horn (Cabo de Hornos) at 56° South Latitude, together with the Western portion of Tierra del Fuego.

Over 10,000,000 acres from 52° South Latitude to about 47° South Latitude are unexplored. The territory is very sparsely inhabited, the total population being under 30,000, of which about 25,000 live in Punta Arenas, the only town and port of any importance. The population has been increasing of late.

NATURAL CHARACTERISTICS.

The topography of Chilean Patagonia is varied. The land is undulating, hilly, mountainous, wooded and well watered by lakes and swamps. Argentine Patagonia is a flat table land, bare of trees, but well watered in parts.

The islands are little known and uninhabited, mountainous, with dense forest intersected by grassy tracts.

The island of Tierra del Fuego has tracts of flat grass land covering an area of millions of acres. Forest country backed by mountains, rises to a height of over 8,000 feet. About three and a half million acres of land are exploited for sheep farming.

The temperature and **climate** vary considerably, and Punta Arenas is probably the most favoured spot. Whilst the low-lying districts near the coast do not get much snow, but farther inland and on the high ground snow lies for many months of the year and very low temperatures are experienced. In Tierra del Fuego, during the summer months, the average temperature varies between 58° F and 45° F., and in winter from 35° F to 46° F

The mean temperatures according to observations taken over a period of thirty years are : Summer average, 51° F , Winter average, 35° F

The summer months are December, January, and February when rains are frequent, although it is not uncommon to have a spell of several weeks of dry weather during this season. For three months of the year snow covers the country, except those parts bordering the sea. The country is more or less impassable, except on horseback, owing to snow and swollen torrents.

Strong, cold piercing winds are experienced throughout the year and particularly during the spring, when they reach a velocity of 70 to 80 kilometres per hour The winds are very dry, and the ground dries in an astonishing manner; their effect is beneficial in drying the country, but detrimental in preventing the growth of the crops, which can only be cultivated in sheltered spots.

Towns :—The only town of size, is Punta Arenas (founded in 1847) with a mixed population of about 25,000 inhabitants. Puerto Natales and Ultima Esperanza have 2,000 inhabitants.

In Chilean Tierra del Fuego the only town is the tiny capital Porvenir, situated opposite Punta Arenas with 800 inhabitants, of which 90 per cent. are Jugoslavs and the remainder British, German, Russian and Chilean.

The chief **ports** are :—Punta Arenas, Puerto Natales, Puerto Porvenir, Tierra del Fuego; and Puerto Harris, Dawson Island, Puerto Bories, Puerto Rio Seco, Puerto San Gregorio, Puerto Sara (all private)

THE BRITISH COLONY

Over one-fifth of the developed land in the Territory belongs to British subjects. At least half the senior staff of the commercial and industrial concerns, as well as a quarter of the working shepherds are British. Ninety per cent. of the large sheep farms are managed by British subjects, chiefly Scotch. One Chilean sheep farming company, which is entirely British managed throughout, employs over 2,000 men, of whom about 500 are British, working in different capacities from general manager down to shepherds.

Amongst the British colony's local institutions are :—The British Club, known as The British Association of Magallanes, the best conducted British club in Chile, with a membership of 240, The Overseas Club (Branch), The Benevolent Society, The Mission School attached to the Protestant Church, The Preparatory School, with 98 pupils, The Anglo-South American Bank, Ltd. (Branch), established in 1894, " The Magellan Times," published by Señor Arturo Riesco M.

Foreign communities include the following nationalities :— British, German, Austrian, Czecho-Slovakian, Argentine, French, Belgian, Spanish, Danish, Brazilian, Panamanian, Greek, Dutch, Russian, Swedish, Polish, Syrian, Persian, Hindu, Italian, Uru-guayan, Portuguese and American, from which it will be seen that very few nations are unrepresented.

NATURAL RESOURCES.

The only **industry** of importance is that of sheep breeding and its by-products wool, frozen meat, canned meat, fat and sheep skins.

All the frozen meat, amounting to between one and a-quarter to one and a half million carcasses, with an equal number of sheepskins, are shipped in British ships and sold in London. London also usually sells the bulk of the wool clip.

The standard type of **sheep** bred in Magellan Territory, Tierra del Fuego, and Southern Patagonia is the Romney Marsh cross merino. The "Corriedale" has been extensively imported.

On the Bradford market grading Punta Arenas wool averages from 40's to 58's in quality

—	1916.	1917	1918.	1919.	1920.
Animals Shorn	1,158,211	1,173,219	1,184,224	1,139,505	1,127,665
Lb. of Wool Shorn	8,565,894	10,420,200	8,547,143	7,961,784	9,115,442
Average per Head, lb.	7.40	8.88	7.22	6.98	8.08
Percentage of Fleeces	73.66	85.93	91.51	94.19	93.41

The total annual production of **timber** amounts to between twenty and thirty million square feet. The export to the Argentine, in normal times, is about half the above-mentioned quantities.

Alluvial **gold** exists in Tierra del Fuego and other districts and has been worked spasmodically for years, but not with success owing to the excessive cost of dredging. A British private company has been founded with a paid-up capital of £125,000. Towards the end of 1920 operations were commenced in the island of Tierra del Fuego, where several claims were marked out in Rio Grande and Rio Verde, when unsatisfactory results obtained.

In 1904 a permit was obtained from the Government for whaling in the Southern Seas. Although satisfactory results were obtained, the company liquidated in 1908. Contemporaneously another company was formed, for whale fishing, and erected a factory for working whales in the Bay of Aquila (Bahia Aquila) In 1906 this company was turned into a limited company under the style of "La Sociedad Ballenera de Magallanes," with a capital of £100,000. The company commenced liquidation in 1913, and the last dividend paid was in 1918.

There is a small lumber industry for local use and export to Argentine.

Small factories exist in Punta Arenas for candles, beer, electric power, alcohol, wood, and coal gas obtained from local coal (lignite) A small lignite mine (Mina Loreto) is worked and the output used locally.

An unpretentious dockyard has three shipways capable of taking ships up to 1,500 tons, and works in conjunction with an iron and brass foundry (managed by British engineers) with repair shops for all classes of machinery.

LAND AND LABOUR.

Magallanes was originally a penal station, as to-day is Ushuaia, the capital of Argentine Tierra del Fuego, but from the year 1853 dates the first colonization scheme under which permission to occupy land was given gratis to any applicant. Gratuitious grants continued until 1884 when the Government held the first auction sale to lease lands for periods varying from five to twenty years. In 1903, the Government decided to put up for sale the first lots of pasture land, followed by others since held. The present total area used for pasture in Magellan Territory exceeds twelve and a half million acres (5,000,000 hectares) of which about five million are held freehold. There has been considerable local agitation against Government action in leasing serviceable land in large blocks to two or three powerful companies, to the exclusion of the small landholder The question of the sale of further tracts of Government land is frequently brought up and pointed out as a means of obtaining ready cash for the depleted exchequer Practically all the Government land suitable for pasture is leased for periods still to run of from seven to 20 or more years.

The Sociedad Explotadora de Tierra del Fuego leases 3,600,000 acres (1,500,000 hectares) expiring September 1928. The Sociedad Ganadera " Gente Grande " leases 240,000 acres (100,000 hectares) expiring the same year The Sociedad Industrial y Ganadera de Magallanes leases 1,200,000 acres (483,700 hectares) expiring January 1940.

The labour question is as acute as in most other industrial centres. Strikes have taken place during the last few years, and on more than one occasion armed forces have had to be employed.

The frontier is patrolled by Chilean Carabineers with the object of preventing the entrance of agitators into the Territory

Local labour is recruited from Chilotes (the inhabitants of Chiloe), some of whom reside permanently in the Territory, and others who travel down for the killing and shearing season, and from Spaniards, Jugoslavs, and Argentines who cross the border

The following statistics show the increase in the **trade** of Magellan Territory in 30 years :—

Year.	Export.	Import.	Total.
	$	$	$
1890	616,000	789,000	1,405,000
1920	49,254,976	15,873,014	65,127,990

A **wireless** station exists at Punta Arenas and another is being erected at Ultima Esperanza, adjoining the Freezer at Puerto Bories, one mile from the village of Natales.

In **Tierra del Fuego** as recently as 1890 exchange was carried on by barter, gold dust being the medium, viz. :—

    40 grms. of gold for 1 quintal (46 kilos) of flour.
    50 „ „ „ „ 1 pair of boots, etc., etc

RAIL ROUTES IN CHILE.

Valparaiso—Santiago :—Trains start in Valparaiso from the Puerto Station and arrive in Santiago at the Alameda or Mapocho Stations. The journey is some 4 hours. The main stations and distances are :—

Valparaiso (Puerto)—

Kilometres.			Kilometres.		
2		Barón.	43	.	. Limache.
9	.	Viña del Mar.	57		Quillota.
13	.	El Salto.	68		La Calera.
22	..	Quilpué.	94		Llay-Llay
31	..	Peña Blanco.	186	.	. Santiago (Alameda or Mapocho).

Santiago—Buenos Aires :—The journey across the continent from Santiago to Buenos Aires occupies 48 hours, or in the contrary direction 38 hours.

The following shows the altitudes in metres, and the distances from Santiago.

	Altitude Metres.		Kilometres from Santiago.
Los Andes .	. . 834	.	. 149
Caracoles	. . 3,185	.	. 218
Frontera	. 3,205		220
Las Cuevas	.. 3,150		.. 224
Mendoza .	767	.	. 398
Buenos Aires	Sea level		1,444

CUSTOMS SEARCH :—The luggage of passengers by Transandine Railway from Chile to Argentina is searched by the Customs in Buenos Aires, not at the frontier

Santiago—Talcahuano :—A daily express in each direction does the journey in 11½-12 hours, leaving the Alameda Station in Santiago and stopping at the following junctions :—Rancagua, Pelequén, San Fernando, Curicó, Talca, Leñares, Parral, Chillán, General Cruz, San Rosendo, and Concepción.

Santiago—Talca :—Trains leave the Alameda Station in Santiago and occupy about 7 hours in reaching Talca.

The main stations and distances are :—

Santiago (Alameda)—

Kilometres.			Kilometres.		
82	..	Rancagua.	185	..	.. Curico.
117	. ..	Pelequeñ.	249	.	.. Talca.
134	..	San Fernando.			

Santiago—Iquique :—A fairly comfortable train service with restaurant and sleeping cars connects Santiago, Valparaiso, and Iquique. Early application for places on the trains is advisable and should be made to the Compañia Trasportes Unidos, Calle Estado Esq. Alameda, Santiago, or Av Brasil Esq. Pudeto, Valparaiso.

The following are the chief stations en route with train distances from Santiago :—

Santiago—
Valparaiso.

Kilometres.		Kilometres.		
118	Calera.	1,147	.	. Pueblo Hundido.
189	Cabildo	1,427	.	Aguas Blancas.
316	Illapel.	1,533	.	Baquedano.
485	Ovalle.	1,629	.	Antofagasta.
593	Serena.	1,687	.	Toco.
811	Vallenar.	1,857	.	Pintados.
985	. . Copiapó.	1,954	.	Iquique.

Trains departing on Saturday mornings arrive at Iquique on Wednesday morning.

Antilhue—Puerto Montt :—From Valdivia for 28 kilometres the route is over the land to Victoria with a change at Antilhue and Puerto Montt is reached in some 7 hours from that point.

Chief stations and distances :—

Valdivia—

Kilometres.		
28	..	Antilhue.
43		Las Lagos.
274	.	Puerto Montt.

Llay Llay—Los Andes :—A change is made at Llay Llay (94 kilos. from Valparaiso, 92 from Santiago) for Los Andes, which station is reached by express in about 1½ hours.

Chief stations and distances :—

Llay Llay—

Kilometres.		
34	.	San Félipe.
49		Los Andes.

Talcahuano—Victoria :—The train journey is some 6 hours. The principal stations and distances follow :—

Talcahuano—

Kilometres.		Kilometres.	
15		113	Coigüe.
85	Concepción.	139	Renaico.
106	San Rosendo.	214	Victoria.
	Santa Fé.		

Victoria—Valdivia :—Trains occupy about 6 hours. The chief stations and distances are :—

Victoria—

Kilometres.		
65	.	Temuco.
208	.	Antilhue.
236	.	Valdivia.

Talca—Talcahuano :—The train journey is some 8 hours. The principal stations and distances are :—

Talca—

Kilometres.		Kilometres.	
50	Linares.	215	Monte Aguila.
90	. Parral.	249	San Rosendo.
148	Chillán.	319	Concepción.
165	Rucapequén.	334	. Talcahuano.
196	.. General Cruz.		

New Transcontinental Railway Project :—A new transandine railway joining Antofagasta with Salta, in Argentina, has been projected, to provide an outlet for the produce of a region in Argentina with an area of 400,000 square kilometres and a million inhabitants. It would serve less directly Catamarca, Formosa, and part of Corrientes, as well as the eastern part of Bolivia. These areas export their produce from Buenos Aires, is 1,685 kilometres away from Salta. Antofagasta is distant only 794 kilometres from Salta. Moreover, Antofagasta is within 4,562 miles of San Francisco. The region is believed to hold enormous mineral wealth, and it is fruitful agriculturally. Irrigation works, which cover an area of nearly 1,000,000 hectares in Jujuy and about 150,000 hectares in Salta, are under construction.

The railway might contribute to appease the feeling which has kept Bolivia estranged from Chile ever since Antofagasta province became Chilean, so landlocking the country Undoubtedly it would increase the trade of Antofagasta, perhaps to a point which would affect considerably the trade of the country as a whole. Possibly, by enabling a larger importation of foodstuffs in Antofagasta and the rest of the nitrate district, it would lower the cost of living. The scheme has opponents, notably among Chilean cattle farmers, who fear Argentine competition.

DISTANCES BY SEA.

	Valparaiso.						
Coquimbo .	198	Coquimbo.					
Antofagasta ..	575	392	Antofagasta.				
Iquique .	769	597	223	Iquique.			
Arica ..	879	697	321	107	Arica.		
Mollendo .	960	778	413	217	134	Mollendo.	
Callao .	1,301	1,128	806	656	581	457	Callao.
Panamá	2,611	2,445	2,137	1,987	1,912	1,788	1,340

THE CHILEAN LAKES.

An Itinerary.

The Chilean Lakes :—From Santiago to Osorno is some 956 kilometres upon the State Railway and the journey can be done in 24 hours.

From Osorno, Puerto Varas is distant 93 kilometres.

The trip can be made in daylight, leaving Santiago upon one of three days in the week, arriving the next evening at Concepción, from which there is a daily service via San Rosendo to Valdivia. An overnight stay in that place is made and Osorno is reached in four hours the next day After another overnight stop Puerto Varas is touched in little over two hours on the train.

A TWO-DAY TRIP

There follows a suggested itinerary from Puerto Varas to San Carlos de Bariloche (about 300 kilometres), crossing Lakes Llanquihue, Todos Santos, and Nahuel Huapi.

FIRST DAY **Puerto Varas Ensenada.** Dep. 7 a.m. by steamer over Lake Llanquhihue. Arr 11.30 a.m. Luncheon is served at the hotel ($3.50) and immediately after luncheon departure is made by motor 'bus for the port 18 kilometres distant, where steamer awaits the arrival of the 'bus. From **Puerto Petrolini** departure is made by steamer over Lake Todos Los Santos for a three hours journey to **Peulla,** arriving about 4 p.m. The Hotel Peulla has a capacity for 40, and provides dinner and lodging. Motor launches are available for excursions on the Lake and several day excursions can be made from this centre, e.g., to Cayatue and Rio Blanco.

SECOND DAY **Peulla** is left by coach or automobile for a run of 20 kilometres to **Puerto Blest** whence a steamer upon Lake Nahuel Huapi leaves for **San Carlos de Bariloche,** which has been likened to a Swiss mountain village. Population 1,200.

Hotels :—Los Lagos and Perito Moreno (Pension $8 Argentine)

Passages by the Express Service need to be booked five days in advance. Tourist Agent, German Wiederhold, Calle del Salvador, Puerto Varas, Casilla Correo No. 150 (Telegrams " TURISMO," Puerto Varas) The fare for the journey is $636 Chilean (exclusive of meals and Hotels) single. The quotation is a maximum.

CHILE

Other excursions can be arranged from Puerto Varas, including Puerto Octay (steamers Fridays outwards, returning Mondays). From **Puerto Varas** there are three departures a week for **Temuco,** an important industrial and agricultural centre. Population 26,500. Hotel Central.

Departure from **Temuco** can be made daily in the early morning for **Talca,** which is reached in the afternoon. Talca, with a population of 36,000, is one of the principal cities, with a large garrison and cathedral and a busy commercial, social, and civic life. Within easy reach is **Constitución,** a fashionable seaside resort on the Rio Maule, very well recommended. Hotel Talca.

Santiago is reached on three days of the week in about five hours from Talca.

THE ARAUCANIAN INDIANS.

When Don Pedro de Valdivia first explored Chile he encountered a race of Indians describing themselves as " Che reché "—the pure people. They inhabited the territory from the river Bio Bio in the centre of Chile to what is now the town of Valdivia, 180 miles farther south.

The Spaniards soon found the futility of attempts at terrorization, for the Indians paid them back in their own coin. Incessant warfare went on between them. Valdivia's native groom—Lautaro—deserted him to become leader of the resisting Indians. He captured his former chief, who was tortured and killed. Lautaro lost his life in battle, and his place was taken by the brave Cacique Caupolican, whose valour is commemorated by statues in Santiago and in the park at Lota. When he was eventually made a prisoner, his wife Fresia reviled him for allowing himself to be taken alive, and destroyed his baby by dashing it on the ground. So vigorously did this race fight for liberty that the Spaniards named them Araucanians from the native word " auca " signifying " free." After fifty years of bloodshed a treaty was made in 1660, and lands were allotted to the Indians, but conflicts continued for more than 200 years.

"PEOPLE OF THE LAND."

The Araucanians were never really conquered, and 100,000 pure Indians still remain in the neighbourhood of Temuco, calling themselves " Mapuchés," meaning " people of the land." Many Chilean families are proud of the Araucanian blood which flows in their veins. The men are of good physique, and of medium height. Their expression is of honest frankness, and sometimes of fierce determination. They look you straight in the face. They live in huts with thatched roofs. Mothers carry their babies in slings on their backs in the usual Indian way. The women are fond of silver ornaments which take the form of a head-band with silver coins attached, and one or more bands made of pieces of beaten silver, suspended from the neck, and reaching almost to the waist. At the lower end is a Maltese cross and several silver coins. The girls wrap their long plaits in silver braid. A woollen girdle woven in different colours is worn round the waist.

In September, when the independence of Chile is celebrated, entertainments are organised, and prizes are offered by the Government. On these occasions the men play a game like hockey, called " la cueca." Bent sticks are used, and the ball must be driven past a small tree at each end of the course to score goals.

Indian dancing, which forms a feature of the entertainments, consists in shuffling round in a circle shoulder to shoulder, the while intoning on two notes, also played on wooden instruments. Army manœuvres as understood by the Indians are rehearsed. Speeches are made in the native tongue, and a banquet of roasted horses and maize cider is provided. Wine and spirits are drunk, often to excess.

The disorders of the body are treated by ' machis," or medicine-women, and there are usually two " machis " in attendance. Each has a drum consisting of a wooden basin about 24 in. in diameter with a piece of hide tightly stretched across the mouth, and a number of little bells like those on a baby's rattle. The drum is struck and the bells rattled to frighten away the devil. The " machi " wears a red shawl. Her house is marked by a post 8 ft. to 10 ft. high with steps cut into it. Tied to the post is a large branch of the sacred tree of the Mapuchés—the canelo—and a sheepskin is often spread on this. The " machi " climbs to the top of the post and flings herself headlong to the ground, as part of the curative practice. A basin containing blood from a sheep is sometimes placed at the top of the post as an offering to their god.

Another ceremony to placate their deity is performed after the " machi " has summoned a number of the Indians by beating her drum. She walks backwards round the post beating her drum and shaking her bells, followed by a young man covered with the skin of a sheep just killed. Others follow, a man blowing a horn, a woman shaking a rattle, and about a dozen men, women, and children all chanting and occasionally giving vent to a shout of exultation.

For many years the South American Missionary Society has had a hospital at Temuco, and dispensaries at other places which Indians readily visit, as they find the " white machi " gives quicker and better results than their own medicine-women. Superstition is prevalent, and a person wearing dark gloves is thought to have dead hands.

The Chilean Government and the British Society mentioned maintain rural schools for the Mapuchés, where the men are taught handicraft, and the women domestic economy as well as reading, writing, and the Spanish language.

Although living in one part of the country only, the Araucanians mingle freely with the Chileans. It cannot be said that they are confined to reservations, though efforts are made to protect Araucanian land-owners whenever they are in danger of victimization. Their huts or " rucas " are often found amongst the habitations of Chilean labourers. A process of assimilation is going on. When completed there will be cause to lament the disappearance of a brave and interesting race.

COLOMBIA

COLOMBIA.

Colombia has ports both upon the Atlantic and Pacific coasts and is more usually approached upon the eastern side through Cartagena or Puerto Colombia (the port for Barranquilla)

Cartagena is one of the most interesting towns in South America, and the entrance to the harbour up the narrow, winding channel is a sight to be remembered. The same forts are to be seen that gave way before the furious onslaught of Drake, and so little changed that the visitor may easily imagine himself back in the days of the pirates and buccaneers of the Spanish Main. The town was founded by Pedro de Heredia in 1533, and stands on a sandy peninsula at the foot of a hill. The white houses of the city appear to rise out of the sea, like the tourist palaces of Venice. Nature has protected it by reefs and the notorious Salmedina sandbanks.

The harbour was once gained by two bocas or mouths, the Boca Grande (the Big Mouth), near the town, and the Boca Chica (or Narrow Mouth), some miles farther south. After an attack by Admiral Vernon in 1740 the Spaniards closed the Boca Grande by sinking old ships, and round these sand has collected, effectively blocking the entrance. Only Boca Chica is available for navigation. Entering the harbour by this narrow strait Fort San José is on the right, and on the left the derelict Fort San Fernando on Tierra Bomba Island. The steamer goes for six or seven miles along a tortuous passage past the mangrove-covered shores of Tierra Bomba, and comes alongside a wharf on Drake's Spit, where Sir Francis Drake and his men passed to the attack on Cartagena in 1585. It was then defended by a ditch and a stone wall with an opening for the cavalry, protected by a barricade of stacked wine butts. The road was commanded by pieces of ordnance, and flanked by two galleons mounting eleven guns. Under cover of the dark, the Englishmen crept silently up and forced an opening at daybreak. The butts were overthrown, the Englishmen drove back their adversaries and captured the town.

A light railway runs along this spit of land to the terminus outside the city walls. Across the open space outside the main gateway is the terminus of the Cartagena (Colombia) Railway Company, Ltd., whose line runs to Calamar, a port on the Magdalena river Cartagena was formerly called by the Indians Calamari or the land of the crawfish, owing to the abundance of those crustaceans.

The houses, generally well and solidly built, have balconies, and the lower windows are barred in Spanish fashion, and all have their cool-looking patios.

A feature of interest is the quaint memorial of the centenary of the liberation of the country; a tall shaft, from the base of which cannons peep from orifices in the concrete base.

The House of the Inquisition, near the principal square, is the residence of a merchant. Cartagena was one of the headquarters of the Inquisition in the New World, and instruments of the terror are said to still lie buried in the patio. An old and worn railing is pointed out in one room behind which the victims are said to have stood to receive their sentences.

The following drive can be recommended to the fortress of San Félipe, and the foot of La Popa Hill, across the bridge to Manga Island, over the Roman Bridge, through Calle Aguada and Calle Larga, and to the market and Independence Square. A visit to the Muralla de la Bovedas, the wall beyond the city, reveals the elaborate nature of the old fortifications. The walk to the summit of La Popa is arduous, and most visitors are content with the drive to the Fortress of San Félipe at its foot.

Landing :—Alongside the wharf. Passengers are conveyed to the city by rail, fare 5 cents.

Hotels :—Walter's, Mariani's, America.

Excursions :—By carriage to Manga, Pie de la Popa, Espinal and Cabrero, 2 hours.

Buildings of Interest :—Palace of Inquisition, Cathedral, San Pedro Claver Church, Santo Domingo Church, San Félipe de Barajas Fort, La Popa Castle, The Tombs, Archbishop's and Government Palaces.

Railway :—Daily to Calamar, a port for the Magdalena River

Fishing :—Excellent sea fishing in the Bay

Mean Temperature :—80° Fahr

Barranquilla is a busy city of some 65,000 inhabitants on the left of the Magdalena River, is distant about 7 miles from the river mouth. The difficulties of navigating the delta of the Magdalena make it the northern terminus of river traffic with the interior of Colombia. There is a large proportion of white inhabitants descended from the old Spanish colonists. Their costumes, old houses with balconies, patios, and brightly painted window shutters recall Spain. There is a handsome cathedral, and in front of it a small statue of Columbus, from whom Colombia takes its name. The market and the wharves are interesting to inspect.

Hotels :—Pension Inglésa, Calle de San Blas (from $3)

Railway from Savanilla (Puerto Colombia), or rail and steamer from Santa Marta.

Puerto Colombia, or Savanilla, the port for Barranquilla, which lies at the head of a large bay and has little to commend it to visitors. It is a collection of huts on a sandy shore. The only feature of interest is the steel railway pier of the Barranquilla Railway and Pier Company, Limited, 4,000 feet long which can accommodate five large steamers at once.

Santa Marta, another Atlantic port, is the capital of the Department of Magdalena. Mean temperature 86° Fahr   Important banana centre. Population (1918), 18,038   Connected with Barranquilla by coastal steamer, and by rail with Ciénaga and Fundación.

Hotels : International, Oriente.

The commercial ports on the Pacific are **Buenaventura** and **Tumaco,** through which pass the commerce of western Colombia.

Buenaventura is the most important Pacific port and entrepôt for a rich valley   It is reached easily from Panamá by steamer (348 miles) and is distant from Bogotá 343 miles.   The population is some 7,000, and the average temperature 80° Fahr   The rainfall is heavy   Coffee, cacao, timber, rubber, and hides are the local produce.

Tumaco is on an island, and ships anchor in face of the town.   It is in steamship connection with Buenaventura (200 miles) and Panamá. It is the most southerly port of Colombia, and has an unfavourable climate and an average temperature of 78° Fahr   Copper, cacao, tobacco, and vegetables are shipped.   Bogotá is distant 531 miles.

Bogotá, the capital of the Republic, stands on a plateau at 2,644 metres altitude.   From the coast it is reached by river steamer to La Dorada (5-7 days), by rail to Beltrán (4-5 hours), river steamer to Girardot (4-7 hours), and by rail to Bogotá (10 hours).   It contains the official residence of the President and the Congress buildings, a Cathedral, a University, an observatory, a national library and museum, the Sociedad de Embellecimiento, Instituto Técnico Central, and Gimnasio Moderno.   The estimated population (1922) is 170,000.

Hotels :—Metropolitano, Atlántico, Continental (catering specially for British and Americans), Regina.

Clubs :—Gun Club, Jockey Club, Anglo-American Club.

Mean Temperature :—59° Fahr

Industries :—Wool weaving and spinning, cement and brick making, leather, beer, and matches.

Medellín, capital of the Department of Antioquía, altitude of 1,541 metres.   Mean temperature is 73° Fahr   Population (1918), 79,146.   Route from coast   river steamer to Puerto Berrio, thence by rail (4-6 days)   The chief industrial and coffee centre of the country, and has over 40 factories—cotton and woollen fabrics, cigarettes and cigars, matches, nails, machinery, carpets, ales, and cider, chocolate, glass and china, etc.

Hotels :—Europa, Wilson, América.

Club :—Unión.

Bucaramanga, capital of the Department of Santander Sur, has an altitude of 925 metres. The mean temperature is 70° Fahr Population (1918), 24,919. The route from the Atlantic Coast is by steamer to Puerto Wilches, thence by mule to Bucaramanga (2½ days) Industries brewing, straw hats, matches, cigars, and cigarettes. Centre of coffee, tobacco, cocoa, and cotton region.

Clubs :—Club del Comercio, Club Garcia Rovira.

Hotel :—Colón.

Calí, capital of the Department of Valle, has an altitude of 1,046 metres. The mean temperature is 78° Fahr Population (1918), 45,525. Route Rail from Buenaventura, to Calí (10 hours) River steamer from Cartago. Industries: brewing, matches, and cigarettes.

Cúcuta, capital of the Department of Santander Norte, is near the Venezuelan frontier. Mean temperature 79° Fahr. Population (1918), 29,490. Route · by steamer from Maracaibo (Venezuela) to Puerto Villamizar, thence by rail.

Hotels :—Continental, Cúcuta.

Clubs :—Club del Comercio, Club Santander.

Manizales, capital of the Department of Caldas; altitude is 2,140 metres. Mean temperature 63° Fahr Population (1918), 42,203. Route from the Atlantic coast · steamer to La Dorado, rail to Mariquita (2 hours), mule to Manizales (2 days) Industries: cotton fabrics, ales and cider, nails, and matches. Important cattle, gold, coffee, cocoa, and sulphur centre.

Hotel :—Europa.

Clubs :—Antioqueno, Manizales.

Mompox, an old town in the Department of Bolívar. Population about 16,000. Noted for cattle, tobacco, Panamá hats. Reached by river steamer from Cartagena or Barranquilla.

Ibagué, capital of the Department of Tolima. Population (1918), 30,255. Centre for cocoa, sugar, çoffee, rice, hats, cattle, and mining.

Popayán, capital of the Department of Cauca. Population (1918), 20,235.

Pasto, capital of the Department of Nariño. Population (1918), 29,035. Noted for hats, wheat, cattle, rice, vanilla, minerals.

Honda formerly a central depot for the transit of European merchandise, has lost in importance since the era of railway construction.

Hotels :—America, Santander.

Ocaña, 3,820 feet above sea-level, is of commercial importance and the natural outlet for the produce of north-eastern Colombia.

PHYSICAL FEATURES.

Colombia has an estimated area of about 440,846 square miles in the north-west corner of South America, stretching from rather north of the equator to the Atlantic, with a coast-line of 1,300 miles on both the Pacific and the Caribbean Sea. Its mountain system falls into three distinct ranges, the Eastern, Central, and Western Cordillera. The first comprises four sections : Miraflores, Sumapaz, Cocuy, and Negra. It attains its highest altitude in the Sierra del Cocuy, about 16,000 feet high, Tama and Cachirí peaks are 13,126 and 13,780 feet respectively

The Central and Western Cordilleras contain the imposing Nevada de Herveo (18,340 feet) and the Tolima peak (18,400), Colombia's highest mountain. Several of these are volcanic. The Choco range—as the Western Cordillera is sometimes styled—attains its highest point in the gold-bearing Cerro Tarra (12,600 feet) The loftier Sierra Nevada de Santa Marta belongs to a different mountain system, and at one point attains over 18,000 feet.

The chief river is the Magdalena, exceeded in length only by the Amazon, Orinoco, and La Plata. It is more than 1,000 miles long, navigable for over 930 miles, and joined by five hundred tributaries. One of these affluents, the Funza, boasts the magnificent Tequendama Falls, 475 feet high. The Magdalena is joined at Tacaloa by the Cauca River Other rivers are the Sinú, Atrato, San Juan, and Patía. Lakes Fuquene and Guatavita are believed to have been much reduced in size since a former geological epoch.

Every variety of **climate** is to be found, from the tropical conditions of the coast to the temperate and cold climate of the mountains.

The eastern and mountainous parts are the most populated and here the climate is temperate or cold. The hot regions are the deep valleys of the Patía and Magdalena Rivers, the Pacific coast Department of Choco and the low lands southward to the frontier of Ecuador There are no regular seasons common to the whole country. Summer is understood to be the dry season and winter the wet season, and as a rule these alternate about every three months, but in the northern and eastern portion the rains last as long as six months. In the Choco district on the Pacific it rains in the afternoon and evening all the year round.

Internal Communications :—Several steamboat companies work on the Magdalena River, from Cartagena and Barranquilla to La Dorada, and up the Cauca, from Calí to Cartago, on the San Juan, from Buenaventura to San Pablo, on the Patía and Telembi, to Barbacoas, on the Zulia, from Puerto Villamizar to the Venezuelan port of Maracaibo, and on the Meta, from Orocue to Ciudad Bolívar in Venezuela.

On the Magdalena River there are about 50 steamers and many barges, with a total tonnage of about 14,000. To La Dorada from Barranquilla,. 600 miles, boats of considerable size and draught can be employed. Beyond the Honda Rapids vessels of smaller capacity can reach Neiva, 150 miles farther   There is a gasoline launch service between Cartagena and the lower Sinú.   The principal navigation companies on the Magdalena River are Compañia Antioquena, Compañia Pérez Rosa, and Colombia Railway and Navigation Company

The engineering difficulties connected with traversing the Cordilleras have hampered railway enterprise.   The total mileage of the railways is some 900 miles.   The main artery of commerce is the Magdalena River, apart from which, and the short railway lines which feed it, travel is slow   The journey to Bogotá, from the coast, may occupy 14 days.   Freightage is costly   Horses and mules are the chief means of getting about where the waterways are not available.   Attempts are being made to introduce the aeroplane to solve a problem which seems almost insoluble by other means.

About one-third only of the area of the country, comprising the north-western and Pacific Department, is inhabited or in any way developed.   The remaining two-thirds form an irregular parallelogram stretching south-eastward into the interior of the continent, and largely consist of comparatively flat country intersected with innumerable tributaries which flow into the Amazon, Putumayo, Yapura, Meta and other rivers which eventually empty into the Orinoco.

The national **religion** is Roman Catholicism.   There are four archbishoprics, viz., Bogotá, Cartagena, Medellín and Popayán. Panamá is under the ecclesiastical control of Colombia, forming a suffragan see of Cartagena.   There is complete freedom for other religious creeds which do not contravene Christian morals or the Law   The Church has control, so far as direction and supervision goes, of practically all the national or partly national secondary schools, and several religious corporations have wide powers in respect of religious teachings.

No specific discriminating laws against **aliens** as such obtain in Colombia.   By a law of 1888, dealing with the subject, aliens are classified as transient or domiciled.   Both enjoy full protection under the law   Residents who have established a business, married a Colombian woman, or done any act which implies an intention to settle definitely in the country belong to the second class, and a formal declaration before two witnesses also suffices to secure this status.   Transient aliens are exempt from all direct taxes.

Naturalization is simple, especially in the case of persons of Spanish-American extraction.   These have only to request the municipal authorities of the place where they reside to duly enrol their names as citizens.   Aliens of other origin apply to the Executive for papers giving the usual particulars as to status, nationality, and financial position.   The oath of allegiance gives full citizenship and confers the same on wife and all children under 21 years.   Such naturalized citizens cannot be compelled to fight thereafter in any war directed against their country of origin.

COLOMBIA.

The **Census** of 1918 gives the population as 5,855,490. Not more than 18 per cent. are classified as white, 18 per cent. as Indians, 14 per cent. as negro and their mixtures with other races, and 50 per cent. as white intermixture with Indians. The census of 1918 showed an increase of 778,658 persons since 1912.

Departments.	Population.	Capital.	Population.
Antioquia	823,226	Medellín	79,146
Atlántico ..	135,792	Barranquilla	64,543
Bolívar ..	457,111	Cartagena .	51,382
Boyacá	657,167	Tunja	10,680
Caldas	428,137	Manizales	42,203
Cauca	238,779	Popayán	20,235
Cundinamarca	812,452	Bogotá	143,994
Huila	183,337	Neiva	24,889
Magdalena	211,395	Santa Marta	18,038
Nariño	340,765	Pasto . .	29,035
Santander Sur	439,161	Bucaramanga	24,919
Santander Norte .	239,235	Cúcuta	29,490
Tolima	328,812	Ibagué	30,255
Valle	271,633	Calí ..	45,525
Intendencies :—			
Chocó	91,383	Quibdó	24,722
Meta	34,071	Villavicencio	4,736
San Andres y Providencia	5,953	San Andrés	5,953
Territories	157,081		
Total	5,855,490		

Currency :—The £1 has been made legal tender and the rate of normal exchange placed at 5 gold pesos, or dollars, to the £1

1 centavo .	100th part of 1 gold dollar
5 gold pesos	£1

The coins actually in circulation are as follows :—

Nickel coins   1, 2, and 5 cents.
Silver coins   10, 20, and 50 cents.
Notes .   50 cents, 1, 2, 5, and 10 gold pesos.
Gold .   5 dollars, 2 50 dollars.

Weights and Measures :—The metric system is in general use, but the following measures are constantly found :—

1 vara cuadrada .		= 0·64 square metres.
1 fanegada	= 6,400 square metres	= 1·5808 acres.
1 vara Granadina		= 0·80 metres.
1 cuadra	= 100 varas	= 80 metres.
1 legua (3 miles)	= 62·50 cuadras	= 5,000 metres.
1 cuarta .		= 0·20 metres.
1 pulgada (inch)		= 0·025 metres.
1 arroba	= 25 libras	= 12·50 kilos.
1 libra	= 16 onzas	= 0·50 kilo.
1 tonelada	= 80 arrobas	= 1,000 kilos.
1 saco .	= 5 arrobas .	= 62·50 kilos.
1 carga .	= 10 arrobas	= 125 kilos.

A COLOMBIAN CALENDAR.

1499. Alonso de Ojeda visits Cape Vela.
1501. Rodrígo Bastidas explores the coast from Riohacha to the Isthmus of Panamá.
1502. Columbus arrives at Colombia.
1508. Ojeda revisits Colombia, obtaining a grant from the King of Spain from Cape Vela to the Gulf of Darien; his companion, Nicuesa, was allotted the territory from the Gulf of Darien to Gracias à Dios.
1514. The two provinces united under Pedro de Avila under the title of Tierra-firma.
1519. City of Panamá founded.
1524. Francisco Pizarro explores the Colombian coast.
1525. Rodrigo de Bastidas lands at Santa Marta, where he establishes a settlement.
1528. The Emperor Charles V grants colonial concession to the German Welsers.
1533. Pedro de Heredia appointed Governor. Founds the city of Cartagena.
1538. Various defeats of Chibcha Indians. City of Bogotá founded, after almost simultaneous arrival on the plain of three expeditions commanded respectively by Quesada, Belalcazar and Federman.
1564. Spaniards proclaim New Granada a Presidency
1596. Porta Bello invaded by Drake.
1610. Tribunal of the Inquisition established.
1668. Porto Bello invaded by Morgan.
1697. Porto Bello attacked by a French fleet.
1708. The Galleons Fleet captured by Admiral Wager.
1713. Great Britain granted exclusive privilege of importing African slaves. Treaty of Utrecht provides commercial concession to the English.
1717. Audience of Santa Fé de Bogotá elevated to a Vice-Royalty, remaining thus for only two years.
1728. Foundation of the Compañia de Guipuzcoa.
1739. Kingdom of Granada formed into a Vice-Royalty.
1740. Porto Bello besieged by Admiral Vernon.
1744. Porto Bello attacked by Admiral Ogle.
1767. Jesuits expelled.
1810. Colombia proclaims its independence of Spain.
1819. Simon Bolívár's victory at Boyacá over the Spanish forces secures Colombian Independence.
1824. Bolívár comes to the assistance of Peru, and overthrows the Spanish at the battle of Junín and Ayacucho.
1825. Independence of Colombia recognized by Spain.
1830. Death of Bolívár.
1831. Ecuador secedes from the Colombian Confederation.
1843. President Alacantara Herran reforms the Constitution.
1850. President Lopez carries out the law passed at the time of the Independence suppressing slavery.
1861. Mosquera Revolution.
1871. New Granada rechristened Colombia.
1878. Boundary dispute with Costa Rica settled.
1883. Boundary dispute with Venezuela submitted to Spain for settlement.
1885. Abortive revolution led by Generals Velez and Reyes. Seventh constitution promulgated.
1886. New Constitution promulgated.
1899–1902. Civil War.
1903. Panamá asserts its independence of Colombia.
1904. Boundary dispute with Ecuador submitted to the arbitration of the German Emperor.
1919. Colombia joins the League of Nations.
1921. Colombia recognizes Panamá as an independent State.

GOVERNMENT

The **constitution** took its present form in 1886. The Republic consists of 14 Departments (subdivided into 796 Municipalities), which enjoy partial autonomy and elect their local legislatures. The whole is under the control of a President elected by popular vote for four years, who is supported by Ministers appointed by him.

COLOMBIA.

The Parliament consists of a Congress of two Chambers, the Senate (34 members) and the House of Representatives (92 members), who are elected by popular vote, the latter every two years and the former for the Presidential term. For election purposes the State is divided into 17 electoral districts, each of which elects six representatives, with the exception of two that each elect four and two others that each elect three. The Intendencies and Commissaries are administered directly by officials appointed by the Executive. The Congress, composed of the two Houses, meets at Bogotá annually on July 20th. There is at present a modified form of minority representation and a tendency towards further developing this ideal. The Departmental Governors, the Intendentes and Comisarios are directly appointed by the President.

PAST PRESIDENTS (SINCE 1870)

General E. Salgar 1870
M. Musillo Foro 1872
S. Pérez 1874
A. Parra 1876
General J Trujillo 1878
R. Nuñez 1880
F J. Zaldúa . . . 1882
General J E. Otálora . . . 1884
R. Nuñez (second term) . .. 1884
C. Holguín 1888
M. A. Caro 1892
M. A. Sanclemente 1898
J. M. Marroquin 1900
Gen. Rafael Reyes 1904
General González-Valencia . 1909
Dr Carlos E. Restrepo . . . 1910
Dr José Vicente Concha 1914
Marco Fidel Suárez 1918
Jorge Holguín 1921

PRESIDENT

In January 1922 General Pedro Nel Ospina was elected to serve as President from August 1922 to 1926.

MINISTRY.

Interior José Ulises Osorio.
Foreign Affairs . Jorge Vélez.
War : Gen. Alfonso Jarmillo.
Agriculture and Commerce : Antonio Paredes.
Public Education : Alberto Portocarrero.
Treasury : Gabriel Posada Villa, Félix Salazar
Public Works : Aquilino Villegos.
Finance : Aristobulo Archila.

NATURAL RESOURCES.

The following list of towns and districts summarizes their chief products :—

Bogotá (Cundinamarca) . Wheat, cattle, horses, agricultural produce, sugar, coffee, coal, salt and emerald mines.

Buenaventura (Valle) Gold, platinum, coffee, dye-stuffs and sugar

Cartagena (Bolivar) · Bananas, sugar, cocoa, cotton, maize, rubber, hardwoods, tortoiseshell, ipecacuanha.

Cúcuta (Santander Norte) Agricultural produce, coffee, tobacco, hides.

Medellín (Antioquía) Gold, silver, sugar, coffee, cotton, Panamá hats.

Neiva (Huila) · Gold, sugar, coffee, cocoa, quinine, Panamá hats, leather-dressing.

Pasto (Nariño) Gold, mica, agricultural produce, cattle, vanilla, aniseed.

Popayán (Cauca) Gold, silver, platinum, rubber, coffee, hides.

Colombia claims to produce the best mild **coffee,** and the quantity is second only to Brazil. Coffee is grown in Santa Marta, Antioquia, Caldas, Santander, Cundinamarca, Tolima, Valle and Cauca. The ports of despatch are Puerto Colombia, Cartagena, Buenaventura, and Santa Marta, except for Cúcuta coffee, the natural port for which is Maracaibo, in Venezuela.

Exports of coffee in bags of 62½ kilos :—

1916	..	1,162,471 bags.	1919 .	1,616,423 bags.
1917	..	1,005,300 ,,	1920 .	1,385,916 ,,
1918	..	1,102,667 ,,	1921 .	2,251,000 ,,

The value of the coffee exported in 1919 was about £11,000,000.

The cultivation of **bananas** is, and has been for the last 30 years, The principal agricultural industry of the Santa Marta district the exportation of bananas in 1919 was 3,000,000 bunches, Colombia. being the third largest exporter

The great **sugar** estate, Ingenio Central Colombia, is situated about 28 miles from Cartagena, and along the Dique Canal connecting this port with the Magdalena River The cultivation is limited to local requirements for the manufacture of rum and raw sugar

The more interesting **fibres** are fique or Colombian sisal, Colombian pita, and Colombian jute. About 200 miles up the Magdalena River there is a pioneer plantation of Colombian jute, with about 380 acres under cultivation.

Tobacco, grows on the plains of Bolivár, Tolima, and Cauca Valley There are in Cundinamarca large numbers of tobacco plants. During 1919, 195,310 kilos. were exported.

Vegetable Ivory, or Tagua, is found on the lowlands of the Caribbean Sea and the Pacific Ocean, and on the banks of the Magdalena, Atrato, and Sinú Rivers.

There are **rubber** forests in the eastern region, but it is found in practically all the Departments.

Wheat and maize are raised in the higher lands.

There is a great amount of arable land.

A great variety of fruits is found, including oranges, mangoes, plums, quince and grapes.

Many medicinal plants such as quinine, sarsaparilla, ipecacuanha, turpentine, palma-christi, copaiba, various plants used for dyes, gums, resins, and balsams are exploited   Cabinet woods are found in considerable varieties.

Cattle, sheep, horses and mules represent a considerable proportion of the wealth of the country   Vast areas are suitable for grazing, and excellent cattle have been introduced. If transport facilities are provided and packing establishments set up, Colombia should become an important source of meat supply   The llanos of Eastern Colombia and the Cauca and Patía valleys have large possibilities. There are computed to be over 8 million head of cattle in the country

Throughout most parts of Colombia there is a great demand for good strains of horses and mules for transport.

In the Eastern Cordilleras there are known to be large deposits of **iron, coal, copper, quartz, asphalt, sulphur, lead, quicksilver, alum, saltpetre, limestone, gypsum** and **marble.**

The **emerald** mines are one of the principal public assets, controlled by the Government, and are among the richest deposits known.   The emerald production is worked at Muzo and Coscuez in the Department of Boyacá.

Salt mines and springs are abundant in Zipaquirá in the Department of Cundinamarca, Bogotá.   The deposits have been worked by the Government since the Colonial days, and the revenues from these mines amount to about $1,000,000 per year

Oil :—The petroleum deposits are considerable and occur in both the cretaceous and tertiary series, from heavy asphalt oils to a light paraffin base oil of $41°$ B. Oil has been found in the vicinity of the Caribbean and Pacific coasts, in the Magdalena Valley, and the Eastern Cordilleras. The petroliferous area is of some 34,000 square miles, some 6,000 are regarded as possible of exploitation. Proven lands exist in the Carere region near Barranca Bermeja. The zones in the mid-valley of the Magdalena are geologically promising.

The fields that have produced the best results are in the Magdalena Valley, especially at the junction of the Upper and Lower Magdalena River, near the Rapids of Honda, where transport is effected by means of the British-owned Dorada Railway   Another important field is in the valley of the Zulia River, on the north-eastern frontier near Venezuela. Large concessions are held in various parts by United States interests. The following United States companies, among others, own properties   The Tropical Oil Company (a branch of the Standard Oil Company), operating near Barranca Bermeja on the Magdalena River; the Colombian Oil Syndicate, the Caribe Oil Company, operating near Honda, and owning land on the Tarra River, the Barco Concession, which has leased an area of 500,000 hectares, bordering northern Venezuela, and the Standard Oil Company, which has claims on the Sinú River and at Cartagena. Several British companies hold extensive concessions. A Canadian company is operating and has a property near Barranquilla. Two Colombian companies have been founded the Compañia Colombiana de Petroleos (capital $1,000,000) and the Compañia Colombiana de Fomento (initial capital, $1,000,000).

LOCAL INDUSTRIES.

Textiles :—There are three well-equipped cotton mills. The larger Barranquilla mill is a modern establishment, owned by Colombians experienced in the Lancashire trade. The mills have about 500 looms and a spinning plant for the supply of 300 looms.

The Medellin mills spin about half their requirements of yarn. The Barranquilla mill imports about two-fifths of its yarn, the third mill imports all its yarns. All three mills do a good business. There are, in addition, three mills making cotton hosiery. There is a small plant in Barranquilla for the spinning of yarns for hosiery purposes.

The Lower Magdalena Valley provides the cotton used by the spinning mills, and none is imported. On the contrary, during heavy crops a small quantity of cotton has been exported to Spain and the United States.

The three cotton weaving establishments produce light drills, and cotton cloth woven in colours, such as is used by the poorer population for dress purposes. The country demand for this class of cloth is met by local production.

There are two modern woollen mills in Bogotá with spinning plant using locally grown wool and making cloth for the working classes.

So far as the ordinary type of suitings and heavier cloths used for "Ruanas," i.e., tweed ponchos, are concerned, the demand is met by local production entirely. The mills make a fairly good blanket, and local mills are now putting out good suitings.

There is a local industry in carpet making, but of an ordinary type. The carpets are made from fique, or local hemp, in various designs.

Panamá hats :—In view of the increasing importance of this industry, especially in La Unión and Sandoná, the Government of Nariño has established schools in the capitals of the provinces.

Boot Manufacture :—The manufacture of boots and shoes is an important industry in Barranquilla. There are three factories producing annually 30,000 pairs, valued at 108,000 pesos, and some 20,000 pairs of hand-made shoes, valued at 60,000 pesos. The production is marketed in Barranquilla, Santa Marta, Cartagena, and district. American styles are copied for men's shoes, and European models for women's. White canvas or white kid low-cut shoes seem more adapted to the climate conditions. There are two tanneries making sole leather and side upper leather.

COLOMBIA.

Foreign Companies :—Under the Colombian Constitution, foreign corporations and the like wishing to establish a permanent business in the country must, before the expiration of six months from commencing operations, file a document attesting their organization and a certified copy of its charter and articles of association in due form (and, where necessary, the State authorization) with the notary of the District. Foreign companies must be permanently represented by a local Agent or Attorney By a law of 1907 the resident General Manager may now assume this responsibility

Under Decree No. 799 of 1923 (dated 26th May), the accounts of foreign limited companies operating in the Republic have in future to be submitted to the scrutiny of the Inspector of Taxes :—

Every foreign limited company established in Colombia is obliged to keep accounts of commercial operations effected within the territory of the Republic in accordance with the provisions of the Commercial Code, and to exhibit their original balances at least once a year

Infringement of the Decree is punishable by a fine of from 200 to 800 pesos.

In the course of a preamble to the Decree it is stated that many limited companies of foreign nationality established in Colombia by legal right, have, with a view to avoid the fiscal duties imposed upon their balances, proceeded to remit their accounts to their head offices, alleging their foreign nationality as a pretext for refusing payment of duties.

Trade marks (Law 110 of 1914), whether of foreign or native origin, can be registered in Colombia, the former enjoying the same status as national trade marks. Failure to use the mark within two years after granting (or a lapse of one year afterwards) terminates the right. Foreign trade marks are exempt so long as their use continues abroad during such period. A stamped application must be made to the Ministry of Agriculture and Commerce. Registration holds good for 20 years and renewal is allowed. The fee is 15 pesos, and for renewal 20 pesos.

COLOMBIAN LEGATION AND CONSULATES IN GREAT BRITAIN

RESIDENCE.	DESIGNATION.	NAME.
London (10 de Vere Gardens, Kensington.)	Envoy Extraordinary and Minister Plenipotentiary ..	Dr. Luis Cuervo Marquez.
	Secretary ..	Dr. Alfonso Delgado.
	Attaché ..	José Medina.
London (7 Sicilian Avenue, W.C.2.)	Consul-General	Joaquin Orrantia.
Birmingham	Consul .	Walter Shirley.
Cardiff . .	Consul .	Abelardo Aldana.
Dundee .	Vice-Consul	S. B. Taylor.
Glasgow .. .	Consul .	J. A. Carswell.
Liverpool . . .	Consul .	Dr. Genaro Payán.
	Vice-Consul .	Th. Delahunt.
Manchester . .	Consul .	Hernán Vélez.
Newcastle-on-Tyne .	Consul .	William H. Harding.

COLOMBIA.

BRITISH LEGATION AND CONSULATES IN COLOMBIA.

The letter (L) denotes that the Consular Officer has authority to register *lex loci* marriages. Members of the Diplomatic Service do not require Warrants.

RESIDENCE.	RANK.	NAME.	CONSULAR DISTRICT.
Bogotá	Envoy Extraordinary, Minister Plenipotentiary, and Consul-General	W. Seeds	Republic of Colombia.
	Vice-Consul	C. C. A. Lee	
	Clerk and Archivist	F V Jelpké	
Honda	Consular Agent	Edward J Hughes	
Medellín	Vice-Consul	C. W Davidson	
Barranquilla	(L) Consul	G. Pycroft	
Calí	Vice-Consul	Valentine Burrowes	
Buenaventura	Consul	G. McCabe	Departments of Cauca, Bolivár, Magdalena, and Atlántico.
Cartagena	Vice-Consul	W J B. Butterfield (Acting)	
Pasto	Vice-Consul	Alfred Hodges	
Santa Marta	Vice-Consul	F G. Maidment	
Tumaco	Consular Agent	William Jarvis	

Customs Duties :—Colombia has a Tariff Law, and the Customs dues form the largest item of the revenue. Imports (with exceptions which pay an ad valorem duty) pay (per kilogram) on the gross weight of the package. The scales of duty vary for different commodities, and in the case of mixed consignments in which the net weight of each class of article is not separately stated in the consular invoice the duty payable on the whole will be that of the article paying the highest scale. Owing to the limitations of mule-traction in the interior, packages must not exceed 150 lbs.

Shipments " to order " are not permitted.

Certificates of Origin as such are not required. Consular invoices, made out in Spanish, are necessary and must be legalized at port of shipment. Fees are charged for legalization, and special forms are obtainable from the Consulate.

The **postal tariff** is that of the Postal Union, viz., 10 cents per letter of 15 grammes or less. The inland rate is 3 cents for a letter and 2 cents for a postcard.

Outward mails are despatched (1) via United States, (2) by Pacific Steam Navigation Line via Panamá, at uncertain intervals, and (3) by Leyland and Harrison Lines, at uncertain intervals. Postage 3d. first ounce, 1½d. each ounce after.

Homeward mails despatched at frequent intervals.

Telegrams are 2 cents per word ordinary despatches, 4 cents urgent, and 8 cents for " extraordinary," with preference over all others. Telegraphic communication is possible between all parts of the country

Cables cost 3s. 5d. per word. There are lines via New York and through Cartagena and Buenaventura.

There is a **wireless** station at Puerto Colombia, and others at Cartagena, Santa Marta, Providencia, Cuento, Bogotá, Medellín and Calí.

The principal **newspapers** are :—

BOGOTÁ : "El Espectador," "El Diario Nacional," "El Diario Oficial," "El Nuevo Tiempo," and "El Tiempo."

MEDELLÍN: "El Colombiano," "El Espectador," and "El Correo Liberal."

BARRANQUILLA . "El Liberal," "La Nación," and "Diario del Comercio."

BUCARAMANGA : "La Vanguardia Liberal."

CARTAGENA : "La Epoca," "El Diario de la Costa."

Aviation :—The configuration of the country is eminently suited for this means of communication Besides various private enterprises, there is a Colombian-German Aviation Company, carrying mails and passengers between Barranquilla and Girardot, following the Magdalena river by hydroplanes as far as Neiva. The Government established in 1921 a school of aviation for the army, with French machines and instructors.

Air Route : Barranquilla—Bogotá.

The difficulty of communications between Barranquilla and the interior is to some extent mitigated by the establishment of a regular system of aviation. The Sociedad Colombo-Alemana de Transportes dispatches air mails carrying passengers twice a week between Barranquilla and Girardot and intermediate points, and two mails weekly on the return journey The flights start every Tuesday and Friday from Barranquilla, arriving at Girardot the same day, stopping to deliver letters at Mompox, Barranca-Bermeja, Puerto Berrio, and Honda. There are departures on Wednesday and Saturday from Girardot. The Wednesday air mail makes connection with the Clyde Line Steamers, sailing on Fridays from Puerto Colombia to New York, and with Elders and Fyffes' steamers, sailing Thursdays and Saturdays from Santa Marta to Rotterdam or Bristol. The Saturday air mail makes connection with the American fruit boats sailing on Sundays from Puerto Colombia to New York, touching Colón.

A passenger writes "I commend this means of locomotion to anyone who values time and comfort. The fare from Barranquilla to Girardot is $250 for 65 kilos, including the weight of the passenger At least eight days are saved by this route. With stops at El Banco, Barranca-Bermeja, Puerto Berrio (for lunch), then on to Honda and Girardot, the trip takes some 7½ hours in actual flight. The average speed is some 135 kilometres per hour, and about 1,300 metres is the highest altitude. The monotony of the river trip, with its heat and mosquitoes, is avoided."

Guidance for Commercial Travellers.

Municipal licences are only required to be taken out in most of the larger towns. They are usually issued for a term of 30 days, but in some towns for longer periods up to three months. The fees vary from 20 to 40 pesos, according to the size of the market. In the larger towns the licence costs 40 pesos and is available for 30 days. Licences are obtained from the municipal authorities. A collector usually visits hotels, calling on travellers for payment. The majority of travellers do not put themselves down as salesmen but as " comerciante," or merchant or trader and as such they are not taxed.

If samples can be put to industrial use or sold, import duty is leviable on them. Refund of duty, with a reduction of 25 per cent. can be obtained, provided that the samples are re-exported within one year. This refund is allowed provided that the entire shipment is re-exported.

A consular invoice is necessary, showing in detail a description of the samples and their weights in kilograms.

Samples of no commercial value and of no industrial use are free of duty. Special definitions are given of such samples.

Exports and Imports.

				Exports.	Imports.
1916	.	..	..	£6,526,655	£6,115,492
1917	..	.	..	6,575,890	4,811,098
1918	..	..	..	7,780,000	4,543,000
1919	..	..	..	17,000,000	10,770,000
1920	..	..	..	15,750,000	22,530,000
1921	..	.	..	12,608,426	6,613,664
1922	..	..	..	13,000,000	6,850,000

Bureau of Information of the Republic of Colombia.

7 Sicilian Avenue, Southampton Row, London, W C.1
Telephone Central 7398.
Director José Medina. Secretary L. Lasprilla.

The Government, through the Ministry of Agriculture and Commerce, has established Bureaux in London, Paris, and New York. The purpose is to encourage the commercial interests of the country, increase the demand for Colombian products abroad, and promote trade by making better known the possibilities and great resources of Colombia.

A Central Department of Information has been created in the Ministry of Agriculture and Commerce at Bogotá so that the Bureau may be kept in touch with all Chambers of Commerce, Agricultural Societies, Statistical Departments, and other important institutions throughout Colombia.

Anglo-Colombian Chamber.

British firms interested in Colombian trade and wishing to foster closer commercial intercourse with that country may become members of the Chamber, membership fee £2 2s. Applications should be addressed The Secretary, 7 Sicilian Avenue, Southampton Row, London, W.C.1

COSTA RICA

COSTA RICA.

Costa Rica means literally "Rich Coast," and it is seen to be rich by the tourist who lands from the steamer at Port Limón where train is taken for San José, the capital, 3,816 ft. above the sea.

From Port Limón, the principal Atlantic seaport, there is a railway to Punta Arenas on the Pacific Coast, passing through Cartago, the former capital, and San José, the present capital. The train climbs from the jungles and fruit plantations of the coastal plain, through tropical valleys and deep ravines, across gorges and along the edges of cliffs, to the plateaux and mountains of the interior, from the tropics to the temperate zone, from sea level to 5,179 ft. altitude—all within a hundred miles or a six-hour journey

Port Limón has a population of 8,000, and a busy trade in bananas, coffee, and produce. It is 107 miles from the capital, and is in daily steamship connection with Colón (Panamá)

Hotels :— United Fruit Company, Limon Lodge ($4–8); Europa ($3–4)

San José, the capital, has a regional population of some 54,000, and stands at an elevation of 3,816 ft. The climate is temperate, but cold in the evenings, the mean temperature being 68° F., with an annual variation of only 5° It possesses a university, an observatory, and a National Opera House. Slight earthquake shocks are frequent. The capital is distant from Limón 107 miles, from Heredia 5½ miles, and Punta Arenas 62 miles.

Rail :—A train for Limón leaves San José daily at 9.30 a.m., arriving 3.50 p.m., in the reverse direction a train leaves 9.40 a.m., and arrives at San José at 4 p.m.

The train for Punta Arenas leaves the Pacific station daily at 9 a.m., and arrives at 2 p.m. In the reverse direction it leaves at 8.30 a.m., arriving San José 2.30 p.m.

There is a local service for Cartago and Heredia and Alajuela and other points, and also a frequent service of motor buses to these towns.

Hotels :—Frances ($4.6); Washington ($4.6), Europa ($3.50-4) (American plan)

Cartago :—The ancient capital is about 12 miles from San José, on the Northern Railway Company's line to Port Limón, at the foot of Mount Irazú (11,200 ft.), a volcanic peak. Population about 19,000. Founded 1553. Destroyed by earthquake in 1823 and 1910, and severely damaged on other occasions. The present town may be said to be earthquake proof, being principally constructed of frame houses.

Hotels :—Frances, Canal.

Heredia :—Chief town of province of same name. Population about 13,000. On railway between San José and Alajuela. Altitude, 3,785 ft.

Hotels :—Central, Italiano.

Alajuela :—Capital of province of that name, 11½ miles W.N.W of San José. Population about 13,000. Altitude, 3,000 ft.

Hotels :—Ramon Aguilar, El Perea.

Punta Arenas :—Population 5,000, on the Pacific, one of the chief ports, is connected by railway with San José.

Hotels :—Europa, Imperial.

CHARACTERISTICS OF THE COUNTRY.

The most southerly of the five Republics of Central America, Costa Rica is bounded by Nicaragua, north-east by the Caribbean Sea, west and south by the Pacific Ocean, and on the south-east by Panamá. The area is about 23,000 square miles. The population is mainly upon the central plateau, of some 3,500 square miles. The country is mountainous, with numerous volcanoes. The Atlantic slopes are covered with dense forests, with large and fertile stretches of pasture and rolling downs on the Pacific side. The interior is traversed by two volcanic Cordilleras, separated by the central plateau and forming a single watershed. The highest peak in the northern range is Irazú (11,200 ft.), whence both the Pacific and Caribbean are visible. The second is Turrialba (10,910 ft.) In the southern range Chiripo Grande attains 11,485 ft. There are few navigable rivers. The San Juan, with a course of less than 100 miles, is the most important. It drains Lake Nicaragua, and has for tributaries the Sarapiqui and San Carlos. On the Pacific coast there are only small rivers, liable to sudden floods.

The **population** was estimated in 1920 at 485,049. Great tracts of country are uncultivated although the State gives facilities for the purchase of land. The proportion of Spanish blood is more considerable than in most other Central American countries. Spanish is the universal language.

The **climate** is temperate. The mean temperature at 3,000 to 6,000 ft. ranges from 57° to 68° F. From the coast inland to a height of 3,000 ft. it ranges from 72° to 82° F Above 7,000 ft. frosts are frequent. There are dry and rainy seasons, the former from December to April and the latter from that month onward.

Currency :—Monetary unit : Gold colon of 100 c. of 778 milligrams of gold, 900 fine, value 1s. 10·9d.

The gold colon has not been in circulation since August 1914. As the privilege of emission by private banks was withdrawn in 1921, the only medium of circulation now existing is the notes of the Banco Internacional de Costa Rica (practically a State bank), which institution's emission amounted to 17,175,000 colones on November 1, 1922 Fractional currency consists of coppers.

In consequence the premium on exchange varies considerably During 1922 and 1923 the fluctuations have not been great. The average for the twelve months ending December 1922 was 435 per cent. New York sight ($1 = 4·35 colones), and the rate current at the end of August 1923 was 450 per cent. ($1 = 4 50 colones), and 410 per cent. for sight sterling (£1 = 20·50 colones)

The metric system is legal and general, certain English **weights and measures** are uséd, and Spanish weights and measures are in common use among the country people.

  1 libra = 1 lb. avoirdupois.   1 quintal = 100 libras.   1 pulgada = 1 inch.   1 pie = 1 foot.   1 vara = 33 inches.   1 yard = 36 inches.   1 arroba = 25 libras = 25 lb.

Lineal and Land Measures :—

  1 vara = 33 pulgadas = 33 inches.
  10,000 sq varas (varas cuadradas) = 1 manzana = 1·72 acres.
  1 hectare = 1 431 manzanas = 2 46 acres.
  64¾ (64·89 exactly) manzanas = 1 caballeria = 111·37 acres.

Dry Measures :—

For beans, maize, etc.—
  4 cuartillos = 1 cajuela.
  24 cajuelas = 1 fanega = 400 litres = 10·9988 bushels.

For coffee and fruit—
  4 cuartillos = 1 cajuela.
  20 cajuelas = 1 fanega = 400 litres = 10·9988 bushels.

Liquid Measures :—

  1 botella = 1·179 pints.
  5 botellas = 1 Spanish gallon = 120 liquid oz.

Sources of Natural Wealth :—Coffee, bananas, gold and silver, hides, timber, sugar, cacao, and rubber Coffee is largely cultivated in the districts of Alajuela, Heredia, San José, Cartago, and on the Atlantic slope. A large banana trade is carried on from Limón or through Panamá from Almirante (Bocas del Toro) with Bristol, New Orleans, New York, and Boston. At the beginning of 1923, a hurricane did damage to a very large number of trees. Gold and silver mining on the Pacific slope, in the Abangarez, Barnanca, and Aguacate districts, ranks fourth in value. Manganese ore exists in the province of Guanacaste. There are about 2,700 acres under tobacco, and mahogany, cedar, rosewood, and other cabinet woods are common. Recently bee-keeping has been introduced.

The export of coffee of the 1920–21 crop amounted to 13,366 metric tons.

The production by districts was as follows in 1921 :—

					Kilogs.
San José	..	..	.	.	. 6,937,028
Heredia .	..	.	.		... 2,529,482
Cartago ..	.			.	.. 1,217,056
Atlantic Slope .		.	.	.	1,219,645
Alajuela	.	.	..	.	.. 1,397,170

Shipments were made through Port Limón to the extent of 62·75 per cent., the balance by Punta Arenas, most of it to San Francisco.

The total export of **bananas** from Costa Rica in 1921, was 8,318,581 bunches as compared with 8,652,473 and 7,270,624 bunches respectively in 1920 and 1919.

Of the total exported in 1921, 2,726,768 bunches were exported from the Sixaola district through Panamá territory and shipped from Almirante (Bocas del Toro), and the remainder from Port Limón. The number of bunches of bananas exported to the United Kingdom, by steamers of British ownership, during 1921 amounted to 1,651,920. There are about 100,000 acres of land under banana cultivation.

The exports of sugar and panela in 1921 amounted to 3,964 metric tons, valued at £125,275, as compared with 5,107 metric tons, valued at £271,660, in 1920. About 38,517 acres (22,407 manzanas) of land are under sugar cane.

The export of cacao amounted to 2,782 metric tons, as compared with 2,154 metric tons in 1920.

The export of cattle during 1921 was 3,121 head, valued at £121,733, of which 1,090 were exported to Mexico, which is a new market.

No distinction is drawn between foreign and native acquisition of **mining rights** and concessions or the administration or distribution of the mineral output. The ownership of the subsoil is vested in the State, and mining rights may only be obtained by purchase or by filing a claim. The judge issues the title to a mine after the preliminary survey and mine work, and this holds good while the mine is being developed, but lapses if the property is abandoned for two years. A mine once delivered to the claimant becomes his property, and he may sell, mortgage, or dispose of it at will.

A COSTA RICAN CALENDAR.

1530. Conquest by Spain completed.
1540. Becomes a province of the Viceroyalty of Guatemala.
1553. Cartago founded.
1666. Pirates raid the coasts.
1821. Costa Rica declares its independence.
1823. Civil war between the Conservative and the Liberal parties. Battle of Ocho-mogo Pass won by the Liberals. Capital transferred from Cartago to San José.
1824-39. Costa Rica a member of the Central American Federation.
1841. Cartago severely damaged by earthquake.
1848. An independent Republic set up.
1863. Costa Rica joins Guatemala and Nicaragua against Honduras and Salvador.
1871. Constitution promulgated.
1885. A defensive alliance made between Costa Rica, Nicaragua, and Salvador against Guatemala.
1897. Costa Rica joins the "Greater Republic" of Central America, of which Nicaragua, Honduras, and Salvador are members.
1898. Secedes from the "Greater Republic." Boundary dispute with Nicaragua settled by arbitration.
1900. Boundary dispute with Panamá (then a province of Colombia) settled by arbitration.
1917. Severed diplomatic relations with Germany.
1918. Declares war on Germany.
1919. Joins the League of Nations.

COSTA RICA.

PRESIDENTS OF THE REPUBLIC.

Rafael Iglesias	1893–1902.
Ascensión Esquivel	1902–1906.
Cleto González Viquez	1907–1910.
Ricardo Jimenez	1911–1914.
Alfredo González Flores	1915–1917
Federico Tinoco Granados	1918–1919 (August).
Francisco Aguilar Barquero	1919 (August) to 1920 (May).

PRESIDENT

Julio Acosta Gárcia . . .. May 1920.

The principal **newspapers** are . At San José, "Diario de Costa Rica," "La Prensa Libre," and the official " La Gaceta y Boletin Judicial."

Costa Rica is in the Postal Union.

There are about 1,500 miles of telegraphs with 130 offices, and 640 miles of telephones.

Wireless messages may be sent from Limón to Bocas del Toro and to Colón in Panamá, and to Bluefields in Nicaragua. There is also a station at Colorado, on the San Juan River

Wireless telegraphs and telephones were declared State monopolies in 1920.

A contract has been made between the Government and the All America Cables (Incorporated) Company for the establishment of a direct cablegram service between Costa Rica and foreign countries. The service is to connect Port Limón with the cables serving the Isthmus of Panamá.

Mails are sent via United States. There is a fortnightly dispatch from London via Avonmouth.

The postage is 3d. the first oz. and 1½d. each oz. after

COSTA RICAN CONSULATES IN GREAT BRITAIN

TOWN.	DESIGNATION.	NAME.
London .. .. . (7 Crosby Square, Bishopsgate, E.C.3).	Consul-General ..	.. Percy Grove Harrison.
Birmingham . ..	Consul . .	John Norman Hotchkiss.
Cardiff	Consul .	——
Falmouth	.. Vice-Consul	.. Howard Fox.
Glasgow ..	. Consul ..	.. Rudolfo Montealegre.
	Vice-Consul	. W A. Moir.
Leeds .. .	——	——
Liverpool ..	——	——
Manchester	Consul ..	. Eduardo Salem.
	Vice-Consul	. William Lloyd Jones.
Southampton	Consul ..	George J Tilling.
Swansea .. .	.. Vice-Consul	.. Fred A. Rees.

BRITISH LEGATION AND CONSULATES IN COSTA RICA.

RESIDENCE.	RANK.	NAME.	CONSULAR LIST.
(See PANAMÁ)	Envoy Extraordinary, Minister Plenipotentiary, and Consul-General.	A. Percy Bennett, C.M.G.	Republic of Costa Rica.
San José .	Consul	Frank N. Cox	.. San José.
Port Limón ..	Consul	Frederick Gordon	.. Province of Limón.

COSTA RICA

Guidance for Commercial Travellers.

Commercial travellers must register, before beginning operations, at the Municipal Offices of the town which they make their head-quarters. They must also take out a licence, the cost of which varies with the municipality. In San José, the municipal tax on commercial travellers is 50 colones and the licence is available for six months. This is the highest fee charged, and on payment of the tax an official receipt is given which has to be produced on demand. No special documents are required, nor have any other formalities to be observed.

If commercial travellers are representatives of their firms as well, and expect to conclude formal contracts on a large scale, or to take legal proceedings, they should as a matter of prudence be provided with a power of attorney.

Samples of commercial value must be declared and the full duty on them deposited at the custom house of entry. A receipt, accompanied by a detailed list of samples, is given, and upon leaving the country within 90 days the traveller receives back the deposit, less an inclusive charge of 5 cents per kilo upon the gross weight of the samples.

No refund is granted in respect of jewellery, or manufactured gold and silver.

PUBLIC HOLIDAYS.

New Year's Day.
March 19 : Dia de San José.   Easter Thursday   Good Friday
April 11 : Battle of Rivas.
May 1 : Opening of Congress.
July 14 : Fall of the Bastille.
September 15 : Central American Independence Day.
October 12 : Discovery of America.
Christmas Day
December 29, 30, 31 : Bank Holidays.
Many feasts of the Roman Catholic Church are also observed.

FOREIGN TRADE.

	Exports. £	Imports. £	Total. £	Balance. £
1911	1,839,215	1,828,492	3,667,707	10,723
1912	2,053,513	2,077,276	4,130,789	*23,763
1913	2,127,205	1,789,941	3,917,146	337,264
1914	2,238,532	1,556,349	3,794,881	682,183
1915	2,055,075	923,046	2,978,121	1,132,029
1916	2,291,997	1,361,024	3,653,021	930,973
1917	2,345,786	1,153,141	3,498,927	1,192,645
1918	1,980,526	768,641	2,749,167	1,211,885
1919	3,652,587	1,696,776	5,349,363	1,955,811
1920	2,563,929	3,645,873	6,209,802	*1,081,944
1921	2,439,619	1,892,804	4,332,423	546,815
1922	2,932,852	1,720,550	4,653,402	1,212,302

*-Adverse.

BANANAS IN COSTA RICA.

Costa Rica holds first place among the Latin American Republics n the cultivation of bananas, raising annually some 11,000,000 bunches of *musa sapientium*. The scientific name arises from a reference of Theophrastus, who said that the ancient sages reposed in the shade of the banana tree and refreshed themselves with its fruit.

The tree grows to a height of from 15 to 40 ft. The trunk, formed of compact sheathing leaf stalks, resembles corn in some degree, but is about 8 in. in diameter and firm in structure. It is endogenous, and increases by internal growth and elongation at the summit. This quality of increasing by internal growth partly explains the development of the newly cut banana stalk, which will be observed to shoot up some inches in a few minutes, while leaves will unfold from the centre of the trunk within 36 hours. The plant takes from seven months to two and a half years before it fructifies.

The bunch of bananas develops from a large, heart-shaped, scaly bud. The scales separate and disclose groups of upward-pointing flowers, sometimes to the number of 150. These are blossoms which turn into fruit. One bunch to a tree is the rule, and they vary in length from 2 to 3 ft., and in weight from 50 to 80 lb., which latter, however, is exceptional. The commercial classification is by "hands," a hand being a cluster which, with the exercise of imagination, may be said to resemble the human hand. Bunches growing nine hands or over command the higher prices and are called "first" by the trade. "Seconds" are from seven to nine hands and bring a lower price. Bunches having less than seven hands are unfit for shipment, and these are the element of loss in banana cultivation. The bunches are cut while green (the greatest care being needed in the operation) and allowed to continue ripening during the voyage to their ultimate destination. Care and experience are necessary in handling bananas during shipment to insure the lowest possible amount of loss from deterioration.

The banana as a food goes back to the very early times. The variety *paradisiaca*, is even claimed by some as the "forbidden fruit" of the Garden of Eden. Nevertheless, there can be no doubt as to the antiquity of its service as an aliment. The banana belt encircles the earth 1,500 miles on either side of the equator Humboldt, in his explorations of the Orinoco basin found a variety of the banana extensively cultivated by the Indians. Garcilaso de la Vega tells us it formed the staple food of the natives in the warmer zones when the Incas reigned. Withal, the plant is rarely found in the wild state. This is due to the fact that bananas are seedless, and propagated by means of shoots or "suckers." The cultivation is not difficult, the hindrances coming from heavy winds, pernicious insects, and sometimes caterpillars.

The by-products of the banana are few, but in the Dominican Republic a delicious sweetmeat is made from ripe fruit. The skins are removed and the banana cut into slices about a quarter of an inch in thickness. The pieces are sprinkled with powdered sugar and placed in the sun on boards or shallow trays. The fruit is turned over several times and dusted with sugar each time turned. It dries within a few days and the result is a delicious crystallized conserve.

Banana flour in time may prove to be of commercial value, for it is very nutritious. It is made by a simple process. Unripe bananas are cut and dried, ground and sifted, and the fruit treated in this way yields 20 to 25 per cent. flour The chief difficulty in flour making is preserving the yellow colour The apparatus used must be either aluminium or silver, for iron turns the flour black. Another by-product is fibre, from which a coarse cloth is woven, and banana vinegar, sugar, and coffee offer other possible ways of utilizing the fruit. In Mexico the fibre is used in making hammocks. The nutritive value of the banana is high, as has already been inferred. One chemical analysis gives the fruit a food value of 460 calories per lb., or more than three times that of cabbage.

There are some 44 varieties of the banana, of which number the plaintain (*musa paradisiaca*) and the abaca (*musa textilis*) deserve further special mention. The former is the platano of Latin America.

CUBA

CUBA.

Havana, the capital, has a population of 360,000. It is 324 nautical miles from Tampa (Florida), and 1,166 from New York whence there are regular steamers. The mean temperature is 76° Fahr., the average rainfall 43 in., and there are normally 106 rainy days in the year The harbour is large and beautiful. The hotels are first-class and the centres of amusement include a fine racecourse.

Havana is a metropolis in which the new merges agreeably with the old—the palaces, plazas, colonnades, towns, churches, and monasteries which moved J. A. Froude to liken the city to Castile. The parks are magnificent and afford an almost continuous drive. The Prado, a central parkway, connects Columbus, India, and Central Parks and beyond are the drives of Paseos La Reina, Carlos III, and Tacon. The Parque Central with its laurels, poncianas, almonds, palms, shrubs, and gorgeous flowers is in the heart of the city and surrounded by clubs, hotels, and cafés.

Effort should be made in Havana to watch the " Jai-Alai " (pronounced high-a-lie) ball game, reputed to be the fastest and most exciting of sports, and one over which Cubans grow excited.

Landing :—Usually alongside.

Hotels :—Inglaterra, Plaza, Telegrafo, Florida, Union, America, Maison Royal, Saratoga, Belvedere, Pasaje, Manhattan, Trianon, Luz, Isle of Cuba, Alcazar.

Points of Interest :—Principe Castle (tramcar), Vedado the finest of the suburbs, Atares Castle (tramcar), Cathedral and numerous churches, Presidential Palace, Morro Castle (built 1587), Cabanas Fortress (built 1763), Plaza de Armas with tomb of Columbus, the cigar factories.

Shopping Centres :—Obispo and O'Reilly Streets.

Theatres :—Nacional, Campoamor, Payra, Polyteama Groude, Polyteama Chico, and Marti.

Golf :—Havana County Club.

Excursions :—MARIANAO, ten miles west by rail or tram, with its beach, La Playa. MATANZAS, sixty miles east by rail, near Yumari Valley, Caves of Bellamar, hermitage of Montserrate. ISLE OF PINES, train to Batabano and steamer (sixty miles) to Nuevo Gerona.

Santiago de Cuba, capital of the province, and the second oldest city in the island, was founded by Velasquez in 1514. Its population was 50,000 in 1908. It was named after the patron Saint of Spain. Santiago is 540 miles from Havana by the Cuba Railroad. The approach by water is through a harbour entrance 180 yds.

wide, beneath the battlements of Morro Castle upon the summit of a rocky point 200 ft. high. The seaward side of the promontory is precipitous, on the inner face, a long flight of crumbling steps, hewn out of the rock, leads to the water's edge.

Opposite Morro on the left is La Socapa, and within the harbour in rear of Morro is the Estrella Battery. Beyond, on the left, is Cayo Smith (Smith Key), a small island once held by the British. It is a home of fisherfolk and pilots, and its red-tiled houses and small ruined chapel are picturesque. In a cove near by Hobson sank the " Merrimac." Farther up the harbour is Cayo Ratones, and a small island formerly the magazine for the ships of the Spanish Navy On the right shore, amidst a grove of coco-nut trees, is the coaling station of Cinco Reales. Opposite are the summer homes of Santiago merchants.

The Santiago Cathedral, the largest church in the Island, is in the Hispano-American style, with two towers and a dome. The nave is very wide, and the side chapels rich in rare marbles and fine mahogany

The principal shopping streets are San Tomad, Enramadas, and Marina. A fine view of the harbour is afforded from the head of Marina Street. The Almeda is a popular avenue and drive in the lower part of the city, along the bay The railway station on this avenue, to the north, is a new, handsome, concrete structure.

HOTELS — Casa Granda ($2 5), Imperial ($2-3), America ($1.50-3), Venus ($1.50-10)

Matanzas one of the chief sugar ports, is on the north coast, about 50 miles east of Havana, and possesses a good sheltered harbour Population 37,000. The town is well laid out, with handsome plazas and boulevards, the Paseo is one of the features. The Bellamar Caves, 1½ mile away, are on a plateau and of a wonderful crystalline formation, with narrow passages and a " Gothic Temple " hall, 250 ft. by 80 ft.

HOTELS :—Louvre, Sevilla, Paris, Golfo de Mexico.

Cienfuegos, 195 miles by rail from Havana, is another principal sugar port, and is a modern city on the south coast, picturesquely laid out. It possesses a magnificent bay, 11 miles long, and one of the finest Plazas on the island. Population 40,000.

HOTELS :—Gran, Ciervo de Oro, Continental, La Suiza, Union.

Camaguey, population 35,000 is 338 miles by rail from Havana, and 200 from Santiago. One of the most picturesque of Cuban towns, it has many mediæval buildings, and a first-class hotel.

HOTELS :—Camaguay, Plaza, Inglaterra, Norman, Grand.

Pinar del Rio, famous for the best cigars and Vuelta Abajo leaf tobacco, is 107 miles by rail from Havana.

HOTELS :—Ricardo, Marina, Sevilla, Globo.

Trinidad, a very picturesque old city founded in 1514, has 12,000 population, and is the centre of a rich agricultural region. It is reached by train (45 miles) from Santa Clara.

HOTELS :—Tuileries, Central, Union.

Guantanamo, with 15,000 inhabitants is reached by rail from Santiago, changing at San Luis. The U.S. Naval Station constitutes an attraction. Many sugar plantations.

HOTELS :—Venus ($1.00-2.00); Washington ($1.50-3.00), La Gran Via ($.75-1.50), La Aurora ($ 75-1.50), Lawley ($1.00-1.50).

Manzanillo, population 18,000, is on the west coast, 487 miles by train from Havana and to be reached also by steamer   Hot and unhealthy

HOTELS :—Edin, Inglaterra, Comercio, La Ferrolana.

Sancti Spiritus, population 18,000, is 240 miles by rail from Havana, a centre of the cattle and sugar trades.

HOTELS :—Perla, Central, Carreo, Plaza.

Cardenas, population 27,000, is 109 miles by rail from Havana and 41 from Matanzas, in a sugar-growing district.

HOTELS :—Europa, Louvre, Isle de Cuba.

PHYSICAL FEATURES.

CUBA is the largest island in the West Indies, with an area of 44,164 miles, and a length, east to west, of 759 miles. The southeast is mountainous and rich in iron and copper, and there are immense forests of hardwoods. The country is open and highly cultivated. The soil is rich and the climate specially favourable for sugar and tobacco, which form the staple industries. There is a large fruit trade, especially in oranges, grape fruit, limes, pine apples, and bananas. Coffee, cocoa, tomatoes, tamarinds, and spices are raised for export, and some districts are suitable for cotton.

The island is well watered, and on the coast are numerous land-locked harbours, several of which could shelter the world's chief navies. As the island lies across the entrance to the Gulf of Mexico, these roadsteads make Cuba of great strategic importance.

Pinar del Rio, in the West, is rich in minerals and grows the finest tobacco, especially in the Vuelta Abajo district. The foot-hills and valleys of the Cordilleras de los Organos are highly productive. The chief port, Bahia Honda, is capable of large development.

Havana province is thickly settled, with flourishing plantations and farms and many prosperous towns. The capital is being modernized with high office buildings and factories, and is extending in pretentious suburbs, parks, and boulevards, to Marianao, the principal coast resort.

Matanzas province is highly cultivated, notably with sugar and well populated. The capital has a large export trade, Cardenas is also an important port. The Yumuri Valley, a reserved area of rich tropical scenery, and the mammoth caverns of Bellamar, attract thousands of tourists.

Santa Clara province has large sugar and tobacco plantations, and rich grazing lands. Cienfuegos, the chief port, has a harbour eleven miles across. Santa Clara, Sancti Spiritus, and Trinidad are important and historic cities. The character of the country changes rapidly farther east. Camagüey has rich grazing lands, important forest areas, and large fruit farms. The capital, Camagüey, is an important city. The chief port is Nuevitas on the north with a large, partly developed harbour

The province of Oriente has flourishing plantations and important fruit industry on the north The Baracoa region is famous for natural wonders, cascades, limestone caverns, and petrified remains. There is a group of ports on the north coast in a large tridented bay Banes, Antilla (the north-eastern terminus of the trunk railroad with fast steamers to New York for fruit and tourists), Nipe, and Cabonico. The southern area of Oriente is heavily wooded and mountainous with the Sierra del Cobre, and virgin forest extending over many rugged peaks of the Sierra Maestre, which are piled in a rugged, picturesque barrier near the coast. Santiago, the capital, and Guantanamo, are based on enormous land-locked harbours shut in by mountains. Jamaica is 80 miles south.

The six provinces are Havana, 3,174 square miles, Pinar del Rio, 5,212 square miles, Matanzas, 3,260 square miles, Santa Clara, 8,260 square miles; Camagüey, 10,070 square miles, Oriente, 14,188 square miles.

The **climate** is equable and generally healthy Defective sanitation and civil war gave Cuba a heavy death-rate during the Spanish administration. Stringent sanitary reforms instituted during American military control and continued by the Republic have made Cuba one of the healthiest countries in the world, with a death-rate of 12 54 per thousand, it is now the most fashionable winter resort for all the Americans. The discovery by an Anglo-Cuban, Dr. Carlos Findlay, that yellow fever was spread entirely by the *stegomia* mosquito led to a successful fight against the scourge by a group of American and Cuban surgeons. The campaign expelled the disease from Cuba and Panamá, and has been extended successfully to other endemic areas.

The heat in Cuba is tempered by the prevalence of the North-East Trade Winds, and the mid-day summer heat gives a lower average than in similar latitudes on the mainland. The nights are generally cool. The summer rainy season is marked by heavy thunderstorms, and periodic deluges with intervals of brilliant sunshine.

GOVERNMENT

The preamble of the **constitution** of 1901 declares the country an independent, sovereign State under the Republican form of government, exerted by three powers, Legislative, Executive, and Judicial. The country undertook to raise no foreign loans beyond the capacity of current revenue, and incorporated certain provisos which granted the United States the perpetual lease of naval stations at Guantanamo and Bahia Honda, the United States undertaking to intervene in the event of the independence of Cuba being threatened by a foreign Power, Cuba assuming all obligations and undertakings which devolved on the United States by the Treaty of Paris. Legislative power is exerted by Congress—the House of Representatives of 120 members elected for four years, and a Senate of four members from each province elected for eight years. The executive power rests in the President, who appoints the Judges of the Supreme Court, and the members of the Diplomatic and Consular Services, subject to approval by the Senate.

PAST PRESIDENTS.

Dr Estrada Palma	..	1902–1906
General J. M. Gomez .. .	..	1909–1913
General Mario G. Menocal .	..	1913
(second term expired May 20, 1921)		

PRESIDENT AND VICE-PRESIDENT

President	Dr. Alfredo Zayas (1921–1925)
Vice-President . .	General Francisco Carrillo.

MINISTRY

Foreign Office .	Carlos Manuel de Céspedes.
Interior .	Francisco Iturralde.
War and Navy	Armando G. Montes.
Public Health and Charity .	Dr Enrique Porto.
Finance . .	Dr Enrique H. Cartaya.
Education	Gonzales Manet.
Justice .	Erasmo Regüoiforos.
Public Works .	Aurelio Sandoval.
Agriculture, Commerce, and Labour	General Pedro Betancourt.
Presidency's Secretary	José M. Cortina.

A CUBAN CALENDAR.

1492. Columbus on his first voyage discovers Cuba, which he named Juana : named Cubanacán by the natives.
1511-24. Diego Velasquez founds settlements.
1516. Las Casas arrives in Cuba as "Protector of the Indians."
1519. Havana founded.
1741. British expedition lands.
1762. Havana captured by the English under Lord Albemarle and Admiral Pocoek.
1763. Havana restored to Spain by the Treaty of Paris.

1818. Cuba opened to the trade of the world.
1850. Invasion by General Lopez and a body of Americans.
1854. Purchase of Cuba recommended by United States envoys.
1868–78. Rebellion against Spanish rule.
1880. Bill for gradual emancipation of slaves promulgated.
1886. Slavery finally abolished.
1895–8. Further rebellion against the Spaniards.
1898. U.S.A. battleship "Maine" blown up in Havana Harbour, Spanish fleet under Admiral Cervera destroyed by United States Navy Havana occupied by United States troops. First Cuban autonomous Congress opened by General Blanco. Capitulation of Santiago de Cuba. The remains of Columbus exhumed and taken to Seville Cathedral.
1899. United States temporarily controls the Cuban Administration.
1902. Cuba declared an independent Republic, and withdrawal of the American authorities.
1903. Permanent treaty between Cuba and the United States signed.
1904. Anglo-Cuban commercial treaty ratified.
1906. Rebellion headed by General Gomez.
1906–8. Intervention by United States at the request of President Palma.
1909. Inauguration of the second Republic.
1917. Cuba declared war on Germany
1919. Joins the League of Nations.

Local Administration :—There are six provinces—Pinar del Rio, Havana, Matanzas, Santa Clara, Camagüey, and Oriente—and 82 municipalities. Each province elects its own governor and provincial councillors. The provinces are divided into municipalities, each governed by a mayor and board of aldermen elected by direct vote. Local rates are based on property valuation. There is no income tax. Revenue is obtained from customs, stamp dues, and on certain commodities.

The Supreme **Court** is in Havana. There is a Court of Appeal at the capital of each province. The provinces are divided into judicial districts, each with judges for civil and criminal actions. In addition, there is in each municipality a corrective court for minor offences.

Article 24 of the Civil Code guarantees foreigners the same rights as Cubans in respect to law, property, and protection of interests.

Naturalisation was granted to foreigners who served in the Cuban army, and to foreign residents, including the large Spanish population, if claimed within six months after the Republic was formed. It can be claimed after five years' residence (and not less than two years after declaration of intention), and is lost by a return of five years for residence in the country of birth unless in the service of the Cuban Government.

Immigration :—A notable feature about the immigrants arriving in Cuba during the fiscal year 1921-22, was the decrease in persons suitable for employment as plantation labourers. Only 20,184 immigrants landed in Cuba during the year 1921-22, whereas arrivals during 1920-21 were 148,361 Spain, which in 1920-21 sent 73,543 immigrants, sent only 11,664 in 1921-22, immigration from Haiti declined from 30,472 to 388, arrivals of Jamaicans from 27,713 to 3,397, and of Chinese from 8,787 to 51. Arrivals from the United States declined from 1,143 to 823, and the number of immigrants from the British Caribbean colonies other than Jamaica fell from 1,274 to 467.

CUBA.

The **population** in 1919 was 2,898,905, of which 74 3 are white and 25·7 coloured. In 1919 there were 80,485 immigrants, including 39,573 Spaniards, attracted by the general prosperity The average population to the square mile is 66.

All **religions** enjoy an equal status. There is no state church. Roman Catholics largely predominate.

The **language** is Spanish, but English is widely understood.

The **monetary unit** is a gold peso of 1 5046 grammes, of the same value as the United States dollar Cuban coinage maintains the same values as American currency, which is legal tender There are gold coins of 20, 10, 5, 4, 2, and 1 pesos. In silver : 1 peso, 40, 20, 10 cents. Nickel : 5, 2, 1 cents. Gold coinage is unrestricted, but the minting of silver·is limited to 12,000,000 pesos. There is no paper money

The **metric** system is in use generally, but the following measures are employed :—

> 1 arroba = 25·366 lb.
> 1 caballería (of land) = 33⅓ acres.
> 1 real = 6¼d. (about)
> 1 ton = 2,240 lb.

Sugar is quoted locally at so many reals per arroba.

Social Life :—There are proportionately more Freemasons in Cuba than in any other country, and there are Lodges in all communities. The Automobile Club has a large membership and a new palatial clubhouse in Havana. The Vedado Tennis Club and the Country Club are important social organisations. The Yacht Club has headquarters at Marianao, the fashionable sea resort of Havana. The Union Club has an influential membership; the Jockey Club, the Athletic Club, the Casino Español, the National Society of Veterans (of the Cuban Army), and the Rotary Club are important. Practically all professions and industries have associations with headquarters or clubhouses in Havana, and clubs in the larger towns. These societies are a marked feature in Cuban life. Spanish residents also have many clubs and associations in the island. The Centro de Dependientes, Centro Asturiano, and Centro Gallego, with more than 50,000 each, have magnificent premises. The American Club with nearly 1,000 members is erecting a residential clubhouse of ten storys and roof garden in Havana. The English Club is well situated at No. 14 Trocadero.

NATURAL RESOURCES.

Trade depends so much on the sugar market that the country's economic prosperity rises and falls with the fluctuation of that commodity The economic, political and geographical ties which link Cuba with the United States are paramount. There exist as bonds between the countries a treaty of reciprocity, a similar coinage, the American capital invested in the island, and the Platt Amendment, which provides for American intervention in case of necessity. These tend to make Cuba dependent to a large degree on the United States.

The chief products of Cuba are sugar and tobacco. The sugar crop of 1922-23 was a small one of 3,650,000 tons. Cuba is said to be able to produce cane sugar a farthing per lb. cheaper than any country in the world. The technical equipment of the sugar mills is first-class. At the end of 1922, Cuba had only 8,500 tons of old crop sugar on hand, a great decrease from the 1,200,000 tons at the end of 1921. This means that Cuba disposed of 5,200,000 tons of sugar during 1922, of which over 4,000,000 tons went to the United States of America.

Associated with the sugar industry is the manufacture of industrial alcohol from molasses. There is a demand for motor spirit cheaper and less uncertain in supply than petrol, and Cuba has at command an abundant supply In the 1920 crop of nearly 4 million tons of sugar, the production of final molasses amounted to over 185 million gallons. The production of alcohol in local distilleries, other than those attached to sugar mills, is about 6½ million gallons.

The greater part of the two thousand motor vehicles which ply for hire in Havana use denatured alcohol as fuel. The mixture known as " Espiritu Motor " is for sale side by side with gasoline in the streets.

Rum, an important adjunct of the sugar trade, was exported by the 2-3,000,000 gallons a year before the adoption of prohibition as the national policy of the United States.

Cuban tobacco, especially in the form of Havana **cigars,** has a matchless reputation. The best tobacco is that of the famous Vuelta Abajo region (Pinar del Rio), but excellent qualities are also grown near and exported from Trinidad, Cienfuegos, and Santiago.

The cedar wood, from which cigar boxes are made, is of local production and there are about 15,000,000 acres of forests rich in hard and cabinet woods. Mahogany and ebony are exported, cedar is abundant, and the acana is used for many industries.

Honey exports exceed a million gallons, and new factories are increasing production of chocolate, confections, guava jellies, and candied fruits, now important industries. Fruit exports are increasing.

Tortoiseshell, sponges, mother of pearl, and beeswax are exported. Brickmaking, tinned fruit, perfume, soap, and fibre fabrics are new industries. New agricultural bureaux have been established with a view to stimulating the production of rice, corn, and other imported food staples.

In January 1919, there were 4,060,000 **cattle** in the island. The succulent parana grass is practically inexhaustible, and there are large ranches in the eastern districts, though cattle and horses are also raised in the other provinces. There were 779,496 horses and 64,570 mules at the last enumeration.

Minerals :—In Oriente the iron mines near the coast export 600,000 tons of ore yearly to the United States. Manganese and copper mines are worked, and new copper deposits have been developed in the Isle of Pines and Pinar del Rio. Petroleum wells have proved disappointing in yield, but are expected to show better returns from deeper borings. Chromium deposits are worked.

COMMERCIAL INFORMATION

Trade Requirements :—The wants of the people in the various districts are singularly uniform. Equipment for portable saw mills, tree felling, etc., is restricted to Camagüey and Oriente. Light cloth, alpacas, and linen suits are worn. English cotton and linen goods have a high reputation. Ore trucks, cane cars, tractors, and oil-burning locomotives are needed, and sugar machinery Miles of cotton cloth are used to protect the tobacco plants, chiefly in the Vuelta Abajo district. Agricultural implements are needed. There is a brisk demand for constructional material, especially tiles, ornamental brick, shop, and office fixtures, and hardware.

Certificates of origin are not required in general, but may be called for to prove special points which may arise.

Consular invoices, to be obtained from a Cuban Consul, are required. They should be made out in Spanish, and certified by a Cuban Consul at the port of shipment, place of sale, or origin of the merchandise. The invoice must be certified by a member of the firm or by an agent duly authorized. A statement as to the rate of exchange ruling at the time of export should be included.

The following declaration in Spanish and signed by the sender is required :—

"Declaro que soy el (fabricante, productor ó vendedor) de las mercancias relacionadas en la presente factura, y que son ciertos los precios y demas particulares que en ella se consignan."

Consular invoices are required for goods sent by parcel post. Fees are leviable for certification.

Commercial Organisations :—There are Chambers of Commerce in practically every town. The Camara de Comercio, Industria y Navegación de la Isla de Cuba has its headquarters at Amargura 11, Havana.

There is a British Chamber of Commerce in Havana.

There has been established in the Cuban Department of Agriculture, Commerce, and Labour a Bureau of the International Encouragement and Promotion of Cuban Commerce and Industry (Seccion para el Fomento y Propaganda Internacional del Comercio y la Industria de Cuba), headed by Dr José T. Pimentel. This new bureau will have at its disposal the services of the Cuban Consular and Diplomatic Officers and Commercial Attachés. In Cuba the bureau deals directly with the public and with national economic organizations and chambers of commerce, serving as a repository for economic and commercial information.

The Press :—There are 81 newspapers and periodicals published in Havana and listed as suitable for foreign advertisers. The list of provincial publications is large and varied. The principal metropolitan dailies are "La Discusion," "El Heraldo," "La Prensa," "La Lucha," "Diario de la Marina," "El Mundo," "La Noche," "El Triunfo," "Diario Español." "The Havana Post" is printed in English. The chief commercial organs are "Mercurio," "Avisador," "Comercial," and "Heraldo Comercial." The chief illustrated papers are "El Figaro," "Social," and "Bohemia." There are excellent monthly reviews devoted to general topics, literature, and art.

Entertainments :—The development of the cinematograph coincided with the restoration of Cuban prosperity, so the dearth of regular provincial theatres was relieved by the erection of a large number of moving-picture houses, and films have an extraordinary hold on the people. There are palatial cinemas in Havana, and the craze has retarded the growth of the legitimate theatre. The National Theatre in Havana is one of the finest in the Americas. There are twelve other theatres, besides numerous music-halls and *cafés chantant*. The Payret, Marti, and Comedia are the best.

Postal Communications :—There are over 600 post offices, and 260 central telegraph offices. The telephone system is well developed, and Havana has an efficient automatic service. Trunk calls to North American cities have been possible since 1921 There is a direct **cable** service with England. The Government maintains several **wireless** stations.

Outward **mails** are dispatched via the United States, and the service is the same as to the United States.
Postage · 3d. for one ounce, and 1½d. each ounce after
Homeward mails are dispatched at irregular intervals.

Air services for mails and passengers are maintained between Cuba and Florida, and Havana and Santiago.

Public Holidays :—January 1, February 24, May 20, October 10, December 7, December 25.

CUBA.

CUBAN LEGATION AND CONSULATES IN GREAT BRITAIN.

RESIDENCE.	DESIGNATION.	NAME.
London (30 York Terrace, Regent's Park, N.W.1.)	Envoy Extraordinary and Minister Plenipotentiary.	General Carlos García-Vélez, K.B.E.
	First Secretary . .	Dr. Rafael Rodriguez Altunaga.
	Second Secretary (Chargé d'Affaires)	Dr. Pedro Rodriguez Capote.
London (46 Kingsway, W.C.2.)	Consul	Rafael Cerviño.
Belfast ..	Consul .	Tomás Estrada Palma y Guardiola.
Birmingham	Consul .	Francisco Sánchez García.
Bristol .	Consular Agent	W. H. Cole.
Cardiff . ..	Consular Agent ..	Algredo John Bovey.
Dover .	Consular Agent	E. T Prescott.
Glasgow (for Scotland)	Consul .	Raoul Mejer y Martin.
Hull .	Consul ..	Julio Brödermann.
Liverpool .	Consul-General	Julian de Ayala y Cruz Prieto.
	Vice-Consul	Salvador Arduín.
Newcastle-on-Tyne ..	Consular Agent . .	——
Nottingham	Consular Agent .	——
Sheffield	Consular Agent	Carlos W. Widmann.
Southampton .. .	Consular Agent	E. H. Dawe.

BRITISH LEGATION AND CONSULATES IN CUBA.

RESIDENCE.	DESIGNATION.	NAME.
Havana . ..	Chargé d'Affaires and Consul-General.	G. D. N. Haggard, O.B.E.
	Vice-Consul	D. St. C. Gainer.
Antilla . .	Vice-Consul .	Wm. L. Macdonald.
Camagüey .	Vice-Consul	Francis Matthews.
Cardenas .	Vice-Consul .	——
Cienfuegos .	Vice-Consul .	J Greentree.
Ruevitao	Vice-Consul	F L. Patten.
Santiago de Cuba	Consul ..	E. D. P. Brice.
Puerto Padre .	Vice-Consul ..	J A. Tannock.

Guidance for Commercial Travellers.

There are no special regulations affecting British commercial travellers, but all persons engaged in industry or commerce are required to take out a licence in each of the municipal divisions of the Republic. These licences are issued free. No special regulations exist in regard to commercial travellers representing more than one firm, or principals of firms travelling to take orders or to visit their customers. Persons selling goods by means of samples are classified as " Commission Agents with samples," and those who sell goods deposited in a warehouse or store are classified as " Commission Agents on account."

The Cuban Customs regulations provide for the free importation of felt samples, wall paper, and textiles when the length does not exceed 0·40 metre. To prevent abuse samples are only admitted free if they have been rendered useless by a cut every twenty centimetres breadthwise. Samples of textiles in which no cuts

241

have been made can be cut at the Custom House. Upon ordinary commercial samples carried by the agent *bona fide* in his baggage, a rebate of 75 per cent. of the duties is allowed on re-exportation within three months, if the total value thereof does not exceed $500. In order to obtain this refund the samples must be imported by the agent as personal baggage and not as merchandise , the traveller must make a verbal declaration of the value, and the Custom House will require the exhibition of consular invoices when the value of the baggage and samples exceeds $50. The samples can be re-exported at other Custom Houses of the Republic. Invoices of commercial travellers' samples should include the gross and net weight of the package and its items, with an exact description of the materials of which the goods are made, and be *visé* by a Cuban consular officer before leaving the country of departure. Samples of textiles should be attached to cards, on which should be shown in red ink, in the handwriting and under the signature of the officer at the port of export, all the particulars shown in the declaration accompanying the goods. Samples of a high value. such as gold, silver, tortoiseshell, should not be attached to cards. Paragraph 345 of the tariff grants free entry to engravings, posters, manufacturers' catalogues, and almanacs for free distribution only , but, in practice, most of the articles mentioned are held to have commercial value and therefore liable to duty.

Commercial travellers should be provided with documents or powers of attorney in order to accredit their profession if necessary Passports are not indispensable, but it is advisable to carry some means of identification. The Cuban Post Office, for a small fee, issues an identification card, which is useful for this purpose throughout the Republic.

DUTCH GUIANA

DUTCH GUIANA

Paramaribo, the capital and chief port, is on the Surinam River, 13 miles from the mouth and 210 miles from Georgetown, British Guiana. It has a population of about 37,000. There is a deep-water frontage of a mile, wharfed for a small portion, and with piers, quays, and warehouses the whole length.

Hotels :—Bellevue, Central Van Emden.

New Nickerie, on the south bank of the Nickerie River, some 3 miles from its mouth, has a population of about 7,000. It can be reached by vessels of moderate draught, and there are facilities for loading and discharging cargoes.

Albina, on the Maroni, is accessible to vessels of moderate size, and has loading and discharging facilities.

Burnside, with a population of about 2,000, **Coronie,** and **Caledonia** (Nassau) are smaller places along the coast.

CHARACTERISTICS OF THE COUNTRY

Dutch Guiana, or Surinam, lies on the north-eastern flank of the South American continent, between 2° and 6° N. lat. and 53° and 58° E. long. To the north it has a coastline on the Atlantic, and it is bounded on the west by British Guiana and on the east by French Guiana, Brazil lying to the south. The area is estimated at about 46,000 square miles. The river Corentyne forms the western and the Maroni and the Itany the eastern border The frontier with Brazil has not been finally delimited and agreed upon by the two Governments, but the Tumuc-Humac mountains form a natural border The principal rivers running between those named are the Surinam (with its tributary the Commewyne), the Coppename, Nickerie, Saramacca and the Cottica. The coastal districts lie low and the country ascends inland to the hills, covered with dense forests, and the savannahs of the interior The districts into which the country is divided are Nickerie, Coronie, Upper and Lower Saramacca, Upper and Lower Surinam, Upper and Lower Para, Upper and Lower Commewyne, Cottica and Maroni.

The **climate** is tropical and moist with temperatures ranging from 70°F to 90°F ; the annual average at Paramaribo being 75°F There is a considerable rainfall on the coast, and this increases in the forest districts. The average inland fall varies from 60 to 80 inches and on the coast is about 100 inches a year After the first dry season, from February to April, comes the first rainy season, from April to August. A second dry season sets in until November, followed by the second rainy season, lasting until February

Among the chief **diseases** are leprosy, ankylostomiasis, filaria, tuberculosis, elephantiasis and tropical fevers. Yellow fever occurs but is not endemic.

The **language** of the colony is Dutch, but English is generally spoken.

All religious beliefs are free and equal before the law The religious bodies include Roman Catholics, Lutherans and Dutch Reformed Church, Moravian Brethren, Hindus, Confucians, Mohammedans, and Jews.

The **coinage** is that of the mother country The florin or gulden equals 1s. 8d., and 5 c. equal 1d., while 12 florins are equivalent to £1 at par

The **metric** system is in general use, but the Flemish ell (27½ inches) and Rhenish foot (12⅜ inches) are in vogue in some districts.

The **population** is estimated at 100,000, but the total cannot be accurately established as regards some of the tribes and negroes of the far inland districts. The nationalities comprise Dutch, British, Dutch Indians, Chinese, Javanese and Hindus, together with a few thousand Bush negroes, the descendants of escaped slaves.

ADMINISTRATION

Dutch Guiana was assured to the Netherlands by the Peace of Breda, in 1667, in exchange for New York to England. The colony again passed under English control from 1799 to 1802, and was restored by the Peace of Amiens. The Convention of London in 1814 finally returned the country to the Netherlands. A long succession of Governors, numbering about ninety, mostly Dutch, have ruled over the colony from 1665, when Maurits de Rama was Commander-in-Chief.

The colony is the only Dutch possession in South America, and is administered by a Governor appointed by the Netherlands Government. It is divided into twelve districts, each under the charge of a Commissary The Governing Council which assists the Governor is appointed by the home Government. The representative body is the Colonial States, elected by qualified electors for a period of six years. The sanction of the Netherlands Government is required before its legislative proposals pass into law.

A Supreme Court of Justice is appointed by the Netherlands Government and the members hold office for life, sitting at Paramaribo. There are, in addition, three cantonal and two circuit courts. The code is Roman-Dutch, and the laws and the system of administration run on the same lines as those of Holland.

TRADE AND INDUSTRIES.

As there is only one short line of railway, inland trade and travel are to a great extent dependent on the rivers, which are deep and navigable by sea-going vessels. The Nickerie takes vessels of 9-feet draught 60 miles inland, the Coppename takes vessels of 15-feet to the Wayombo, and the Corentyne can be navigated 70 miles inland. There is a Government service of steamers and motor-boats on various rivers, and a few privately-owned schooners and cutters.

The agricultural parts of the country lie along the rivers and the coast, and the area cultivated is estimated at 62,000 acres. The hinterland furnishes timber and minerals.

In the list of **agricultural** products, sugar is the most important, bananas and coffee, rice and maize coming next. Cacao is assuming increasing importance. Rum and molasses are considerable products. Balatá is a species of gutta percha, taken from the tree of that name. Over 1,000 tons of balatá, of the value of £250,000, are exported on the average, or double the export of that material from British Guiana. Fish glue, hides and various kinds of wood are among the usual exports.

The **foreign** trade is not extensive : imports £1,143,000, exports £623,000 in 1920. Sugar, rum, cocoa and gold are the principal exports.

Important deposits of bauxite are known to exist on the Cottica, and the mineral is worked at Mungo.

COMMUNICATIONS.

The **postal** rates are the same as those in the Postal Union. Registration is not accepted for parcels in the colony

INLAND RATES:—Letters, 20 grammes or less, 5 cents, to 200 grammes, 10 cents, increasing to a maximum of 2,000 grammes at 30 cents. Postcards, 2½ cents.

The **cable** service outward is controlled by the Compagnie Française des Câbles Télégraphiques, with an office at Paramaribo. Messages can be sent to Albina, St. Laurent du Maroni, Nickerie, etc.

Outward **mails** (i) by sea direct at frequent intervals, (ii) via United States, and (iii) by French packet at uncertain intervals. Postage, 3d. first ounce, and 1½d. each ounce after. Homeward mails are despatched at frequent intervals.

The chief **public holidays** are New Year's Day (1st January), Good Friday, Easter Monday, the Ascension, Whit Monday, 21st August (Queen of Holland's birthday), Christmas Day and the day after.

Press :—"De Suriname," "De Surinamer," "De West," published at Paramaribo, are the principal papers printed in Dutch; they appear twice a week. The " New Paramaribo Times " appears weekly and in English.

Guidance for Commercial Travellers.

Only travellers representing liquor firms are required to take out licences. Samples of no commercial value may be imported, and also dutiable samples on guarantee of re-exportation. The moisture of the climate demands special care in the packing of samples and luggage. Agencies may usefully be established in Paramaribo, but some firms cover British Guiana, Dutch Guiana, and French Guiana from Georgetown.

ECUADOR

ECUADOR.

Guayaquil, the chief seaport and commercial city, is some thirty miles from the bar of the River Guayas. Its site, the pleasant valley of the Guayas, literally "Vale of Lamentations," recalls a defeat which befell Spanish arms in the early days of colonization. The harbour is two and a half miles long, with one and a half mile of quays, the town is bustling and prosperous. Steam sawmills, foundries, machine-shops, and breweries indicate the busy activities of to-day, and a few yards' progress across the Plaza to the inside of the cathedral carry the traveller back to the leisure of mediæval Spanish churchmen. Population about 100,000. Yellow fever has been eradicated. There are two theatres, the Almedo and Eden, and several clubs, including the Club de la Unión, Jockey, Metropolitano, and Nacional. There is a Municipal Museum.

Landing :—Shore boat.

Conveyances :—Electric and horse trams.

Hotels :—Wellington, Plaza de Rocafuerte; Paris, Calle Gral Elizalde No. 5, Victoria, Calle 9 de Octobre No. 104; Guayaquil, Calle Bolivar No. 215 y 217.

Rail :—To Quito (290 miles).

Quito, the capital, with a population of 100,000, is in a picturesque valley 9,350 ft. above sea-level, and is connected with Guayaquil by a mountain railway It possesses a university with a museum, and the Jesuit and Dominican orders also have museums. There is a State theatre, the Sucre, with seating accommodation for 2,000. The Government subsidy for the theatres of the Republic amounts to $25,000 annually There are tramways and taxi-cabs.

HOTELS :—Gran Hotel Continental, Royal Hotel, Hotel Ecuador, and Hotel Metropolitano.

Cuenca, capital of the province of Azuay, stands 9,000 ft. above sea-level, 70 miles from Guayaquil, and 190 miles south of Quito. Population, 80,000. It is the third town in importance of the Republic. Railways are in construction to Sibambe and Puerto Bolivár.

HOTEL :—Continental.

Latacunga, capital of the province of Léon, on the Patate river, is 64 miles north-east of Quito and 220 from Guayaquil. Population, 36,500.

HOTEL :—Italia.

Riobamba, capital of the province of Chimborazo, is 140 miles north-east of Guayaquil, with which it is connected by rail. Population, 52,000.

HOTELS :—Metropolitano, Ecuador

Ambato, capital of the province of Tunguratua, on the Ambato river, is 75 miles from Quito, and is the junction for Guayaquil. Population, 115,000.

HOTEL :—Victoria.

Manta, in the same province, on the Pacific, with a population of 3,000, is 40 miles from Puertoviejo, and the port for Jipijapa and Monte Christi, centres of Panama hat manufacture.

Esmeraldas, principal port and capital of the province of the same name, situated at the mouth of the River Esmeraldas; 90 miles north-west from Quito and 300 from Guayaquil. Population, 14,000.

Bahia de Ceraquez, on the Pacific, in the province of Manabi, with a population of 5,000, is 28 miles north of Manta.

HOTELS :—Alejandro Santos, Gregorio Usivoviela.

Ibarra, 60 miles north of Quito, has a population of about 20,000.

Puerto Viejo, on the river of the same name, is 100 miles from Guayaquil and 400 from Quito.

Machala is joined by rail with Pasaje (11 miles distant) and with Puerto Bolívar (4 miles). Population, 16,000.

Guaranda, on the Llangama river, is an import point for transhipment, between Quito (110 miles) and Guayaquil.

CHARACTERISTICS OF THE COUNTRY

Ecuador is situated approximately between latitudes 1° 40′ north and 6° south, and longitudes 69° 20′ east and 90° west. It is bounded on the north by Colombia, on the east and south by Peru, and on the west by the Pacific. It has benefited from the opening of the Panamá Canal.

The area is given roughly as 276,000 square miles, but definite figures cannot be given as a large part of the territory is in dispute. The Andes traverse the country from north to south in two parallel ranges. Between the mountains and the Pacific Ocean is a narrow stretch of coast plain; to the east stretches the vast and well-watered plain of the region called the Oriente. Of the rivers, those flowing through El Oriente and Loja in the Amazon basin are important, the Napo constitutes the frontier with Colombia, and others are the Curaray, Nigre, Pastaza, Morona, Paute, and Zamora. Among those flowing to the Pacific from the Andes are the Mira, Esmeraldas, Chones, Daule, and Guayas.

Originally the country was the home of the Quichua Indians. The chief Indian tribes to-day are the Zaparos, Jivaros, Iquitos, and the Mazanes.

Although Ecuador is well watered, few of its **rivers** are navigable. The Guayas and its tributaries form the principal waterways. There are practically no lakes, and no canals have been constructed.

ECUADOR.

The principal public **road** from the capital to a point called Babahoyo, on a tributary of the Guayas, is the one over which traffic between Guayaquil and the interior formerly passed. It was destroyed in parts by the construction of the Guayaquil and Quito Railway, and has since been abandoned. There are practically no cart roads, transport being effected on muleback over rough trails.

The varying altitudes afford many varieties of **climate**, from the tropical climate of the coast region to the temperate and cold climates of the higher mountain ranges. The average temperature of the littoral between the Andes and the sea is 82° to 84° F., and the mean temperature of Guayaquil is given as 78° F The temperature falls with the altitude from 79° F upon the plains to 43° F. on the Cordillera at a height of 13,200 ft. The dry season is from June to November, and the rainy from December to May On the whole the climate is healthy for the tropics.

The country is divided into seventeen provinces and one territory. The Oriental Region was divided into two provinces (Napo-Partaza and Santiago-Zamora) by Legislative Decree of 25 November 1920. The population is variously calculated as between 1,500,000 and 2,000,000.

Provinces.	Area Square Miles.	Population.	Capital.
Carchi	1,494	100,000	Tulcan (15,000)
Imbabura	2,394	150,000	S. Miguel de Ibarra (15,000)
Pichincha	6,219	300,000	Quito (100,000)
León	2,595	150,000	Latacunga (16,500)
Tungurahua	1,686	100,000	Ambato (25,000)
Chimborazo	2,990	200,000	Riobamba (22,000)
Bolivár	1,160	80,000	Guaranda (6,000)
Cañar	1,755	100,000	Azógues (35,000)
Azuay	3,874	250,000	Cuenca (40,000)
Loja	25,096	150,00	Loja (15,000)
El Oro	2,340	80,000	Machala (6,000)
Guayas	8,215	400,000	Guayaquil (110,000)
Los Ríos	2,296	150,000	Babahoyo (5,000)
Manabí	7,893	250,000	Puertoviejo (8,000)
Esmeraldas	5,464	100,000	Esmeraldas (4,000)
Napo-Partaza		40,000	
Santiago-Zamora		40,000	

The territory previously named is the Galapagos Islands, called the Archipelago of Colón, situated in the Pacific Ocean about 600 miles west of Ecuador

The population of the two provinces last named and of the Galapagos Islands is unknown, and consists principally of savage Indian tribes, mostly nomads.

NATURAL RESOURCES.

The principal agricultural products are cacao, ivory nuts, rubber, coffee, tobacco, cinchona bark, hat straw (called "Toquilla"), and tropical fruits. Other products, produced in smaller quantities, are sugar, rice, cotton, aloe fibre (Cabuya), maize, wheat, barley, potatoes, vegetables of all kinds, cabinet woods and timber generally

The estimated stocks of produce on hand in 1922 were Cacao, 1,630,825 lb., cinchona bark, 35,000 lb., coffee, 400,000 lb., cotton, 1,400,000 lb., hides, 75,000, kapok, 60,000 lb.

Cacao is the principal export.

The principal oil regions are on the coast at Salinas and Santa Elena, situated on the Gulf of Guayaquil. A British company produces oil for local consumption and larger developments are intended.

While there are evidences of the existence of mineral deposits, such as coal, manganese, quicksilver, petroleum, sulphur, etc., these are almost entirely undeveloped. The only mining industry worthy of note is at Zaruma, where gold is extracted.

Included in the **fauna** of the republic are the jaguar, puma, tapir, and several kinds of monkeys, the armadillo, ant-bear, squirrel, porcupine, peccary, various kinds of deer, and many rodents, including the guinea-pig. There are also tortoises, lizards, and iguanas. Among the snakes are the boa-constrictor and the anaconda, and the alligator is also met. The bird-life comprises the condor of the Andes, falcons, kites, macaws, owls, toucans, parrots, ibises, cranes, and storks.

CONSTITUTION

Since the proclamation of the Republic in 1830, Ecuador has had eleven constitutions, the last dating from 1906. The executive power is vested in the President, who is elected for a period of four years, and cannot be re-elected until after a period of eight years from his retirement.

The legislative power is in the hands of the National Congress, which consists of a House of Senators and a House of Deputies. It meets every year at Quito on August 10 and sits in session for sixty days, which term can, however, be extended. There is also a Council of State, with fifteen members, which includes the five Cabinet Ministers. The suffrage is extended to all literate male adults.

PAST PRESIDENTS.

General Juan José Flores	1830
Dr. Vicente Rocafuerte	1835
General Juan José Flores	1839
Vicente Ramón Roca	1844
Diego Noboa	1851
General José Maria Urvina	1852

ECUADOR.

General Francisco Robles	1856
Dr Gabriel Garcia Moreno	1861
Jerónimo Carrión	1865
Dr. Xavier Espinosa	1868
Dr. Gabriel Garcia Moreno (second term)	1869
Dr Antonio Borrero	1875
General Ignacio de Veintimilla	1876
Dr. José Maria Plácido Caamaño	1884
Dr Antonio Flores	1888
Dr Luis Cordero	1892
General Eloy Alfaro	1897
General Leonidas Plaza	1901
Lizardo Garcia	1905
General Eloy Alfaro (second term	1906
Emilio Estrada	1911
General Leonidas Plaza (second term)	1912
Dr Alfredo Baquerizo Moreno	1916
Dr José Luis Tamayo	1920

PRESIDENT.

Dr José Luis Tamayo (1920).

MINISTRY

Home Office and Public Works : General Delfin Freviño.
Foreign Office and Justice : Dr. Clemente Ponce.
War Office and Admiralty : Octavio Icaza.
Finance . Dr. Larrea.
Education and Agriculture : Pablo Vasconez.

The **administration** is by the Governors of the provinces, who are appointed by the Executive. The departments of each province are administered by Jefes Politicos, and the municipal areas by Tenientes Politicos.

The Galapagos Islands are governed by a territorial chief, and Chatham Island, which is a penal settlement, by special laws.

Judicial power is exercised through the Supreme Court; superior or divisional courts, and other tribunals and courts of law established by the constitution. The Supreme Court sits at Quito and has jurisdiction over the whole Republic. The divisional courts are in Quito, Riobamba, Cuenca, Loja, Guayaquil, and Portoviejo.

Freedom of worship obtains, there is no State religion. The predominating belief is Roman Catholicism.

The language of the country is Spanish, but Quichua is spoken to some extent in the interior.

There are universities at Quito, Guayaquil, and Cuenca.

ECUADOR.

AN ECUADOREAN CALENDAR.

1533. Pizarro conquers Quito for the Spanish Crown.
1564. Quito promoted to a Presidency, under Peruvian Viceroyalty.
1710. Transferred to the Viceroyalty of Santo Fé.
1719. The Vice-Royalty of New Granada created.
1721. The Presidency of Quito made part of the Vice-Royalty of New Granada.
1722. Again incorporated with Peru.
1809. Unsuccessful attempt at revolt on the part of the Patriots.
1811. Open state of war between Ecuadoreans and Spanish troops.
1822. General Sucre, after defeating the Spaniards, assumes charge of Ecuador. Union of Quito with New Granada and Venezuela, the new Confederation taking the name of Colombia.
1828-9. Peru goes to war with Ecuador, capturing Guayaquil and Cuenca, Ecuador defeats the Peruvians near Tarqui.
1830. Peace with Peru.
1831. Secedes from the Colombian Confederation and proclaims itself an independent republic, with General Juan Flores as its first President.
1861. Unsuccessfully attacks New Granada.
1866. Alliance with Peru and Chili against Spain; Spanish subjects banished from Ecuador.
1868. Quito and other towns devastated by earthquake.
1875. President Morena murdered at Quito.
1876. His successor, Dr. Borrero, displaced by a revolution.
1877. Eruption of Cotopaxi.
1987. General Alfaro heads a revolution and became President.
1899. The Guayaquil-Quito Railway begun. Rebels routed at San Ancaja.
1904. Boundary dispute with Colombia submitted to the arbitration of the German Emperor.
1906. Revolutionary rising suppressed by Alfaro, who again becomes President.
1917. Ecuador severs diplomatic relations with Germany
1919. Joins the League of Nations.

The unit of currency is the **Sucre**, at par equal to two shillings. Coins, with English equivalents :—

			£	s.	d.
1 Condor (gold)	=	10 sucres =	1	0	0
1 Sucre (silver)	=	..		2	0
½ Sucre (silver)	=	=		1	0
1 Peseta	=	$\frac{1}{5}$ sucre =			5
1 Real (silver)	=	$\frac{1}{10}$ sucre =			2½
1 Medio (silver)	=	$\frac{1}{20}$ sucre =			1¼

There has been an issue of nickel coin consisting of "Reales" and "Medios."

The **metric system** is legal but not general. Spanish measures are more generally used :—

				English lb.
Weights.—1 Libra	= 16 onzas	=		1·0147
1 Arroba	= 25 pounds	=		25 36
1 Quintal	= 100 pounds	=		101 47
1 Kilo	..	.	..	2·2

Length.—1 Vara = 3 Pies = 36 Pulgadas = 32·875 in. to 33 43 in. (variable.)

Surface.—1 Vara Cuadrada = 0·859 sq. yd.

Capacity.—1 Arroba (Dry) = 6·70 gallons.
1 Galón (Liquid) = 0·74 gallon.

ECUADOR.

The principal **newspapers** are "El Comercio" and "El Dia," published at Quito, and "El Diario Illustrado," "El Guante," and "El Telégrafo," published at Guayaquil.

Guayaquil and Quito have telephone systems.

There are about 5,400 miles of telegraphs, with 188 offices, and a **cable** office (Central and South American Telegraph Company) at Salinas. There are wireless stations at Guayaquil and Quito, and on the Galapagos Islands as well as at other points.

Outward **mails** are dispatched via the United States, and at intervals by the Pacific Steam Navigation Line, via Panamá.

Postage 3d. first ounce, and 1½d. each ounce after

Homeward mails are despatched at irregular intervals.

LEGATION AND CONSULATES IN GREAT BRITAIN

RESIDENCE.	DESIGNATION.	NAME.
London ..	Envoy Extraordinary and Minister Plenipotentiary	Enrique Dorn y de Alsúa (resident at Paris, 91, Avenue de Wagram).
	Attaché ..	L. A. Guzmán.
London .. (23 College Hill, E.C.4.)	Consul-General .	G. H. Wright.
Birmingham	Consul	Juan Norman Hotchkiss.
Cardiff ..	Consul .	Abelardo Aldama.
Glasgow . .	Consul	Juan de Elizalde.
Liverpool .	Consul-General .	Eduardo Wright.
Southampton	Consul	Carlos Stagg Aguirre.

PUBLIC HOLIDAYS.

New Year's Day
February 14 : National Holiday
May 24 : Battle of Pichincha.
August 10 : Independence of Quito Opening of Congress.
October 9 : Independence of Guayaquil.
October 12 : Discovery of America.
Christmas Day.
The usual feast days of the Roman Catholic Church are also observed.

BRITISH LEGATION AND CONSULATES IN ECUADOR.

The letter (M) denotes that the Consular Officer holds a Marriage Warrant. Members of the Diplomatic Service do not require Warrants.

RESIDENCE.	RANK.	NAME.	CONSULAR LIST.
(See PERU)	Envoy Extraordinary, and Minister Plenipotentiary	Lord H. A. R. Hervey	
Quito	(M) Consul-General	R. C. Michell	Republic of Ecuador
Guayaquil	(M) Consul	W. G. Graham	Provinces of Esmeralda,
Bahia de Caraquez.	Consular Agent	Pierre Discomps	Manabá, El Oro,
Cuenca	Vice-Consul	E. Malo	Guayas and Los Ráos.

I

EXPORTS AND IMPORTS.

Year.	Exports. £	Imports. £	Total. £	Balance. £
1921	3,396,889	2,348,619	5,745,508	1,048,270
1920	4,989,193	4,017,451	9,006,644	971,742
1919	4,322,055	2,400,769	6,722,824	1,921,286
1918	2,834,179	1,720,700	4,554,879	1,113,479
1917	3,368,635	2,102,218	5,470,853	1,266,417
1916	3,628,989	1,927,131	5,556,120	1,701,858
1915	2,653,306	1,730,991	4,384,297	922,315
1914	2,687,565	1,728,958	4,416,523	958,607
1913	3,248,841	1,818,798	5,067,639	1,430,043
1912	2,816,809	2,130,568	4,947,377	686,241
1911	2,611,571	2,324,013	4,935,584	287,558
1910	2,806,236	1,647,660	4,453,896	1,158,576

Consular invoices are necessary for imported goods. They must be in Spanish and presented to the Consul at the port of shipment for certification. Special forms are obtainable at the Consulates, and fees are charged. Certificates of origin are not required.

Guidance for Commercial Travellers.

Commercial travellers are liable to a tax of 100 sucres (£10) each time they enter Ecuador. The tax is levied at the Custom House on arrival and a receipt is given, which, in the event of the traveller moving from one port of the Republic to another by sea, should be produced at each port called at for endorsement by the maritime authority. Commercial travellers can make purchases or take orders from merchants or manufacturers, but if they sell their goods are liable to municipal pedlar's taxes in addition to the tax mentioned above. Commercial travellers must register their names at the local Magistrates' Office in accordance with Police Regulations.

Samples of fabrics, small articles of no value, and articles rendered unfit for use, are exempt from Customs duty.

Samples of value are entitled to free temporary admission if a guarantee is given by a merchant of standing in the Republic. The samples are then invoiced on paper stamped for 30 centavos. No other Customs formality is necessary.

FALKLAND ISLANDS

FALKLAND ISLANDS.

The Falkland Islands are inhabited almost exclusively by people of pure British descent, and descendants of the early pioneers own the greater part of the land. The Colony is entirely dependent on the sheep industry The total number of sheep in the country in 1920 was 667,677. As many as 800,000 have been carried, but this was probably overstocking the pasturage. The inhabitants are hard-working and thrifty They numbered at 31 December, 1920, 2,271, viz., 1,285 males and 986 females. The birth-rate was 21·5 and the death-rate 9·5. The general health is good and there is no doubting the salubrity of the climate.

Stanley, in the north-east corner of the group of islands, is the only town of importance. It has a fine inner and outer harbour, and is visited occasionally by P.S.N steamer The population of Stanley is about 900, and its houses are mostly wood and iron. There are several small hotels and boarding-houses offering fair accommodation. The port is a convenient coaling station for vessels passing through the Straits of Magellan. The bay, surrounded by low-lying hills covered with brown moss and grass, has a very home-like appearance to the native of Great Britain.

Landing by shore-boat.

Currency and Language :—English.

East Falkland is of about 3,000 square miles, and West Falkland about 2,300 square miles. The remaining islands to the number of about 100 have a total area of over 1,000 square miles. The situation is between lat. S. 51° and 53° and between long. W. 57° and 62°, approximately 1,000 miles due south of Montevideo and 480 miles north-east of Cape Horn. Physically the Falklands bear a marked resemblance to some parts of the north-west coast of Scotland or the Shetland Islands. The highest peak, Mount Adam, is 2,315 ft. above sea-level.

East Falkland :—The country is wild moorland, interspersed with rocks and stones. Building-stone is found in different parts of the island of Devonian and Gondwana formations. The soil is chiefly soft peat, making travelling difficult. There are no roads except within the limits of Stanley, and communication is by sea or horse-back. The islands are so well adapted for sheep-farming, that the whole acreage has been devoted to that industry The tussac, which grows to the height of 7 ft., and affords fattening food for cattle, has disappeared from the East and West Falklands, but abounds on the smaller islands. Celery, scurvy grass and sorrel are plentiful, besides a small plant called the tea plant, much used formerly by the sealers and Gauchos. The cultivation of fruit and vegetables is made difficult by the damp, cold nature of the soil and the winds. Trees are completely absent.

Meat is cheap, and fresh milk is bought for 4d. a pint in summer but cannot be obtained in winter Apples and oranges, imported from Chile and Uruguay, sell at 2d. each.

The Dependencies, as distinct from the Colony, are inhabited almost exclusively by foreigners. The Norwegians were first in the field, and credit must be given to their initiative and energy The personnel of the whale and seal oil factories and whale-catchers is almost entirely foreign.

Of these Dependencies the principal is :—

South Georgia :—A group of islands $54\frac{1}{2}°$ S. and $36°$ to $38°$ W It was discovered by Antony La Roche in 1675, and explored and taken possession of by Captain Cook in 1775 It has an area of about 1,000 square miles, and is a centre for whaling. It is almost perpetually icebound. The snowstorms in the winter are numerous and heavy The island is mountainous, with inconsiderable lowland areas round the coast, divided by high ridges into small valleys. There are considerable areas of bog.

Other Dependencies include the South Shetlands, Graham's Land, the South Orkneys (on which the Argentine Government maintain a meteorological station), and the Sandwich group.

The climate is severe but healthy, except for those predisposed to pulmonary affections. The mean temperature is $42°$ The thermometer ranges between $30°$ and $50°$ in winter, and between $40°$ and $65°$ in summer The cold is intensified by high winds which prevail, especially in the summer, rising about 10 a.m., and falling away between 4 and 5 p.m. The annual rainfall seldom exceeds 25 in. In the summer the atmosphere is remarkably dry, and evaporation rapid.

Farming methods are said to be far behind those prevailing in South America. The poverty of the soil, the isolation of the Colony, the intemperance of the climate, and the lack of capital make progress difficult.

The breed of sheep is a cross-bred Romney There were in 1906 only two pure-bred flocks in the Islands, one Romney Marsh, the other Lincolns. The imports between 1902 and 1912 give a fair indication of the cross—584 Romney Marsh rams, 75 Border Leicester rams, 35 Lincoln rams, 69 Merino rams.

Small quantities of oats and potatoes are grown.

Efforts are in progress to develop the resources of the country in pasturage, peat, penguin and seal oil, fisheries and guano. The growing of trees and the discovery of payable minerals and mineral oils are hoped for It would be a great boon could trees be grown for shelter. Government officers have been appointed to conduct research. Mutton is canned for export at Goose Green, East Falkland.

There were in 1920 eight leases of land sites for whaling purposes in South Georgia, and in addition, some twenty floating factories and sixty whale-catchers. The whale-catchers are small steam vessels which kill whales and bring them to the mother ship or land station.

There is at present no fur seal industry in the Dependencies. The only company with a licence for taking seals killed 1,527 sea elephants and 18 sea leopards in South Georgia in 1920, 2,269 barrels of oil, value £11,345, were obtained.

The opening of the Panamá Canal has prejudiced the ship-repairing business, once a valuable local industry. A long list of damaged vessels used to put into Stanley for repairs, but casualties are now happily few and far between.

WORK OF THE PIONEERS.

The group is said to have been visited by Davis in 1592, and Hawkins in 1594. In 1690 Captain Strong sailed between the East and West Falklands and gave the name of Falkland's Sound to the Channel, it is probable that the islands came to receive their title from this survey. They were, and are, known to the French as the Isles Malouines and to the Spaniards as Islas Malvinas, from visits paid to the group in the eighteenth century by vessels from St. Malo. In 1764 they were taken by France, and Bougainville planted a small colony at Port Louis. Two years later France admitted Spain's prior claim and ceded her rights. In 1767 England asserted her dominion, and a post was established in the West Falklands with the object of surveying the group. This was driven out by the Spaniards in 1770 and restored in the following year, after threat of war The post was abandoned in 1774, and there was no further formal occupation until 1820, when the "United Provinces of South America" hoisted their flag at Port Louis. This settlement was broken up in 1831 by an American warship owing to the illegal imprisonment, by a German in charge of the settlement, of some American sealers. In the following year the British flag was restored and there has been no change of ownership since. From 1833 to 1842, continuous Admiralty surveys were made round the coast-line. On 23 June, 1843, a Charter under the Great Seal was issued defining the constitution of the Colony and its Dependencies, Richard Clement Moody (afterwards General Moody) being the first Governor.

The regions of the Dependencies were visited by a number of navigators in the sixteenth, seventeenth and early part of the eighteenth centuries, in endeavours to round Cape Horn or pass through the Straits of Magellan. Captain Cook took possession of South Georgia and the Sandwich group in 1775. The large number of whales was especially mentioned. Mr. William Smith took possession of the South Shetlands in 1819. The South Orkneys were annexed by Captain George Powell in 1821. Mr. Edward Bransfield, R.N., under whom Mr. William Smith sailed in 1819–1820, discovered the first part of Graham's Land, and Mr. John Biscoe discovered the west coast in 1832

ADMINISTRATION

The Colony is administered for the Crown by a Governor, aided by an Executive and Legislative Council. The Legislative Council is composed of the Governor, the Colonial Secretary, the Treasurer, and the Colonial Surgeon, together with two unofficial members appointed by warrant for five years.

The Governor is ex officio Chief Justice, there are magistrates for East and West Falkland, and two for South Georgia.

The Colonial Secretary for Stanley acts as Imperial Trade Commissioner

Owing to the opening of the Panamá Canal there is no direct homeward mail service. Steamers proceed to the United Kingdom via the west coast of South America.

There is a **wireless service** with Montevideo, whence messages are cabled at 3s. 9½d. per word for messages of over ten words. A small wireless station in the West Falkland maintains communication with Stanley. There is no shore wireless station in the Dependencies, but communication is occasionally established with ships carrying installations.

IMPORTS AND EXPORTS.

The total value of **imports** during 1920 was £916,769. Of this, £210,002 represented the share of the Colony and £706,767 the Dependencies.

The principal articles imported were :—

	Value. £		Value. £
Groceries	138,315	Hardware, machinery	64,776
Corn and fodder	6,875	Drapery, fancy goods	22,230
Tobacco	8,139	Paints and oils	21,058
Coal and coke	443,528	Ships, fittings	13,843
Empty barrels	14,245	Wearing apparel	28,697
Timber	46,456	Wire fencing materials	4,308
Canvas, rope, etc.	19,288	Live stock	12,251
Boots, shoes, saddlery	11,421		

There are no import duties except on wine, malt liquors, spirits and tobacco.

The total **exports** were valued at £3,132,909 in 1920. Produce to the value of £363,998 was shipped from the Colony and £2,768,911 from the Dependencies.

The following is a comparative table :—

Article.		1910. lb.	Value. £	1920. lb.	Value. £
Falkland Islands—					
Wool		4,828,109	161,666	4,510,607	269,170
Tallow		481,173	8,439	535,360	21,798
		No.		No.	
Sheepskins		—	—	86,447	36,200
		Cases.		Cases.	
Tinned meat		33,198	4,138	4,794	23,127
Dependencies—		Tons		Tons.	
Whale oil		6,433	120,995	41,892	2,748,852
Whale bone		51	2,280	55	1,730
		Bags.		Bags.	
Whale guano		—		18,579	17,273

FRENCH GUIANA

FRENCH GUIANA.

Cayenne, the capital of the colony and its chief port, is on the island of the same name at the mouth of the river Cayenne. The population is about 13,000. It is distant some 470 miles from Georgetown (British Guiana) and 260 miles from Paramaribo (Dutch Guiana) by sea. Ships discharge into lighters.

Hotels :—Grand, De France, De l'Avenir.

St. Laurent du Maroni, on the Maroni, with about 1,300 inhabitants, is an important town. Other towns are **St. Georges de l'Oyapok,** with about 1,000 inhabitants, **Sinnamarie,** with the same number, **Mana,** with 800, **Iracoubo,** with 500; and **Guizanbourg,** with 600.

Places of less importance include : **Touat** (Macouria), **Mont-Sinery** (300), **Kourou** (600), **Roura, Caux,** and **Approuague.**

On the **Iles du Salut** ("Devil's Island,"), 27 miles north-west of Cayenne, stands the celebrated convict settlement where Dreyfus and other French prisoners have been interned.

CHARACTERISTICS OF THE COLONY

The land is the only French possession in South America. It lies to the north of Brazil, its eastern frontier being formed partly by the river Oyapok and the southern by the Tumuc-Humac mountains. The western frontier line with Dutch Guiana is constituted by the rivers Maroni and Itany   The northern boundary is the Atlantic coastline of about 300 kilometres.

The area is estimated at 34,000 square miles. The land rises gradually from the coastal regions to the higher slopes and plains about 50 miles inland. Forests cover the hills and valleys of the interior, and they are succeeded by savannahs.

The colony is well watered, for over twenty rivers run to the Atlantic. Besides those named are the Mana, Cayenne, the Sinnamarie, with its tributary the Coureibo, the Marouini, Oyack, and the Approuague. Smaller rivers and tributaries are the Inini, Ardoua, and Camopi.

The only mountain range of importance is the Tumuc-Humac, and among the higher peaks are Mounts Mitarka, Temorairem, Leblond, and Timotakem, the latter in the extreme south on the Brazilian frontier.

The islands include the Enfant Perdu, the Malingre, and Rémire islands.

The **climate** is tropical with a very heavy rainfall. The rainy seasons are approximately from May to August and November to February   An average annual rainfall of 100 inches is recorded for Cayenne. The mean annual temperature of that city is 80° F. Tropical diseases, dysentery, malaria, etc., occur

FRENCH GUIANA.

The **population,** inclusive of natives, was estimated in 1911 at 49,000, of which 6,465 were convicts and persons deported from the mother country and her colonies. The prisoners reside in a Penal Settlement and are not kept in confinement, but employed in the gold-mining area.

The **language** of the colony is French.

The **religion** is predominantly Roman Catholic.

The weights and measures are, of course, metric.

The **currency** is based on the French unit of value, but the coins and bank notes differ in design.

ADMINISTRATION.

Awarded to France by the Peace of Breda in 1667, French Guiana was twice thereafter attacked, first by the British in the same year and later by the Dutch in 1676, when the Governor was taken a prisoner to Holland. In the same year the French retook possession and remained undisturbed until 1808 In that year a combined Anglo-Portuguese naval force captured the colony, which was handed over to the Portuguese (Brazilians) Though the land was restored to France by the Treaty of Paris in 1814, the Portuguese remained in possession until 1817 Gold was discovered in 1853 and disputes arose respecting the frontiers of the colony with Dutch Guiana and Brazil and these were settled by arbitration in 1891, 1899, and 1915.

The Governor is assisted by a small Council, and there is a General Council of sixteen elected members possessing powers of local administration. The colony sends a deputy to the Legislative Assembly at Paris. The country is divided into fourteen communes, which have the right to elect their municipal councils. The Penal Settlement has its own administration.

The chief Courts sit at Cayenne.

NATURAL RESOURCES.

The **agricultural** products are few and of no great importance for export, the principal being sugar, coffee, and cacao. These are cultivated for domestic consumption, sweet potatoes, bananas, manioc, maize, and tobacco.

Various timbers, including rosewood, are derived from the forest regions, and factories exist for the production of rosewood extract, which is exported to France. Balata is collected for export, but the forests are practically unexploited.

The **gold** mines yield an annual production of about £400,000. Other minerals found include silver, copper, iron, lead, mercury, and phosphates.

Individuals and companies established under French law, may prospect for and work minerals under a State concession. A committee of official, technical, and commercial experts assists the Government in mining matters.

Customs Duties :—With certain specified exceptions, goods of foreign origin pay the same duties as in France. Most goods, whether liable to import dues or not, also pay octroi and other charges, and there are, in addition, tonnage and pilotage dues. An ad valorem duty of 8 per cent. is levied on gold exports, and a tax of 10 francs per kilogramme on declaration at Cayenne.

The **postal** rates are those of the Postal Union.

The principal towns are connected by telegraph and telephone. The Compagnie Française des Câbles Télégraphiques has lines to Paramaribo and the Antilles and to Pará. Cayenne and the Maroni are connected by telegraph, operated by the Penal Settlement, by way of Macouria, Roches, Sinnamarie, and Mana.

Telephones operate in Cayenne, St. Laurent du Maroni, and other centres. Lines connect the capital with Montjoly, Rémire, Le Rorota, and Fouillée Creek, and one links up Matoury, Stoupan, and Roura.

Outward **mails** are dispatched by various routes at frequent intervals.

Postage, 3d. first ounce, 1½d. each ounce after

Homeward mails, irregular

GUATEMALA

COMMERCIAL BANK

OF

SPANISH AMERICA, L^TD.

Affiliated to

THE ANGLO-SOUTH AMERICAN BANK, LTD.

Head Office—
9 Bishopsgate, LONDON, E.C.2.

Branches in—

NEW YORK: SAN FRANCISCO, CALIFORNIA:
49 Broadway.   465 California Street.

and in the Republics of—

COLOMBIA, NICARAGUA, PERÚ (Iquitos), ECUADOR,
VENEZUELA, SALVADOR, GUATEMALA.

EVERY KIND OF BANKING BUSINESS TRANSACTED

by our Branch in

Address.
CIUDAD DE GUATEMALA .. 7a Avenida Sur No. 8a.

GUATEMALA.

Guatemala ("Guatemala la Nueva") :—Before the destruction caused by the earthquake of 1918 the capital city was the largest and most important in Central America, finely situated on a plateau 4,880 ft. above the sea, 200 miles from Puerto Barrios on the Atlantic and 75 from San José, the principal port of the Pacific, with both places connected by rail. The population is some 91,300, and it speaks well for local enterprise, for the whole city has been rebuilt since the disaster already named. The earliest capital, now Ciudad Viejo, lies between Fuego and Agua, and was destroyed by an eruption of 1524, it has a considerable Indian population. The second of the capitals of the country, Guatemala la Antigua ("Old Guatemala"), twenty miles from the new town, had 100 churches and 60,000 inhabitants when, in 1773, it also was wrecked by earthquake. Belgian financiers have obtained (1923) a concession for establishing an electrical tramway system in Guatemala City and the distribution of electrical energy in the town and district. The company has a capital of 10,000,000 francs.

Hotels :—Palace, Grace Gran, Gran Central, Gran Royal Union, Italia Hamilton Delmonico, Continental Iberia, Paris. Rates $2–6 per day

San José, on the Pacific side, is the principal port of the country It is connected with the capital by 75 miles of narrow-gauge rail, with a daily service, and has good telegraphic communication with all parts of Central America and a submarine cable to all parts of the world. It has an iron wharf 900 ft. long by 25 ft. wide, with a depth of 35 ft. at pier-head. Here there is storage room for 8,000 sacks of coffee, capable of being shipped in twelve hours. There are facilities for receiving 600 tons of merchandise per day, and for handling weights up to 16 tons. The chief exports are coffee, rubber, hides, deer-skins, mahogany, cedar, horns, essence of lemon, and grass.

Hotels :—Marina, Solorzano.

Quezaltenango, chief town of department of the same name, is about 75 miles from Champerico and 160 miles from Guatemala. It stands at an elevation of 7,350 ft., in the centre of the coffee planting district. Industries · cotton cloth and thread. Population, 35,000. Transit is by motor from the railway at Retalhuleu.

Hotels :—Paris, Unión.

Champerico :—The Pacific port has a daily train service during the coffee season to the capital and intermediate places, and from May to November a service of three trains weekly There is an iron wharf 1,777 ft. long by 22 ft. wide (with storage room for 6,000 sacks of coffee), fitted up for handling 400 tons of cargo per day. The pier is connected with warehouses on land by two tracks of narrow-gauge railway The chief exports are coffee, rubber, hides, and mahogany; 155 miles from Guatemala City.

Ocos :—A Pacific port, is 22 miles west of Champerico and a few miles from the Mexican frontier It is connected by rail with Retalhuleu. The principal exports are coffee, hides, and rubber.

Hotel :—Bella Vista.

Livingston :—On the left bank of the Rio Dulce; is some 12 miles north-west of Puerto Barrios on the Gulf of Amatique. Its principal trade is in bananas, boat-building, and mahogany cutting; trade in indiarubber and sarsaparilla is also carried on.

Hotels :—Modelo ; Rio Dulce ($2.00); Vernons ($1.00).

Puerto Barrios :—In the large landlocked Gulf of Amatique, on the Pacific coast, is the terminus of the Guatemala Railroad. It is connected with the capital, distant about 200 miles, by a daily train service; the journey takes some twelve hours. From Puerto Barrios tourists may ascend the Rio Dulce as far as Lake Izabal and the old Spanish fort, San Felipe , it is among superb river and lake scenery Sixty miles out of Puerto Barrios is Quirigua, where are the wonderful Maya ruins, relics of a prehistoric race. There are temples, monoliths and columns covered with baffling inscriptions.

Hotels :—Italia, Del Norte.

Retalhuleu :—A town of 7,000, on the International Railway, is reached from Champerico or Mazatenango , connected by road with Quezaltenango.

Hotels :—Gran, Nuevo, Salon Club.

Coban :—85 miles north of Guatemala. Crayons are manufactured from neighbouring chalk mines. Altitude, 4,010 ft. Population, 30,770.

Hotels :—Verapaz, Victoria.

Totonicapan :—Chief town of that department, is about 65 miles north-west of Guatemala. Altitude, 7,894 ft. Manufactures native cloth and pottery.

Hotel : Central.

Zacapa has a population of 15,000.
The **Customs** houses are at Champerico, Guatemala City, Livingston, Ocós, Puerto Barrios, Retalhuleu, San José, and are classified as houses of transit, clearance, etc.

CHARACTERISTICS OF THE COUNTRY

Guatemala is the chief commercial country of Central America and has a land surface of 42,456 square miles. It stretches from Mexico and British Honduras in the north to the boundaries of Honduras and Salvador in the south, with an Atlantic seaboard of 70 miles and a Pacific coast-line of some 200 miles. About two-thirds of the country—the western and southern areas—is mountainous and volcanic. The altitude of the towns is from 1,000 to 8,000 ft. and the climate is healthy and of an even spring-like warmth. The coast lands and northern region, low-lying and tropical, are covered with dense vegetation. There are two seasons —wet, from May to October, and dry, from November to April.

Of the numerous volcanoes several are still active, although the highest, Fuego (12,075 ft.) has been extinct for 150 years. A new and active volcano, Santa Maria, burst out in 1902 and gives continual evidences of activity, it is close to Quezaltenango. Agua, which destroyed the first capital of Guatemala in 1541, has been long extinct. There are many sulphur and other hot springs.

The important rivers include the Usumacinta, which enters Campeche Bay in Mexico, and the Motagua and Polochic, which have a course of about 300 miles before flowing into the Gulf of Honduras.

The larger lakes are Izabal (36 miles in length), Petén (27 miles), Atitlán (17 miles), and Amatitlán (9 miles)

Population :—Guatemala has a population of 1,600,535 (1921 Census), of which at least 60 per cent. are Indians, speaking native dialects. The remainder are of mixed Indian and Spanish descent (ladinos), with a small proportion of pure European origin. The density of population averages 14 per sq km. (37·7 per sq mile) The religion is Roman Catholic and the language of commerce Spanish.

Currency :—The unit of currency is the paper peso with, in 1923, a value of one-sixtieth of a Guatemalan dollar Notes are issued for 500, 100, 50, 25, 20, 10, 5, 2 and 1 pesos, and there are also fractional bronze coins in reals (1 real=12½ centavos=⅛ peso) 50 cent., 1 dollar, and 5 dollar metal pesos have been issued recently

The American dollar is legal tender and universally used in foreign commerce and retail trade in imported articles in the capital. Government employees are paid in dollars. In the territory from Zacapa to Puerto Barrios only dollar currency is used. According to a decree of 1921, two American cents are legally equivalent to one Guatemalan peso, but the market rate of exchange varies daily and hourly.

Weights and Measures :—The metric system is used officially, but certain Spanish standards are current. Land is reckoned by caballerias. Cloth is sold by varas. Coffee and sugar are weighed by quintals.

```
1 league = 3 miles
1 vara = 32 in.
1 manzana of land = 100 varas square.
1 caballeria of land = 100 manzanas = 45 hectares.
1 libra (Spanish) = 16 oz. Spanish
1 arroba = 25 lb. = 25·35 lb. English.
1 quintal = 100 libras = 101·4 lb. English.
1 tonelada = 20 quintals = 18·10 cwt. English.
```

NATURAL RESOURCES.

The staple product is **coffee,** mostly a fine quality and grown on volcanic soil in a warm climate at altitudes of 2,000 to 8,000 ft. The chief coffee districts are in the highlands on the Pacific slope from Guatemala City to the Mexican border and on the Atlantic side around Coban. Most of the coffee goes to San Francisco. In 1921 the export was 938,555 quintals (101 4 lb.)

After coffee the chief product is **sugar.** The plantations are chiefly along the railway on the Pacific slope and at an altitude of 1,000 ft. About 80 per cent. of the sugar is white and goes mainly to San Francisco and New Orleans. The exports were, in 1920, 214,075 quintals, and in 1921, 145,819 quintals.

Guatemala has an effective monopoly of the **chicle** gum extensively used for chewing in North America. Large quantities of chicle are gathered in the Peten province and exported through British Honduras. In 1920, 7,877 quintals were sent to the United States market by this route.

The United Fruit Company own large **banana** plantations on the Atlantic slope near Puerto Barrios. The total production in 1920 was 2,179,943 bunches, valued at nearly one million dollars, and shipped to the United States.

The country is rich in **timber,** notably mahogany and cedar The northern provinces contain vast areas of virgin forest largely unexplored. At present no exploitation on a large scale is carried out owing to the absence of railways and road communications, except in the Peten region, which is richest. The total exported in 1920 was under 10,000,000 ft.

Other Products :—Coconuts, hides (19,928 quintals in 1920), skins, rubber, horn, honey, and beans. Rice and cotton are grown for local consumption.

That Guatemala is not more productive is due to lack of capital, shortage of labour, and the want of communications. The coastlands are very fertile. The highlands from the capital to Quezaltenango could grow maize, wheat, and other cereals more than sufficient for the population. Along the Pacific coast the wild Manaco palm gives large quantities of nuts, at present allowed to waste, from which oil could be extracted. Large areas along the Northern railway need only an irrigation scheme for development, and there are enormous tracts of uncleared lands in the north.

There is one modern brewery, as well as flour mills, furniture factories, and a cotton factory In 1915 over 12,500,000 bottles of aguardiente were distilled, value $1,500,000 (gold)

GUATEMALA.

Mineral Wealth :—There is not much mining activity, but a few small silver and lead mines are worked.

There are possibilities of oil resources, and geologically the conditions are favourable in certain districts. A Decree of 10 December, 1915, reserves ownership of mineral oil to the State, leases of oil-bearing lands being granted only to Guatemalan citizens and for a period not exceeding ten years, for this reason interested parties have been reluctant to disclose the whereabouts of supposed oil lands.

The lower cretaceous deposits of Coban in the East Verapaz district are said to be saturated with bitumen. The district of greatest interest lies in the square between Coban, Huehuetenango, Quiché and Salamá. The district north-east of Jalapa, near the Honduras border, and the Petén province towards the border of Tabasco in Mexico are reputed to be promising areas.

A GUATEMALAN CALENDAR.

1522-4. Spanish conquest of Guatemala under Pedro de Alvarado.
1541 Guatemala City destroyed by volcanic eruption.
1821 Revolts against Spanish rule, and joins the Central American Federation.
1839. Dissolution of the Central American Federation.
1840. Rafael Carrera elected President.
1846. Carrera wins a victory at La Arada over the armies of Salvador and Honduras.
1847 Guatemala declares itself an independent republic.
1851. New constitution proclaimed.
1854. Carrera appointed President for life.
1863. Guatemalan army defeated at Coatepeque by General Barrios of Salvador
   Costa Rica and Nicaragua becomes allied with Guatemala, and Honduras with Salvador
   The ultimate victory is with Carrera, who occupies Salvador.
1865. Death of Carrera ; succeeded as President by General Cerna.
1871 Cerna deposed by the Liberal Party; succeeded as President by Justo Rufino Barrios.
1872. Alliance with Honduras against Salvador.
   Expulsion of the Jesuits.
1879. Constitution promulgated.
1885. Barrios declares himself the supreme head of the five Central American States.
   A defensive Alliance made between Nicaragua, Salvador and Costa Rica.
   Barrios invades Salvador and is killed in battle.
1886. The new President, General Manuel Barillas, makes peace.
1897. Revolution in the west suppressed by the Government forces.
1898. President José Barrios assassinated.
1898-1902. Manuel E. Cabrera occupies the Presidential chair
1902. Quezaltenango and other towns destroyed by earthquake.
1903. Railway, joining up the central, southern and western departments, opened.
1917. Diplomatic relations with Germany severed.
1918. War on Germany declared.
1919. Joins the League of Nations.
1921. Joins the Central American Federation.
1922. Secedes from the Central American Federation and a Republic again proclaimed.

277

GUATEMALA.

PAST PRESIDENTS.

Rafael Carrera	..	..	1840.
General Cerna ..	..	.	1865 (deposed 1871)
Justo Rufino Barrios ..		..	1873–85.
General Manuel Barillas		..	1886.
José M. Barrios	..	..	1892 (assassinated 1898)
Manuel E. Cabrera	..	..	1898.
Carlos Herrera	..	..	1920.

PRESIDENT
General José Maria Orellana.

MINISTRY

Interior	..	..	Rodolfo Sandoval.
Foreign Affairs	..	..	Roberto Lowenthal.
Finance	..	..	Don R. Felipe Solares.
Propaganda	..	..	Rafael D. Ponciano.
War	..	..	General Francisco Fuentes.
Education ..	..	..	H. Abraham Cabrera.
Agriculture	..	..	Salvador Herrera.

GUATEMALAN LEGATION AND CONSULATES IN GREAT BRITAIN.

RESIDENCE.	DESIGNATION.	NAME.
London (11 Queen Victoria Street, E.C.4.)	Minister ..	Dr. Manuel Arroyo.
London (11 Queen Victoria Street, E.C.4.)	Consul	David Bowman.
Birmingham..	Consul	John Hotchkiss.
Cardiff	Vice-Consul ..	John Bovey
Glasgow	Consul	Patrick Smith Dunn.
	Vice-Consul ..	James Shaw Nowery.
Grimsby	Consul	Tom Sutcliffe.
Liverpool	Consul-General ..	José Azurdia.
	Vice-Consul ..	Ralph H. Baker.
Manchester	Consul	Julio Garcia Salas.
Newport (Mon.)	Consul	Samuel D. Williams.
Southampton	Consul . ..	A. C. Dunlop.

BRITISH CONSULATES.
The letter (M) denotes that the Consular Officer holds a Marriage Warrant.

RESIDENCE.	RANK.	NAME.
Guatemala	(M) Vice-Consul	Herbert Apfel.
Livingston and Port Barrios	Vice-Consul .. .	——
Quezaltenango	Consul	Hugo Fleischmann.
San José	Vice-Consul . ..	David Savage.

MAILS.

There are wireless towers, but these are not in operation at the time of going to press.

Mails are sent via United States, and homeward mails are dispatched every Thursday

An ordinance of 1923 provides that a copy of invoice, duly legalized by the Guatemala Consular Officer at the place of dispatch, must be presented in order to secure Customs clearance of goods sent to Guatemala by parcels post. A fee of 2 per cent. ad valorem will be charged for the Consular visa.

PRESS.

The principal daily papers published in Guatemala are as follows ·
Guatemala City—"La Compaña," "El Nacional," "La República."
Quezaltenango—"El Bien Publico," "El Comercio," "El Pais."
Guatemala is in the Postal Union.

The telegraphs and telephones are a State monopoly Messages in code or any other language than Spanish are charged double rates. Salvador is the cable station.

RAILWAYS.

The Guatemala, Guatemala Central, Occidental, Ocos, and Pan-American lines constitute the International Railways of Central America. They connect with Atlantic and Pacific steamers at San José, Champerico, Ocos, and Puerto Barrios, and at Ayutla, on the Mexican frontier, with the Ferrocarril Nacional de Mexico.

IMPORTS AND EXPORTS.

The following table gives statistics of exports and imports, converted from American dollars to sterling at $4.85 to the pound :—

	Exports. £	Imports. £	Total. £	Balance. £
1922	2,395,137	2,216,837	4,611,974	+ 178,300
1921	2,501,214	2,807,513	5,308,727	— 306,299
1920	3,732,557	3,782,363	7,514,920	— 49,806
1919	4,622,501	2,931,106	7,553,608	+1,691,396
1918	2,333,892	1,367,752	3,701,644	+ 966,140
1917	1,634,538	1,483,146	3,117,684	+ 151,392
1916	2,189,314	1,386,721	3,576,035	+ 802,593
1915	2,384,862	1,045,871	3,430,733	+1,338,991
1914	2,629,696	1,923,941	4,553,637	+ 705,755
1913	2,979,366	2,074,700	5,054,066	+ 904 666

Guidance for Commercial Travellers.

No special regulations exist affecting commercial travellers. No fees are payable, nor are they required to take out licences. Travellers are not subject to income tax on sales effected. Travellers are not required to produce certificates or powers of attorney, but it is better that they should have with them documents establishing their right to act, in case of eventualities. Fire-arms and ammunition and electrical apparatus are liable to seizure.

Travellers have no special privileges on the railways.

There are no special provisions in the Customs Tariff with regard to the importation of samples, which are subject to duty according to their classification in the tariff. Samples without value do not pay duty   Samples intended for re-exportation can be cleared without payment of duty provided the Customs can identify them on re-exportation. In such cases a bond is required for the value of the duties chargeable thereon, and the Customs appoint terms up to two months within which the interested party may re-export them through the same Custom House.

PUBLIC HOLIDAYS.

New Year's Day
June 30 : Reform Day
September 15 : Independence Day
October 12 : Discovery of America.
Christmas Day

The principal feast days of the Roman Catholic Church are also observed.

HONDURAS

HONDURAS.

La Ceiba, upon the Atlantic coast, is some 225 miles from Teguci-galpa and 33 from Tela. It is the terminus of a railway running through the banana country and is of considerable commercial importance. The average annual rainfall is about 120 in., and temperature ranges between 78° to 88° Fahr. Population, 7,000.

HOTELS :—Americano, Paris, Cosmopolito, Delmonico, Roma, Internacional.

Trujillo (or Truxillo), was formerly the chief trade centre on the Central American Atlantic coast. The trade has declined, but may be expected to revive with the completion of the railway Principal products, fruits, cattle, rubber, hides, mahogany, and other woods. The Trujillo Railway is to connect that port with Juticalpa and Tegucigalpa. Population, 4,000.

HOTEL :—Codin.

Puerto Cortes, 38 miles from San Pedro Sula and 207 from Tegucigalpa, stands near the mouth of the Ulua river, which affords water communication via the Rio Blanco to the Lake of Yojoa. The largest port on the Atlantic coast, and only three days' steam from New Orleans, it is the port for all the produce grown on the Puerto Cortes-Pimienta Railway line. Climate is torrid , rainfall averages 90 in. annually Population, 4,000.

HOTELS :—Italia, Lefevre, The Palms.

Amapala, is the only port of Honduras on the Pacific coast with a good anchorage. It supplies the Departments of Teguci-galpa, Paraiso, and La Paz. Population, 2,500. Vessels lie off shore and small boats are used for transfer of passengers. About 114 miles from Tegucigalpa, its principal products are cattle, cacao, hides, sugar-cane, rubber, rice, with gold and silver mines.

HOTELS :—Palacios, Morazan.

Tegucigalpa, the capital of the Republic, has a population of 35,000. It stands on the River Choluteca, 114 miles from Ama-pala and 207 miles from Puerto Cortes. The climate is sub-tropical. Chief industries : mining of gold, silver, marble, and mica ; also agriculture. Tegucigalpa is difficult to reach from the Atlantic coast. From Amapala it is approached by San Lorenzo. Roads are being constructed to the north-west through Comayagua and to the north-east to Juticalpa.

HOTELS :—Jockey Club, Agurcia, New York, Progreso.

Juticalpa is the second city in population, 17,800. It is 99 miles from Tegucigalpa, on the bank of the Guyape river, and connected with the capital and with Trujillo by cart road.

San Pedro Sula, in the fertile and extensive Sula valley, is served by the National Railway of Honduras. It is 40 miles from Puerto Cortes, and 216 from Tegucigalpa. It is the centre of the banana-growing industry, and an important distributing point for the interior of northern and western Honduras. Population, 8,000.

HOTELS :—International, Washington.

Choluteca is between Tegucigalpa and Amapala. Population, 18,000. Vanilla, coffee, sugar-cane, and cattle centre.

Comayagua, population about 10,000, stands on the river Ulua, 35 miles north-west of Tegucigalpa. The nearest railway station is La Pimienta, 124 miles distant.

HOTELS :—Colón, Comayagua.

Santa Rosa de Copán, the largest city in the northern part of the Republic is the centre of a rich mining and cattle-raising district. It is 125 miles south-west from San Pedro Sula and 249 miles from Tegucigalpa. Population, 10,000.

PHYSICAL FEATURES.

Honduras, the second largest Central American Republic, has an area of about 45,000 square miles. It has a coast line on the Atlantic Ocean of 400 miles, and on the Pacific Ocean, of 60 miles. The Republic lies between latitudes 13° and 16° north of the Equator, and longitudes 86° and 92° west. On the east it is bounded by Nicaragua, and on the west by Guatemala and El Salvador The country is mountainous, richly timbered, and it abounds in minerals, the principal of which so far developed, are silver and gold. Fertile valleys and pine-clad tablelands afford continuous panoramas of magnificent scenery Volcanoes are unknown, but slight and harmless seismic shocks are occasionally felt. The volcanic chain, which periodically causes havoc in Salvador and Guatemala, breaks off at Honduras, and is marked by volcanic islands in the Gulf of Fonseca on the Pacific coast.

Along the Atlantic (Caribbean) and Pacific coasts the **climate** is generally torrid, but modified by trade winds and heavy rainfall. At the higher altitudes the climate is temperate, pleasant and healthful. The temperature in the neighbourhood of Tegucigalpa averages about 74 degrees. On the Pacific coast the dry season begins in November and ends in May : on the Atlantic it lasts from March or April to early November.

Road and Rail :—An interoceanic road between the Atlantic and Pacific is under construction. A survey has been made with the object of extending the national railway from Potrerillos to the northern shores of Lake Yojoa, connecting with a launch service on the lake, and with an automobile service from the southern end of the lake via Comayagua to Tegucigalpa and Amapala.

The fruit companies on the north coast have extended their railway systems in opening up new banana plantations.

Honduras suffers from the lack of roads. There are good roads from San Lorenzo to Tegucigalpa (130 kilometres), and from the capital to Comayagua (102 kilometres) The latter road is to be continued to the railway terminus at Potrerillos. The Honduras Petroleum has made a road from Siguatepeque, via Taulabé to Pito Solo on the southern shores of Lake Yojoa, so that there only remains to be constructed a road from Comayagua to Siguatepeque on the south, and from Lake Yojoa to Potrerillos on the north, to complete direct communication between the north and south coasts. A road is under construction from the capital to Juticalpa.

POPULATION AND COINAGE.

The **population** (1920) was estimated at 637,114, of which 314,528 were males and 322,846 females. The distribution is shown below :—

DEPARTMENT.				CAPITAL AND POPULATION
Tegucigalpa	.	.	.	Tegucigalpa (35,000).
Choluteca	..			Choluteca (18,000)
Copán	..	..	..	Santa Rosa (10,000)
Gracias		.	.	Gracias (6,000)
Olancho		..	.	Juticalpa (17,800)
Santa Barbara	.			Santa Barbara (6,000).
El Paraiso		..	.	Yuscaran (5,000)
Cortes	.	.	..	San Pedro Sula (8,000).
Intibuca	.	..	.	La Esperanza (2,150)
Comayagua	..	..	.	Comayagua (10,000).
Ocotepeque	..	..	..	Ocotepeque (7,500).
Valle	.	..	..	Nacaome (1,500).
Atlantida	.		.	La Ceiba (7,000).
Colón	..	.	..	Trujillo (4,000)
Yoro	.	.	..	Yoro (4,800)
Islas de la Bahia		..	..	Roatan (2,000).

The **language** in general use is Spanish. English is freely spoken on the north coast.

The Roman Catholic is the prevailing **religion,** but the State guarantees freedom to all creeds and contributes to the support of none.

The **metric** system is the legal standard, but merchants import goods by the pound and yard. Spanish equivalents are in common use, for example :—

  1 League = 3 miles = 4¾ kilometres.
  1 Vara = 32 inches = 83·59 centimes.
  1 Manzana = 100 Varas square (land measure)
  1 Caballeria = 100 Manzanas.
  1 Lb. (libra) = 16 oz.
  1 Arroba = 25 lb.
  1 Quintal = 100 lb.

The nominal **currency** is silver, consisting of the silver peso, with fractional coins of 50, 25, 12½, 10 and 5 cents pieces, and 2 cents and 1 cent copper. On account of heavy clandestine shipments of silver, silver currency has been replaced almost entirely by American paper money. By decree of September 12, 1919, a fixed rate of exchange of 2 to 1 was made, i.e., 2 Honduras pesos equals 1 American dollar Local Bank notes pass at the same rate of exchange, viz. : a five peso Bill equals $2.50 U.S.A. currency

A HONDURANEAN CALENDAR.

1498. Americo Vespucci explores the Honduranean coast.
1502. Columbus lands at Cape Honduras and annexes the country on behalf of Spain.
1524. Cristóbal de Olid sent by Cortés to exploit the colony, establishes himself as an independent ruler.
1525. Cortés reaches Honduras and displaces Cristóbal de Olid.
1539. Honduras included in the Captaincy-General of Guatemala.
1821. Honduras declares its independence. Joins the Central American Federation.
1839. Dissolution of the Central American Federation.
1859. Great Britain cedes the Bay Islands to Honduras.
1871. War with Guatemala.
1894. War with Nicaragua.
1897. Joins the "Greater Republic" of Central America, of which Costa Rica, Nicaragua, and Salvador are members.
1907 Honduras and Salvador at war with Nicaragua.
1919. Joins the League of Nations.
1921. Joins the Central American Federation.

GOVERNMENT.

The Republic declared its independence on September 15, 1821. The **Legislature** consists of a single Chamber, the Congress, composed of 42 Deputies elected in the ratio of one per 10,000 inhabitants, for four years. Congress assembles annually on January 1st, and the Sessions last for 60 days. The executive Authority rests with a President, elected also for four years, assisted by a Cabinet of six Ministers representing the Departments of Foreign Affairs, Government and Justice, War and Marine, Finance, Public Works and Agriculture, and Public Instruction. For administrative purposes the country is divided into 17 Departments which are sub-divided into 62 Districts.

There is a Supreme Court with five judges chosen directly by popular vote for four years. There are also four Appeal Courts and departmental and local judges.

HONDURAS.

PAST PRESIDENTS.

General J. M. Medina (first term)	1864
(second term)	1869
C. Arias	1872
Marco Aurelio Soto (first term)	1874
P. Leiva	1875
M. A. Soto (second term)	1877
(third term)	1880
General Luis Bogran (first term)	1883
(second term)	1887
General Pariano Leista	1891
General Vasquez	1893
General Sierra	1899
General Manuel Bonilla (first term)	1903
General Miguel R. Dávila	1907
General Manuel Bonilla (second term) (died 1913)	1911
Dr. Francisco Bertrand (first term)	1913
(second term)	1916

PRESIDENT AND VICE-PRESIDENT.

President .. .. General Rafael López Gutierrez.
Vice-President .. .. .. José Maria Ochoa Velasquez.

MINISTRY.

Foreign Affairs .. .. .. Romuld E. Duron.
Justice .. .. J M. Guillen Velez.
War .. .. General Salvador Cisneros.
Treasury and Public Credit .. Trinidad E. Rivera.
Public Works and Agriculture .. Marcial Logos.
Instruction .. .. .. Federico C. Canales.

NATURAL RESOURCES.

The principal source of wealth is the banana in which there is a large export trade with the United States. The coco-nut is of growing importance. Large tracts of cheap land are available on the Atlantic coast for planting. The country abounds in vegetable oils, the chief being that extracted from the corozo nut. The mountain slopes produce good sugar-cane, coffee, maize, and tobacco. The uncultivated lands are covered with fine timber, such as mahogany, pine, cedar, oak, and ebony , as grazing lands they are unrivalled. The country is well watered and excellent for cattle raising. Sarsaparilla, hides, and rubber are also produced. Among local industries may be mentioned straw hats, cigars, soap, shoes, ice, soda water, and aguardiente.

Although rich in minerals, the greater part of the country remains unexploited. The most important mining concern is the New York and Honduras Rosario Mining Company, Inc., which has been producing gold and silver for many years. The minerals include silver zinc, copper, iron, lignite and coal.

MAHOGANY IN HONDURAS.

The mahogany tree growing in splendid isolation, rears its branches crown-like above the surrounding growth. The trees are cut in the rainy season. A man climbs to the highest limbs that will afford him a view of the forest. He marks down the mahogany by its conspicuous yellow-reddish leaves, then descends and leads the cutters through the jungle, hacking a road till the tree is found. Saws and axes are plied, always at the time of the waning moon, for experience has shown that the mahogany tree is then freer from sap, sounder, and of a richer colour, as the cool of the night offers the best time for the work, the wisdom of the custom is apparent.

True mahogany is the familiar dark-coloured hardwood largely used for household furniture and supplied by a tree native in Mexico, Central America, Panamá, Colombia, Venezuela, and the Islands of the Caribbean Sea. In botany it is known as *Swietenia mahogani*, a designation combining an honour to Baron Van Swieten (court physician to Maria Theresa, Empress of Germany and mother of Marie Antoinette) with the original native name. The mahogany bears imparipinate leaves similar to those of the ash. It sometimes grows to the height of 100 ft., with a diameter of 12 ft. Frequently trees are found that five men joining hands cannot circle. Its period of growth covers perhaps 200 years.

The wood is noted for hardness, durability, beautiful colour, and grain, and in these qualities lies the value of the hewn trunk. There are two main differences in grain pattern, the close-grained mahogany, the best of which comes from Cuba and Jamaica, and the wide-grained, also known as baywood, the mahogany of Honduras. The ease with which mahogany can be veneered makes for its extended use, and modern machinery can cut a mahogany board 1 in. thick into 200 sheets. Much of Honduras formerly growing the precious trees has been deforested, but the principles of conservation have spread to all the Republics. In Honduras are thousands of acres where mahogany grows in primal isolation.

Mails for the capital and southern districts are brought from Puerto Cortes by rail to Potrerillos, and thence by mule to Tegucigalpa.

Letter post from London to Tegucigalpa, via New York and New Orleans, takes 25 to 30 days , newspaper and parcel post, via France and the Panamá Canal, takes three to four months to the capital. Parcels from the United States for Tegucigalpa arrive via the Panamá Canal.

Telegrams are $7\frac{1}{2}$ cents gold for five words, address and signature free, for any part of the Republic, or of Central America.

The principal **newspapers** are published at Tegucigalpa : "El Cronista," "El Nuevo Tiempo," and "La Patria," "El Renacimiento" is a monthly review issued at Amapala.

HONDURAS.

BRITISH LEGATION AND CONSULATES IN HONDURAS.

The letter (M) denotes that the Consular Officer holds a Marriage Warrant.
Members of the Diplomatic Service do not require Warrants.

RESIDENCE.	RANK.	NAME.	CONSULAR DISTRICT.
(See GUATE-MALA).	Envoy Extraordin-ary, Minister Ple-nipotentiary, and Consul-General.	—	
Tegucigalpa	(M) Consul Vice-Consul	G. Lyall J. Walter	Republic of Honduras.
Amapala	Vice-Consul	P. Casanova	—
Omoa and Puerto Cortes	Consul	John Hepburn (acting)	Omoa and Puerto Cortes.
Trujillo	Consul	Alfred Edward Melhado	Trujillo and the Bay Islands.
	Pro-Consul	Albury H. Tatem	

PUBLIC HOLIDAYS.

January 1 : New Year's Day
July 14 : Fall of the Bastille.
September 15 : Independence Day
October 12 : Discovery of America.
Many of the feast days of the Roman Catholic religion are observed.

CONSULATES IN GREAT BRITAIN.

RESIDENCE.	RANK.	NAME.
London (4 Lloyd's Avenue, E.C.3.)	Consul-General	Arthur Breen Ryde.
Birmingham	Consul	Philip Cohen.
Cardiff	Consul	Alfred John Bovey
Grimsby	Consul	Jack Sutcliffe.
Liverpool Manchester	Consul-General	Antonio Rosa.
Newcastle-on-Tyne	Consul	William Dodds.
Glasgow	Consul	Archibald Craig.

IMPORTS AND EXPORTS.

In the following table the values have been calculated at the rate of exchange of $2 silver for $1 gold in 1918-19 and 1919-20 , $2.50 silver for $1 gold in the other years, the sterling value being reckoned at 6s. to one dollar gold 1913-14 and at 5s. to the gold dollar since :—

Year.	Exports. £	Imports. £	Total. £	Adverse Balance. £
1912-13	954,290	1,539,803	2,494,093	585,513
1913-14	1,026,399	1,987,479	3,013,878	961,080
1914-15	1,037,354	1,752,439	2,789,793	715,085
1915-16	1,257,169	1,335,632	2,592,801	78,463
1916-17	1,606,035	1,887,948	3,493,983	281,913
1917-18	1,376,079	1,435,334	2,811,413	59,255
1918-19	1,799,322	2,079,412	3,878,734	280,090
1919-20	2,083,418	3,858,228	5,941,646	1,774,815
1920-21	1,357,147	4,180,675	5,537,822	2,823,528
1921-22	1,346,601	3,201,065	4,547,666	1,854,464

HONDURAS.

Guidance for Commercial Travellers.

Commercial travellers are not required to take out licences. No fees are collected. Travellers are not required by law to produce certificates or powers of attorney authorising them to act for the firms they represent.

The municipal tax for Commercial travellers in the city of Tegucigalpa has been increased to 50 pesos, valid for one year

Samples without value, when of a weight not exceeding 25 lb. are subject to duty of 0·01 pesos per ½ kilo (gross weight)

In entering samples of value the commercial traveller or his agent must present an examination permit for his samples in quadruplicate, costing $2.50. The Customs give the traveller one copy of the receipt accompanied by a transit permit for the re-embarkation of the goods. This can take place through any Custom House. Deposit may be required of the amount of duty.

MEXICO

MEXICO.

Mexico City, capital of the Republic and of the Federal District, with a population of about 500,000 for the city and over 700,000 for the district, stands at an altitude of 7,400 ft. on a small plain in an agricultural and manufacturing district near Lake Texcoco. It is the commercial centre of the country   Most of the city stands on ground reclaimed from swamps and lakes, and has been inundated more than once.   Except for a few days in midwinter the climate is agreeable, and the average temperature is 60° Fahr

The city is reached by train from El Paso, upon the United States frontier, in 48 hours (Mexican Central Railway), or via Eagle Pass (Mexican International Railway), or from the port of Vera Cruz by Mexican or Interoceanic Railway

In the more important districts the streets are forty to fifty feet wide, the Avenida Cinco de Mayo being the widest.   Other chief streets are the Avenida de San Francisco, Plaza de la Constitución, and Avenida 16 de Setiembre.   On the north of the Plaza stands the cathedral, the finest church in Mexico, dating from 1573, which possesses a fine Murillo, on the east is the National Museum, in the old National Palace, and on the south the Municipal Palace and the Flower Market.   There is a good collection in the National Picture Gallery of San Carlos, behind the National Palace.   In the centre of the city is the Alameda, a large park, with the National Theatre on its east side.   The Mexican Country Club is housed in a large building near Churubusco, south of the city

HOTELS :—Iturbide, Lascurain, Isabel, St. Frances, Porter, Alameda, Regis.

Conveyances :—Electric tramways, motors.

Suburbs :—

COYOACAN, the oldest, contains the old Cortes Palace, and lies about eight miles south of Plaza.

GUADALUPE-HIDALGO, 2½ miles north-east, contains a large church with a miraculous portrait of the Virgin, the most popular shrine in the Republic, visited by enormous numbers of Indians.

MIXCOAC, nine miles south-west, with large nursery gardens and brickworks.

SAN ANGEL, nine miles south-west of Plaza, a fruit-growing centre, on the southern slope of the mountains.

TACUBAYA, seven miles south-west, is one of the most populous and fashionable suburbs, with large country houses and the National Astronomical Observatory

TLALPAN, eleven miles south of Plaza, the farthest out and most picturesque of all, with a modern municipal palace and various factories.

Vera Cruz, the chief port of Mexico, and some 264 miles from Mexico City is on a low alluvial plain bordering the Gulf coast. It has a splendid breakwater built by the English firm of Pearson who also effected the sanitation, paving and water supply of the city. Population about 40,000. The town has been modernized but retains many picturesque and old-fashioned buildings. It is a gay and pleasing town and healthy despite its warm climate. It has a large trade with the interior, and has numerous wholesale houses of importance.

Landing :—Custom-house wharf, alongside.

HOTELS :—Diligencia, Universal, Mexico, Colón, Jardin Astoria, Buena Vista, Oriente.

Rail :—To Mexico City, Tehuantepec and Puerto Mexico (Coatzacoalcos), Acapulco, Alvarado, for steamers to points on Papaloapam River.

Coatzacoalcos (Puerto Mexico), with a harbour built by the Mexican Government, is in Vera Cruz State, and is 188 miles from Salina Cruz. An eastern terminus of the Tehuantepec National Railway, it has a considerable body of trade, notably in hides, coffee, sugar, rubber, and dyewoods. The climate is hot and not healthy

Landing :—Steamer to wharf.

HOTELS :—Colón, Two Republics, California.

Acapulco, on the Pacific and 320 nautical miles from Manzanillo, has a population of 7,000 and a trade in fruits, vegetables, cereals, tobacco, and cotton. It is a place of call for San Francisco steamers. Vessels anchor offshore.

Mazatlan, with a population of 30,000 inhabitants, is the chief industrial and commercial port on the Pacific Coast of Mexico. It stands at the mouth of the Gulf of California, and has a large export and import trade and a number of wholesale merchant houses.

HOTELS :—Central, Francia, Felton, Mexico.

Tampico, population 20,000, is on the Gulf of Mexico and six miles from the mouth of the Panuco River It is 600 miles from Mexico City and is the terminus of two branches of the National Railways. Important as an oil port it is second only to Vera Cruz in general importance. The atmosphere is hot and damp.

Landing :—To wharf.

HOTELS :—Imperial, Southern, Palacio, Bristol, Continental.

Local Steamers :—Weekly up Panuco River

Tehuantepec, on the river of the same name, is a port of Salina Cruz, upon the Pacific side of the narrow isthmus (13 miles distant), and situated in a rich agricultural district. The word Tehuantepec signifies in the Aztec tongue " Mountain of the Man Eaters," and was given because the hills in rear of the town were infested with man-eating beasts.

The population consists largely of Indians of the Zapotecan tribe, descendants of the Aztecs, who have retained the language, dress, and customs of their progenitors. They are healthy and hardy, and the native women are well formed, and fine-looking people, some are strikingly handsome, and their physique is fully revealed by the costumes worn by the Zapotecan Indians. A few hours may be well spent in the markets, the old mission church, and in watching the laundresses in the river

Guadalajara, capital of State of Jalisco, stands at an altitude of 6,100 ft., 381 miles from Mexico City, 223 from Manzanillo. Population 140,000. One of the finest and cleanest of Mexican towns, regularly built, resembling the towns of southern Spain. The chief shops are in or near the Plaza Mayor and the Calle de San Francisco. The Plaza Mayor, sometimes called de la Constitución or de Armas, is flanked by the Government palace and the cathedral, which contains Murillo's picture of the Assumption. Guadalajara is a rich agricultural and manufacturing centre : the chief industries are breweries, textile and flour mills, foundries, and hosiery works.

HOTELS :—Fenix, Frances, Roma, Cosmopolita, Garcia.

Rail :—To Manzanillo via Colima extension ; Mexico City (National Railways)

Excursion :—Lake Chapala, the largest lake in Mexico, is seventy miles long and fifteen to twenty miles wide. The principal village is Chapala, where there are some hot springs, and a good hotel. Ribera on the lake shore, reached via Ocotlán, and three miles distant, has an hotel. These resorts are convenient to Guadalajara. A trip around Lake Chapala makes a charming excursion. There is water-fowl shooting during the autumn and winter, and there are sailing and bathing all the year. The climate is really semi-tropical.

León is a large town (population 64,000) in the State of Guanajuato, 259 miles from Mexico City, situated in a fertile valley of the Gomez river. There are many shaded plazas and gardens, and the streets are well-kept. The chief streets are Real, de Guanajuato, los Pachecos, and de la Condeza, with the business centre in the Plaza de la Constitución. There is a striking municipal palace, a cathedral with two towers and a dome, a theatre, and a hospital. The chief manufactures are of leather goods, spurs, hats, shawls, and pottery, and there are cotton and wool mills.

HOTELS :—Guerra, Hidalgo, Mexico, Colón.

Rail :—Mexican Central.

Mérida, capital of State of Yucatan, 770 miles east of Mexico City, stands in a very flat agricultural country, almost entirely devoted to the production of henequen. Population, 62,000.

Massively built after the Spanish fashion, the town is healthy, clean, and well-paved. Calle 65 is the chief street for shops. Among the buildings are a beautiful cathedral, bishop's palace, Government palace, model penitentiary, a large hospital, and theatre. Besides the henequen and sisal industry, there are soap, chocolate, and hemp factories.

HOTELS :—Alameda, Francia, Gran, Bazar, Paris.

Rail :—United Railways of Yucatan, four lines and four stations

Salina Cruz :—Important as a port of entry and Pacific terminus of the Tehuantepec National Railway, population 6,000.

Landing :—Steamer to wharf.

HOTELS :—Salina Cruz, Terminal.

Campeche, on the western coast of Yucatan in south-eastern Mexico, has a population of 20,000. It is 820 miles from Mexico City and 576 from Vera Cruz. Logwood, sisal, hides, and produce are its chief exports. New York steamers call.

HOTELS :—Betancourt, Marforte, Campechano.

Local Steamers :—To Vera Cruz.

Chihuahua, capital of State of same name in northern Mexico, 1,000 miles from Mexico City, stands on a level site on east bank of Chubiscar river With a population of about 40,000, it possesses a number of good buildings, including the municipal and Government palaces and a cathedral. The chief business centres are the Plaza de la Constitución and the Aldama, de la Libertad, and de la Victoria streets. It is a distributing centre for a large mining, agricultural, and cattle-raising district, and has a corn mill, cotton mills, and brewery in the Avenida Juaréz also railway shops, hat and candle factories. The climate is excellent.

HOTELS :—Ahuamada, Francia, Vidal, Colón, Palacio.

Rail :—Mexico North-Western (to Juaréz), Mexican Central (to Mexico City), by Kansas City, Mexico and Orient; and Ferrocarril Mineral de Chihuahua (to Santa Eulalia).

Puebla, capital of State of Puebla, population 110,000, altitude 7,200 ft. on the Sierra Madre foothills, in an important agricultural and manufacturing district. The city is the third in size in Mexico, and the seat of an archbishop. It is well built, clean and healthy, and the streets are paved with asphalt. There are over 60 churches, and the cathedral contains fine pictures and marqueterie. The architecture is largely Andalusian, with considerable use of coloured Moorish tiles. Puebla was the first city to manufacture the celebrated Talavera ware. The chief industry is cotton-spinning, among local manufactures are included brandy, chocolate, cigar, hat, clothes, match, glass and shoe factories, flour mills and sugar factories, and breweries. The chief products are beans, maize, sugar and fruits. Electric trams run to all parts of the city and suburbs.

HOTELS :—Español, American, Barcelona, Pasaje, Francia, Inglés.

Rail :—Interoceanic Railway (158 miles from Mexico City); Mexican Southern, Mexican.

Monterey, capital of State of Nuevo León, has a population of 85,000 and lies in a fertile valley of the Santa Catarina river One of the most important and progressive towns in North Mexico, it dates from the earliest Spanish times. The majority of the buildings are massively built. It is the seat of a bishop. The Government palace stands in Plaza Cinco de Mayo and the cathedral in the Plaza de Zaragoza. The town has iron and steel works, brewery, flour and cotton mills, soap and tobacco factories, mineral-water works, and cement works. Monterey is sometimes called the Chicago of Mexico. The Topo Chico hot springs, a favourite bathing resort, lie four miles north-west of the town, and the suburban town of Bella Vista stands a little farther to the north.

HOTELS :—Iturbide, Independencia, Continental, Aurora, Gulf, Bridges, Monterey, Windsor

Rail :—National Railway to Tampico (322 miles) and Mexico City

San Luis Potosí, capital of State of same name, stands 327 miles north of Mexico City, altitude 6,100 ft., climate temperate. Silver, gold, and lead mines are near by The chief shops are in Calle Hidalgo, there is a fine cathedral, a theatre, a Government palace, and two markets. The chief industries are tanning, flour mills, mining, smelting, match, candle, wool, and sweetmeat factories.

HOTELS :—Internacional, Progreso, Sauz, Comercio, Jardin.

Rail :—National Railway to Mexico City and Tampico; Mexican Central to Aguascalientes, Potosí and Rio Verde Railway to Aguacatal.

Aguascalientes, capital of State of same name, 364 miles north-west of Mexico City, has a population of 56,000 and stands at an altitude of 6,280 ft. on the left bank of the Aguascalientes river among volcanic hills. As the name of the town would indicate, there are hot springs in the vicinity. The climate is very mild and the death-rate low Wool and cotton mills, tobacco factories, potteries, brewing and distilling.

HOTELS :—Washington, Francia, Paris, Moore, Bellini.
Rail :—Central Railway, four hours to Mexico City, 19 hours to Tampico by branch line, via San Luis Potosí.

PHYSICAL FEATURES.

The area of Mexico, 767,168 square miles, is almost equal to that of Great Britain, Ireland, France, Germany, and Austria combined. The Republic is between Guatemala and the United States, it extends for an extreme length of nearly 2,000 miles, and of a breadth from 1,000 to 130 miles. The coast-line is 6,000 miles. The greater part of the country is a tableland, commencing in Colorado in the United States. Its elevation is 3,700 ft. at El Paso on the northern frontier, but over 8,000 ft. at Marquez, 76 miles from Mexico City. The greatest range is the Sierra Madre Occidental on the west, rising to over 10,000 ft., and extending from Tehuantepec to the United States, while parallel run the Sierra Madre Oriental on the east and the mountains of Lower California. Among the highest peaks are the Nevado de Toluca (14,950 ft.), the Pico de Orizaba (18,250 ft.) and Popocatepetl (14,950 ft.). In this elevated region the climate is almost that of spring, and most of the volcanoes are extinct, though Colima was in eruption in 1909, when the towns of Acapulco and Chilpancingo were destroyed.

The lowland regions between the sierras and coast are sandy along the seashore, with a higher and fertile belt of land rising to 3,000 ft. The Mexican coast has no large islands, but there are several off Lower California and in the Gulf of California.

The largest rivers are the Rio Grande de Santiago, which flows to the Pacific, with a total length of 540 miles, the Rio de las Balsas, which also enters the Pacific, after a course of 426 miles, the Yaqui (390 miles), which joins the Gulf of California, the Grijalva (350 miles), which enters the Gulf of Mexico, the Fuerte (340 miles), the Usumacinta (330 miles), and the Pánuco, also flowing to the Gulf of Mexico. The lakes, few and small, consist of those of the plateau region and the coastal lagoons. In the Valley of Mexico are the Lakes Chalco, Texcoco, Zumpango, and San Cristóbal, of which Texcoco has an area of 11½ square miles. In south-western Coahuila a group of lakes or lagoons occupy a large, isolated drainage-basin.

Acapulco is by far the best of the harbours. There are no bays of importance along the south-west part of the Gulf of Mexico or Gulf of Campeche, and only one natural harbour, that of Carmen. Vera Cruz is an open anchorage with a breakwater. On the east coast of Yucatan are the large and deep bays of Asunción and Espiritu Santo. The Gulfs of Tehuantepec and of California present two large indentations in the coast-line, the latter penetrating the continent for 740 miles. The bays of the mainland— Olas Atlas (the port for Mazatlán), San Blas and Tonalá—are being improved.

There is a great range of **climate.** Although a large portion of the country is in the torrid zone, much of this is temperate, owing to the altitude. From Tampico southwards, at or slightly above sea-level, the climate is generally tropical . north of this point, at about the same elevation, it is semi-tropical, as also southward at elevations of from 1,000 to 6,000 ft. In the centre of the country, extending from Mexico City to the northern border, is a central plateau with an altitude of 3,500 ft. in the north, and 7,000 ft. in the south, with a temperate climate. The air is dry and bracing, and especially good for bronchial, pulmonary, and rheumatic troubles. The air is remarkably free from moisture on the plateau, which has four seasons in the north, and a wet and a dry season south of about 28° N. The rainfall varies by districts from 8 to 40 in. Mexico as a whole has a very even climate.

CLIMATIC TABLES.

Average monthly temperature (Fahrenheit) :—

	January	February	March	April	May	June	July	August	September	October	November	December	Elevation Above Sea-level
Mexico .	53.8	56.7	60.4	64.0	64.6	63.7	62.4	61.9	62.1	58.5	55.6	53.4	7,349 feet
San Juan del Rio	59.2	61.5	65.5	70.5	71.2	70.5	66.9	67.5	65.7	64.8	58.5	56.8	6,245
Queretaro ..	60.1	61.5	65.3	71.1	72.3	70.9	67.5	68.9	64.2	63.0	59.5	56.7	5,975
Silao	59.2	61.2	63.3	70.2	74.7	74.3	69.4	69.6	68.9	64.8	59.7	57.7	5,828
Guanajuato	56.8	62.4	61.7	69.3	71.1	71.1	68.2	66.0	63.3	62.2	62.1	57.9	6,583
León . . .	58.3	61.2	63.1	70.9	74.3	74.8	68.7	68.9	67.6	63.7	58.3	56.8	5,859
Aguascalientes .	55.0	61.2	60.3	68.5	73.9	74.4	71.4	69.4	68.9	64.0	61.5	55.9	6,181
San Luis Potosi .	57.0	59.7	63.3	68.9	71.8	71.6	68.2	68.5	67.8	62.2	56.8	54.3	6,123
Pachuca	54.5	58.6	60.1	61.3	61.0	61.9	66.9	61.3	62.2	59.5	53.2	54.1	7,828
Zacatecas	54.5	56.1	58.6	66.0	70.0	68.4	62.1	62.8	62.2	60.6	55.4	55.6	8,012
Guadalajara ..	59.5	62.6	69.8	70.9	73.6	73.6	73.4	69.8	69.8	66.4	62.8	60.4	5,053
Lagos	60.6	61.0	62.4	63.9	69.3	68.7	69.8	68.7	66.4	60.6	59.4		6,134
Tampico	..	....	..	75.0	77.7	82.4	81.1	81.5	80.1	77.4	69.1	71.2	Sea-level, Gulf Port

Public Health :—Of the two coastal areas, the Pacific is more healthy than the Gulf. Much of the central plateau is healthy, but in the low, hot lands tropical diseases are prevalent. Generally, the medical profession is efficient.

Malaria is perhaps the commonest ailment, appearing in various mild forms. Mosquitoes have unlimited breeding grounds in the lagoons and marshes of the coast, and most foreigners experience mild fever Yellow fever was formerly a scourge on the Gulf Coast, and appeared also at Salina Cruz and elsewhere. The late President Diaz set up a Board of Health which dealt successfully with this and other epidemic diseases. Small-pox, typhus, and tuberculosis have increased with the relaxation of precautionary measures.

Of the total **population** of some 16 million, the whites amount to about 20 per cent., the Indians to 38 per cent., the residue are mestizos.

States :					Population (estimated, 1921).	Capital.
Aguascalientes	..	..	..	..	125,000	Aguascalientes.
Campeche	..	.	..	..	90,000	Campeche.
Chiapas	..	..	.	..	..	560,000	Tuxtla Gutiérrez.
Chihuahua	..	..	..	..	500,000	Chihuahua.
Coahuila	..	..	..	..	400,000	Saltiollo.
Colima	..	..	..	.	80,000	Colima.
Durango	..	..	..	..	500,000	Durango.
Guanajuato	.	..	..	..	1,100,000	Guanajuato.
Guerrero	..	..	..	..	750,000	Chilpancingo.
Hidalgo	..	..	..	..	750,000	Pachuca.
Jalisco	..	..	..	..	1,280,000	Guadalajara.
Mexico	..	..	..	..	1,100,000	Toluca.
Michoacán	..	..	..	..	1,050,000	Morelia.
Morelos	..	..	..	..	210,000	Cuernavaca.
Nayarit	..	.	.	.	200,000	Tepic.
Nuevo León	..	.	..	..	420,000	Monterey.
Oaxaca	..	..	..	..	1,100,000	Oaxaca.
Puebla	..	.	..	..	1,100,000	Puebla.
Querétaro	.	..	.		260,000	Querétaro.
San Luis Potosí	..	..	..	..	700,000	San Luis Potosí.
Sinaloa	..	.	.		400,000	Culiacan.
Sonora	..	.			350,000	Hermosillo.
Tabasco			.		210,000	Villa Hermosa.
Tamaulipas	.		..		400,000	Ciudad Victoria.
Tlaxcala	.				210,000	Tlaxcala.
Vera Cruz	..	.			1,400,000	Córdoba.
Yucatan	..	.			390,000	Merida.
Zacatécas	..	.	.		500,000	Zacatécas.
Territories :						
Lower California		.	.		60,000	La Paz.
Quintana Roo	..	.	.	.	10,000	Santa Cruz de Bravo.
Federal District	.	.	..	..	800,000	Mexico City.

The residents include about 20,000 persons of foreign birth : 12,000 Spaniards, 3,000 North Americans, 2,700 French, 1,300 Syrians, and 1,200 Germans.

Constitution :—On February 5, 1917, a new Constitution of Mexico was promulgated, superseding that of 1857 Mexico was proclaimed a Federal Republic, the States having the right to manage their local affairs. The powers of the Supreme Government are divided into the legislative branch, the executive, and the judicial. Congress, the legislative branch, consists of a House of Representatives and a Senate. Representatives are elected for a term of two years. There is universal suffrage, and one member for 60,000 inhabitants. The Senate consists of fifty-eight members, two for each State, elected in the same manner as the deputies. The President, holding the executive power, is elected by direct vote for a four years' term.

PAST CHIEFS OF STATE.

General Agustin Iturbide		..		..	.	.	..	1821
Crowned Emperor ; abdicated		..		..	..	.	1822
Vicente Guerrero	..	..		..	..	..	1831
General Antonio Lopez de Santa Anna			..		..	1833
General Anastacio Bustamente		..		..	..	.	1837
General José [Herrera	..		.		..	..	.	1848

General Mariano Arista	.		.		.	1851
General Antonio Lopez de Santa Anna (second term)				..		1851
Benito Juaréz	.	.	.	..	..	.. 1858
Archduke Maximilian (crowned Emperor)		.	..	..		.. 1864
Benito Juaréz (second term)	..	.	..	..		.. 1867
Sebastian Lerdo de Tejada	.	..	.	..		.. 1872
General Porfirio Diaz	..	.	..	.	..	... 1877
Manuel González	..	..	..	..	..	.. 1880
General Porfirio Diaz (second term)			.	..		.. 1884
Francisco de la Barra	.	.	..	.	..	.. 1911
Francisco I. Madero	..	.	..	..	..	.. 1911
Pedro Lascurain	..	..	..	.	..	.. 1913
General Victoriano Huerta	.	.	.	.		. 1913
Venustiano Carranza	.	..	..	..	..	.. 1915
Adolfo de la Huerta	..	.	..	..	..	.. 1920

PRESIDENT.
General Alvaro Obregon (Dec. 1, 1920)

MINISTRY.

Foreign Affairs .	.	..	Ing. Alberto Pani.
Interior ..	..	..	Gen. Plutarco Elias Calles.
Public Education	.		Lic. José Vasconcelos.
Finance and Public Credit	..		Adolfo de la Huerta.
War and Marine .	..	..	Gen. Francisco Serrano.
Communications .	..	.. ⎱	Ing. Amado. Aguirre.
Public Works ..	.	.. ⎰	

NATIONAL REVENUE AND EXPENDITURE.

Revenue.

						1922.
Foreign Commerce	.	.		.	..	$101,190,358.06
Internal Commerce	.		.		..	139,431,955.89
Public Services	..	.	.	.	..	15,720,628.24
National Properties	.	.	..		..	1,258,668.02
Sundry Sources	.	.	..		.	19,965,408.02
						$277,567,019.15

Disbursements.

Legislative	.	.	..	.	.	$5,820,858.88
Executive	..	.		..	.	6,201,924.46
Judicial..				.	..	2,448,579.97
Secretary of Gobernación (Interior)				.	..	. 4,598,205.85
Department of Health	..	..		.	..	. 3,492,518.06
Secretary, Foreign Relations		..	..		..	. 6,036,293.23
Secretary of Hacienda (Finance)	.			..	..	39,628,900.34
Department of Control of Finances			..		..	4,097,409.90
Secretary of War and Marine	.		..		..	111,021,291.48
Department of State Factories		..			.	12,917,432.78
Secretary, Agriculture and Development..					.	13,147,457.83
Secretary, Industry Commerce and Labour			.		.	4,658,734.83
Secretary, Communications and Public Works		..				29,855,462.79
Secretary, Public Instruction	.			.		21,558,953.17
Attorney-General's Office				..	.	1,203,409.54
Department of General Supplies	.		..		.	350,030.74
						$267,137,468.85

IMPORTS AND EXPORTS.

Imports.					1922.
Animal Matter and Materials	..	..	..	..	$41,138,533.13
Vegetable Matter and Materials	..	..	..	..	45,911,554.22
Minerals	..	..	..	..	56,408,829.43
Woven Goods and Manufactures of Same		..	..	40,028,612.19
Chemical and Pharmaceutical Products	..		..	..	21,493,330.08
Drinks, Spirituous and Others	..	..	..	..	5,117,114.75
Pulp, Paper, Manufactures and Appliances		.	.	11,039,987.65
Machinery and Apparatus	..	..	..	..	34,979,651.63
Vehicles	.	..	..	.	.	19,038,226.77
Arms and Explosives	..	.	..	.	..	5,527,081.16
Sundries	..	..	..	.	..	23,125,448.65
				TOTAL	$303,808,369.66

Exports.					
Animal Matter and Materials	..	..	..	..	$4,307,548.47
Vegetable Matter and Materials	..	..	..	..	65,576,487.64
Minerals	..	..	.	..	..	111,651,005.92
Sundry Manufactured Products	..	..	..	..	4,520,776.04
Petroleum and Products	..	..	..	..	679,877,433.85
				TOTAL	$865,933,251.92

A MEXICAN CALENDAR.

1503. Montezuma becomes Emperor.
1519–21. Conquest by Spain under Hernando Cortés.
1530. Mendoza, first Viceroy of New Spain.
1543. Campaign of Las Casas against oppression of the Indians results in promulgation of the New Laws.
1771–9. Ursúa, Viceroy.
1789–94. Revillagigedo, Viceroy
1810–11. Rising under Hidalgo in Querétaro.
1821. Plan of Iguala promulgated by General Iturbide (establishment of Mexico as a limited monarchy under a Bourbon prince). Captain General O'Donoju withdraws Spanish troops to Vera Cruz. Mexico declared independent by Treaty of Córdoba.
1822. Augustin Iturbide declares himself Emperor.]
1823. Iturbide compelled to abdicate.
1824. Iturbide shot. Federal Consitituency promulgated.
1825. Treaty of commerce with Great Britain.
1829. Spanish attempt to reconquer Mexico defeated by Santa Anna at Tampico. Expulsion of the Spaniards decreed. Revolution. President Guerrero deposed.
1830. Independence of Mexico recognized by Brazil.
1833–7. Santa Anna, President.
1835. Texas declares its independence.
1836. Independence of Mexico recognized by Spain.
1845. Texas admitted into the American Union.
1845–8. War with United States.
1847. Mexico City captured by the American troops.
1848. Treaty of Peace signed with United States.
1854. Santa Anna forced to leave Mexico.
1855. War of the Reform.
1857. New Constitution promulgated.
1858. Conservative *oup d'état* drives the Liberals from Mexico City.
1858–9. Benito Juaréz head of the State.
1859. Reform Laws prohibit the Church or any religious corporation to hold property; religious orders and lay confraternities dissolved.
1861. Vera Cruz occupied by a Spanish force, which is soon joined by British and French contingents.
1862. British and Spanish forces withdrawn.

1863. General Forey enters Mexico City   Archduke Maximilian becomes Emperor.
1864. Archduke Maximilian arrives in Mexico.
1867. French troops withdrawn. Successful campaign headed by General Diaz, the Republican Leader. Emperor Maximilian shot. Juaréz re-elected President.
1868. Maximilian's body buried at Vienna.
1872. Lerdo de Tejado elected President.
1873. Vera Cruz Railways opened. Protestant Missions established in Mexico. Diplomatic relations reopened with France and Spain.
1876. General Porfirio Diaz heads a revolt, and defeats Presidential forces at battle of Tecoac.
1877. General Porfirio Diaz elected President.
1880. Manuel González elected President.
1884. Diplomatic relations with Great Britain resumed. Completion of Central Railway, connecting Mexico and the United States.
1884-1911. Diaz's second term of office as President.
1887. Law against re-election of President repealed.
1895. Treaty with Guatemala over boundary question. Mexico announces its adhesion to the Monroe Doctrine.
1897 Boundary dispute with Great Britain settled.
1901. First Pan-American Congress held at Mexico City.
1907. Earthquake in South Mexico.
1908. Represented at the Central American Court of Arbitration. Earthquake shocks in Mexico City
1909. Conference between President Diaz and President Taft.
1911. Diaz overthrown, leaves the country (d. 1913). Francisco I. Madero, President (d. 1913).
1912. Carranza, leader of the Revolutionaries.
1913. General Victoriano Huerta, President.
1914. United States troops occupy Vera Cruz.
1915. Carranza, President (d. 1920).
1916. Hostilities with the United States averted by negotiations.
1917. New constitution promulgated.
1920. Adolfo de la Huerta, Provisional President. General Obregon elected President.

Local Administration :— Besides one Federal District, there are twenty-eight States, and two Territories, each a separate entity so far as government and laws are concerned, inter-State customs duties are not permitted. States can levy their own taxes, and each State has its governor, legislature, and judicature popularly elected in the same fashion as those of the Federation. The Federal District and Territories have their governors appointed by the President. Laws made by the Federal Government are binding on the various States, which can, however, supplement them with laws of their own.

The **judiciary** consists of a Supreme Court and various circuit and district courts. The fifteen judges of the Supreme Court are at present chosen for a period of six years; tenure of office for life will come into force in 1923. Mexican law contains a unique feature in the writ of amparo (protection), which combines the essential elements of our writs of habeas corpus, certiorari, and mandamus. It affords redress when any of the fundamental rights of man are infringed by any authority

The **language** of the country is Spanish. English is spoken, but a knowledge of Spanish is essential for business purposes.

The Church is independent of the State, and there is tolerance of all **religions, but** Mexico is still one of the great strongholds of Roman Catholicism. There are about 8,800 churches and chapels, and the Roman Catholic population in 1910 numbered 15,000,000 as against 69,000 Protestants and 33,000 of other faiths. All places of worship are under State supervision monastic orders are prohibited, and churches are forbidden to hold real property or loans. Only Mexicans by birth may be ministers of any religious creed.

The **monetary** unit was the silver dollar or peso, divided into 100 centavos, until the rise in silver caused Mexican silver coins to disappear from circulation. A law, passed on November 13, 1918, decreed that gold should be the monetary unit.

There are gold coins of $20, $10, $5, $2.50, $2, silver coins of $1, 50 and 20 centavos, a nickel coin of 5 centavos, and bronze coins of 20, 10, 5, 2, and 1 centavos.

The **metric** system is official. Old Spanish measures are used, especially among the lower classes and Indians. The more important of these are :—

Linear.			Measures of Area.		
1 legua	=	5,000 varas	1 manzana	=	1·66 acres
1 vara	=	3 piés	1 fanega	=	8·81 acres
1 pié	=	12 pulgadas	1 caballeria	=	105·75 acres
1 pulgada	=	12 lineas			

Dry Measures.

1 carga	=	2 fanegas	181·63 litres	=	5·15 bushels
1 fanega	=	12 almudes	90·81 litres	=	2·58 bushels
1 almud	=	4 cuartillos	7·57 litres	=	0·86 peck.

Liquid Measures.

1 cuartillo of oil	0·51 litre	=	0·89 pint.
1 cuartillo of wine	0·46 litre	=	0·80 pint.

Commercial Weights.

1 carga (freighting)	=	12 arrobas	=	138·07 kilogrammes	=	303·75 lb. av
1 quintal	=	4 arrobas	=	46·02 kilogrammes	=	101·24 lb. av
1 arroba	=	25 libras	=	11·51 kilogrammes	=	25·32 lb. av

Land Tenure :—Until recent years the desirable agricultural lands of Mexico were held in large tracts by a comparatively small number of owners. The system of ownership dates back to the sub-division of the lands of New Spain by the Spanish crown among the soldiers and adventurers who aided in the conquest. Each hacendado (proprietor) had to rely almost entirely upon the products of his own estate for subsistence, and a large area was put under cultivation in order that he might accumulate a surplus for his necessities in periods of internal disorder or whenever his crops might fail. The great haciendas have remained for many generations in possession of the descendants of the original owners.

The Spanish Government early set aside certain sections for the use of the Indian population. These sections, called " congregaciones," exist in nearly all the fertile sub-tropical districts. Titles to these lands are possessory, the fee simple being vested in a grant owned by the pueblo, or community   Transfer of title is made by a bill of sale acknowledged by the cacique (chief) of the village. The title lapses through abandonment of the land or non-payment of taxes. Many tracts of good land are held in " condueñazgos," which are grants made by the King of Spain to individuals. These grants have never been sub-divided by the heirs of the original owners, and are owned by all heirs in common.

Municipal lands are owned by the various municipalities. Tracts of these lands may be " denounced " by any one who will pay to the municipality the price set upon it. The deed is confirmed by the State Government and becomes an absolute title. This land is forfeited by abandonment and by non-payment of taxes. When forfeited it reverts to the municipality, and may be " denounced " again.

The titles of most of the large farms, or haciendas, are perfect, being grants from the King of Spain, confirmed by the Federal Government.

Irrigated lands in Mexico are difficult to purchase and command high prices, or prices that appear high when compared with those for unirrigated lands in the same vicinity   As a rule irrigated lands are not on the market, but opportunities occur to secure properties containing a small area under irrigation. The yield on irrigated lands in Mexico is so large that it requires but a small portion of this land to produce a good income.

Opportunities of Sport :—Yurécuaro, La Barca, and Ocotlán on the Guadalajara branch of the National Railways of Mexico are close to marshes which are the winter resort of aquatic birds, from snipe to swans. Pelican, swan, geese, brant, ducks of every variety, snipe, curlew, and sandhill cranes are found in immense numbers in the region known as the Lake Chapala district.

There is good deer shooting about Villar, east of San Luis Potosí, also between Tamasopo and Tampico and in the vicinity of Jimulco on the main line, also north of Tampico.

About twenty miles south from San Bartolo, on the Tampico branch, are swamps formed by large springs, where in the winter season great numbers of aquatic birds are found. To the south are mountains in which deer, wild pig, and an occasional Mexican lion are seen. Farther east, south of the Tampico line, in the foothills between the mountains and the gulf, game is abundant. The alligator and the manatee abound along the rivers near the gulf, in the mountains are panthers, tigers, and wild pig, in the hills are pheasants, of five varieties, varying from the size of a pigeon to that of a turkey

In the vicinity of Tampico there is fine sea fishing. In the River Panuco the tarpon, the pargo, and the curel are caught by trolling, by still fishing, by spearing, and occasionally with the fly. There is good beach fishing from the jetties, and fish weighing four ounces to a hundredweight can be caught. A few miles from the mouth of the Panuco are the red-snapper banks, where the fish are large and abundant. In the little streams and rivers threading the tropical forests of the region muscovy duck are to be had. The birds are large, brilliant of plumage, and good eating.

The States of Vera Cruz, Oazaca, and Chiapas offer excellent sport with wild turkeys, water and other fowl, lions, wild cats, jaguars, wild pig, ant-eaters, deer, and alligators. There is no "closed season", shooting is allowed at any time of the year

Lake Pátzcuaro, reached by the National Railways, is on the Pacific slope. It is a winter home of birds. Seven thousand feet above sea-level, Lake Pátzcuaro is high among the clouds in the Sierras. The lake is twenty miles long by ten wide, and its islands, populated by Tarascans, who speak little Spanish, are highly picturesque. Teal, spoonbills, mallards and canvas-backs are the chief families of duck, and the lake teems with fish.

Importation of Arms :—No permit or licence is now required for the importation into Mexico of saloon pistols, calibre ·22, including revolvers, or the requisite cartridges, shotguns and cartridges, cutlasses or cane-knives, and hunting knives, powder for shotguns, lead ammunition for sporting purposes, except buckshot and mould shot, cartridge cases and percussion caps.

NATURAL RESOURCES.

It was estimated in 1918 that the area under cultivation was 14,634,848 hectares out of the total 198,309,800 hectares, or 7·37 per cent. The principal crops are Indian corn, sugar cane, barley, wheat, henequen hemp, and beans.

Maize furnishes one of the chief foods of the people, and the tortilla, made of this grain, is universally eaten in all the States. Maize is chiefly grown south of latitude 21° N., and Jalisco and Yucatan are the two chief producing States. The production is not as a rule sufficient for the local demand, and quantities have to be imported.

The **wheat** supply is almost always insufficient. The chief productive areas are the States of Michoacan, Guanajuato, Chihuahua, Sonora, Puebla, Coahuila, Querétaro, Tlaxcala, and Durango. Uncertain rainfall and lack of irrigation make the crop very variable. In years of scarcity it is always necessary to import from the United States or Argentina.

A small quantity of oats and rye is grown, chiefly in Mexico and Lower California. Rice is grown in almost all the coastal States and some of the interior, but in quantities not sufficient for the needs of the country Several kinds of beans afford a staple article of food to the people; the frijol, or Mexican bean, is the commonest. Other principal products are coffee, vegetable oils (including castor-oil), and cotton and tobacco. Guano is found at several points.

Large areas are suitable for **sugar** production, and especially the " tierras calientes " of the Atlantic belt. There is room for development in this industry, which dates back to the earliest years of the Spanish Conquest. In 1921 the sugar production was over 81,000 tons. The chief producing State was Vera Cruz with 29,000 tons, and the next Sinaloa, with nearly 24,000 tons.

Coffee grows in great perfection on the mountain slopes, and the production in 1921 was 34,500 tons. Vera Cruz contributed nearly 14,000 tons and Chiapas (bordering upon Guatemala, a producer of exquisite high-grade coffee) nearly 13,000 tons. Mexican coffee fetches a high price, and is highly esteemed by connoisseurs. Coffee can be cultivated in almost any part of Vera Cruz at an altitude not lower than 1,000 ft. The best coffee is produced at about 2,500 to 4,000 ft. The number of coffee trees to the acre varies from 500 to 1,000 trees, but they produce better coffee, and more of it, with not over 600 trees per acre. The usual life of the tree is about 40 years, but it is considered to be at its prime from the sixth to the thirteenth year.

Cotton grows in practically all parts, but the bulk is derived from four States : Durango, Coahuila, Chihuahua, and Lower California. In 1921 the Mexican cotton crop was 32,000 tons.

Other agricultural products of importance are enumerated below with estimates of the production in 1921 :—

	Tons.		Tons.
Garlic	81,097	Canary seed	860
Banana	54,641	Pea-nuts	1,120
Cocoa	3,251	Coco-nuts	16,500
Peas	10,334	Beans	71,053
Hemp	115,684	Alfalfa.	766,500
Mangoes	5,674	Onions .	34,180
Sweet potato	102,000	Capsicum	40,730
Potatoes	42,231	Tobacco	6,548
Tomatoes	23,520	Cassava	6,220

Ixtle :—One of the principal plants producing textile fibres is the lechuguilla, belonging to the great agave family. The plant thrives even in the sandiest and most barren districts of the northern part of the republic. It is almost an air plant, seeming to take very little nourishment from the soil.

Henequen has for many years been the principal source of wealth in the peninsula of Yucatan, and has been introduced in the region tributary to Victoria, in the State of Tamaulipas. On semi-arid lands in Tamaulipas and Nuevo León, it has been found that henequen is a successful crop.

Zapupe, a new fibre-producing plant, growing especially in Tuxpan (Vera Cruz), seems to be a first cousin of henequen, over which it has some advantages. On well-drained soil and with decent care, one-year plants from the nursery produce leaves for fibre in their third year. The plants produce for 12 to 15 years.

Mexico has been said to have more sugar-cane land than Cuba, more citrus-fruit land than the United States and Italy combined, more pineapple land than Hawaii, more tobacco land than the West Indies, more coco-nut land than the Philippine Islands, more banana land than Central America, more corn land than any country except the United States. It produces more coffee than any country outside Brazil.

Fruit-farming :—Oranges, lemons, grape-fruit, bananas, mangoes, zapotes, mamayes, aguacates, granadillas, chirimoyas, granadas, guavas, papayas, pineapples, and practically all other tropical fruits are, for the most part, indigenous. When not found growing wild, as are all except the grape-fruit, pineapples, and bananas, they grow, when cultivated, to high perfection.

Navel oranges grow wild in great perfection.

The **aguacate** (alligator pear) is capable of profitable development. The aguacate grows almost wild and has many varieties. It is a green or greenish-purple pear-shaped or round fruit with a glossy skin, inside is a stone varying in size with the variety, and between the stone and the skin is the meat, a substance of buttery consistency and of a greenish cream colour The meat is either eaten from the shell or scooped out, generally it is dressed with salt and pepper, or with a regular salad dressing, and frequently is mixed with lettuce or tomato, or both, to form a salad, in flavour it is rather nutty and rich, for those who cannot eat starchy foods the aguacate is excellent.

The **papaya** or tree melon is cultivated in the tropics. It is propagated by seed planted in rows eight feet apart and cultivated like corn or vegetables. After sending up a single stalk from four to eight feet high (it may reach twenty feet), it commences to bear at about one year of age. Some plants have been known to have as many as 75 melons at one time; it lasts for about three years, bearing continuously A rich well-drained sandy soil is best adapted to this plant. The fruit is a long green or yellowish melon weighing from five to twenty pounds, the flesh red or yellow in colour and very firm, the interior contains many black seeds. The papaya contains a large percentage of papein, a chemical substance almost identical with pepsin, and possessing the same qualities. The green fruit while still on the plant is cut on four sides through the skin only and the white juice which exudes is collected and evaporated. The residue, a white powder, is used by druggists in the manufacture of pepsin gum. The flavour of this fruit is very fine, and its qualities make it ideal for dyspeptics.

Live Stock :—Ranching is of importance, and Mexican cattle have been improved by the introduction of foreign breeds. Zacatécas is the principal sheep-rearing State. Durango has the greatest number of horses. Before the Revolution there had been a continuous increase in the number of head.

Large quantities of eggs, milk, butter, cheese, and lard are imported into the country Cheese is made in Hidalgo and Mexico States.

MEXICO.

The best **woods** are found along the coast, and in the Southern States. The supply includes dye-woods, oak, pine, cedar, ebony, mahogany, sandal wood, and rosewood.

MINERAL RICHES.

There is hardly a region, except in the lowlands along the coasts where gold or silver is not found. When the Spaniards came to Mexico they found silversmiths and goldsmiths displaying articles of fine and intricate workmanship.

Nearly all the gold used by the Aztec and Maya jewellers was obtained from the sands of rivers, but it was known that the mother-lode of gold came from the rocks, and in specially rich regions the rock was broken up and crushed.

It has been computed that between 1521 and 1921 the quantity of silver produced was 141,400,000 kilos, worth £600,000,000 sterling.

The mining code was made more liberal and protective some 30 years ago, and between 1892 and 1921 thousands were added to the number of silver-mining claims in force. Altogether there are over 75,000 mining claims, but the Government regards only 28,000 as in force, since they alone are paying taxes regularly Of these, 3,800 are in production, and from them Mexico produces the quantity that makes her to-day the greatest producer of silver in the world, with 40 per cent. of the world's output to her credit. During 1921 Mexico, despite the internal troubles, produced 62,000,000 oz. of silver, as against 50,000,000 in the United States.

The most important mineral region is enclosed in a rough parallelogram extending from north-west in Sonora to south-east in Oaxaca, following the direction of the Sierra Madre Cordillera, about 1,600 miles long and 250 broad. The principal mining States are Chihuahua, Guanajuato, Oaxaca, Sonora, Durango, Jalisco, Michoacán, Zacatécas, Hidalgo, Querétaro, and Mexico, but there are also mineral potentialities in Vera Cruz, Lower California, and other States.

The principal minerals are silver, gold, copper, lead, iron and zinc, with coal, platinum, mercury, manganese, antimony, sulphur, bismuth, tin, graphite, and salt.

A recent table shows the following mines and minerals :—

State.	Mines.	Minerals.
Aguascalientes	1	Silver and copper.
Coahuila	3	Silver, copper, iron, lead, and zinc.
Chihuahua	16	Gold, silver, lead, copper, and manganese.
Durango	1	Gold and silver.
Hidalgo	5	Gold and silver.
Jalisco	5	Gold, silver, copper, and lead.
Mexico	1	Gold and silver.
Michoacán	1	Silver and copper.
Nayarit	4	Gold, silver, and copper.
Nuevo León	1	Silver, lead, iron and zinc.
Querétaro	4	Silver, lead, iron, gold, and opals.
San Luis Potosí	1	Silver and copper.
Sinaloa	12	Gold, silver, copper, and lead.
Sonora	19	Gold, silver, copper, lead, and graphite.
Zacatécas	7	Gold, silver, copper, lead, sulphate of mercury.

309

Great possibilities of exploitation remain. Present and past records of output are not necessarily the measure of the potentialities. Although Mexico ranks next to the United States in the production of copper, the largest sulphur deposits in the world are lying idle, and valuable tin beds and coal-fields await development. Some authorities have expressed the opinion that the lead mines are near exhaustion, but others hold that there still remain millions of tons of rich ore which can be worked at low cost.

The most important **coal deposits** are at Sabinas and Coahuila. About 1,000,000 tons per annum were produced before the Revolution. An interesting development has occurred in the Ciudad Juarez district. A large seam of coal has been discovered in the foothills of the Sierra Paso del Norte. The vein is between lime shales and sandstone, and five or six feet thick. Analysis of the coal shows 45 per cent. fixed carbon with 20 to 30 per cent. of volatile combustibles.

The annual coal consumption in Monterey is about 7,500 metric tons, and the annual consumption of coke about 100,000 tons; the steel plants and smelters being the principal consumers.

Owing to the proximity of Salina Cruz to the oil-fields, petroleum is there the cheaper fuel. Consequently the coal consumption is low The industrial establishments and railways use oil, water power, or wood. In Chihuahua, where about 50,000 tons of coal are consumed annually, the needs are supplied from the United States, and Coahuila.

Mining Concessions :—Under the Constitution of 1917 the ownership of lands and waters, mineral resources, petroleum, salt, and so forth is inalienably vested in the nation. Concessions can be granted by the Federal Government to private parties or to commercial corporations on condition that the natural resources are regularly developed. Only Mexicans by birth or naturalization have the right to acquire such concessions, and when the nation grants these rights to foreigners it is only with the proviso that they agree to be regarded as Mexicans and not to invoke the protection of their Governments. It is provided that within a zone of 100 kilometres from the frontier and 50 kilometres from the seacoast no foreigner shall under any conditions acquire direct ownership of lands or waters.

An extra session of Congress unanimously approved in March 1923 a Bill for the retaining State ownership of the subsoil. The articles passed say that petroleum is the inalienable, imprescriptible property of the nation.

The **oil** production in 1921 amounted to 26 per cent. of the world's output, and the remaining resources are believed to be the greatest extant. The three chief zones are Tampico, Tuxpán, and Manitatlán. The domestic consumption of petroleum being small, the greater part of the production is exported in tank steamships to the United States and Europe. The potential production of existing wells has been estimated at nearly two million barrels daily.

Local Industries :—Mexico is not primarily a manufacturing country, but certain industries are carried on. The cotton mills are numerous and important, as are the sugar refineries. Cigarettes are manufactured in about 40 factories. Cigars are made at Vera Cruz. There are 170 soap, tallow, and glycerine factories, perfume factories, sweetmeat, biscuit and chocolate factories, breweries, distilleries, and mineral-water factories; and potteries (especially in Guadalajara), glass and mirror factories (several in Puebla), tanning yards, and printing offices. Straw hats, boots, and woollen goods are manufactured.

The metal manufactures include iron, nickel, tin, and copper articles like bedsteads, boxes, safes, clock and watch cases, hardware, and pins, under the ownership chiefly of Mexican and Spanish subjects.

Public Holidays :—The feast days of the Church are carefully observed. Other holidays are :—

January 1 : New Year's Day.
February 5 : Anniversary of the Constitution.
May 5 : Anniversary of the Triumph in 1862.
September 16 : Anniversary of Independence.
December 25 : Christmas Day

Certain States and cities have also their own holidays.

Press :—All the more important newspapers are published in Mexico City The chief daily is " El Universal," with a very large circulation. Next comes "Excelsior," representing more conservative views. Other papers are " El Nacional Courrier de Mexique," " Democrata," " El Mundo," " La Defensa," " La Rendición," " La Cauterio," " La Boletin de la Guerra," and " El Pueblo."

Immigration :—Circular 998 of the Mexican Government decrees that any alien (aliens holding certificates showing employment are exempt) who cannot show ticket through to final destination, plus $50.00 Mexican Currency, will not be allowed to land at any Mexican port.

POSTAL COMMUNICATION

The **postage** rates on letters not exceeding 20 grammes in weight are . for urban or suburban service, 2 centavos, to other points in Mexico and to the United States, Canada, and Cuba, 5 centavos, to other countries, 10 centavos. Maximum weight, 5 kilogrammes (11 lb.).

Parcel post rates are 12 centavos for 500 grammes, maximum weight, 5 kilogrammes. Parcels for foreign countries are usually detained for several days by the Customs authorities.

There is a fairly extensive system of telegraph lines in addition to the railway telegraphs, and various wireless stations.

Outward **mails** are dispatched via the United States, and the service is the same as to the United States.

Postage . 3d. first ounce and 1½d. each ounce after.

Homeward mails are dispatched at frequent intervals.

LEGATION AND CONSULATES IN GREAT BRITAIN

LEGATION.

(London 48 Belgrave Square, S.W.1)—
In charge of Señor Alberto Mascareñas, Consul-General.
Financial Agency In charge of Señor Rafael Manzo.

CONSULATES.

Residence.	Designation.	Name.
London	Consul-General	Alberto Mascareñas.
(Bush House, Aldwych, W.C. Tel. Victoria 7807.)		
Birmingham	Consul	Gustavo Shurhoff.
Cardiff	Consul	Joseph Piffaretti.
Glasgow	Consul	Filiberto Valero.
Liverpool	Consul	Rafael Aveleyra.
Newcastle-on-Tyne	Consul	John Avery

BRITISH LEGATION AND CONSULATES IN MEXICO

The letter (L) denotes that the Consular Officer has authority to register lex loci marriages, the letter (M) that he holds a Marriage Warrant. Members of the Diplomatic Service do not require Warrants.

RESIDENCE.	RANK.	NAME.
Mexico City	Envoy Extraordinary and Minister Plenipotentiary	—
	Chargé des Archives	H. Cummins, C.M.G., O.B.E.
	Translator	Capt. R. Hollocombe.
	(M) Consul-General	Norman King.
	Vice-Consul	C. G. Rickards.
Chihuahua	Vice-Consul	Thomas Dale.
Chinipas	Vice-Consul	G. E. Stephenson.
Durango	Vice-Consul	Wm. W Graham.
Ensenada	Vice-Consul	Wm. David Madden.
Gomez Palacio	Vice-Consul	Patrick A. O'Hea.
Guadalajara	Vice-Consul	Capt. P G. Holms.
Guanajuato	Consular Agent	William Hislop.
Mérida and Progeso	Vice-Consul	W J Cameron.
Monterey	Vice-Consul	J B. Sanford.
	Pro-Consul	James M. L. Mackay
Orizaba	Vice-Consul	S. W Stacpoole.
Puebla	Vice-Consul	William Hardaker
Zacatécas	Consular Agent	James Caldwell.
Salina Cruz	Vice-Consul	F R. Crowther.
	Pro-Consul	—
Soconusco. (Tapachula)	Vice-Consul	Robt. O. Stevenson.
Tampico	(M) Consul	A. J de E. Rivers.
	Vice-Consul	Robert G. Pulford.
Colima	(L) Consul	Douglas G. C. MacNeill.
La Paz	Vice-Consul	Frank W Moore.
Mazatlan	Vice-Consul	George E. S. Watson.
Ciudad del Carmen	Vice-Consul	J A. Cué (acting).
Saltillo	Vice-Consul	R. H. Jeffery
	Pro-Consul	—
San Luis Potosi	Vice-Consul	Dr. Harry E. Nolan.
Tuxpán	Vice-Consul	E. G. S. Strong.
Vera Cruz	(M) Consul	J S. Hutchison.
	Vice-Consul	Arthur R. Hogg.
	Pro-Consul	—
Puerto Mexico	Vice-Consul	J J Sparks.

MEXICO.

Guidance for Commercial Travellers.

There are no special regulations for foreign commercial travellers, but the treatment accorded to travellers is not uniform. The practice most prevalent is the imposition of a State tax (derecho de patente), equivalent to a right or a licence to trade, payable monthly, and assessed according to tariffs varying considerably in different States. The actual assessment of a traveller or commission agent is left to the revenue officer. As a general rule, a commercial traveller, on arrival, is obliged to present himself at the office of the Collector of Revenue—in some cases before the Jefe Politico (Prefect of Police)—and make a declaration setting forth the name of the firm or firms he represents, their importance and standing, and the nature of the goods in which he proposes to deal.

Foreign commercial travellers are not required by State laws to be furnished with special certificates or powers of attorney, but their customers may call for credentials, and in the State of Mexico the traveller must produce his credentials to obtain his licence.

Besides State and municipal taxes, foreign travellers are subject to the Federal contribution of 20 per cent. additional on all taxation. This tax is levied in the form of stamps. If a commercial traveller actually delivers goods, he has to pay the interior stamp tax (Renta Interior del Timbre) of one half per cent. on the value of all sales. This is also a Federal tax and the stamps are affixed to the receipts. It is the usual practice for salesmen in Mexico to charge these stamps to the purchaser. Foreign travellers must be prepared to pay in some States a local stamp tax on the value of the sales they effect, even where no mention of such a tax is made. The State and municipal taxes are imposed under budget or revenue laws and are liable to periodical revision

TRAVEL IN MEXICO.

South of Mexico City, crossing the mountains at an elevation of 10,000 ft., and winding down to Cuernavaca, the train journey is wonderfully picturesque and interesting At the City of Mexico, in the highest of the great valleys of North America, 7,349 ft. above sea-level, the line winds westward by Chapultepec and Molino del Rey, through and above battlefields where Toltecs, Aztecs, Spaniards, French, and Americans have fought for the possession of the great valley

MOUNTAIN SUMMITS,

In the climb over the mountains one of the great views of the world unfolds itself. The line crosses the battlefield of Contreras and climbs towards Monte de las Cruces—Hidalgo's great victory, which should have ended the Mexican War of Independence. In the distance to the east, at the foot of a little hill, can be seen church domes and towers, the Shrine of Guadalupe, the most venerated in the republic. Here the patroness of the Indians appeared to Juan Diego. Here also the treaty of Guadalupe Hidalgo, which legalized the possession by the United States of about a third of her present territory, was signed. To the right, near the foot of the mountains, in the edge of a grove of trees, the brown walls of Churubusco can be seen, and far away, almost at the foot of the range which closes the valley, can be discerned the church spires and whitewashed walls of Texcoco and the Puente de los Bergantines, where Cortez built his little warships and sailed away to the siege of Tenoxtitlan.

At the top of the hill, among the pines, are the stations of Ajusco, La Cima (the Summit), the highest point on the line, 9,895 ft. above sea-level, Toro (the Bull), and Tres Marias (Three Marys), so called from the three pine-covered peaks at whose base the station is located. On one of them is an ancient ruin which may have been a small temple or more probably an ancient watch tower overlooking the valley

Grey and craggy Ajusco, over 13,000 ft. high, forms a culminating point of the ridge, before descending to the valley of Cuernavaca to the south. There is another view, with fields of cane, rolling hills, lava flows miles in length and hundreds of feet high, little lakes, villages, cities, sugar mills, and Indian pueblos are dotted through the valley or almost hidden in the nooks of the mountains, till on the southern horizon the coast range, forest-crowned, cuts off the view

One great zigzag and then a curve or two brings the train to Cuernavaca, the capital of the State of Morelos. Thence southward, lower and lower, winding among fields of cane, orchards of oranges, mangoes, and bananas, past sugar mills, among rice fields, the descent is into the tropical State of Guerrero, rich in mines, jungle, forests, hills and mountains.

On the Southern Railway :—The Mexican Southern Railway is a narrow gauge line connecting Puebla and Oaxaca cities, 228 miles apart. There is an extension from Oaxaca to Taviche, and one from Oaxaca to Esperanza, and a branch building from Taviche to Tlacolula.

From Puebla the railway descends by easy grades to Tehuacán, passing a number of picturesque Indian villages. Tehuacán is the first town of importance, settled by the Indians long before 1520. Tehuacán has been termed the Carlsbad of the New World, as its mineral waters effect wonderful cures.

From Tehuacán the descent commences to the hot country At Sanchez the shaggy heads of date palms can be seen—an unmistakable indication of lower altitude and warmer climate. Farther south, near Venta Salada and Aldama, the train runs through fields of sugar cane, and near Tecomavaca an amphitheatre of lofty mountains, on whose sides may be seen little Indian villages.

From Quiotepec the line begins an upward climb, passing little plantations between precipitous hillsides. The summit is reached at Las Sedas, 6,304 ft. above sea-level, from which point the road descends to Oaxaca. The most beautiful scenery on the line commences at Tomellín and continues almost as far as Las Sedas. The Tomellín canyon is one of the sights of the republic. Before reaching Huitzo on the other side of the Las Sedas divide, the country assumes a pastoral beauty and fertility surpassing anything since leaving Puebla.

Oaxaca and its suburbs has an elevation of 5,069 ft. above sea-level, population 40,000. The city was founded in 1486. Oaxaca is an especially pretty city, with parks and gardens, and is neither extremely hot nor cold.

The ruins of Monte Alban within four miles, are among the most notable in the world, and held by competent authorities to be at least 2,000 years old. The mountain on which they are situated is covered with remains of temples, sepulchres, platforms, open squares, and other ruins, bearing some resemblance to those of Egypt.

At Mitla, 25 miles south-east of Oaxaca, the ruins are of still more interest. Practically nothing is known of the prehistoric city The walls and their mosaics stand as mute evidence of past greatness. They are reached from Oaxaca by a 25-mile coach journey

Across the Isthmus :—The Tehuantepec National Railway proper extends across the Isthmus from Puerto Mexico (Coatzacoalcos), on the Gulf of Mexico, to Salina Cruz on the Pacific Ocean (190 miles) There is a through Pullman service between Salina Cruz and Mexico City, taking 36 hours only for the through journey

MEXICO.

A regular steamship service has been established by the Salvador Railway Company between Salina Cruz and Central American ports as far south · as Corinto, including a fast service between Acajutla and Salina Cruz without intermediate calls, and occupying 36 hours only The journey from Acajutla to Mexico City need not exceed four days.

From Puerto Mexico south for more than a hundred miles the line is flanked by dense tropical vegetation. As the train ascends to higher ground the vegetation thins gradually, and its character changes completely on the Pacific slope, where the air is dry and rains infrequent.

The Malatengo Cañon, with its deep cuts and ravines, affords a pretty scenic change just before reaching Rincon Antonio. Another interesting break is given by the Chivela Pass, where the railway crosses the back of the Cordilleras at an elevation of about 750 ft.

NICARAGUA

NICARAGUA.

Bluefields, the principal port on the Atlantic coast, is near the mouth of Bluefields River With a population of about 4,000, it is 187 miles from Managua and 185 from Cape Gracias. Bluefields handles about 75 per cent. of the Atlantic coast trade. Small vessels carry on a coasting trade with other points on the east coast.

Hotels :—Peterson, Atlántico, Tropical.

Greytown (San Juan del Norte), a port of fair importance at the mouth of the San Juan river, is on the Caribbean Sea. Vessels lie about a mile offshore and lighters are used. There is a good steamship connection with Granada via the river and Lake Nicaragua. Population 2,600.

Hotel :—Central.

Corinto, 87 miles from Managua and 13 from Chinandega, is an important port on the Pacific, doing about 65 per cent. of the foreign trade of the country. Population 3,500.

Hotels :—Boston, Corinto, American, Lupone.

Served by the Pacific Railway.

Managua, the capital, with a population of about 45,000, stands on the southern shore of Lake Managua, 187 miles from Bluefields and 52 from León. The principal products are coffee, cacao, cattle, and sugar. The chief buildings are the President's Palace and the National Palace. There is a fine park.

Hotels :—Gran, Italia, America, Estrella, Lupone.

Rail :—Pacific Railway (from Corinto, León, or Granada)

León, the former capital, with a population of over 70,000, is one of the most important cities in the republic, standing in a rich agricultural district 35 miles from Corinto and 52 from Managua. It is the principal distributing centre for the departments of Nueva Segovia, Esteli, Jinotega, and Matagalpa. There is a fine cathedral.

Hotels :—Metropolitano, Lupone, Roma.

Served by the Pacific Railway.

Granada on the shore of Lake Nicaragua, has a population of about 30,000. The town is 36 miles from Managua and 118 from Corinto. It is the third city of the republic, and has a large business. The chief products are sugar, coffee, cacao, fruit, alcohol, hides, cotton, indigo.

Hotels :—Colón, Ascarate, La Alambra.

Matagalpa, 103 miles from Managua, 120 from León, has a population of about 16,000, and is the centre of an important

coffee, cattle, and mining district. It has no communications
by rail or water, and is reached by mule or on horseback.
Hotels :—Setentrional, Casino.

Masaya, with a population of 13,000, stands 106 miles from
Corinto, 13 miles from Granada, in a rich agricultural district
growing tobacco, corn, rice, sugar, coffee, and vegetables.
Hotel :—Josefina Ascarate.
Served by the Pacific Railway

Jinotega, population 14,000, 136 miles from Managua, 14 from
Matagalpa. Products. coffee, cacao, sugar, manilla, rubber, tobacco,
and tropical fruits.
Reached from Matagalpa by pack-animal.

Chinandega is reached from Corinto or Managua by the Pacific
Railway. The centre of a large agricultural district, it contains
the largest sugar mill in Central America. 74 miles from Managua,
13 from Corinto. Population 30,000.
Hotel :—La Unión.

CHARACTERISTICS OF THE COUNTRY.

Nicaragua, the largest of the Central American Republics, is
bounded on the north by Honduras, on the east by the Caribbean
Sea, on the south by Costa Rica, and on the west by the Pacific
Ocean. The superficial area is about 49,200 square miles, and
the population estimated at 750,000. The longest coast-line
is 300 miles, on the Atlantic, and the Pacific coast-line is 100 miles
shorter The fact that Nicaragua is traversed by two mountain
ranges causes considerable diversity of climate and products. The
plateau and uplands are healthful and fertile, and the lowlands
tropical. Several of the mountain peaks are extinct volcanoes.
There are two fine lakes. Lake Nicaragua, the larger, is about
110 miles long and 45 wide, and navigable throughout, while
Lake Managua, connected with it by the river Tipitapa, is some
38 miles long and varies from 10 to 16 miles in width. Of rivers
the best known are San Juan, connecting Lake Nicaragua with the
Atlantic, on which a regular steamship service runs between Greytown and Granada; and the Bluefields river, navigable for 65
miles or more from Bluefields to the city of Rama. The western
half of Nicaragua contains three-fourths of the population, chiefly
of mixed Spanish and Indian blood, with many Nicaraguans of
pure Spanish descent. The eastern half, containing the banana
plantations, has a number of negroes from the West Indies, also
natives of mixed negro and Indian blood.
Rain is very frequent during practically the whole year in the
eastern part of the country In the western half there are wet
and dry seasons, from May to November, and December to April
respectively. The prevailing winds are from the north-east, laden
with moisture from the Atlantic.

ADMINISTRATION.

The country is divided into 13 departments, and 2 comarcas, each under a military commandant, who has supervision of finance, public instruction, and other matters. There are 105 municipalities in the Republic.

Besides a Supreme Court, there are three courts of second instance, and several inferior tribunals.

Roman Catholicism is the prevailing religion. There is an archbishop, with his seat at Managua, and three bishoprics, at León, Granada, and Bluefields.

Spanish is the language of the country

The gold standard is in force, and the unit of the currency is the cordoba, divided into 100 centavos, equivalent to the United States dollar. Fractional coins are the 5-, 10-, and 50-cent pieces in silver, and copper coins of half a cent and one cent.

The metric system is official; but in domestic trade local terms are in use, for example the media, which equals a peck, and the fanega of 24 medias. These are not used in foreign trade. The principal local weight is the arroba=25 lbs.

GOVERNMENT.

The Constitution of April 5, 1913, provides for a Congress of two houses, consisting of 40 deputies, elected every four years by popular vote, and 13 senators elected for six years. The executive power is vested in a President, appointed for four years. Earlier Constitutions were promulgated in March 1905 and March 1912.

PAST PRESIDENTS.

Frutos Chamorro	1855
T. Martinez (first term)	1859
(second term)	1863
Fernando Guzman	1867
Vicente Quadra	1871
P. J. Chamorro	1875
Joaquin Zavala	1879
Dr. Adam Cárdenas	1883
Evaristo Carazo	1887
Dr. Roberto Sacasa (deposed 1893)	1889
General José Zelaya (first term)	1894
(second term)	1898
(third term)	1906
Dr. José Madriz (provisional)	1909
Juan J. Estrada	1910
Adolfo Diaz (provisional)	1910
Adolfo Diaz	1913
General Emiliano Chamorro	1917

PRESIDENT AND VICE-PRESIDENT.

President	Diego M. Chamorro (1921).
Vice-President . ..	B. Martínez.

MINISTRY

Interior	Humberto Pasos Diaz.
Foreign Affairs	Carlos Cuadra Pasos.
War and Marine . .	Narciso Lacayo.
Finance	G. A. Arguello.
Public Instruction .. .	Mariano Zelaya B.
Posts and Telegraphs ..	P Solorzano.
President Supreme Court of Justice	Dr. Santos Flores López.

A NICARAGUAN CALENDAR.

1502. Discovered by Columbus.
1522. The Indian Chief, Nicaras, received into the Roman Catholic Church.
1524. Granada founded.
1610. León founded.
1685. León plundered by Dampier and his buccaneers.
1821. Nicaragua declares itself independent of Spain.
1823–9. A member of the Central American Federation.
1856. William Walker proclaims himself President.
1860. Walker shot at Trujillo, Honduras.
1863. War between Nicaragua, Salvador, and Costa Rica against Guatemala and Honduras.
1885. A defensive alliance made between Nicaragua, Salvador, and Costa Rica against Guatemala.
1886. Peace signed with Guatemala.
    Treaty by which the United States may construct canal from San Juan to Brito rejected by United States Legislature.
1889. Nicaragua Canal Bill passed.
1891. Insurrection in Granada suppressed.
1894. War with Honduras.
1895. British Vice-Consul at Bluefields, Hatch, and other British subjects expelled for alleged conspiracy. British squadron occupies Corinto until indemnity paid.
1897. War with Honduras. Zelaya declares himself Dictator. Joins the "Greater Republic" of Central America, of which Costa Rica, Honduras, and Salvador are members.
1898. Boundary dispute with Costa Rica settled by arbitration.
1900. Nicaragua Canal Bill passed by United States Senate.
1901. Hay-Pauncefote Canal Treaty signed.
1905. Constitution promulgated. Commercial treaty with Great Britain.
1907. War with Honduras and Salvador. Peace signed.
1909. Rising against Zelaya. Government forces captured by General Estrada. President Madriz succeeds Zelaya.
1912. New commercial treaty with Great Britain.
1916. United States Treaty to acquire rights on the Nicaraguan Canal Route, etc.
1919. Joins the League of Nations.
1921. Joins the Central American Federation.

NICARAGUAN LEGATION AND CONSULATES IN GREAT BRITAIN

RESIDENCE.	DESIGNATION.	NAME.
London . . (49 St. James's Street, S.W.1.)	Chargé d'Affaires . .	Eduardo Pérez-Triana.
London .. . . (65 Bishopsgate, E.C.3.)	Consul	Esteban Vargas.
	Vice-Consul	W B. Gauld.
Birmingham . .	Vice-Consul	John Hotchkiss.
Liverpool	Consul	Ernesto Bermudez.
	Vice-Consul	E. A. Barker.
Manchester . ..	Consul-General (for Great Britain).	Jorge Lacayo.
	Consul	Ernesto Bermudez.
Nottingham . ..	Consul	Max Frank.
Southampton ..	Consul	W. J. Warren.
Cardiff	Consul	A. J Bovey.

BRITISH LEGATION AND CONSULATES IN NICARAGUA.

The letter (M) denotes that the Consular Officer holds a Marriage Warrant. Members of the Diplomatic Service do not require Warrants.

RESIDENCE.	RANK.	NAME.	CONSULAR DISTRICT.
(See Guatemala).	Envoy Extraordinary, Minister Plenipotentiary, and Consul-General.	—	—
Managua ..	(M) Consul	T I. Rees	} Republic of Nicaragua.
Corinto ..	Vice-Consul .	John L. Griffith ..	
Matagalpa .	Vice-Consul .	Alex. Potter ..	
Leon . .	—	W. P. Labero ..	Atlantic Coast of Nicaragua, including the Department of Bluefields and the Districts of San Juan del Norte, Siquia, Rio Grande, Prinzapolca, and Cabo Gracias à Dios, and for the Department of Chontales.
Granada .	Consular Agent ..	T. Cranshaw ..	
Bluefields .	(M) Consul	E. C. Rees (acting) ..	

Natural Resources :—Nicaraguan products are chiefly agricultural, including coffee, cacao, sugar-cane, rice, and tobacco. Bananas are the chief item of export in the eastern half of the country. Mahogany, logwood, and pitch-pine are found, as well as rubber. Tropical fruits and medicinal plants exist in great variety, Nicaraguan coffee is exceptionally good, the best grades coming from the Matagalpa and Jinotega districts. Coconut plantations have in many cases superseded bananas on the Atlantic coast.

Cattle raising is carried on extensively. In the western half of the country there are sugar mills, sawmills, shoe factories, electrical plants, and ice factories. A contract has been approved between the Government and a private contractor for establishing a new industry for making glassware and china.

Gold mining is an important industry in the eastern section, especially in the region of Nueva Segovia. Among the most active districts are Cuicuina and Mico. The principal mines in the west are the Santa Francisca, San Lucas, Amaya, and San Cristobal. The Leoncas mine is near Matagalpa.

Nicaragua imports breadstuffs (corn, macaroni, rice and wheat flour), soap and candles. Cotton, linen, and woollen goods are always in demand. The United States has the bulk of the boot and shoe trade in her hands, as also the trade in chemicals. Glass and glassware, iron and steel goods, tools and machinery are all a good market. A large number of jute bags are imported. Paints, paper, rubber goods, and toilet preparations find a ready sale.

Mails from the United Kingdom to Nicaragua are sent via Panamá, and take about four weeks. They are dispatched irregularly, as opportunity offers.

The Republic belongs to the Postal Union and has a parcel post. The letter rate is 5 cents for the first ounce, and 3 cents for each additional ounce. Telegraph and telephone lines are owned by the Government, and worked well and at a reasonable rate. There is cable connection over the lines of the Central and South American Co., via San Juan del Sur A private **wireless** station is maintained at Bluefields, on the Atlantic coast, and others are being provided.

Press :—Managua . ''El Comercio,'' ''El Heraldo,'' ''Nicaragua Informativa,'' ''La República,'' ''La Tribuna,'' ''La Noticia'', Granada : ''El Pais,'' ''El Correo'', León . ''El Centro-Americano,'' ''El Eco Nacional,'' ''El Independiente '' , Bluefields ''La Información.''

IMPORTS AND EXPORTS.

The unit of value in Nicaragua is the cordoba, equivalent to the United States dollar Converted into sterling at $4.85 to the £, the following are the trade totals for ten years past :—

	Exports. £	Imports. £	Total. £	Balance. £
1913	1,590,112	1,189,691	2,779,803	400,421
1914	1,021,660	852,437	1,874,097	169,223
1915	941,690	651,385	1,593,075	290,305
1916	1,089,662	985,072	2,074,734	104,590
1917	1,232,011	1,318,158	2,550,169	*86,147
1918	1,598,956	1,222,639	2,821,595	376,317
1919	2,558,654	1,631,474	4,190,128	927,180
1920	2,224,889	2,859,529	5,084,418	*634,640
1921	1,509,615	1,094,825	2,604,440	414,790
1922	1,629,576	1,056,392	2,685,968	573,184

ИОМЬ   * Adverse.

NICARAGUA.

Guidance for Commercial Travellers.

No special regulations exist affecting commercial travellers ; they are not required to take out licences nor are any fees collected except in Managua. Travellers are not required to produce certificates or powers of attorney, but it is better that they should carry documents establishing their right to act. Travellers who sell samples of the goods they carry are not subject to a special licence and are not considered as hawkers.

A municipal tax of 10 cordobas is levied on each occasion that a traveller visits Managua with samples. For a traveller in one particular article, the tax is 5 cordobas per visit.

Samples of no value are not liable to duty, but duty is collected on those of commercial value. In the latter case, the samples must be examined and the duties deposited in the custom house, together with a declaration of the intention of the traveller to re-export them. (A bond is accepted in lieu of cash for deposit of duties.) Samples must be re-exported from the port of entry if advantage is to be taken of this arrangement and re-exportation must take place within six months. The importation of catalogues brought by commercial travellers is free, and there are no regulations affecting their use, distribution, or sale.

Public Holidays :—Most of the feast days of the Roman Catholic Church are observed. Other holidays are :—

January 1   New Year's Day.
July 4 .   Independence of the United States.
July 14   Feast of France.
September 14 and 15 .   Independence of Central America.
October 12   Columbus or Discovery Day

THE
SOUTH AND EAST AFRICAN
YEAR BOOK AND GUIDE

Edited annually for **The Union-Castle Mail Steamship Co., Ltd.,** by

A. SAMLER BROWN, F.R.M.S., and
G. GORDON BROWN, F.R.G.S.

Crown 8vo.   *Nearly 1,000 pages.*

With Plans and Diagrams, and a Specially prepared Atlas of 64 Pages of Maps in Colour, containing the finest Atlas of South and East Africa available.

THOSE requiring detailed information about South and East Africa will find the above publication of considerable help and interest.

This work is divided into three sections. Part I. deals with South Africa, Part II. with East Africa, and Part III. with Sport and Research.

FOR THE BUSINESS MAN.—As a Gazetteer for Office use this work is without a rival, the Index contains over 2,000 place names. Imports and exports, means of transport and communication, etc., are dealt with in considerable detail, together with the rapid growth in manufacture, which is the last phase in South African development.

FOR THE IMMIGRANT OR SETTLER.—There is no concise Publication extant in which will be found more correct, more useful, or more practical Information on such subjects as the following :—Immigration, Acquisition of Land, Land Laws, Agriculture generally, tropical or otherwise (including special articles on subjects so diverse as the cultivation of Sugar, Tea, Cotton, Cereals, Timber, Fruit, &c., and the manufacture of the resultant products, such as Wines, Spirits, &c.), the Pastoral Industry (in conjunction with articles on the Breeding of Live Stock, such as Horses, Oxen, Sheep, Ostriches, &c., and on Diseases affecting Stock), The Mining Industry, and the Laws by which Prospectors and Miners are governed, &c., &c.

FOR THE SPORTSMAN.—A special section of the book gives, as far as is possible, the latest and most authentic information obtainable on the Habitats of Game and of Fish, the means of reaching the Best Hunting Fields; the Game Laws of the various territories, &c., &c.

FOR THE TOURIST.—The description of the Towns and of the Country of the Through Routes and of the Side Connections are thorough and exact. An effort has also been made, by means of historical and other Notes, to give the traveller an active interest in what he sees.

FOR THE INVALID.—There are lengthy articles on Climate, both general and local, so embodied in the book as to aid the Immigrant in choosing the situation and occupation best adapted to his special needs.

The Price is 5/- nett.

PANAMÁ

HOTEL TIVOLI
ANCON, C.Z.

"Panama's Distinctive Hotel"

Where comfort and refinement combined with moderate charges are at your convenience.

Overlooking the City of Panama and the Pacific Ocean.

European Plan.

Excellent cuisine and Prideful Service.

Room without bath, one person,	**$2.50** and up, per day.
,, with ,, ,, ,,	**4.00** ,, ,,
,, without ,, two persons,	**6.00** ,, ,,
,, with ,, ,, ,,	**7.00** ,, ,,

ANDREW JOHNSTON, *Manager.*

328

PANAMÁ.

Panamá, the capital of the Republic, with a population of about 70,000, is upon the Pacific Coast, 45 miles from Colón. The town was built in the seventeenth century near the site of an earlier city The ruins of Old Panamá are about half an hour's motor drive from the modern city by a concrete road. The town was captured, sacked, and destroyed by Morgan, the buccaneer The climate is somewhat variable; mean temperature about 80° Fahr.

The Cathedral possesses twin towers and the domes are encased in mother-of-pearl. It stands in the Avenida Central, facing it are several public buildings, and the Episcopal Palace and old Government Palace. At the lower end of the Avenida, behind a group of Government buildings, stands the National Theatre—one of the finest of its kind. A noteworthy new building is the Palacio Municipal or City Hall. At the foot of Ancón Hill stands the Institute Nacional, the University of Panamá.

Excursions :—By motor to Ancón, Balboa, Yacht Club, Miraflores and Pedro Miguel Locks or to Old Panamá by way of Bella Vista. Time, about four hours. Cost, about $3.00 per hour (four passengers and driver).

Bathing :—Bella Vista Beach and Taboga Island.

Golf :—Panamá Golf Club.

Shopping :—Chinese and Hindoo stores for silks, laces and ivory curios.

Markets :—Panamanian and Chinese.

HOTELS :—Tivoli (at Ancón, distant one mile), International, Metropole, Central, Continental, American, France, Europa.

Ancon :—An agreeable point at which to stay while visiting the Isthmus, has first-class hotel accommodation.

HOTEL :—Tivoli (overlooks Pacific), fishing, bathing, tennis, golf, shooting, European plan.

Points of Interest on the Pacific side in or near Ancón :—
Hospital, Fort Amador, Baseball Park, Balboa Swimming Pool, Administration Building, Chorrera Falls, Corozal Farm, Gaillard Cut, Juan Diaz Village, Old Panamá, Cocoa Plantation, Las Cascadas, Miraflores Locks, Pedro Miguel Locks, Military Road to Culebra, Panamá City, Bella Vista Bathing Beach, Cathedral and Plaza, Exposition Grounds, Market, National Institute, National Palace and Theatre, Old French Administration Building, Pearl Islands, Taboga Island, Summit Poultry Farm.

Taboga Island, Panamá Bay. One hour from Balboa by launch, is an extinct volcano rising from the waters of Panamá Bay. There is a village on the island and a 300-year-old church.

HOTEL :—Aspinwall , bathing, fishing, boating; American plan.

Points of Interest :—Church (300 years old); Morro Island, Fishing Village, Taboguilla Island, Old Spanish Cemetery.

Colón, capital of province, population about 35,000. On the Panamá Railroad, 45 miles from Panamá City. The town was formerly called Aspinwall, after one of the founders of the Panamá Railroad. It stands on Manzanillo Island, separated from the mainland by mangrove swamps. Formerly a hotbed of yellow fever, the campaign against the mosquito has improved it out of all recognition.

HOTELS :—Washington, Aspinwall, Grand Hotel Imperial, Cosmopolitan, Park.

Points of Interest, Atlantic side :—New Cristobal, Radio Station, Coco Solo Naval Station, Colón Hospital and Grounds, Gatun Locks, Fort San Lorenzo, Tarpon Club, Gatun, Spillway, Military Camp, Cold Storage Plant, Mount Hope Cemetery.

Cristóbal, in the Canal Zone, is practically a part of Colón.

Excursions :—From Cristóbal trips may easily be made to Mount Hope Cemetery, France Field Army Air Station, Coco Solo Submarine Base, and New Cristóbal ; fares about $3.00 per hour (four passengers and driver).

Fishing :—Tarpon fishing at Gatun Dam.

Golf :—At Gatun.

Bocas del Toro, capital of the province, stands on an island of the same name in Chiriqui Lagoon. It is a picturesque town and port, chiefly important as a banana-exporting centre, 161 miles from Colón. Population, 10,000.

HOTELS :—Washington, Central.

David, capital of the province of Chiriqui, one of the largest and richest provinces. Population 15,500. Situated on the David river, about five miles from Pedregal, its port. Distant 310 miles from Panamá City, with which a regular weekly steamship service is maintained.

HOTEL :—Santiago Lombardi.

Santiago, capital of Veraguas province, lies 155 miles from Panamá City Rather difficult of access, it can be reached from Panamá by steamer via Puerto Mate or Aguadulce, thence by cart road for 27 miles. Population 5,000.

Aguadulce, a seaport on the Pacific in the province of Coclé, is about 28 miles from Penenomé and 113 miles from Panamá City. It is reached by steamer. Population about 8,000.

El Porvenir, in the Bay of Mandinza, is the latest port on the Atlantic, opened in 1916.

PHYSICAL FEATURES.

The Republic is bounded on the north by the Caribbean Sea, on the east by Colombia, on the south by the Pacific Ocean, and on the west by Costa Rica. It contains the Panamá Canal. Zone, a strip of land 10 miles wide occupied by the United States. The total area is 32,380 square miles, about one-fourth of which is inhabited. The density of population is calculated to be about 14 persons per square mile. The coast-line is 477 miles on the Atlantic and 767 miles on the Pacific side. The two mountain ranges traverse the country, enclosing a number of valleys and plains with excellent pasturage for cattle. There are extensive forests on the slopes of the mountains, and numerous banana plantations along the Atlantic coast.

The **climate** is tropical, with a heavy rainfall, especially on the Caribbean coast. In the interior, at the higher altitudes, the temperature averages about 66° Fahr. On the coast the mean temperature is about 80° Fahr The dry season extends from January to April. The heaviest rains occur during October and November. On the Atlantic coast the average annual rainfall is about 140 in, on the Pacific, 60 in.; and in the interior, 93 in.

Constitution :—After Panamá asserted its independence of Colombia (November 3, 1903), a Constitution was adopted providing for a Chamber of 33 members and for a President elected for four years. The President is not eligible for a succeeding term unless he has resigned from power at least eighteen months before the day of election. There are three Vice-Presidents.

PAST PRESIDENTS.

Dr. Manuel Amador Guerrero ..	.. ..	1904
José Domingo de Obaldia	. .. .	1908
Carlos A. Mendoza	.. ..	1910
Pablo Arosemena	.. ..	1910
Rodolfo Chiari .	.. . .	1912
Belisario Porras ..	.. . .	1912
Ramón Valdés ..	. .. .	1916
Dr. Belisario Porras	.. ..	1918
Ernesto Lefevre ..	. . ..	1920

PRESIDENT AND VICE-PRESIDENTS.

President	Dr. Belisario Porras.
Vice-Presidents	Rodolfo Chiari, Ignacio Quinzada and Nicanor de Obarrio.

MINISTRY.

Interior and Justice .. .	Rodolfo Chiari.
Foreign Affairs	Narciso Garay.
Finance	Dr. Eusebio A. Morales.
Public Instruction	Octavio Mendez Pereira.
Public Works	Juan Antonio Jimenez.

PANAMÁ.

A PANAMIAN CALENDAR.

1501. Rodrigo Galvan de Bastidas discovers Panamá. Colombus, on his fourth voyage, reaches Porto Bello.
1513. Vasco Nuñez de Balboa crosses the Isthmus and discovers the Pacific Ocean.
1514. Pedro Arias de Avila arrives as Governor of the Gulf of Uraba.
1519. Balboa beheaded.
1546. La Gasca arrives at Nombre de Dios.
1595-6. Drake captures Nombre de Dios, and starts overland for the city of Panamá, but is driven back.
1597. The Spaniards fortify Porto Bello.
1602. William Parker's freebooting expedition.
1670-1. The pirate Henry Morgan burns and loots Panamá.
1673. The present city of Panamá founded.
1698. William Patterson's attempt to colonize the Isthmus of Darien.
1700. Patterson surrenders to the Spaniards and leaves the colony
1821. Panamá declares its independence. Union with Colombia.
1850. Railway to link up Colón and Panamá City begun.
1855. Railway linking up Colón and Panamá City opened.
1888. Lesseps plans the Panamá Canal.
1900. Boundary dispute with Costa Rica settled by arbitration.
1903. Panamá asserts its independence of Colombia.
       The de facto Government recognized by the Government of the United States, and by the other Powers soon after.
1903. Treaty between Panamá and the United States for the Panamá Canal.
1904. Dr. Manuel Amador Guerrero elected first President of the new-born Republic.
1904. Constitution promulgated.
1914. Opening of Panamá Canal to commercial traffic.
1919. Joins the League of Nations.
1921. Panamá recognized by Colombia as an independent State.

ADMINISTRATION

The eight provinces, with their capitals, are Bocas del Toro (Bocas del Toro), Coclé, (Penonomé), Colón (Colón), Chiriqui (David), Herrera (Chitré), Los Santos (Las Tablas), Panamá (Panamá), Veraguas (Santiago)

The **language** of the country is Spanish, but English is understood by the majority of commercial men in Panamá and Colón.

The people include elements of Spanish, Indian, and negro blood. The number of pure whites is small. The **population,** according to the census of 1920, is 434,786.

Roman Catholicism is the religion of the Republic. Protestantism has a large following in the Canal Zone.

The **metric** system is official. The vara is in use, and English weights and measures are commonly understood.

The standard of **currency** is the balboa, legally equivalent to the United States gold dollar, but balboas are not actually coined. The following silver coins are current. Peso, or half-balboa ($0.50); 50-centavo, 20-centavo, 10-centavo, 5-centavo and 2½-centavo pieces. There is no paper money

The silver peso is of the same value as 50 cents American money, whereas in other countries the peso consists of 100 cents, whether called centavos, centimos, or centesimos. The misnamed Panamá " peso " is divided into 100 imaginary cents, two of which are equal to one cent in gold. All legal prices are quoted in American gold terms these include prices of railway tickets, hotel rates, postage and telegraph charges. Commercial charges are quoted in terms of the local peso. The legal charge for a carriage is 15 cents, but the price stated by the driver is 30, to which he may add the word " plata " (silver) when addressing a stranger

NATURAL RESOURCES.

The country is rich in natural products, and the resources have barely been tapped. Bananas, coconuts and sugar cane are leading products, to which must be added rubber, balata, ivory nuts, coffee, cacao, maize, rice, nispero (a kind of medlar), and all the tropical fruits and vegetables. There are over 50 species of timber of from fair to excellent commercial value, and many varieties are used in the shop and building work of the Canal. Many medicinal plants and roots are also found. A short-fibred tree variety of cotton grows wild, and it is considered possible that a longer staple cotton might be easily grown. Cattle and hogs are raised in considerable quantities, principally in the Province of Chiriqui.

The banana and the coconut have been developed chiefly by foreign capital, and the native capitalist has devoted himself almost exclusively to cattle raising. The lumber trade is almost entirely in the hands of an American corporation, who have installed a large mill on the Rio Congo. Sugar, coffee and cocoa are produced, chiefly with native capital.

Coconuts are produced chiefly on the Atlantic seaboard and on the coral islands and coasts of the Gulf of San Blas. The nuts from this district have an excellent reputation.

The production of **sugar** is steadily increasing and in the near future the country ought to be self-supporting in this respect. There are over eight plantations with sugar mills. Of this the Santa Rosa mill at Aguadulce in the Province of Coclé produced more than half. The consumption of the Republic is estimated at about 80,000 bags annually

A good grade of coffee is grown in Chiriqui and supplies a large part of the local demand.

There is a small output of rubber, Mahogany and other valuable tropical woods are also grown. Copaiba, sarsaparilla and ipecacuanha are exported, and tobacco in moderate quantities, as well as balata, mother-of-pearl, and tortoiseshell. Cattle rearing and the export of hides are increasing. Livestock was estimated (1916) at 200,000 cattle, 15,000 horses, 2,000 mules, and 30,000 pigs.

Brewing and the manufacture of soap and candles are conducted on a minor scale, and there is a small tobacco factory.

Mining :—The Government allows concessions for coal and salt mining, oil wells, and water-power under fixed conditions. The applicant must give notice of his desire to exploit, accompanying his notice with plans or sketches of the proposed site, and applying within 60 days to the Department of Finance and Treasury for a licence. The application is published in a local paper, 30 days being allowed for objections. In the case of oil wells the successful exploiter has the privilege of free export of the product and the right to import, duty free, necessary machinery. He has preferential rights as regards the purchase of national lands and the right to carry his pipe lines through private property.

The exploitation of gold, silver, copper, etc., mines is dealt with in the Mining Code of 1917 The general tendency of successive decrees with reference to mining and the development of new industries is favourable.

There are **manganese** deposits at Mandinga Bay in the San Blas Gulf, and in the Boqueron Valley near Nombre de Dios. The latter is claimed to be one of the largest surface deposits discovered up to the present time, with about 150,000 tons of surface ore.

POSTAL COMMUNICATIONS.

Panamá is in the Postal Union.

Foreign letters 5 cents per 20 grammes, 3 cents each additional 20 grammes. Postcards 2 cents.

Inland letters (including Canal Zone and U.S.A.) 2 cents for 20 grammes. Postcards 1 cent.

There are 25 telegraph and 130 national telephone offices, and various wireless telegraph stations.

Tariff :—Inland telegrams 10 cents for ten words, with 5 cents for each additional ten words.

Outward **mails** are sent via United States, by Pacific Steam Navigation Line via Panamá, and by Leyland and Harrison Lines. Despatches for the first route as for United States, for the other, uncertain.

Postage :—3d. first ounce and 1½d. each ounce after.

Homeward mails are irregular

Press :—" Star and Herald " (Panamá), published daily, has the largest circulation of any paper in the Republic, and issues also a Spanish section called " La Estrella de Panamá." Other papers are " El Diario de Panama " (daily) , " The Central American Express " (weekly) ; " El Tiempo " (daily, Spanish) ; " Ecos del Valle " (daily, Spanish) ; " El Mundo " (weekly, Spanish) , " Motivos Colombianos " (fortnightly, Spanish) , " The Independent " (weekly, English and Spanish).

Public Holidays :—
January 1 : New Year's Day
February 15 : Signature of the National Constitution.
May 1 : Labour Day.
July 4 : American Independence Day.
July 24 : Birthday of General Bolivar.
October 12 : Thanksgiving Day.
November 3 : Anniversary of separation from Colombia.
November 28 : Anniversary of separation from Spain.
December 25 : Christmas Day.
The chief feast days of the Catholic Church are scrupulously observed.

PANAMÁ.

BRITISH LEGATION AND CONSULATES.

The letter (M) denotes that the Consular Officer holds a Marriage Warrant.
Members of the Diplomatic Corps do not require Warrants.

RESIDENCE.	RANK.	NAME.	CONSULAR DISTRICT.
Panamá	Envoy Extraordinary, Minister Plenipotentiary, and Consul-General	A. Percy Bennett, C.M.G.	Republic of Panamá.
Bocas del Toro	(M) Vice-Consul	R. Keith Jopson.	Republic of Panamá, and the Panamá Canal Zone.
Colón	Vice-Consul	William H. Ponton	
	(M) Consul	Constantine Graham	
	Vice-Consul	H. W. Border (acting)	

Trade Information :—Certificates of origin are not required, but goods shipped to Panamá must be accompanied by a Consular invoice certified by the Consul at the port of shipment. Fees are payable. An original bill or invoice from each of the manufacturers, merchants, or companies who sold the different articles to be exported, has to be presented at the port of origin, together with the invoice to be certified.

The foreign trade depends almost entirely on the retail trade within the Republic. The imports are largely food, clothing and luxuries. The value of the imports is about five times that of the exports and the balance is paid for by the wages of the canal worker, the money of the tourist, and the receipts from sales to shipping.

The following figures shows some of the principal imports during 1921 :—

	Balboas.
Rice	390,157
Flour (wheat)	541,523
Milk (tinned)	297,288
Sugar	106,996
Spirituous liquors	143,773
Wooden articles	473,805
Mineral oil and its derivatives	510,264
Leather	352,766
Cement	131,224
Cotton fabrics	1,044,758
Woollen fabrics	75,109
Rubber goods	160,858
Hemp fabrics	255,420
Iron and steel goods	774,046
Sugar refining machinery	95,130
Automobiles	169,280

The country has only recently begun to figure as an agricultural and manufacturing producer The demand from the Canal Zone, for the employees and for the passing steamships, offers inducements for the development both of agriculture and manufacture.

In the neighbourhood of the chief towns, Panamá, Santiago, Colón, there is a growing demand for imported wearing apparel, millinery and hosiery; and an excellent market for ornamental and fancy articles and objets d'art. The chief opportunities for trade, in addition to cottons and linens, lie in provisions, chinaware, soaps and perfumery, drugs and patent medicines, paints (especially prepared) and varnishes, paper and stationery, and toys.

Panamanian merchants buy only a few weeks' or at most three or four months' supply of goods. Merchants do not have to cater to seasonal demands as there is little seasonal change, and the income from bananas, coconuts, and other crops, is spread over the year.

EXPORTS AND IMPORTS.

	Exports. £	Imports. £	Balance. £
1916	1,135,407	1,896,365	— 760,958
1917 . .	1,159,624	1,901,684	— 742,060
1918 ..	597,846	1,612,713	—1,014,867
1919	774,645	2,351,934	—1,577,289
1920	728,090	3,418,454	—2,690,360
1921 . ..	—	—	—
1922 .. .	497,495	1,922,814	—1,425,319

British trade with Panamá has fallen in ten years from 24 per cent. of the total imports to 1 per cent., although the foreign trade of the Republic has continued to increase.

EXPORTS, 1922.

	Kilos.	Balboas.
United States . ..	116,066,351	2,160.581.62
England	252,927	131.332.03
Germany	682,453	128.255.88
Holland . ..	100,142	25.380.00
Spain . ..	126,846	16.632.00
Italy .. .	361,538	12.527.00
France .	119,135	5.838.00
Panamá Canal Zone	31,768	3.378.00
Jamaica .	192	1.164.00
Japan . .	39,928	896.00
Chile . .	19,786	557.50
Colombia ..	64	400.00
Costa Rica .	450	300.00
Guatemala .	46,440	236.25
Total .	117,848,020	2.487.478.28

PANAMÁ.

IMPORTS, 1922.

Paises.	Kilos.	Balboas.
United States	38,945,113	6,663.951.77
England	1,524,463	912.023.05
China	4,895,115	508.395.02
Germany	2,276,759	286.606.18
Perú	3,193,238	277.822.77
France	225,922	251.761.73
Japan	458,197	157.101.80
Holland	623,610	95.444.37
Chile	2,140,537	84.464.46
Spain	120,862	66.542.36
Italy	59,755	55.592.49
Colombia	81,881	46.019.76
Jamaica	60,212	42.893.40
Ecuador	225,402	37.221.89
Cuba	37,697	33.639.58
Norway	1,164,583	32.751.55
Sweden	769,362	20.813.41
Belgium	57,900	9.922.25
El Salvador	27,749	9.296.64
Costa Rica	2,720	6.418.64
Nicaragua	8,352	5.172.56
Curazao	4,525	4.590.93
Haiti	3,425	2.634.29
India	26,784	1.354.26
Guatemala	519	550.00
Honduras	320	350.00
Trinidad	—	336.00
Puerto Rico	94	300.00
Venezuela	100	101.90
Total	56,935,232	9.614.073.06

LEGATION AND CONSULATES IN GREAT BRITAIN

RESIDENCE.	DESIGNATION	NAME.
London (232 Finsbury Pavement House, E.C.2.)	Chargé d'Affaires	Carlos R. Zachrisson Vallarino.
	Attaché	Enrique Stagg.
	Attaché	Robert John Turner.
London	Consul	Carlos R. Zachrisson Vallarino.
Birmingham	Consul	Sergio S. Sauri.
Cardiff	Consul	Alfred J Bovey.
Glasgow	Vice-Consul	Charles John Cleland.
Liverpool	Consul-General	Archibaldo E. Boyd.
	Vice-Consul	Miguel Diaz.
Manchester	Consul	
Newcastle-on-Tyne	Vice-Consul	T F Weidner
Nottingham	Consul	Henry W Krabe.
Southampton	Consul	Juan Vallarino.
	Vice-Consul	
Swansea	Vice-Consul	Alfred Rhode.
London	Vice-Consul	C. J Dunbar MacConnell.

Guidance for Commercial Travellers.

Commercial travellers are not required to register, but municipal taxes for licences available for one month are payable by commercial travellers in Panamá. A separate licence is required for each municipal district. Travellers who visit only their own customers, or come for the special purpose of collecting debts, are not subject to any charges.

Municipal tax in Colón, $12.50 , Bocas del Toro, $10 for six months , Panamá, $25 for 30 days.

Agents of foreign firms permanently residing in Panamá are subject to a graduated tax.

Samples of no value are not liable to duty, but this fact should be stated in the invoice. In the case of samples of value, foreign commercial salesmen bringing samples with them must make a declaration of the samples and their value. A bond must be deposited covering the import duty, and it is desirable that the bond should be certified by the Consul for Panamá in the country whence the traveller comes. The bond is returned when the traveller leaves the country, on the presentation of a Custom House certificate stating that no part of the samples has been sold by the salesman during his stay in the Republic. Samples must be re-exported through the original port of entry unless notification is given to the Collector of Customs.

There are no restrictions upon commercial travellers in the Canal Zone, provided a traveller takes orders from samples. One who disposes of his samples must take out a pedlar's licence costing $2 per month.

THE PANAMA CANAL.

The length of the canal from the entrance to the dredged channel in the Atlantic to that in the Pacific is 43·84 nautical miles. The general direction is north-west to south-east. The main feature of the work is the triple flight of locks at Gatun and a dam constituting a lake, occupying about 164 square miles, formed by impounding the waters of the Chagres river. From here the Culebra Cut (or Gaillard Cut) is entered—a cutting 300 ft. wide, 6·97 miles long, and 45 ft. deep. From this there are changes of level at Pedro Miguel Locks and Miraflores, and thus into another artificial sheet of water

Canal History :—The idea of constructing a canal to unite the Atlantic with the Pacific was already old when Ferdinand de Lesseps arrived in Panamá in 1881 and started his preliminary surveys. Canals—open, level, through tunnels, or with locks—had been planned along various routes, but that fixed upon by de Lesseps was from Limón Bay to Panamá by the Chagres and Rio Grande. A company was formed to carry out this scheme in 1881, with a capital of £53,000,000. Nineteen miles were prepared before the crash in 1891.

The chiefs of the French Canal Company, convinced of their inability to complete the work, started negotiations with the United States and Colombian Governments. Eventually by the Herran-Hay Treaty they were authorized by Colombia to sell all rights and properties to the American Government. This treaty was strongly opposed in Colombia, and its ultimate rejection led to Panamá proclaiming her independence in 1903, and signing the Canal Treaty in November of the same year.

The price paid by the United States Government to Panamá for construction rights was ten million dollars. The French company received forty millions for its rights and properties. The total cost amounted at completion to $375,000,000. The canal was opened to commercial traffic August 15, 1914.

It was announced in August 1923 that the Canal was earning profit at the rate of about $500,000 a month, or at the rate of 3% upon its cost.

The seat of government of the Canal Zone is at Balboa Heights. The building containing the offices of the Governor and the higher officials is on a slight bluff on the western side of Ancón Hill, overlooking the surrounding country from Ancón to the canal entrance. The private residences of the higher officials surround the administrative offices, and the quarters of other officials are in Ancón or Balboa, and along the slopes of Sosa Hill.

The Panamá Canal has an office in Washington, D.C., the cable address of which is " Pancanal, Washington," and the mail address " Chief of Office, The Panamá Canal, Washington, D.C."

PANAMÁ.

This office provides information about the canal, and its rules and regulations. Matters referring to individual ships passing through the canal should be addressed to the Marine Superintendent at the Canal.

COMPARATIVE DISTANCE (IN NAUTICAL MILES) AND DIFFERENCE IN DISTANCES VIA PANAMA CANAL AND OTHER ROUTES.

To	Via	From					
		New York.	New Orleans.	Liverpool.	Hamburg.	Suez.	Panamá
Seattle ..	Magellan	13,953	14,369	14,320	14,701	15,397	—
	Panamá	6,080	5,501	8,654	9,173	10,447	4,063
Distance	saved	7,873	8,868	5,666	5,528	4,950	—
San Francisco	Magellan	13,135	13,551	13,502	13,883	14,759	—
	Panamá	5,262	4,683	7,836	8,355	9,629	3,245
Distance	saved	7,873	8,868	5,666	5,528	4,950	—
Honolulu .	Magellan	13,312	13,728	13,679	14,060	14,756	—
	Panamá	6,702	6,123	9,276	9,795	11,069	4,685
Distance	saved	6,610	7,605	4,403	4,265	3,687	—
Guayaquil	Magellan	10,215	10,631	10,582	10,963	11,659	—
	Panamá	2,810	2,231	5,384	5,903	9,192	793
Distance	saved	7,405	8,400	5,198	5,060	2,467	—
Callao .	Magellan	9,613	10,029	9,980	10,361	11,057	—
	Panamá	3,363	2,784	5,937	6,456	7,730	1,346
Distance	saved	6,250	7,245	4,043	3,905	3,327	—
Valparaiso	Magellan	8,380	8,796	8,747	9,128	9,824	—
	Panamá	4,623	4,054	7,207	7,726	9,000	2,616
Distance	saved	3,747	4,742	1,540	1,402	824	—
Wellington	Magellan	11,344	11,760	—	13,353	9,694	—
	Suez ..	—	—	12,989	—	—	—
	Panamá	8,857	8,272	11,425	11,944	9,205	6,834
Distance	saved	2,493	3,488	1,564	1,409	489	—
Melbourne	C. of Good Hope ..	13,162	14,095	—	11,845	8,186	—
	Suez ..	—	—	11,654	—	—	—
	Panamá	10,392	9,813	12,966	13,452	10,713	8,342
Distance	saved	2,770	4,288	1,312	1,607	2,527	—
Manila .	Suez ..	11,589	12,943	9,701	9,892	6,233	—
	Panamá	11,548	10,969	14,122	14,608	11,869	9,370
Distance	saved	41	1,974	4,421	4,716	5,636	—
Hong Kong	Suez .	11,673	13,031	9,785	9,976	6,317	—
	Panamá	11,691	11,112	13,957	14,443	11,704	9,173
Distance	saved	18	1,919	4,172	4,467	5,887	—
Yokohama	Suez	13,566	14,924	11,678	11,869	8,210	—
	Panamá	9,798	9,219	12,372	13,858	11,119	7,660
Distance	saved	3,768	5,705	694	1,989	2,909	—
Panamá ..	.. .	2,017	1,438	4,591	5,110	6,387	—

PANAMÁ CANAL ZONE.

The Panamá Canal Zone, a strip ten miles wide, extends from the Atlantic to the Pacific across the Isthmus. It includes the waters of Gatun Lake and the land round it within the 100-ft. contour line from mean sea-level. The canal runs through the centre of the zone, its ports being Colón and Cristobal on the Atlantic, Balboa and Panamá on the Pacific. This territory is administered by the United States, through the Governor of the Panamá Canal, but the cities of Panamá and Colón, with their harbours, are excluded from his jurisdiction and remain under the Republic of Panamá. Cristobal and Balboa, the only harbours that need be used by ships passing through the canal, are under United States rule.

Postal Service : — There is a regular mail service to and from the United States several times a week, and from other countries according to steamship service. Mail from the United States is received approximately one week after posting. Mail for officers or crews of vessels passing through the canal or calling at terminal ports, unless specially addressed to a local steamship agency, is forwarded to the postmaster at Cristobal for delivery The Cristobal post office is officially advised of the

A Bird's-eye View of the Canal, its Locks, the famed Culebra Cut, and the great Gatun Lake

341

movements of vessels, and mail is forwarded in the most expeditious manner, by rail or launch. Cristobal and Balboa have become the terminal ports of the canal, in place of Colón and Panamá, and letters addressed to agents of steamship lines at the latter places frequently fail to be delivered in time.

The letter rate from the Canal Zone to the United States, Canada, Cuba and Mexico is 2 cents an ounce or fraction : to all other countries, 5 cents for the first ounce and 3 cents for each additional ounce or fraction. Postcards, 1 cent to the United States, Canada, etc., and 2 cents to other countries.

Parcel post rate between the Canal Zone and the United States and other countries of the Postal Union is 12 cents per pound or fraction of a pound. The limit of weight is 22 pounds.

There are direct **cable** connections between the Isthmus and New York; also to the west coast of Central and South America, and to Mexico. Cable messages requiring an answer should be prepaid or covered by deposit.

The United States Government controls wireless service in the Republic of Panamá and contiguous waters.

Customs Regulations :—Vessels may enter either at Balboa or at Cristobal. A vessel arriving for passage through the canal, with through clearance from port of departure to port of final destination, and not stopping at either terminal port, is not required to enter or clear. A vessel stopping at either or both terminal ports is required to enter, and clearance is issued from the last port at which the vessel stops.

The **quarantine** regulations and requirements in brief summary are :—

The quarantine officer will board vessels on the Atlantic side anywhere in the bay; on the Pacific side between San José rock and the entrance of the channel. No vessel is allowed to go to a wharf without authority from the quarantine officer. Boarding hours are from sunrise to sunset on the Pacific terminal and from sunrise to 10 p.m. on the Atlantic. The office on the Pacific side is at the inshore end of the breakwater near the radio station; on the Atlantic side it is in the same building as that of the captain of the port.

All vessels from foreign ports are subject to inspection, and all vessels so subject shall be considered in quarantine until granted free pratique, and shall fly a yellow flag from the foremast head from sunrise to sunset.

One crew list and one passenger list must be handed to the quarantine officer when he comes aboard. Vessels must not proceed until these lists have been produced. This does not apply to troopships, men-of-war, or ships carrying contract labourers.

Masters of vessels will be held strictly responsible that no unauthorized person leaves the ship while in the terminal ports, passing through the locks, or in canal waters. Any violation of this law will subject the vessel to delay and the master to a heavy penalty

Standard time, 75th meridian, is kept throughout the Canal Zone. Under the direction of the Naval Radio Service, a time ball is dropped at 1 p.m. daily, 75th meridian time, from the mast over the centre of the signal station on Sosa Hill, Balboa Harbour.

Hotels :—The Washington at Colón and the Tivoli at Ancón are owned and maintained by the United States Government, and are both good, with modern improvements and charges fixed under Government direction.

Steamship connections :—From Cristobal there are fortnightly departures for Valparaiso and intermediate ports (Cia Sud Americana) ; for Peruvian ports (Cia Peruana), San Francisco and intermediate ports (Pacific Mail), Buenaventure and Tumaco (Colombian Maritime)

From Panamá there is a weekly steamer (National Navigation Co.), to the Panamá Pacific ports.

The Pacific Steam Navigation vessels, Liverpool—Valparaiso, and the Grace Line steamers, New York—Valparaiso, call regularly at Cristobal.

Press :—"The Panamá Canal Record," the official publication of the Canal Zone, is published once a week. All vessels passing through are furnished with a current copy. The paper contains official information and statistics, as well as weather probabilities and tide predictions.

Sanitation :—When the United States undertook the construction of the canal in 1904, Panamá was one of the most unhealthy spots in the world. Yellow fever and malaria had been endemic for years, and these, rather than engineering difficulties, had been responsible for the failure of the French engineer, Ferdinand de Lesseps. Yellow fever has been stamped out, and malaria has been diminishing ever since Colonel Goethals, the first Governor of the Zone, started his campaign.

At Ancón, a fine tropical hospital, with 800 beds, has the most modern equipment, and there are good hospitals at Colón and Panamá City

The **Panamá Railroad** runs from Colón to Panamá City (48 miles)

The old Panamá Railroad followed the valley of the Chagres River from Gatun to Gamboa, but this part is now submerged in Gatun Lake, the canal following the route of the old railway very closely From Gamboa it crossed the Divide through the present site of Culebra, thence through Paraiso and the bed of what is now Miraflores Lake to Panamá. It was not found possible to utilize much of the old road when the canal was made, and it was mostly relaid to run roughly parallel with the canal to the eastward.

There is a frequent train service across the Isthmus and between local points. Between the canal and the railroad there is strong community of interest. The management and direction of both are vested in the Governor, and many officials and employees are common to both. Fare, 1st class return, Panamá-Colón, $4·80. There are stations at Mount Hope, Fort Davis, Gatun, Monte Lirio, Frijoles, Darien, Gamboa, Summit, Pedro Miguel, Red Tank, Miraflores Locks, Fort Clayton, Corozal, and Balboa. There are three daytime passenger trains each way daily. The crossing of the Isthmus by train takes two hours.

PANAMÁ.

Canal Traffic.

Commercial traffic through the Panamá Canal for the fiscal year ending June 30, 1923, was approximately one-half greater than in any preceding year :—

Fiscal year			No. of vessels.	Panamá Canal net tonnage.	Tolls.*	Cargo tonnage.
1920			2,478	8,546,044	$8,513,933	9,374,499
1921		..	2,892	11,415,876	11,276,889	11,599,214
1922	.	.	2,736	11,417,459	11,197,832	10,884,910
1923		..	3,967	18,605,786	17,508,199	19,567,875

* Exclusive of launches.

344

PARAGUAY

PARAGUAY.

Paraguay has no seaboard of its own and its capital city, **Asunción,** may be reached either by rail or steamer from Buenos Aires. The train journey is 1,514 kilometres over the Paraguay Central Railway and its connections. The capital has a population of 75,000 and is seated on the east bank of the Paraguay river, 1,200 miles from the sea, 132 from Concepción and 93 from Villa Rica. The elevation is 200 ft. above sea-level. Among its chief buildings are the Government Palace, the Palace of Congress, and the National Library. The industries include sugar refineries, cotton and woollen mills, tanneries and distilleries.

Hotels :—Cosmos, Hispano-Americano, Italia, Roma, Gran Hotel del Paraguay, Parque.

Cab fares :—6 a.m. to 8 p.m., 7 pesos any distance; from 8 p.m. to 6 a.m., 15 pesos. Fares to the outskirts vary up to 25 pesos.

House rents at Asunción are high, having regard to the accommodation and the conveniences provided. A small four-roomed house of the better class, with the usual offices, could not be obtained for less than £160 a year, unfurnished. There is no public water service, drainage, or gas, but electric current is available at a charge of 9d. per kilowatt-hour. The wages of native domestic servants run from £15 to £30 a year exclusive of food, which can be taken as equivalent to a further £35 a year per head.

Concepción, capital of department of the same name, also on the east bank of the Paraguay river, is reached by steamer from Asunción. An agricultural centre, it is one of the centres for yerba maté growing. Population, 35,000.

Hotels :—Central, Frances, San Martin, Aurora, Victoria.

Encarnación, capital of the department of Encarnación, is on the Alta Paraná river, 230 miles from Asunción and 136 from Villa Rica. The centre of a rich agricultural and grazing district, it produces maté, tobacco, hides and timber A ferry connects the town with Posadas, on the Argentine North-east Railroad, whence there is good communication with Buenos Aires. Population, 33,000. Terminus of the Paraguay Central Railway.

Hotels :—Palmas, Universal, Engelsbourg.

Villa Rica, with a population of 44,500, is in the department of Guaira, 93 miles from Asunción and 136 from Villa Encarnación. The district produces yerba maté, tobacco, hides, sugar-cane, and timber, and the chief industries are brickworks, saw-mills, and distilleries. Served by the Paraguay Central Railway.

Hotels :—Central, Español, Franco Suizo.

Villa del Pilar, a port on the Paraguay river, opposite the mouth of the Bermejo, has a population of about 15,000 and stands in a district producing tobacco, yerba maté, hides, and oranges. Served by steamer and the Paraguay Central Railway

Hotel :—Paris.

PHYSICAL FEATURES.

Paraguay is 290,000 square miles in extent, or considerably larger than Great Britain and Ireland. It is divided into two portions by the river of the same name. Eastern Paraguay is some 100,000 square miles in area, and borders upon Argentina and Brazil. It is bounded on the north by the rivers Apa and Estrella, on the east by the mountain-chains of Amambay and Mbaracayú and by the river Paraná, and on the south also by the Paraná. Western Paraguay, or the Chaco, is a quadrilateral, one side being formed by the Paraguay river between the mouths of the Rio Negro and the Pilcomayo. It is watered by the latter and by the Bermejo, a river which in 1870–2 opened a new channel, known as the Teuco, for some 200 miles. The land is well wooded, and the annual rainfall (between May and November) about 80 in. The climate is equable, and agriculture is carried on under most favourable conditions.

The mountain-chain of the Sierra Amambay runs through Paraguay from north to south and, separating to east and west under the name of Sierra Mbaracayú, divides the tributaries of the Paraná river from those of the Paraguay. The northern portion of the Republic is undulating, with long grass plains. The southern part is fertile, undulating, richly wooded, well watered, and intersected by alluvial plains. The most noteworthy sheet of water is Lake Ypoá.

The Paraguay river rises in Brazil, and is for a considerable distance the boundary line between that country and Bolivia. It flows south-west through Paraguay to its junction with the Paraná, a little above Corrientes. Its principal tributaries are the Cuyabá, Mondego, Tacuary, Apa, Jauru, Pilcomayo, and Bermejo. Its whole length is 1,800 miles. It is navigable to the mouth of the Cuyabá, and both banks are well timbered. The Paraguay is an affluent of the Paraná, it rises in Brazil and has a total length of 2,000 miles. It separates the State of Paraná from that of Matto Grosso and from Paraguay, and it passes on its junction with the Paraguay around the southern border of the Republic. The chief means of communication are the Paraná and Paraguay rivers. The Republic is well served by various lines of steamers. The Compañia Argentina de Navegación (Mihanovich Line) steamers leave Buenos Aires for Asunción three days a week, calling en route. The Upper Paraguay River Line leaves Buenos Aires once a month for Bella Vista, Villa del Pilar, Asunción, Concepción. The Corrientes-Posadas Line leaves Corrientes twice a week, and the Alto Paraná Line sails from Buenos Aires to Villa Encarnación and Posadas.

The greater part of the **population** is of Indian descent, with a comparatively slight intermixture of alien blood. The total population is not precisely known as it is some twenty-five years since any attempt was made to take a census. It is usually placed at about 800,000, but the figure by some is placed as low as 600,000.

The language of the country is Spanish, but Guaraní (Indian) is spoken generally outside the towns.

The **climate** is hot, without being unhealthy The lower two-thirds of the Republic are within the temperate zone, and the upper third in the tropics. The rivers and mountains affect the climate.

The year is divided into two seasons, the hot lasting from October to March, and the cold from April to September. The mean temperature is 81° for summer, and 71° for winter, the annual rainfall is 46 in., very equally distributed. The heaviest rainfall occurs during August, September, and October

A PARAGUAYAN CALENDAR.

1515. Juan Diaz de Solis reaches the coast of La Plata.
1527. Sebastian Cabot sails up the Paraguay
1535. Founding of Asunción.
1537. Irala assumes charge of the new colony.
1542. Cabeza de Vaca arrives at Asunción.
1545. Cabeza de Vaca sent a captive to Spain.
1550. First Catholic missionaries arrive.
1557. Death of Irala.
1570. Villa Rica founded.
1591. Hernandarias becomes the first colonial Governor of the Rio de la Plata (Paraguay and Argentina).
1610. First arrival of the Jesuits in Asunción.
1617. Separation of Paraguay from Rio de la Plata; subject to the Vice-Royalty of Peru.
1641. Beginning of the dispute between the Governor Hinestrosa and Bishop Bernadino Cardenas.
1648. Beginning of conflict between Bishop Cardenas and the Jesuits.
1769. Expulsion of the Jesuits.
1776. Establishment of the Vice-Royalty of Buenos Aires, with jurisdiction over the present Republics of Bolivia (part), Uruguay, Paraguay, and the Argentine Confederation.
1810. The Paraguayans repulse Argentine troops under General Belgrano.
1811. Paraguay declares its independence of Spain. First Paraguayan Junta established.
1814-1840. Dr. Francia, Dictator of Paraguay.
1844. Carlos Antonio López elected President. (d. 1862.)
1845. Appearance of the first newspaper.
1853. Francisco Solano López despatched on a mission to Europe.
1854. Construction of first railway line begun.
1861. Opening of the railway line between Asunción and Paraguarí.
1862. Francisco Solano López named President in succession to his father
1865. Outbreak of war with Argentina, Brazil and Uruguay
1870. Death of López in the battle of Aquidaban. Conclusion of war.
1870. The present Constitution promulgated.
1877 President Bautista Gil assassinated.
1879. Delimitation agreement signed with Bolivia.
1891. Revolutionary rising under Major Vera suppressed.
1893. Establishment of the colony of "New Australia."
1902. Revolution at Asunción President Aceval deposed. Hector Carvalho elected President.
1908. Coup d'état. Emiliano González Navero made President.
1916. Congress increased to a strength of 20 Senators and 40 Deputies.
1919. Joins the League of Nations.

GOVERNMENT.

PAST PRESIDENTS (since 1906).

The Republic had six provisional Presidents between November, 1906, and August, 1920, owing to the deaths and retirements from office of the Chiefs of State.

General Benigno Ferreira (provisional), November, 1906–July, 1908.

Dr. Emiliano González Navero (provisional), July, 1908–November, 1910.

Dr. Manuel Gondra, November, 1910–January, 1911.

Colonel Albino Jara (provisional), January–July, 1911.

Dr. Liberato M. Rojas (provisional), July, 1911–February, 1912.

Dr. Pedro Peña (provisional), February–March, 1912.

Dr. Emiliano González Navero (provisional), March–August, 1912.

Dr. Eduardo Schaerer, August, 1912–August, 1916.

Dr. Manuel Franco, August, 1916–June, 1917 (when he died).

Dr. José P Montero, June, 1917–August, 1920.

Dr. Manuel Gondra (second term), August, 1920–October, 1921

PRESIDENT.

Provisional President : Eligio Ayala.

MINISTRY.

Interior	Modesto Guggiari.
Foreign Office	Rogelio Ibarra.
Finance	Dr. Luis Riart.
Education and Justice ..	Dr. Lisandro D. Leon.
War	Colonel Manlio Schenone.

The established **religion** is Roman Catholicism, but universal toleration is the rule. The only episcopal diocese is Asunción, and the Bishop is suffragan to the Archbishop of Buenos Aires. The civil ceremony alone renders marriage valid, but religious ceremonies are permitted.

There are a Supreme Court, two Courts of Appeal (civil and commercial and criminal), ten judges of first instance, and three metropolitan police magistrates. In the provinces justice is administered by justices of the peace, who also act as registrars.

Currency :—The unit of value is the gold peso, which is based on the Argentine coin of the same name. The actual currency is depreciated paper, varying widely in value. There are no gold or silver coins current, and only a few nickel coins.

The metric system is in use, but the following **local measures** are commonly found :—

Linear Measure.

100 varas = 1 cuadra = 97 yards (about).
50 cuadras = 1 league Paraguayan = 2⅔ miles (about).

Square Measure.

1 cuadra = 2 acres (nearly).
2,500 cuadras = 1 league Paraguayan = 7¼ square miles (about)

NATURAL RESOURCES.

Much of the country is admirably suited to pastoral purposes, while other parts yield such forest products as quebracho, maté, and various timbers, which can be produced without cultivation. The inadequacy of available labour and the primitive character of communications render scientific agriculture at present a rather difficult problem. A far greater productive power may be expected to take place as capital is applied to the development of the country. Tobacco-growing is becoming more important, and orange groves are being planted in many places. Coffee, rice, cotton, and sugar are increasingly cultivated. Yerba-maté, or Paraguayan tea, is the most important product. With the exception of tanneries and breweries there are few factories.

Yerba-maté :—The tree grows wild in the forests of the north-east, and the gathering, preparation, and transport of the product constitutes one of the most lucrative industries in the country. The immense number of trees over an area of 15,000 to 20,000 square miles are a most valuable asset. The industry is carried on by a few large companies, of which the most important is La Industrial Paraguaya. Owing to the vast extent of the forests, their surreptitious exploitation by unauthorized persons is common.

The total average registered production is about 10,000 tons a year, and the average quantity exported during seven recent years is 3,680 tons. The selling price is some £50 and £60 a ton.

It is estimated that there are some 2,000,000 plants, two to four years old, and new plantations are continually being set up. In six to eight years the average amount of yerba obtainable per tree should be about six kilos. Upon the plantations the trees are set in rows so that systematic pruning is facilitated.

Sugar :—The cultivation of cane has received an impulse in face of the high prices ruling for the imported article. The area under cane is reported to be about 11,000 acres, and the production of sugar in 1920 about 3,800 tons, as against 2,505 in 1919, and 562 in 1918. The average consumption of sugar is estimated at 3,000 tons a year. Of the seven factories in present operation, the largest is the Azucarera Paraguaya, with eight or ten miles of metre-gauge railway running through its estates. Unrefined sugar is produced by these factories, and there should be room for the establishment of a refinery.

Timber :—Timber is available of the finest quality and in practically unlimited quantities. Thousands of miles of forests remain untouched. Many rare and valuable woods are still largely unknown in foreign markets, since lumbermen obtain larger profits by cutting and shipping the common kinds used for railway sleepers.

In the Chaco Territory practically the only timber cut is quebracho, and the forests are being rapidly depleted of the larger trees, which are taken in thousands to the tanning factories to be broken up.

The lumbering industry offers a good field for enterprise. Prime timber land, in blocks of 10 to 50 square leagues or more, can be purchased at the present time for £1,000 to £2,000 a square league (about 5,000 acres). The forests in the vicinity of the railway or the semi-navigable streams, down which rafts can be floated, are being depleted of the finest trees, compelling lumbermen to go farther afield. There are several sawmills along the Paraguay Central Railway, and at Concepción, Encarnación, Pilar, with three or four at Asunción, where the smaller logs are cut into boards and scantlings for shipment to the Argentine.

Cotton :—Due to the praiseworthy efforts of the Banco Agricola in encouraging cultivation of cotton as a domestic industry there is some hope that the product may at no distant date figure regularly as an article of export. The cotton is said to be of very fine quality, and the difficulties originally experienced in regard to the irregular ripening of the bolls are being overcome by selection of seed. The quantities bought by the Banco Agricola, the only purchaser, are · 1919, 363 tons, 1920, 432 tons; 1921, 900 tons.

Rice :—The production of rice, estimated at 1,000 tons in 1914, has increased largely. The crop was 2,800 tons in 1919 and 2,000 tons in 1920.

Cattle and Meat Packing :—Stock-breeding has always been one of the staple industries. Before the war Paraguay depended on the Argentine as a market for her surplus production, and the position was somewhat insecure, as the quality of Paraguayan stock was considerably lower than that raised in the Argentine. The war created a sudden demand for meat, with the result that three meat-packing companies were established in Paraguay (1917–18). Soon after the cessation of hostilities in Europe it became apparent that Paraguayan meat products could not compete with those of the Argentine, and first one and then another of the packing houses were forced to close.

The boom nevertheless had a permanently beneficial effect on the stock-breeding industry Efforts had been made from the commencement to improve the type of cattle, and numbers of Shorthorn, Hereford and Polled Angus bulls were imported.

Mineral Wealth :—The extent of the mineral resources is largely unknown. There is no question that large and workable deposits of rich iron ores exist in many parts of the country. Several mines exist which were worked in the time of López, whose foundries and shops turned out cannon, cart axles and tyres, beams and plates. As far as it is known, the richest deposits of magnetic iron, hydric oxides and brown hematite are in the neighbourhood of Ibicui, Quiquyo, Caapucú and the surrounding district, but iron exists practically all over the country. Pyrites and peroxide of manganese abound. Copper is known to exist in many parts.

Limestone, marble, granite, porphyry, serpentine and kaolin are found in many places. Only the limestone is worked to any extent, but the export of kaolin to the Argentine is being attempted. Large beds of excellent lithographic stone were discovered a few years ago. Salt is obtained at Lambaré.

No coal has yet been found, though some authorities believe it to exist. There is an inexhaustible supply of hard wood for fuel. Petroleum is also believed to exist in Paraguay Proper, and in the Chaco Territory bordering upon Bolivia, but no systematic prospecting has been done.

POSTAL COMMUNICATION.

Paraguay is in the Postal Union, and the usual rates for foreign letters apply in communications between it and the United Kingdom.

Outward and Homeward mails are despatched with the mails to and from Argentina.

Cable rates :—The ordinary rate per word to Paraguay is 2s. 9d. and the deferred rate half the ordinary.

There are **wireless** installations at Asunción, Concepción, and Encarnación.

PUBLIC HOLIDAYS.
January 1 : New Year's Day.
February 3 : San Blas Day.
May 14 and 15 : Independence Days.
August 15 (at Asunción only) : Founding of the City (1536).
October 12 : Columbus Day.
November 25 : Adoption of Constitution.
December 25 : Christmas Day.

Sports :—Football was introduced some twenty years ago, and has become remarkably popular. Almost every town and village in the country has one or more clubs. At the capital the League comprises some thirty clubs, some with seating accommodation for 8,000 to 10,000 people. International matches with teams from Uruguay and Argentina are of yearly occurrence. There are three or four tennis clubs at Asunción, and the game has been taken up at some of the towns in the interior. There is at Asunción a rowing and swimming club with some 300 members, and a motor-boat club with about 150 members and 25 to 30 motor-boats.

Commercial Information :—Country of origin must be stated on bills of lading and invoice, but Certificates of Origin, as such, are not required.

No special form of Consular invoice is required, but merchants' invoices in Spanish must be presented in triplicate with bills of lading for visa. Special particulars must be inserted, details of which are obtainable from the Paraguayan Consulates. In the case of goods transhipped at Buenos Aires or Montevideo, documents must be produced at those ports to show the country of origin. If the goods are not sent on a through bill of lading the consular requirements either of Uruguay or Argentina have also to be complied with.

Trade Marks :—As Paraguayan law takes no cognisance of the fact that a trade mark may have been registered elsewhere, anyone may appropriate a mark that has not hitherto been registered in the country and without adducing any proof of rightful ownership. Exporters of goods bearing a mark should therefore register as soon as possible.

IMPORTS AND EXPORTS.

	Exports. £	Imports. £	Total. £	Balance. £
1922	1,963,469	1,127,934	3,091,413	835,535
1921	1,848,556	1,658,515	3,507,071	190,041
1920	2,968,090	2,602,890	5,570,980	365,200
1919	3,588,297	3,167,194	6,755,491	421,103
1918	2,279,942	2,210,324	4,490,266	69,618
1917	2,341,002	1,835,490	4,176,492	505,512
1916	1,770,384	1,404,007	3,174,391	366,377
1915	1,778,199	625,531	2,403,730	1,152,668
1914	1,111,761	1,029,893	2,141,654	81,868
1913	1,126,186	1,623,999	2,750,185	*497,813

* Adverse.

CONSULATES IN GREAT BRITAIN.

RESIDENCE.	DESIGNATION.	NAME.
London (14 Chiswell House, Finsbury Pavement, E.C.2.)	Consul-General (for Great Britain and Ireland).	Captain Ernesto Ibañez.
Birmingham	Consul	Alfred S. Chovil.
Bradford	Consul	James Edward Bottomley
Cardiff	Consul	Alfred John Bovey.
Glasgow	Consul	Sir Thomas Dunlop.
Liverpool	Consul	Alfred Stephen Collard.
Manchester	Consul	Walter Beer.
Southampton	Consul	Col. Joseph Edward Dawe.

Guidance for Commercial Travellers.

The only licence required by commercial travellers in Paraguay is municipal. The fee payable ranges from $1,200 currency to $7,000 currency for each half year, and the precise sum is fixed according to the importance or scope of the traveller's business as assessed by the Municipal Authorities. A separate licence must be taken out in each municipality and the charge is equal as between municipalities of the 1st and 2nd Grade ; in municipalities of the 3rd Grade, the charge is one-third. The licence needs renewal on January 1st or July 1st, if the traveller continues to carry on business after the end of the term.

In practice, and with a view to encouraging foreign trade, the regulations affecting commercial travellers within the municipality of Asunción are not strictly enforced. The fee for the lowest class of licence is usually charged, viz., $1,200 for the half year ; and, should the licence be applied for after the commencement of a term, only a proportion is charged. A traveller applying for a licence in November, pays for the months of November and

December, at the rate of $200 currency a month, not for the entire six months. The same practice is adopted by most other Paraguayan municipalities.

The various municipalities are graded as :—

1st Grade : ASUNCIÓN.

2nd Grade : Concepcion, Pilar, Villarrica, Encarnacion, Villa San Pedro, Caazapa, Carapegua, San Juan Bautista, San Ignacio, Luque, Paraguari, San Estanislao.

3rd Grade : All other Municipalities in Paraguay.

The fees payable per half year are :—

1st Class $7,000 , 2nd Class $5,500 ; 3rd Class $3,800 ; 4th Class $2,500 , 5th Class $1,200.

THE IGUAZU FALLS.

The Falls and Cataracts of Iguazu exert a first claim upon the attention of the sightseer They are in the Misiones Territory, in the wild country abutting upon Argentina and Brazil. They rank in grandeur with Niagara and the Victoria Falls and their reputation arises in part from their great size and partly from the beauty of the great number of cascades.

COMPARATIVE DIMENSIONS.

		Height.	Breadth.	Flow of Water.
Iguazu Falls	..	760 ft.	13,000 ft.	28,000,000 c.f. per minute.
Niagara Falls	..	160 ft.	4,726 ft.	18,000,000 c.f. per minute.
Victoria Falls	..	387 ft.	5,300 ft.	variable.

The most favourable season for a visit is May to November The journey is made by rail and river steamer or by steamer, and may be combined with visits to Asunción and other points in a round trip from Buenos Aires.

The several falls possess distinctive names. Of those on the Argentine side the Two Sisters are the chief, and the Bossetti, the most turbulent and picturesque, is usually crowned by a rainbow, as are the smaller San Martin Falls. Mitré, the Three Musketeers, and the Devil's Throat, are best seen from an island, reached by canoe.

To see the falls on the Brazilian side, it is necessary to cross from Puerto Aguirre to Foz de Iguazu, and traverse Brazilian territory

Waterproofs and sandals are requisite in making close inspection and especially for those who undertake the rope ladder descent.

The Iguazu River is a tributary of the Paraná, from which the Falls are 19 kilometres. The word is Guarani for "Great Waters."

By Steamer from Buenos Aires two itineraries are offered to the tourist .

1 Via the River Paraná and the Upper Paraná.

2. Via River Uruguay to Salto, Concordia to Posadas by train, thence by river steamer to the Falls, returning via Corrientes.

Sailings are made from Buenos Aires (South Dock) via the Paraná every Sunday and Thursday Transhipment is made at Corrientes whence steamers leave on Monday and Thursday mornings, arriving at Posadas in the afternoon of the following day Steamers depart from Posadas about twice a week. These steamers disembark passengers at Puerto Aguirre, and the journey is continued up-river to the Falls, returning to Puerto Aguirre in about fifty-six hours. From Puerto Aguirre the transit is by coach or horse for the remaining 17 kilometres. There is a boarding house in Puerto Aguirre and an hotel in Iguazu, both comfortable. The climate is salutary and temperate.

ITINERARY.

From Buenos Aires to Corrientes .	3 days	(River Paraná).
,, Corrientes to Posadas . .	36 hours	
,, Buenos Aires to Concordia .	26 hours	(River Uruguay).
,, Posadas to Puerto Aguirre . .	48 hours	

Approximate Fares
    Route No. 1 $315.
    Route No. 2 $340.
Including Hotel Accommodation.

By Rail from Buenos Aires :—The itinerary combines the Entre Rio and North-eastern Argentine systems. The journey is comfortable, economical, and picturesque. The trains have sleeping and restaurant cars, good meals and wines.

The train leaves Lacroze station, Buenos Aires, westward, passing Lynch, Caseros, and a series of small stations on the way to Zarate, a port on one of the arms of the Paraná. There passengers alight and ferry across to Ibicuy The journey continues through the Gualeguaychu plains to the heart of the province of Entre Rios, nearly parallel with the River Gualeguay, afterwards north-east to Concordia on the Argentine bank of the River Uruguay. Thence the North-east Argentine Railway runs close by the river through Monte Caseros, Paso de los Libres, Yapeyu, Santo Tome Apostoles to Posadas, so crossing the Province of Corrientes.

Posadas, reached after thirty-six hours' rail journey from Buenos Aires, is the capital of Misiones. Posadas is not a modern town, but it has fine buildings and good hotels.

A visit to the Guarani ruins in the region of Misiones is very interesting, and should be undertaken. The zone of the old Missions begins at Yapeyu. Traces of the Guarani are visible on both sides of the River Uruguay, in Santo Tome Apostoles, and also to the south-east and north-east of Posadas between the Upper Paraná and Upper Uruguay Tourists cannot visit them all but should not voluntarily omit a visit to the **Ruins of San Ignacio,** which are reached by special launch from Posadas (50 kilometres) After five kilometres by horseback or coach, the remains of four squares, a cathedral, and a seminary are reached.

The **Ruins of Santa Maria** are inviting, and to visit them one returns to Posadas and re-embarks for San Javier on the Upper Uruguay, near which is the chapel of "Cerro the Monk" and a curative spring.

From Posadas there are capital steamers for Iguazu. The banks of the Paraná are well wooded, and present a memorable picture. From Posadas one can continue by rail to Asunción in Paraguay, or alternatively, without returning to Posadas, one may leave Iguazu for Villa Encarnación, on the Paraguayan side, thence over the Paraguayan Central Railway through fertile country to the foot of the Cordilleras, where the route inclines to the west, leading to Asunción.

PARAGUAY.

Villa Encarnación resembles Posadas. It has a telegraph office, and various branch banks.

Before arriving at Asunción, the beautifully wooded Lake Iparcaray is passed—a favourite summer resort for Paraguayan families.

San Bernardino village is the fashionable summer resort of Paraguayan society, and has fine hotels.

In **Asunción,** although the principal streets are well paved, the rest leave much to be desired. The main street is the "Uruguaya." The public buildings include the Ministry of the Interior, the Governor's Palace, Superior Tribunal, Mail and Telegraph Office, and Legislative Palace. There are also neat chalets, and elegant mansions.

The "Itinerario" of the Express Internacional, Buenos Aires, Montevideo, and Rio de Janeiro, can be consulted with advantage for the purpose of studying the alternative combined tickets available for round trips from Buenos Aires to Iguazu. Tickets include the passage on the steamers of the Mihanovitch Line, rail fares and hotel charge.

PERU

PERU.

Callao, the chief port and the main approach to the capital of the country, is distant only 8 miles from Lima. The harbour works cover 250 acres. The town is a busy one and nearly 400,000 tons of cargo are dealt with yearly The population is some 53,000. The barren island of San Lorenzo protects the roadstead to the south, and in the opposite direction stretches the green Rimac Valley. The distant towers of Lima's churches and hills make a pleasing sight as the vessel steams into the harbour No movement is allowed in the port after 6 p.m., a point worth noting by passengers in transit.

Landing :—Shore boat.

Hotels:—Universal ($2–$3), without meals, Italia ($2–$3), without meals.

Conveyance :—Electric cars to Lima, journey about thirty-five minutes.

Excursion :—To Ancón (bathing).

Lima, at one period the capital of Spanish South America, owes its creation to Pizarro the conqueror " Amidst the woe and destruction which Pizarro and his followers brought on the devoted land of the Incas," wrote Prescott, " Lima, the beautiful City of the Kings, survives as the most glorious work of his creation, the fairest gem on the shores of the Pacific." Its cathedral was founded by Pizarro in the year 1535, and there his remains rest. It has excellent hotels and good modern conveniences. The wide and fertile plain on which it stands slopes gently to the sea. The Andes, whose higher ranges are within fifty miles' distance, send their foothills to the gates of the city The hills keep off the colder winds, and the ocean breezes temper the sun. The town is built in the shape of a triangle, and the streets run straight and intersect at right angles. Well-kept squares or plazas vary the plan. Old Spanish houses, with carved doors and overhanging balconies, breathe an old-world charm which is echoed by the convents and churches. The streets abound with life, and many of the new buildings are fine. The old Spanish buildings contrast with modern ferro-concrete structures built to resist earthquakes. The population is some 220,000. The situation is on the Rimac river, eight miles from the port, 110 miles from Cerro de Pasco, and 600 from Cuzco. The temperature averages about 66° Fahr. Altitude 500 feet. The ruins and relics of Inca and pre-Inca times in the neighbourhood deserve a visit.

Hotels :—Maury, Francia-Inglaterra, Cardinal, Americano, Gran, Central.

Restaurant :—" Botanical," Zoological Gardens.

Conveyances :—Electric cars, motors, and cabs.

Points of Interest :—The Cathedral, with the remains of Pizarro, the Senate, the old Hall of the Inquisition, with a fine carved roof, the Bolognesi and Bolivar Monuments, Zoological Gardens, Paseo Colón, the fashionable promenade.

Curios :—Inca pottery, etc., from Brignardello, Portal de Escribanos.

Excursions :—Bathing and pleasure resorts (by electric railway) Miraflores, Barranco, Chorillos, Magdalena, La Punta, Chosica.

Railways :—Central Peruvian Railway to Oroya and Cerro de Pasco, three times a week. Lima to Huacho, three times per week upon the highest railway in the world.

Arequipa, 107 miles from the sea, stands at an altitude of 7,600 feet, in a beautiful valley at the foot of the mountain "El Misti" (17,934 feet), guarded on either hand by the Pichu Pichu and Chachani mountains. It has quaint old Spanish buildings and many ancient and interesting churches. The streets present as strange a panorama as those of any city in the world, with the crowd of Spanish-descended Peruvian hidalgos, half-breeds, and Indians of different tribes. Some walk, others ride donkeys, mules, or horses. All are picturesquely dressed. Population 50,000. Mean temperature 58° Fahr Subject to earthquakes.

Hotels :—Central, Royal, Panamá, Francia-Inglaterra, Internacional, Grand.

Restaurants :—Parodi and Morosini.

Conveyances :—Trams, cabs.

Buildings of Interest :—Cathedral and churches.

Excursions :—Harvard Observatory, half an hour's ride; Tiabaya and Tingo, suburbs of Arequipa.

Rail :—Mollendo and La Paz. (See page 88.)

Mollendo is the port for through traffic for Bolivia. It lies between the Tambo and Camara rivers. The urban population is 7,000 with 2,000 or more in the suburbs, British colony 20.

South-bound passengers wishing to see the interior of Peru and Bolivia do well to disembark at Mollendo and proceed via Lake Titicaca to La Paz, the capital of Bolivia. The round trip can be completed by returning to the steamer at Antofagasta, or Arica, with which La Paz is connected by rail. (See page 88.)

A shorter trip can be made by the Southern Railway to Arequipa, and thence to Juliaia and Cuzco, the most ancient city upon the Southern Continent, with magnificent temples, churches, and Inca ruins. The journey of five hours is varied and interesting, and the scenery increases in beauty as Arequipa is approached.

Landing :—Shore boat.

Hotels :—Gran and Ferrocarril.

Cuzco was the capital of the Inca Empire. It stands 11,440 feet above sea-level. Intensive cultivation, combined with a cast-iron rotation, enabled the terraces, scooped from the mountain slope, to support a teeming population under the old régime. Now the population is scanty and the plateaux are out of cultivation. The terraces on the hillside, the road, aqueducts, bridges, the temple, and walls, with their gigantic stones, bear witness to the splendour of the elder civilization.

Cuzco has some 30,000 inhabitants, mostly Indians. Many old families of pure Spanish descent live in and around the town. The town is the collecting centre for the departments of Cuzco, Apurimac, and part of Madre de Dios. It is remarkably fertile and has a considerable trade, but owing to lack of roads and railways has not developed of late years in proportion to the rest of the country The greater part of the traffic out of the railway sphere is over mountain trails by mules and llamas.

There are two or three breweries with a fairly large output, and there are woollen mills at Lucre and Marangani, producing a fair grade of cloth and suitings.

The town is remarkable for its churches and convents, dating from the early times of the Spanish conquest, possessing in their day great wealth in gold and silver and jewels. Many of the carvings of the wood work are worth inspection. One of the main attractions are the ruins : fortifications and irrigation works of the Inca and pre-Inca or Cyclop periods. These are a source of increasing interest to travellers and archæologists. Of recent years the Government has made efforts to prohibit excavations or the removal of any portion of the ruins or antiquities. Laws exist impeding the export of antiquities—pottery (huacos), mummies, silver or gold ware of either Inca or colonial origin, church furniture, etc.

Cuzco Cathedral (Renaissance style) was built at the beginning of the 17th century. The high altar is covered with silver, and amongst many original paintings the Cathedral contains one attributed to Van Dyck.

Hotels :—Colón, Angel, Gasco, Maury, Pullman, Central, Europa.

Rail :—Southern Railroad.

From Cuzco a narrow-gauge line is under construction to **Santa Ana,** capital of the province of Convencion, covering the fertile valley of that name, watered by the river Urubamba and its tributaries. Santa Ana (altitude 1,205 metres) is an outpost of civilization for the vast foreign region stretching to the Brazilian frontier and to the river Ucayali. The building of the line makes slow progress. About 40 kilometres have so far been completed of the total distance from Cuzco to Santa Ana of about 200 kilometres. The roads are merely trails.

Ayacucho, capital of department, population 20,000, altitude 9,200 feet, 360 miles from Lima, 162 from Huancayo. A mining centre, producing gold, silver, copper, cobalt, besides coffee, cacao, sugar, cotton, tobacco, grain and alfalfa. Industries : Pottery making and stock raising.

Hotel :—Colón.

Rail :—Central Railway

Cerro de Pasco, capital of department of Junin, altitude 14,380 feet, 110 miles from Lima, 81 from Oroya. Population about 15,000, a great centre of copper mining.

Hotels :—Universo, Ibero-Americano.

Rail :—Central Railway.

Chiclayo, capital of department of Lambayeque. Population 15,000. About 514 miles from Lima and 12 from the Pacific port of Eten. Industries Textile mills, straw hats, distilleries, chocolate factories, rice mills. Sugar, rice, cotton, and cacao centre.

Hotels :—Gran, Royal, Internacional.

Rail :—Connected with Eten (Ferrocarril Muelle de Eten) and Lambayeque (Ferrocarril de Chiclayo)

Chala, a minor port, south of Callao, which ships large numbers of cattle from the pampas of the interior. The coast is rocky and a favourite haunt of cormorants. Large numbers of sharks, bonitos, and seals are to be seen.

Landing :—Shore boat.

Chimbote, a minor port north of Callao, whence a railway (32 miles) runs tb Suchiman. It is an outlet for the mining hinterland and has a small trade in sugar

Huaráz, the capital of the department of Ancachs, altitude 9,932 feet, on the Santa river, 216 miles from Lima and 64 from Casma, its port. Silver, cinnabar, coal, wheat, and potatoes centre.

Hotels :—Italia, Ancachs.

Ica, capital of department, on the Ica river, 92 miles from Lima, 46 from Pisco. Population 15,000. Industries : Distilleries, textile mills. Wool, cotton, cacao, silver and copper centres.

Hotel :—Americano.

Rail :—Pisco and Ica Railway.

Iquitos, the capital of Bajo Amazonas de Loreto, is a port on the left bank of the Upper Amazon, 2,300 miles from the mouth and 1,268 from Lima. It has regular steamship connection with Pará, Brazil, by which route it is generally reached, being difficult of access from western Peru. Population 20,000. Industries : Saw-milling, chocolate making, preparation of rubber Rubber, tobacco, coffee, and ivory nuts centre.

Hotels :— Continental, Loro, Malican, Bella Vista, Colón, Unión.

Steamers :—To Pará, Europe, United States.

Ocoña, the town and valley, in the department of Arequipa, is 65 miles by sea from Mollendo, but the heavy surf makes it inaccessible. At a small cove, Chira, a few miles to the south, cargo can be landed from tugs or lighters, but there is no wharf. The valley though extensive and fertile is sparsely populated. Cotton and sugar are grown, but the difficulty of transport arrests development. There have been repeated attempts to establish shipping facilities at Ocoña by means of andarivél or overhead cable line, but none has been successful. The population of the valley is said to be between 2,000 and 3,000. There is an ample supply of water.

Piura, capital of department. Population 11,000. Stands on left bank of Piura river, 60 miles by rail from the port Paita. The town is chiefly famous for Panama hats, the largest cotton plantations in Peru are in its immediate vicinity

Hotels :—Gran, Colón.

Rail :—Paita-Piura Railway.

Paita, a port of Northern Peru exporting sugar and Panama hats. Although possessing a population of only 2,000, it ranks third in importance in Peru, for it taps the chief cotton-growing districts. The town has an old-fashioned Spanish appearance, and is worth inspection. The structures are principally wood. Despite proximity to the Equator the climate is healthy. The ancient church contains a miraculous statue of the Mother of Christ.

Hotels :—Pacific, at Paita. Gran, and Colón, at Piura.

Landing :—Shore boat.

Excursion :—Piura, sixty miles distant by rail, was founded three years before Lima and is the capital of one of the richest districts on the coast. The cotton-growing land in the vicinity consists largely of the alluvial deposit of the river Piura, and is marvellously rich.

Rail :—To Piura.

Pisco, major port, south of Callao, which taps an agricultural hinterland. Passengers by ship going north see a green valley and bright vegetation, making a welcome relief from the general barrenness of the coast.

Pacasmayo is a little north of Salaverry The port has a good pier, and exports sugar, rice, silver, hides and copper. A short railway runs into the interior, branching into two about ten miles from Pacasmayo, north-east to Guadalupe, and east to Paypay

Puno, capital of the department, altitude 12,648 feet, population 11,000, stands on the north-west shore of Lake Titicaca, about 218 miles from Arequipa, 820 miles from Lima, and 171 from La Paz, Bolivia. Industries, chiefly agricultural.

Hotel :—Comercio.

Rail :—Southern Railway

Quilca, 34 miles by sea north of Mollendo, is a smooth-water port, deep, well-protected and safe at all times, but suitable only for small vessels and tugs. It has a good wharf for cargo. It is served by weekly services of two motor tugs from Mollendo. The roads throughout this region are very poor The port serves the Camana Valley, a centre of the cotton-growing industry Sugar is grown in moderate quantities, other products being cereals, wine, and cattle. Oil, a by-product of cotton, has of late years become a staple industry in Camana, largely used in the Arequipa and local soap factories, and for the adulteration of olive oil. The population of the valley is from 8,000 to 9,000. Attempts have been made here to establish communication with the sea by means of andarivéls. The valley is about 20 miles distant from Quilca over a steep, hilly coast road.

Trujillo, capital of department of La Libertad, has a population of 22,000 and stands at an altitude of 200 feet on the Moche river, some 300 miles from Lima and nine from Salaverry Founded by Pizarro in 1535. Three miles north-west are the ruins of the ancient town Chimu, of which the walls remain. Industries Soap and candle factories and tanneries. Sugar, rice, coffee, cotton, cacao, hides and minerals centre.

Hotels :—Central, Cosmos, Italia, American, Arco, Gran.

Rail :—Salaverry and Trujillo Railway. 35 minutes from Salaverry

PHYSICAL FEATURES.

Peru has an area, exclusive of Tacna and Arica, of 439,014 square miles, and a coast line of 1,248 miles. It is divided naturally into three well-defined regions, the coast, the sierra, and the " montaña." Of these, the coastal area stretches from the base of the West (Maritime) Cordillera to the Pacific, and is a sandy desert intersected by rivers flowing to the sea through fertile valleys. The sierra, or region of the Andes, is about 250 miles wide, and contains immense chains of mountains and high table-lands. The montaña is a land of tropical forests along the valley of the Amazon.

The coast has few safe anchorages. Of the numerous islets may be mentioned Foca, San Lorenzo, San Francisco, Lobos de Tierra, and Lobos de Afuera, which possess rich deposits of guano. Piura, the great desert-region of the coast, extends for 200 miles from the Gulf of Guayaquil to the Morope Valley, and here rain falls at intervals of three and four years. The second section of the coast country, also about 200 miles in extent, includes several well-watered valleys. In a third coast section occurs the River Santa, which, rising in the Lake of Conococha nearly 13,000 feet above sea-level, has a course of 180 miles. The fourth section, of some 300 miles, contains the great valley of Cañete, famed for its sugar-cane. The fifth, the Arequipa and Tacna area, covering 350 miles, includes numerous smiling valleys. Arequipa, 7,000 feet above the sea and 107 miles from the coast, was destroyed by an earthquake in 1868, while Callao was similarly destroyed in 1746.

The great **Cordilleras** of the Andes are divided into three chains —the Western or Maritime Cordillera, the Central Cordillera, and the Andes. The former has a system of volcanic peaks (rarely in eruption), including the Misti volcano (17,934 feet) and Sarasara (19,500 feet) On the Nevada, a still higher altitude is obtained by the peaks of Huascan (22,051 feet) and Huandoy (21,088 feet) The Central Cordillera consists largely of crystalline and volcanic rocks, connecting with the eastern Andes of the mountain-knot of Vilcañota (17,651 feet), forming the great inland expanse of Lake Titicaca. The magnificent Eastern Andes, in South Peru, are penetrated by the rivers Marañon and Huallaga, the Mantaro, Perene, Vilcanayu, Paucartambo, and Apurimac, and their most commanding peaks are Illampu (21,709 feet) and Illimàni (21,014 feet).

The great **rivers** of the Peruvian sierra are the Marañon, the Huallaga, and several tributaries of the Ucayali. Most of these run through great gorges in a tropical climate, above them is a comparatively temperate zone, and still higher a cold and freezing plateau. The tropical forests at the foot of the Andes are traversed by navigable streams. The Marañon and the Huallaga unite near the Brazilian frontier to join the Ucayali, which has a course of 600 miles; the forests traversed form the northern section of the Peruvian montaña. The southern half has rivers coming from the Eastern Andes, which help to form the Madre de Dios. This fertile region covers 800 miles from the Marañon to the frontier of Bolivia, and divides itself naturally into the sub-tropical forests east of the Andes, and the tropical forests in the plains of the Amazon.

The **climate** varies greatly according to the altitude. Along the Pacific coast it is tropical, cool all the year round on the inland plateaux, and very hot in the eastern Amazon district. There is practically no rain on the coast, but the heat is moderated by the Humboldt current. At times in the winter, when heavy fogs come inland from the Pacific, it is uncomfortably cool on the coast.

POPULATION.

The **population** is estimated at six millions, with 13 per cent. of whites, 57 per cent. Indians, and the residue mixed nationalities.

There are 18 departments and three provinces—Callao, Moquequa, and Tumbes. The following give the names, with those of the capital cities and the latest available estimates of population :—

Puno (Puno)	538,000
Cajamarca (Cajamarca)	443,000
Cuzco (Cuzco)	550,000
Ancachs (Huaraz)	428,000
Junín (Cerro de Pasco)	395,000
Lima (Lima)	450,000
Ayacucho (Ayacucho)	303,000
Liberdad (Trujillo)	250,000
Arequipa (Arequipa)	230,000
Huancavelica (Huancavelica)	224,000
Piura (Piura)	214,000
Apurimac (Abancay)	178,000
Huanuco (Huanuco)	145,000
Lambayeque (Chiclayo)	124,000
Loreto (Iquitos)	200,000
Ica (Ica)	90,000
Amazonas (San Carlos)	100,000
Madre de Dios (Maldonado)	46,000

The three provinces have a population of about 250,000.

The above figures are estimates in the absence of recent census returns.

A PERUVIAN CALENDAR.

1526. Francisco Pizarro makes his first landing on the coast.
1529. Pizarro granted the right of discovery and conquest in Peru.
1530. Pizarro and Almagro begin the occupation of Peru. The Inca Atahualpa defeated and captured by Pizarro.
1533. Execution of Atahualpa. Capture of Cuzco by the Spaniards.
1534. City of Lima founded.
1537. Pizarro gains a victory over Almagro, who is beheaded.
1542. Assassination of Pizarro.
1544. Rebellion of Gonzalo Pizarro.
1548. La Gasca defeats Gonzalo Pizarro, who is beheaded.
1551. Antonio de Mendoza made Viceroy.
1560. First olive tree planted in Peru.
1567. Jesuits arrive in Peru.
1570. Tribunal of the Inquisition founded.
1571. Execution by the Viceroy, Francisco de Toledo, of "the last of the Incas," Tupac Amaru.
1574. System of galleons introduced.
1579. Drake harries the coast.
1582. System of runner posts introduced.

1624. Callao attacked by Dutch squadron.
1632. Naval battle of Lake Titicaca between Royal forces and rebels.
1796. Ambrose O'Higgins made Viceroy of Peru.
1819. Navy organized for the liberation of Peru, under Lord Cochrane, arrives off Callao.
1820. San Martin's expedition lands at Pisco.
1821. San Martin proclaims the independence of Peru.
1822. San Martin withdraws from Peru.
1823. José de la Riva Agüero elected President. Simon Bolivár with a Colombian army attacks the Spaniards who are overthrown at the battles of Junín and Ayacucho.
1824. Bolivár elected President.
1826. Bolivár returns to Colombia.
1827. General de Lamar succeeds Bolivár.
1828. Constitution promulgated.
1829. War with Colombia. Lamar deposed.
1835. Santa Cruz intervenes in Peru and establishes the Peru-Bolivian Confederation.
1836. War between Chile and the Peru-Bolivian Confederation.
1839. Peru-Bolivian Confederation defeated by Chile.
1846. Exportation of guano begun.
1847. Unsuccessful invasion of Peru by the Bolivian General Ballivián.
1855. Slavery abolished.
1856. New Constitution promulgated.
1860. Constitution modified.
1866. Peru joins Chile, and declares war on Spain. Callao bombarded by Spanish fleet.
1868. Treaty of peace with Spain.
1876. Peruvian-Brazilian frontier dispute settled.
1879. Outbreak of the Nitrate War.
1881. Lima occupied by the Chileans.
1884. Peace signed with Chile.
1884-5. Insurrection under General Cáceres.
1886. General Cáceres elected President.
1892. Great fire at Callao.
1895. Lima besieged by insurrectionists under General Pierola. President Cáceres takes refuge on a French man-of-war at Callao. General Pierola elected President.
1903. Boundary dispute between Peru and Bolivia submitted to the arbitration of Argentina.
1908. Abortive revolution in Peru.
1917. Peru severs diplomatic relations with Germany
1919. Joins the League of Nations.

GOVERNMENT

The Constitution of January 18, 1920, vests legislation in a Senate of 57 members and a House of Representatives of 128. The latter has one deputy for each 30,000 inhabitants, and the former one to four senators for each department according to size. Both senators and deputies are elected by direct vote. Every two years one-third of the members of each Chamber retire by lot. The President, to whom is entrusted the executive power, is elected for five years and is not re-eligible until after another five years. There are two vice-Presidents. All three are elected by direct vote.

PAST PRESIDENTS.

José de San Martin	1821
José de la Mar	1822
J de la Riva Agüero	1823
Simon Bolivár	1824
General J de Lamar	1827
General Agustin Gamarra	1829

Luis José Orbegoso	1833
Félipe Santiago Salaverry	1835
Andrés Santa Cruz	1836
General Agustin Gamarra (second term)	1839
Manuel Menendez	1842
Manuel Vivanco	1843
Ramón Castilla (first term)	1845
General J. Echenique	1851
Ramón Castilla (second term)	1855
Miguel San Ramón	1862
General Pezet	1863
General Canseco	1865
General Mariano Ignace Prado	1867
José Balta	1868
Manuel Pardo	1872
General Mariano Ignace Prado (second term)	1876
Nicolás de Pierola	1879
Francisco Garcia Calderón	1881
Admiral Montero	1881
Miguel Iglesias	1883
General A. Cáceres	1886
Morales Bermudez	1890
Justiniano Borgoño	1894
General A. Cáceres (second term)	1894
Nicolás de Pierola (second term)	1895
S. Romaña	1899
Manuel Cándamo	1903
Serapio Calderón	1904
José Pardo	1904
Augusto B. Leguía	1908
G. E. Billinghurst	1912
General O. R. Benavides	1914
José Pardo (second term)	1915

PRESIDENT AND VICE-PRESIDENTS.

President : Augusto B. Leguía (1919) second term.
Vice-Presidents : General César Canevaro, Dr. Agustin de la Torre González.

MINISTRY.

Interior	Dr P. J. Roda y Gamio.
Foreign Office	Dr. Alberto Salomón.
War Office	B. Huamánde los Heros.
Navy	Capitán de Navío N. Vallerriestra.
Finance	Dr Abraham Rodríguez Dulanto.
Justice and Education	Dr J. Ego Aquiare.
Agriculture	Dr. P. Max Medina.

ADMINISTRATION

There are ten judicial districts in which justice is administered by superior and minor courts, and there is also a Supreme Court at Lima, the judges of which are chosen by Congress.

The departments are divided into provinces (113 in number) and the provinces into 873 districts. Each department is administered by a Prefect, and each province by a Sub-Prefect. Municipal councillors are elected by direct vote, and foreigners are eligible.

The Constitution guarantees complete religious liberty The **religion** of the Republic is Roman Catholicism. The churches and convents are the property of the State. Lima is the seat of an archbishop, under whom are 13 bishops.

The language is Spanish, but the Kechua and Aimara dialects are spoken among the Indian population.

The **metric** system of weights and measures is general along the coast and in the more populous centres.

Other weights and measures used in the interior are the :—

Onza	=	1·014 oz. avoirdupois.
Libra	=	1·014 lb. ,,
Quintal	=	101 44 lb. ,,
25 libras	=	1 arroba.
1 vara	=	0·927 yard.
1 square vara	=	0·859 square yard.
1 Peruvian gallon of wine	=	6·70 imperial gallons.

Currency :—The monetary unit of Peru is the sovereign. The gold coins are the Peruvian sovereign and half-sovereign and the British sovereign and half-sovereign, both of the same value and standard. The silver coins are the sol, the half-sol (50 centavos), the peseta (20 centavos), the real (10 centavos), and the medio (5 centavos) Ten sols are the equivalent of the sovereign. The copper coins are the 2-centavo and 1-centavo pieces.

NATURAL RESOURCES.

Sugar is the chief agricultural crop. The plantations lie mainly in the irrigated section of the country west of the mountains. Salaverry and Trujillo are the centres of the industry, there are also plantations near Chimbote. Some 100,000 acres under sugar-cane give a crop of probably under 300,000 tons. Sugar at 12s. 6d. a quintal f.o.b. Peruvian port is understood to leave a small margin of profit to the producer

Cotton ranks next in importance. Three varieties are grown, greatly differing from each other in their general characteristics :—

PERUVIAN SEA ISLANDS :—Is an inferior Sea Islands cotton. Though it has a fairly long staple and a silky appearance, it is more irregular, both as to colour and length of staple, than the pure Sea Islands grown in the United States. It has a length of about 1⅜ inch.

ROUGH PERUVIAN :—Is a harsh, wiry cotton, with a staple of about 1¼ inch. It is an indigenous variety, and the product of a perennial plant, which attains a height of about 10 ft. On account of its very harsh fibre this cotton is used chiefly for mixing with wool, with which fibre it has certain properties in common.

SMOOTH PERUVIAN :—Is a soft cotton, similar to American, from which it is not improbably descended. It constitutes about 70 per cent. of the crop. Staple, about 1⅛ inch.

In some respects Peru resembles Egypt as a cotton-growing country. In the hot season the melting of the snows causes an overflow of the rivers, which deposits a rich mud over the cotton fields.

The total production of cotton is not known exactly, but was about 36,000 tons in 1921 The production of Tangüis (a hybrid of rough and smooth) has noticeably increased, while that of Mitafifi (long staple) has decreased. The imposition by the United States of a duty on long staple cotton has made this grade relatively unsaleable. On the Amazon side of Peru, cotton-growing assumes some importance.

The area under cotton in Peru was, in acres, for 1915, 138,860 ; for 1917, 160,175 , for 1919, 222,160. The production of ginned cotton for the same years was, in tons, 24,600, 27,125, and 33,558. Peruvian smooth cotton corresponds approximately to American Middling. Since the collapse of wild rubber, formerly the chief product of the Amazon basin district of Peru around Iquitos, attention has been turned to cotton planting as an alternative.

The **wool** business is the life-blood of Arequipa, Cuzco, and other large towns. The Government has a model farm in the Department of Puno for the improvement of the national breeds of sheep.

Before the advent of plantation **rubber,** wild rubber collected in the Peruvian Orient was one of the principal exports. It has now decayed to insignificant proportions. In 1921, the rubber produced in the Madre de Dios district (southern region) was exempted from export tax, as a measure of relief to the collectors.

Large quantities of tobacco are grown, and other products include rice (on the northern coast), cacao, coffee, yucca and hides. Alpaca, sheep and llama wool are exported in considerable quantities. Many other products are being exploited, including grapes, olives, and wheat. The Government assists by furnishing large quantities of guano, which is found on the many islands bordering the coast. Limited quantities of this manure may be exported after the needs of the country are supplied.

Sisal hemp is not at present cultivated in Peru, though it is found in a wild state. There is much land suitable to this product on the eastern slopes of the Cordillera which could be obtained very cheaply.

The **castor oil** plant grows wild in the cotton districts wherever there is water.

Coca is grown in the Cuzco, Ayacucho and Huánuco districts, coca being a necessity to the Indian population. Coca in the leaf is consumed locally, but cocaine is made at Huánuco and about 3,300 pounds are exported annually, principally to Japan.

The cultivation of **Vanilla** offers profitable ground for investigation.

MINERAL RICHES.

Although the mineral wealth of Peru is proverbial, capital has been timid and tardy in its exploitation, and this despite steps to clear away difficulties and smoothe the path for capital. In 1876 a School of Mining Engineers was founded. This was quickly followed, in 1877, by the reformed administration of mining property and the promulgation of a liberal mining code. In November 1890 a bolder law was passed, relieving mining from taxation for twenty-five years. A famous corps of mining engineers, under such leaders as Rizo Patron, Balta, Denegri and Bravo, have carried out the survey and estimation of the mineral wealth of the country Notwithstanding, capital has so far attempted to exploit only one or two products in one or two regions. However, the mining companies of to-day are double in number those operating twenty years ago, and their capital is much larger The Cerro de Pasco Copper Corporation has a capital of £6,000,000, and the International Petroleum Company £4,000,000. The coal measures are scientifically estimated at six thousand million tons.

The production of **copper** has latterly been some 30,000 tons a year The richer lodes have been largely exhausted, but modern smelting plant is employed to secure the most economical results in working the poorer ores.

The production of **silver** rose from 300 metric tons in 1918 to 306 in 1919, and fell to 286 in 1920. The Peruvian-owned Salpo mine, in the Libertad Department, inland from Trujillo, is at present the most important producer.

Peru has produced latterly an annual average of 1,419 kilograms of pure **gold.** The principal source is the Cotabambas Auraria mine, near Abancay The New Chuquitambo mine, to the north of Cerro de Pasco, is now producing, though not on a large scale. The Inca or Santa Domingo mine, to the east of the Puno-Cuzco railway and near the Inambari River, has had large sums spent on its development. Placer beds have been tested on the river Napo in the eastern tropical part of the country, but the prospects are not called encouraging.

The principal **vanadium** mine in the world, known as Minas Ragras, lies to the west of Cerro de Pasco. The approximate production of vanadium concentrates in previous years has been as follows :—1912, 3,000 , 1917, 4,000 , 1920, 9,700 metric tons. The mine is owned by the Vanadium Corporation of America, and closely connected with the United States Steel Corporation. The most valuable and accessible ore is believed to be exhausted.

Bismuth is found and smelted at San Gregorio, near Cerro de Pasco, Tungsten, Molybdenum, antimony, and mercury are all worked and so is borax.

There are fields of **anthracite** at Huayday, inland from the port of Chimbote, and at Paracas, near Pisco. The first is a very extensive deposit, the quality of which has been proved n smelting work. If the railway construction in the region continues, it should soon be accessible from the coast. The second would be valuable if made available at the port, as the harbour is one of the best in the country and well situated for a coaling station. The third is a partially investigated field situated to the south of Pisco on the coast. The coal is bituminous and of good quality. At present, Peru does not produce enough coal for her own use. If later a surplus for export were available it could be taken by Bolivia and Ecuador

PETROLEUM `LANDS.

The discovery of oil extends back to the days of the Incas, when it was obtained from shallow hand-dug pits situated along the outcrop of the oilsands. These pits were visited by Pizarro, and must have been used by the early Spanish conquerors, as some of their old cannon have been found in their vicinity.

The first oil wells were drilled near Negritos, 15 miles south of Talara, towards the end of last century, but it was not until 1904 that the Peruvian oil industry began to make rapid progress. In 1920 the production of crude oil amounted to 400,000 tons, and in 1921 exceeded 500,000 tons. The oil is of high grade and contains from 15 per cent. to 40 per cent. of petrol.

Only one field is exploited, that of the north near the Ecuadorian frontier. Petroleum is proved in the Huancané district, between Lake Titicaca and Cuzco. Indications have been found in many parts of the country east of the Cordillera.

Oil is found in the Sierra, at Abancay and Ayacucho; in the central provinces of Yauli, Jauja, and Huancavelica; in the south at Canas, Lampa, Azangaro, and Huancané by the waters of lofty Titicaca. The Montana is possibly the richest oil land of Peru. Oil may be seen floating on the surface of the rivers. The prospector has confined his efforts largely to northern Peru.

Application for concessions must be made to the Ministry of Fomento. A pertenencia, or concession, is defined as a superficial area of 40,000 square metres. Companies holding concessions are subject to the provisions of the Commercial Code, and have a duly authorized representative of Lima. Foreigners may not acquire claims within fifty kilometres of the frontier, nor may any concessionaire make contracts with foreign Governments, nor with companies associated with or controlled by such Governments, nor may claims be transferred without the permission of the Executive.

On application for an exploration concession, a guarantee deposit must be made of £200 on the coast, £80 in the Sierra, and £40 in the Montana for each 1,000 pertenencias or fraction thereof. Before the concessionaire can export the oil, he must satisfy pro rata the needs of the country in petroleum and its derivatives. Companies exploiting petroleum deposits and hydrocarbons must offer 25 per cent. of their shares for sale to the State or to Peruvian capitalists, and native labour must be employed, not only in the technical and administrative spheres, but also in the working force, and in each case in the proportion fixed by the Executive.

The product is subject to an export tax.

Foreign Capital :—In the five years 1916-20, some twenty millions of capital have been invested in Peru. The total amount invested by all nations is about sixty millions, the heaviest participator being Great Britain. Although Peru's natural wealth —the bedrock upon which the future prosperity of the nation will be built—cries aloud for capital, there are other outlets for investment. A great livestock industry looms on the horizon, while needs awaiting fulfilment include electrical goods of all kinds, glassware, canning factories, cement plants, building accessories, toilet articles, rope and twine, hotels, sanitary fittings, enamelled baths and lavatory appointments, paper mills, and additional cotton mills. The consumption of articles of luxury, of mechanical parts, and of domestic equipment, should draw capital to Peru for the erection of factories to produce these commodities.

Speaking generally, **Labour** in Peru is not possessed of even elementary notions of economics, and, being temperamentally open to the influence of oratory, is easily persuaded to unreasonable action by interested propagandists. There is a law enjoining compulsory arbitration before striking, but, as is to be expected, it proves difficult of application.

PERUVIAN LEGATION AND CONSULATES IN GREAT BRITAIN.

RESIDENCE.	DESIGNATION	NAME.
London .. . (28 Holland Park, W.11. Tel. Park 3644.)	Chargé d'Affaires .. .	Dr. Ricardo Rivera Schreiber.
	First Secretary	
	Civil Attaché .	Señor Juan Fry
	Air Attaché .	Comandante Juan Leguía S., D.F.C.
	Naval Attaché ..	Comandante Federico Taboada.
London (36/37 Queen Street, E.C.4.)	Consul-General Vice-Consul .	Oscar Victor Salomón. Gerardo Vargas.
Belfast .	Consul	Raymond Augustine Burke.
Birkenhead	Vice-Consul .	John Weston.
Birmingham .	Consul .	John Hotchkiss.
Brighton	Consul'	
Cardiff . .	Consul Vice-Consul	Carlos A. Mackchenie. Alfred F. Bovey.
Chatham .	Consul	
Edinburgh .	Consul . ..	Hon. James Montague Balfour.
Glasgow	Consul .. .	Bruno E. Bueno.
Hartlepool	Vice-Consul ..	L. K. Fawcitt.

RESIDENCE.		DESIGNATION.				NAME.
Huddersfield	..	.. Consul	..	..	.	John Arthur Freeman.
Liverpool ..	..	.. Consul	..	..	.	Guillermo Leguía.
Manchester	.	Consul	.	.		——
Newcastle-on-Tyne	.	Vice-Consul	.			E. P. Deas.
Newport (Mon.)	..	Consul	.	..	..	——
Plymouth	..	.. Consul	..	.		Arthur Bellamy
Queenstown	..	.. Consul	.			James Charles Rohan.
Sheffield	..	.. Consul	.			William Ernest Wheatley
Southampton	.	.. Consul	.	.	.	——

POSTAL COMMUNICATIONS.

In 1921 the **postal,** telegraph, and radio-telegraph services of Peru were handed over for twenty-five years to Marconi's Wireless Telegraph Company, Ltd. Sir William Slingo, late engineer-in-chief of the British Post Office, was appointed Administrator-General on behalf of the Company

Peru is in the Postal Union. The tariff for inland letters is 5 cents for 15 grammes or any fraction thereof. There is a parcel post.

There are about 8,000 miles of State telegraph line and 3,000 miles of telephone system in the country.

There are three submarine cables between Peru and Chile, and two between Peru and the northern republics. Wireless stations have been established at Iquitos, Putumayo, San' Cristóbal, Lima, Callao, and other places.

Outward **mails** are dispatched (i) via the United States; (ii) via Buenos Aires; and (iii) by Pacific Steam Navigation Line via Panamá, at uncertain intervals.

Postage: 3d. first ounce and 1½d. each ounce after.

Homeward mails are dispatched at irregular intervals.

BRITISH LEGATION AND CONSULATES IN PERU.

The letter (M) denotes that the Consular Officer holds a Marriage Warrant. Members of the Diplomatic Service do not require Warrants.

RESIDENCE.	RANK.	NAME.	CONSULAR DISTRICT.
Lima	Envoy Extraordinary and Minister Plenipotentiary	Lord H. A. R. Hervey	——
	(M) Vice-Consul ..	A. R. Gilzean (acting)	
Callao	(M) Consul	J P. Trant. . ..	
	Vice-Consul ..	A. J. Hill . ..	Republic of Peru, with the exception of the Department of Loreto.
	Vice-Consul (temp.)	Acting Captain Ernest Henslowe, O.B.E., R.N.	
	Pro-Consul ..	H. E. Young ..	
Arequipa ..	Vice-Consul ..	Reginald W. Stafford	
Mollendo ..	Vice-Consul ..	G. H. J Marshall ..	
	Pro-Consul	——	
Payta ..	(M) Vice-Consul ..	R. Antram ..	
Salaverry and Trujillo.	Vice-Consul ..	H. E. Lawson	
Iquitós ᴇ.	Consul ᴇ. ..	J. W. Massey ..	Department of Loreto.

Public Holidays :—The chief feast days of the Roman Catholic Church are observed. The following are official holidays :—
July 28, 29, 30—Commemoration of National Independence.
August 30—Santa Rosa de Lima.
September 24—Our Lady of Ransom.
October 12—Discovery of America.
Press :—The principal daily papers published at Lima are : "El Comercio," "La Crónica," "El Excelsior," "La Prensa," "El Tiempo," and "La Unión."

Commercial Travelling in Peru.

No special regulations exist affecting the operations of commercial travellers and no registration or licences are required. The Municipality of Lima has, however, recently imposed a tax payable once only upon all established businesses, in addition to the yearly " patente de Comercio." Amongst the different categories appears " Commercial travellers with samples," and the tax amounts to £.P.40, 35, or 30 according to the goods and the importance of the business. The rate is determined by the officials of the Municipality and the tax is personal. Travellers carrying catalogues only would be exempt. No other municipality in the Republic levies a tax upon commercial travellers. Commercial travellers' samples are governed by a law of June 26, 1912, containing the following provisions :—

1 The importation of sample cases through the Customs of the principal ports of the Republic is subject to the following regulations.

2. The interested parties must present in each case in duplicate a detailed inventory containing the following particulars :—

(A) Mark, number, and gross weight of the case.

(B) Individual numbering of each article which the case may contain, giving the tariff classification and the number of the tariff corresponding thereto, and also a description of the article, gross weight, legal and net weight, and dimensions, should occasion require.

(c) The importation of more than one specimen of each article is not permitted, it being allowed only in the event of their being different in quality, form, size, weight, and colour

(D) The articles, which are free of duty under the Tariff, may be imported without any of the preceding requirements.

(E) The articles, the importation of which may not be allowed under section (c) (of this article), may be stored in the Customs, the dues for packing and storage being charged to the interested parties in accordance with the respective tariffs.

3. In respect of the goods referred to in the previous article, Sections (A) and (D), bonds must be presented in triplicate, which are to remain subject to the procedure established therefor by the Commerce and Customs Regulations.

4. The duties owing on the articles entered must be paid in cash, or in bank drafts, and will be returned at the time of the re-exportation of the merchandise, after deduction of the amount due in accordance with Section (E) of Article 1.

5. The Customs shall fix in each case a reasonable time, which must not exceed three months, for re-exportation, and if the term shall lapse without such re-exportation there will not be any ground for a claim for the return of the duties, nor will there be any reason why the bank draft shall not be presented by the Customs.

6. In order to re-export a sample case or part of its contents, the interested parties must present the case to the Customs beforehand, in order that its contents may be compared in detail ; no responsibility attaching to the Customs for delay in its re-embarkation unless it is presented within reasonable time.

7. If the result of examination shows that any article is missing, that it has been changed in weight or measure, or replaced by some other article, the double duty corresponding must be paid and the substituted article shall be confiscated.

8. Sample cases imported on observance of this resolution may be transported throughout the rest of the Republic subject to the dispositions of the Commerce and Customs Regulations in the matter of national merchandise.

9. The Superintendent-General of Customs shall make suitable provision to facilitate the examination of sample cases, for their storage and re-embarkation.

In the case of samples which the importer wishes to remain entire and re-ship, the importation will be allowed without payment of duty, when it is possible to identify the goods on exportation from the country. In this case the interested party must make a deposit equal to twice the amount of duty chargeable on the merchandise which he may re-ship through the same Customs House during a period not greater than six months. If at the end of the period allowed the importer tenders the amount of the corresponding duty the draft deposit will be returned to him, but if during the period allowed the goods are not exported or the duties paid, the draft will be collected.

Travellers would be well advised to bring a letter of recommendation to some known resident in the port through which they enter the country.

Should a commercial traveller enter **Bolivia** through Mollendo with samples, he must see that a detailed list of his samples is made out, and that by means of an agent a bond for the full value of the Customs duty is put up. Should the traveller not leave Peru within a certain period, this bond is forfeited. On leaving Peru within the stipulated period, the traveller can have a revised list of his samples made out by the Peruvian Custom House at Puno, and this on being sent to Mollendo, enables the agent to withdraw his bond , if more convenient the list may be revised by the Custom House at La Paz, when it must be signed and viséd by the Peruvian Consul. The responsibility of the agent at Mollendo then ceases and he can withdraw the bond he has given, there being no duties leviable in Mollendo on articles in transit to Bolivia.

There is no Government tax on commercial travellers, but taxes are imposed by certain municipalities. Arequipa imposes 25 soles (about £2 10s.) quarterly, and Cuzco 50 soles for each visit. The best times for visits are from August to October and during April and May The rainy season lasts from November to April. The railways do not grant any special concessions as regards luggage.

A limited amount of advertising matter may be carried, such as calendars, but if these appear to have a definite value the appraiser may demand payment of duty on them. The best selling times in Peru are for some weeks preceding the national holiday (July 28), the Christmas season, and the weeks before Easter

Import Formalities :—Certificates of origin are not required for exports to Peru.

Consular invoices, made out on special forms, obtainable at a Peruvian Consulate, and drawn up in Spanish, must be presented with all goods. These have to be submitted in quadruplicate to the Consul of Peru at the port of shipment for legalization, together with a copy of the bill of lading. Fees are payable for legalization.

IMPORTATION OF FIREARMS :—New regulations for the import, sale, and use of firearms, ammunition, and weapons were made June 29, 1923. Licences and permits are required in each case, and Callao is the only port through which such goods are permitted to enter the country Applications must be addressed to the police at Lima or Callao. The general prohibition on firearms does not apply to "Winchester" carbines for farms and mines, hunting arms, saloon arms up to calibre ·22 revolvers and pistols, and firearms of historical value. Members of the army and navy and the National Target Shooting Association of Peru, are given special permits under the new regulations.

PERUVIAN RAIL ROUTES.

The Central Railway is a standard-gauge line from Callao to Huancayo, 217 miles distant, on the Atlantic side of the Andes, with branches to Morococha (9 miles) and to Ancón (24 miles).

There are sixty-five tunnels and sixty-seven bridges. Sixteen "switch-backs" exist at points where the steepness of the mountain sides permits of no other means of ascent. Chosica, a favourite winter resort near Lima, stands at an elevation of 2,800 feet, Matucana, where there is a good hotel, at 7,799 feet, Tamboraque, Rio Blanco, and Casapalca, important smelting centres, are at 9,826, 11,500 and 13,606 feet respectively At Oroya, the junction of a railway leading to Cerro de Pasco, are the largest copper mines in the world, at 12,178 feet.

From Oroya the Huancayo section branches off to the town of that name, the centre of a flourishing grain and livestock district, and the point of departure for the Huancavelica, and other mining regions. The town of Jauja has a wide and growing reputation as a resort for consumptives. The short branch from Ticlio to the mining camp of Morococha, beautiful with its lakes and glaciers, crosses the range at 15,865 feet above sea level, or somewhat higher than Mont Blanc. The Central Railway of Peru is the highest railway in the world. The ascent into the clouds is accomplished without the use of a rack line. On the downward journey all passenger trains are piloted by a hand car, equipped with most powerful brakes.

From Oroya station the Perené Colony is reached, an important agricultural settlement controlled by the Peruvian Corporation.

Trains run between Callao, Chosica, and Ancón two or three times daily, according to season, and from Callao to Oroya and Huancayo every Monday, Wednesday and Friday, returning the following days. Return fares, Oroya, 29 soles (say £2 18s.), Huancayo, 43.80 soles (say £4 7s. 6d.)

The Paita to Piura Railway is a well-kept standard-gauge line sixty miles in length, passing through a fertile district famous for high-grade cotton and the manufacture of Panama hats. Paita, one of the most northerly ports in Peru, is third in importance in exports and imports. Large oilfields and sulphur deposits are situated in the neighbourhood, as well as vast tracts of virgin land suitable for agriculture.

Trains leave at 1 p.m. on Mondays, Wednesdays and Fridays, and at 2 p.m. on Saturdays, for Piura (fare 2.91 soles), returning on Tuesdays, Thursdays, Saturdays and Sundays at 8 a.m. Piura was the first town established by the Spaniards, and to-day has an industrious and progressive population of some ten thousand.

The Pisco to Ica Railway, forty-six miles, is the highway by which the products of the departments of Ica, Ayacucho, and

Huancavelica reach their coastal outlet at Pisco, one of the oldest
of the Peruvian ports. After traversing the plain of Chunchanga,
between the Ica and Pisco rivers, the line changes its direction
at the village of Guadalupe, where it crosses the Ica valley and
reaches the city of that name. The Ica valley, with its smiling
vineyards, is celebrated for its wines and aguardiente (native
brandy). Several varieties of grapes are successfully grown, those
chiefly favoured being the Quebranta, Moscatel, Albilla and Italia,
from all of which wines of excellent quality are produced. A
short distance from Ica stands the pretty town of Huacachina,
a health resort, famous for its medicinal baths.

Ilo to Moquegua Railway :—The line is some 100 kilometres
in length, linking the fine port of Ilo with Moquegua, the capital
of its province. The district is an agricultural one, its principal
exports being wine, olives, and olive oil for domestic use. The
Government of Peru has evinced an active interest in promoting
the wine industry of the Moquegua Valley and has imported cuttings
from the best French vineyards and engaged an expert to instruct
the growers.

The **Pacasmayo Railway** connects the port of that name with
the towns of Guadalupe (42 kilometres) and Chilete (105 kilometres),
traversing a productive district chiefly devoted to the cultivation
of rice. The mole is 775 metres long, and has a double line of
rails.

There is a daily service of trains to Guadalupe, and a bi-weekly
service to Chilete, the first-class fares being respectively 1.20
soles and 5 soles. From various points on the line easy horseback
journeys can be made to other centres, for instance, to Chocope,
Chiclayo, and Cajamarca.

The **Chimbote Railway** :—The port of Chimbote, situated on
one of the most magnificent natural harbours in the world, is
reached from Callao by steamers leaving every Thursday, arriving
at Chimbote shortly after mid-day on Saturdays. Steamers for
the return journey call at Chimbote at 8 a.m. on Sundays. The
railway runs inland 57 kilometres to Tablones (fare 3.40 soles).
The principal productions are sugar, grown at Tambo Real (Cambio
Puente station), cotton and rice, grown at Suchiman and Vinzos,
and grapes, grown at Tablones.

The **Trujillo Railway** :—Its coast terminus is at the port of Salaverry, which possesses a well-equipped mole with excellent landing
facilities.

Trujillo, the capital of the department of La Libertad, 14½
kilometres inland, is a picturesque old town founded by Pizarro,
and so named by him in honour of his birth-place. It has a
population of about 10,000, and contains many imposing buildings.
A few miles north are the ruins of Chanchan, an Inca town of
great archæological interest. The ruins cover a large area of
desert, and antiquities of great value have been unearthed. There
are four trains daily each way from Salaverry to Trujillo.

LIMA TO THE AMAZON RIVER.

A route, practicable but not recommended for comfort, leads from **Lima** to **Iquitos** on the Amazon River via the Central Railroad of Peru:—

		Transit.	Hours.	Days.	Km.
Rail	.	Lima to Oroya	10	1	206
Mule	.	Oroya to Tarma	5	1	30
,,		Tarma to Huacapistana, via Acobamba Pampa and Carpata	10	1	44
,,		Huacapistana to La Merced, via Libertad and San Ramón	6	1	34
,,	..	La Merced to Vista Alegre, via Perené and San Luis	6	1	34
,,		Vista Alegre to Tambo Eneñas	6	1	42
,,	.	Eneñas to Tambo, kilometre 93 ..	6	1	42
,,	.	Tambo, kilometre 93, to Azupizú via San Nicolas	8	1	50
,,		Azupizú to Puerto Yessup, via Puerto Ibarra	6	1	42
Mule or Canoe	.	Puerto Yessup to Puerto Bermuder	4	1	20
Steamer		Puerto Bermuder to Puerto Victoria and Masisea	50	5	1,500
		TOTALS .	117	15	2,044

PORTO RICO

Porto Rico

PORTO RICO.

The Island, more properly called Puerto Rico, passed into the ownership of the United States after the war with Spain in 1898. It forms part of the Greater Antilles group of the West Indies, and lies between 17°50′—18°30′N and 65°30′—67°15′W. The total area is 3,606 square miles and the population 1,297,770 in 1920. The situation is 1,400 miles from New York, and 980 from Key West. The island is rectangular in shape and some 40 miles wide by 100 miles long.

There is one mountain range with a peak, El Yuque, 3,700 ft. above sea level, and some 1,200 streams, the chief being the Loiza, de la Plata, Manati, and Arecibo.

San Juan, the capital, with some 71,000 inhabitants, is approached oftenest by steamer from New York.

The approach by sea affords a good view of the high battlements of Morro Castle with fortifications which were formerly the most formidable of Spanish strongholds in the New World. The city is compact and about a mile and a-half long by a quarter of a mile in width. It has narrow streets and their high points overlook the sea and harbour. The sea wall is of interest, and at some points rises to 300 ft. above sea-level, and the width allows several persons to walk abreast.

A drive through the principal street—Calle Tetuan—brings the traveller to the Plaza, with the Governor's Palace, first occupied by Ponce de Leon; the Hall of the Legislative Assembly, the Alcaldia, or town hall, the club houses of the Spanish casino, the Atenec, and the Forteleza, an old fortification built in 1532. A fifteen-minute tram ride leads to Santurce, a suburb with a park and excellent bathing beach and other seashore attractions.

Hotels :—Condado, Vanderbilt (golf, tennis, etc.), Eureka, Miramar, Inglaterra, Comercio.

A TOUR OF THE ISLAND

Sixteen-day cruises sail from New York every Saturday, the steamer reaching San Juan the following Wednesday or Thursday, leaving on Friday evening. The next port of call is Ponce, the second largest city On the Saturday evening, the voyage is continued to Mayaguez, where Sunday is spent. The vessel remains at San Juan until the following Wednesday afternoon.

Ponce has a district population of 68,000 and is 81 miles by road from San Juan.

Hotels :—Frances, Melia, Leon-Oro, Inglaterra.

Mayaguez has a bay in which large vessels anchor and a regional population of 42,500. It is 117 miles from San Juan.

HOTELS :—Inglaterra, Paris, Palmer, Pinar.

Caguas, in the midst of an upland tobacco district, is a sleepy town, with buildings that might have been transported from old Spain. Its macadam streets are lit by electricity.

HOTELS :—America, Filo.

Cayey, 37 miles from San Juan, has large military barracks, and a regional population of 19,000. The altitude is 2,300 ft.

HOTELS :—La Esperanza, Gloria, Inglaterra, Frances.

Along the military road, past dense jungles, is **Aibonito,** at 2,200 ft. elevation. The road dips in curves to **Coamo,** where there are famous springs and a capital hotel.

The **climate** is temperate for the tropics, with a summer mean of 79° Fahr., and winter mean of 73° Fahr The nights are cool and the humidity high. There are no definite wet or dry seasons. February is the driest month, and March-May the months of greatest rain. March is the best time for a visit and is the normal end of the cool season, beginning November.

AVERAGE TEMPERATURES.

	Mean Daily Maximum.	Mean Daily Minimum.	Mean Annual.	Mean Daily Range.
San Juan	83·4°	72·6°	78·2°	10·8°
Ponce	88·2°	68·8°	78·5°	19·3°
Mayaguez	88·7°	65·7°	77·2°	23·0°
Cayey	84·0°	63·0°	73·5°	21·0°
Aibonito	81·0°	61·6°	71·3°	19·4°

Spanish is most spoken but English is taught in the schools. United States **currency** is used.

Sale of liquor is prohibited as in the United States.

The chief **products** are tobacco, sugar, coffee, rice, corn, oranges, pineapples, bananas, cotton, cattle, coconuts, cacao, **ginger,** divi-divi, patchouli, sisal, annatto, turmeric, hides. Gold, silver, copper, iron, petroleum, and marble are found in small quantities.

SALVADOR

SALVADOR.

La Unión, capital of the Department of that name, the only port of consequence, stands on the Bay of Fonseca, across which there is a steamer or motor-boat service to Amapala, Honduras. In 1914 the population was 5,679. It is 137 miles from San Salvador and 37 from San Miguel. The port of shipment for San Miguel and other places in eastern Salvador.
Hotels :—Central, Ferrocarril.
Rail :—International Railway of Central America.

La Libertad is the second port of the Republic, 25 miles from San Salvador Steamers discharge by lighter Population, 3,000.

Acajutla, in the Department of Sonsonate, is a port with open roadstead. Landing is difficult and accommodation not good. It is 12 miles from Sonsonate and 65 from San Salvador Pacific Mail steamers from San Francisco and Panamá call.
Hotels :—Occidental, Las Americas.

San Salvador, the capital of the Republic, is a city of considerable commercial importance, with a population in 1921 of 80,900. It stands at an altitude of over 2,000 feet near the foot of the supposedly extinct volcano of San Salvador. It is 65 miles from Acajutla, 25 from La Libertad, and 137 from La Unión. The climate is semi-tropical, and the temperature averages about 76° Fahr Originally founded on a site some 20 miles away by Jorge Alvarado in 1528, it has been ruined several times by earthquake, the latest occasions being 1917 and 1919. Cotton goods, soap, and cigarettes are manufactured. The chief products are coffee, beans, rice, sugar, and tobacco.
Many of the wealthier inhabitants have houses in the suburb of Santa Tecla (Nueva San Salvador), ten miles away. The volcano of Ilobasco, near the capital, is worth visiting, also Lake Ilopango, reached by a motor drive of some ten miles.
Hotels :—Hotel Nuevo Mundo (from $10) ; Hotel Italia (from $8), Pension España (from $8), Boarding House, 8a Calle Pontiente (from $6)
Rail :—Salvador Railway, from Acajutla.

Santa Ana, capital of the Department of that name, is 48 miles from San Salvador and 66 from Acajutla, with a population in 1921 of 59,815. The second city of the Republic, it is an important business centre. Its chief products include cigars, textiles, coffee, sugar, cattle.
Hotels :—Oriental, La Florida, Colombia.
Rail :—Salvador Railway, from San Salvador and Sonsonate.

San Miguel, capital of the Department of the same name, with a population in 1921 of 30,406, stands at the foot of the San Miguel volcano, 107 miles from San Salvador, 37 from La Unión, and 63 from San Vicente. It manufactures shoes and other leather goods. The chief products are agricultural—coffee, cattle, and cereals.

Hotels :—Hispano, Americano.

Rail :—International of Central America.

Ahuachapán, capital of the Department of the same name, with a population in 1921 of 24,683, stands 72 miles from San Salvador, and 22 from Sonsonate. One of the most important distributing centres in the south-west of the Republic. Chief products coffee, cereals, tobacco, sugar. There is a good deal of mining in the neighbourhood.

Hotel :—The American.

Reached by motor from Santa Ana and Sonsonate.

San Vicente, capital of the Department of the same name, on the Ahuachapán river near the foot of the San Vicente volcano, stands 40 miles from San Salvador and 63 from San Miguel. Shawls and other woollen goods are manufactured as well as hats, cigars, and sugar. The chief products are corn, tobacco, indigo, coffee, fruits, sugar-cane. In 1921 the population was 30,080.

Hotel :—Italia.

Rail :—International of Central America. The connection with San Salvador is by motor.

Sonsonate, capital of the Department of the same name, with a population in 1914 of 15,000, stands on the Salvador Railway, 53 miles from San Salvador and 12 from Acajutla, in the centre of a rich agricultural district, producing coffee, sugar, hides, tobacco, rice, and various woods. It manufactures mats, baskets, cigars, and coarse cotton cloth. An important market is held here every Sunday

Hotels :—Gran Hotel, Internacional.

CHARACTERISTICS OF THE COUNTRY

Salvador, the smallest but most densely populated of the Central American Republics, is bounded on the north-west by Guatemala, on the north and east by Honduras, on the south-east by the Gulf of Fonseca, and on the south by the Pacific Ocean. Its total area is about 7,225 square miles. The Pacific coast line is 160 miles long. Two mountain chains cross almost the entire country, sending out numerous spurs enclosing valleys of great fertility The most important valley is that of the River Lempa. Violent earthquakes are frequent.

In the lowlands the **climate** is tropical, but pleasant and healthful in the higher altitudes. The summer lasts from May to October. Rain is almost continuous during September and October.

The **population** estimated in 1921 was 1,501,000. The distribution of the population is suggested by the following particulars (1914) :—

Department.				Capital.				
Santa Ana	.	..	142,211	Santa Ana	.		..	59,421
Ahuachapán	..	.	78,877	Ahuachapán	..	..	.	24,151
Sonsonate	.	..	87,907	Sonsonate	.		..	15,002
La Libertad	..	.	95,416	Nueva San Salvador			..	22,101
San Salvador	.	.	146,540	San Salvador	.	..	..	64,694
Chalatenango	..	.	79,377	Chalatenango		..	.	9,122
Cuscatlán	;	.	80,237	Cojutepeque	.		.	12,071
La Paz	:	..	87,500	Zacatecoluca	.	..	.	25,964
San Vicente	..	.	71,687	San Vicente	.	..		25,370
Cabañas	..	..	47,448	Sensuntepeque	.			15,548
San Miguel	.	.	105,569	San Miguel	.	..		29,874
Usulután	.	.	102,068	Usulután	.	.		15,729
Morazán	..	..	68,723	San Francisco		.		8,930
La Unión	.	..	60,591	La Unión	..	..	..	5,679

On August 11, 1920, a decree came into force establishing a gold standard for **currency.**

Previously the coinage was on a silver basis, the standard being the colon or peso, of 100 centavos, the rate of exchange for which was fixed by law in September, 1919, at 2 pesos for each U.S.A. gold dollar   Other silver coins are 50 centavos, 25 centavos (2 reals), 20 centavos, 12½ centavos (1 real), 10 and 5 centavos. Nickel coins are issued for 1 and 3 centavos.

Coined American gold and silver are legal currency in the proportion of two colons to one dollar, whilst national money is coined in sufficient quantities.

The language of the country is Spanish.

The prevailing religion is Roman Catholicism. An archbishop has his seat in San Salvador, and there are episcopal sees at Santa Ana and San Miguel.

The **metric** system was made obligatory in 1886, but in the more remote districts the old Spanish units linger.

GOVERNMENT.

Legislation is in the hands of a congress of 42 deputies, 3 for each department, elected for one year by universal suffrage.   The President, who wields the executive power, holds office for four years, and carries on the administrative business of the Republic assisted by a Vice-President and a Ministry of four.

PAST PRESIDENTS (since 1895).

General Rafael A. Gutiérrez	1895
General Tomás Regalado	1899
General Pedro J. Escalon	1903
General Fernando Figueroa	1907
Dr Manuel Araujo	1911-Feb. 1913.
Dr. Carlos Melendez	Feb. 1913-Oct. 1918.
Dr. Alfonso Quiñonez	Oct. 1918-March 1919.
Dr Jorge Melendez	March 1919.

PRESIDENT AND VICE-PRESIDENT

President	Dr. Alfonso Quiñonez.
Vice-President	Dr Pio Romero Bosque.

MINISTRY.

Interior	Dr. Rodolfo Schönenberg.
Finance and Agriculture	Marcos A. Letonia.
Health	Dr Carlos Guillen.
Foreign Affairs, Education, and Justice	Dr. Reyes Arrieta Rossi.

There are a Supreme Court, several courts of First and Second Instance, a Court of Third Instance, and a number of minor courts. All judges of First Instance are appointed by the Supreme Court for a term of two years; those of Second and Third Instance are elected by the National Assembly for a similar period.

A SALVADOREAN CALENDAR.

1526. Conquest of Salvador completed by Pedro de Alvarado.
1822. Declares itself independent of Spain.
1823-39. A member of the Central American Federation.
1859. Declares itself an independent republic. Constitution promulgated.
1863. General Barrios defeats the Guatemalan Army at Coatepeque. Honduras joins Salvador against Costa Rica, Nicaragua and Guatemala. The ultimate victory is with President Carrera of Guatemala, who occupies Salvador.
1885. A defensive alliance made between Salvador, Nicaragua and Costa Rica against Guatemala. President Barrios invades Salvador and is killed in battle.
1886. Peace made with Guatemala.
1889-90. Insurrection under General Rivas suppressed by Government forces.
1890. War with Guatemala and Honduras. Peace signed. Salvador joins the "Greater Republic" of Central America, of which Costa Rica, Nicaragua, and Honduras are members.
1898. President Gutiérrez deposed because of his proposed federation with Honduras and Nicaragua.
1899. External debt of £720,000 taken over by the Salvador Railway Company, in exchange for concessions.
1907. Salvador and Honduras at war with Nicaragua.
1908. Represented at the Central American Court of Arbitration.
1919. Joins the League of Nations.

NATURAL RESOURCES.

Salvador is almost entirely **agricultural,** and coffee is the chief crop. The Government offers a bounty on cotton exports. Other products are sugar, balsam, indigo, rubber, rice, cacao, beans, and tobacco. Such manufactures as exist are only on a small scale and for home trade. Cigars, leather goods, and a little coarse linen or cotton cloth, with hats and shawls, constitute most of the industries.

Gold, silver, copper, and lead exist in considerable quantities in Salvador, as well as iron and mercury. Several United States and British companies are engaged in the business. The chief mining departments are Morazán, Cabañas, La Unión, Santa Ana, and Chalatenango.

The **roads** are better than most of those in the Latin-American countries, and as a rule are fair even in the rainy season. The 25 miles stretch between San Salvador and La Libertad is an excellent road for motor traffic. The chief highway is the main road eastward from Ahuachapán to La Unión, and from this are various by-roads, north and south, affording good connection with places not reached by rail.

SALVADOREAN LEGATION AND CONSULATES IN GREAT BRITAIN.

RESIDENCE.	DESIGNATION.	NAME.
London (7 Union Court, E.C.2, pro tem.).	Chargé d'Affaires	Dr. Pio Romero Bosque.
London (7 Union Court, E.C.2).	Consul-General	Dr. Pio Romero Bosque.
	Vice-Consul	G. Le Bourdonnec.
Aberdeen	Consul	A. Norman Davidson.
Birmingham	Consul	Frederick Hickinbotham.
Brighton	Consul	Francis Geo. Horne.
Glasgow	Consul	Archibald Craig.
Liverpool	Consul	Dr. Carlos Varaona.
	Vice-Consul	Carlos Varaona V
Newport	Consul	Eduardo P Lawlor.
Southampton	Consul	Archibald Claude Dunlop.

BRITISH LEGATION AND CONSULATES IN SALVADOR.

The letter (M) denotes that the Consular Officer holds a Marriage Warrant. Members of the Diplomatic Service do not require Warrants.

RESIDENCE.	RANK.	NAME.	CONSULAR DISTRICT.
(See GUATEMALA)	Envoy Extraordinary, Minister Plenipotentiary, and Consul-General.	—	—
San Salvador	(M) Consul	J D. Scott	Republic of Salvador.
	Vice-Consul	William Gibson	
Acajutla	Vice-Consul	Thomas Massey	

Outward **mails** are sent via New Orleans and Puerto Barrios, and also via New York and Panamá. They are dispatched with the mails to the United States.

Postage, 3d. first ounce; and 1½d. each ounce after Homeward mails are irregular.

Salvador is a member of the Postal Union, and has a parcel post. The rates are 5 cents for the first ounce or fraction thereof and 3 cents for each additional ounce. There are 220 telephone stations, and more telegraph offices, owned and operated by the Government. A wireless station has been installed at the capital.

Public Holidays :—The feast days of the Roman Catholic Church are observed. Other holidays generally observed are as follows :—

January 1 : New Year's Day
March 1 : Civic holiday.
March 15 : National holiday commemorating General Morazan.
August 29 : National holiday commemorating General Gerardo Barrios.
September 15 . Independence Day.
October 12 Columbus Day.

EXPORTS AND IMPORTS.

	Exports. £	Imports. £	Total. £
1912	2,050,000	1,397,000	3,447,000
1913	1,857,961	1,257,419	3,115,380
1914	2,226,081	1,022,396	3,248,477
1915	2,178,076	829,313	3,007,389
1916	2,392,732	1,200,746	3,593,478
1917	2,206,240	1,416,345	3,622,585
1918	2,556,660	1,266,536	3,823,196
1919	3,499,845	3,083,752	6,583,597
1920	3,699,758	2,603,787	6,303,545
1921	1,748,360	1,746,081	2,494,441

Guidance for Commercial Travellers.

No special regulations exist affecting commercial travellers merely canvassing for orders. Commercial travellers, carrying samples for sale to wholesale merchants pay a tax of 100 pesos if their stay does not exceed two months ; for every month beyond this period they are charged 25 pesos (about £2), the amount being collected by the Administrator of Customs at the time of their departure. In addition, in the municipality of Salvador, a tax of 50 dollars is levied on commercial travellers and representatives of foreign business houses, whether they do business or not. Commercial travellers are not subject to income tax on sales.

All samples are liable to duty whether or not of commercial value. If the goods are intended for re-exportation the duties may be deposited with a view to their return when the traveller leaves. Guarantees from responsible merchants are also accepted. Ordinary goods thus re-exported must be shipped from the port of entry, but they may be shipped from any other port provided a Ministerial order is obtained, a requirement which presents no difficulty

Duty of $0.03 per kilog. is levied on samples of no commercial value.

Certificates of origin are not required for goods dispatched to Salvador

Consular invoices are needed in quintuplicate, on special forms, which must be purchased at a Salvadorean Consular Office. These invoices must be certified by the Consul and for this fees are charged. The origin of the goods must be declared on all documents.

URUGUAY

URUGUAY.

Montevideo, the capital of the Republic (formerly known as the Banda Oriental) is one of the great cities of the continent. It was founded 1726, and has a population of nearly 400,000. Originally built on a low promontory between the ocean and Horseshoe Bay, the city stretches into the flat country behind, and round the Cerro, the lofty isolated cone to which Montevideo owes its name. The city is well built with flat-roofed houses, above which towers the cathedral, to a height of 133 ft., flanked by two side turrets and surmounted by a dome. There is a large Italian colony, and a British community of about 900, with a British Hospital and King Edward VII Sanatorium. Montevideo is the chief rail centre, all lines radiating outward therefrom. Points of interest include the Cathedral, the Plaza Constitución, the Cabildo, the Bourse, and the new University There are two seaside resorts, now very popular, Poçitos and Playa Ramirez, within four miles of the town, and reached by tramway. There is a good race course.

Landing :—Steamers normally go alongside. Motor launches are usually available.

Hotels :—Grand Hotel Lanata ($5-10) , Hotel del Globo ($2.50-5) ; Hotel La Alambra ($5-7) , Hotel Pyramides ($3-6) , Hotel Poçitos ($5-8.50) ; Hotel Rio Branco ($2.50-4.50) , Palacio Florida Hotel ($3-5) , Palace Hotel Poçitos ($5-8) , Hotel Colón ($3.50-8) ; Hotel Severi ($2.50-4.50) , Hotel Campiotti ($3-4.50) , Hotel Barcelona ($3-4.50) , Parque Hotel ($7-10) , Hotel Camino Carrasco ($15).

Theatres :—Solis, Urquiza, 18 de Julio, Casino, Royal, Colón, Politeama, Cataluña, and Stella d'Italia.

Clubs :—English, French, German, Italian, Spanish, Press and Jockey Clubs, Club Oriental, Club Uruguay, and the Circulo de Armas.

Local Steamers :—To Buenos Aires daily ($17.80 first, return). To Salto, weekly. To Rio Grande, Belatas, Porto Alegre, Florianopolis, San Francisco, Paranagua, Antonina, fortnightly.

Rail :—Through trains to San Paulo (Brazil) leaving Saturdays ($47) Trains to Salto and Paysandú, and all parts.
Travellers visiting Montevideo and its neighbouring seaside resorts during the summer (December to March), are advised to book rooms at the hotels in advance.
Restaurant cars are provided on all long-distance trains. It is usually necessary to book sleeping berths beforehand.

Paysandú, on the east bank of the Uruguay River (navigable to vessels of 14-ft. draught), is the second town in order of importance, and has a population of about 30,000. It is the head-quarters of the Midland Railway, and the centre of the meat-packing and frozen-meat industry

HOTELS :—Concordia, Splendid, Paris, Bayonne, Del Vapor.

RAIL :—To Salto, 3½ hours ; to Montevideo, $15.

LOCAL STEAMERS :—Mihanovitch Line to Buenos Aires and Montevideo.

Fray Bentos, a port on the Uruguay, some 120 miles above Buenos Aires, and about 250 miles from Montevideo by river, has a population of 14,000, and is almost wholly concerned with the same industries as Paysandú, with which town and Montevideo it is connected by rail. The Liebig factories are established here. There is a depth of 30 ft. at the port, and about fifty ocean-going steamers call annually

LOCAL STEAMERS :—Mihanovitch Line from Buenos Aires.

Salto, an important port on the Uruguay River, has a population of 35,000, and is a centre of the livestock and agricultural interests. It is connected by rail and steamer with the capital, and by rail with Brazil.

HOTELS :—Comercio, Uruguay, Concordia, Oriental, Americano, Salto, De los Amigos.

Maldonado, a port on the Atlantic, with a population of about 4,000, is about 90 miles east of Montevideo, and is connected therewith by rail and steamer The principal industry is seal-fishing on the Lobos and Castelles Islands.

RAIL :—Montevideo, 5½ hours.

San José, on the river of the same name, is one of the most important provincial towns, with a population of about 15,000, and is connected by the Central Railway with the capital, which is 70 miles distant.

HOTEL :—Londres.

Colonia, a pleasure resort on the River Plate, with a casino and bull-fighting ring, has a population of 15,000, and is about 60 miles from Montevideo, with which it is connected by rail and steamer. There is a boat service to Buenos Aires.

HOTELS :—Del Ruso, Esperanza, Garden, Brighton, Casino.

Durazno, on the Yi River, 127 miles from Montevideo, is the capital of the department of the same name, and has a population of about 17,000. It is on the Central Uruguayan line from Montevideo.

HOTELS :—Bulo, Ferrocarril, De la Hermosa.

San Eugenio, the capital of Artigas, on the Brazilian frontier, 508 miles from Montevideo, with which it is connected by rail, has a population of about 5,000.

Mercédes, an agricultural and livestock centre, with a population of 15,600, is connected by rail with San José and the capital.
HOTELS :—Comercio, Franco-Español, Paris, Universal, Navarro.

Rocha is the capital of the province of the same name, and has a population of about 12,000.
HOTELS :—Uruguayo, Roma.

Minas, about 90 miles by rail from Montevideo, with about 15,000 inhabitants, is a copper ore centre.
HOTELS :—Garibaldi, Oriental.

Florida, about 80 miles from Montevideo, has a population of 12,000.
HOTELS :—Pastorizo, Fernandez, Anchustequi.

Artigas, a small town near the Brazilian frontier, with about 3,000 inhabitants.

Canelones (or Guadeloupe), a railway centre, 36 miles from Montevideo, has a population of about 10,000.

Melo, capital of the department of Cerro Largo, is about 300 miles from Montevideo on the Eastern Extension Railway, and has 16,000 inhabitants.

San Carlos, 9 miles from Maldonado on the railway to the capital, has a population of about 7,000.

Tacuarembó, in the province of that name, has over 9,000 inhabitants. Products · timber, tobacco, yerba maté.
HOTELS :—Central, Español, Internacional.

Trinidad, has a population of about 10,000 and is connected by rail with Durazno.
HOTELS :—Comercio, Esperanza.

Rivera (with 10,000 inhabitants) is the Northern terminus of the Central Uruguayan Extension Railway , this line continues in Brazil to Santos and Rio de Janeiro.
HOTELS :—Brazil, Central.

Treinta y Tres is the terminus of a branch line of the Central Uruguay Railway, 192 miles from Montevideo, and has a population of 7,700.

PHYSICAL FEATURES.

With its area of 72,210 square miles, Uruguay is the smallest Republic in South America. It is separated from the Brazilian province of Rio Grande do Sul by Lake Mirim, the Santa Ana hills, and the rivers Quarahy, Chuy, and Jaguarao. Its sea line stretches along the Atlantic for 120 miles, while the shore-line follows the course of the Uruguay River for some 270 miles eastward. That stream is navigable all the year round as far as Salto, where there are rapids. The River Negro and its tributary the Yi cross Uruguay from north-east to south-west, the Negro's principal port being Mercédes. Lesser rivers include the Santa Lucia, Queguay, and Cebollati, but these are not navigable, or only for short distances. The mountains are of no great altitude, none of the peaks attaining 2,000 ft. ; on the west and north they are distinguished as the Cuchilla de Haedo, and on the south and east as the Cuchilla Grande.

Uruguay possesses over 700 miles of navigable **rivers,** more than 500 miles of which are contributed by the Uruguay and the Plata. Other rivers are the Rio Negro, traversing the centre of the country, with its tributary the Yi, and the Rio San Salvador. The Uruguay is navigable as far as Paysandú for vessels of 14-ft. draught and for vessels of lesser draught as far as Salto, where falls interrupt navigation.

The **climate** is one of the best and healthiest in the world. Epidemic diseases are rare, and the Atlantic breezes temper the summer heat delightfully. The annual rainfall amounts to 43 in., and the lowest temperature is 35°.

POPULATION AND IMMIGRATION

The Republic has a **population** of 1,500,000. The majority of those of foreign extraction are Spanish and Italian.

Department.	Area. Square Miles.	Population.	Capital.
Artigas	4,394	37,500	San Eugenio.
Canelones	1,834	112,100	Guadalupe.
Cerro Largo	5,763	56,300	Melo.
Colonia	2,193	80,300	Colonia.
Durazno	5,525	53,800	Durazno.
Flores	1,744	22,700	Trinidad.
Florida	4,673	60,000	Florida.
Maldonado	1,587	39,000	Maldonado.
Minas	4,819	65,900	Minas.
Montevideo	256	500,000	Montevideo.
Paysandú	5,115	66,000	Paysandú.
Rio Negro	3,269	35,700	Fray Bentos.
Rivera	3,793	44,824	Rivera.
Rocha	4,280	45,400	Rocha.
Salto	4,865	74,400	Salto.
San José	2,688	59,500	San José.
Soriano	3,560	54,000	Mercédes.
Tacuarembó	8,112	58,700	San Fructuoso.
Treinta y Tres	3,682	39,200	Treinta y Tres.

Immigration :—In 1921 there were 1,575 male immigrants, 491 women, 347 children, making a total of 2,413. In the same year there were 2,391 emigrants. According to nationality the largest numbers were :—

Spanish	1,055	Portuguese		80
Argentine	325	English		51
Brazilian	255	Roumanian		50
Italian	253	German		37
Russian	202			

GOVERNMENT

The **Legislature** consists of two Houses, the Senate and the Chamber of Representatives, the former containing 19 senators and the latter members in proportion to the population , one member being chosen for every 12,000 qualified electors for a term of three years. An electoral college set up by popular vote elects the senators, one for each Department, for a term of six years, one-third retiring every two years. Congress sits from February 15 to June 15 annually, and in the interval a committee of two senators and five representatives administers affairs. The President, elected by direct popular vote, holds office for four years, assisted by a National Administrative Council. There is no Vice-President. On March 1, 1919, a new constitution came into force, which, besides considerably reducing the prerogatives of the President, introduced the ballot (secret voting), which was operative at the last general election on November 30, 1919. This will also apply to the election of President after 1923. The franchise is open to all qualified men of 18 and over In 1921, the right of suffrage was accorded to women. In 1923 a movement was begun with the object of giving women all civil and political rights possessed by men.

PAST PRESIDENTS.

General F Rivera	1830
General M. Oribe	1835
General F Rivera	—
B. P Berro	1851
A. Aguirre	1864
General V Flores	1865
D P Varela	1868
General L. Batlle	1869
T. Gomensoro	1872
General J. D. Ellauri	1875
Dr Varela	1875
Colonel Latorre	1876
Dr F A. Vidal (died in office)	1880
General M. Santos	1882
M. Vidal F.	1886
General M. Tajes	1887
J. Herrera y Obes	1890
J. Idiarte Borda	1894
Juan L. Cuestas	1897
Juan L. Cuestas (second term)	1899
J Batlle y Ordoñez	1903
Dr Claudio Williman	1907
J. Batlle y Ordoñez (second term)	1911
Dr Feliciano Viera	1915
Dr Baltasar Brum	1919

PRESIDENT
Ingeniero Don José Serrato.

MINISTRY.

President of the National Administrative Council	Señor Julio M. Sosa.
Foreign Affairs	Dr Pedro Manini y Rios.
Interior	Dr Lorenzo Vincens y Thiviens.
War and Marine	Coronel Riverós.
Education	Dr. Pablo Blanca Acevedo.
Industry	Dr José F. Ariás.
Public Works	Ingeniero S. A. Colcagno.
Finance	Dr. Ricardo Vecino.

AN URUGUAYAN CALENDAR.

1515. Juan Diaz de Solis lands on coast and is killed by the Charrúas.
1518. Ferdinand Magellan visits the coast.
1526. Sebastian Cabot visits Uruguay.
1573. Zárate, the third Adelantado, endeavours unsuccessfully to establish a port in Uruguay.
1580. Hernandarias fails in an attempt to conquer Uruguay. Sends cattle into the country.
1680. Colonia founded by the Portuguese.
1726. Montevideo founded by Zavala, Governor of Buenos Aires.
1729. First Cabildo established at Montevideo.
1750. Spain agrees to exchange the Seven Missions for Colonia.
1762. The Governor of Buenos Aires attacks Colonia.
1776. Uruguay included in the new Vice-Royalty of Buenos Aires.
1777. By the Treaty of San Ildefonso, the Seven Missions remain Spanish, and the Portuguese are deprived of the southern half of the great lagoon and of Colonia.
1807. (February). Montevideo captured by the British.
(September). Montevideo evacuated by the British.
1811. After Revolution in Buenos Aires, seat of Vice-Royalty transferred to Montevideo.
1814. Montevideo captured by the patriot, General Alvear. Spanish garrison expelled from Montevideo.
1817. The Portuguese capture Montevideo, which temporarily becomes Brazilian territory
1821. A Uruguayan Congress declares the country incorporated with the Portuguese dominions under the name of the Cisplatine Province.
1825. Disembarkation of the thirty-three Orientals in Uruguay
1827. Brazilians defeated by Alvear at the Battle of Ituzaingo.
1830. Constitution promulgated. Rivera declared first President.
1843-51. Intervention of the Dictator Manuel Rosas leads to siege of Montevideo by his troops and those of General Oribe.
1863. Civil war breaks out in consequence of the invasion of General Venancio Flores.
1864. Brazil invades Uruguay Aguirre elected President.
1865. General Flores becomes President.
1868. The Republic divided into two parties, the Blancos and the Colorados. General Flores assassinated during an insurrection. The leader of the Blancos, Berro, shot. F A. Vidal elected President. Construction of the Central Uruguay Railway begun.
1870. Conclusion of the Paraguayan war.
1872. Blanco insurrection ended.
1875. President Ellauri overthrown. Succeeded by Pedro Varela.
1885. Treaty of commerce with Great Britain.
1886. Unsuccessful insurrection under General Arredondo.
1891. Attempted revolution by the Blancos.
1894. The Colorado Juan Idiarte Borda elected President.

1897. The Blancos revolt under the leadership of Aparicio Saraiva. Borda assassinated at Montevideo. Juan L. Cuestas succeeds him.
1898. Cuestas declares himself Dictator, suspends the Constitution, and dissolves the Chambers. New Council of State appointed.
1899. Treaty of Commerce with Great Britain renewed.
1901 New port works at Montevideo begun.
1903. Civil war breaks out on the election of José Batlle y Ordoñez as President.
1904. The leader of the rebels, General Saraiva, mortally wounded. Peace restored.
1907. Capital punishment abolished.
1910. Treaty with Argentina concerning the navigation of the River Plate.
1917 Diplomatic relations with Germany severed.
1919. Amended Constitution comes into force. Uruguay joins the League of Nations.
1921. Introduction of women's suffrage.

Local Administration :—Each Department is governed by a Council, consisting of at least three and not more than seven members, who are elected by direct popular vote for a period of three years. The Departments are autonomous, collecting their own revenue and controlling their own expenditure. Taxes are levied on properties and the various industries, business houses, commercial concerns, etc., according to graduated tables of values.

There are a Supreme **Court,** two Courts of Appeal, and several inferior courts. The judges of the Supreme Court are elected by Congress, and those of other courts are appointed by the Supreme Court. The death sentence has been abolished.

Currency :—Gold is not minted in Uruguay, but the currency is based on a gold standard. The circulating medium is paper notes issued by the Bank of the Republic, normally convertible into gold in the case of notes of \$10 and over, but temporarily inconvertible. Smaller units of currency are notes of \$5 and \$1, silver coins of 50 centesimos and 20 centesimos, and nickel coins of 5 centesimos, 2 centesimos and 1 centesimo.

The par rate of exchange is $51\frac{1}{16}$ pence to the dollar (peso) or \$4·70 to the £ sterling.

The **language** of the country is Spanish.

The majority of the population are Roman Catholics, but no religion is established by the State, and all beliefs are free.

A foreigner capable of exercising some industry or practising some science or art, or owning property, or possessing capital invested in the Republic, is eligible for **naturalization,** if married after three years', and if single, after four years' residence in the country. Naturalization is bestowable upon foreigners by Congress for notable services rendered to the nation.

The **metric** system is established and enforced by law, any infraction being punished by fine.

NATURAL RESOURCES.

Livestock constitutes the main source of the wealth of the Republic. According to the census of 1916 the livestock in Uruguay was : head of cattle, 7,802,442; sheep, 11,472,852, mules and donkeys, 16,663, horses, 567,154, pigs, 303,958, goats, 12,218.

URUGUAY.

During the season 1921-1922, 200,000 animals were killed for jerked beef, half of which amount was exported to Cuba.

Marked preference is shown for Hereford cattle, the Durham breed is well known, but demand is comparatively small for Short-horn pedigree stock.

The Romney Marsh sheep is sought, and the Lincoln breed is popular. Buyers of pedigree sheep pay much attention to the wool-bearing qualities of the animal.

Wool in Montevideo is quoted per 10 kilos, and in the following main varieties. Crossbreds, special fine, medium; and coarse. Merinos, ''supras''; ''primeras''; and ''segundas.''

The greatest precautions are taken to prevent disease, travelling inspectors, sanitary police, and district commissioners being appointed, who report cases of sheep scab and other infections and supervise curative measures. Formerly sheep-dip prepara-tions came from abroad, but some years ago their importation was highly taxed, and plant set up in the country supplies domestic requirements. A veterinary school has been established, and educational propaganda among breeders is having good effect in the scientific propagation and care of livestock.

The principal agricultural **crops** are wheat, oats, barley, linseed, maize, fruit, olives and vegetables.

The wheat harvest in 1921-1922 was the best for many years, the yield per hectare being 823 kilogs. In 1919 maize was produced to the extent of 170,000 tons. In 1922-1923 there were 328,650 hectares under wheat, 24,660 under linseed, 43,260 under oats, and 1,100 under barley.

Seals are caught in large numbers on the Uruguayan coast, and it appears that the flesh can be put to profitable use in the preparing of emulsions, polishing pastes, metal polish, lubricating grease, furniture polish, soap, etc.

Montevideo is the anchorage during the winter months of various **whaling** flotillas owned by British and Scandinavian firms operating in the South Atlantic. Up to 77,000 barrels of whale oil has been secured in a season.

Afforestation is carried out upon an important scale by the departments and stimulated by an Arbour Day holiday and Government prizes.

Nutria or otter **skins**, valued by furriers and hat makers, are an important product of the Republic.

Among **local industries** are weaving and flour-milling, glass, cordage, cement, footwear, leather and tanning, tobacco, wine, brewing, ostrich feathers, etc.

The manufacture of chemicals has been fostered, and among products on sale are alcohol, sulphate, chloride and carbonate of soda, chloroform, collodions, sulphuric ether and acid, commercial sulphate of iron, benzol, toluol, and naphthaline, nitric acid, hydrochloric acid, caustic soda and ammonia The range is being extended.

There are very few **gold-mines** ; the San Gregorio in Cuñapiru is owned by British interests, and there are other mines in the department of Rivera, which send their mineral for crushing to the stamps at San Gregorio. In the Montevideo department there is the manganese mine, Adelaide, and the talc-mines, Yacimiento N and Maruja, in the Minas department, are active.

In 1922 **coal** was discovered in the Department of Cerro Largo, but its industrial importance has yet to be ascertained.

Building Materials :—Stone is plentiful in the country, but preference is shown for brick, plastered to imitate stone. Reinforced concrete construction is used, and the locally made cement is well spoken of. Most of the wood used comes from neighbouring countries. Buildings in Montevideo call for large quantities of glass for floor lights, sky lights, doors, windows and fanlights. Much use is made of tiles for roofing, flooring and for walls, and of marble for halls and staircases. Mortice locks with long bolts and lever handles are preferred. Espagnolette bolts are much used in double-leaved doors and casements, and the keys and handles are usually nickelled. Ornamental ironwork of a medium class is employed for balcony and stair railings.

Labour Laws :—In 1920, the National Administrative Council issued a decree establishing an eight-hour working day for labourers and employees. In exceptional cases the working day may be lengthened, provided that the working hours do not exceed 48 every six days.

A law was promulgated 10th December, 1920, enacting that the personnel of all industrial or commercial establishments and branches are to be allowed one day's rest every six days. Weekly rest is compulsory for drivers of motor cars and carriages, and domestic servants.

Free Zones :—A project has been approved for the establishment of " free zones " at Colonia and Nueva Palmira. The creation of free zones without Custom House, to serve as distributing points of commerce, should be a boon to merchants in Uruguay who import for exportation to Paraguay, and ought to stimulate trade with that country, Boliva and Brazil.

Postal Rates :—Letters, Inland   City, every 20 grammes or fraction, 2 cts.   Country, 5 centisimos.

Abroad : South American States, every 20 grammes or fraction, 5 cts.   Brazil and Venezuela, 5 cts. , other countries, 12 cts.

Outward **mails** are despatched at frequent intervals by the Royal Mail, Pacific Steam Navigation, Nelson, Houlder, Lamport and Holt, etc. Lines, and by French Packet at uncertain intervals.

Postage · 3d. first ounce and 1½d. each ounce after

Homeward mails are despatched at frequent intervals.

Telegrams :—Inland, ordinary telegrams, first 10 words, 40 centisimos , every additional word, 3 cts. Urgent telegrams, triple rates.

There is a large **wireless** station at Cerrito, near Montevideo. Other stations are at Rivera, Lobos Island, Paso de los Toros, and English Bank.

PUBLIC HOLIDAYS.

February 3 : Battle of Monte Caseros (1852).
February 28 : Proclamation of Independence.
April 18 : Landing of the Thirty-three Uruguayan Patriots.
May 1   Labour Day
May 18 : Battle of Las Piedras (1811).
May 25 : Revolution of May, 1810.
July 4 : American Independence Day
July 14 : Democracy Day (French National Feast) (1789).
July 18 : Proclamation of the Constitution (1830).
August 25 : National Independence Day (1825).
September 20 : Italian National Feast.
October 12   Discovery of America Day (1492).
The feast days of the Roman Catholic Church are observed.

PRINCIPAL EXPORTS.

Commodity	Value, 1921. $	Value, 1922. $
Cattle	736,410	599,761
Sheep	34,844	38,155
Horses	5,162	5,238
Canned Beef	1,709,495	6,979,871
Frozen Beef	11,004,994	6,524,391
Chilled Beef	3,066,650	8,063,381
Frozen Mutton	1,759,780	2,144,415
Frozen Pork	48,432	39,982
Jerked Meat	2,670,112	5,555,030
Meat Extract	338,347	1,178,273
Preserved Tongues	208,396	347,339
Fats (including Tallow)	1,527,253	3,241,199
Wool, raw, washed, combed, etc.	31,723,538	21,322,238
Tanned Hides	178,937	229,832
Sheep Pelts	1,190,279	1,591,340
Salted Ox-hides	2,575,788	6,454,913
Dry Ox-hides	2,610,081	3,216,972
Salted "frigorifico" hides	3,980,073	4,506,985
Horsehair	207,731	241,600
Horns and Bones	136,884	215,501
By-products	135,493	207,792
Flour	358,708	192,506
Oats	16,996	69,916
Linseed	1,214,795	934,940
Wheat	156,239	448,426
Maize	186,277	110,252
Olives	5,141	2,417
Garlic	13,686	31,597
Oranges	13,771	6,599
Stone, common	332,391	331,799
Sand ..	431,752	535,314

Newspapers :—MONTEVIDEO . " El Bien," " Publico," " El Dia," " El Diario del Plata," " El Diario Español," " La Mañana," " Montevideo Times," " El País," " El Plata," " La Razón," " El Siglo," " El Telégrafo," " La Tribuna Popular," " Uruguay Weekly News," " La Democracia," " The Sun."

PAYSANDU : " El Diario," " La República," " El Telégrafo."
SALTO : " El Diario Nuevo," " Ecos del Progreso," " La Tarde,"
" Tribuna Salteña."

A special edition of the morning daily paper, ' La Nación,"
published at Buenos Aires, is sent by aeroplane to Uruguay.

LEGATION AND CONSULATES IN GREAT BRITAIN

RESIDENCE.	DESIGNATION	NAME.
London .. .. .. (3 Elvaston Place, South Kensington, S.W.7).	Envoy Extraordinary and Minister Plenipotentiary	Federico R. Vidiella.
	First Secretary . .	Carlos de Santiago.
London .. . .. (57–58 Chancery Lane, W.C.2).	Consul-General	Juan C. Muñoz.
Cardiff	Consul	Arturo Pratto.
Glasgow	Consul	Carlos A. Sermite.
Liverpool	Consul	Eduardo Martinez.
Manchester ..	Consul	Geoffrey Simpson.
Newport .	Consul .	Luis Uriarte.

BRITISH LEGATION AND CONSULATES IN URUGUAY.

The letter (M) denotes that the Consular Officer holds a Marriage Warrant
Members of the Diplomatic Service do not require Warrants.

RESIDENCE.	RANK.	NAME.	CONSULAR DISTRICT.
Montevideo .	Envoy Extraordinary, Minister Plenipotentiary, and Consul-General.	Sir Claude C. Mallet, C.M.G.	
	(M) Vice-Consul	E. A. Cleugh	Republic of
	Vice-Consul .	Colonel De S. Dobrée, R.M.A.	Uruguay.
Fray Bentos	Vice-Consul	L. A. Gepp (acting)	
Maldonado	Vice-Consul .	Henry W Burnett	
Paysandú	Vice-Consul	Alexandra M. Dick	
Salto . .	Vice-Consul	G. W Teague .	

Guidance for Commercial Travellers.

Commercial travellers must obtain a licence, costing 100 dollars
annually The licence expires 31st December, and the full annual
charge must be paid, regardless of the period at which the licence
is taken out. Persons desirous of obtaining a licence must apply
in writing, on paper bearing a stamp of 50 centavos, to the Chief
of Police, Montevideo, who will grant a certificate, which the
applicant must present at the office of the Director-General of
Indirect Taxes in order to obtain the required licence. Travellers
handling jewellery, timepieces and similar classes of goods pay
a tax of 500 dollars.

Commercial travellers carrying samples should on arrival in
Uruguay declare to the Customs officials the number of packages,
description of contents, weight and value. If the samples have

been mutilated in such a way as to make them unsaleable and therefore of no commercial value, they are passed without further trouble, otherwise the officials assess the lot and a Custom House Agent is called upon to guarantee payment of the import duty, in the event of any of the samples being left in the country. The Commercial Traveller in turn must satisfy the Custom House Agent whom he has engaged to conduct the clearing of the samples, and should furnish the Agent with the name of a local bank or business house which may be prepared to back his undertaking.

If during his stay in the Republic the traveller disposes of any of his samples these must be detailed in the Customs declaration made by the Custom House Agent when his client leaves the country and duties are levied on the goods short shipped.

It is advisable that Commercial Travellers who may bring samples with them should be provided with several copies of the packing lists of the sample case or cases. If the samples are saleable articles the traveller should engage a Custom House Agent to effect the clearance of the goods and attend to the other formalities mentioned.

FARMING LANDS AND FARMING LIFE IN URUGUAY.

Uruguay, although so near Argentina, is a land of widely different character. Argentine country is mostly flat. In Uruguay one finds rolling, rocky ridges, not very high, sometimes tree crowned. The climates are much the same. Uruguay is in the warm temperate zone, and oranges grow over practically all of the Republic. There is less arable farming practised in Uruguay than in Argentina. The soil is not so well adapted to the plough and there has been less immigration. It is a land devoted to sheep and cattle fed on native pastures.

Upon an Uruguayan estancia, the first thing that impresses the stranger is the excellence of the fences. These are of wire, not barbed, tightly stretched, with posts 40 feet or more apart. Posts are obtained from the northern forests, or more rarely cut from neighbouring tracts of small timber. They are usually crooked and made of hard and durable wood, " namdebay " and quebracho woods being most used. Between the posts are wooden stays to keep the wires properly spaced to prevent the sheep creeping through between them.

ROADS AND FENCES.

The roads are often 100 yards wide and sometimes widen out to several times that width to afford grazing for travelling flocks and herds. The estanciero owning the land left outside of his pastures is in the habit of charging a small fee for animals stopping there to rest and graze.

The roads are commonly good. The nature of the earth makes it easy to have good roads, and the Government is energetic in building needed bridges and approaches.

The country undulates without being actually hilly. Ledges of rock protrude along the summits of the ridges, sometimes on the slopes, and even on the lowlands. On the high parts are often wide level areas, free from stone and with a good depth of soil. The rocks are often granites, sometimes sandstones. Layers of soft limestone are found—a chalky substance called " tosca." The word " tosca " is much used in South America to denote a hard substance in the subsoil.

The soil is almost uniformly black and full of humus, rich in nitrogen, though said to be poor in phosphorus and bone material. It is much improved by the use of bone meal. The land is not well adapted to the plough, for ploughed slopes are apt to erode, but there are wide areas well fitted for tillage.

The soil is not so absorbent of moisture as that of alluvial Argentina. Streams abound and springs are common.

The whole country is covered with native perennial grasses. Some are coarse, and others short and fine. There are good growths of wild native clovers. The "burr clovers" and the very fattening alfilaria are seen. Uruguay is more richly supplied with grasses than is Argentina.

A TYPICAL ESTANCIA.

The typical Uruguayan estancia is set within a grove of high trees. At or near the gate is a small house, brick or adobe, with a roof often of thatch. This is the home of one of the puesteros, or pasture tenders, whose duty is to look after one of the large potreros, or pastures, and to keep the gate.

Entering the pasture and driving through, one follows a cart track or an avenue of eucalypti. The pasture may be of 100 or even 5,000 acres. Well-managed estancias make rather small enclosures, the better to arrange their stock—from 200 to 500 acres in the main pastures, with smaller paddocks of from 40 to 100 acres, more or less, near the headquarters.

The estancia headquarters gleam white through the trees. There are the galpones, or barns, for shearing and possibly storing the wool, stables for horses and perhaps for cattle, small houses for the peons, or labourers, and last the house of the estanciero himself, which may be large, but is usually a rambling, roomy, one-story brick building, plastered on the outside, and roofed with tiles. It is probably surrounded with a garden yielding oranges, peaches, apricots, figs, plums, roses and other flowers, and vegetables. These oases show what Uruguay might become, given skilled labour and small holdings.

The number of peons, or labourers, required varies somewhat. On one estancia raising pure-bred sheep 5 men care for 6,000 head. Another uses 5 men to care for 14,500; another has 4 men for 11,000, another 6 men for 7,500, another 30 men for 55,000 sheep; and yet another 15 men for 19,000 sheep, or an average of about 1,750 sheep per man.

In ordinary weather when there is little to do to the sheep, the men employ themselves in perfecting the fences, repairing the houses, getting up the sheep for assorting or culling, or work with the cattle, of which there are always a number on the place. The fences are inspected at short intervals and there is a rigid scrutiny of every sheep for scab disease.

Lambing begins in April, May, or June, and lambs born then get a good start during winter and grow rapidly in August and September, when the spring comes. Other estancieros have all the lambs born in August and September, or sometimes as late as October.

Droughts in Uruguay are possibly less severe than in Argentina, though there is probably little difference in this respect. Locusts come in swarms from the north, settle over the lands, strip trees of their leaves, gardens of their plants, orchards of their fruit, consume even the grass and the very weeds. Few species of trees and plants are untouched by the destroyers. They come at irregular periods, and after a time disappear for another period.

There is a custom somewhat prevalent in South America of placing the flocks in charge of puesteros, who take all care of them and receive as payment a share in the wool and lambs. At one estancia the puestero receives 25 per cent. of the wool and the same of the increase, valuing lambs at 88 cents each. The scheme proves, on the whole, more economical than to hire the men. In good years they make good profits, in bad years very little. It is notable that the estancias with the highest labour costs have often returned the largest profits.

WAGES OF SHEPHERDS AND PEONS.

In Uruguay, as in Argentina, the superintendents of estancias are often paid large salaries and are very skilled, intelligent men, often British or American in origin. The peons are native, and the superintendent's salary is often as much as the combined wages of the peons.

It is customary in South America to furnish food to the labourers on estancias, who are often married men, living in small houses with their families. The food is chiefly mutton.

On every estancia there is set apart a flock of sheep to be eaten.

A noted estanciero gave a Government agent in 1911 the following diet and costs for 20 men for one day. Meat, $2.50; coffee, 9 cents, sugar, 16 cents, biscuits, 72 cents, yerba maté (tea), 64 cents, macaroni, 24 cents, farina, lard, salt, 15 cents; total, $4.50.

This estimate made the food of a man cost $82 12 for one year, and other estancieros called this too low.

Another estanciero furnishes the following estimate of food required for a peon keeping a puesto, or pasture, living with his family, per month : Thirty-three pounds of yerba maté; six to eight sheep, according to size of family; galletas (hard biscuits), about six per day, or 33 pounds of farina; salt. The home consumption of meat is large, and a man with his family may consume 70 to 100 sheep in a year. The ordinary estancia has at least four peons and a manager, and the five families consume about 400 sheep in a year.

VENEZUELA

VENEZUELA.

Caracas, the capital, was founded in 1567, and has a population of some 100,000. The city is regularly laid out, with streets at right angles to each other, on the southern slopes of the coast range. The northern part of the city has an altitude of over 3,000 feet; the southern is some 400 feet lower. Although in the torrid zone, the temperature is that of perpetual spring, the maximum temperature being 82° Fahr. and the minimum 48°. The town has broad and shady avenues and squares, excellent water supply, a good tramway and telephone service. Caracas is 23 miles from La Guaira, 112 miles from Valencia, and 29 from Charallane. A very important commercial centre, it has paper, cement, and textile factories, with soap and candle works; its chief products are cacao, coffee, tobacco. Served by the Central Railway of Venezuela (Valencia and Puerto Cabello) and by the Caracas-La Guaira Railway

Points of Interest :—The Pantheon, Government Palaces, Municipal and National Theatres, Cathedral.

There are several beautiful squares, the principal being the Plaza Bolívar, with a statue of the Liberator, Simon Bolívar.

Hotels :—Grand Hotel Klindt, Gran Hotel, Hotel Saint Armand, Gran Hotel Continental, Alemania, America, New, Universal, Italia.

Excursions :—Round Drive. La Vega, Antimano, Sabana Grande and El Valle, 2½ to 3 hours.

Rail :—La Guaira and Caracas Railway. A list of stations, their altitudes and distances from La Guaira follow. The fares are : first-class single, bs. 7, return, bs. 10.50, second-class single, bs. 5, return, bs. 7.50.

STATIONS.			MILES.	HEIGHT.	HOURS.
La Guaira	.		—	6 ft.	—
Maiquetia			1·30	50 ft.	—
El Rincon		..	2·46	300 ft.	0.15
Curucuti	.	.	6·97	1,078 ft.	0.40
Zig-Zag	.	.	9·89	1,533 ft.	1.00
Boqueron	..	..	11·80	1,955 ft.	1.10
Pena de Mora	.	..	14·00	2,295 ft.	1.27
Cantinas	.	..	18·00	2,903 ft.	1.46
Caracas	..	..	23·00	2,984 ft.	2.08

La Guaira is the principal port, and practically all business for the central part of the Republic passes through it. La Guaira is the shore end of the submarine cable to Florida via Curaçao, Santo Domingo, and Cuba. The breakwater which has transformed La Guaira from an open roadstead into a commodious harbour was built by British enterprise. Adjoining La Guaira are Maiquetia and Macuto, the latter of which is the Brighton of Venezuela. Population about 14,000.

Landing :—Alongside wharf.

Excursion :—Rail to Caracas. The mountain railway is one of the most wonderful in the world.

Hotels :—Neptuno, Español, Alemania, Familia.

Puerto Cabello, in the State of Carabobo, is the second port of the Republic, and has a population of nearly 20,000. It is on a narrow peninsula 65 miles west of La Guaira, 34 from Valencia, 40 from Tucacas. It has an excellent harbour and good communication with the rest of Venezuela. Chief products : coffee, cacao, copra, woods, hides; and the industries, corn mills, cotton mills, sawmills, marble works, and cigarette factories.

Hotels :—Universal, Baños, Hotel de France.

Rail :—Central Railway of Venezuela (12 hours to Caracas); Puerto Cabello and Valencia Railway, Bolívar Railway (Barquisimeto).

Ciudad Bolívar, capital of Bolívar State, on the right bank of the Orinoco and 372 miles from its mouth. Population about 20,000. Formerly known as Angostura, it received its present name in 1846 in honour of General Simon Bolívar. There are several buildings of note. The town is the centre of the Orinoco river trade.

Hotels :—Bolívar, Gran, Venezuela, Central, Unión, Manoni.

Barquisimeto, the capital of Lara, has a population of about 25,000, and is the centre of a large and flourishing trade. It is at an altitude of about 1,700 feet, on the Barquisimeto river, 164 miles from Caracas and 90 from Puerto Cabello. The chief products of the district are coffee, cacao, sugar, copper and other minerals, and cattle. Fibre hammocks and bags are manufactured.

Hotels :—Sucre, Vesubio.

Rail :—Bolívar Railway de Tucacas (via Tucacas to Puerto Cabello)

Valencia, capital of the State of Carabobo, has a population of about 30,000, and stands on the west bank of Cabriales river, three miles from its mouth, near Lake Valencia. It is 34 miles from Puerto Cabello, 56 from Tucacas, and 112 from Caracas. The climate and situation are delightful. The principal products are coffee, cacao, sugar, hides, tobacco, and beans; the industries : cattle-raising, sawmills, foundries and cotton mills.

Hotels :—Lourdes, Olivares, Ottolina.

Rail :—Central Railway of Venezuela and the Puerto Cabello Railway.

Maracaibo, capital of State of Zulia, has a population of over 46,000, and stands on the western shore of the lake. It is 572 miles from Caracas. One of the most important and progressive cities of the country, it exports large amounts of coffee. Large steamers carry on an active trade between Maracaibo and La Ceiba. Products coffee, cinchona, sugar, marble, and asphalte. Industries : rum, sugar, flour, and chocolate.

Hotels :—Bismarck, Colón, Los Andes, Zulia.

Steamer from La Guaira, calls at Puerto Cabello and La Vela ; a service to Encontrados, on the Catatumbo river, and to San Carlos on Escalante river by way of the lake.

Barcelona, capital of Anzoategui, has a population of about 16,000, and lies on the west bank of the Neveri river, 3 miles from the ocean, and 155 miles from Caracas. It is connected by rail with the port of Guanta, 11 miles away, and is a good trading centre. There are coal and salt mines, and a large amount of livestock in the district. Products · cattle, cotton, sugar, cacao, tobacco.

Hotels :—Oriental, Nacional, Vesubio.

Served by the Guanta-Naricual railway

Other important towns are **San Cristobal,** with a population of 22,000, and **Cumaná, Coro, San Félipe, Maturin,** and **Mérida,** each with a population of over 14,000.

PHYSICAL FEATURES.

Venezuela occupies the extreme northern part of South America and is altogether within the tropics. It is bounded on the north by the Caribbean Sea, on the east by British Guiana and Brazil, on the south by Brazil, and on the west by Colombia. The area is estimated at 398,594 square miles. The western boundary has been in dispute with Colombia.

There are three principal chains of mountains. The first, formed by a branch of the Andes where it divides at Pamplona (Colombià), may be called the alpine region, a broad and compact mass with its summits perpetually covered with snow The second chain, the coast range, intersects the Andes near Barquisimeto, and runs in parallel ridges to the Caribbean Sea. The third is the Parima range, differing from the two others in geological formation. The region of Venezuelan Guiana which it occupies is a convex table-land of an elongated shape running from east to west, in which rise at intervals large mountains separated by plains crossed by the principal rivers of the eight great watersheds of Venezuela. The country is well watered, no fewer than 1,059 rivers and streams of varying size being found, of which 436 are affluents of the Orinoco, 230 discharge into the Caribbean Sea, 124 into the Gulf of Paria, 200 into Lake Maracaibo, and 22 into the Lake of Valencia. The principal navigable rivers are the Orinoco, Apure, Meta, Cauca, Negro, Guárico, and Zulia-Catatumbo.

The Orinoco and its tributaries are navigable during the rainy season some way into Colombia. Navigation is restricted to boats flying the Venezuelan flag and owned by Venezuelans. The waterway is practically a monopoly of the Compañia Venezolana de Navegación.

The rich Cúcuta district in Colombia is dependent upon Venezuela for the transit of merchandise by rail and by the Catatumbo River flowing into the Lake of Maracaibo.

Climate :—There are three well-marked zones, varying in temperature according to their height above sea level, and classified as torrid, temperate, and cold. The torrid zone begins at the coast and extends to an altitude of about 1,750 feet, with a temperature ranging from 78° to 90° Fahr. The temperate zone, from altitudes of 1,750 up to 6,500, has readings from 64° to 77°, and the cold region, above 6,500 feet, from 35° to 38° Fahr. The rainy or winter season on the llanos lasts from April to October, the dry season from November till March. In the temperate zone the climate is healthy and pleasant and the seasons are not so definitely marked as in the lowlands.

Population :—In addition to pure whites, there is a considerable mixed Spanish and Indian population and also an admixture of negro blood.

The population is estimated at 2,800,000. The population of the principal towns is : Caracas (100,000), Maracaibo (46,706), Valencia (29,466), Barquisimeto (23,943), San Cristóbal (21,385) and Ciudad Bolívar (19,712) The only other towns with a population of over 14,000 are Cumaná, Coro, San Félipe, Maturin, and Mérida.

GOVERNMENT

The present **Constitution** dates from June 13, 1914. The legislative authority is entrusted to two Chambers of Congress, a Senate of 40 members and a Chamber of Deputies of about twice as many Senators are elected for three years, each State being represented by two. Deputies are elected also for three years, each State choosing one for every 35,000 inhabitants.

The States compose the Federal Union of Venezuela, each State having its own constitution. The national constitution provides three powers with which the government is entrusted : the legislative, the federal, and the judiciary.

The President is elected by Congress for seven years; there is at present no restriction as to re-election.

Each State has a Supreme Court under three officers, also superior courts, courts of first instance, district and municipal courts. State judicial appointments are held for three years. There is a Federal Court, also acting as Court of Cassation.

VENEZUELA.

Political Divisions :—The country is divided into twenty States, two Territories, and the Federal District :—

State.	Capital.
Anzoategui.	Barcelona.
Apure.	San Fernando.
Aragua.	Maracay
Bolivár	Ciudad Bolivár
Carabobo.	Valencia.
Cojedes.	San Carlos.
Falcon.	Coro.
Guárico.	Calabozo.
Lara.	Barquisimeto.
Mérida.	Mérida.
Miranda.	Ocumare del Tuy
Monagas.	Maturin.
Nueva Esparta.	Asunción.
Portuguesa.	Guanare.
Sucre.	Cumaná.
Táchira.	San Cristóbal.
Trujillo.	Trujillo.
Yaracuy	San Félipe.
Zamora.	Barinas.
Zulia.	Maracaibo.
Territories.	
Amazonas.	San Fernando de Atabapo.
Delta Amacuro.	Tucupita.
Cristóbal Colón.	Cristóbal Colón.
Federal District.	Caracas.

The various States are self-governing and politically equal, each has a legislative assembly of its own, a President, and a General Secretary The States are divided into districts and municipalities. The President of the Republic appoints governors for the Federal District and the Territories.

PRINCIPAL PAST PRESIDENTS.

General José Antonio Páez	1829
General José G. Monagas ..	1849
General José Falcón	1863
General José R. Monagas	1868
General Guzman Blanco	1870
Andueza Palacio	1890
General Crespo	1891
General Andrade	1898
General Castro ..	1900
General Juan Vicente Gómez ..	1908
Dr. V Marquez Bustillos (provisional) ..	1914

PRESIDENT AND ACTING PRESIDENT

President : General Juan Vicente Gómez.
Acting President : Dr. V. Marquez Bustillos.

VENEZUELA.

MINISTRY.

Interior : Dr. F Baptista Galindo.
Foreign Affairs : Dr P Itriago Chacín.
War and Marine : Carlos Jimenez Rebolledo.
Finance : M. Centeno Grace.
Education : Rubén González.
Public Works : Tomás Bueno.
Improvements : Dr. Antonio Alama.

A VENEZUELAN CALENDAR.

1492. Columbus lands on the island of Guanabaní.
1498. Columbus sights the Venezuelan coast just south of the Windward Islands.
1499. Alonso de Ojeda lands on the Peninsula of Paria.
1500. First Spanish settlement on the island of Cubagua.
1502. The *Real Audiencia y Casa de la Contratación de las Indias* is established.
1508. The name America is confirmed by Papal Bull.
1520. Cumaná founded.
1525. Asunción (on the island of Margarita) founded.
1528. Cubagua raided by French filibusters. The coast between Cabo de la Vela and the Gulf of Paria leased to the Welsers.
1529. The city of Maracaibo founded.
1551. City of Barquisimeto founded.
1556. End of the rule of the Welsers. Dutch establish themselves in Demerara.
1567. The Spaniards establish their power in the valley of Caracas.
1595. Sir Walter Raleigh sails up the Orinoco River in search of El Dorado; Caracas sacked by the British buccaneer Amyas Preston.
1617. City of Barcelona founded.
1618. Sir Walter Raleigh again explores Venezuela in search of El Dorado.
1629. Dutch sack and burn Santo Tomé.
1637. Dutch sack and burn Santo Tomé.
1654. The French repelled in an attack on Cumaná.
1669. Morgan sacks Maracaibo.
1679. The French pillage Caracas.
1696. A priests' school established in Caracas.
1730. First arrival of the vessels of the Guipuzcoa Company Venezuela raised to the dignity of a Captaincy-General.
1742. Province of Venezuela made independent.
1749. Insurrection under a Creole leader, León.
1762. The Government of Guiana separated from that of Cumaná.
1764. City of Angostura (now Ciudad Bolívar) founded.
1777. The provinces of Cumaná, Guiana, Maracaibo, and the islands of Trinidad and Margarita separated from the Kingdom of Granada and included in the Captaincy-General of Venezuela.
1778. Guipuzcoa Company liquidates.
1796. Republican outbreak.
1806. Francisco Miranda leads the patriot expedition from New York to Venezuela. After capturing Coro he is defeated.
1810. Spanish Captain-General exiled and Junta established at Caracas.
1811. Independence proclaimed.
1812. Defeat of patriot forces. Miranda is sent to prison in Spain. Caracas destroyed by earthquake.
1813. After some successes Spanish forces severely defeated at Maturin.
1821. Patriot victory of Carabobo under the leadership of Simon Bolivár.
1829. Part of the Republic of Colombia declares itself an independent republic.
1841. The introduction of "Schomburg Line" to define the boundaries of Guiana and Venezuela.
1845. Independence recognized by Spain.
1850. New boundary delimitation introduced.
1858. New constitution promulgated.
1870. General Guzman Blanco captures Caracas and becomes President.
1876. Renunciation of Papal authority.
1883. Boundary dispute with Colombia submitted to Spain for settlement.

1887. Diplomatic relations with Great Britain broken off.
1892–4. Civil War.
1895. Diplomatic differences with Great Britain.
1896–7. United States commission on boundaries. Arbitration with Britain and the United States.
1897 Diplomatic relations with Great Britain resumed. Anglo-United States-Venezuelan boundary treaty Abortive revolutionary outbreak.
1899. Conclusion of arbitration on the boundary question between Venezuela and Britain.
1899–1903. Rebellion.
1902. Great Britain and Germany present ultimatum. Blockade of ports.
1903. British and German claims referred to The Hague. Blockade of ports raised.
1904. Decision of the Arbitration Court at The Hague.
1905 Diplomatic relations with France severed.
1908. President Castro expels the Dutch Minister.
1909. Settlement with Holland arranged.
1914. Present constitution promulgated.
1919. Joins the League of Nations.

ADMINISTRATION

The unit of **currency** is the gold bolivar (grammes 0·290323 fine gold) Bolivares 25.25 equal £1 sterling normal.

Banknotes are Bs. 1,000, Bs. 800, Bs. 500, Bs. 400, Bs. 100, Bs. 50, Bs. 20 and Bs. 10.

Gold coins are Bs. 100 (morocotas) and Bs. 20.

Silver coins in current circulation are : Bs. 5, Bs. 2.50, Bs. 2, Br 1, Br. .50 (real), Br. .25 (medio).

Nickel : Bs. 0.125 (locha), Bs. 0.05 (centavo)

In remote districts, especially in the Eastern provinces, currency calculations are still sometimes in pesos (Bs. 4) or pesos fuertes (Bs. 5) and cents (Bs. 0.05) There is no State Bank and no Government paper money in circulation. Silver is legal tender up to 500 bolivares in five-bolivar coins, up to 50 bolivares in smaller coins, and up to 10 bolivares in nickel coins.

The circulation of foreign bank notes is prohibited, such notes introduced by travellers should be declared at the Customs and can only be exchanged at an establishment holding a Government licence for such operations, on production of a certificate issued by the Customs Authority at the port of entry

Metric **measures and weights** have been adopted by law and have now almost universally replaced the old Spanish measures and weights : Leguas (leagues), varas (yards), fanegas (bushels), arrobas (twenty-five pounds, equal to 11.502 kilograms), libras (sixteen onzas) and onzas (ounces)

NATURAL RESOURCES.

The greater part of the population is engaged in agricultural pursuits, principally the cultivation of coffee, cocoa, and sugar, and cattle raising.

Cotton, tobacco, and maize are cultivated, chiefly for home consumption, with a varying margin for export. The native mills are entirely supplied by home-grown cotton, which is of good quality.

The forest regions, mainly those of the south-east and north-west, produce balatá, rubber, copaiba, chicle, tonka beans, and tanning barks, as well as various kinds of valuable timber

Balatá :—Balatá gum, an important article of national produce, is largely employed in the manufacture of driving belts for machinery Exports averaged 1,368 tons, valued at Bs.7,162,500 between 1911 and 1920, and were in 1921, 979 tons, valued Bs.5,121,000.

The extensive plains known as the Llanos, watered by the Orinoco and its tributaries, are well suited for raising cattle, but the pasture is decidedly inferior to that of the Argentine Pampas. A British concern, which owns large areas of land in the State of Apure, has imported numbers of pedigree Shorthorn bulls and some rams, with a view to improving native breeds. The total head of cattle in Venezuela may be estimated at about 3,000,000.

A recent estimate of the distribution of capital in Venezuela gives £14,000,000 engaged in agriculture and stock raising, £14,000,000 in industry, and £16,000,000 in trade.

The centre of the trade in **Egret feathers** is San Fernando de Apure. Exports have been Bs.1,591,370 in 1919, Bs.1,488,763 in 1920; and Bs.313,000 in 1921

There are **Pearl fisheries** in the neighbourhood of the island of Margarita, under Government control. Fishing is allowed during the first seven months of the year, and no one is allowed to fish without having obtained a Government licence. The value of pearls exported was Bs.429,403 in 1919, Bs.631,805 in 1920, and Bs.421,000 in 1921

Gold mining is not in a flourishing condition. The Gold Fields of Venezuela, Limited, is the most important company in operation.

Some 11,300 tons of **copper** ore were mined by the South American Copper Syndicate in 1921, and a smelting plant has been erected at the mines. A copper mining company " La Cumaragua," near Aroa, a native concern, is in liquidation.

Petroleum :—Important developments have taken place recently in the oil-fields. Production from nine wells in 1921 was 218,246 tons of crude oil, compared with 69,539 tons in 1920. Of the production in 1921 5,599 tons were consumed by the company, 61,389 tons were refined at San Lorenzo on the Lake of Maracaibo, and 151,158 tons were exported to Curaçao. Nearly seven million litres of gasolene, kerosene, mineral turpentine, and benzine were refined and put on the home market during 1921. Payment of taxes and royalties to the Government amounted for the same period to over £60,000.

The law governing oil concessions has been amended, and great activity is shown by powerful corporations.

It is calculated that the wells so far discovered in Venezuela will produce more than 6,000,000 tons per annum.

Coal is got at Naricual from State coal mines, equipped with briquetting plants.

Asphalte is exported.

INTERNAL COMMUNICATION

Roads available for **motor traffic** are :—

Caracas, La Guaira, and Macuto (38 kilometres),
Caracas, La Victoria, Maracay, and Valencia (160 kilometres),
Caracas, Guatiré (50 kilometres),
Caracas, Charallave (52 kilometres),
Turmero to Calabozo—" Carretera del Llano " (178 kilometres),
Maracay to Ocumaré de la Costa (59 kilometres),
Táchira Station to San Cristóbal (86 kilometres),

as well as a number of roads branching off from Valencia and Barquisimeto.

There are many motor cars in the country and some motor lorries. Carts, mules and donkeys are extensively used, even in competition with the railways. During the rains (May to October), when trade by cart over the Llanos of the Guarico and Orinoco is impossible, owners bring in their vehicles to Caracas and other places served by railways and accept freight at rates below those charged by the railway companies.

POST AND TELEGRAPH.

Postal rates :—Minimum for foreign letters, 50 centimos, for inland letters, 25 centimos.

Telegrams :—10 words, 1 bolivar, 20 words, 1.50 bolivars. Double on Sundays, holidays, and at night (7 p.m. to 6 a.m.).

Cable communication by the Cie. Française des Cables Télégraphiques.

There are **wireless** stations at Caracas, La Guaira, San Cristóbal, Ciudad Bolívar, Puerto Cabello, and Maracaibo.

There are **telephones** in the more populous districts.

Outward **mails** are sent via the United States, and by Leyland and Harrison Lines, French or Dutch Packets.

Postage, 3d. first ounce, and 1½d. each ounce after
Homeward mails irregular

PUBLIC HOLIDAYS

The feast days of the Roman Catholic Church are unofficially observed. In addition, the following are legal holidays :—

January 1 : New Year's Day
April 19 : First Movement for Independence.
June 24 : Battle of Carabobo.
July 5 : Independence Day.
July 24 : Bolivár Day.
December 19 : National Holiday.
December 25 : Christmas Day.

VENEZUELA.

VENEZUELAN LEGATION AND CONSULATES IN GREAT BRITAIN

RESIDENCE.	DESIGNATION.	NAME.
London (Waldorf Hotel, Aldwych, W.C.2.)	Envoy Extraordinary and Minister Plenipotentiary	Dr. Diógenes Escalante.
	First Secretary	Julio F. Mendez.
	Acting Secretary and Commercial Attaché.	Dr. E. Arroyo Lameda.

London (104 High Holborn, W.C.1.)	Consul	Pablo Heyden Altuna.
	Vice-Consul	Carlos Heyden Altuna.
Birmingham	Consul	Henry George Petersen.
Cardiff	Consul	Abelardo Aldana.
Glasgow	Consul	E. Radonicich.
Hull	Acting Consul	E. Olhson.
Liverpool ..	Consul	Segundo Antonio Mendoza.
	Vice-Consul	Thomas Albert Nickels.
Manchester	Consul	Pedro Rivero.
Newport (Mon.)	Consul	Samuel Dickinson Williams.
Southampton	Consul	Hilario Gimón.
	Vice-Consul	A. C. Dunlop.

BRITISH LEGATION AND CONSULATES IN VENEZUELA.

The letter (L) denotes that the Consular Officer has authority to register *lex loci* marriages. Members of the Diplomatic Service do not require Warrants.

RESIDENCE.	RANK.	NAME.	CONSULAR DISTRICT.
Caracas	Envoy Extraordinary and Minister Plenipotentiary	Henry H. D. Beaumont.	United States of Venezuela, with the exception of the States of Bolívar, Apure, Monagas the Districts of Cajigal, Freites, Independencia, Miranda, and Monagas, in the State of Anzoategui; and the Territories of Delta - Amacuro, and Amazonas.
	(L) Vice-Consul ..	R. J Fowler	
Carupano	Consular Agent	Albert Franceschi ..	
La Guaira	Vice-Consul	M. Brewer .	
Maracaibo	Vice-Consul	R. Cameron	
Puerto Cabello	Vice-Consul	H. F Worth ..	
Bolívar	(L) Consul	F J de Bossière .	States of Bolívar, Apure, Monagas; the Districts of Cajigal, Freites, Independencia, Miranda and Monagas, in the State of Anzoategui; and the Territories of Delta - Amacuro and Amazonas.
San Felix (Puerto Tablas)	Consular Agent	Edward Mathison ..	
Barrancas ..	Consular Agent	S. Palacio	

Guidance for Commercial Travellers.

The possession of a selling licence is not always insisted upon, but in any case the cost is not exorbitant. Commercial travellers are not subject to income tax in respect of the sales they effect.

All persons entering Venezuela are required to produce a certificate of vaccination legalised by a Venezuelan Consular Officer ; no charge is made for such legalisation.

According to the Venezuelan Customs Tariff, samples of cloths, in small strips, in quantities not exceeding 25 kilogrammes in weight, and of wall paper not exceeding 50 centimetres in length, or of all other articles imported in such condition as to be unsaleable, are exempt from duty Excess weight above 25 kilogrammes is liable to duty under Class 3A of the Tariff at the rate of 25 centimes of a bolivar per kilogramme.

The " Codigo de Hacienda " provides that collections of samples, made up of small pieces, or of pieces or objects rendered useless so that they cannot be offered for sale, nor classed under any heading of the Customs Tariff, are likewise exempt from duty, even when their weight exceeds that specified as free by the Tariff, provided that on importation they are declared as " Muestras sin valor " (samples without value), and are destined to be re-exported. The interested party must provide a surety for the duty leviable on the excess weight. Re-exportation must take place within a year

Samples other than those above specified and samples which form entire articles or pairs of articles, for exhibition, must be entered by the importer with the usual invoices, and he must also present to the Customs Authorities a special detailed list, in triplicate, in which he must specify the number of manufacture (" número de fabricación ") of each article, the material of which it is composed, the dimensions, and any other details which distinguish it from other articles of the same class, number or kind. The Customs will then assess the samples according to the Tariff and hand them over to the importer, who will be required to furnish securities for the amount of duty payable and the interest which the delay in payment represents. The samples must be re-exported within a year from the date of inspection by the Customs, and must be verified by the presentation of that copy of the detailed list which the importer has retained. If any articles are missing, the duty payable, plus interest, will be met out of the security furnished, which will be entirely forfeit if the samples are not presented to the Customs within the stated time.

Arrangements can be made for the re-exportation of the samples from a Custom House of the Republic other than that at which they were entered.

Trunks, portmanteaux, or other cases containing samples are subject to duty, and there is no provision for refund. It is understood, however, that in practice plain wooden cases are not considered dutiable.

VENEZUELA.

Transport inland being mainly by mule pack it follows that packages should be of a size and weight suited to that mode of carriage. The packing should be strong without being heavy, because duties are assessable upon the gross, not the net, weights of packages. The gross weight needs to be marked legibly upon each package.

SPORT IN SOUTH AMERICA

SPORT IN SOUTH AMERICA.

SPORT ON THE PAMPAS.

Estancieros have tried more than once to introduce pheasants, but without success, and the reason is a mystery   It is not for lack of cover that the pheasant perishes, nor because of foxes, for the pheasant is a tree-roosting bird, and has an advantage over the partridge.

The killing of partridges and other game is lawful from April to September, and shooting picnics are organized. The accommodation and the hospitality are likened to those encountered in the wilder parts of Ireland. The parties are chiefly confined to the Anglo-Saxon element with occasionally a Basque or an Italian neighbour The native partridge is plentiful, noisy, and conspicuous in the open.

FAMILIAR GAME BIRDS.

The so-called partridge of the Pampas is a species of francolin (*Nothura maculosa*) existing in very large numbers. The species is less prolific than the English partridge. When disturbed the birds run, uttering a shrill piping note, and allow the gun to come within easy range before taking flight, which is seldom of more than three or four hundred yards. After being flushed for the second time they refuse to rise again, hiding in the long grass until pushed out or even seized by a dog. A common device of the natives is to ride them down and catch them with a noose at the end of a pole. In times of drought the birds perish for want of food , and they have countless enemies—hawks, owls, and other birds of prey, foxes, weasels, and skunks. A party of five guns without dogs has been known to kill over a hundred brace in a morning. In the vicinity of the railway, whence game can be sent in cool weather to Montevideo, birds are scarcer , but even near that city Italian and French sportsmen are met returning by train from Sunday outings with a pointer and a bag of partridges.

Another bird, larger, more succulent, and even more stupid than *Nothura maculosa*, was once common in Uruguay, but is now only found in districts where thick reed-beds or large tracts of maize and oats afford good cover. This is the martinetta (*Rhynchotus rufescus*), generally called a partridge in the Chaco and other parts of the Argentine , a big lumbering bird about the size, and something of the shape, of a hen pheasant. In the wilderness of the Chaco this toothsome fowl may avert extinction, but it is quite incapable of doing so in any region where man pursues it with a keen-nosed dog, for its only resource after being flushed is to hide in the nearest cover.

There is good snipe shooting throughout the winter in the " camp," wherever low-banked *canadas* make marsh lands in the little valleys. When flushed, the birds circle round and about their feeding-grounds, making their curious drumming sound as they come up against the wind. A number of snipe breed in the country, and two or three species of duck are permanent residents.

SNIPE AND DUCK.

Wild-fowl shooting is good throughout the winter wherever there is marshy ground with reed-beds, and very pleasant sport it is in the bright sunshine of a June day with the air crisp and nipping after a morning frost, and the south wind blowing. Teal and spoonbill are commonest, and the mallard is fairly plentiful. The only drawback to the sportsman's pleasure lies in the lack of consumers for his game. The peons have little fondness for wild-fowl, though they will condescend to partridges. As to hares, with which the " camp " abounds, the peons regard them as unfit for human food. Hares must be shot, or coursed with hounds, because of the damage they do to the crops and young trees.

The English sparrow, of comparatively recent importation, is making himself very much at home, and ousting the dainty little crested sparrow of Uruguay. The first English sparrows were brought to Montevideo, they say, by an Italian emigrant as pets.

FOUR-FOOTED GAME.

The Pampas deer have disappeared since the introduction of wire fencing, but wherever there is timber or thick cover on the river banks the amphibious carpincho (*Hydrochœrus capyraba*) may be seen or heard, granted woodcraft and patience. A strangely uncouth beast, this river hog is quick of hearing and fleet of foot; at the first alarm he makes straight for the water, where he remains with the tip of his snout projecting.

The lagunas and deep pools of the river teem with animal and bird life. Otters are fairly plentiful, in spite of the value of their skins in the Montevideo market, for trappers are scarce, and shooting at them in the water is useless killing, for the body sinks. Along the untimbered *canadas*, where the stream runs between high shelving banks and there is good grass in the open, are colonies of nutrias (*Myopotamus coypu*), busy beaver families, harmless small deer that make their homes by the river's edge and play at evening like rabbits on the greensward. Nutria is valued as a fur for garments and by felt hat manufacturers.

The native method of killing nutrias is singularly lacking in business foresight. Instead of trapping the full-grown animals in the winter, when their fur is long, the skin-hunters dig out an entire colony with dogs and spades, exterminating the lot, regardless of age and sex, and probably spoiling half their skins in the process. The nutria at bay in his warren is a match for most

terriers, and many a good dog has been badly mauled in subter-
ranean fights. The female nutria carries her young on her back,
where Nature has placed her teats.

The skunk has suffered some diminution of numbers from
drought. The fur-hunter is on his trail more actively, so that
the midnight raids on ducks and poultry are fewer. A fearless
and attractive little beast, his skin is less dark and glossy than that
of the skunk of the northern continent.

Foxes are plentiful and do a good deal of damage in the lambing
season. They make their habitation amongst the holes of the rocks
down by the river, and are seldom seen by day Hares, partridges,
molitos, and other groundlings provide them with prey

BIRDS OF PREY.

The birds of prey are formidable, and include eagles and
harriers, kites and owls, carrion-feeding carancho (*Polyborus
tharus*) and cuervos (*Cathartes aura*) One of the carancho's
favourite devices is to pick the eyes out of sick or wounded sheep.
The reputation of the cuervo is as evil as his vulture-like appearance.
There are neither crows nor rooks.

A bird of very brilliant plumage is the bien-te-veo—one of the
noisiest members of the *Tyrannidæ* family—and his incessant
call, like that of the teru-teru, becomes associated in mind with the
daily life of the " camp." Wood-pigeons murmur at dawn in
the eucalyptus trees. *Paloma grande*, the biggest species of pigeon,
affords good flight shooting towards sunset, when the birds make for
their roosting places along the river A smaller species, varying
from the size of an Antwerp carrier to little larger than a robin,
occurs in vast numbers wherever cultivation provides them with
food. When the thistle seed ripens they descend upon it in great
flocks. There are two humming-birds, great green wood-peckers,
and bands of green parrots, that seem to know to a nicety the range
of a gun.

In " Men, Manners and Morals in South America " (Heinemann,
12s. 6d.), Mr J O. P Bland gives a graphic account of the kind of
shooting to be enjoyed under the hospitality of British estancieros
in Argentina and Uruguay. To his book we are indebted for most
of the particulars given above, and to its pleasant pages readers are
referred for more extended information.

TACKLE FOR SOUTH AMERICA.

Sporting Guns :—" For use in Southern Argentina, Chile, and the River Plate country in general, 12- and 16-bore calibres are favourites," write Messrs. W W. Greener, Ltd., the well-known Birmingham gun makers, out of the fruits of long experience. The usual light-weight 16-bore, made with swivels for carrying by a sling in the Continental manner, is in popular use and ammunition of this size is easily procurable. Twelve-bores are used for pigeon shooting by the better-class sportsmen.

In the Brazils a different type of gun is popular, hammerless and with hammers—the latter preferred. Small calibres such as 24-, 28-, and 32-bore are sought, and this because of the climate which makes a light gun a necessity, and because of the relative scarcity of big game. The 28- and 32-bores are the more general sizes. Hammerless and ejector guns are occasionally demanded by the better-class buyers. These small guns have to be properly proportioned to be satisfactory, and the cheapest ones are not recommended. A hammer-gun costing from £15 to £25 is the cheapest that should be taken.

In the zone north of the Amazons the weapons more generally used are of the European sporting sizes such as 12- and 16-bore. The natives employ muzzle-loaders of small calibre, and these weapons have almost superseded the blowpipe except against the very smallest of birds.

Rifles are little used except by people going upon expeditions into the interior, and then a good shotgun with ball cartridges suitably loaded is regarded as more to the purpose.

Anglers' Outfits :—The type of rod most useful in trout and general river fishing is such as would be used for fly and for spinning in English waters. Messrs. Hardy Bros., the well-known fishing-rod makers, recommend fly rods 10 ft. or 10 ft. 6 in. in length and in three joints, for convenience in travelling.

The reel should be of contracted form to carry as much line as possible, and give a quick recovery when winding-in the line; the more so, because one hardly knows exactly what fish may be hooked in some of the waters.

The usual patterns of flies are satisfactory, but an assortment of gaudily-dressed flies, with silver bodies and bright-coloured feathers, should be taken.

In spinning for trout, a rod 8 ft. or 8 ft. 6 in. in length is preferable. The " Victor " casting type, fitted with a " Silex " casting reel and a suitable line, is good. Artificial baits are generally the most successful, but if natural baits are used, then spinners of the "Crocodile" pattern are necessary upon which to mount the bait used.

For large game fish, like the dorado, a fairly strong rod and a reel for about 120 yards of line are required. An outfit resembling that supplied for heavy salmon fishing in British waters or in Norway is needed with a rod 10 ft. 6 in. or 11 ft. 6 in. long and a 4 in. to 4½ in. "Silex" pattern reel, a good line is required, preferably oiled silk dressed, as the "Alnwick" spinning line. A spoon is the most successful bait for these large, strong-fighting fish. Hooks need to be stoutly made and very strong.

GAMES IN ARGENTINA.

Golf in Argentina :—The finest course in the Republic is at Mar del Plata, the seaside resort, distant seven hours by Southern Railway from the capital. Many others are near at hand and the Argentine Club (Palermo) is only ten minutes by motor-car from the centre of Buenos Aires. Others which offer good opportunities of practice and pleasure are the San Andrez (25 minutes on the Central Argentine Railway), San Isidro (30 minutes by Central Railway), Hurlingham (45 minutes by Pacific Railway), Saenz Peña (30 minutes by Pacific Railway), Links (35 minutes by Southern Railway), and Itzuaingo (40 minutes by Western Railway)

Visitors furnished with letters of introduction are made free of the club, and balls and supplies can be purchased from the clubs in the same way as at home.

Polo in Argentina :—Both the British v American International Polo Championships were won in 1922 by Argentina, a fact which sufficiently illustrates the high class both of the players and their ponies. As a great horse breeding country with a turf and climate favourable to the game, Argentina possesses natural advantages, and to these are added zest in competition and love of horsemanship.

Swimming in Argentina :—Upon August 12, 1923, an Argentine swimmer, S. Tiraboschi, set up a new record in long distance swimming by crossing the English Channel. Starting from the French coast he swam the course in 5 hours 12 minutes less than the time taken by the famous Captain Webb (who started from the English shore) The following gives details and similar performances up to the date of Tiraboschi's feat :—

	H.	M.
Capt. Webb, August 24-25, 1875	21	45
T W Burgess, September 6, 1911	22	35
H. Sullivan, August 6, 1923	26	50
S. Tiraboschi, August 12, 1923	16	33

The first three swam from the English coast.

WITH ROD AND GUN.

Fishing at Iguazu :—The Alto Paraná, in the experience of one who made the transit to Iguazu leisurely by launch, teems with fish. Although a novice, he landed specimens up to 13 lb. A more expert member in a short time took 17 dorado (a fish not unlike salmon, but golden), including one of 40 lb. These fish are powerful enough to snap a strong hook. In return for a present of fish natives of these quarters have been known to insist upon the acceptance of native-made curios, like Indian bows and arrows.

Fishing in British Guiana :—Especially good sport is to be had on the Essequebo and Mazaruni rivers from August and October, when the waters are low. Lukanani, belonging to the perch family, abound. Capital lukanani fishing can be had about the same season on the Lamaha Canal, near Georgetown. Fly, minnow, and spoon baits are all used.

Tarpon-fishing, for which many anglers make special expeditions to Florida, can be enjoyed in British Guiana, where the fish is known as "cuffum." There are big fish and good sport on the east of Demerara and in the Canje Creek, a tributary of the Berbice, cuffum haunt the mouths of the large creeks where fresh and salt water meet. Specially strong line is necessary, and live or spoon bait.

The arapaima, one of the largest fresh-water fish in the world, is common in the Rupununi and higher Essequebo. There are reports current of specimens 15 ft. long and weighing over 400 lb. The fish is often harpooned by the Indians, but it takes the hook readily

Shooting in British Guiana :—The waters of British Guiana also offer sport with the gun. There are two small varieties of alligator on the coast, and the large alligator, or cayman, infests the upper reaches of the Essequebo. Duck, plover, pigeon, snipe, and spurwing, are found on the coast. The largest birds are the jabiru and the harpy, the most plentiful are the gaily plumed birds of the interior
There are regulations for the protection of wild birds. Under the Wild Birds Ordinance, it is made illegal to kill or wound certain specified wild birds, and anyone knowingly killing or wounding them, or selling or exporting parts of them, is liable to a penalty of $24 (£5) for each bird.

The following are protected only during the close season (from April 1 to September) : The bitten, curlew, douraquara, dove (not being ground dove), ibis, hannaqua, maroudi, maam, negro cop or jabiru, plover, parrot, powis, pigeon, quail, spurwing, and trumpet-bird; the curri-curri from January 1 to July 1. Anyone killing or wounding these birds during the close season is liable to the same penalty of £5 per bird. Wild birds may be killed at any time for food, if at a spot distant more than ten miles from a sugar plantation. The Governor may authorize persons to kill wild birds and to export skins, subject to such conditions as he thinks fit.

The sportsman has a choice between the rivers and the dense forests. By day he has little choice of marking quarry in the forest, but at night many animals come out to seek food and drink, and at sunrise make their way back to their lairs. The largest animals are the tapir and the manatee, the first amphibious, and the latter aquatic. Other game animals are peccaries, deer, and various cavies. Baboons and monkeys are plentiful, and tigers varying in size from the cat to the jaguar are fairly common.

A gun licence, available for two months, can be obtained for $1 (4s. 2d.).

THE BULLFIGHT IN PERU.

Lima is one of the places in South America where bullfights are held of the kind familiar in Spain.

In Lima the temporado de toros (season for bull-fighting) is during the hottest weather, from Christmas to Easter   There are bull-fights almost all the year round, but it is during the summer that famous bull-fighters from Spain are engaged, often at salaries as high as those of the stars of the music-hall or cinema.

Peru is not noted for its punctuality, but a bull-fight begins promptly at the hour named. The bugle sounds, the big doors on the right are thrown open, and the cuadrilla of bull-fighters, in their gaily-coloured, bejewelled costumes, advance down the centre of the arena in line, the capa in their hands, accompanied by the picadores carrying long wooden lances with steel points, and mounted on blindfolded hacks. Applause breaks out as they enter, and then falls a hush of expectancy as they take up their positions round the ring near the little wooden shelters behind which they can retreat if necessary from the bull's onslaught.

TOREROS AND PICADORES.

Again the bugle blows and a large iron door on the left is thrown open. Immediately a black-and-white bull dashes into the ring, stops and gazes about in uncertainty for a moment till the flick of a cape in the hands of a bull-fighter catches its eye. Head down it makes a dash for the man, who deftly eludes its charge, and as another bull-fighter catches the bull's eye by waving his cloak the performance is repeated. In this way the bull is kept running round the ring two or three times to take the breath out of it. Then one of the chief toreros draws the bull by flicking his cape, passing the bull backwards and forwards in front of him, twists the cape round the bull's head out of its reach. When the infuriated beast is so bewildered that it hesitates, the man, with a last flick of his cape, turns his back on it and walks with exaggerated carelessness back to the sides of the ring amidst a prolonged tribute from the audience.

Next comes that surgical operation on the bull's neck known as the pica, which is the main basis of most of the accusations of barbarism levelled against the bull-ring and its practices.

A picador, his lance outstretched before him, legs and body protected by leather, and mounted on an old broken-down cab-horse bandaged over the left eye, is pushed by certain attendants, told off for the purpose, in the direction of the bull, always carefully keeping the horse's blinded eye on the side facing the animal. The bull paws the ground in doubt: and, lowering its head and exposing its neck to the thrust of the lance, it hurtles full against the blind flank of the unfortunate horse, goring it with its horns and lifting it and the rider into the air, to fall in a seething mass,

437

from which each separate entity is extracted with the help of two attendants, while the bull's attention is drawn elsewhere with the waving of capes.

It is a loathsome spectacle to those unaccustomed to the sight, but the aficionado will tell you that it is absolutely necessary for the success of the bull-fight, as some of the superfluous strength of the bull is thus expended and its temper worked up and its head down.

BANDERILLERAS.

The sound of the bugle announces the commencement of another suerte, the banderillas. The bull-fighter holds above his head a pair of steel-tipped wooden darts covered with coloured crinkled paper The remainder of the men run to the side of the ring and the main performer, standing well out in the open, brandishes his darts, shouts, and stamps his feet. The bull lowers its head, sets its cumbrous body in motion, and the bull-fighter runs lightly forward to meet it. Both gather speed, the distance between them shortening, until it appears that the man is about to impale himself on the horns of the charging animal. At the psychological moment, he steps swiftly aside, and leaning forward, deftly lodges the pair of gaudy banderillas in the bull's neck as the latter charges past, unable to check its pace or alter its course. The trick is very neat and effective. It is repeated two or three times until the bull has a sheaf of darts hanging from its neck on either side, irritating it with every movement, while the blood flows down its flank, its struggles causing much amusement to the spectators.

Again the bugle sounds, and now comes the serious business with the muleta. This consists of a red cloth stretched over a wooden stick, and with this the bull-fighter, sword in hand, plays the now tired bull to and fro, and making passes to the right and left, and occasionally kneeling on one knee while the bull charges past, or even turning his back on it completely This suerte is the test of the finest qualities of the bull-fighter, and each movement has its technical name. According to his skill in this act, the bull-fighter makes or mars his reputation, and it is at this stage that most of the serious accidents occur.

Finally, when the man has dominated the animal and has proved his valour and dexterity, the bugle blows the signal for the coup-de-grace—the kill. Holding the muleta in the left hand but in front of the bull, with the right hand he aims the sword at a fixed spot on the top of the bull's neck. As the animal charges the red cloth, the man leans swiftly forward and thrusts his sword to the hilt in the animal's body, leaping back lightly to one side from the on-coming horns. The beast hesitates, stumbles, gasps, and blood pours from its mouth and nostrils. Its legs weaken, and it falls heavily to the ground. Round upon round of applause, shouts, yells, shrill whistles and a shower of straw hats follow the successful torero as he walks round the ring acknowledging with a nod, a wave of the hand, a smile, the ovations that greet him.

HORSEMANSHIP UPON THE PAMPAS.

The Lasso and the Bolas :—The skill of South American horsemen in the use of the lasso is very well known. The true lasso consists of a very strong, but thin, well-plaited rope, made of raw hide. One end is attached to the broad surcingle, which fastens together the complicated gear of the recado, or saddle, used in the pampas, the other ends with a small metal ring upon which a noose is formed. The gaucho, when he is going to use the lasso, keeps a small coil in his bridle hand, and in the other holds the running noose, which has generally a diameter of about 8 ft. This he whirls round his head, keeping the noose open , by the dexterous movement of his wrist in throwing it, he causes it to fall on the spot that he chooses. The lasso, when not in use, is tied up in a small coil to the after part of the saddle. Exhibitions of skill with this appliance are always of interest.

Less known to the untravelled than the lasso, but not less formidable as a weapon or as a means of throwing down horses, are the bolas, or balls, which appear to have been used time out of mind in the southern part of the continent. They are of two kinds, and Darwin reported that the type chiefly used for catching ostriches consisted of two round stones, covered with leather, and joined by a thin plaited thong about 8 ft. long. The other kind differs in having three balls united by the thongs to a common centre. The gaucho held the smallest of the three balls in his hand, and whirling the other two round his head, sent them hurtling like a chain shot through the air.

The balls no sooner strike an object than, winding round it, they cross each other and become firmly hitched. The size and weight of the balls varies, according to the purpose for which they are made ; when of stone, although not larger than an apple, they can be sent with such force as sometimes to break the leg of a horse. The balls may be made of wood, and as large as a turnip, for the sake of catching horses without injuring them. The balls when made of iron can be hurled to a great distance.

In using either lasso or bolas one should ride well enough to be able, even at full speed, and while suddenly turning about, to whirl the weapon steadily round the head and take accurate aim. Darwin wrote " One day, as I was amusing myself galloping and whirling the balls round my head, by accident the free one struck a bush, and its revolving motion being thus destroyed, it immediately fell to the ground, and like magic caught one hind leg of my horse , the other ball was then jerked out of my hand, and the horse fairly secured. Luckily he was an old practised animal, and knew what it meant , otherwise he would probably have kicked till he had thrown himself down. The gauchos roared with laughter ; they cried out that they had seen every kind of animal caught, but had never before seen a man caught by himself."

NATIVE WEAPONS IN THE GUIANAS.

Shot-guns have largely replaced the blowpipes and poisoned arrows used by the tribes of the Guianas as weapons in bringing down their prey It may be long however before the use of these traditional weapons and the manufacture of "wourali" poison becomes extinct. The preparation of this poison, not indeed in accordance with the recipe of "a nobleman of the country," but in a method at least one century old, is described by Waterton in his "Wanderings," who writes :—

POISON BREW FOR ARROWS.

"A day or two before the Macoushi (or Macusi) Indian prepares his poison, he goes into the forest in quest of ingredients. A vine grows in these wilds which is called "wourali." It is from this that the poison takes its name, and it is the principal ingredient. When he has procured enough of this he digs up a root of very bitter taste, ties them together, and then looks about for two kinds of bulbous plants, which contain a green and glutinous juice. He fills a little quake, which he carries on his back, with the stalks of these, and, lastly, ranges up and down till he finds two species of ants. One of them is very large and black, and so venomous that its sting produces a fever, it is most commonly to be met with on the ground. The other is a little red ant, which stings like a nettle, and generally has its nest under the leaf of a shrub. After obtaining these, he has no more need to range the forest.

"A quantity of the strongest Indian pepper is used, but this has already been planted round his hut. The pounded fangs of the Labarri snake and those of the Counacouchi are likewise added. These he commonly has in store, for when he kills a snake he generally extracts the fangs and keeps them by him.

"Having thus found the necessary ingredients, he scrapes the wourali vine and bitter root into thin shavings, and puts them into a kind of colander made of leaves; this he puts over an earthen pot, and pours water on the shavings, the liquor which comes through has the appearance of coffee. When a sufficient quantity has been procured the shavings are thrown aside. He then bruises the bulbous stalks and squeezes a proportionate quantity of their juice through his hands into the pot. Lastly, the snakes' fangs, ants, and pepper are bruised, and thrown into it. It is then placed on a slow fire, and as it boils more of the juice of the wourali is added, according as it may be found necessary, and the scum is taken off with a leaf, it remains on the fire till reduced to a thick syrup of a deep brown colour. As soon as it has arrived at this state a few arrows are poisoned with it to try its strength. If it answers to the expectations it is poured out into a calabash or little pot of Indian manufacture, which is carefully covered with a couple of leaves, and over them a piece of deer's skin tied round with cord. They keep it in the dryest part of the hut, and from time to time suspend it over the fire to counteract the effects of dampness.

"The women and young girls are not allowed to be present lest the Yabahou, or evil spirit, should do them harm. The shed under which it has been boiled is pronounced polluted and abandoned ever after. He who makes the poison must eat nothing that morning, and must continue fasting as long as the operation lasts. The pot in which it is boiled must be a new one and must never have held anything before, otherwise the poison would be deficient in strength add to this that the operator must take particular care not to expose himself to the vapour which arises from it while on the fire.

"Though this and other precautions are taken, such as frequently washing the face and hands, still the Indians think that it affects the health, and the operator either is, or what is more probable, supposes himself to be, sick for some days after

THE INDIAN BLOW-PIPE.

"When a native of Macouschia goes in quest of feathered game or other birds he seldom carries his bow and arrows. It is the blow-pipe he then uses. This extraordinary tube of death is perhaps one of the greatest natural curiosities of Guiana. It is not found in the country of the Macoushi. Those Indians tell you it grows to the south-west of them in the wilds which extend betwixt them and the Rio Negro. The reed must grow to an amazing length, as the part the Indians use is from ten to eleven feet long, and no tapering can be perceived in it, one end being as thick as the other It is of a bright yellow colour, perfectly smooth inside and out. It grows hollow, nor is there the least appearance of a knot or joint throughout the whole extent. The natives call it "ourah." This, of itself, is too slender to answer the end of a blow-pipe, but there is a species of palm, larger and stronger, and common in Guiana, and this the Indians make use of as a case in which they put the ourah. It is brown, susceptible of a fine polish, and appears as if it had joints five or six inches from each other. It is called "samourah," and the pulp inside is easily extracted by steeping it for a few days in water

"Thus the ourah and the samourah, one within the other, form the blow-pipe of Guiana. The end which is applied to the mouth is tied round with a small silk-grass cord to prevent its splitting, and the other end, which is apt to strike against the ground, is secured by the seed of the Acuero fruit, cut horizontally through the middle, with a hole made in the end, through which is put the extremity of the blow-pipe. It is fastened on with string on the outside, and the inside is filled up with wild-bee's wax.

"The arrow is from nine to ten inches long. It is made out of the leaf of a species of palm tree called "coucourite," hard and brittle, and pointed as sharp as a needle. About an inch of the pointed end is poisoned. The other end is burnt to make it still harder, and the wild cotton is put round it for about an inch and a half. It requires considerable practice to put on this cotton well. It must just be large enough to fit the hollow of the tube, and taper off to nothing downwards. They tie it on with a thread of the silk-grass to prevent its slipping off the arrow.

ARROWS AND QUIVERS.

"The Indians have shown ingenuity in making a quiver to hold the arrows. It will contain from five to six hundred. It is generally from twelve to fourteen inches long, and in shape resembles a dice-box used at backgammon. The inside is prettily done in basket-work with wood not unlike bamboo, and the outside has a coat of wax. The cover is all of one piece, formed out of the skin of the tapir Round the centre there is fastened a loop, large enough to admit the arm and shoulder, from which it hangs when used. To the rim is tied a little bunch of silk-grass, and half of the jawbone of the fish called pirai, with which the Indian scrapes the point of his arrow.

"Before he puts the arrows into the quiver he links them together by two strings of cotton, one string at each end, and then folds them round a stick, which is nearly the length of the quiver. The end of the stick, which is uppermost, is guarded by two little pieces of wood cross-wise, with a hoop round their extremities, which appears something like a wheel; and this saves the hand from being wounded when the quiver is reversed in order to let the bunch of arrows drop out.

USING THE BLOW-PIPE.

"There is also attached to the quiver a little kind of basket to hold the wild cotton which is put on the blunt end of the arrow. With a quiver of poisoned arrows slung over his shoulder, and with his blow-pipe in his hand, in the same position as a soldier carries his musket, the Macoushi Indian advances towards the forest in quest of powises, maroudis, waracabas, and the other feathered game.

"These generally sit high up in the tall and tufted trees, but still are not out of the Indian's reach, for his blow-pipe, at its greatest elevation, will send an arrow three hundred feet. Silent as midnight he steals under them, and so cautiously does he tread the ground that the fallen leaves rustle not beneath his feet. His ears are open to the least sound, while his eyes, keen as that of a lynx, are employed in finding out the game in the thickest shade. Often he imitates their cry and decoys them from tree to tree till they are within range of his tube. Then, taking a poisoned arrow from his quiver, he puts it in the blow-pipe and collects his breath for the fatal puff."

PRODUCTS OF SOUTH AMERICA

PRODUCTS OF SOUTH AMERICA.

NITRATE.

The production of nitrate of soda, perhaps better known as saltpetre, has grown to immense proportions. The consumption in agriculture increases year by year and it is also required in many manufacturing processes. Nitrate of soda is the principal source of combined nitrogen, and it is derived from a saline mineral found in the elevated desert districts in the northern provinces of Chile, viz., Tacna, Tarapaca, Antofagasta, and Atacama.

Rain rarely falls in the nitrate zone, and the region is desolate and devoid of beauty Such vegetation as exists is confined to certain valleys and ravines, chiefly in the Andean Cordillera. The possession and working of the nitrate fields caused friction between the three Republics, culminating in a fierce warfare, as the result of which Chile acquired in 1881, from Bolivia and Peru, possession of the whole zone. Since then the nitrate industry has progressed remarkably

LIFE IN THE NITRATE ZONE.

The industry began in 1830, when 813 tons were exported to Europe, whereas over 2,700,000 tons were shipped in 1913. Nitrates support, directly and indirectly, the bulk of the population of a region inhabited by 250,000 people, having no vegetation, virtually no water, and situated far from all the necessaries of life. Foods for man and beast, apparel, building material and machinery, fuel, and even water, have all to be imported. Even the soil has been imported for making public and private gardens.

There are 170 factories producing nitrates, employing over 40,000 persons.

Though the nitrate country is devoid of natural beauty, the climate is healthy and for the most part neither excessively hot nor cold. The deposits never occur near the sea, nor on the Western or Pacific Ocean slopes of the coastal Cordillera, but at varying distances, usually from 30 to 45 miles, inland. The deposits exist in some instances in small folds on the eastern side of the coastal hills, extending eastward across the deserts or " pampas " of Tamarugal. Farther south the deposits extend eastward into the desert plains of Atacama.

The mineral is mostly found at altitudes from 3,000 to 5,000 feet above sea-level.

The crude material or caliche undergoes treatment in the factories, or oficinas, to purify or concentrate it.

" Caliche " is the name given to deposits containing workable quantities of Nitrate. It is found :—

    As bedded or stratified deposits, and in pockets covered with layers of conglomerated salts, gravel, and earth.

    As impregnations in decomposed surfaces of volcanic rocks.

    As efflorescences on the surface of salt-fields.

    As cavities in calcareous formations.

LAYER UPON LAYER.

The " Chuca " consists of a top layer of about from 10 to 16 inches of loose sand and earth containing some anhydrous sulphates of soda and lime. The " Costra " is a mixture of disintegrated feldspar and porphyry, common salt, etc., cemented together into a hard mass by calcareous and other salts to a thickness of from one to ten or more feet, merging into the " Congelo," a somewhat similar congested, solid mass several feet in thickness, containing varying amounts of nitrate, not rich enough to extract under present conditions. Below the " Congelo " is found the " Caliche." Except in the richest beds, the " Caliche " is composed of materials similar to the beds above it. The thickness of the " Caliche " varies from 18 inches to 12 feet. The best quality contains 40 to 50 per cent of nitrate. The average quality worked contains 30 to 40 per cent and the poorest workable quality 17 to 30 per cent. Under ordinary conditions nothing under 30 per cent. is profitable.

The colour of " Caliche " varies from white, yellow, orange, grey, blue, violet, to brown.

ANALYSES OF TYPICAL " CALICHE " AND " COSTRA."

	Caliche per cent.	Costra per cent.
Nitrate of Soda ..	36	17
Chloride of Sodium	32	2
Sulphate of Sodium	8	72
Sulphate of Lime	8	2
Insoluble Matter	14	1
Other Salts, including Magnesia, Potash, Iodine, Iron, etc.	2	6
	100	100

The " Caliche " in the more northern fields, contains chloride of sodium as the predominating impurity, farther south, however, this is replaced by sulphate of sodium, with chloride present only in small quantities.

Beneath the " Caliche " exists a bed called " Coba," over a solid volcanic rock and below the " Coba " no nitrate is found.

The **origin** of the Chilean saltpetre beds have long been a puzzle to geologists and scientists, and many theories have been propounded to explain their origin.

Noellner and Darwin considered them due to the decomposition of seaweed which had grown on the site before isolation by upheaval from the sea. The presence of iodine, would seem to favour this theory Muntz and Plagemann attributed the deposits to the work of nitrifying bacteria. Ochsenius attributed the presence of nitrogen to the Guano, which occurs largely along the Pacific Coast. Williams, Pissis, and Sundt ascribe the material to atmospheric origin, caused by the union of nitrogen and oxygen in the air under the influence of electric discharges.

The absence of rain has preserved the deposits, and the condensation of moisture from sea breezes on the hills might account for the accumulation in beds. The unique situation of this rainless tract in proximity to the coast gives Chile a virtual monopoly of the supply of natural nitrate.

MINING AND REFINING.

In mining, bore-holes are put down to test the deposits, and the ground is often blasted to enable a more thorough inspection. A trench is opened by blasting. Holes are bored through to the bedrock, and sufficiently enlarged for a boy to be lowered to the bottom. A cavity is made in the " Coba," and a charge of blasting powder is placed in position. Thus the whole face of the trench is broken, and workmen pick out by hand blocks of " Caliche " from the débris. Experience enables them to select the right material, and they employ crude tests to aid them in determining the percentage of nitrate.

The blocks are conveyed by trams or mule carts to the " Oficinas," to be crushed by machine. The crushed " Caliche " is conveyed to boiling tanks, or " Cachuchos," in which solution of the nitrate is effected. These tanks, are about 30 feet long, 6 to 9 feet wide, and about the same depth, and are heated by steam pipes. A series of six or eight " Cachuchos " constitutes a battery.

The extraction of nitrate consists in a lixiviation of the crushed " Caliche " for 20 to 24 hours at a temperature between 110 and 120 degrees C., when the contents of the boiling tank are discharged into a settling tank or a " Chullador," for 15 to 30 minutes. The soluble salts are thus separated from the insoluble matter The solubility of nitrate of soda increases with the temperature, whereas that of chloride of sodium remains about the same, and that of sulphate of soda diminishes. By gradual cooling, the nitrate can be separated by crystallisation from the other salts. Although theoretically a simple process, difficulties occur in actual practice, for the soluble salts so vary in amounts that they affect the solubility of the nitrate.

After the insoluble matter (or " Ripio ") has subsided, the solution is conveyed through pipes to the crystallising tanks, or " Bateas." These tanks, of a size about 16 x 16 x 3 ft., are usually about six inches deeper at one end, from which part the mother liquor is drawn off, to be used again in the boiling tanks;

iodine having first been extracted by precipitation. The crystallisation usually takes five or more days. The nitrate is then dug out and dried for about two weeks in the open, before being bagged ready for shipment.

The " Oficinas " have a large number of these crystallising tanks all uncovered, for roofing is unnecessary in the absence of rain. Some " Oficinas " produce as much as 250,000 tons of nitrate per annum, and according to their situation, the water needs to be pumped for many miles. The " Oficinas " are equipped with the best technical outfits, and the operations are controlled by chemists and the machinery is mostly driven by imported coal.

The nitrate thus produced is the commercial article, and is exported with a guaranteed minimum contents of 95 per cent. Nitrate of Soda.

An average analysis gives :—

	Per cent.
Nitrate of Soda (containing a little Nitrate of Potash)	95.0 (Nitrogen 15.6 per cent.)
Chloride of Sodium (Common Salt)	2.0
Sulphate of Sodium	0.5
Other Salts (Magnesia, Lime, etc.)	0.4
Insoluble Matter	0.1
Moisture	2.0
	100.0

This material is a white, grey, yellowish, or slightly brown-coloured material, resembling coarse kitchen salt.

Nitrate guaranteed to contain over 96 per cent. nitrate of soda and under 1 per cent. of common salt is prepared by allowing the hot lye from the boiling tanks to stand in a steam-heated pan before transferring to the crystallising pans for an extra half-hour or more, when fine crystals of sodium chloride and other foreign matters are precipitated. Material of this higher-grade is used largely in the chemical trades.

The nitrate, dried and bagged, is conveyed by rail to the ports. Self-acting cable railways, where the full descending truck pulls up the more lightly-loaded ascending truck, are used in some places. In other instances the railroads zig-zag up the hills to obtain the necessary gradients suited to the power of the locomotives.

DEMAND AND SUPPLIES.

It was at one time supposed that the nitrate fields would be exhausted by 1923. However, the Chilean Government proved in 1908 that a minimum quantity of 220 million tons was immediately available and this computation does not make any allowance for the discovery of new deposits. Recent computations estimate the total at 720 million tons. Thus, the deposits are likely to last for 300 years at the present rate of consumption.

Nitrate of soda contains ordinarily 15·6 per cent. of the plant food nitrogen. It gives the best results when the requisite quantities of the other foods necessary for plant growth are present in the soil. Nitrogen is the most necessary of constituents and before it can be absorbed by the roots, it must be applied in the form of a nitrate. This is one reason why nitrate of soda is so highly esteemed as a fertiliser Organic compounds of nitrogen are comparatively of little value to plant growth.

Nitrate of soda has virtues as an insecticide, especially in helping to check eel worm, wire worm, and other grubs which attack plants. Club root in cabbages is said to be less pronounced on plots manured with nitrate of soda.

(Indebtedness is expressed to the Chilean Nitrate Committee, Friars House, New Broad Street, E.C.2, for the information upon which the foregoing article is founded.)

CACAO.

The dense forests that fringe the river Amazon are the original home of the cacao plant. Here it flourishes in all its pristine luxuriance.

From an ancient MS. in the British Museum, entitled "A Voyage to the West Indies and New Spain (Yucatan) made by John Chilton in the year 1560" comes the following extract :—

"So we were provided of victualls till we came where Townes were in the province of Soconusco, where groweth cacau, wch the Christianes carrye from thence unto Nova Hispaniola because y^t will not growe in a cold countrye . . their chiefest marchandize is Cacau."

Thus early, at least, had the cacao bean become an article of commerce, and the culture is now distributed over a great portion of the tropical world. The plant thrives within twenty-three parallels of latitude and luxuriates within fifteen. It is cultivated at an average altitude of 1,700 ft. above sea-level, but not successfully over 1,000 ft.

According to the author of "Cocoa · All about it" (Sampson Low, 1896) . "A healthy cocoa tree in good soil yields from 50 to several hundred pods a year The average for well-cultivated trees, at seven years old, should be between 80 and 100 pods. It requires about 11 pods to yield one pound of cocoa, it follows that a good mature tree, under favourable conditions, might yield, on an average, not less than 7 lb. of cured cocoa. "An estate of 300 acres, averaging 2 lb. or 3 lb. a tree might yield a return of between 4 and 6 cwt. of cured cocoa per acre."

The Cacao Tree :—With its abundant red flowers and golden yellow fruit the tree forms a conspicuous ornament of tropical vegetation. It attains a height of about 24 ft., and a considerable diameter Its wood is light and porous. The bark is cinnamon-coloured , and the leaves are bright green on the upper, and dull green (and slightly hairy) on the lower

The flowers occur not only on the thicker branches, but also on the stem , but the formation of fruit only comes from the flowers growing on the thicker parts. Thus, for a thousand flowers there is but a single fruit. The flowers are small and reddish-white in colour

The fruit is green when young, later turning yellow, and not infrequently tinged with red. It has somewhat the appearance of a cucumber, and is of variable size, but generally some 9½ in. long. A rather thin shell covers the fruit, beneath which is a soft sweetish pulp, within which are ranged from twenty to forty almond-shaped seeds lying close together in five longitudinal rows.

Gathering and Preparing :—The gathering of the fruit is done by means of a long rod at the end of which is a semicircular knife for cutting through the stalk. The fruits are then split in two, the beans separated from the surrounding pulp and spread out on screens to dry gradually upon a bamboo floor exposed to the sun. The beans are then transferred to wooden troughs or to large vessels made of rough earth (called Tinajás) with wide openings. Covered with leaves they are allowed to stand for twenty-four or forty-eight hours. The leaves are removed and the beans exposed to the sun for three to five days, after which they are either packed into covered receptacles or carefully piled up into heaps and kept at a moderate heat for four days, or packed in casks and buried in the earth. After either process they are again exposed to the sun until perfectly dry

After the fermentation it is usual in most plantations to remove the adherent portions of pulp by washing. The beans are then allowed to dry in the air, and finally packed into sacks. Contact with metal is carefully avoided throughout the operation. The practical result of the process of fermentation is to convert the colour of the beans from a harsh red to a chocolate hue, to harden the shells, and to improve the colour and flavour, besides destroying the fermenting power of the seed.

A machine for drying by means of hot-water pipes is considered superior to the open-air method. The pipes are arranged in a long square iron box over which the beans travel slowly forward on a band of belting. At the same time they are stirred by a series of arms as they move along.

Varieties of Cacao :—The cacaos of Venezuela and Ecuador are the finest in the world, the best samples are not imported into Europe, but retained for home consumption. The kind known as Soconusco was at one time used entirely by grandees of the Spanish Court, and it sells for extremely high prices.

Venezuela also produces the famed Caracas cocoa, well-known as one of the most delicate brands and employed in the manufacture of the finest qualities of chocolate used in Europe. This kind is exported in great quantities. The shells are marked by a reddish-brown earthy crust.

The credit for fostering the industry in Venezuela is largely due to the Jesuit missionaries. They engaged the natives to form small plantations on the river Orinoco and to gather wild cacao. Father Gumilla, in his "History of Orinoco" says " I have seen in these plains, forests of wild cacao trees laden with bunches of pods supplying food to an infinite number of monkeys, squirrels, parrots, guacamayas, and other animals."

Puerto Cabella cacao is mostly consumed by France and Spain. Esmeraldos is the name most famous amongst the Ecuadorean varieties. It is said that the finer sorts of this bean are never imported into Europe.

The valleys of Guayaquil and Quito produce the largest quantities of any district in the world. The Guayaquil variety has an individuality of its own, both in shape and aroma, and is easily distinguished from that of other districts. Because the finer beans contain a large percentage of " theobroma " they are much valued.

Ecuador stands second both in point of quality and quantity of cacao exports.

Colombia, from the earliest times, produced large quantities, and the material has become a source of great wealth to the country Maracaibo—as it is known—is of a reddish-brown colour and extremely rich in fat, and probably for this reason the beans are seldom met in Europe. It is customary to blend this cocoa with other less strongly-flavoured varieties.

The generic name of " Surinãm " is given to all the cacaos deriving from the Guianas (French, Dutch, and British) as well as that from Colombia. The points of difference between the several kinds would only be appreciated by an expert.

British, Dutch, and French Guianas grow cacao, but the sorts partake so much of the nature of Colombian (Maracaibo) variety that they deserve but little mention. Berbice and Essequebo are the two standard species—the former being a rather larger bean than the latter; both are so fat that they are used to mix with other kinds. Beans from Dutch Guiana are occasionally in the open market; Holland is the principal consumer

Brazilian cacaos have assumed a new importance. Recent experiments in the artificial drying of Bahia sorts have resulted in a great improvement in the ·quality The artificially-dried kind, called " Estufa," commands a good market. This is the more notable because formerly Bahia cacao was distinctly inferior, no doubt, because of careless cultivation and indiscriminate mixing with " wild " kinds from the interior This state of things is altered and Bahia cacao is yearly advancing as to quantity and quality

The cacao of Pará and Maranhão differs from all other growths, the bean is smaller, rounder, and more elongated, but when well cured is mild in flavour, and on that account highly valued by manu-facturers.

Cuban cacao is usually classed with Brazilian.

COFFEE.

Coffee is a tropical product, and a large portion of the tropical belt around the earth is potentially a coffee-growing area. The chief seat of production is South America, and of the South American republics Brazil comes by far the first in importance.

About a million tons of coffee are consumed yearly, and it is probable that Brazil produces 70 per cent. of the whole. During the last two decades there has been an expansion of the areas of production in South America and a contraction in India and Java.

The world-war has considerably affected consumption, and Great Britain, Spain, and the Netherlands are consuming less than in 1913, and Germany very much less.

In Brazil there are under coffee cultivation some eleven hundred thousand (1,100,000) square miles. The area reaches from the Amazon to the southern border of the State of São Paulo, and from the Atlantic coast to the western boundary of the State of Matto Grosso.

The best coffee is grown in a specially suitable earth called "Terra Roxa." Near to this soil is found the second best, called "Massape." The former is practically confined to the São Paulo district, which is the premier coffee growing State. The "terra roxa" is a dark red earth, "massape" is sometimes dark red but generally yellow and often black. The chief plantations are on plateaux about 1,800 ft. above sea-level, they rise even to 4,000 ft. The temperature averages 70° Fahr

From September to December the coffee trees are in bloom, and the blossoms only last about four days. In unseasonable weather the blossoms are frequently damaged, and damage also occurs to the young green berries before their hold upon the parent branches is well established. From April to August is the extreme limit of the harvest. About 25 per cent. of the coffee plantations in São Paulo are cultivated by machinery

A recent registration of labourers in the State last-named showed the total number of labourers to be 450,000, of whom 420,000 were employed in growing or handling coffee. During 1922-23 there were 764,969,500 coffee trees in bearing in São Paulo. One plantation near Ribeirao Preto has over five million trees and requires an army of 6,000 labourers.

Brazil is said to possess the largest coffee plantations in the world. One of them was valued in 1915—including cost of land improvements—at nearly £1,250,000. Several plantations have over a million trees. The quality of Brazilian coffee is excellent, although some special varieties are never highly esteemed.

In Venezuela coffee has been cultivated since the late eighteenth century, and the output has reached 100,000,000 lb. Venezuela is favourably placed, for much of its territory is along the slopes and foot-hills of the Maritime Andes, strictly eastward over the continent. A zone of the Equatorial Andes, between 4,000 and 6,000 ft. high is the best coffee land.

The finest grades are grown in the localities known as "Tierra Templada." In these regions the equable climate, the constant moisture, the rich well-drained soil, and the protecting shade of the forests afford the most suitable conditions for coffee culture. About a quarter of a million acres were under cultivation during the opening years of this century, and the average yield per acre was 250 lb. The chief enemy of the crop is the hosts of tropical weeds. The land is measured into "Fanegadas" (about 1¾ acre) It is calculated that the average yield for a "fanegada," should be about 20 quintals, or 2,000 lb.

In Colombia the finest coffee is grown in the foot-hills of the Andes, and in this respect the country resembles Venezuela. Coffee is produced in all departments, that of Cundinamarca producing the best grades. Antioquia province produces the largest quantity Native trees form the "wind-break," and 700 trees are planted to the acre. One pound per tree per year is the average yield.

The Namay plantation may be taken as typical. Half a day's travel by rail and horse from Bogotá, it stands some 5,000 ft. above sea-level. There are over 1,000 acres on this plantation, carrying a quarter of a million trees. On an estate of this size about 200 families are needed during harvesting periods.

In Guatemala about 75,000,000 lb. of coffee is raised annually It is a country of magnificent table-lands, 2,500 to 5,000 ft. above sea-level, with a temperate climate. The lower ranges, being somewhat exposed, require protection from the heat of the sun and banana trees are used for this purpose. They serve the double purpose of a wind-screen and a profit-bringer. The harvesting season lasts from August to January. All work is done by Indian labourers working under a system of peonage.

In Salvador coffee has been cultivated since 1850. Large plantations have been established in the state of La Paz, which has become the leading coffee district of the country Salvadorean planters largely own the plantations that they work. Native Indian labour is employed and a large part of the work of preparing the berry for shipment is done by hand. It is estimated that about 166,000 acres are under cultivation.

In Mexico coffee growing is not nearly so old an industry as in some other parts of tropical America. In the Coatepec district trees were planted about 1808. The plants thrived; and so began the coffee industry of that famous district. Having been started in Coatepec and Córdoba, the new industry spread to the mountains of the neighbouring regions of Oazaca and Pueblo, where it was taken up by the Indians who still carry it on.

The principal coffee territory is in the State of Vera Cruz. Soconusco is one of the most prolific districts in the Republic and also the youngest, having been developed within the last 30 years. This region is near the border of Guatemala, and the quality of its coffee resembles that of the neighbouring country

A sub-variety of "arabica" is the kind most cultivated, but in the flatter and warmer parts of the country what is called the "myrtle" is mostly grown. From October to February is the harvesting season. Trees begin to yield when two years old and reach full production at the age of six.

In Porto Rico the climatic conditions are ideal. No plantation on the island is more than 20 miles from the sea. Less labour is required for the culture of coffee than in many other countries. The guama, a big tree of dense foliage, is a beautiful wind-break, and the guaba—a sturdy shrub—furnishes shade to the plantation. The average yield per acre is between 200 and 300 lb. Yet expert opinion has ventured the conjecture that under better methods of cultivation it could be increased to 800 or 900.

In coffee-culture **Costa Rica** ranks next to Guatemala and Salvador in Central America. The San José and the Cartago districts are the best for this particular crop. The soil is an exceedingly rich beach loam, made up of continuous layers of volcanic ashes 3 to 15 ft. deep. Its annual yield in recent years has reached 35,000,000 lb.

In Nicaragua poor and costly transportation on the Atlantic slope has operated against the industry, but from the provinces of Mangua, Carazo, Matagalpa, Chontales, and Jinotega the annual crop has reached dimensions that make it the chief agricultural product of the country

In Panamá the local supply does not meet the domestic demand. A considerable amount has to be imported from neighbouring countries. No ploughing is necessary, no wind-breaks, no shade bushes.

In Ecuador coffee is grown on the mainland and the islands. About 32,000 acres are under cultivation, with an aggregate of 8,000,000 trees.

In Bolivia coffee is frequently grown as a hedge plant, otherwise it is cultivated in small patches. Little attention is given to its culture. The Yungas and the Apulobamba districts of La Paz are the chief sources.

GROWERS' COSTS IN CENTRAL AMERICA.

The cost of a Central American plantation producing 1,000 quintals (100 lb. each) of coffee is $35,000 to $50,000, write L. R. Grace & Co., of San Francisco. Money costs an average of 10 per cent., and most planters borrow to the limit of their credit facilities. Take the average of an investment of $40,000. An initial overhead cost is thus created of $4,000, or 4 cents a pound. The cost of raising a pound of coffee, including picking and cleaning is close to 5 cents. It thus costs 9 cents net to raise a pound of coffee on the average plantation in Central America. Freight, export duty, and expenses to the nearest market, say San Francisco, average $3\frac{1}{2}$ cents, making a total of $12\frac{1}{2}$ cents net cost to the planter Some low-grade coffees average slightly less, but many cost considerably more.

To give the producer an income of $4,000 per annum the price realized should thus be $16\frac{1}{2}$ cents per lb.

It must be remembered that $40,000 invested in a plantation does not every year render 1,000 quintals, and very rarely more, nor does the average producer possess a plantation as large. The majority of plantations in Central America produce 200 to 700 quintals. The average planter does not prosper unless he averages 16 to 17 cents for good to fine varieties and 14 to 15 cents for low and medium varieties.

RUBBER.

The marketing of Pará rubber is more than two centuries old. The preparation of the commodity is still mainly conducted upon primitive lines. The forests of the Amazon and its tributaries are the main source, and many of the trees are of great age. The methods of preparation, primitive as they are, yet produce a material well suited to the requirements of the manufacturer "Fine hard Pará," obtained from the wild trees of the Amazon regions, is still the market standard for rubber

Hevea brasiliensis is the botanical name of the tree yielding the finest rubber It often attains a height of 100 ft., and has a well-developed trunk, some 10 or 12 ft. in circumference. The flowers are small, green, and sweet-scented. The fruit is a three-celled triangular capsule, containing a single oval seed. The Hevea sheds its leaves annually, but remains leafless only for a short time.

Its habitat comprises portions of Brazil, Bolivia, and Peru. Dr Jacques Huber, of the Museu Gœldi, Pará (a great authority upon this subject), states that the shores and islands of the River Amazon, the valleys of the Xingu, Tapajoz, and Madeira rivers, the Acre territory, and the valleys of the Purus, Jurua, Jutahy, Javary, and the Ucayali, are the regions where *Hevea brasiliensis* is most abundant. In these districts the mean annual temperature is between 76° and 81°F., and the annual rainfall is usually 80 to 120 in.

A number of other species of Hevea occur in South America, some of which yield quite good rubber, and that of *H Benthamiana* and *H Duckei* is nearly equal to *H brasiliensis*

Second quality rubber (known in Brazil as "Borracha Fraca" or "weak rubber") is produced by a group of some half-dozen trees, which do not grow in the same districts as *H brasiliensis*, and are so scattered that the natives do not trouble seriously with them.

The **latex** from which commercial rubber is derived is a fluid not unlike milk in appearance, and cream-coloured or yellowish, or more seldom pink or pale reddish-brown. It is an emulsion, holding minute globules of rubber in suspension. The specific gravity of latex is usually below that of water It has been found that if Pará trees are regularly tapped at frequent intervals, the percentage of rubber in the latex is sensibly diminished, while if longer intervals are allowed the diminution is less marked.

The most important constituents of latex other than the caout-chouc are resin and protein, which substances are always found in the coagulated product.

The following note is taken from Brown's "Rubber, its Sources, Cultivation, and Preparation" (Murray, 5s.) :—

"It has been suggested that the latex serves for the purpose of storing water for use by the plant during drought, and this may perhaps be true of those laticiferous plants which inhabit countries having a well-marked dry season. Many laticiferous plants, however, are found in countries and situations where there is always abundant moisture, and in those cases it would appear unnecessary for the plant to secrete latex in order to have a reserve supply of water

"Another suggestion is that the latex forms a reserve food supply and that it serves to conduct food materials in the plant. In support of this view it is pointed out that latex usually contains protein and carbohydrates, and that in certain cases it is known to contain a proteolytic ferment capable of rendering the protein soluble so that it can be utilized as food by the plant.

"Other views are that the latex serves for the storage of waste products—the rubber being regarded in this case as a waste product —or that it forms a protection to the plant by sealing incisions made in its bark, thus preventing the entry of insect or fungoid pests.

"None of these views has received general acceptance."

Spence believes that caoutchouc is a reserve food for the plant, and bases his theory on the hydrocarbon nature of this substance and the presence of oxidizing enzymes in the latex. He states that caoutchouc is a "reserve food-stuff for the plant at certain stages of its growth, which is broken down as circumstances demand by the enzymes associated with it in the living protoplasm, into the simple food-stuffs, the sugars, from which the caoutchouc is almost certainly formed by the plant." (Wright's "Hevea Brasiliensis." Maclaren.)

Petch observes that if a fallen Hevea leaf be taken, and a thin layer of the midrib on the back of the leaf be slowly peeled off, strands of rubber appear between the midrib and the strip that is being peeled off. Rubber can also be extracted from fallen leaves with carbon bisulphide. Now when a tree sheds its leaves all the potash, phosphoric acid, starch, etc., in them has been absorbed. The dead leaf contains only waste products, therefore, rubber is probably a waste product.

Rubber Collection :—The system of gathering the latex from the rubber trees is the following   Early in the morning the *seringueiro* (rubber gatherer) starts out from his hut, which forms a rallying point in the forest, carrying with him a *machadinha* (tapping axe) and several hundred tin cups. Thus he sets out for his *estrada* —which might be translated "milk-round."

Arrived at the tree he attaches a circle of cups, making an incision in the bark as high as he can reach. He attaches the cups directly under the cuts with a little finely-kneaded clay, if clay cups are used. If tin ones are employed, he fastens these on by bending them under the bark. From tree to tree he goes till all in his *estrada* have been tapped.

The gatherer is now back at his hut, and discarding his *macha-dinha*, he takes a large receptacle—such as a kerosine can—and again sets out to collect the latex. There is much difference in the productivity of the trees, some bleed freely, others reluctantly The quality of the latex varies greatly, some give thick creamy latex, others thin, and a few none at all. The latex from his first tree has probably ceased running, and the cups may be nearly full. So he goes on till he has completed his round. Then he prepares breakfast.

Smoking the Latex :—After breakfast comes the smoking of the rubber On the fire smouldering in his hut he heaps some of the heavy oily nuts of the " urucuri " palm. Over this he places a truncated-conelike funnel, with a cut-out of the lower edge to furnish a draught. The best sort are made of clay, inferior ones of sheet-iron, which the old *seringuieros* hate, because when they get hot they are so uncomfortable to work with.

When the smoke is coming thick and hot from the funnel, the *seringuiero* takes a piece of wood shaped something like a paddle, and thoroughly dries it in the smoke. This he dips into the latex, holding it again over the smoke until that film is dried. So the process goes on, the ball of rubber increasing in size with every dipping Frequently he brings to his aid a home-made bit of machinery A rest is made by driving two forked sticks into the ground with a cross-piece connecting them, in the middle of which is a loop of bush-rope into which one end of the pole holding the rubber is thrust. By this device the *seringuiero* moves it easily

Having finished his week's work the *seringuiero* takes his balls of rubber to the *seringal*, where he is credited with the number of pounds he has gathered at some 50 per cent. of the market value, the other 50 per cent. is to reimburse the *seringal* for freight, shrinkage, and so on. Each rubber bale is then branded with the mark of the *aviador* and stored awaiting shipment. A *seringal* is practically a centre, or village, where the representative of the *aviador* lives in the largest hut, which is also a store.

The manager of the *seringal* makes his profit out of what he sells to the *seringuiero*. The latter is obliged to buy what he requires at his store, the owner of which must assume his debt (should he want to leave for another *seringal*), with a 20 per cent. increase for the transfer Economic serfdom appears to be the fate of the rubber-gatherer, he is held captive by the "truck-system."

Systems of Recovery :—The native method of smoking the rubber is not always followed in Brazilian forests. Reagents in the form of acids, salts and alkalis being chiefly used , spontaneous coagulation involving the dilution of latex with water and allowing it to stand, a similar method with "creaming" superimposed, and centrifugal action, all have been tried, and some of them answer well upon certain kinds of latex. The heat cure is probably as good as any for *H brasiliensis*

The native method (i.e., smoking) is considered to have a better effect on the physical properties of the finished product.

Ceara Rubber :—The different species of the Ceara rubber tree have only been discovered and accurately tabulated within the last twenty years. *Manihot Glaziovii* is the botanical name of the most famous kind, but there are three or four others. Professor Ule, who investigated the question on the spot at the request of the Bahia Rubber Syndicate, was able to establish, in 1906, the existence of three new rubber-yielding *Manihots* in North-Eastern Brazil.

The tree is 30 to 50 ft. high, with an erect stem 8 to 20 in. in diameter It is abundant in the Brazilian states of Ceara, Piauhy, and Bahia. It has been found growing under a variety of conditions, on the desert plains, where the rainfall is said to be less than 50 in. and vegetation is scorched for the greater part of the year, and on hill-sides, in poor and rocky soil, at elevations of about 3,500 ft., where the rainfall is over 100 in. a year and the temperature at night falls as low as 60° F It is reputed that the Ceara will grow and flourish in a dry or humid atmosphere provided the soil is not wet.

The Ceara tree is more difficult to tap than the Para tree. In dry countries the latex does not flow freely when incisions are made in the bark, it coagulates on the stem, and rubber is obtained in the form of scrap. In this case a series of small cuts are made without removal of the bark. In wetter districts the trees can be tapped by the "herringbone" or some similar system. The incision system in use for Ceara trees is known as the "hevea" method, in which the bark is stripped from one-fourth of the circumference of the stem to a height of 6 ft. and the acid of some citrus fruit used to moisten the stripped surface. The tree is then stabbed with a thin-bladed knife, the cuts being in vertical rows 2 or 3 in. apart. The latex, exuding from the cuts, coagulates on mixing with the acid and is then peeled off in thin sheets.

Where the latex flows more freely the "herringbone" system is usually employed, after the removal of the outer bark. Half the tree is usually tapped at a time to a height of 6 ft., the lateral incisions being 1 ft. apart. The flow of latex is sometimes helped by allowing a slow stream of water, containing a little ammonia, to run down the incisions from drip-tins.

The latex of the Ceara is easily coagulated. It is first strained to remove impurities, then diluted with water and allowed to stand until complete coagulation has taken place. If ammonia has been used in the collection a little acetic acid is mixed with the water. The average yield of rubber from cultivated Ceara trees in Brazil has been given as 300 kilograms per hectare. As some 2,500 trees are planted to the hectare, this is equivalent to a little more than 4 oz. per annum per tree. As a rule the latex of the Ceara tree contains more protein and mineral matter than plantation Para. The best qualities realize prices equal to those given for plantation Para.

Central American Rubber : *Castilloa elastica* grows wild in Mexico, south of latitude 22° N., and extends thence through all the states of Central America to Colombia. It is also found on the western slopes of the Andes in Peru and Ecuador During recent years large plantations of castilloa trees have been made in Southern Mexico, chiefly in the state of Chiapas. The trees abound in British Honduras, and are cultivated there. On both eastern and western sides of the mountain chain through Central America, along the valley of the Magdalena river in Colombia, and on most of the islands of the British West Indies is the castilloa to be found. This variety does not grow successfully on swampy land nor on a stiff clay soil, nor does it thrive in a dense forest, liking better open situations where it is found in groups. The trees occur at low elevations, and are seldom found higher than 2,000 ft. above sea level.

Pittier has recorded the opinion that the yields of rubber from cultivated castilloa trees in Mexico have been exaggerated. According to him trees which give 500 grammes (equal to 1 1lb.) of rubber at one tapping are not uncommon, but the number yielding only 50 grammes is legion.

A very large proportion of pure caoutchouc is got from cultivated trees by the "Empire" separator, amounting to about 93·9 per cent. From wild trees it is only 2 points less.

YERBA MATÉ

Yerba Maté (or simply Maté) in its infused state is to a great part of South America what tea is to England. The tree belongs to the ilex family In form and foliage it resembles an orange tree, though larger, and the leaves softer. The flowers are small and white with a calyx of five petals, the seeds resemble "American pepper," except that three or four small, whitish, oblong kernels are visible through the skin. The seed is covered with a gluten which prevents germination. In the wild state this gluten is removed by the passage of the seed through the bodies of certain birds, principally the Paraguayan pheasant, Jacú. It is stated that this gluten is removed by careful washing, and the seed sown very deep in ground drenched with water and almost reduced to mud.

In using the leaf, the main principle is as follows A small quantity of the Yerba is placed in a narrow-mouthed receptacle, usually a gourd, and hot, but not boiling, water is poured on it. The infusion is then imbibed through a cane or silver tube, with a strainer at the end, in order to prevent the smaller particles of the crushed leaf from entering the mouth. The gourd can be refilled several times with water before all the flavour is extracted from the leaf. The almost universal name for the cup is Maté, a Kechua word, meaning simply "cup." Apart from the specific terms Caamini, Caaguazú, the generic term for the drink has come to be "Yerba Maté" practically throughout the whole of South America, or simply "Maté." In Brazil the receptacle, at any rate at first, was known as "Cuia," also meaning simply "cup." The name for the tube is Bombilla, a Spanish word.

The aroma of the leaf is improved by sprinkling, during the curing process, with the leaves or rind of the Quabira-miri. Ilex-leaves so treated fetch a higher price. The Paraguayans frequently add sugar to the infusion, but the lower order of Spaniards and the Indians drink it without, the vessel in which it is taken is made of hide, or a gourd split in half, and, among the higher orders, mounted in silver In this a tablespoonful of the leaf is placed, mixed with sugar and cold water, hot water is added, and often citron or lemon juice.

In Buenos Aires in nearly all native houses the maté circulates continuously, it is the offering made to all guests, and the same maté and bombilla serve for all; to refuse it would be an act of impoliteness. A Gaucho will take a maté or two in the early morning, and gallop all day long, requiring no more food or drink until nightfall. In it the caravan-drivers find the same resource. In all the public offices, both of the nation and of the province, the hours of siesta are set apart to a great extent for an indiscriminate bout at the maté-cup. All employés, from the grave minister of government to the porter who guards the door, taking their turn at the bombilla, much to the delay, sometimes, of those who have business to be dispatched. In some cases the leaf is simply mixed with cold water, when it is called Terreré. So mixed it serves to sweeten water which is foul and proves very refreshing after a journey The use of cold water appears to be on the increase, being much encouraged by employers of labour, since less time is wasted in the preparation of the beverage.

QUININE.

Quinine is the best known and most widely used of the alkaloids obtained from the various species of cinchona.

Cinchona bark was originally found in South America, and was formerly called "Peruvian Bark" from its natural habitat. Its name is derived from the Countess of Cinchon, wife of a Viceroy of Peru, who was cured of fever by the bark in 1638. Not until the beginning of the nineteenth century was quinine at all generally used. Since that time it has entirely taken the place of cinchona.

The plant is an important genus of *Rubiaceæ* The trees seldom exceed 50 ft. in height, have simple leaves and small flowers. It inhabits chiefly the east side of the Andes, in Peru, Bolivia, Ecuador, and Colombia.

Three species of this genus yield the so-called "Peruvian Bark," viz., *Calisaya*, *Loxa*, and *Succirubia*. The *calisaya* is richest in alkaloids. From the wasteful methods employed in cutting down trees to procure the bark it was feared that there would soon be a dearth of the drug. Steps have been taken to plant cinchona in different tropical countries, and to protect the gathering of it in its own so that now its future is assured. The bark is taken off in strips longitudinally and in time it grows again.

The method of obtaining quinine is the following First the bark is dried, then finely ground and mixed with lime. It is extracted with hot, high-boiling paraffin oil. The solution is then filtered, shaken up with sulphuric acid—the latter neutralized with sodium carbonate—and on cooling quinine sulphate crystallizes out.

Quinine is used in malaria, and is one of the most effective remedies in that disease. It is said to be one of the best examples of the specific action of a drug in therapeutics, as it causes the malarial organism in the blood to break up and disappear

LOGWOOD.

The logwood tree is smallish and bears purple flowers with three stamens, the fruit is encased in a prickly pod. The heart-wood constitutes the commercial logwood, which is chiefly used in dyeing

The tree belongs to the natural order *Leguminosæ*, which grows in moist and swampy places in Central America, particularly round the Bay of Campeche. It is usually from 40 ft. to 50 ft. high. The wood is red in colour, tinged with orange and black, so heavy as to sink in water, and capable of receiving considerable polish. It is used chiefly as a dyewood, the trees being cut down, the bark and albumen removed, and the hard centre parts cut into logs 3 ft. long.

In extracting the colouring matter it is hewn into much smaller pieces, and ground or rasped to small chips or to a coarse powder The aqueous extract is muddy and of a reddish-brown colour By using acids the colour is made paler, and by alkalies it is converted to purple. By mordanting the fabric with iron, black is produced, with alumina, violet and lilac, with copper, blue, and with chromium a black and green.

The colouring power of logwood depends chiefly on a crystalline ingredient called hæmatoxylin. It is used in calico-printing to give a brown or black colour, also in the preparation of some talcs. An extract of logwood is medicinally used as an astringent. It is on occasion concentrated into crystals or made into logwood extract.

INDIGO.

The blue colouring principle called indigo is obtained from herbs which are indigenous to the tropical parts of South America, and is prepared by extracting the leaves with water.

Indigofera tinctoria is the species most largely cultivated and highly valued. It is of a perennial habit, but is usually grown from seed sown twice each year. The dye is present in the form of a complex glucoside indican, from which it is obtained in a free state by fermentation.

The cut plant is steeped in vats for some twelve hours, and the fermented extract, which is of a yellowish green colour, is then run off into free vats and agitated with air The liquid turns green and finally blue with the deposition of the indigo in the form of mud. This is boiled up with water, allowed to settle, pressed, and cut into cubes which are dried and sent to market. Thus obtained, indigo forms dark blue to purplish violet lumps which show a bronzy lustre when rubbed.

In addition to the essential constituent, indigo-blue, which is present to the extent of about 60 per cent., natural indigo contains indigo-red and indigo-brown, together with a small proportion of mineral matter and moisture. Natural indigo has a formidable competitor in the synthetic indigotin now produced in large aniline colour factories in various countries.

TOBACCO.

The botanical name for tobacco is *Nicotiana*, so called after Jean Nicot, a French diplomat, who was thought to have introduced tobacco into Europe about 1530.

The species of tobacco most usually cultivated is the *N tabacum*, Linn., which grows to the height of from 4 ft. to 6 ft., and produces several clusters of white or beautiful pink flowers.

The tobacco plants are all natives of America, and the use of tobacco was widespread at the time of its discovery in 1492. Cuba and Brazil are celebrated both for the quality and quantity of their tobacco crop. Cuba is, above all, noted for the quality of its cigars, which take the name of Havanas, from their place of export. The tobacco grown in the district known as Vuelta Abajó, west of Havana, is of a high aromatic grade.

Tobacco can be grown anywhere in the tropics. The period within which it comes to maturity varies according to circumstances, and the limitation of its range arises principally from the necessity of protecting it during growth against frost. This is particularly necessary in the early stages, when a single white frost is sufficient to spoil the whole crop.

PANAMA HATS.

The straw hats which have earned a deserved celebrity under this name are rarely manufactured in Panamá, but are made in the neighbouring States. Ecuador was the original, and is still the chief source of production. The name originated during the gold rush to California, when returning prospectors purchased the hats in Panamá. Hats made from toquilla straw are now made in Colombia, Panamá, and in Central America, and all of them, together with the Ecuadorean and Peruvian hats, are indiscriminately known as "Panama."

In Ecuador the hats are made chiefly in the Province of Manabi, where they are known as jipijapa. The *Carludovica palmata* furnishes the straw from which the hats are woven, and it grows chiefly in Ecuador, although it is also found in Colombia and in the forests of the upper Amazon. The shrub is 6 to 10 ft. high, and thrives best in hot and humid regions. It is fan shaped, resembling the saw palmetto. The price of the raw material depends upon the place of production, colour, length, thickness, and number of threads to the strand or skein. The fan-shaped leaves need to be cut from the trunk of the shrubs before they open, or just as they ripen. They are then stripped of their outer filaments, dipped for a few seconds in boiling water, withdrawn for a moment to be again immersed for an instant, taken out and shaken vigorously, hung to dry in the shade, and a day or two later put out in the sun to be bleached. A little lemon juice added to the hot-water bath gives a much whiter straw. In a day or two the sprouts shrivel into a cylindrical form, like string, when the straw is ready for weaving. It was formerly believed that Panama hats were woven under water, which is not strictly true, although the straw must be kept thoroughly moistened while in the hands of the weaver. Native women and children make the most skilful weavers, although men sometimes possess deftness enough to be successful in the art.

QUEBRACHO.

Quebracho, valuable as timber and a source of tannin, derives its name from a colloquial Spanish and Portuguese term quiebra-hacha, or "axe-breaker." From this the hardness of the wood can be inferred.

Species of quebracho grow in the Chaco of Paraguay, Brazil, and northern Argentine Republic. The red variety is the one containing tannin used to make an extract valuable in tanning hides. The wood furnishes railway sleepers for a large part of South America, and is used also for furniture and fencing. Every portion of the tree is utilized for the extraction of tannin.

In Paraguay and the Argentine Republic land bearing the trees sells from $3,000 upward per square league. Paraguay manufactures annually many thousand tons of extract. In 1918 the output amounted to 23,180 tons. Quebracho gathering is an industry, so extensive that railways are pushed into the wilderness to facilitate the marketing of the wood. Ocean steamers travel up the rivers emptying into the Paraná to receive the wood or the extract as it comes from the forest. Whole settlements gather and leave permanent traces over the immense tract of Paraguay where quebracho grows. Quebracho can be cultivated, but the tree is of slow growth.

The extraction of tannin from quebracho had its origin in France, where a consignment of logs was sent in 1874. The first factory in South America for the manufacture of the extract was erected at Puerto Casado, Paraguay, in 1889.

GOLD.

The lure of gold led Columbus to America. Images and gold dust were found in the possession of native tribes, and soon the galleons of the King of Spain were crossing the seas, laden with the yellow metal. Much of this supply came from Nicaragua. Other Spanish colonies contributed their share, and gold was found in the lands and river beds of Mexico, Panamá, Peru, and Colombia. Not until modern times was the richest South American gold deposit found, the Callao mine, in Venezuela, south of the Orinoco, which produced a value of $25,000,000 in the twenty years of its most prosperous working.

Modern explorers of the eastern Andean slopes report many indications of gold-bearing quartz, only waiting the attention of man. Bolivia holds a vast treasure of gold in her mountain fastnesses. Chile produced over $235,000,000 in gold during the eighteenth century In Argentina the gold mines in La Rioja are worked successfully, and only lack of transport interferes with the exploitation of many other regions.

TIN.

Bolivia is one of the few countries of the world possessing really rich veins of tin, but, although the chief, it is not the only Latin-American source of this indispensable mineral. There are smaller deposits in Mexico, Colombia, Peru, and even in the mineral region of Argentina.

In extracting the metal the first process is the grinding of the ore, which is then washed to remove impurities. The earthy matter and some of the foreign metallic ores present are easily eliminated in this process. The ore is then roasted in a reverberatory furnace and the sulphur and arsenic are expelled. The roasted ore is mixed with fuel and limestone and again subjected to great heat in the reverberatory furnace to bring the whole into a state of fusion, which should continue for about eight hours. The lime unites with the remaining earthy matters and flows off as slag, and the coal reduces the oxide tin to its metallic state. The tin thus obtained needs to be further refined in order to command the highest price.

The tin zone in Bolivia has four districts—La Paz in the north, Oruro in the centre, Chorolque in the south, and Potosi in the east. The city of Oruro is the tin metropolis. Much of the mining country is in the Cordillera Real Range, and the lodes are found at altitudes of from 11,000 ft. to 16,000 ft.

SILVER.

The production of silver in *million ounces, fine,* is thus given in the Report of the United States Mint for 1919 :—

Mexico ..	. 62·68
Peru	. 9·78
South America and West Indies	2·80
Bolivia .	2 44
Chile ..	1·90

Silver ores generally occur in veins or irregular deposits. But it is important to note that the silver-lead ore sometimes occurs in great quantity in pockets or cavities in limestone rocks. These are for a time very productive, but generally are soon exhausted. The extraction of silver from lead is a most important subsidiary branch of the lead industry, as a certain proportion is nearly always contained in galena—the chief lead ore.

SUGAR.

The chief area of cane-sugar production, so far as the commerce of the world is concerned, is the West Indies, Guiana, and Brazil. By far the largest producer is Cuba, where the industry has greatly increased of late years. Sugar-cane is, next to rice, the bulkiest of tropical commodities in proportion to its value, and demands a large amount of shipping.

Cane sugar possesses advantages over beet sugar, in that it is easier of culture and richer in sugar, also it grows in tropical countries where labour is at its cheapest. The stems of the plant are crushed between rollers. Cane sugar is usually exported in an unrefined condition. It is called "raw sugar," and is further treated and refined, more syrup flowing away from it in the process. Until recently the cane-growers relied solely upon the greater richness of their raw material to enable them to compete with the producers of beet sugar An economy has been effected by a change of system in some cane-growing districts. Instead of each planter extracting the sugar from his own cane, different estates are connected with a single sugar factory, the juice from the canes being pumped through pipes leading to reservoirs belonging to the factory This is known as the *usine,* or factory system. Even this method does not result in the greatest economy unless the separate estates are large enough for equipment with the best crushing machinery

SARSAPARILLA.

The *Smilax medica* yields the Mexican or Vera Cruz sarsaparilla. It is slightly different from *Smilax officinalis,* which yields the native Jamaica sarsaparilla. In appearance the latter are similar to the plant which yields the Peru sarsaparilla. A plant called *Smilax ornata,* growing in Costa Rica, is known to the British pharmacopœia officially as sarsaparilla. Little is definitely known of the plant that gives Honduras sarsaparilla, though the product has been used for over 400 years. The plants have long roots, and these are the parts used in medicine.

GUM CHICLE.

This is a gum somewhat resembling caoutchouc, and is obtained from the sapodilla tree. The gum is known in commerce as Gum Chicle, and comes from Yucatan. It is whitish, brittle, aromatic, and yet somewhat elastic, and contains 45 per cent. of a colourless crystallizable resin, which is soluble in alcohol and ether It is used in large quantities for the making of chewing gum.

FUSTIC.

Fustic-wood, or Cuba-wood, is the wood of the *Chlorophora tinctoria,* a tree of the mulberry order, growing in South America. It is a large and handsome tree, and the timber—though, like most dye-woods, brittle or, at least, easily splintered—is hard and strong. Chips of fustic are extensively used as an ingredient in the dyeing of yellow, and the wood is exported for that purpose.

KAPOK.

The tree *Bombax ceiba,* Linn., a native of tropical America, is commonly known as the "silk-cotton" tree. It furnishes a soft silky wool which, like the true cotton, is an investment of the seeds. The fibre is little used for spinning.

It derives its commercial name—Kapok, or vegetable down—from the Eastern Archipelago, whence it has been largely exported by the Dutch. On account of its extreme buoyancy it is largely used in making life-saving waistcoats and the like. The main use is as a stuffing for cushions, quilts, and so forth, and ordinarily it requires cleaning by machine to rid it of the large proportion of dust found in the crude material.

GUANO.

Guano is an animal product, consisting of the droppings of birds accumulated through the ages in regions where there is little or no rain to wash away the valuable manurial salts.

The Lobos Islands, on the west coast of Peru, are rich in a light phosphatic product. Guano is worked as a mineral, and may be described as an earthy nitrate or combined nitrate and phosphate rock.

ANIMALS AND BIRDS

ANIMALS AND BIRDS.

Tropical South and Central America afford the richest variety of animals. Northward and southward of the tropics the variety of animal life diminishes.

"There is a great variety of mammals, birds and reptiles," wrote Bates in his "Naturalist on the River Amazon," "but they are widely scattered, and excessively shy of man. The region is so extensive and uniform in the forest clothing of its surface, that it is only at long intervals that animals are seen in abundance, when some particular spot is found which is more attractive than others. Brazil is poor in terrestrial mammals, and the species are of a small size. They do not form a conspicuous feature in the forests."

MEMBERS OF THE CAT FAMILY

Jaguar :—Largest and strongest of the cats of the New World, it inhabits South and Central America. It is a near relative of the leopard, which it resembles in appearance, but is somewhat larger It is of great strength and most agile, and is able to kill beasts greatly exceeding itself in size. It is the personification of concentrated force, swimming and climbing with equal ease. It is seldom encountered by white men. It inhabits the forests running from Central America to Southern Brazil.

Humboldt declares that at one period 4,000 jaguars were killed annually, and 2,000 skins exported from Buenos Aires alone.

Waterton says: "The word tiger does not mean the Bengal type, it means the jaguar, whose skin is beautifully spotted, and not striped, like that of the tiger of the East. It is in fact the tiger of the New World, and receiving the name of 'tiger' from the discoverers of South America it has kept it ever since. It is a cruel, strong, and dangerous beast, but not so courageous as the Bengal tiger"

Pampas Cat, also called the "Straw," or "Grass" cat, is generally found in the open country of the Argentine and Patagonia. It is stoutly built and very savage.

Tiguire Cat is a small spotted form which ranges from Guiana to Paraguay It is arboreal in its habits and is marked by bright colouring.

Heusat's Cat is the smallest of the species of ocelot cats, is found in the forests of Brazil.

Salt Desert Cat belongs to the Ocelot group of tiger-cats, and lives in the higher altitudes of the Argentine.

Jaguarondi and the **Eyra** are two peculiarly South American wood-cats, long in body and tail, short legged, the jaguarondi being dark grey and the Eyra tawny The Jaguarondi is the larger of the two, the Eyra being about the size of the tame cat and is elongated in form as one of the weasel tribe.

The Jaguarondi is found in Paraguay, Guiana, Brazil, and Mexico.

Geoffrey's Cat is found in most parts of South America, varies greatly in colour and markings, is rather smaller in size than the common domestic cat.

THE MONKEY TRIBE.

Monkeys : — The principal kinds are the Capuchins, woolly monkeys, woolly spider monkeys, spider monkeys, Douroucoulis, squirrel monkeys, Titi, Saki and Howler monkeys, and Uakaxis, the short-tailed marmosets and the long-tailed marmosets.

The Capuchins and the Spider monkeys have a prehensile tail and are the two most typical. The range of these two species is from Mexico to Paraguay They are easy to train and gentle in disposition. The coaita, or red-faced spider monkey, is much liked by the Brazilians, who keep it as a pet. It is vegetarian in its habits and amiable in its disposition.

Woolly monkeys inhabit the forests of Amazonia. By the Brazilians they are called Carrigudos, or " big-bellied," and are larger and less active than the Capuchins. This animal was first introduced into Europe by Humboldt who saw it in the cabin of an Indian on the Orinoco. It dislikes people in soiled or dirty working clothes.

" The total number of species of monkeys I found inhabiting the margins of the Upper and Lower Amazons," says Bates, " was thirty-eight. They belonged to twelve different genera, forming two distinct families. .   .   All the New World genera of apes, except one, are represented here. . . .   One of the two American families (Cebidæ) has 36 teeth. This important characteristic is constant throughout all the varied forms of which the Cebidæ family is composed. .   The second American family, the Marmosets, have 32 teeth, like the Old World monkeys and man."

The " Howlers " are a genus of monkeys which every traveller to South America knows. Their cry has been described as a "harrowing roar " They are chiefly found in Brazil. The "Red Howler" belongs to Colombia, the Amazon Valley, Bolivia and Guiana.

The Douroucoulis are found in Nicaragua and Eastern Peru Squirrel monkeys inhabit the forests from Costa Rica to Brazil and Bolivia. The Marmosets range as far North as Mexico.

Bears :—Two kinds are found in Colombia, a black variety in the lowlands, and one with a white face in the Eastern Cordilleras of Colombia.

The Spectacled Bear is small for a bear   Its habitat is the higher Andes. It is marked by great width and shortness of skull. It is black in colour with tawny semi-circles round the eyes, which give it its name.

MEMBERS OF THE DOG FAMILY

Maned Wolf (or Aguara-guaza) is the largest of the South American wild dogs, and inhabits Paraguay. In colour it is chestnut-red, with black feet. Inside the noticeably large ears and on the throat the hair is white. This dog has long limbs, and is as tall as the true wolf, but is less heavy and powerful. Although fleet-footed it is not dangerous.

Azara's Dog (sometimes called " fox ") is about the size and colouring of that animal. It is found from Brazil to Terra del Fuego.

Colpeo ranges from Chile to Terra del Fuego, and in the south is as big as a coyote, it is there called the Magellanic wolf.

Solenedon :—Found in mountains in South and West of Cuba, lives on grubs, insects and reptiles. Is yellowish or tawny on the head and neck, and dark brown on the body.

Bush Dogs :—One kind is found in Guiana and Brazil, the other sort in Ecuador. They are fierce and usually hunt in packs, and for their size they display great ferocity   The Guiana bush dog is a long-bodied animal with short limbs, small ears, and short tail. The Ecuador bush dog resembles a badger in appearance.

FUR-BEARING SPECIES.

Skunk are found from Mexico to Patagonia. They differ from the North American skunk in being of a heavier build. Their nostrils open downwards and forwards instead of at the side of the muzzle.

Coypu inhabits Chile and Peru. It is one of the largest of the rodents, sometimes being as much as two feet without the tail. It is an aquatic animal making its home on the banks of lakes and rivers. They are said to be mainly vegetarian in their habits, but frequently feed upon molluscs. In colour coypu are dusky and brownish-looking with a white chin. Their fur is long and harsh, and is known to commerce as **Nutria.**

When eating the coypu holds its food in its fore paws like a rat or squirrel. Usually they associate only in pairs but are sometimes seen in larger parties on the banks of a quiet lake or river.

Chinchilla :—This animal lives in lonely burrows on the higher slopes of the Andes. It displays extraordinary agility in climbing up and down the faces of almost perpendicular rocks. Chinchilla are seen in great numbers, are rather like squirrels, about 10 in. long, and their brown fur is highly valuable.

Viscacha is an animal of much stouter build than the Chinchilla, to which it is nearly related. It is the commonest animal of the Argentine pampas. In colour it is grey above, of a whitish-yellow beneath, the head striped with black and white. Its burrows are deep, and at the head of each is a curious mound whereon is a collection of rubbish, from thistle stalks to ostrich bones.

Ocelot :—This animal is found only in the tropical parts of Central America, is of a tawny or grey colour and is one of the most beautifully marked of all animals. The ground tint of the fur is a smoky pearl colour, spotted black, but it varies considerably in colour and markings. It is a tree-dweller, and lives upon smaller animals and birds. The ocelot can be tamed and almost domesticated when taken young, and is occasionally kept as a pet by the forest Indians.

Puma (also called Cougar)—Has quite a wide range of habitat, extending almost over the whole continents of North and South America. It has the widest range of any beast of prey in the Western Hemisphere. Amongst horses and other domestic stock it plays great havoc, but it does not seem to be a natural enemy of man.

It is a beautiful animal, resembling the leopard in form, but without its distinctive markings. It has a long and very curly tail. When young pumas are marked with solid black spots which gradually fade away as the adult coat appears. They purr like domestic cats when pleased, and caterwaul in the breeding season.

Opossum :—Many species are found in Guiana, in Brazil, and the valley of the Amazon. Bates says. " One kind of these rat-like opossums is aquatic and has webbed feet. The terrestrial species are nocturnal in their habits, sleeping during the day in hollow trees and only coming forth at night to prey on birds in their roosting places. It is very difficult to rear poultry in this country on account of these small opossums."

Crab-Eating Racoon is larger in size than the common species. Its habitat is entirely South America, but it is commonest in Panamá, Colombia, and Guíana. Its fur is shorter and its teeth larger than in the common racoon.

Cavy is common, in various species, to South America. One is found in the grass lands east of the Andes, another, from Brazil, lives in rocky crevices.

The Mara—or Patagonian Cavy—unlike the other sorts, has longer ears and limbs, it is between two and three feet in length, with a grey upper-body and whitish under-parts. It differs from the other cavies in being diurnal in habit. Cultivation has greatly reduced their numbers.

Another sort of cavy, the Lesser Mara, comes from the dried salt-marshes of Southern Argentina. Though of the same genus as the Patagonian cavies it is smaller in size.

CHARACTERISTIC SPECIES.

The **Tapir** is found in the Amazon Valley It belongs to the odd-toed group of mammals, and chiefly inhabits swamps and low ground near rivers. In the paranas of Colombia the animal is shy and of nocturnal habit. Its hide is useful for making saddles and harness, and its flesh is palatable.

The **Iguana** is fairly common throughout South America. This large lizard grows to a length of five feet and becomes enormously fat. Its skin changes colour like that of the chameleon. It has a high serrated crest on the back. It lives in trees on the banks of rivers, and its flesh is said to be more delicate than chicken.

" The Iguana," says Bates, " is one of the stupidest animals I ever met with. The one I caught dropped helplessly from a tree just ahead of me it turned round for a moment to have an idiotic stare at the intruder, and then set off running along the pathway I ran after it and it stopped, as a timid dog would do, crouching down, and permitting me to seize it by the neck and carry it off."

Armadillo :—Seven species are found in Argentina, running from the Giant Armadillo to the small Pichiciego.

Porcupines :—In the forests on the East Coast of Mexico lives a tree-porcupine, distinguished by its long hair, black in colour, which often conceals the species. On the lower part of the body are bristles. Young shoots of trees, bark, and similar sorts of vegetables, are its food.

In Brazil there flourishes another kind known as the Guianian tree-porcupine. It has a long, prehensile tail which curls upwards round a bough, not downwards as the spider-monkey's. It usually lives alone and is nocturnal in its habits.

Aguti, of which there are several species, is found in most regions of Central and South America. Its long slender limbs give it a most graceful appearance. The colour is usually orange brown, with paler tints on the hind quarters and a pale line underneath. The West Indian aguti is essentially a forest dweller and lives among the roots of trees. The aguti feed upon grass and leaves and are very swift in their movements.

Coatis (or Coatimundis) are found in Mexico and Central America. In appearance they are generally brown, splashed with white. Coatis are especially fond of young birds and eggs, and frequently climb trees in search of them. They wage an unrelenting war on the Iguana; some chase it along the boughs while others run below ready to catch the animal if it drops. They are easily recognized by the prolongation of the muzzle into a long upturned snout.

Kinkajou:—Inhabits tropical America from the Isthmus to Brazil. It is remarkable as a carnivore, possessing a prehensile tail, but its manner of life is similar to the racoons. One of its most characteristic features is its long tongue, with which it can lick out insects from crevices of trees. Birds, small animals, bananas and oranges are included in its diet.

Peccari (or Bush Hog)—Abounds in the Guianas. There are two species, the collared peccari—about the size of a small pig, which ranges the forest in small parties, and the white lipped peccari, which is rather larger, has a white spot on the lower jaw, and hunts in herds of a considerable size.

Sloth :—Lives amongst the highest trees of dense forests. It walks and sleeps suspended beneath the boughs, securing itself by means of its hooked claws, which are immensely powerful. In Costa Rica a sort called the "two-toed" sloth is found; this probably refers only to the fore feet, the hind feet have three toes.

Waterton was the first correctly to describe the habits of the sloth and to recognize that it is an animal admirably adapted to its surroundings. He says " The sloth, in its wild state, spends its whole life in trees and never leaves them but through force or by accident."

Paca :—This animal is found over the whole of South America, except west of the Andes. It is about 2 ft. long, adorned over the whole of the body with light spots upon a black and fawn ground, but the colour varies in different regions.

Dinomy (or Branich's Paca)—Is a remarkable Peruvian animal related to the Paca, but distinguished by its cleft upper lip, rather long bushy tail and the presence of four toes upon each foot.

The **Labba** is yet another species. It somewhat resembles a large guinea-pig.

WOOL-BEARING ANIMALS.

Llamas are found in flocks on the puno, a comparatively level plateau, between two main lines of the Cordilleras. " The Indians of Peru, whose more favoured home contained the Llama, were enabled to reach a high degree of civilization, a great help thereto being this priceless animal, which served as a beast of burden, yielded wool for clothing, milk, cheese, and flesh for nourishment. In the plains of Tropical America there exists no wild animal comparable to the ox, the horse, the sheep, or the hog." [Bates.]

Alpacas are found in flocks on the Peruvian puno. "The Alpaca, or paco, has a long fleece, usually black. The fibre is strong and lustrous and is used for making blankets (ponchos) It is shorn every two years, giving a yield of six to nine pounds. It depends for protection partly on its speed and partly on its faculty of ' spitting '—the accurately aimed projection of a mass of peculiarly unpleasant saliva. The diminishing number of these animals has rendered necessary measures of Government protection." [Vivian, " Peru " , Pitmans 1914.]

Guanaco (or Huanaco) :—The largest of the wool-bearing family of Peru, it has never been domesticated, but is an important source of food to Indian hunters. It roams the uplands in herds as large as 500 to 800.

Vicuña, a native of Peru. It is growing scarce and is hunted for its fine and valuable wool.

ANT-EATERS AND ALLIGATORS.

Alligators frequent especially the rivers of the Amazon valley " One day I amused myself," reports Bates " by taking a basketful of fragments . . and drawing the alligators towards me by feeding them. They behaved pretty much as dogs do when being fed. . The enormous gape of their mouths, with their blood-red lining and long fringes of teeth, and the uncouth shape of their bodies, made a picture of unsurpassable ugliness."

Ants abound all over the continent. The white ants, or " termites," have a habit of shedding their wings round the lamps at night. The animal known as the **Ant-Eater** is not uncommon in the Amazon forests. It is one of the edentates and is a survivor of the gigantic mammals which formerly inhabited the Amazon valley.

" In the far extending wilds of Guiana," said Waterton, " the traveller will be astonished at the immense quantity of ants he perceives in the trees and on the ground. They have nests in the branches, four or five times as large as that of the rook, and they have a covered way from them to the ground. . . . Other species of ants have no covered way, but travel, exposed to view, upon the surface of the earth."

TROPICAL AND OTHER BIRDS.

Humming Bird :—Several species are found in Brazil, but they occur in the forests throughout the tropical regions of the continent.

"The humming birds are chiefly to be found near the flowers at which each of the species of the genus is wont to feed." [Waterton.]

"Of all animated beings the humming bird is the most elegant in its form and the most brilliant in its colours." [Buffon.]

Toucan is abundant near Para. It is also found on the lower islands of Rio Negro, near Barra, and does not seem to range much farther west. It is called by the natives " Tocáno pacovo," from its beak resembling a banana or " pacovo." Five species are found in the woods. All the family are large birds, having enormous beaks and are quite characteristic of tropical America.

"Fruit is undoubtedly the chief food of the toucans, and it is in reference to their mode of obtaining it that the use of their uncouth bills is to be sought." [Bates.]

"The singular form of the toucan makes a lasting impression on your memory There are three species of toucans in Demerara, and three diminutives, which may be called toucanets. The largest of the first species frequents the mangrove trees on the sea coast. He is never seen in the interior till you reach Kiacoushia, where he is seen in the neighbourhood of the river Tacatore." [Waterton.]

"To what purpose is a bird placed in the woods of Cayenne with a bill a yard long, making a noise like a puppy dog, and laying eggs in hollow trees ? The toucans, to be sure, might retort, to what purpose were gentlemen in Bond Street created ? To what purpose were certain foolish prating Members of Parliament created ? There is no end of such questions. So we will not enter into the metaphysic of the toucan ! " [Sidney Smith on Waterton's " Wanderings."]

Flamingo, found in the Amazon valley Waterton also mentions it as being seen in Guiana. It is a tall, bulky, and beautiful bird. Its body is scarlet and of about the size of a swan's. Its legs and neck are of such extraordinary length that when it stands erect it is quite six feet high. The flamingo lives near salt water lakes and swampy islands.

Parrots are found in Colombia, Northern Brazil, Chile, and in Argentina. There are ten distinct species in the last-named country.

Paroquet :—Abundant in Brazil, these little birds are fairly common over the whole continent. Green, with a patch of yellow on the forehead, they will feed quietly, chattering in subdued tones, but set up a harsh scream and fly off on being disturbed.

Macaw, found in the valley of the Amazon, sitting on the topmost branches of trees.

Umbrella Bird :—Its habitat is the forests of the Upper Amazon. In size, colour, and appearance it resembles the common crow   At the top of its head it wears a crest of long curved hairy feathers which, when raised, spread themselves out into the form of a sunshade.   A thick pad of glossy steel-blue feathers depends from its neck, hanging on to a long fleshy lobe.

Organ Bird (or " realejo "), is the most remarkable songster of the Amazon forests.   Bates writes   " When its singular notes strike the ears for the first time the impression cannot be resisted that they are produced by a human voice.   No bird is to be seen, however closely the surrounding forest may be scanned.   .   .   But the end of the song is rather disappointing. it sounds like a barrel organ out of wind and tune."

Jacamar, common in Amazon forests, where there are two kinds, viz., the Great Jacamar and the Green Jacamar, clothed in beautiful golden-bronze and steel-coloured plumage.

Bates says, " I sometimes saw two or three together seated on a slender branch, silent and motionless with the exception of a slight movement of the head.   When an insect flew past within a short distance, one of the birds would dart off, seize it and return again to its sitting place."

Tanager :—This is the modern form of a name used by Buffon and Brisson which they spell " tangara."   The tanagers represent a large family of small birds restricted to the tropical regions of America.   They have most brilliant colourings.

Trogon :—Inhabits the forests of tropical America.   It is a beautiful bird with glossy green back and rose-coloured breast. It is dull and inactive, and not very ready to take flight.

Heron :—The smaller variety of this genus was found by Bates in his travels on the Amazon.   It is of graceful shape and mien, its plumage variegated into bars and spots of many colours.   Its long-drawn whistle generally betrays its presence.   It is a favourite pet-bird of the Brazilians.

Carashué is a species of thrush, inhabiting the forests of the Amazon valley   It is a smaller and plainer coloured bird than the English thrush, and the song is neither so long nor so loudly sustained.   Several allied species are known in Brazil.

Cassique abounds in Guiana and Northern Brazil.   They are a family of birds that may be considered as taking the place of starlings in Britain.   Brisson uses the French name ''troupiale'', others are called ''hanquests.''   The principal kinds found in South America are commonly called the ''Mocking Bird'', the ''Red-Rumped Hanquest'', the ''Crested Hanquest '', and the ''Green Hanquest.''   The ''troupiale,'' also called the ''Nightingale of Guiana,'' is the ''Yellow Hanquest.''

479

Ostrich :—The species is properly called the Rhea, or American ostrich, it is a native of Brazil. Two species are known, one named after Darwin is found in Patagonia.

Eagle :—Buffon's " Great Eagle of Guiana " , also the " Destroying Eagle," " White," and " Royal " sorts are found in Colombia. It builds its nest on lofty mountains and inaccessible cliffs, employing in the construction the bones of animals it has slaughtered and some dry branches of trees. The materials are enough to fill the body of a cart.

Andine Condor :—Habitat Chile, where it is represented in the national arms. It is more frequently seen in Peru than elsewhere, but abounds in other parts of South America. During the season in which they lay their eggs the condors sit on the leaves of the trees watching the coming of the female alligator to deposit its eggs. When these have been covered with sand to hide them, the birds swoop down, tear away the sand and devour the eggs.

Vulture :—The ''King Vulture'' is a native of Northern Brazil, but is found all over the tropical parts of the continent. The Portuguese call them corvos or crows. Somewhat resembling rooks in appearance, they are much larger and have black, wrinkled skin about their faces and throats.

Ibis :—Probably a bird of the vulture kind. If it is the same bird as was worshipped by the Ancient Egyptians it is almost certainly not confined to that country. (See Buffon.) Its plumage is a reddish white, inclining to red or black at the wings and back.

CARRION BIRDS.

Many references have been made to the carrion-feeding hawks of South America, whose "number, tameness, and disgusting habits" impressed Charles Darwin. We quote the great naturalist from " The Voyage of the Beagle," who notes four species of the Caracara or Polyborus, the Turkey buzzard, the Gallinazo, and the Condor

The Caracaras are, from their structure, placed among the eagles. In their habits they well supply the place of carrion-crows, magpies, and ravens, a tribe of birds widely distributed over the rest of the world, but entirely absent in South America.

The Polyborus Brasiliensis · this is a common bird, and has a wide geographical range, it is most numerous on the grassy savannahs of La Plata (where it goes by the name of **Carrancha**), and is far from unfrequent throughout the sterile plains of Patagonia. Although common in dry and open countries, and likewise on the arid shores of the Pacific, it is nevertheless found inhabiting the damp impervious forests of West Patagonia and Tierra del Fuego. The Carranchas, together with the Chimango, constantly attend in numbers the estancias and slaughtering-houses.

If an animal dies on the plain the Gallinazo commences the feast, and then the two species of Polyborus pick the bones clean. These birds, although thus commonly feeding together, are far from being friends. When the Carrancha is quietly seated on the branch of a tree or on the ground, the Chimango often continues for a long time flying backwards and forwards, up and down, in a semi-circle, trying each time at the bottom of the curve to strike its larger relative. The Carrancha takes little notice, except by bobbing its head. Although the Carranchas frequently assemble in numbers, they are not gregarious, for in desert places they may be seen solitary, or more commonly by pairs.

The Carranchas are said to be very crafty, and to steal great numbers of eggs. They attempt, also, together with the Chimango, to pick off the scabs from the sore backs of horses and mules. These false eagles must rarely kill any living bird or animal, and their vulture-like, necrophagous habits are very evident to anyone who has fallen asleep on the desolate plains of Patagonia, for when he wakes he will see, on each surrounding hillock, one of these birds patiently watching him with an evil eye it is a feature in the landscape of these countries which will be recognized by every one who has wandered over them. If a party of men go out hunting with dogs and horses, they will be accompanied during the day by several of these attendants. After feeding, the uncovered craw protrudes, at such times, and indeed generally, the Carrancha is an inactive, tame, and cowardly bird. Its flight is heavy and slow like that of an English rook. It seldom soars, but I have twice seen one at a great height gliding through the air with great ease. It runs (in contradistinction to hopping), but not quite so quickly as some of its congeners.

At times the Carrancha is noisy, but not generally so : its cry is loud, very harsh and peculiar, and may be likened to the sound of the Spanish guttural *g*, followed by a rough double *r r*, when uttering this cry it elevates its head higher and higher, till at last, with its beak wide open, the crown almost touches the lower part of the back. This fact, which has been doubted, is quite true, I have seen them several times with their heads backwards in a completely inverted position. To these observations, I may add, on the high authority of Azara, that the Carrancha feeds on worms, shells, slugs, grasshoppers, and frogs, that it destroys young lambs by tearing the umbilical cord, and that it pursues the Gallinazo till that bird is compelled to vomit up the carrion it may recently have gorged. Azara states that several Carranchas, five or six together, will unite in chase of large birds, even such as herons. All these facts show that it is a bird of very versatile habits and considerable ingenuity

The Polyborus **Chimango** is considerably smaller than the last species. It is truly omnivorous, and will eat even bread, and I was assured that it materially injures the potato-crops in Chiloe, by stocking up the roots when first planted. Of all the carrion-feeders, it is generally the last which leaves the skeleton of a dead animal, and may often be seen within the ribs of a cow or horse like a bird in a cage. Another species is the Polyborus Novae Zelandiae, which is exceedingly common in the Falkland Islands. These birds in many respects resemble in their habits the Carranchas. They live on the flesh of dead animals and on marine productions, and on the Ramirez rock their whole sustenance must depend on the sea. They are extraordinarily tame and fearless, and haunt the neighbourhood of houses for offal. If a hunting party kills an animal, a number soon collect and patiently await, standing on the ground on all sides. After eating, their uncovered craws are largely protruded, giving them a disgusting appearance. They readily attack wounded birds a cormorant in this state having taken to the shore, was immediately seized on by several, and its death hastened by their blows.

We have now only to mention the **Turkey-buzzard** (*Vultur aura*), and the Gallinazo. The former is found wherever the country is damp, from Cape Horn to North America. Differently from the Polyborus Brasiliensis and Chimango, it has found its way to the Falkland Islands. The turkey-buzzard is a solitary bird, or at most goes in pairs. It may at once be recognised from a long distance by its lofty, soaring, and most elegant flight. It is well known to be a true carrion-feeder On the west coast of Patagonia, among the thickly-wooded islets and broken land, it lives exclusively on what the sea throws up, and on the carcasses of dead seals. Wherever these animals are congregated on the rocks, there the vultures may be seen.

The **Gallinazo** (*Cathartes atratus*) has a different range from the last species, as it never occurs southward of lat. 41° Azara states that there exists a tradition that these birds, at the time of the conquest, were not found near Montevideo, but they subsequently followed the inhabitants from more northern districts. The Gallinazo generally prefers a humid climate, or rather the neighbourhood of fresh water, hence it is extremely abundant in Brazil and La Plata, while it is never found on the desert and arid plains of Northern Patagonia, excepting near some stream. These birds frequent the whole pampas to the foot of the Cordillera, but I never saw or heard of one in Chile . in Peru they are preserved as scavengers. These vultures certainly may be called gregarious, for they seem to have pleasure in society, and are not solely brought together by the attraction of a common prey On a fine day a flock may often be observed at a great height, each bird wheeling round and round without closing its wings, in the most graceful evolutions.

BIBLIOGRAPHY

BIBLIOGRAPHY

OF WORKS IN THE ENGLISH LANGUAGE ON SOUTH AMERICA FROM 1870.

1870 Resources of the Argentine Republic. By MAJOR RICKARD.
Letter of Columbus, with other Original Documents Relating to his Four Voyages to the New World. Translated by R. H. MAJOR. (Hakluyt Society.)
The Andes and the Amazon. By JAMES ORTON
Letters from the Battle Fields of Paraguay By SIR RICHARD BURTON.
Pioneering in the Pampas. 2nd Edition. By R. A. SEYMOUR.
Seven Eventful Years in Paraguay By G. F MASTERMAN.
Ten Months in Brazil, with Notes on the Paraguayan War. By J CODMAN
Flint Chips A Guide to Prehistoric Archæology, as Illustrated by the Collection in the Blackmore Museum, Salisbury By T STEVENS.

1871 Emigration to the River Plate, Success of British Subjects in Buenos Aires, List of Landowners, Description of the City and Province of Buenos Aires. By S. WEBSTER.
Notes on the Natural History of the Straits of Magellan and West Coast of Patagonia. By R. D. CUNNINGHAM.
Three Years' Slavery among the Patagonians. By A. GUINNARD.
The Coolie, his Rights, Wrongs Notes of a Journey to British Guiana. By EDWARD JENKIN.
At Home with the Patagonians. By COMMANDER G. CHAWORTH MUSTERS, R.N.
Travels in Uruguay By J H. MURRAY

1872 Rough Notes on a Journey through the Wilderness, from Trinidad to Pará, Brazil, by way of the Great Cataracts of the Orinoco and Rio Grande. By H. A. WICKHAM.
Round the World in 1870 : An Account of a Brief Tour made through India, China, Japan, California, and South America. By A. D. CARLISLE.
Reports on the Discovery of Peru by Pizarro and Others. Translated and edited by SIR CLEMENTS R. MARKHAM. (Hakluyt Society.)

1873 Two Years in Peru : with Exploration of its Antiquities. By T J HUTCHINSON
British Guiana, the Essequibo and Potaro Rivers, with an Account of a Visit to the Recently Discovered Kaieteur Falls. By LIEUT.-COLONEL WEBBER.
Brazilian Colonisation from an European Point of View By JACARÉ ASSU
The Amazons : Diary of a Twelvemonth's Journey on a Mission of Enquiry up the River Amazon. By R. S. CLOUGH.
Reports respecting the Condition of British Emigrants in Brazil.
Narratives of the Rites and Laws of the Yncas. Translated and edited, with Notes and an Introduction, by SIR CLEMENTS R. MARKHAM. (Hakluyt Society.)
Life and Missionary Travels of the Rev. J F Ogle. Edited by WYLIE.
A Journey Across South America. By PAUL MARCOY

1874 The Western World : Picturesque Sketches of Nature and Natural History in North and South America. By W H. G. KINGSTON.
Memoir of Lady Ana de Osorio, Countess of Chinchon and Vice-Queen of Peru. By SIR CLEMENTS R. MARKHAM.

1875 Explorations made in the Valley of the River Madeira, from 1749 to 1868. Published for the National Bolivian Navigation Company
Geological Survey of British Guiana. By C. B. BROWN and J G. SAWKINS.
The Amazon and Madeira Rivers. By FRANZ KELLER.
History of British Guiana. By GEO. W BENNETT.

1876 The Argentine Republic. By RICHARD NAPP.
Handbook to the River Plate. By M. G. and E. T MULHALL.
Sporting Adventures in the Pacific whilst in Command of the "Reindeer." By W R. KENNEDY
Recollections of Four Years in Venezuela. By C. D. DANCE.
Dutch Guiana. By W G. PALGRAVE.
Canoe and Camp Life in British Guiana. By C. BARRINGTON BROWN
Over the Sea and Far Away. By T. W HINCHLIFF.

BIBLIOGRAPHY

1877 The Two Americas. By MAJOR SIR R. LAMBART PRICE.
      Peru and its Creditors. By W. CLARKE.
      Brazil and the River Plate, 1870–76. By W. HADFIELD.

1878 Fifteen Thousand Miles on the Amazon and its Tributaries. By C. B. BROWN
        and W LIDSTONE.
      The English in South America. By M. G. MULHALL.
      Pioneering in South Brazil. By T. P BIGG-WITHERS.
      Visit to South America, with Notes and Observations, etc. By EDWIN CLARK.
      The Land of Bolívar; or, War, Peace, and Adventure in the Republic of Vene-
        zuela. By J M. SPENCE.
      Peru : Incidents of Travel and Exploration in the Land of the Incas. By E.
        GEORGE SQUIRE.
      On the Supply of Nitrate of Soda and Guano from Peru.

1879 Wanderings in Patagonia, or, Life among the Ostrich Hunters. By JULIUS
        BEERBOHM.
      Notes by a Naturalist on the "Challenger." By H. N MOSELEY.
      Roraima and British Guiana, with a Glance at Bermuda, the West Indies, and
        the Spanish Main. By J W. BODDAM-WHITHAM.
      Waterton's Wanderings in South America. Edited by the Rev J. G. WOOD.
      Brazil, the Amazons, and the Coast. By H. H. SMITH.
      Report of Robert Cross's Mission to South America in 1877–8 to Collect Plants
        of the Quinine Bark Tree, etc.
      Up the Amazon and Madeira Rivers. By EDWARD D. MATHEWS.
      Brazil and the Brazilians. (9th edition.) By J. C. FLETCHER and D. P KIDDER.

1880 Voyages of the Elizabethan Seamen to America. By E. J PAYNE.
      Eight Months on the Gran Chaco of the Argentine Republic. By GIOVANNI
        PELLESCHI.
      The Natural and Moral History of the Indies. By FATHER JOSEPH DE ACOSTA.
        Edited by SIR CLEMENTS R. MARKHAM. (Hakluyt Society.)
      Legends and Myths of the Aboriginal Indians of British Guiana. By W. H.
        BRETT.
      South America. By A. GALLENCA.
      Six Weeks with the Chilean Army, being a Short Account of a March from Pisco
        to Lurin, and the Attack on Lima. By COMMANDER WILLIAM ACLAND, R.N.
        (Privately printed at the Melanesian Mission, Norfolk Island.)
      Across Patagonia. By Lady FLORENCE DIXIE.
      Peruvian Bark : A Popular Account of the Introduction of Cinchona Cultivation
        into British India. By SIR CLEMENTS R. MARKHAM.

1881 The Prospects of Peru, the End of the Guano Age and a Description Thereof,
        etc. By A. J DUFFIELD.
      Between the Amazon and Andes, or, Ten Years of a Lady's Travels in the
        Pampas, Gran Chaco, Paraguay, and Matto Grosso. By M. G. MULHALL.
      Chapters from a Guianese Log-Book. By the Rev C. D. DANCE.
      Sketches of Chile and the Chileans during the War 1879–1880. By R. W
        BOYD.
      Cameos from the Silver Land; or, The Experiences of a Young Naturalist in the
        Argentine Republic. By E. W. WHITE.

1882 A Year in the Andes, or, A Lady's Adventures in Bogotá. By ROSA CARNEGIE-
        WILLIAMS.

1883 Among the Indians of Guiana. By EVERARD F. IM THURN.
      The Geology of the Goldfields of British Guiana. By J. B. HARRISON.
      The Colony of British Guiana and its Labouring Population. By the Rev.
        H. V. P. BRONKHURST.
      Researches into the Lost Histories of America; or, The Zodiac shown to be an
        old Terrestrial Map in which the Atlantic Isle is delineated, etc. By W S.
        BLACKET.
      The Republic of Uruguay. (Stanford.)
      The War between Peru and Chile, 1879–82. By SIR CLEMENTS R. MARKHAM.

488

BIBLIOGRAPHY.

1884 Spanish and Portuguese South America. By R. G. WATSON.
The Peruvians at Home. By GEORGE R. FITZ-ROY COLE.
The Temple of the Andes. By RICHARD INWARDS.
Across the Pampas and the Andes. By ROBERT CRAWFORD.
The Origin and Growth of Religion as illustrated by the Native Religions of
Mexico and Peru. By ALBERT RÉVILLE.
A Naturalist on the River Amazon. By N W BATES.
The Cruise of the "Falcon." By E. F KNIGHT.

1885 Central America, the West Indies, and South America. (Stanford's Compen-
dium of Geography and Travel.) Edited and extended by H. W. BATES.
Brazil and Java. Report on Coffee Culture. By C. F. LEARNE.
Ascent of Mount Roraima. By SIR EVERARD IM THURN.
Sketches of African and Indian Life in British Guiana. By IGNATIUS SCOLES.
Description of the Collection of Gold Ornaments from the "Huacas" or Groves
of some Aboriginal Races of the North-Western Provinces of South America,
belonging to Lady Brassey. By BRYCE-WRIGHT.

1886 A Year in Brazil, with Notes on the Abolition of Slavery, etc. By H. C. DENT.
Venezuela A Visit to the Gold Mines of Guiana, and Voyage up the River
Orinoco during 1886, etc. By WILLIAM BARRY
Travels in Guiana and Venezuela. By H. TEN KATE.
Travels in the Wilds of Ecuador and the Explorations of the Putumayo River
By ALFRED SIMSON.
Exploring and Travelling Three Thousand Miles through Brazil. By J W
WELLS.

1886–89 History of America. By J WINSOR.

1887 Notes of a Naturalist in South America. By JOHN BALL.
The Apostle of the Indians. By W H. BRETT.
Zephyrus : A Holiday in Brazil and on the River Plate. By E. R. PEARCE
EDGECUMBE, LL.D.
The Great Silver River; Notes of a Residence in Buenos Aires in 1880–81. By
SIR HORACE RUMBOLD.
Sketch of the City of Iquique, Chile, South America Its Past and Present
during the last Fifty Years. By CAPTAIN W M. F. CASTLE.

Undated. Missionary Pioneering in Bolivia, with some Account of Work in Argentina.
By W. M. PAYNE.

1888 The Amazon Provinces of Peru as a Field for European Emigration, and the
Gold and Silver Mines. By H. GUILLAUME.
Three Cruises of the United States Coast and Geodetic Survey Steamer "Blake"
in the Gulf of Mexico, Caribbean Sea, etc., 1877–1880. By ALEXANDER
AGASSIZ.
The Venezuela Central Railway and its Sources of Traffic. By G. E. CHURCH.
Prospects of Gold Mining in Venezuela. By W G. WEARS.
Among the Hindus and Creoles of British Guiana. By the Rev H. V. P. BRONK-
HURST.
The Capitals of Spanish America. By W E. CURTIS.
Annals of Guiana : Chronological History of its Discovery and Settlement.
By JAMES RODWAY and THOMAS WATT.

1888–89 Argentine Ornithology By P. L. SCLATER and W. H. HUDSON.

1889 Recollections of Travel Abroad. By A. J DUFFIELD.
Textile Fabrics of Ancient Peru. By W. H. HOLMES.
From Peru to the Plate Overland. By PATRICK A. EVANS.
1890 A Visit to Chile and the Nitrate Fields of Tarapacá. By WILLIAM H. RUSSELL.
The Great Silver River : Notes of a Residence in Buenos Aires in 1880–81.
Second edition, with an additional chapter on the present commercial position
of the country By SIR HORACE RUMBOLD.

BIBLIOGRAPHY

1891 The Conquest of the River Plate, 1535–1555. Translated by LUIS L. DOMIN-
GUEZ. (Hakluyt Society.)
Twelve Months in Peru. By E. B. CLARK.
History of the Buccaneers of America. By B. J BURNEY.
Story of the Filibusters, etc. By JAMES J ROCHE.
Adventures amidst the Equatorial Forests and Rivers of South America, West
Indies, and Florida. By VILLIERS STUART.
Travels and Adventures of an Orchid Hunter. By ALBERT MILLICAN
A Winter's Cruise in Summer Seas. By C. C. ATCHISON.

1892 Sporting Sketches in South America. By SIR W. R. KENNEDY.
Paraguay By Dr. E. DE BOURGADE LA DARDYE.
The South American Republics. By THEODORE CHILD.
The Naturalist in La Plata. By W H. HUDSON
The Discovery of America with Account of Ancient America and the Spanish
Conquest. By JOHN FISKE.
The Voyage of the "Nyanza" Three Years in the Atlantic and Pacific. By
J CUMMING DEWAR.
Writings of Colombus, Descriptive of the Discovery and Occupation of the New
World. Edited, with Introduction, by P L. FORD.
Career of Colombus. By CHAS. J ELTON.
Life of Colombus. By C. K. ADAMS.
Life and Labours of John Wray, Pioneer Missionary in British Guiana. Compiled
by THOMAS RAIN.
Notes on British Guiana. By SIR EVERARD IM THURN.
Argentina and the Argentines. By T A. TURNER.
Travels among the Great Andes of the Equator. By EDWARD WHYMPER.

1892–4 History of the New World called America. By E. J PAYNE.

1893 An Enumeration of the Plants Collected in Bolivia by Miguel Bang, with de-
scriptions of New Genera and Species. By H. H. RUSBY
The South American Republics. By T C. DAWSON.
Handbook of British Guiana. By JAMES RODWAY.
Idle Days in Patagonia. By W H. HUDSON.
Christopher Colombus : His own Book of Privileges, 1502, etc. With historical
introduction by H. HARRISSE, the whole compiled and edited, with preface,
by G. F STEVENS.
History of Chile. By A. M. HANCOCK.
Journal of Colombus, during his First Voyage, 1492–3, and Documents Relating
to the Voyages of John Cabot and Gaspar Corte Real. Translated, with
notes, etc., by SIR CLEMENTS R. MARKHAM. (Hakluyt Society.)
Tropical America. By L. N FORD.
The History and Present State of the Sheep-Breeding Industry in the Argentine
Republic. By HERBERT GIBSON.
The State of Pará : Notes for the Exposition of Chicago, as authorized by the
Governor of Pará, Dr. Lauro Sodri.
Argentine, Patagonian, and Chilean Sketches. By C. E. AKERS.

1894 Travels of a Naturalist. By A. BOUCARD.
By Order of the Sun to Chile to see his Total Eclipse. By J J AUBERTIN.
China to Peru over the Andes. By LADY HOWARD VINCENT.
In the Guiana Forest. By JAMES RODWAY, F.L.S.

1895 The Gold Diggings of Cape Horn A Study of Life on Tierra del Fuego and
Patagonia. By J R. SPEARS.

1896 Venezuela : or, Two Years on the Spanish Main. By W E. WOOD.
Over the Andes, from the Argentine to Chile and Peru. By MAY CROMMELIN.
John Cabot. By HENRY HARISSE.
Documents and Maps on the Boundary Question between Venezuela and
British Guiana from the Capuchin Archives in Rome. By J. STRICKLAND.
The West Indies and Spanish Main. By JAMES RODWAY
Venezuela A Land where it's Always Summer. By W E. CURTIS.
Three Gringos in Venezuela and Central America. By RICHARD HARDING
DAVIS.

490

BIBLIOGRAPHY

1897 Records of the Scottish Settlers in the River Plate and their Churches. By
JAMES DODDS.

1898 Boundary Agreement in Force between Argentine Republic and Chile. By
Dr. EMILIO LAMARCA.
Twenty-five Years in British Guiana. By HENRY KIRKE.
South American Sketches. By ROBERT CRAWFORD.
Spanish America. By J W ROOT.
Bibliography of the Anthropology of Peru. By GEO. A. DORSEY.
The Establishment of Spanish Rule in America. By BENJAMIN MOSES.
The Dwarf Tribe of the Upper Amazon. By D. G. BRINTON
Spain and Her Colonies. By J W ROOT.

1899 Temperate Chile. By W A. SMITH.
Notes on the Natural History of the Aconcagua Valleys, from Fitzgerald's
"Highest Andes." By PHILIP GOSSE.
The Highest Andes : A Record of the First Ascent of Aconcagua and Tupungato
in Argentina, and the Exploration of the Surrounding Valleys. By E. A.
FITZGERALD.
The Ores of Colombia. By H. W NICHOLS and O. C. FARRINGTON.

1900 Electrical Enterprise in Argentina. By ERNESTO DANVERS.
South America. By F G. CARPENTER.
The Colombian and Venezuelan Republics. By WM. L. SCRUGGS.
Argentine-Chilian Boundary Report, presented to the British Arbitration
Tribunal on behalf of the Argentine Government.
Travelling Impression in, and Notes on, Peru. By F SEEBEE.

1900-4 The Spanish Conquest in America in Relation to the History of Slavery and
of the Government of Colonies. New edition, with Introduction and Notes,
by M. OPPENHEIM.

1901 The Bolivian Andes : Climbing and Exploration in the Cordillera Real in 1898-
1900. By SIR MARTIN CONWAY.
The Land of the Amazons. By BARON DE SANTA-ANNA NERY Translated by
GEORGE HUMPHREY.
Through Patagonia. By W D. CAMPBELL.
A. H. Keane's Central and South America. Edited by SIR CLEMENTS R. MARK-
HAM.
The South American Republics. By W F. MARKWICH and W. A. SMITH.
Peru History of Eoca. By W E. MORTIMER.
The Question of the Pacific. An edition in English of Dr. Maurtua's work.
By F. A. PEZET.
A Vanished Arcadia. By R. B. CUNNINGHAME GRAHAM.

1902 The Great Mountains and Forests of South America. By PAUL FOUNTAIN.
Ancient Peruvian Art. By A. H. KEANE.
Notes on Bolivia. By COLONEL PEDRO SUAREZ.
The Caura. By E. ANDRÉ.
Aconcagua and Tierra del Fuego a Book of Climbing, Travel, and Exploration.
By SIR MARTIN CONWAY.
Climate of the Argentine Republic, compiled from observations made to the
end of the year 1900. By WALTER G. DAVIS.
Down the Orinoco in a Canoe. By S. PÉREZ-TRIANA.
Through the Heart of Patagonia. By HESKETH H. PRICHARD.

1903 Great Argentina. By FRANCISCO SEEBEE.
The Independence of the South American Republics. By F. L. PAXON.
To the Falls of Iguazú. By W. S. BARCLAY.
Trade and Travel in South America. By F. ALCOCK.

1903-4 Christopher Columbus, his Life, his Work, his Remains, as revealed by
Original Records, with Essay on Peter Martyr and Las Casas. By J. B.
THACHER.

BIBLIOGRAPHY

1904 A Naturalist in the Guianas. By E. ANDRÉ.
The Great Mountains and Forests of South America. (2nd edition.) By PAUL FOUNTAIN.
South American Sketches. By W. H. HUDSON.
An Account of the Spanish Settlements in South America. Anonymous.
A History of South America (1854–1904). By C. E. AKERS.
Argentine Shows and Live Stock. By Professor ROBERT WALLACE.
The Countries of the King's Award. By Col. SIR THOMAS HOLDICH.
Among the Indians of the Paraguayan Chaco. By W B. BARBROOKE GRUBB.

1905 Brazilian Mines and their Laws. By Dr. PANDIA CALOGENAS.
The Republic of Chile. By M. R. WRIGHT.
Through Five Republics of South America. By PERCY F. MARTIN.

1906 Panamá to Patagonia. By C. M. PEPPER.
The Republic of Colombia. By F L. PETRE.
Bolivia. By MARIE ROBINSON WRIGHT.
Christopher Colombus, and the New World of his Discovery. By FILSON YOUNG.

1907 Modern Argentina. By W H. KOEBEL.
The Birds of Tierra del Fuego. By R. CRAWSHAY
Humboldt's Voyage. Translated and edited by T ROSS.
The Continent of Opportunity, the South American Republic. By F. E. CLARK, D.D.
Chile. By G. F. SCOTT-ELLIOT.

1908 Richard Spruce. Notes of a Botanist on the Amazons and Andes. Edited and condensed by A. R. WALLACE. ·
American Supremacy The Rise and Progress of the Latin American Republics, and Relations to the United States under the Monroe Doctrine. By GEORGE W CRICHFIELD.
A Bibliography of Sir Walter Raleigh, Knight. By T N. BRUSHFIELD.
A Pleasure Pilgrim in South America. By D. C. MACKELLAR.
The Andes and the Amazon Life and Travel in Peru. By C. R. ENOCK.
Peru. By C. R. ENOCK.

1909 Explorers in the New World, before and after Colombus, and the Story of the Jesuit Missions of Paraguay. By MARION MCMURROUGH MULHALL.
The Argentine Year Book. By H. W FARRELL.
Bartholomew de Las Casas. By F A. MACNUTT.
Yachting in the Pacific. Notes of Travel in Peru, Ecuador, etc. By A. MANN.
The Great Pacific Coast. By C. R. ENOCK.
Argentine Republic : Agricultural and Pastoral Census.
The Journal of an Expedition across Venezuela and Colombia. By HIRAM BINGHAM.
Peru, its Story, People, Religion. By GERALDINE GUINNESS.

1910 Brazil : Its Natural Riches and Industries. Published by the Brazilian Mission of Economic Expansion.
Official Handbook of British Guiana.
Argentina : Past and Present. By W H. KOEBEL.
Manual of Argentine Railways. By S. H. M. KILLIK. (Annual.)
Ups and Downs of a Wandering Life. Roaming Adventures in Argentine, Paraguay, Venezuela, etc. By WALTER SEYMOUR.
On Sea and Land. By H. W CASE.
The Argentine Republic. By A. STUART PENNINGTON.
Our Search for a Wilderness : An Account of Two Ornithological Expeditions to Venezuela and to British Guiana. By M. B. and C. W BEEBE.
Simon Bolivár, "El Libertador" By LINDON BATES.
Up the Orinoco and Down the Magdalena. By H. J MOZANS.
Life of Sir Woodbine Parish, or, Early Days in Argentina. By the HON. NINA KAY SHUTTLEWORTH.
The United States of Brazil, with a Chapter on Uruguay By C. W. DOMVILLE-FIFE.
The Other Americans. By A. RUHL.
The Amazons in Antiquity and Modern Times. By G. C. ROTHERY
Argentina. By W A. HIRST.
Brazil. By P DENIS.

1911 Early Spanish Voyages to the Strait of Magellan. Translated and edited, with a preface, introduction and notes, by SIR CLEMENTS R. MARKHAM. (Hakluyt Society.)

An Unknown People in an Unknown Land. By W BARBROOKE GRUBB.

The Family and Heirs of Sir Francis Drake. By LADY ELLIOT DRAKE.

A Woman's Winter in South America. By CHARLOTTE CAMERON

Uruguay. By W H. KOEBEL.

The Argentine in the Twentieth Century By ALBERT B. MARTINEZ.

Under the Roof of the Jungle. By CHARLES LIVINGSTON BULL.

The Ten Republics. By ROBERT P PORTER.

Peru of the Twentieth Century. By PERCY F. MARTIN.

The Wilds of Patagonia. By CARL SCOTTSBERG.

South America To-day By GEORGES CLEMENCEAU.

Through the Wilderness of Brazil. By W A. COOK.

Picturesque Paraguay. By A. K. MACDONALD.

In the Guiana Forest. (2nd edition.) By JAMES RODWAY, F.L.S.

Argentine Plains and Andine Glaciers. By WALTER LARDEN.

Wheat Growing in Canada, the United States, and the Argentine. By W P RUTTER.

The Rise of British Guiana. Compiled by C. A. HARRIS and J A. J DE VILLIERS. (Hakluyt Society.)

Along the Andes and Down the Amazon. By H. J MOZANS.

Adventures in Search of a Living in Spanish America. By "VAQUERO."

The Argentine Republic. By A. J PENNINGTON.

Across South America. By HIRAM BINGHAM.

Old Panamá and Castillo del Oro. By R. D. JOHNSON.

The Incas of Peru. (2nd edition.) By SIR CLEMENTS R. MARKHAM.

1912 The Putumayo, the Devil's Paradise. By W. E. HARDENBURG.

The Sea and the Jungle. By H. M. TOMLINSON.

Venezuela. By LEONARD V. DALTON.

Early Man in South America. By ALES HRDLICKA, in collaboration with H. M. Holmes, B. Willis, Fr. E. Wright, and Clarence N. Fenner.

South America. By W H. KOEBEL.

Where Socialism Failed. By STEWART GRAHAME.

The Secret of the Pacific. By C. R. ENOCK.

The Conquest of New Granada. By SIR CLEMENTS R. MARKHAM.

Chile : An Account of its Wealth and Progress. By J PÉREZ CANTO.

Aborigines of South America. By COLONEL CHURCH.

South American Archæology By THOMAS A. JOYCE.

In Jesuit Land : The Jesuit Missions of Paraguay By W. H. KOEBEL.

The Independence of Chile. By A. S. M. CHISHOLM.

South America. Observations and Impressions. By JAMES BRYCE.

In the Amazon Jungle. By A. LANGE.

The Path of the Conquistadores. By L. BATES.

South America To-day By GEORGES CLEMENCEAU.

Guiana British, French, and Dutch. By JAMES RODWAY.

High Mountain Climbing in Peru and Bolivia. By A. S. PECK.

1913 South America. (The Making of the Nations Series.) By W H. KOEBEL.

The Lords of the Devil's Paradise. The Putumayo Atrocities. By G. SIDNEY PATERNOSTER.

Illustrated South America. By W. D. BOYCE.

The Putumayo Red Book. By "N. T "

The River Plate and Back. By J W HOLLAND.

Bibliography of South America. By T P O'HALLORAN.

Latin America : Its Rise and Progress. By F GARCIA CALDERON.

The Venezuelan Boundary Controversy By GROVER CLEVELAND.

Panamá : The Creation, Destruction, and Resurrection. By BUNAU-VARILLA.

Colombia. By PHANOR J EDER.

South America : A supplementary Geography By J F and A. H. CHAMBERLAIN.

Observations on the Natives of the Patagonia Channel Region. By CARL SCOTTSBERG.

Across Unknown South America. By A. HENRY SAVAGE LANDOR.

The Travels of Ellen Cornish.

BIBLIOGRAPHY

A Tour through South America. By A. S. FORREST.
In the Wonderland of Peru. By HIRAM BINGHAM.
Brazil in 1913. By J C. OAKENFULL.
Brazil and Portugal in 1809. (Manuscript Marginalia.) By GEORGE W. ROBIN-SON
O'Higgins of Chile. By J. J MEHEGAN.

1914 Ecuador. By C. REGINALD ENOCK.
Bolivia. By PAUL WALLE.
Chile. By GEORGE J MILLS.
Argentina. By G. J MILLS.
North Brazil. By E. C. BULEY
South Brazil. By E. C. BULEY
Peru. By E. CHARLES VIVIAN.
New Light on Drake. By ZELIA NUTTALL. (Hakluyt Society.)
The Romance of the River Plate. By W H. KOEBEL.
The Beautiful Rio de Janeiro. By A. BELL.
The Upper Reaches of the Amazon. By JOSEPH F WOODROFFE.
The River Amazon from its Sources to the Sea. By PAUL FOUNTAIN.
The Spanish Dependencies in South America. By B. MOSES.
The Amazing Argentine. By JOHN FOSTER FRASER.
A Walloon Family in America. Lockwood de Forest and his Forebears, 1500–1848. Together with a Voyage to Guiana, being the Journal of Jesse de Forest and his Colonists. By Mrs. ROBERT W DE FOREST.
Under the Southern Cross in South America. By WILLIAM BUCKMAN.
The Scottish National Antarctic Expedition. The Whale Fisheries of the Falkland Islands and Dependencies. By THEODORE E. SALVESEN.
The Lower Amazon. By ALGOT LANGE.
South America as an Export Field. By OTTO WILSON. (Issued by the U.S. Department of Commerce.)
The South American Tour. By A S. PECK.
Northern Patagonia Character and Resources. By BAILEY WILLIS.
Mysterious South America. By A. HENRY SAVAGE LANDOR.
Through the Brazilian Wilderness. By THEODORE ROOSEVELT.
The New Brazil. (2nd edition.) By MARIE ROBINSON WRIGHT.
The Timbers of British Guiana. By HERBERT STONE and Dr. W G. FREEMAN.
West Indies and Guiana. By ALGERNON E. ASPINALL.
Chile : Its Land and People. By F J G. MAITLAND.
Colombia. By V LEVINE.
The Two Americas. By GENERAL R. REYS.
Forty Years in Brazil. By FRANK BENNETT.
A Church in the Wilds : The South American Mission to the Paraguayan Chaco. By W B. GRUBB.

1915 Brazil and the Brazilians. By G. J. BRUCE.
South of Panamá. By Dr. EDWARD ALSWORTH ROSS.
The Rubber Industry of the Amazon and how its Supremacy can be Maintained. By JOSEPH F WOODROFFE and HAROLD HAMEL SMITH, with a Foreword by VISCOUNT BRYCE.
The Real Argentine. By J A. HAMMERTON.
A Guide to South America. By A. W HIRST.
The North-West Amazons. Notes of Some Months Spent Among Cannibal Tribes. By CAPTAIN THOMAS WHIFFEN.
Mineral Resources of Minas Geraes (Brazil). By ALBERT F CALVERT.
The Amazon as a River, a Problem, and a Call. By the Rev. O. R. WALKEY
The South Americans. By W H. KOEBEL.
The Plateau Peoples of South America. By ALEXANDER A. ADAM.
Colombia and the United States. By NORMAN THOMSON

1916 Through South America's Southland. With an Account of the Roosevelt Scientific Expedition to South America. By the Rev J A. ZAHM (H. J MOZAMS)
Arequipa Pyrheliometry By CHARLES GREELEY ABBOT.
South America Pilot. Issued by the Admiralty
Our Hispanic South-West. By E. PEIXOTTO.

BIBLIOGRAPHY

Bolivia. By W REID.
Big Game Fields of America, North and South. By DANIEL J SINGER.
The Birds of North and Middle America. Vol. 7 By R. RIDGWAY
North and South America : their Geography, Resources, and Commerce. (Meiklejohn.)
The Future of South America. By ROGER W BABSON.
Senior Geography of South America. By G. C. FRY

The Literary History of Spanish America. By ALFRED COESTER.
A Brief Bibliography of Books in English, Spanish, and Portuguese relating to the Republics commonly called Latin American. By PETER H. GOLDSMITH.
The Americas. Macmillan's Geographical Exercise Books. By B. C. WALLIS.
The Americas. Beginners' Regional Geography By J B. REYNOLDS.
A Regional Geography of the Americas. By LEONARD BROOKS.
Pampas and Wilds of the South the Argentine and Patagonia. (Little People in Far-off Lands.) By FLORENCE A. TARBELL.
Baedeker of the Argentine Republic. 4th edition. By ALBERT B. MARTINEZ.
The Argentine through English Eyes. By J A. HAMMERTON.
The Black Princess and other Fairy Tales from Brazil. By CHRISTIE T YOUNG.
The Neutrality of Latin-America. By SANTIAGO PÉREZ-TRIANA.
The Pan-American Financial Conference of 1915. By SANTIAGO PÉREZ-TRIANA.

1917 Paraguay. By W H. KOEBEL.
Argentina. By H. STEPHENS.
Brazil, To-day and To-morrow. By L. E. ELLIOTT.
Latin America and the United States. Addresses by ELIHU ROOT, collected and edited by R. BACON and J. B. SCOTT.
Argentina and Uruguay By H. J GORDON ROSS.
Quito to Bogotá. By C. VEATCH.
The Pacific Ocean in History : Papers and Addresses presented at the Panama-Pacific Historical Congress, 1915. Edited by H. MORSE STEPHENS and H. E. BOLTON.
Spanish Reader of South American History Edited, with Notes, Exercises and Vocabulary, by EDWARD WATSON SUPPLE.
Distribution of Bird Life in Colombia. By F M. CHAPMAN

1918 South America and the War. By F A. KIRKPATRICK.
South America, an Industrial and Commercial Field. By W H. KOEBEL.
Rise of the Spanish American Republics as told in the Lives of their Liberators. By WILLIAM SPENCE ROBERTSON
Understanding South America. By C. SEDGWICK COOPER.
My Life in the Argentine Republic. By CHARLES DARBYSHIRE.
The Brazilian Green Book consisting of Diplomatic Documents relating to Brazil's Attitude with regard to the European War, 1914–1917 Authorized English Version, with Introduction and Notes. By ANDREW BOYLE.
Medical Report of the Rice Expedition to Brazil. By W T. COUNCILMAN and R. A. LAMBERT.
Far Away and Long Ago : A History of My Early Life. By W H. HUDSON.
Manual of Argentine Railways for 1918. By STEPHEN H. M. KILLIK.
Argentina Commercially Considered. (Syren and Shipping.)
Brazil. By J D. McEWAN
Recommendations on International Law and Official Commentary thereon of the Second Pan-American Scientific Congress, Washington, 27 December 1915 –8 January 1916. Edited by JAMES BROWN SCOTT.
The Quest of El Dorado, the Most Romantic Episode in the History of the South American Conquest. By JOHN AUGUSTINE ZAHM.

1919 South America Pilot. Revised Supplements. Issued by the Admiralty
British Mission to South America. Correspondence. H.M. Stationery Office.
In the Wilds of South America. By LEO E. MILLER.
Vagabonding down the Andes, being the Narrative of a Journey, chiefly Afoot, from Panama to Buenos Aires. By HARRY A. FRANCK.
Arbitration Treaty between the United Kingdom and Uruguay, signed at Montevideo, 18 April 1918. H.M. Stationery Office.
The Great South Land The River Plate and Southern Brazil of To-day By W H. KOEBEL.

BIBLIOGRAPHY.

The Battle of the Falkland Islands : Before and After. By COMMANDER H. SPENCER-COOPER.
Falklands, Jutland, and the Bight. By COMMANDER HON BARRY BINGHAM.
Brazil : Past, Present, and Future. By J C. OAKENFULL.
Early Effects of the War upon the Finance, Commerce, and Industry of Peru. By L. S. ROWE.
The Economic Development of the Argentine Republic in the last Fifty Years. (Ernesto Tornquist & Co., Ltd.)
The Mystery of Easter Island : The Story of an Expedition. By Mrs. SCORESBY ROUTLEDGE.
The Pacific : its Past and Future, and the Policy of the Great Powers from the Eighteenth Century. By GUY H. SCHOLEFIELD.
Rise of the Spanish Empire in the Old World and the New. By ROGER BIGELOW MERRIMAN.

1920 Men, Manners, and Morals in South America. By J O. P. BLAND.
The Royal Mail War Book. By H. W. LESLIE. With Foreword by LORD KYLSANT, G.C.M.G.
Spanish America : its Romance, Reality, and Future. By C. R. ENOCK.
Cartagena and the Banks of the Sinu. By R. B. CUNNINGHAME GRAHAM.
Birds of La Plata. By W H. HUDSON.
The Brazilians and Their Country. By C. S. COOPER.
Bolivia's Case for the League of Nations. By JOSÉ CARRASCO. With an Introduction by ANDREW BOYLE.
Antorio Conselheiro (Brazilian Mystic). By R. B. CUNNINGHAME GRAHAM.
Argentines of To-day   Edited by WILLIAM BELMONT PARKER.
Chilians of To-day   Edited by WILLIAM BELMONT PARKER.
Peruvians of To-day   Edited by WILLIAM BELMONT PARKER.

1921 Argentine International Trade under Incontrovertible Papèr Money, 1880–1900. By JOHN H. WILLIAMS.
The States of South America. By C. W DOMVILLE-FIFE.
Studies in Spanish-American Literature. By I. GOLDBERG.
Pan-Americanism : Its Beginnings. By J R. LOCKLEY.
Casual Letters from South America. By WILLIAM BELMONT PARKER.
El Inca Garcilasso de la Vega. By JULIA FITZMAURICE-KELLY.
Paraguayans of To-day   Edited by WILLIAM BELMONT PARKER.
Uruguayans of To-day   Edited by WILLIAM BELMONT PARKER.
Bolivians of To-day. Edited by WILLIAM BELMONT PARKER.
Anglo-South American Handbook for 1921. Edited by W H. KOEBEL.
Collection Tariff Exchange Tables. Issued by the Anglo-South American Bank, Ltd.

1922 Working North from Patagonia. By HARRY A. FRANK.
The Argentine Republic Its Development and Progress. By PIERRE DENIS. (Trans. JOSEPH MCCABE.)
Conquest of New Granada. R. B. CUNNINGHAME GRAHAM.

1923 The New Argentina. By W. H. KOEBEL.
Quito to Bogotá. By A. G. VEATCH. With introduction by LORD MURRAY OF ELIBANK.
Hispanic-American Relations with the U.S. By WM. SPENCER ROBERTSON Edited by DAVID KINLEY.
South American Jungle Tales. By H. QUIROGA.
Admirals of the Caribbean. By FRANCIS RUSSELL HART.
Inca Land. By HIRAM BINGHAM.

STEAMSHIP SERVICES

STEAMSHIP SERVICES.

BRITISH.

Argentine Navigation Company (N. Mihanovich), Ltd.

Head Office   35 Lime Street, E.C.3.

Buenos Aires Office : 25 de Mayo 199, Buenos Aires.

Branches at Asunción, Montevideo, Rosario.

Directors . London   Lord Kylsant, G.C.M.G. (Chairman), John C. Gibson, C.B.E., Arthur Cook, T H. Carlton Levick, C.B.E., Comm. Mario Perrone. Buenos Aires—Alberto A. Dodero (Chairman), Luis Dodero, José A. Dodero, Hilary H Leng, F l'Estrange Wallace.

South American Fleet   33 passenger steamers, 24 cargo vessels, 55 tugs, also steam launches, lighters, etc.

Fares   Buenos Aires to Asunción—1st class, $120, 3rd class, $60. Montevideo to Salto—1st class, $20, 3rd class, $10.

Service   Nightly in either direction between Buenos Aires and Montevideo. Bi-weekly   Alto Paraná service between Montevideo and Buenos Aires and Corrientes and Posadas.   Paraguayan bi-weekly service to Asunción and fortnightly to Corumbá.

Booker Line.

Head Office : Booker Bros., McConnell & Co., Ltd., 77 The Albany, Liverpool.

Sailings from Liverpool to British Guiana, about every three weeks.

The Booth Steamship Company, Ltd.

Head Office : Cunard Building, Liverpool.

London Office   11 Adelphi Terrace, W.C.2.

Directors   Charles Booth (Chairman), Sir Alfred Booth, Bart., George Macaulay Booth, Enfield Emile Fletcher, Wynn Harold Tregoning, C.B.E., Clement W Jones, C.B.

Correspondents   Argentina—Buenos Aires (Wilson, Sons, & Co., Ltd.), La Plata (Wilson, Sons, & Co., Ltd.).

Brazil : Bahia (Wilson, Sons, & Co., Ltd.), Cabedello (Julius von Söhsten & Co.), Camocim (Nicolau & Carneiro), Ceará (Booth & Co. [London], Ltd.), Itacoatiara (Isbar Perez & Co.), Florianopolis (Guilherme H. Chaplin), Maceió (R. W B. Paterson & Co.), Manáos (Booth & Co. [London], Ltd.), Maranhão (Booth & Co. [London], Ltd.), Natal (Julius von Söhsten), Pará (Booth & Co. [London], Ltd.), Parnahyba (Booth & Co. [London], Ltd.), Paranaguá (Empreza de Melhoramentos Urbanos de Paranaguá), Pernambuco (Julius von Söhsten & Co.), Rio de Janeiro (Wilson, Sons, & Co., Ltd.), Rio Grande do Sul (Wilson, Sons, & Co., Ltd.), São Francisco (R. O'N Addison), Santos (Wilson, Sons, & Co., Ltd.), Victoria (Arbuckle & Co.).
Uruguay : Montevideo (Williams & Co.).
Panamá   Panamá City (W Andrews & Co.).
Peru   Iquitos (Booth & Co. [London], Ltd.).

Services   (1) Liverpool to Pará and Manáos via Havre, Vigo, Leixões (Oporto), Lisbon, and Madeira ; returning via Madeira, Lisbon, and Leixões. Sailings : monthly Duration of voyage, 2 months.

(2) Liverpool to Maranhão, Tutoya Bay (Parnahyba), and Ceará via Leixões and Lisbon; returning via Portugal and Continental ports. Sailings : monthly. Duration of voyage, 2¼ months.

(3) New York to Maranhão, Pará, and Manáos via Barbados, returning to New York, via Barbados. Sailings : monthly Duration of voyage, 2 months.

(4) New York to Pará, Ceará, Maceió, Pernambuco, and Cabedello; returning to New York via Ceará and Pará. Sailings monthly Duration of voyage, 2 months.

(5) New York to Rio de Janeiro, Santos, and Rio Grande do Sul, returning to New York via Santos and Rio de Janeiro. Sailings : monthly Duration of voyage, 3 months.

The British and Argentine Steam Navigation Company, Ltd.

(Furness, Withy & Co., Ltd., managers.)

Head Office : 53 Leadenhall Street, E.C.3.

Cables : "Uruguayo, London."

Telegrams : "Uruguayo, Fen, London."

Telephones : Avenue 5504.

Branch Office 201 Royal Liver Building, Liverpool.

Cables and Telegrams : "Uruguayo, Liverpool."

Telephone : Bank 8890.

Directors : Sir Frederick William Lewis, Bart (Chairman), R. E. Burnett, Sir John Esplen, Bart., K.B.E., F H. Houlder, W C. Warwick, M. C. Houlder, S. J. Forster.

Manager and Secretary : J P Stewart.

Assistant Secretary : W P Watson.

Agents : Furness, Withy & Co., Ltd., at Cardiff, Newcastle, etc.; Houlder Bros. & Co., Ltd., at Buenos Aires and other River Plate ports, Liverpool, etc.

South American Fleet : The British and Argentine Steam Navigation Co., Ltd., 3 steamers, of a total gross tonnage of 29,500 tons; the associated Furness-Houlder Argentine Lines, Ltd., 6 steamers, of a total gross tonnage of 61,000 tons.
Regular services between London and Argentine, Uruguayan, and Brazilian ports; and Liverpool and Argentine and Uruguayan ports. Intermediate sailings between Newport, Mon., etc., and Argentine and Uruguayan ports.
Sailings from London and Liverpool fortnightly, intermediate services monthly.
Passenger fare to Argentine ports, £45 single, £76 return. First-class passengers only carried.
Duration of voyage by London and Liverpool services, 19–20 days.

Donaldson South American Line, Ltd.

Head Office 14 St. Vincent Place, Glasgow

London Office : Donaldson Bros., Ltd., 16 Gracechurch Street, E.C.

Liverpool Office : Donaldson Bros., Ltd., Cunard Building, Water Street.

Buenos Aires Office : J E. Turner & Co., Casilla 905.

Montevideo Office : J. R. Williams & Co., Calle Cerrito, 382.

Santos Office G. C. Dickinson & Co.

Joint Managers : Donaldson Bros., Ltd.; John Black & Co., Ltd.

Routes : Glasgow and Liverpool to Montevideo and Buenos Aires.

Sailings : Approximately three-weekly No passengers are carried.

Elders and Fyffes, Ltd.

Head Office 31–32 Bow Street, Covent Garden, London, W.C.

Branch Offices : Avonmouth Dock, Bristol, and at Birmingham, Brighton, Cardiff, Chatham, Glasgow, Hull, Leeds, Liverpool, Manchester, Newcastle-on-Tyne, Plymouth, Portsmouth, Sheffield, Southampton, Woolwich, Rotterdam, Las Palmas, Teneriffe, Jamaica, Costa Rica, Cristóbal, and Santa Marta.

Directors : A. H. Stockley, A. R. Ackerley, H. Stockley, R. Clark, A. W Preston, M. C. Keith.

Fleet : Bayano (6,500 tons), Camito (6,500), Coronado (6,500), Changuinola (6,000), Motagua (6,000), Patuca (6,000), Chirripo (5,500), Zent (5,500), Manistee (5,500), Patia (5,500), Reventazon (5,500), Tortuguero (5,500), Greenbrier (4,800), Miami (4,600), Manzanares (4,200), Barranca (4,100), Nicoya (3,900), Pacuare (3,900), Matina (3,870). Building Cavina (6,500), Aracataca (5,500), Aguan (5,500).

Services Avonmouth, Liverpool, and Hull to Bermuda, Kingston, Jamaica, Barbados, Trinidad, Port Limón (Costa Rica), Cristóbal (Panamá), Santa Marta (Colombia), and Tela (Honduras).

Fares : From £30 single, £50 return. Duration of voyage To Kingston, 14–15 days; to other ports, 18–19 days; round trip, 34–35 days.
The fleet does not carry cargo outwards.

The Furness-Houlder Argentine Lines, Ltd.

(See The British and Argentine Steam Navigation Company, Ltd.)

Furness, Withy, & Co., Ltd.

(See The British and Argentine Steam Navigation Company, Ltd.)

Gulf Line.

Proprietors : Nautilus Steam Shipping Company

Directors and Managers : F & W Ritson, 30 West Sunniside, Sunderland, the Head Office.

AGENTS IN THE UNITED KINGDOM AND IN EUROPE.

London : C. Howard & Sons, 45–6 Leadenhall Street, E.C.3.
Liverpool Wm. Nicol & Co., 18 James Street.
Glasgow : Gulf Line Agency, 29 Waterloo Street.
South Wales : F & W Ritson, 50–51 George Street, Cardiff.
Tyne : Sharp & Co., Milburn House.
Antwerp : Wescott & Co., 21 Canal des Brasseurs.
Hamburg : D. Fuhrmann, Alsterthor 21.

Agents : Chile—Corral, C. Prochelle, Lebu, Cia. Carbinifera los Rios de Curanilahue; Coronel, Franklin and Co.; Lota, Jorge Walker; Talcuhuano and Penco, Talcahuano Agencies Co.; Tomé, Antofagasta, Mejillones, Caleta, and Coloso, Gibbs & Co.; Valparaiso, Allardice & Co., Los Vilos, H. C. Streeter; Guayacan, Fundicion Guayacan, Coquimbo, Jenkins & Co.; Huasco, Craig, Vance & Co.; Carrizal Bajo, Soc. Minas y Fundiciones, Caldera, H. B. Beazley; Chanaral, Sheriff Hnos; Taltal, Williamson, Balfour & Co., Tocopilla, Anglo-Chilian Nitrate & Railway Co., Ltd., Iquique and Caleta Buena, Buchanan Jones & Co.; Junin, Cia. de Salitres y F C. de Junin; Pisagua, L. J Garratt; Arica, Thomas Bradley

Ecuador : Guayaquil, Soc. Comercial Anglo-Ecuatoriana Ltda.

Peru : Ilo, Agencia Maritima Peruana, Mollendo, Mollendo Agencies Co.; Pisco, Tomas Bull & Co., Tambo de Mora, T C. Conroy, Cerro Azul, Agencia Maritima y Commercial, de C. A., Ltda., Samanco, Soc. Agricola Nepeña, Ltda.; Callao, Paita and Huacho, Duncan, Fox & Co.; Casma, Juan E. Reyra, Supe, E. Ayulo & Co.,

Chimbote, Agencia Juan Dalman; Salaverry and Guanape, Gonzales Larranga Hnos, Pacasmayo, C. G. Salas y Salinas, Eten, F C. de Eten, Talara, London and Pacific Petroleum Co., Lobitos, Lobitos Oilfields, Ltd., Chicama, Gildemeister & Co.; Pimentel, Vda. de Piedra é hijos.

Services   About every three weeks, from Glasgow, Liverpool, and South Wales, and also from Tyne, Antwerp, and London, also from Hamburg and Rotterdam to Chile, Peru, and Ecuador. Some steamers proceed via Panama Canal and others via the Magellan Straits.

Cargo vessels with limited passenger accommodation.

Thos. & Jas. Harrison.

Head Office   Mersey Chambers, Liverpool.

London Office   Dock House, Billiter Street, E.C.

Loading Berth   Brunswick Dock, Liverpool.

Fleet   50 steamers, with total gross tonnage of 246,943.

Services   To Pernambuco, Maceió, Cabedello, Arucaju, Natal, Barbados, Trinidad, and other West Indies. Demerara, La Guaira, Puerto Cabello, Curacao, Puerto Colombia, Cartagena, Cristóbal (with transhipment via Panama Canal to West Coast Central, and South America and Mexico), Puerto Cortes, Puerto Barrios, Livingston and Belize, Kingston (Jamaica), Bermuda, and Nassau.

Harrison " Direct Line " Steamers.

Agents : Prentice, Service & Henderson, 175 West George Street, Glasgow

Regular fortnightly sailings from London and Glasgow to Barbados, Trinidad, Grenada and other West Indian Islands, and Demerara.
(See also Thomas and James Harrison.)

Houlder Brothers and Company, Ltd.

(See also The British and Argentine Steam Navigation Company, Ltd.)

Head Office : 53 Leadenhall Street, London, E.C.3.

Offices   Argentina—Buenos Aires, Rosario de Santa Fé, La Plata, Bahia Blanca; Uruguay : Montevideo.
Brazil : Rio de Janeiro, Santos.

From London and Liverpool to Montevideo and Buenos Aires. Passage 20–21 days. Also South Wales and Antwerp to River Plate ports. Homewards from Patagonia and River Plate to London, Liverpool and other ports with frozen and chilled meat and general cargo.

Passenger Fares   To Buenos Aires, £45, from Buenos Aires, £40, or £76 return. Between September 1 and December 31, outwards, and March 1 and June 30, homewards, single fares are subject to an increase of £5.   Children   1 child under 2 years, free, between 2 and 6 years, a quarter fare is charged, and 6 to 12 years, half fare.

Lamport and Holt Line.

Head Office : Royal Liver Building, Liverpool.

Telegrams : "Lamport, Liverpool." Telephone : Bank 8850.

London Office : 36 Lime Street, E.C.3.

Telegrams : "Lamport, Led., London." Telephone : Avenue 6550.

Manchester Office : York Buildings, 21 York Street.

STEAMSHIP SERVICES.

Telegrams   "Lamport, Manchester."   Telephone : City 2100.

New York Office   42 Broadway

Telegrams   "Lamport, New York."

Rio de Janeiro Office   Avenida Rio Branco.

Telegramas :   "Lamport "

Buenos Aires Office   Edificio Britanico.

Telegramas :   "Lamport."

Directors   Lord Kylsant, G.C.M.G. (Chairman) , The Right Hon. Viscount Pirrie, K.P., P.C., The Most Hon. the Marquess of Carisbrooke, G.C.V.O., George H. Melly, Arthur Cook (Managing Directors).
There are agents in the principal towns of Argentina and Brazil, and also at Valparaiso and Lima.

Fleet   49 steamers of a gross tonnage of 320,039 tons (excluding tugs, etc.).

Routes   (1) From Liverpool, Glasgow, and Manchester to Brazil, via Portugal.

(2) From Liverpool and Glasgow to the River Plate, via Spain.

(3) From Middlesbrough, Hamburg, Antwerp, London, and Cardiff to the River Plate.

(4) From New York to North Brazil, and vice versa.

(5) From New York to Central and South Brazil.

(6) From New York to River Plate ports.

(7) From Brazil to New York.

(8) From Brazil to New Orleans.

(9) From Buenos Aires and Brazil to the United Kingdom and Continent.

(10) From Buenos Aires to Brazil and New York.

(11) From New Orleans and the River Plate.

The chief passenger service is that between New York, Brazil, and the River Plate, calling at the West Indies.
Sailings   The service from the United Kingdom to South America and from New York to South America is fortnightly
Voyage from the United Kingdom to Buenos Aires (via Brazil), about 24 days; from New York to Buenos Aires (via Brazil), about 21 days.
Fares   New York to Rio de Janeiro—1st class, $160, 2nd class, $125, 3rd class, $75. New York to Montevideo—1st class, $200, 2nd class, $160; 3rd class, $95. New York to Buenos Aires—1st class, $200, 2nd class, $160; 3rd class, $100.
Suites and staterooms from New York to South American Atlantic ports from $590 to $1,450.
[See Index to Advertisers.]

Leyland Line.
Frederick Leyland and Company, Ltd.

Head Office : 27 and 29 James Street, Liverpool. (Telegrams   "Leyland.")

London Offices : 38 Leadenhall Street, E.C.3. (Telegrams   "Lerum, Led, London"); 1 Cockspur Street, S.W.1. (Telegrams   "Vessels, Westrand, London.")

Directors : Charles Franklin Torrey (Chairman), The Right Hon. Viscount Pirrie, K.P., P.C., W Roberts, O.B.E., H. A. Sanderson.

Agents : La Guaira—Anglo-Venezuelan Trust & Agency, Ltd. Puerto Cabello : Boulton & Co.   Barranquilla : Cia-Anglo-Colombia de Comisiones.   Cartagena Pombo Hnos & Co. Cristóbal : W Andrews & Co. Port Limón : Maduro and Sons, Ltd. Vera Cruz (Mexico) : J H. Drake. Tampico Pulford Bros.

Fleet : 42 steamers, gross tonnage, 288,251 tons.

Sailings   Fortnightly to Barbados, Trinidad, La Guaira, Puerto Colombia, Curaçoa, Cartagena; Colón and Cristóbal for Pacific ports, Kingston (Jamaica), Vera Cruz , Tampico, Progreso, and Puerto Mexico.

Lloyd Royal Belge (Great Britain), Ltd.
Late Brys & Gylsen, Ltd.

Head Office : 101 Leadenhall Street, London, E.C.3.

Telegrams : "Llodroybel."

Telephone : Avenue 3712–3713.

Directors : Senator Arthur Brys (Chairman), H. M. Gylsen (Managing Director), Arm Grisar.

For further particulars, see Lloyd Royal Belge.

MacIver Line.

Head Office : 31 James Street, Liverpool.

London Office : 6 Lloyd's Avenue, E.C.3.

Buenos Aires Manager : W Allinson Bell, 240–50 Reconquista, Buenos Aires.

Directors : The Right Hon. Lord Kylsant, G.C.M.G.; Sir Charles MacIver; Charles Livingston, Edward S. MacIver (Managing Directors).

Fleet : 6 steamers; dead weight capacity, 36,142 tons.

Routes : Liverpool to Montevideo, Buenos Aires, and Rosario (without transhipment).

Average passage, about 24 days. Special attention to shipments of pedigree livestock.
[See Index to Advertisers.]

Nautilus Steam Shipping Company.
(See Gulf Line.)

H. & W. Nelson, Ltd.
Managers of the
Nelson Line (Liverpool), Ltd.,
and the
Nelson Steam Navigation Company, Ltd.

Head Office : 98 Leadenhall Street, London, E.C.3.

Cables and Telegrams : "Nelsonian, Fen, London."

Telephone : Avenue 5070.

Liverpool Office : 20 Water Street.

Cables and Telegrams : "Nelsonian, Liverpool."

Buenos Aires Office : Edificio Britanico, Reconquista, 314.

La Plata Office : Gran Dock.

Agents : Rio de Janeiro—Royal Mail Steam Packet Co.; Wilson, Sons, & Co. Montevideo : Christophersen Hnos.

Routes : London and Liverpool to Canary Islands, Brazil, River Plate, via French, Spanish, and Portuguese ports.

Sailings : Alternate Thursdays from London. Frequent service from Liverpool.

The steamers have accommodation for the finer descriptions of cargo, and, having mail packet privileges at Buenos Aires, proceed direct to the mail berths and discharge there. Limited accommodation on the outward voyage for pedigree livestock.
[See Index to Advertisers.]

Nelson Line (Liverpool) Ltd.
(See H. & W Nelson, Ltd.)

STEAMSHIP SERVICES.

The Nelson Steam Navigation Company, Ltd.
(See H. & W Nelson, Ltd.)

The Pacific Steam Navigation Company.
(See The Royal Mail Steam Packet Company.)

Prince Line, Ltd.

Head Office : 56 Leadenhall Street, London, E.C.3.

Directors : Sir Frederick Wm. Lewis, Bart., R. E. Burnett, S. J. Forster, H. E. Weddell, N. Stockdale, H. C. Blackiston.

Agents : Middlesbrough—Furness, Withy & Co., Ltd., Zetland Buildings.

Antwerp : The Furness Shipping and Agency Co., Ltd.

United States : Furness, Withy & Co., Ltd., New York; M. & R. Warriner, Inc., New Orleans.

Argentina : Houlder Bros. & Co., Ltd., Buenos Aires, Rosario, La Plata, Bahia Blanca.

Brazil : Higson Brooks & Co., Pará, Logan Griffith, Pernambuco, Conde & Co., Bahia; Hard, Rand & Co., Victoria; Houlder Bros. & Co., Ltd., Rio de Janeiro and Santos; Ed. Wigg & Sons, Rio Grande do Sul.

Uruguay : Houlder Brothers & Co., Montevideo.

Fleet : 38 steamers ranging 5,000–10,000 tons dead weight.

South American Services : Middlesbrough, Antwerp, and London to River Plate ports, monthly; New York to Brazil and River Plate ports, fortnightly; River Plate to Brazil, monthly; Brazil to New Orleans and New York, fortnightly

Steamers running on these services have only limited passenger accommodation.

Nitrate Producers' Steam Ship Co., Ltd.

Head Office : Billiter Street, London, E.C.3.

Directors : Sir John Latta, Bart. (Chairman), Thomas S. Short, J.P., Robert A. Lawther, Gilbert G. Blane, J.P

Managers : Lawther, Latta & Co., Ltd.

Routes : (1) Clyde and Bristol Channel ports to the West Coast of South America, via the Magellan Straits, and thence to the United States, (2) West Coast of South America to Australia.

Cargo : Nitrate.

The Royal Mail Steam Packet Company.
(Established by Royal Charter, 1839.)

[See Index to Advertisers.]

The Pacific Steam Navigation Company.
(Established by Royal Charter, 1840.)

[See Index to Advertisers.]

The Royal Mail Steam Packet Company.

Head Office : Royal Mail House, Moorgate, London, E.C.2.

Telegrams : "Omarius Ave," London.

Telephone : London Wall 6460 (10 lines).

Directors . Lord Kylsant, G.C.M.G. (Chairman and Managing Director), The Duke of Abercorn, K.P., John William Clark, A. Nevile Lubbock, Sir Leslie Scott, K.C., M.P.

General Manager : P G. M. Mitchell. Assistant Managers J Allsop and H. A. P. Cotton. Secretary D. I. Conradi.

Fleet : 48 vessels, with a gross tonnage (including tugs, launches, etc.) of 379,490 tons. The fleets of the companies closely affiliated with the management of the R.M.S.P. Co. represent a gross tonnage 1,774,122 tons.

[See Index to Advertisers.]

STEAMSHIP SERVICES.

The Pacific Steam Navigation Company.

Head Office   Goree, Water Street, Liverpool.

Telegrams   "Pacific," Liverpool.

Telephone   Bank 9150 (14 lines).

Directors   Lord Kylsant, G.C.M.G. (Chairman), The Duke of Abercorn, K.P., A. Nevile Lubbock, J G. Nicholson, Viscount Pirrie, K.P., P.C., Thos. Rome , J W Clark.

General Manager   William Lewis. Assistant Managers   Albert Whiteside and Ed. James. Secretary   Thos. T Ford.

Fleet : 32 vessels, with a gross tonnage of 189,210 tons (including tugs, launches, etc.).

SOUTH AMERICAN ROUTES

of the R.M.S.P. and P.S.N.C.

East Coast :—

Via France, Spain, Portugal, and Atlantic Islands.

(1) Fortnightly by "A" Steamers from Southampton and Cherbourg. Usual ports of call : Coruña, Vigo, Leixoes (Oporto), Lisbon, Madeira, St. Vincent (C.V.), Pernambuco, Bahia, Rio de Janeiro, Santos, Montevideo, and Buenos Aires for West Coast Ports (via Andes).

(2) Fortnightly by "D" Steamers from Liverpool and Cherbourg. Usual ports of call : Coruña, Villagarcia, Vigo, Leixoes (Oporto), Lisbon, Bahia, Rio de Janeiro, Santos, Montevideo, and Buenos Aires (for West Coast Ports via Andes).

(3) By "O" Steamers—Liverpool, La Rochelle-Pallice, Coruna, Vigo, Leixoes (Oporto), Lisbon, Rio de Janeiro, Montevideo (for Buenos Aires) Port Stanley (F.I.), Punta Arenas, Coronel, Talcahuano, Valparaiso, Antofagasta, Iquique, Arica, Mollendo, Callao, Panamá, Cristobal, Havana, Spanish Ports, La Pallice, Liverpool.
(4) Intermediate Service from Glasgow, Liverpool, Hull, London, and Continental Ports, as inducement offers, for France, Spain, River Plate, Bahia Blanca, Port Stanley, Punta Arenas, and West Coast Ports.

West Coast :—

(5) From Liverpool to La Rochelle-Pallice, Coruña, Vigo, Havana, Cristóbal, Balboa, Callao, Mollendo, Arica, Iquique, Antofagasta, Coquimbo, Valparaiso, Talcahuano, and Coronel, and other South Pacific and Central American Ports by transhipment at Isthmus.

(6) By"E" Steamers from New York to Havana, Cristóbal, Balboa, Callao, Mollendo, Arica, Iquique, Antofagasta, and Valparaiso, also other South Pacific and Central American Ports by transhipment at Isthmus.

(7) From New York via Panamá Canal to Guayaquil.

Local Services :—

(8) Between Cristóbal and Central American (Pacific) Ports up to Champerico.

(9) Between Cristóbal (Atlantic and Pacific) and Colombian and Ecuadorian Ports.

(10) Between Cristóbal and Guayaquil and intermediate ports.

(11) Regular sailings from England via Coruña and Vigo to Havana (Cuba) and Galveston.

(12) From Hamburg, Southampton, and Cherbourg to New York by the "O" Steamers.

(13) From Europe to North Pacific Ports.

(14) Between Canada (Halifax, N.S.) and Demerara (British Guiana) via Bermuda.

R.M.S.P. Meat Transports, Ltd.

Head Office : 17–18 Telegraph Street, London, E.C.2.

The Directors, Secretary, Branch Offices, and Agents are the same as those of the Royal Mail Steam Packet Company

Fleet : 4 vessels, of a total gross tonnage of 35,048 tons. Cargo ships only

Routes   United Kingdom to River Plate.

Sailings : Fortnightly

ARGENTINE.

Braun and Blanchard Line.

About every three weeks from Buenos Aires to Punta Arenas, Talcahuano, and intermediate ports.

Compañia Importadora y Exportadora de la Patagonia.

Fortnightly sailings from Buenos Aires to Punta Arenas, calling at intermediate ports.

Compañia Mercantil y de Transportes "Domingo Barthe."

Head Office   Avenida de Mayo, 490 Buenos Aires.

Directors : Jorge Barthe (President), Rodolfo Barthe (Vice-Chairman), Raúl Barthe, Manuel Patiño, Anibal Barthe, Hector Carvallo.

Passenger and cargo-boats, between Buenos Aires and Asunción, Posadas, and the Falls of Iguazú.

Dodero Hnos., Ltda.

Steamship Owners, Brokers, and Custom House Agents.

Established 1873.

Head Office   Calle 25 de Mayo, 267 Buenos Aires.

Branches at Bahia Blanca, Rosario, Montevideo.

Lloyd Americano.

Soc. Anon. de Navegación.

Head Office   Calle 25 de Mayo, 267 Buenos Aires.

Regular services to the United Kingdom, French, and Italian ports.

BELGIAN.

Lloyd Royal Belge.

Capital   Frs. 5,000,000

President   A. F Brys.   Vice-President : H. Gylsen.

Head Office   24 Longue Rue Neuve, Antwerp.

London Office   See Lloyd Royal Belge (Great Britain), Ltd.

Rio de Janeiro Office : Avenida Rio Branco, 47.

Santos Office   Rua San Antonio, 25.

Bahia Office : Rua São João.

São Paulo Office : Rua Alvares Penteado, 35.

Buenos Aires Office   Calle 25 de Mayo, 214, Cangallo, 215.

Fleet   82 steamers with a tonnage of 550,000 tons. Regular cargo service to all parts of the world from Antwerp and other Continental ports. Passenger and mail service from Antwerp to Brazil and Argentina started in September, 1920.
(See also Lloyd Royal Belge (Great Britain), I,td.)

BRAZILIAN.

Amazon River Steam Navigation Company (1911).

Caixa Postal 469, Pará, Brazil.

Head Office   Pará.
Directors   Dr. Samuel Macdowell (President), F F Urbano Leitao, Dr. Guilherme Paiva (Secretary).
London Correspondents   Binder, Hamlyn & Co., 80 Bishopsgate, E.C.2.

Commercio e Navegação.

Head Office   Rio de Janeiro.
Service between Brazil and Europe, local service between Rio de Janeiro and Manáos, via Victoria, Bahia, etc.

Companhia de Navegação de Maranhão.

Maranhão to Pará, Maranhão to São Bento, Maranhão to Pernambuco, calling at intermediate ports.

Companhia de Navegação S. João da Barra e Campos.

Service on the Parahyba River, calling at ports in States of Rio de Janeiro and Espirito Santo.

Companhia de Viação São Paulo-Matto Grosso.
Established 1908

Head Office : 45 Rua Jose Bonifacio, São Paulo.
500 kilometres trade route between São Paulo and Matto Grosso. Ferry-boat across the Paraná River at Porto Tibiriçia. Regular steamship navigation on the Paraná and tributary rivers.

Companhia Nacional de Navegação Costeira.

Head Office : Caixo do Correio 1032, Rio de Janeiro.
Freight and General Offices   Avenida Rodiques Alves, 303-331 Rio de Janeiro.
Passenger Department : Avenida Rio Branco, 27 Rio de Janeiro.
Telegrams : Costeira.
Under the same administration as Lage Irmãos.
Directors : Henrique Lage (President), Gentil de Mello Araujo (Treasurer), Codrato de Vilhena (Director of Traffic).

STEAMSHIP SERVICES.

AGENTS.

Victoria (Antenor Guimãraes), Ilheus (Luiz da Silva Pinto), Bahia (Isaias de Andrade), Aracjú (Carlos Cruz), Macció (Manoel Ramalho), Recife (Ulysses de Faria Correa), Parahyba (Manoel Raymundo Ferreira Farias), Macau (Vitoldo Zaremba), Areia Branca-Mossoró (Tertuliano Fernandes), São Sebastião (Hilarião Amancio de Moraes), Santos (Alberto Rebustillo), Paranaguá (Euripedes Branco), Antonyna (Joaquim Cardozo), São Francisco (Antonio P de Oliveira), Itajahy (Jayme Silva), Florianopolis (Leonel H. da Luz), Imbituba (Alvaro Catão), Rio Grande do Sul (Pedro Fernandes Braga), Pelotas (Francisco A. Gomes da Costa), Porto Alegre (Mario Murillo Barbosa), São Paulo (Alfredo Freire).

Sailings to all ports bi-weekly

Fleet   22 steamers, with a total tonnage of 28,000 tons.

Companhia Navegação Bahiana.

Service from Bahia north to Sergipe and Pernambuco.

Companhia Pernambucana de Navegação.

Service from Pernambuco to Maranhão; to Bahia; and to Rocca.

Lage Irmãos.

(Companhia Nacional de Navegação Costeira.)

Lloyd Brazileiro.

Head Office   Rio de Janeiro.

Service from Rio de Janeiro   North Line, between Rio de Janeiro and Manáos. South Line, between Rio de Janeiro and Buenos Aires.   Weekly sailings on Fridays and Thursdays respectively   The Company operates many other small lines.

Lloyd Nacional.

Head Office : Rio de Janeiro.

CANADIAN.

Canadian Mexican Pacific.

From Victoria, B.C., monthly to Salina Cruz, calling at Mazatlan, Manzanillo, and Acapulco.

CHILEAN.

Borquez & Cia.

Local service to north and south of Valparaiso.

Compañia Sud-Americana de Vapores.

(The South American Steamship Company.)

Established 1872.

Head Office   Valparaiso.

Services between Valparaiso and Cristóbal, touching at the main intermediate ports; and between Valparaiso and Pimentad (North of Peru), and intermediate ports.

STEAMSHIP SERVICES.

Gonzales, Soffia & Cia.

Weekly service between Valparaiso and Arica, calling at Coquimbo, Huasco, Caldera, Taltal, Antofagasta, Tocopilla, and Iquique.

Soc. Anon. "Menendez Behety."

Regular service between southern Chilean ports and Patagonia.

COLOMBIAN.

Anglo-Colombia Navigation Co.

Buenaventura to San Pablo.

Colombia Railways and Navigation Co., Ltd.,

Between Barranquilla, Cartagena, and La Dorada.

Compañia Antioqueña de Trasportes.

Barranquilla and La Dorada.

Compañia de Navegación del Rio Atrato.

Monthly service between Cartagena and Quibdo.

Compañia de Navegación del Rio Cauca.

Between Calí and Cartago.

Compañia Pérez Rosa.

Navigating the Magdalena River.

Empresa de Navegación F. A. Scharberg.

On the Sinú and Atrato rivers between Cartagena and Quibdo : between Cartagena and Monteria.

Empresa Hanseatica.

Barranquilla and La Dorada.

Empresa Nacional de Los Rios Sinú y Atrato.

Fortnightly service to Sinú and Atrato rivers, and from Cartagena to Monteria.

Empresas Aliadas.

Between Barranquilla and La Dorada, and up the Cauca river.

COSTA RICAN.

Empresa de Trasportes Maritimos del Golfo de Nicoya.

Serves points in the Gulf of Nicoya.

CUBAN.

Empresa Naviera de Cuba, S.A.

Head Office : Havana.
Regular service Havana to other Cuban ports; also to Porto Rico and Dominican Republic.

Isle of Pines Steamship Co.

Daily service between Isle of Pines and mainland. Outwards on Mondays, Wednesdays, and Fridays; inwards on Tuesdays, Thursdays, and Sundays.

DANISH.

Baltic South-American Line.

Head Office : C K. Hansen, Amaliegode, 29B., Copenhagen K.

Regular freight service between Denmark, the Baltic, and Brazil, Uruguay, Argentina, and vice versa.

Det Forenede Dampskibs-Selskab Aktieselskab.
(Copenhagen.)

Directors : A. O. Andersen and Kay Reinhard (Mercantile Directors), J A. Körbing (Technical Director).

Agents :—
London : The United Shipping Co., Ltd., 108 Fenchurch Street, E.C.3.
Telegrams : " Neutral."
Liverpool : N. Johansen & Dahl.
Telegrams : " Dahlia."
Bahia : Schwarz & Brusell.
Telegrams : " Brusell."
Buenos Aires : Scandinavian South-American Shipping Co., Ltd.
Telegrams " Scandship."
Rio de Janeiro : Cumming Young.
Telegrams : " Young."
Santos : G. C. Dickinson & Co.
Telegrams : " Dickinson."
The fleet consists of 118 vessels with a gross register tonnage of 211,581

Det Sydamerikanske Plantageselskab.

(South American Forest Industry Shipping Co.)
Copenhagen.

DUTCH.

Koninklijke Hollandsche Lloyd.
(Royal Holland Lloyd.)

Head Office: Post Handelskade 12, Amsterdam.

London Agents: Wainwright Bros. & Co., 21 Fenchurch Street, E.C.3. D. H. Drakeford, 60 Haymarket, S.W.1.

Directors: M. H. de Beaufort, J Foudraine, L. A. Hissink.

Agencies in South America :—

Argentina :—Buenos Aires (Lloyd Real Holandés, 240 Reconquista 250). Rosario (J C. Lea.)

Brazil Pernambuco and Cabedello (Julius von Söhsten & Co.), Bahia (Conde & Co.); Rio de Janeiro (Sociedade Anonyma Martinelli, 106 Avenida Rio Branco); Santos (Sociedade Anonyma Martinelli, Rua 15 de Novembre, Caixa 166), Ceará (Leite Barboza & Co.), Rio Grande do Sul (E. Wigg & Sons.).

Uruguay Montevideo (Antonio Piaggio, 425 Piedras).

Fleet: 16 steamers, with gross tonnage of 141,503.

Passenger and Freight Services: three-weekly to Brazil, Uruguay, and Argentina.

Freight Services: Fortnightly to South America.

Koninklijke West-Indische Maildienst.
(Royal Netherlands West-India Mail.)

Head Office: Amsterdam.

Directors: E. Heldring, P Den Tex, J van Hasselt, D. Hudig, S. M. D. Valster

Fortnightly service of passenger steamers from Hamburg, Amsterdam, Dover, and Boulogne to Barbados, Trinidad, La Guayra, Puerto-Cabello, Curaçao, Puerto Colombia, Cartagena, Cristóbal, Puerto Limón, and back to Plymouth, Hâvre, Amsterdam, and Hamburg.

Four-weekly service of passenger steamers from Amsterdam to Madeira, Paramaribo, Demerara, Barbados, Trinidad, Carupano, and back to Hâvre and Amsterdam.

Weekly service of passenger and cargo steamers New York to Haiti, Venezuela, and Curaçao and vice versa.

Three-weekly service of cargo steamers from Hamburg, Bremen, and Amsterdam to Cap Haitien, Puerto Plata, Sanchez, San Pedro de Macoris, San Domingo City, Jacmel, Aux Cayes, Port au Prince, Santiago de Cuba, Puerto Cortez, Puerto Barrios, and Livingston, and back via Kingston, Haitien, Dominican ports, and San Juan de Porto Rico to Hâvre, Amsterdam, and Hamburg.

Fortnightly service of cargo steamers from Hamburg, Amsterdam, Rotterdam, Antwerp, and London to Kingston, via Panamá Canal to the Pacific ports of South America, and back to European destinations.

DUTCH GUIANA.

Government steamship service between Paramaribo, Burnside, Nickerie and Georgetown; sailings weekly

FRENCH.

Chargeurs Réunis.

Head Office (Administration, Booking, and Freight): 3 Boulevard Malesherbes, Paris.

Telegrams · "Chargeurs."

Telephone: Elysées 69–29A, 69–35.

STEAMSHIP SERVICES.

Directors : Denis Perouse (Chairman), Léon Fould (Vice-Chairman), Ch. Ledoux, H. de Clermont, E. de Sincay, J de Sayve, J Boissonnas, J Exbrayat, A. Celier, Gaston Breton (Managing Director).

Agents or Representatives in most towns in Argentina, Brazil, Chile, Paraguay, Peru, and Uruguay.

Routes and Sailings :—

Accelerated services : Hamburg to River Plate. Every fourteen days from Hamburg, Antwerp, Hâvre, La Rochelle-Pallice, for Bilbao, Coruña or Villagarcia, or Vigo, Leixoes or Lisbon, Dakar, Rio de Janeiro, Montevideo, Buenos Aires.

Regular services : Antwerp to River Plate. Every 28 days from Antwerp, Dunkirk, Hâvre, Teneriffe, Montevideo, Buenos Aires.

Antwerp to Brazil-River Plate. Every 28 days from Antwerp, Hâvre, Bordeaux, Leixoes, Lisbon, Maceió, Rio de Janeiro, Santos, Buenos Aires.

Hamburg to Brazil. Every 28 days from Hamburg, Antwerp, Dunkirk, Hâvre, Leixoes, Lisbon, Pernambuco, Bahia, Rio de Janeiro, Santos, Rio Grande do Sul.

Compagnie de Navigation Sud-Atlantique.
(3 Boulevard Malesherbes, Paris.)

Mail Service : Every 28 days from Bordeaux to Vigo, Lisbon, Rio de Janeiro, Santos, Montevideo, Buenos Aires (passengers, all classes).

Cargo and Passenger Service : Every 28 days from Bordeaux to Coruña, Oporto (Leixoes), Lisbon, Dakar, Pernambuco or Bahia (alternately), Rio de Janeiro, Santos, Montevideo, Buenos Aires.

Compagnie Générale Transatlantique.

Head Office : 6 Rue Auber, Paris.

Agent General : P Le Brun, 22 Pall Mall, S.W.1.

Chairman : John dal Piaz.

This Company has agents in most cities in Central and South America, including Barranquilla (Banque Dugand), Bogotá (Ruperto Campos), Callao (Colonia Rehder et cie.), Cayenne (M. Magny), Concepción (M. Gibbs), Demerara (Wieting and Richter), Guatemala City (Beyré & Co.), Guayaquil (Reyre), Havana (Ernest Gaye), Maracaibo (M. Roche), Mexico City (F. Burgunder), Rio de Janeiro (D'Orey & Co.), San José de Costa Rica (MM. Tournon), San Miguel (M. Meardi), Santiago and Valparaiso (F Broom).

Services include : Hâvre, Plymouth, and Bordeaux to Colón (passengers and freight —15 to 18 days) ; Anvers-Hâvre-Cuba-Mexico (freight) ; Antwerp-Hâvre-Bordeaux-South and North Pacific (freight), Saint Nazaire-Colón (passengers and freight—15 to 18 days) ; Saint Nazaire-Havana-Vera Cruz (passengers and freight—12 to 15 days, Le Hâvre, Spanish ports, Havana, New Orleans (passengers and freight).

Société Générale de Transports Maritimes a Vapeur.
5 Rue de Surène, Paris.

Directors : André Babeau (President), Hubert Giraud, Paul Daher, Brenier.

Agents in South America : Argentina—Luis Nicol, Reconquista 433, Buenos Aires.

Brazil : Companhia Commercial et Maritima, Avenida Rio Branco 14-16, Rio de Janeiro, and Caixa de Correio 202, Santos ; Wildberger & Co., Bahia.

Uruguay : Luis Nicol, Montevideo.

Services, (1) Thrice-monthly, calling at Las Palmas or Santos or Dakar, Rio de Janeiro, Santos or Montevideo, and Buenos Aires, returning to Marseilles ; (2) monthly cargo-boats from Marseilles to La Plata via Genoa and Spanish ports ; (3) monthly steamers for passengers and cargo sailing to Rio de Janeiro via Genoa, Spanish ports, and Gibraltar.

FRENCH GUIANIAN.

Tancy & Cie.

Coastal service; also between Cayenne, Paramaribo, Demerara, Trinidad, and Martinique.

GERMAN.

Hamburg-Sudamerikanische Dampfschffahrts-Gesellschaft.

Head Office : Holzbrücke 8, Hamburg.

Telegrams : "Columbus."

Fortnightly services to Montevideo and Buenos Aires; monthly services to South Brazil ports (including Pelotas and Porto Alegre); fortnightly services to Mid-Brazil ports.

ITALIAN.

Lloyd del Pacifico.

Head Office : Genoa.

Lloyd Italiano.

Head Office : Naples.

Lloyd Sabaudo.

Head Office : Palazzo della Meridiana, Piazza Meridiana, Genoa.

Director : Marchese Renzo de la Penne.

Fleet : 6 passenger steamers, 53,489 tons; 12 cargo steamers, 54,854 tons.

Services : Genoa to Rio de Janeiro, Santos, Montevideo, and Buenos Aires, via Barcelona; Genoa and Naples to New York; Genoa and Naples, etc., to Australia, via Suez Canal Ports and Colombo.

Navigazione Generale Italiana.

Head Office : Genoa.

Societá di Navigazione a Vapore.

Head Office : 21 Piazza della Borsa, Naples.

Transatlantica Italiana.

Head Office : 40 Via Balbi, Genoa.

La Veloce.

Navigazione Italiana a Vapore.

Head Office : Genoa.

JAPANESE.

Nippon Yusen Kaisha.

Head Office : Tokyo.

London Branch : 4 Lloyds Avenue, E.C.3.

Directors : Yonejiro Ito (President), Yúkichi Nagatomi, Shigetarö Nakajima, Akira Ishii, Masaki Yasuda, Hampei Fujishma, Asao Shimamura, Fukuta Mizukawa, Nisuke Nagata, Motoomi Yukawa, Sadae Yeguchi, Kikusaburo Fukui, Masayasu Naruse.

Agents : Argentina—Lamport and Holt, Buenos Aires.

Brazil : Lamport and Holt, Antunes dos Santos & Co., Santos and Saô Paulo.

Service : Two-monthly; Kobe, Moji, Singapore, South African ports, Rio de Janeiro, Buenos Aires.

[See Index to Advertisers.]

MEXICAN.

Compañia Mexicana de Navegación.

Calls at Tampico, Vera Cruz, Puerto Mexico, etc., four times a month.

Compañia Naviera del Pacifico.

Calls frequently at Pacific ports (Guaymas, Mazatlan, etc.).

Vapores Correos Mexicanos.

To Frontera, Jonuta, Amatitlan, and other points from San Juan Bautista.

NORWEGIAN.

Det Nordenfjeldske Dampskibs-Selskab.

Head Office : Trondhjem.

Telegrams : "Nordenfjeldske," Trondhjem.

London Office: Nordenfjeldske Steamship Services, Ltd., 353 Strand, London W.C.2, and 4 Cullum Street, E.C.3.

Christiania Agents : S. O. Stray & Co., Ltd.

Agents on the Pacific Coast : Chile—Nordenfjeldske South Pacific Line, Calle Blanco, 620 Casilla 910, Valparaiso.
Ecuador: Sociedad Commercial Anglo-Ecuadoriana, Guayaquil.
Peru   Milne & Co., Lima and Callao.

Norwegian South American Line.

The Steamers, "Rio de la Plata" and "Rio de Janeiro," are employed in the South American trade, running regularly between Norway and River Plate, calling at Santos, Bahia, Buenos Aires, and Rosario. There is accommodation on each vessel for about eight first-class passengers.
Agents in South America : Buenos Aires, Christian Bugge; Bahia, Schwarz and Brussell; Santos and Rio de Janeiro, Fredrik Engelhart; Pernambuco, Julius van Söhsten & Co.

Nordenfjeldske South Pacific Line.
S. O. Stray & Co., Ltd., Christiania.

Agents : Brazil—Schwarz and Brussell, Bahia, Fredrik Engelhart, Santos and Rio de Janeiro.
Chile   Mr. Riso, Electro Quimica, Valparaiso.
Ecuador : Sociedad Commercial Anglo-Ecuadoriana, Guayaquil.
Peru: Milne & Co., Lima (Callao).
United States : S. O. Stray Steamship Corporation, 11 Broadway, New York.

Den Norske Syd-Amerika Linje.
(The Norwegian South-American Line.)

Head Office : Prinsensgt. 1, Christiania.
London Agents : Fred Dessen & Co., 6–8 Lime Street Square, E.C.3.
Agencies in South America : Argentina—S. O. Stray & Co., A/S., Buenos Aires.
Brazil : Stray, Engelhart & Co., Rio de Janeiro and Santos; Schwarz and Brussell, Bahia; Julius von Söhsten & Co., Pernambuco; Hermogenes & Co., Paranagua; Edward Wiij and Sons, Rio Grande do Sul.
Uruguay : S. O. Stray & Co., A/S.

STEAMSHIP SERVICES.

..Directors Einav Engelsen, Kristofer Lemkuhl, Joh. L. Müller, Th. Thoresen, Oivend Lorentzen (Managing Director).

Fleet : 8 Diesel motor ships and steamers of a total dead-weight of 52,000 tons.

Service : Fortnightly or three-weekly from East and West Norway to Brazil, Uruguay, and Argentina; regular sailings from South Finnish ports and Copenhagen to Bahia, Rio de Janeiro, Santos, Rio Grande do Sul, Montevideo, and Buenos Aires.

Duration of voyage from Scandinavian ports to Buenos Aires, via Brazil, 30 days.

Passengers : No steamer has accommodation for more than eleven.

Fares : Brazil, £40; Buenos Aires, £45.

The North and South Atlantic Line, Ltd.

Head Office : Lodin Leppsgt. 2, Bergen.

Branch Offices : Raadhusgt. 2, Christiania; 11–19 Moore Street, New York.

London Agents : H. Clarkson & Co., Ltd.

Agents in South America : Argentina—Buenos Aires and Rosario, Christophersen Hnos.

Brazil : Rio de Janeiro and Santos, Armando Lichti, Pernambuco, A. Goncalves & Cia.; Agents at Bahia and Rio Grande do Sul.

Uruguay : Montevideo, Christophersen Hnos.

Services : Loading at Scandinavian ports for the East Coast of the United States; loading there (especially New York) for Rio de Janeiro, Santos, and Buenos Aires, and vice versa.

Duration of the round trip—Scandinavia, United States, South America, and back, approximately, 4–4½ months.

Fred. Olsen & Co.

Head Office : Christiania.

Partners : Fred. Olsen, Rudolf Olsen, Johan L. Müller.

Services : Norway to Newcastle (Tyne Dock), Grangemouth, London, Rouen, Hâvre, Dunkirk, Calais, Antwerp, Garston, Amsterdam, Rotterdam, Buenos Aires, Brazilian ports, North and South Pacific Coast, and Baltic ports.

Fleet : 44 steamers and Diesel motor ships, cf a total dead-weight of about 133,000 tons.

Skogland's Line.

Regular South American service.

PARAGUAYAN.

Alto Paraná Line.

From Buenos Aires to Ita-Ibate, Villa Encarnación, and Posadas.

Corrientes-Posadas Line.

From Corrientes to Posadas twice weekly.

Upper Paraguay River Line.

Between Buenos Aires and Rosario, Paraná, etc., on the 15th of each month.

PERUVIAN.

Compañia Peruana de Vapores.
(Peruvian Steamship Company.)

Head Office : Plaza Grau, Callao, Peru.

Branch Office : Colón and Balboa, Panamá.

Weekly service between Cristóbal, Guayaquil, Callao, and intermediate and southern ports.

516

STEAMSHIP SERVICES.

SPANISH.

Compañia Transatlántica de Vapores Correos Españoles.

Head Office : 14 Apartado, Barcelona, Spain.
Liverpool Agents : Larrinaga & Co., Ltd., 30 James Street.
Sailings from Spain to Puerto Rico, Havana, New York, Vera Cruz, Colón, Montevideo, Buenos Aires, Fernando Po, Manila.

Pinillos, Izquierdo & Cia.

Agents   Zenha, Ramos & Co., 1 de Marco 73, Rio de Janeiro.
Sailings from Spain to Santos, etc.

SWEDISH.

Rederiaktiebolaget Nordstjernan.
(Johnson Line.)

Head Office : Stureplan 3, Stockholm.
London Agents : A. Johnson & Co. (London), Ltd., 101 Leadenhall Street, E.C.3.
Agencies in South America : Argentina—Buenos Aires (W. Allinson Bell, 240 Reconquista).
Bolivia : La Paz (W. R. Grace & Co.).
Brazil : Pernambuco (Williams & Co.), Rio de Janeiro (Luiz Campos); Bahia (H. Enedeville & Co.), Santos (Johnson Line Agencies).
Chile : Punta Arenas (Braun & Blanchard), Corral (W. R. Grace & Co.), Talcuhuano (The Talcuhuano Agencies Co.), Valparaiso (W R. Grace & Co.), Coquimbo (The Coquimbo Agencies Co.), Taltal, Antofagasta, Tocopilla, Iquique, Arica, Pisagua (Nitrate Agencies, Ltd.).
Ecuador : Guayaquil (The Guayaquil Agencies Co.).
Guatemala : Guatemala City (W. R. Grace & Co.).
Panamá : Panamá City, Colón (Panamá Agencies Co.).
Peru : Mollendo (Mollendo Agencies, Ltd.), Pisco (Pisco Agencies, Ltd.), Callao (W. R. Grace & Co.), Salaverry (Salaverry Agencies Co.).
Salvador : San Salvador (Agencia W R. Grace & Co.).
Uruguay : Montevideo (Antonio Piaggio).
Fleet : 11 steamers, with dead weight tonnage of 81,480 tons.
Regular services between ports in Sweden and Finland (Gothenburg, Malmö, Stockholm, and Helsingfors), and (1) Pernambuco, Bahia, Rio de Janeiro, Santos, Rio Grande do Sul, Montevideo, and Buenos Aires; and (2) between ports in Sweden, Finland, and Norway (Gothenburg, Malmö, Stockholm, Helsingfors, and Christiana), and Puerto Colombia, Panamá, Acajutla, Champerico, Guayaquil, Callao, Iquique, Antofagasta, and Valparaiso, etc.

UNITED STATES.

Blue Diamond Line.

Head Office : New York.

Bluefields Fruit and Steamship Co

Head Office : New Orleans, La.
Direct Freight and Passenger Service between New Orleans and Kingston, Jamaica, and outports; direct Freight and Passenger Service between New Orleans and Bluefields, Nicaragua.

STEAMSHIP SERVICES.

Caribbean Steamship Company, Ltd.

Head Office : 8-10 Bridge Street, New York City.
Service between New York, New Orleans and Kingston, Santiago, Ports of Colombia (Atlantic and Pacific), Venezuela, Ecuador, Curaçao, and Trinidad.

Cuyamel Fruit Co. Steamship Service.

Head Office : New Orleans.
Semi-weekly departures for Puerto Cortes and Omoa, Honduras.

Independent Steamship Line.

Agents : Vaccaro Bros. & Co., New Orleans.
Weekly departures for Ceiba, Honduras.

Isthmian Lines.

Managers and General Agents : Norton, Lilly & Co., 26 Beaver Street, New York.
Service : New Orleans to Montevideo, Buenos Aires, Rosario.
Sailing : Monthly.

Massey Steamship Company.

Head Office : New York.

Norton, Lilly and Company.
26 Beaver Street, New York.
Established 1843.

Partners : Skeffington S. Norton, Joseph T Lilly, John B. O'Reilly, John J Farrell, Edward J. Brandreth, W. J. Edwards.
Managers of the Norton and the Isthmian Lines (q.v.).

Norton Line.

Managers and General Agents : Norton, Lilly & Co., 26 Beaver Street, New York.
Branch Offices : Boston, Philadelphia, Baltimore, Norfolk, Newport News, New Orleans, Chicago, Los Angeles, San Diego, San Francisco, Seattle, Portland, Oregon.
Argentine Agents : J. R. Williams & Co., Buenos Aires.
Sailings : About every three weeks to Montevideo, Buenos Aires, and Rosario; making the voyage from New York to Montevideo in about 23 days, and carrying general merchandise.
Fares : New York to Montevideo, $175, to Buenos Aires, $185 and upwards.

Panamá Rail-Road Steamship Line.
24 State Street, New York.

Weekly departures from New York for Port-au-Prince, Haiti, and Cristóbal, Panamá Canal Zone.

STEAMSHIP SERVICES.

Trinidad Line.

Head Office: Furness, Withy & Co., Ltd., 34 Whitehall Street, New York City.

Sailings from Pier 24, Brooklyn, every two weeks for Grenada, Trinidad, and Demerara.

United Fruit Company Steamship Service.

Head Office: 131 State Street, Boston, Mass., U.S.A.

President: Andrew W. Preston. Secretary: Bradley W. Palmer.

General European Agents: A. J. Shepherd & Co., Dashwood House, 9 New Broad Street, London, E.C.2.

Agents in South and Central America and Mexico—Argentine: Buenos Aires (Express Villalonga, American Express Co.).

Bolivia: La Paz (Thomas Bradley).

Chile: Valparaiso (G. C. Kenrick & Co.), Tocopilla (Anglo de Vapores), Santiago (Spencer & Waters, G. C. Kenrick & Co.), Iquique (Carlos H. Lemare), Antofagasta (Le Mare & Co.), Arica (Tomas Bradley).

Colombia: Cartagena (Rafael del Castillo & Co.), Barranquilla (Alzamora, Palacio & Co.).

Costa Rica: Port Limón (G. P Chittenden), San José (Sasso and Pirie).

Cuba: Havana (W M. Daniel), Santiago de Cuba (L. Abascal y Sobrinos).

Ecuador: Guayaquil (Andean Trading Co.).

Guatemala: Guatemala City (P A. Bruni), Puerto Barrios (J. C. Fluker), Livingston (D. E. Rayor).

Honduras (British): Belize, C. V Freeman.

Honduras (Spanish): Tela (Tela Railroad Co.), Puerto Cortez (S. Culotta).

Mexico: Mexico City (Berea O'Kelly & Co.).

Panamá: Panamá City (Thomas H. Jacome).

Panamá Canal Zone: Cristóbal (M. C. O'Hearn).

Weekly Services: (1) New York-Jamaica-Panamá-Colombia; (2) New York-Havana-Panamá-Costa Rica; (3) New Orleans-Havana-Panamá; (4) New Orleans-Honduras-Guatemala; (5) New York-Havana-Jamaica-British Honduras-Guatemala-Honduras.

Ward Line.
Foot of Wall Street, New York.

Services: (1) New York to Cuba, Mexico, and the Bahamas; semi-weekly to Havana; weekly to Progreso, Vera Cruz, Tampico, Cienfuegos, Manzanillo, Naval Station, Santiago, and Guantanamo, monthly to Puerto Mexico and Frontera; fortnightly to Nassau.

(2) New Orleans to Cuba and Mexico: fortnightly to Havana, Matanzas, Cardenas, Sagua, Caibarien, Neuvitas, Antilla, Santiago, Guantanamo, Cienfuegos, Manzanillo, Tampico and Vera Cruz; monthly to Puerto Mexico.

(3) Orange, Beaumont, Port Arthur, and Galveston to Mexico: monthly to Tampico and Vera Cruz.

Windward Islands Line.

Head Office: Mobile, Alabama.

STEAMSHIP SERVICES.

URUGUAYAN.

Uruguay River Line.

Between Montevideo and Buenos Aires and Salto, three times a week.

VENEZUELAN.

Compañia Anonima de Navegación Fluvial y Costanera.

Service between La Guayra, Curaçao, and Maracaibo. Connects with lake steamers at Maracaibo.

Compañia Anonima Venezolana de Navegación.

Fortnightly service between Ciudad Bolivar and Port of Spain, Trinidad.

Red " D " Line.

Fortnightly service between La Guayra and Curaçao.

THE ROYAL MAIL
& PACIFIC LINES

"The Comfort Route."

TO

EAST & WEST COASTS OF
SOUTH AMERICA

TOURS ROUND SOUTH AMERICA

BETWEEN HALIFAX (N.S.), NEW YORK & SOUTH AMERICA

The Royal Mail Steam Packet Co.
The Pacific Steam Navigation Co.

LONDON—LIVERPOOL.

Glyn, Mills, Currie, Holt & Co.

Glyn, Mills, Currie, Holt & Cia.

CABLE AND WIRELESS
SERVICES

CABLE AND WIRELESS SERVICES.

Cable Charges :—The following rates prevailing at July, 1923, apply to dispatches from any part of the United Kingdom to the named places. Complete particulars are obtainable at British Post Offices and from the official "Post Office Guide."

Rates from South America to the United Kingdom, except that they are collected in local currency, are practically identical.

	Ordinary Rate per word. s. d.	Deferred Rate per word. s. d.
ARGENTINE REPUBLIC :		
Eastern Co.—Madeira		
Direct Spanish Co.—Madeira		
Eastern Co.—Teneriffe—Noronha		
Via France—Teneriffe—Noronha and Western Cables		
Via France and Dakar	2 9	1 4½
Anglo-American Co.		
French Co.		
Western Union Co.		
Commercial Co. ..		
Via France—Teneriffe—Noronha and Brazilian Land Lines	2 6	1 3
Marconi Co.	2 6	1 3
AZORES :		
Eastern Co.		
Direct Spanish Co.	0 9	—
Via France		
BOLIVIA :		
To all places except Riberalta and Trinidad :		
(1) Eastern Co.—Madeira		
(2) Direct Spanish Co.—Madeira		
(3) Eastern Co.—Teneriffe—Noronha		
(4) Via France—Teneriffe—Noronha		
(5) Via France and Dakar	2 9	1 4½
(6) Anglo-American Co.		
(7) French Co. ..		
(8) Western Union Co.		
(9) Commericial Co.		
(10) Marconi Co.	2 5	1 2½
Riberalta and Trinidad :		
By routes (1) to (9) above	3 9	2 4½
By route (10) above	3 3	2 3

The words "Wireless via Viacha" must also appear in the route instructions of telegrams for these places.

BRAZIL :		
Places other than Pernambuco (Town) and Fernando Noronha, and other than Offices of the Amazon Co., and the Acre District :		
(1) Eastern Co.—Madeira		
(2) Direct Spanish Co.—Madeira		
(3) Eastern Co.—Teneriffe—Noronha		
(4) Via France—Teneriffe—Noronha and Western Cables		
(5) Via France and Dakar	2 7	1 3½
(6) Anglo-American Co.		
(7) French Co.		
(8) Western Union Co.		
(9) Commercial Co.		
(10) Via France—Teneriffe—Noronha and Brazilian Land Lines	2 4	1 2
Marconi Co.	2 3	1 1½

BRAZIL—*cont.*

	Ordinary Rate per word.	Deferred Rate per word.
	s. d.	s. d.
Offices of the Amazon Co. :		
1st Zone :		
By the routes numbered (1) to (9)	3 10	1 11
By the route numbered (10)	3 7	1 9½
Marconi Co.	3 6	1 9
2nd Zone :		
By the routes numbered (1) to (9)	5 0	2 6
By the route numbered (10)	4 9	2 4½
Marconi Co.	4 9	2 4½
Offices in the Acre District :		
Eastern Co.—Madeira.		
Anglo-American Co.		
French Co.	4 7	—
Western Union Co.		
Commercial Co.		
Marconi Co.	4 4	2 2

The words " Belem Radio " must also appear in the route instructions of telegrams for places in the Acre District.

CHILE :

	Ordinary Rate per word.	Deferred Rate per word.
All places except Punta Arenas :		
Anglo-American Co.		
French Co.		
Western Union Co.		
Commercial Co.		
Eastern Co.—Madeira.	2 9	1 4½
Direct Spanish Co.—Madeira.		
Eastern Co.—Teneriffe—Noronha		
Via France—Teneriffe—Noronha and Western Cables		
Via France and Dakar		
Marconi Co.	2 6	1 3
Punta Arenas :		
Routes as above (except Marconi)	2 9	1 4½
Via France—Teneriffe—Noronha and Brazilian Land Lines	2 6	1 3
Marconi Co.	2 6	1 3

COLOMBIA, Republic of (South America) :

	Ordinary Rate per word.	Deferred Rate per word.
All places except Buenaventura and Cartagena :		
Imperial	3 2	1 7
Anglo-American Co.		
French Co.		
Western Union Co.	3 2	1 7
Commercial Co.		
Marconi Co.		
Buenaventura and Cartagena :		
Routes as above	2 6	1 3

COSTA RICA :

	Ordinary Rate per word.	Deferred Rate per word.
Imperial	2 7	1 3½
San José, Costa Rica :		
(1) Anglo-American Co.	2 7	1 3½
(2) French Co.		
Limon, Costa Rica :		
(3) Western Union Co.		
(4) Commercial Co.	2 7	1 3½
(5) Marconi Co.		
Other places :		
Imperial	2 11	1 5½
By routes (1) to (5) above	2 11	1 5½

CABLE AND WIRELESS SERVICES.

—	Via Imperial.		Via Anglo-American Co., French Co., Western Union Co., or Commerical Co. (via Key West, via Hayti, or via New York and Havana Cable)			Via Marconi Co.	
	Ordinary.	Deferred.	Preferred.	Ordinary.	Deferred.	Ordinary.	Deferred.
1.	2.	3.	4.	5.	6.	7.	8.
CUBA :	s. d.	s. d.	s. d.	s. d.	s. d.	s. d.	s. d.
Havana	1 5	0 8½	1 8	1 5	0 8½	1 5	0 8½
Santiago de Cuba	1 5	0 8½	—	1 5	0 8½	1 5	0 8½
All other Places	1 7	0 9½	—	1 7	0 9½	1 7	0 9½

ˎ	Night Letter Telegrams.		Week-end Letter Telegrams.	
—	20 words or less (including the indication TLT).	Each word after 20.	20 words or less (indication TWT).	Each word after 20.
1.	2.	3.	4.	5.
CUBA :	s. d.	s. d.	s. d.	s. d.
Havana	10 0	0 6	8 4	0 5
Santiago de Cuba	11 8	0 7	9 2	0 5½
All other Places	11 8	0 7	9 2	0 5½

	Ordinary Rate per word.	Deferred Rate per word.
	s. d.	s. d.
ECUADOR :		
Imperial .	2 6	1 3
Anglo-American Co.		
French Co.		
Western Union Co. }	2 6	1 3
Commercial Co. .		
Marconi Co. ..		
FALKLAND ISLANDS :		
Port Stanley:		
Eastern Co.—Madeira		
Direct Spanish Co.—Madeira		
Via France and Dakar		
Anglo-American Co. . }	3 11	—
French Co. .		
Western Union Co. .		
Commercial Co..		
Marconi Co. ..	3 8	
Fox Bay :		
Routes as above (except Marconi) ..	4 5	—
Marconi Co. . .	4 2	—

		Ordinary Rate per word. s. d.	Deferred Rate per word. s. d.
FRANCE :			
Via Cable Marconi Co.	.. ..	0 2½	—
GUATEMALA :			
San Jose de Guatemala :			
Imperial ..	.	2 7	1 3½
(1) Anglo-American Co.			
(2) French Co. .			
(3) Western Union Co.	.	} 2 7	1 3½
(4) Commercial Co.	.		
(5) Marconi Co.	.		
Other Places :			
Imperial	. .	2 10	1 5
By routes (1) to (5) above	.	2 10	1 5
GUIANA, BRITISH :			
Imperial . ..	.	2 8	1 4
Anglo-American Co. .	(via Key West		
French Co.	{ via Bermuda or	} 2 8	1 4
Western Union Co. .	via New York		
Commercial Co. .	(and Havana Cable.		
Marconi Co.	..	2 8	1 4
GUIANA, DUTCH :			
Imperial .		6 6	3 3
Anglo-American Co. .	(via Key West)		
French Co.	{ or } 6 6	3 3
Western Union Co.	{ via Hayti. }		
Commercial Co. .			
Marconi Co. .	.	6 6	3 3
GUIANA, FRENCH :			
Imperial ..	..	5 7	—
Anglo-American Co. ..	(via Key West)		
French Co.	{ or } 5 7	2 9½
Western Union Co. ..	(via Hayti.)		
Commercial Co. ..			
Marconi Co. ..	.. . ..	5 7	2 9½
HONDURAS, BRITISH :			
Imperial .. .		2 4	—
Anglo-American Co.			
French Co.	}		
Western Union Co.	.	} 2 4	—
Commercial Co.	..		
Marconi Co. ..	. .		
HONDURAS, REPUBLIC OF			
Imperial .		2 10	1 5
Anglo-American Co. .	)		
French Co. ..			
Western Union Co.	.	} 2 10	1 5
Commercial Co...	. .		
Marconi Co. ..	. ..	)	
NICARAGUA :			
All places except San Juan del Sur :			
Imperial .	.	2 10	1 5
(1) Anglo-American Co.	.		
(2) French Co. .	..		
(3) Western Union Co.	..	} 2 10	1 5
(4) Commercial Co.	.		
(5) Marconi Co.	.		
San Juan del Sur :			
Imperial ..	. .	2 7	1 3½
By routes (1) to (5) above ..	. . . ..	2 7	1 3½

—	Via Imperial.	Via Anglo-American Co., French Co., Western Union Co., or Commercial Co.		Via Marconi Co.
I.	Ordinary. 2.	Preferred. 3.	Ordinary. 4.	Ordinary. 5.
MEXICO :	s. d.	s. d.	s. d.	s. d.
All places except the following :	1 10	2 1	1 10	1 10
Altar de Sonora				
Arizpe ..				
Banamichi				
Chihuahua (City)				
Cuauhtemoc				
Guaymas ..				
Hermosillo	1 3	1 6	1 3	1 3
Matamoros de Tamaulipas				
Monterrey de Nuevo Leon				
Sabinas Villa				
Saltillo de Coahuila				
Sauz ..				
Coatzacoalcos (Puerto Mexico)				
Mexico (City)				
Salina Cruz ..	1 9	2 0	1 9	1 9
Tampico de Tamaulipas .				
Vera Cruz de Vera Cruz ..				

	Ordinary Rate per word. s. d.	Deferred Rate per word. s. d.
PANAMA, Republic of :		
All places except Colón, Panamá, Bocas del Toro and Almirante :		
Imperial	2 6	1 3
(1) Anglo-American Co.		
(2) French Co. ..		
(3) Western Union Co.	2 6	1 3
(4) Commercial Co.		
(5) Marconi Co. ..		
Colón and Panamá :		
Imperial	2 5	1 2½
By routes (1) to (5) above ..	2 5	1 2½
Bocas Del Toro and Almirante :		
Imperial	3 6	—
By routes (1) to (5) above . ..	3 6	—
PARAGUAY :		
Eastern Co.—Madeira		
Direct Spanish Co.—Madeira.		
Eastern Co.—Teneriffe—Noronha ..		
Via France—Teneriffe—Noronha and Western Cables .		
Via France and Dakar .	2 9	1 4½
Anglo-American Co. ..		
French Co. .. .		
Western Union Co. .		
Commercial Co... . .		
Via France—Teneriffe—Noronha and Brazilian Land Lines	2 6	1 3
Marconi Co.	2 6	1 3

CABLE AND WIRELESS SERVICES.

	Ordinary Rate per word. s. d.	Deferred Rate per word. s. d.

PERU :
All places except El Encanto, Iquitos, Leticia, Masisea, and Puerto Maldonado :

Imperial	2 9	1 4½
(1) Anglo-American Co.		
(2) French Co. ..		
(3) Western Union Co.		
(4) Commercial Co. ..		
(5) Eastern Co.—Madeira	2 9	1 4½
(6) Direct Spanish Co.—Madeira		
(7) Eastern Co.—Teneriffe—Noronha		
(8) Via France—Teneriffe—Noronha		
(9) Via France and Dakar ..		
(10) Marconi Co. ..	2 6	1 3

El Encanto, Iquitos, Leticia, Masisea, and Puerto Maldonado :

Imperial	3 2	1 9½
By routes (1) to (9) above .	3 2	1 9½
By route (10) above . ..	2 10	1 8

PORTUGAL :

Eastern Co. .. .		
Direct Spanish Co. .. }	0 3	—
Via France .		

PORTO RICO :

Imperial and Bermuda .	2 5	1 2½
By routes (1) to (4) on previous page { via Key West, via Bermuda, via Hayti or via New York and Havana Cable }	2 5	1 2½
Marconi Co.	2 5	1 2½

SALVADOR :
All places except Libertad :

Imperial	2 10	1 5
(1) Anglo-American Co. .		
(2) French Co. .		
(3) Western Union Co. . }	2 10	1 5
(4) Commercial Co. .		
(5) Marconi Co. ..		

Libertad :

Imperial	2 7	1 3½
By routes (1) to (5) above .	2 7	1 3½

SPAIN :

Direct Spanish Co. .		
Eastern Co. . }	0 3	—
Via France .		
Via Marseilles Cable .	0 5	—
Marconi Co. . .	0 2½	—

URUGUAY :

Eastern Co.—Madeira		
Direct Spanish Co.—Madeira.		
Eastern Co.—Teneriffe—Noronha .. .		
Via France—Teneriffe—Noronha and Western Cables		
Via France and Dakar .. .. . }	2 9	1 4½
Anglo-American Co.		
French Co. . .		
Western Union Co. .		
Commercial Co.		
Via France—Teneriffe—Noronha and Brazilian Land Lines	2 6	1 3
Marconi Co.	2 6	1 3

		Ordinary Rate per word. s. d.	Deferred Rate per word. s. d.
VENEZUELA :			
Imperial	.	4 10	2 6
(1) Anglo-American Co.			
(2) French Co. . .			
(3) Western Union Co.		4 10	2 6
(4) Commercial Co.			
(5) Marconi Co.			
Imperial ..	Via Trinidad and Wireless.	3 4	—
By routes (1) to (5) above		3 4	—
By routes (1) to (4) above .	Via New York and Wireless.	2 6	—

Radio-telegrams between ship and shore are transmitted at long range from the Oxford Radio station at 1s. 2d. a word, plus a ship charge of usually 4d. per word.

To coast radio stations in South and Central America the charge is usually 6d. per word apart from ship charge. The precise rates are ascertainable on shipboard.

CABLE COMPANIES.

Cable, wireless, and **telegraph companies** serving South and Central America, Mexico, and Cuba include :—

ALL AMERICA CABLES, INC., 89 Broad Street, New York. Services Direct cable to South America via All America, direct to Mexico and Central America via Galveston.

THE AMAZON TELEGRAPH COMPANY, LTD., Finsbury Pavement House, London, E.C.2. Service : Brazil (Amazon region). Branches and Agents at Soure, Mosqueiro, Pinheiro, Cameta, Curralinho, Antonio Lemos, Breves, Macapa, Chaves, Mazagao, Gurupa, Prainha, Monte-Alegre, Santarem (first Zone); Alemquer, Obidos, Parintins, Itacoatiara, Amatary, Manáos (second Zone).

ANGLO-AMERICAN TELEGRAPH COMPANY, LTD., Winchester House, Old Broad Street, London, E.C.

CENTRAL AND SOUTH AMERICAN TELEGRAPH COMPANY

COMPAGNIE FRANÇAISE DES CABLES TÉLÉGRAPHIQUES.

THE CUBA SUBMARINE TELEGRAPH COMPANY, LTD., 58 Old Broad Street, London, E.C.2. Connects Havana with Santiago de Cuba, with stations also at Cienfuegos and Manzanillo.

MARCONI'S WIRELESS TELEGRAPH COMPANY, LTD., Marconi House, Strand, W.C.2, and its subsidiaries THE COMPAÑIA MARCONI DE TELEGRAFIA SIN HILOS DEL RIO DE LA PLATA, and the COMPANHIA RADIOTELEGRAPHICA BRASILIERA.

MEXICAN TELEGRAPH COMPANY

PAN-AMERICAN WIRELESS TELEGRAPH AND TELEPHONE COMPANY, 233 Broadway, New York.

RIVER PLATE TELEGRAPH COMPANY, LTD., 5 Royal Bank Place, Glasgow; Electra House, Moorgate, E.C.2.

SOUTH AMERICAN TELEGRAPH CO., U.S.A.

THE WEST INDIA AND PANAMÁ TELEGRAPH CO., LTD., Spencer House, 4 South Place, London, E.C.2.

THE WESTERN TELEGRAPH COMPANY, LTD., Electra House, Moorgate, E.C.2, with European Agencies at PARIS : 37 Rue Caumartin (9ième Arrt); BRUXELLES : Société Anonyme Belge des Cables Télégraphiques, 93 Rue de la Toison d'Or; HAMBURG Monckebergstrasse, Caledonia Haus.

The collection and delivery of South American telegrams in Great Britain is made on behalf of the Western Telegraph Company, Ltd., by the Eastern Telegraph Company, Ltd., at their various offices.

RAILWAYS OF
LATIN-AMERICA

RAILWAYS OF LATIN-AMERICA.

ARGENTINA.

Argentine Great Western Railway Company, Ltd.
Dashwood House, 9 New Broad Street, London, E.C.2.

(Administered by the Buenos Aires and Pacific Railway Company, Ltd.)
Mileage: 982. Gauge, 5 ft. 6 in.
Passengers (1921-1922): 2,905,150.
Area: Part of the Buenos Aires and Pacific Co.'s system.
Chief traffic: Wheat, hay, wine, grapes, firewood, live stock.

Argentine North-Eastern Railway Company, Ltd.,
River Plate House, Finsbury Circus, London, E.C.2.

Mileage: 752. Gauge, 4 ft. 8½ in.
Rolling Stock: 68 locomotives, 1,195 goods stock, 82 coaching stock.
Floating Plant: 2 ferry boats.
Passengers (1921-1922): 233,026.
Area: Provinces of Corrientes, Misiones, connecting with the Paraguay Central Railway in the north and the Entre Rios Railways in the south.
Chief traffic: Live stock, wool, wheat, oranges, fruit and vegetables, yerba maté, firewood, tobacco.

Argentine Railway Company.
Serves Provinces of Santa Fé and Territory of the Chaco. Metre gauge.

Argentine Transandine Railway Company, Ltd.,
Dashwood House, 9 New Broad Street, London, E.C.2.

Rolling Stock: 29 locomotives, 28 passenger cars, 24 vans, 134 wagons, general service stock, 48.
Gauge: Metre.
Area: Connecting link across the Andes between the Argentine Great Western Railway and the Chilean Transandine Railway
Chief traffic: Live stock, general.

Argentino del Norte Railway.
Created by the fusion of several local railway systems. By purchase of the Córdoba and North Western Railway this railway has access to Córdoba and to the port of Santa Fé. The La Rioja section was originally known as the " Dean Funes and Chilecito Railway "
Starting at Santa Fé, it serves the Provinces of Santa Fé, Córdoba, La Rioja, San Juan, and Catamarca.
Metre gauge.

Bahia Blanca and North-Western Railway Company, Ltd.,
Dashwood House, 9 New Broad Street, London, E.C.2.

(Worked by the Buenos Aires and Pacific Railway Company, Ltd.)
Mileage: 763. Gauge, 5 ft. 6 in.

Buenos Aires and Pacific Railway Company, Ltd.,
Dashwood House, 9 New Broad Street, London, E.C.2.

(Includes the Villa Maria and Rufino Railway   The Company also works the Argentine Transandine Railway Company, Ltd.)
Mileage: 3,428. Gauge, 5 ft. 6 in.
Area: Provinces of Buenos Aires, San Luis, Mendoza, Territories of La Pampa and Rio Negro.
Chief traffic: Wheat, barley, oats, linseed, hay, live stock, wine, grapes, firewood, wool.

Buenos Aires Central Railway.

(Inc. under the laws of the Argentine Republic as the Ferro Carril Central de Buenos Aires, Limitada.)
Mileage: 280. Gauge, 4 ft. 8½ in.

Buenos Aires, Ensenada and South Coast Railway Company, Ltd.
River Plate House, Finsbury Circus, London, E.C.2.

(Worked by the Buenos Aires Great Southern Railway.)
Mileage: 109. Gauge, 5 ft. 6 in.
Passengers (1921–1922): 175,434.
Area   Connecting the ports of Buenos Aires and Ensenada.
Chief traffic: Live stock, wheat, maize, barley

Buenos Aires Great Southern Railway Company, Ltd.
River Plate House, Finsbury Circus, London, E.C.2.

(The Company also works the Buenos Aires Ensenada and South Coast Railway Co., Ltd. Jointly with the Buenos Aires Western Railway, Ltd., it operates the Buenos Aires Midland Railway Co., Ltd.)
Mileage owned: 3,948. Gauge, 5 ft. 6 in.
Passengers (1921-1922): 32,116,000. Goods, 4,538,325 tons. Animals, 6,615,078.
Area: Province of Buenos Aires, Territories of La Pampa, Rio Negro, and Neuquen.
Chief traffic: Wheat, linseed, maize, oats, flour, frozen beef and mutton, wool, hides and skins, dairy produce, potatoes.

Buenos Aires Midland Railway Company, Ltd.
River Plate House, Finsbury Circus, London, E.C.2.

Mileage: 322. Gauge, 3 ft. 3 in.
Area: From the Capital to Carhue, Province of Buenos Aires.
Chief traffic: Cereals, flour, linseed, frozen meat, hides, agricultural and dairy produce.

Buenos Aires Port Lines.

A line of 4,689 metres, which links up the Central Argentine with the Great Southern systems. Gauge, 5 ft. 6 in.

Buenos Aires Western Railway, Ltd.
River Plate House, Finsbury Circus, London, E.C.2.

Rolling stock: 371 locomotives, 391 passenger cars, 7,870 general traffic wagons.
Mileage: 1,882. Gauge, 5 ft. 6 in.
Passengers: 11,125,543.
Area: Provinces of Buenos Aires, San Luis, and Mendoza, Territory of La Pampa.
Chief traffic: Wheat, oats, maize, hay, live stock, wool, flour, linseed.

Central Argentine Railway, Ltd.
3A, Coleman Street, London, E.C.2.

Mileage 3,305. Gauge, 5 ft. 6 in. (including 27 miles mixed 5 ft. 6 in., and 1.00 metre gauge).

Passengers (1921–1922): 27,189,212.

Area: Provinces of Buenos Aires, Santa Fé, Córdoba, Santiago del Estero, Tucumán.

Chief traffic: Maize, wheat, linseed, sugar and sugar cane, flour, charcoal, firewood, timber, limestone, lime, live stock, wool.

Central Norte Argentino Railway.

The main line is from Santa Fé to Tucumán, and thence to the Bolivian frontier. The line was purchased by the Government from the Argentine French Railways Co., in 1896. It serves the provinces of Santa Fé, Santiago del Estero, Tucumán, Salta, and Jujuy. Among the towns served besides Santa Fé and Tucumán, are San Cristóbal, Rosario de la Frontera, Perico, and Jujuy.

The line opens up the territories of the Chaco and Formosa Governments, much of which are primeval forest. It has two branches from the banks of the Paraná, from Resistencia to Salta, and from Formosa to Embarcación, and a third branch starting from Quimili.

Metre gauge. Mileage: 4,916 kilometres.

Central Railway of Chubut Company, Ltd.
River Plate House, 13 South Place, London, E.C.2.

Mileage: 65. Gauge, metre.

Passengers (1919–1920): 32,004.

Area: Districts of Viedma, Rawson and Gainan Park; Territory of Chubut, ocean port Puerto Madryn.

Chief traffic: Alfalfa, wool, hides, skins.

Compagnie du Chemin de fer de Rosario-Puerto Belgrano (Soc. Anonyme).
22 Rue Caumartin, Paris, and Rosario de Santa Fé.

Rolling stock: 45 locomotives, 39 passenger cars, 1,084 goods and other wagons.

Mileage: 826 km. Gauge, 5 ft. 6 in.

Passengers (1921–1922): 212,768.

Area: The western portion of the Province of Buenos Aires and Santa Fé.

Chief traffic: Cattle, cereals, wool, timber and general merchandise.

Compagnie Française des Chemins de fer de la Province de Santa Fé (Société Anonyme),
66 Rue de la Chaussée d'Antin, Paris.

Rolling stock: 187 locomotives, 161 passenger cars, 5,693 general traffic wagons.

Mileage: 1,911 km. Gauge, 3 ft. 3 in.

Passengers (1921–1922): 728,138.

Area: Province of Santa Fé.

Chief traffic: Cereals, timber and cattle.

Córdoba Central Railway Company, Ltd.
River Plate House, Finsbury Circus, London, E.C.2.

Rolling stock: 315 locomotives, 352 passenger cars, 6,620 general traffic wagons.

Mileage: 1,206. Gauge, 3 ft. 3 in.

Passengers (1921–1922): 2,590,993.

Area: Provinces of Buenos Aires, Santa Fé, Córdoba, Santiago del Estero, Catamarca, and Tucumán.

Chief traffic: Firewood, sugar and sugar cane, maize, wheat, linseed, hay, wine, fruit and vegetables, salt, lime and limestone, live stock.

Entre Rios Railways Company, Ltd.
River Plate House, Finsbury Circus, London, E.C.2.

Mileage : 729.   Gauge, 4 ft. 8½ in.

Rolling stock : 90 locomotives, 123 coaching stock, 2,136 goods stock.

Floating plant : 3 train ferry steamers.

Passengers (1921–1922) : 396,350.

Area : Province of Entre Rios connecting with Buenos Aires, and with the Argentine North-Eastern at Concordia (whence connection with Paraguay).

Chief traffic : Live stock, wool, hides and skins, wheat, maize, linseed, flour, timber, firewood, charcoal, oranges, tobacco.

Ferro Carril Puerto Ocampo.
Alsina 261, Buenos Aires.

Serves the Province of Entre Rios, from Las Palmas to Paraná and Concordia. Metre gauge.

Patagonia State Railways.
(i) San Antonio to Nahuel Hapi.

(ii) Puerto Deseado to Nahuel Hapi.

(iii) Comodoro Rivadavia to Lago Buenos Aires.

Gauge, 5 ft. 6 in.

Province of Buenos Aires Railway.
Buenos Aires to Villegas.   Metre gauge.

Provincial Government Railway.
Province of Buenos Aires, from La Plata to Sundblad and Mari Lauquen.   Metre gauge.

Rosario—Mendoza Railway.
Province of Buenos Aires.   Metre gauge.

Santiago del Estero Railway.
Province of Santiago del Estero.   Metre gauge.

Strategical Railway (Naval Port).
Serves the naval port to the east of Bahia Blanca.   Gauge, 5 ft. 6 in.   Length, 20 km.

Union Railway.
Bartolomé Mitre, 430, Buenos Aires.

Province of Mendoza, from Mendoza to La Guevas.   Metre gauge.

BRAZIL.

Alagôas and Northern Railway Company, Ltd.
River Plate House, Finsbury Circus, London, E.C.2.

Formed 1912, to build a one-metre gauge railway in the State of Algôas, construction postponed.

Brazil North-Eastern Railways, Ltd.
Taken over by Brazilian Government in 1915.

Area : That covered by the Sobral Railway and the Baturité Railway in the State of Ceará, and extensions.

Brazil Great Southern Railway Company, Ltd.
14 Queen Victoria Street, London, E.C.4.

Rolling stock (1920) : 8 locomotives, 12 passenger cars, 112 general traffic wagons.
Mileage : 186. Gauge, Metre.

Area   Quarahim (connecting with the North Western of Uruguay Railway) to Itaqui, with extension to São Borja through the western districts of Rio Grande do Sul, a connection at Uruguayana with the State Railway of Rio Grande do Sul.

Chief traffic : Hides, wool, lime, salt, matte, sugar, cereals, alcohol, flour, dried meat, grease, coal and timber.

Great Western of Brazil Railway Company, Ltd.
River Plate House, Finsbury Circus, London, E.C.2.

Rolling stock : 164 locomotives, 270 passenger cars, 2,325 general service wagons.
Floating plant : 6 lighters, 1 steam tug.

Mileage : 1,011. Gauge, Metre.

Area : States of Pernambuco, Parahyba, Alagôas and Rio Grande do Norte.

Passengers (1922) : 3,056,045.

Chief traffic : Sugar-cane, sugar, cotton-seed and cotton, maize, castor seed and oil, mandioca, hides, alcohol, tobacco and coffee, building materials, imported food-stuffs, kerosene and general goods.

Leopoldina Railway Company, Ltd.
3 Lombard Street, London, E.C.3.

Rolling stock : 247 locomotives, 324 passenger cars, 2,556 general traffic wagons.
Floating plant : 5 launches, 2 lighters, 4 pontoons.

Mileage : 1,831. Gauge, Metre.

Area : States of Rio de Janeiro, Espirito Santo, and Minas Geraes, including ports of Rio, São João da Barra, and Victoria.

Chief traffic : Coffee, sugar-cane, sugar, flour, alcohol, rice, salt, timber and building materials, tobacco, and imported goods.
[See Index to Advertisers.]

Leopoldina Terminal Company, Ltd.
3 Lombard Street, London, E.C.3.
(Controls the Companhia Cantareira e Viação Fluminense.)

Operates tramways at Nictheroy, a ferry boat system, and has warehouses i   Rio de Janeiro.

Madeira-Mamoré Railway Company.
(Incorporated, 1907, under the Laws of Maine, U.S.A.)
Friars House, New Broad Street, London, E.C.2.

Mileage : 226. Gauge, Metre.

Area : West Brazil and North-east Bolivia.

Chief traffic : Rubber, agricultural products, general merchandise.

Mogyana Railways and Navigation Company.
(Companhia Mogyana de Estradas de Ferro e Navegação.)

Mileage : 1,194. Gauge, Metre.

Area : Districts of Campinas, Ribeirão Preto, Franca, Uberaba, Catalão Guaxupe, and southern parts of Minas Geraes.

Chief traffic : Coffee, cattle, cereals and general merchandise.

Quarahim International Bridge Company, Ltd.
London Office : River Plate House, 10–11 Finsbury Circus, E.C.2.

A bridge to link the North Western of Uruguay line with the Brazil Great Southern, opened for traffic in 1915. Consists of 19 spans of 33˙730 metres (steel superstructure on concrete columns), with a total length of 640˙87 metres.

San Paulo (Brazilian) Railway Company, Ltd.
111 Gresham House, Old Broad Street, London, E.C.2.

Rolling stock   Main Line, 113 locomotives, 197 passenger cars, 4,100 general traffic wagons; (Bragantina section), 9 locomotives, 11 passenger cars, 122 general traffic wagons.

Mileage : Main Line, 86½; gauge, 5 ft. 3 in. Bragantina section, 67; gauge, 3 ft. 3 in.

Area : Santos, via São Paulo, to Jundiahy and the towns of Bragança, Atibaia and Piracaça, including the most important coffee-producing districts.

Passengers (1922) : 5,373,699.

Chief traffic : coffee, cereals, cotton, salt, sugar, coal, building materials.

Sorocabana Railway Company.
(Inc. 1907, under the Laws of the State of Maine, U.S.A.)
281 St. John Street, Portland, Maine, U.S.A.

Southern San Paulo Railway Company, Ltd.
80 Bishopsgate, London, E.C.2.

Rolling stock (end 1919) : 6 locomotives, 9 passenger cars, 56 general traffic wagons.
Mileage : 105. Gauge, Metre.
Area : The coffee-producing districts of the State.
Chief traffic : Firewood and timber, rice and cereals, building materials and general goods.

State of Bahia South Western Railway Company, Ltd.
8 Arthur Street, King William Street, London, E.C.4.

Rolling stock : 7 locomotives, 11 passenger cars, 69 general traffic wagons.
Mileage : 89 kilometres. Gauge, Metre.
Area : The cocoa-producing area between the port of Ilheos and Itabuna and the Almada and Mucambo valleys.
Passengers (1920) 165,060.
Chief traffic : Cocoa, foodstuffs, building materials, dried meat and sugar, kerosine, and general merchandise.

Sul-Mineira Railway (Rede Sul-Mineira).
Area : State of Minas Geraes.
Mileage : 12,000 kilometres.
Chief traffic : Coffee, live-stock (pigs and cattle), potatoes, butter and cereals.

BRITISH GUIANA.

Demerara Railway Co.
London Office : 110 Cannon Street, E.C.

Two lines : Demerara and Berbice (Georgetown to Rosignol), 60¼ miles; West Coast Railway (Vreden Hoop to Parika), 18¼ miles.

BRITISH HONDURAS.

Stann Creek Railway.

Inland from Commerce Bight, Stann Creek, for 25 miles; 3 ft. gauge.
Chief traffic: Bananas and produce.

COSTA RICA.

Costa Rica Railway Company, Ltd.
Dashwood House, 9 New Broad Street, London, E.C.2.

Leased to the Northern Railway Company of Costa Rica.
Mileage   189.   Gauge, 3 ft. 6 in.
Area : Port Limón to San José and Alajuela.
Chief traffic   Coffee and bananas.

Northern Railway Company of Costa Rica.
Mileage : 140.
Main Line : Port Limón to San José and from that town to Alajuela.

The Estrella Valley Railway,
with about 12¾ miles of railway, is owned by the United Fruit Company

CUBA.

The Cuba Railway Company.
52 William Street, New York City.

Mileage   685,066. Gauge, 4 ft. 8½ in.

The Cuban Central Railways, Ltd.
(Controlled by the United Railways of Havana, q.v.)
Dashwood House, 9 New Broad Street, London, E.C.2.

The Havana Central Railroad.
(Controlled by the United Railways of Havana.)

The Havana Terminal Railroad.
(Controlled by the United Railways of Havana.)

The Marianao and Havana Railway Co., Ltd.
270 Dashwood House, New Broad Street, London, E.C.2.

(Leased to and worked by the United Railways of the Havana and Regla
Warehouses, Ltd.)
Mileage : 19.   Gauge, 4 ft. 8½ in.
Area : Havana to Marianao and La Playa.

Matanzas Terminal Railroad.
(Controlled by the United Railways of Havana, q.v.)

United Railways of the Havana and Regla Warehouses, Ltd.
Dashwood House, 9 New Broad Street, London, E.C.2.

The Western Railway of Havana and the Cuban Central Railways are amalgamated with the United.

Mileage : 1,210. Stations, 111.

Passengers (1921–1922) : 17,303,729.

Rolling stock : Engines, 381; passenger stock, 240; baggage and parcels stock, 78, goods stock, 10,669, service stock, 347

The Western Railway of Havana, Ltd.
(Controlled by the United Railways of Havana.)

COLOMBIA.

Amagá Railway.
Connects Medellín with Caldas.

Antioquia Railway.
From Puerto Berrio to Cisneros on the eastern side of the Cordilleras (116 kilometres); on the west from Medellín (74 kilometres). The estimated length of tunnel to unite the sections is 3,700 metres.

The Barranquilla Railway and Pier Company, Ltd.
615–616 Salisbury House, Finsbury Circus, London, E.C.2.

Mileage : 18½. Gauge, 3 ft. 6 in.

Pier at Puerto Colombia, 4,600 ft.

Passengers (1921–1922) : 237,643. Goods, 159,048 tons. Specie, $6,664,130.

Chief traffic   Coffee, hides, tobacco, cotton-seed, machinery, ivory, nuts, mineral and general merchandise.

Area : From Puerto Colombia Pier (Savanilla Bay) to Barranquilla.

The Colombia Railways & Navigation Co., Ltd.
Finsbury Court, Finsbury Pavement, London, E.C.2.

Mileage : 65. Gauge, 3 ft.

Connects Cartagena with the River Magdalena. The Company owns a fleet of steamers on the River Magdalena.

Chief traffic : Coffee.

The Colombian National Railway Company, Ltd.
52 Bedford Street, London, W.C.2.

Mileage : 82. Gauge, 3 ft.

Passengers (1920) 272,438.

Chief traffic : Livestock, coffee. and general goods.

Area : Department of Cundinamarca, from Girardot to Facatativá, a city on the Sabana Railway, to Bogotá.

The Colombian Northern Railway Company, Ltd.
9 Bishopsgate, London, E.C.2.

Mileage : 43 kilometres. Gauge, 3 ft. 3 in.

Area : Savanna of Bogotá, connecting the capital, Bogotá, with Zipaquira, a salt-mining centre on the Colombian Central Railway.

Chief traffic : Agricultural produce and foodstuffs.

Cúcuta Railway Company.
(Incorporated under the Laws of Colombia, 1865.)

Capital authorized and issued   . $1,800,000

Area : Cúcuta Valley districts extending to Puerto Villamizar on the Zulia River.

Mileage : 55 kilometres. Gauge, 3 ft.

Chief traffic : Timber, hides, live stock, salt, and coffee.

The Dorada Extension Railway, Ltd.
Moorgate Hall, London, E.C.2.

Mileage : 70. Ropeway to Frutillo, 23¼, operated by agreement with the Dorada Railway (Ropeway Extension), Ltd. Gauge, 3 ft.

Area   Connects Ambalema with La Dorada.

Chief traffic : Coffee, hides, machinery, provisions, salt, soap, and sugar.

The Dorada Railway (Ropeway Extension), Ltd.
(Operated by the Dorada Extension Railway, Ltd., q.v.)
Moorgate Hall, London, E.C.2.

The Ropeway is completed across the Andes via Cajones and Esperanza stations to Manizales and extends about 44½ miles.

The Great Northern Central Railway of Colombia, Ltd.
130 Dashwood House, London, E.C.2.

Owned by the Colombian Government. Works the system of the Great Northern Central Railway Company

Mileage : 90. Gauge, metre.

Pacific Railway.

From Cali and Buenaventura on the Pacific to Girardot. The property of the Government.

Puerto Wilches Railway.

From Puerto Wilches, on the Magdalena River, in the direction of Bucaramanga.

The Sabana Railway.

Bogotá to Factativá, to El Dintel-Sabaneta and Buena Vista in progress.

The Santa Marta Railway Company, Ltd.
57½ Old Broad Street, London, E.C.2.

Mileage · 99. Gauge, 3 ft.

Rolling stock : 20 locomotives, 16 passenger cars, 281 general traffic wagons.

Floating plant : 2 steamboats.

Serves the banana-growing district between Santa Marta and Fundación. About 80 per cent. of the income is derived from bananas.

CHILE.

Aguas Blancas Railway Company.
See Antofagasta (Chile) and Bolivia Railway Co., Ltd.

Anglo-Chilian Nitrate and Railway Company, Ltd.
4 London Wall Buildings, London, E.C.2.

Mileage, 95. Gauge, 3 ft. 6 in.

Passengers (1922) : 16,285. Traffic : 238,494 tons

Antofagasta (Chili) and Bolivia Railway Company, Ltd.
1 Broad Street Place, London, E.C.2.

Connects the nitrate ports Antofagasta, Mejillones and Coloso with the principal towns of Bolivia. The Company operates under leases the lines of the Bolivia Railway Co., and Aguas Blancas Railway Co. It also, works the Chilian Northern Longitudinal Railway.

Mileage (own and leased lines), 1,810. Gauges, 2 ft. 6 in. and metre.

Chief traffic : Nitrate of soda, of which over 1,000,000 tons were carried in 1920. Fuel, bar copper, borate of lime. Tin is important on the Bolivian section, and about 70,000 tons per annum of concentrates are carried.

Arica and Tacna Railway Company.
London Office : 132 Dashwood House, 9 New Broad Street, London, E.C.2.

From the port of Arica to Tacna.

Mileage, 40. Gauge, 4 ft. 8½ in.

Passengers (1921) : 17,870; goods, 20,804,394 kilogrammes; specie, value, $97,688.

Chief traffic : Vegetables, fruits, live stock, flour, hay, salt, and general merchandise.

Caleta Buena and Agua Santa Railway.
See Compañia de Salitres y Ferrocarril de Agua Santa.

Carrizal and Cerro Blanco Railway Company.
Offices : Valparaiso, and 34 Castle Street, Liverpool.

Mileage, 126. Gauge, 4 ft. 2 in.

Line was leased to the Sociedad de Minas y Fundiciones de Carrizal for five years from 1917, with the option of purchase.

Last Dividend (May 1922) : 4 per cent.

Chilian Eastern Central Railway Company, Ltd.
Capel House, New Broad Street, E.C.

Chilian Northern Railway Company, Ltd.
1 Broad Street Place, London, E.C.2.

Chilian Transandine Railway Company, Ltd.
147 Leadenhall Street, London, E.C.3.

Capital authorized	.	.	£1,500,000
Capital issued		.	£1,500,000

Mileage, 44. Gauge, metre.

From Los Andes (Chile) to the Argentine frontier, connecting with the Argentine Transandine (metre gauge) Railway Portions of the track are on the " rack " system.

Compañia de Salitres y Ferrocarril de Agua Santa.
Iquique.

Area : Districts of Huara and Negreiros, in the province of Tarapacá.

Chief traffic : Nitrates and petroleum machinery, coal, hay, barley, and foodstuffs. Caleta Buena, the port, is connected with the railway by inclined planes of 2,400 ft. high. The line runs inland to Negreiros, about 50 kilometres. The farthest point is Huara, 60 kilometres. The elevation of the oficinas served is between 3,500 and 3,750 ft.

Rolling stock : 19 locomotives, 1,112 cars, 110 petroleum tanks, 13 passenger cars.

RAILWAYS OF LATIN-AMERICA.

Nitrate Railways Company, Ltd.
110 Cannon Street, London, E.C.4.

Rolling stock : 73 locomotives, 64 passenger cars, 1,471 general traffic wagons.
Mileage, 393. Gauge, 4 ft. 8½ in.
Passengers (1922): 246,989.
Area : The line connects the nitrate oficinas of the province of Tarapacá with the ports of Iquique and Pisagua.
Chief traffic : Nitrates, coal, oil, and stores for oficinas.

Taltal Railway Company, Ltd.
River Plate House, 10 and 11, Finsbury Circus, E.C.2.

Rolling stock : 50 locomotives, 18 passenger cars, 1,128 general traffic wagons.
Mileage, 172. Gauge, 3 ft. 6 in.
Passengers (1922): 44,147.
Chief traffic : Nitrates, copper ore, hides, oil fuel, coal, timber, fodder, foodstuffs, iodine.

BOLIVIA.

Antofagasta (Chili) and Bolivia Railway Company, Ltd.
See Chile.

Southern Railway of Peru.
See Peru.

ECUADOR.

Ambato-Curaray Railway.
Under construction by the Government. Total length 182 kilometres.

Bahia-Chone Railway.
(Bahía de Caráquez to Quito Railway).

A Government line of some 60 miles.
Gauge 0·75 metre.

Central Railway of Ecuador, Ltd.
55 London Wall, London, E.C.2.

Mileage : 130 kilometres.
Area : A narrow gauge line from the port of Manta to Santa Ana (Province of Manabi), through coffee, cacao, ivory nut, and Panamá hat-making districts.
The Government has assumed control.

Guayaquil and Quito Railway Company.
25 Broad Street, New York.

Rolling stock : 16 locomotives, 21 passenger cars, 147 general traffic wagons.
Floating plant : 1 ferry-boat, 1 tug, 4 lighters.
Mileage : 464 kilometres. Gauge, 3 ft. 6 in.
Area : The towns of Durán, Bucay, Guamote, Luisa, Riobamba, Ambato, and Quito.

Puerto-Bolívar Railway.

A short ine partly constructed and working between Puerto Bolívar and Pasaje, about 18 miles.

Quito-Esmeraldas Railway.

To connect Esmeraldas with Quito, a distance of about 230 miles; under construction.

Salinas Railway.

To connect Guayaquil with Salinas, under construction by the Government. Total ength 174 kilometres.

Sibambe-Cuenca Railway.

Construction of this line undertaken by the Government, total length 150 kilometres. Gauge, 1·067 metres.

Transamazonic Railway.

Under construction by the Government from Puerto Bolívar, through Cuenca and Loja, to Zamora in the Oriental Region, 300 kilometres.

GUATEMALA.

International Railways of Central America.
17 Battery Place, New York City, U.S.A.

London Agents : Hambros Bank of Northern Commerce, 70 Old Broad Street, London, E.C.2.

Rolling stock : 75 locomotives, 110 passenger cars, 1,424 general traffic wagons. Mileage (Guatemala and Salvador), 632. Gauge, 3 ft.

Area : Main line from Puerto Barrios, via Guatemala City, to San José and various points in the west, including the ports of Champerico and Ocós (Guatemala). The Salvador division, with mileage of 135, from the port of La Unión on the Pacific towards the city of San Salvador.

Chief traffic bananas, also coffee, sugar, firewood and lumber, flour, garden produce, hardware, cereals, hides, rubber and general goods.

HONDURAS.

	Kilometres.
National Railway	95
Matâ de Guineo Branch	21
Tela Railroad Co.	245
Trujillo Railroad Co.	119
Vaccaro Bros. & Co.	203
Cuyamel Fruit Co.	80

NICARAGUA.

Ferrocarriles Internacionales de Centro-America.
(International Railways of Central America.)

Projected to connect Honduras, Salvador, and Nicaragua frontiers, known also as the Pan-American Railway.

Pacific Railroad of Nicaragua.
(Ferrocarril del Pacifico de Nicaragua.)

Mileage : 165. Corinto, on the Pacific coast, to Chinandega, and thence to León, Managua, Masaya, Granada, and Diriamba.

Pearl Lagoon Railway, on the Atlantic coast, under construction.

RAILWAYS OF LATIN-AMERICA.

MEXICO.

El Oro Mining and Railway Company, Ltd.
24 Lombard Street, London, E.C.3.

Mileage : 38. Gauge, 3 ft.

Ferro Carril Hidalgo y Nordeste.
Operated by the National Railways.

Mexico City to Pachuca, via Gran Canal, San Augusta and Tepa, 68 miles; and from Tepa to Huauchinango, 67 miles. Gauge, 3 ft.

Ferro Carril Pachuca à Tampico.

From Pachuca to Ixmiguilpan, 51'5 miles, will proceed North-east to Zacualtipan and thence to Tampico. Gauge, 4 ft. 8½ in.

Ferro Carril Rafael y Atlixco.

Runs from Mexico City to Ozumba, 52'1 miles; Atlanta to Apapasco, 18 miles; and Santa Catalina to Atlixco, 19'8 miles. Gauge, 3 ft.

Interoceanic Railway of Mexico (Acapulco to Vera Cruz), Ltd.
240 Finsbury Pavement House, London, E.C.2.

(Leases the Mexican Eastern Railway and Mexican Southern Railway.) Operated by the National Railways of Mexico.

Mileage (including leased lines) 1,047. Gauge, 3 ft.
Area : Vera Cruz to Mexico City and branches.

Kansas City, Mexico and Orient Railway Company.

In 1918, the Mexican section was taken over and operated by the Mexican Government under contract for a term of years. Will connect Kansas City, U.S.A., and Topolobampo on the Pacific, a distance of 1,659 miles, lines from Marquez to Chihuahua, and to Sanchez in operation.

Mileage 285. Gauge, 4 ft. 8½ in.

Mexican Central Railway.

Incorporated in 1880, under the Laws of Massachusetts, U.S.A.; in 1909, merged in the National Railways of Mexico.

From El Paso, State of Texas, U.S.A., and crosses the frontier at Ciudad Juarez, thence via Chihuahua, Jimirez, Escalon, Bermejillo, Terreon, Gutierrez, Zacatecas, Aguascalientes, Salamanca, Celaya, Querétaro and Tula to Mexico City

Mileage 1,224. Gauge, 4 ft. 8½ in.
There are branches, including one from San Luis Potosí to Tampico.
Mileage : 275'3. Gauge, 4 ft. 8½ in.

Mexican Eastern Railway Company, Ltd.
Finsbury Pavement House, London, E.C.2.
(Leased in 1903 to the Interoceanic Railway of Mexico.)

Mileage : 140. Gauge, 3 ft.
Area : From Oriental to Iturbe with a branch to Teziutlan.

Mexican International Railway Company.

Incorporated in 1882 under the Laws of the State of Connecticut, U.S.A.; now part of the National Railways.

The object was to connect Mexico and the United States and to provide an outlet on the Pacific coast at Mazatlan. Starting at Eagle Pass, State of Texas, U.S.A., it crosses the frontier at Piedras Negras, and runs to Sacramento, Durango, Canitas, and Tepehuanes. Serves the coalfields of Coahuila. The mineral traffic is considerable.

Mileage : 683. Gauge, 4 ft. 8½ in.

RAILWAYS OF LATIN-AMERICA.

Mexican Northern Railway Company.
Escalon, Mexico.

Mileage 89. Gauge, 4 ft. 8½ in.
Area : Escalon to Carrillo and Sierra Mojada.

Mexican Railway Company, Ltd.
1 Broad Street Place, London, E.C.2, Buena Vista Station, Mexico City
(Taken over by the Mexican Government.)

Mileage : 628 kilometres. Gauge, 4 ft. 8½ in. 130 kilometres, narrow gauge.
Passengers (1922) : 2,749,962. Goods traffic, 425,358 tons.
Area : Mexico City to Vera Cruz, through the provinces of Vera Cruz, Puebla,
Tlaxcala and Mexico. Branches to Huatusco, Puebla, Pachuca, and Huajuapan.

Mexican Southern Railway, Ltd.
Finsbury Pavement House, London, E.C.2.

(Leased in 1909 to the Interoceanic Railway of Mexico (Acapulco to Vera Cruz),
Ltd.)
Operated by the National Railways of Mexico, before the seizure by the Government
in 1914; still in Government possession.
Mileage : 320. Gauge, 3 ft.
Area : Puebla to Oaxaca.

Mexico North-Western Railway Company.
(Inc. 1909 under the Laws of Canada.)

603 Dominion Bank Buildings, Toronto, Ciudad Juaréz, Chihuahua, Mexico.
Mileage : 495. Gauge, 4 ft. 8½ in.
Area : Ciudad Juaréz to La Junta, thence to Chihuahua, from where a branch runs
to Santa Eulalia, the largest silver-lead mines in Mexico.

Michoacan Railway and Mining Company, Ltd.
17 Ironmonger Lane, London, E.C.2.

Mileage : 60. Gauge, 3 ft.

Nacozari Railway Company.
The Mexican border is crossed at Agua Prieta by the Nacozari Railway Co., which
has its headquarters at New York. It runs from Douglas, Arizona, to Nacozari, the
centre of a large mining district, via Esqueda, for the El Tigre mine and Pilares de
Teras, the latter containing large deposits of low grade sulphide copper.
Mileage : 75. Gauge, 4 ft. 8½ in.

National Railways of Mexico.
London Representative : E. J Bray, Palmerston House, Old Broad Street, E.C.2.
Embraces several systems, including the Interoceanic Railway, the Mexican Central
Railway, and the Mexican International Railway Co.
Mileage : 6,468 miles, standard gauge, 387 miles, narrow gauge.

Pan-American Railway.
Starts from Gamboa, State of Oaxaca, and runs South-east to the Guatemalan
frontier, via Jalisco, Tonala, Pijijiapan, Huixtla and Tapachula.
Mileage : 284·3. Gauge, 4 ft. 8½ in.

South Pacific Railway Company of U.S.A.
This company has 928 miles of track in Mexico. It runs from Nogales on the American
frontier, and goes through the west of Mexico so far as Tepic, whence a line is in course
of construction to Guadalajara, to provide through communication to Mexico City.
This railway, of which the Mexican section was taken over in 1917 by the Government,
leased in 1898 the Sonora Railway.
Mileage (Nogales to Tepic) : 931. Gauge, 4 ft. 8½ in.

RAILWAYS OF LATIN-AMERICA.

Tehuantepec National Railway.

Puerto Mexico to Salina Cruz.
Mileage : 188·5. Gauge, 4 ft. 8½ in.

United Railways of Yucatan.

Area : (1) Northern Division : Merida to Progreso and Izamal. Mileage, 66 kilometres. Standard gauge. (2) Eastern Division : Merida to Valladolid. Mileage, 181 kilometres. Narrow gauge. (3) Western Division : Merida to Campeche. Mileage, 173 kilometres. Narrow gauge. (4) Southern Division : Merida to Peto. Mileage, 153 kilometres. Narrow gauge.

Vera Cruz and Isthmus Railway.

Vera Cruz to Santa Lucrecia, 206·6 miles; and Córdoba to Tierra Blanca, 57·7 miles. Gauge, 4 ft. 8½ in.

Vera Cruz Terminal Company, Ltd.
1 Broad Street Place, London, E.C.2.

Handles the import and export traffic of the Mexican Railways Co., Ltd., the Interoceanic Railway of Mexico (Acapulco to Vera Cruz), Ltd., the Vera Cruz (Mexico) Railways, Ltd., and the Vera Cruz and Isthmus Railway
Area : The port of Vera Cruz.
Mileage : 63. Gauge, 4 ft. 8½ in. and 3 ft.

PERU.

Central Railway of Peru, Ltd.
(Including the Morocacha Branch and the Oroya-Huancayo Extension.)
Owned by the Peruvian Corporation Ltd.

Chimbote Railway.

Owned by the Peruvian Corporation, Ltd.
Passengers (1919–1920) 9,578.
Chief traffic : Sugar, cotton, guano, coal.

Guaqui-La Paz Railway.

Owned by the Peruvian Corporation, Ltd.
Passengers (1920–1921) 51,284.
Connects La Paz, Bolivia, with Southern Railway of Peru by way of the Titicaca Lake steamers.

Ilo-Moquegua Railway.

The property of the Government of Peru.

Pacasmayo and Guadalupe Railway, Ltd.
(With the Chilete Extension.)
Owned by the Peruvian Corporation, Ltd.
Passengers (1920–1921) : 263,236. Freight, 33,267 tons.
Chief traffic : Animals, sugar, maize, barley, rice.

Paita-Piura Railway, Ltd.
Owned by the Peruvian Corporation, Ltd.
Passengers (1920–1921) : 230,927. Freight, 81,677 tons.
Chief traffic : Cotton, cotton-seed, charcoal, firewood, wheat and maize, rice, flour,

Pisco-Ica Railway.
Managed by the Peruvian Corporation, Ltd.
Chief traffic : Principally cotton and cotton-seed.

Southern Railway of Peru, Ltd.
(Including the Cuzco Extension.)

Owned by the Peruvian Corporation, Ltd.
Passengers (1920–1921): 326,366. Freight, 131,516 tons.
Chief traffic : Wheat, maize, flour, wool, sugar, minerals.

Trujillo Railway, Ltd.

Owned by the Peruvian Corporation, Ltd.
Passengers (1920–1921): 797,885. Freight, 148,117 tons.
Chief traffic Guano, sugar, rice, minerals.

PANAMÁ.

Bocas del Toro Railway.

Belonging to the United Fruit Company Mileage, 144 miles; carries fruit and passengers to Almirante.

Chiriqui Railroad.

Narrow-gauge from Pedregal to Boquete via David.

Darien Railroad.

38 miles long, a Decauville railway.

Panamá Railroad.

Panamá City and Colón (part of the Canal undertaking).

PARAGUAY.

The Paraguay Central Railway Company, Ltd.
80 Bishopsgate, London, E.C.2.

Rolling stock : 23 locomotives, 63 passenger cars, and 512 general traffic wagons, ferry slip cranes, etc.
Mileage, 274. Gauge, 4 ft. 8½ in.
Area : From Asunción, via Paraguarí, Villa Rica, and Pirapó, to Encarnación, where there is a train ferry across the Río Paraná to Posadas (Argentina), whence there is direct communication with Buenos Aires (966 miles) via the Paraná ferry at Zárate.
Passengers (1921): 512,383.
Chief traffic : Timber, quebracho extract, meat, hides, building materials, sugar-cane tobacco, oranges, hay, cereals and flour, cattle, and general goods.

SALVADOR.
International Railways of Central America.

See Guatemala.

The Salvador Railway Company, Limited.
7 and 8 Idol Lane, London, E.C.3.

Mileage, 100. Gauge, 3 ft. 6 in.
Chief traffic : Coffee, sugar-cane, sugar, salt, cereals, timber, building materials, agricultural produce, liquors, drugs and chemicals.

URUGUAY.

Central Uruguay Eastern Extension Railway, Ltd.
River Plate House, Finsbury Circus, London, E.C.2.

Mileage   311. Gauge, 4 ft. 8½ in.

Passengers (1921-1922): 185,584.

Area : Provinces of Florida, Minas, Treinta y Tres, Cerro and Largo.

Chief traffic : Cereals, stock products, timber and firewood, building materials, livestock.

Central Uruguay Northern Extension Railway Company, Ltd.
River Plate House, Finsbury Circus, London, E.C.2.

Mileage : 185. Gauge, 4 ft. 8½ in.

Passengers (1921-1922) : 47,873.

Area : The provinces of Durazno, Tacuarembó, and Rivera.

Chief traffic   Cereals, stock products, timber and firewood, building materials, livestock, canned meats.

Central Uruguay Railway Company of Montevideo, Ltd.
The lines worked by this Company are (1) The Central Uruguay Eastern Extension Railway, Ltd., (2) The Central Uruguay Northern Extension Railway Company, Ltd., (3) The Central Uruguay Western Extension Railway, Ltd., (4) The North Eastern of Uruguay Railway Company, Ltd.

Mileage 197   including extensions, 980. Gauge, 4 ft. 8½ in.

Passengers (1920-1921) : 2,701,795.

Area : From Montevideo (San José) and via Florida and Durazno to Rio Negro (Province of Durazno), where it joins the Northern Extension.

Chief traffic : Wheat, maize, and other cereals, linseed, wool, hides, timber and firewood, building materials, limestone, coal, salt, agricultural produce, and live-stock.

Central Uruguay Western Extension Railway, Ltd.
River Plate House, Finsbury Circus, London, E.C.2.

Mileage   211. Gauge, 4 ft. 8½ in.

Passengers (1922) : 75,647

Area : The provinces of San José, Colonia, Soriano, and Flores.

Chief traffic   Cereals, stock products, timber and firewood, building materials and livestock.

Midland Uruguay Extension Railway Company, Ltd.
River Plate House, Finsbury Circus, London, E.C.2.

Operated by the Midland Uruguay Railway Co., Ltd.

Area   Eastern portion of province of Paysandú from Tres Arboles (Midland Uruguay Railway) to Piedra Sola (Central Uruguay Northern Extension Railway).

Midland Uruguay Railway Company, Ltd.
River Plate House, Finsbury Circus, London, E.C.2.

Works the Midland Uruguay Extension Company, and the Uruguay Northern Railway Company, Ltd.

Mileage   317 kilometres. Gauge, 4 ft. 8½ in.

Passengers (1920-1921)   81,790.

Area : The provinces of Rio Negro, Paysandú, and Salto, with a branch to Fray Bentos.

Chief traffic : Cattle (for Liebig factories at Fray Bentos), building materials, wool, hay, cereals, and agricultural produce, general goods.

RAILWAYS OF LATIN-AMERICA.

North Eastern of Uruguay Railway Company, Ltd.
River Plate House, Finsbury Circus, London, E.C.2.

Area : Provinces of San José and Minas.

North Western of Uruguay Railway Company, Ltd.
20 Copthall Avenue, London, E.C.2.

Mileage : 113. Gauge, 4 ft. 8½ in.
Passengers (1920–1921) : 21,929.
Area : Follows the Rio Uruguay from the Midland Railway at Salto to Quarahim to connect with the Brazil Great Southern Railway.

Uruguay East Coast Railway Company, Ltd.
1 Broad Street Place, London, E.C.2.

Transferred to the Uruguayan Government.

Uruguay Northern Railway Company, Ltd.
River Plate House, Finsbury Circus, London, E.C.2.

Worked by the Midland Uruguay Railway Company, Ltd.
Mileage : 114 kilometres. Gauge, 4 ft. 8½ in.
Passengers (1920–1921) : 10,832.
Area : The province of Artigas.
Chief traffic : Saladero products, wool, flour, cereals, cattle and general goods.

VENEZUELA.

Bolivar Railway Company, Ltd.
Dashwood House, 9 New Broad Street, London, E.C.2.

Rolling stock (Dec. 31, 1920) : 16 locomotives, 19 passenger cars, 72 goods wagons, 244 general traffic wagons, 4 motor-cars.
Floating plant : 1 iron steamer, 1 wooden steam launch, 1 iron steam launch, 4 lighters, 7 rowing boats.
Area : Tucacas, on the coast, to Barquisimeto, with branches to Aroa and San Felipe, with extension from San Francisco de Yare to Ocumare del Tuy.
Mileage : 136. Gauge, 2 ft.
Chief traffic : Coffee, maize, salt, lard, cement, country produce.

La Guaira and Caracas Railway Company, Ltd.
Finsbury Pavement House, London, E.C.2.

Rolling stock : 13 locomotives, 28 passenger cars, 117 general traffic wagons.
Passengers (1920) : 92,399.
Mileage : 23. Gauge, 3 ft.
Chief traffic : Coffee, cocoa, coal, timber, salt, sugar, tobacco, provisions, agricultural produce, and general goods.

Puerto Cabello and Valencia Railway Company, Ltd.
Finsbury Pavement House, London, E.C.2.

Rolling stock (1920) : 11 locomotives, 13 passenger cars, 98 general traffic wagons.
Passengers (1920) : 57,993.
Mileage : 34. Gauge, 3 ft. 6 in.
Chief traffic : Firewood, meat, coal, coffee, sugar, salt, timber, building materials, maize, general goods.

556

BANKING FACILITIES.

BANKING FACILITIES.

INTERNATIONAL BANKS.

Head Offices, London.

The Anglo-South American Bank, Limited.
Established 1888.

Capital authorized ..		£10,000,000
Capital subscribed		£8,733,750
Issued and paid up		£4,366,875

Head Office: 62 Old Broad Street, London, E.C.2.

Directors: Robert John Hose, Esq. (Chairman and Managing Director), Sir Robert Harvey (Vice-Chairman), Sir Clarendon Golding Hyde, Edward Exton Barclay, Edward Bunge, Baron Emile Beaumont d'Erlanger, Alfred George Gumpert, Andrew Geddes, James Alfred Goudge, Charles Eugene Gunther, William Herbert Hollis, Auguste de Lantsheere, Alfred Naylor, Harry William Patrick, Thomas Woodsend.

General Managers: William E. Wells, Augustus C. E. Kimber, and David G. Davidson.

Local Branches—Argentina Buenos Aires, Bahia Blanca, Comodoro Rivadavia, Mendoza, Puerto Deseado, Rio Gallegos, Rosario de Santa Fé, San Julian, San Rafael, Santa Cruz, Trelew.

Chile: Antofagasta, Concepción, Copiapó, Coquimbo, Iquique, Punta Arenas, Santiago, Talcahuano, Valparaiso.

Mexico: Mexico City.

Peru: Lima.

Uruguay: Montevideo.

The Bank has branches in Bradford and Manchester, New York (Agency), Paris, Barcelona, Bilbao, Madrid, Valencia, Vigo, and Seville.

The Bank is represented in Brazil by the British Bank of South America, Ltd., and in the Central American countries by the Commercial Bank of Spanish America, Ltd., in which institutions the Anglo-South American Bank holds 99½ per cent. and about 97 per cent. respectively of the issued share capital.

Dividends: 1909-10, 1910-11, 10 per cent.; 1911-12, 1912-13, 12 per cent.; 1913-14, 10 per cent.; 1914-15, 8 per cent.; 1915-16, 9 per cent.; 1916-17, 10 per cent., 1917-18, 12½ per cent.; 1918-19, 15 per cent.; 1919-20, 15 per cent., in addition to a special interim dividend of 10 per cent.; 1920-21, 15 per cent.

For the first half of 1921-22 an interim dividend at the rate of 12 per cent. per annum was paid.

[See Index to Advertisers.]

The British Bank of South America, Limited.
Established 1863.

Capital subscribed		£2,000,000
Capital paid up		£1,000,000

Head Office: 4 Moorgate, London, E.C.2.

Manchester Office: 2 Norfolk Street.

Directors: Robert John Hose (Chairman), William Herbert Hollis (Deputy Chairman), Frederick R. S. Balfour, Rt. Hon. Sir Maurice W E. de Bunsen, Bart., G.C.M.G., G.C.V.O., C.B., Raoul Hector Foá, Edward Greene, Frank Henry Houlder, Frederic Lubbock, John Edward Mounsey.

Manager: Henry Probyn Roberts.

Local Branches—Argentina: Buenos Aires (six sub-branches), Rosario, Pergamino.

Brazil: Bahia, Rio de Janeiro, São Paulo, Porto Alegre, Rio Grande, Pernambuco, Santos.

Uruguay: Montevideo (two sub-branches), Mercedes.

Dividends: 1918, 14 per cent., 1919, 15 per cent., 1920, 15 per cent.; 1921, 12 per cent.; 1922, 10 per cent.

[See Index to Advertisers.]

The Colonial Bank.
Established 1836.

Capital authorized	. . . .	£5,000,000
Capital subscribed		£3,000,000
Capital paid up	.	£900,000

Head Office: 29 Gracechurch Street, London, E.C.3.

Directors: C. F Wood (Chairman), Cyril Gurney (Deputy Chairman), C. A. Campbell, George Cyril Cassels, Thomas du Buisson, G. W Fox, Sir Herbert Hamblin, Olive V G. Hoare, The Rt. Hon. Sir F. J. D. Lugard, R. Rutherford, The Rt. Hon. Lord Wargrave, Col. C. W Sofer Whitburn.

Joint General Managers: C. H. Hewett, E. H. Bell.

Secretary: J D. Race.

Branches in British Guiana: Demerara, Georgetown, Mahaica, Berbice, New Amsterdam.

Dividends: 1918, 8 per cent.; 1919, 9 per cent.; 1920, 10 per cent.; 1921, 10 per cent.; 1922, 8 per cent.

Commercial Bank of Spanish America, Limited.
Established 1904.

Capital authorized and issued	. . ..	£500,000

Head Office: 9 Bishopsgate, London, E.C.2.

Branch Office: 42 Whitworth Street, Manchester.

Directors: W E. Wells (Chairman), J A. Goudge, A. G. Gumpert, P C. Matts, S. R. Pryor.

Manager: Geo. Williams.

Assistant Manager and Secretary E. A. Green.

Local Branches—Colombia Bogotá, Medellín, Barranquilla, Santa Marta, Cartagena.

Ecuador: Guayaquil, Manta.

Guatemala: Guatemala City

Nicaragua: Managua.

Peru: Iquitos.

Salvador: San Salvador.

United States: New York, San Francisco.

Venezuela: Caracas, Puerto Cabello.

[See Index to Advertisers.]

Erlangers.
Established 1859.

8 Crosby Square, London, E.C.3.

General banking, commercial, and financial business.

Glyn, Mills Currie, Holt & Co.
Established 1753.
Registered with unlimited liability 1885.

Capital	£1,000,000
Reserve Fund	£500,000

Head Office: 67 Lombard Street, E.C.3.

Managing Partners: Lord Wolverton, Laurence Currie, Lord Hillingdon, General The Hon. Sir H. A. Lawrence, K.C.B., Brig.-General A. Maxwell, C.M.G., D.S.O., Eric Gore Browne, D.S.O.

Secretary: Hubert Bartlett.

[See Index to Advertisers.]

Huth (Frederick) & Co.
London and Manchester.
Established 1809.
Private firm.

Head Office: 12 Tokenhouse Yard, London, E.C.2.

Partners: Edward Huth, Lewis Huth Walters, Louis Ernest Meinertzhagen, The Acorn Trust, Ltd.

Foreign Houses: Huth & Co., New York; Huth & Co., Valparaiso; with branches in Santiago, Concepción, and Coquimbo.

BANKING FACILITIES.

London and Brazilian Bank, Limited.
Established 1862.

Capital subscribed	£3,000,000
Capital paid up	£1,500,000
Reserve Fund	£1,500,000

Head Office : 7 Tokenhouse Yard, London, E.C.2.

Directors : William Douro Hoare, C.B.E. (Chairman), Edward Anthony Benn (Managing Director), Max Julius Bonn, Leonard Daneham Cunliffe, Sir H. H. I. W Drummond, Bart., C.M.G., Charles Seymour Grenfell, John Kenneth Henderson, Wynn Harold Tregoning, C.B.E.

Joint Managers : T. J Finnie, H. P Caley

Bankers : The Bank of England, Messrs. Glyn, Mills, Currie, Holt & Co., The National Provincial and Union Bank of England, Ltd.

Local Branches—Brazil : Rio de Janeiro, Manáos, Pará, Maranhão, Ceará, Pernambuco, Bahia, Santos, São Paulo, Curityba, Rio Grande do Sul, Pelotas, Porto Alegre.

Argentina : Buenos Aires, Rosario.

Uruguay : Montevideo.

[See Index to Advertisers.]

The London and River Plate Bank, Limited.
Established 1862.

Capital authorized	£4,000,000
Capital paid up . .	£2,040,000

Head Office : 7 Princes Street, London, E.C.2.

Manchester Office : 86 Cross Street.

Bradford : 35 Hustlergate.

Directors : J W Beaumont Pease (Chairman), Richard Foster, Follett Holt, Kenneth Mathieson, Lambert W. Middleton, Herman B. Sim, Robert A. Thurburn (Managing Director).

Dividends : 1905-1913, 20 per cent. per annum; 1914-1919, 15 per cent. per annum, 1920, 15 per cent.; 1921, 12 per cent., 1922, 10 per cent.

Local Branches—Argentina : Buenos Aires (Sub-offices : Barracas, Boca, Once, Calle Santa Fé, Calle B. de Irigoyen), Rosario, Mendoza, Córdoba, Bahia Blanca, Paraná, Concordia, Tucumán.

Brazil : Rio de Janeiro, Santos, São Paulo, Porto Alegre, Bahia, Pernambuco, Maceió, Pará, Victoria, Curityba, Pelotas, Rio Grande, Manáos (Agency).

Chile : Valparaiso, Santiago, Antofagasta.

Colombia : Bogotá, Medellín, Manizales.

Paraguay : Asunción.

Uruguay : Montevideo, Paysandú, Salto, and Rivera.

Paris, Antwerp, and Lisbon, and an agency at New York.

[See Index to Advertisers.]

The National Bank, Limited.
Established 1835.

Subscribed Capital	£7,500,000
Capital paid up . .	£1,500,000
Reserve Fund .	£1,125,000
Deposits, etc. (as at June 30, 1923)	£42,011,746

Head Office : 13–17 Old Broad Street, London, E.C.2.

Directors : James Blackader Meers, Esq., C.B. (Chairman), Sir Thomas Henry Grattan Esmonde, Bart. (Chairman of Irish Board and Deputy Chairman of the Bank), Rt. Hon. Lord Macdonnell of Swinford, G.C.S.I., K.C.V.O. (Deputy Chairman of London Board).

Branches : London, Liverpool, Manchester, Bristol, Dublin, South Wales (127 Branches and 90 Sub-Offices in the U.K.).

[See Index to Advertisers.]

INTERNATIONAL BANKS.

Head Offices in U.S.A.

American Foreign Banking Corporation.

Capital $5,000,000

Head Office : 56 Wall Street, New York City

Local Branches.—Cuba : Havana.
Panamá : Panamá City
Panamá Canal Zone : Cristóbal.

Chairman of Board of Directors : A. H. Wiggin.

President : John H. Allen.

Secretary and Treasurer : E. P Sine.

Assistant Secretary : C. B. Holt.

Assistant Treasurer : W B. Sullivan.

Directors : John H. Allen, Robert I. Barr, J P Butler, Jr., Gerhard M. Dahl, H. G. P Deans, Charles L. Farrell, Oliver C. Fuller, Hayden B. Harris, Harris Nesbit, Levi L. Rue, John Sherwin, John W Staley, E. V. R. Thayer, A. H. Wiggin, Henry B. Wilcox.

London Agents : London Joint City & Midland Bank, Ltd.; Lloyds Bank, Ltd.

American Trading Company.

Established July 1900, under the laws of the State of Maine, U.S.A., being the amalgamation of the firm of Flint, Eddy & Co. (formed in 1870) and the American Trading Company (formed 1878).

Capital authorized $\begin{cases} \$5,000,000 \text{ preferred shares.} \\ \$7,500,000 \text{ ordinary shares.} \end{cases}$

Capital subscribed and paid up $\begin{cases} \$3,591,600 \text{ preferred shares.} \\ \$4,499,730 \text{ ordinary shares.} \end{cases}$

Head Office . New York.

London Office : 90 Fenchurch Street, E.C.3.

Directors : O. G. Jennings, H. P McCullough, G. S. Brewster, R. S. Brewster, G. M. Woolsey, M. N. Buckner, Lansing P Reed, James R. Morse (President), Alfred Debuys, P. H. Jennings, Daniel Warren, E. M. Sutliff, George S. Franklin, D. H. Blake, Walter S. Franklin (Vice-Presidents), Gardner B. Perry (Treasurer).

London Agent : F. Wallin.

Local Branches—Argentina : Buenos Aires, Bahia Blanca, Rosario.
Brazil : Bahia, Pernambuco, Porto Alegre, Rio de Janeiro, São Paulo.
Mexico : Mexico City.
Uruguay : Montevideo.
Venezuela : Caracas.

Bank of Central and South America, Inc.

Capital $5,000,000
Surplus . $2,500,000

Head Office : 44 Pine Street, New York.

Directors : Arthur M. Anderson, James Brown, W Palen Conway, Walter E. Frew, R. F McCreery, Gates, W. McGarrak, J. McHugh, H. Esk Moller, M. A. Oudin, William C. Potter, J Louis Schaefer, S. Stern, E. R. Stettinius, Albert Strauss.

Affiliated Banks—Colombia : Banco Mercantil Americano de Colombia, Medellín.
Costa Rica : Banco Mercantil de Costa Rica, San José.
Nicaragua : National Bank of Nicaragua, Managua.
Peru : Banco Mercantil Americano del Peru, Lima.
Venezuela :—Banco Mercantil Americano de Caracas, Caracas.

Foreign Office—Bank of Central and South America, Inc., Ecke Monckeberg and Paulstrasse, Hamburg.

London Correspondents : Guaranty Trust Company of New York.; Brown, Shipley & Co.

The Bank has agencies in Paris, Milan, Madrid, and Barcelona.

First National Bank of Boston.

Established 1864.

Capital $15,000,000

Head Office : Federal, Franklin and Congress Streets, Boston.
Local Branches : Buenos Aires and Havana.
Special Representative : London, 24 Old Broad Street, E.C.2.
Directors : Daniel G. Wing (President), Charles G. Bancroft (Chairman, Executive Committee), Robert Amory, Calvin Austin, Frederick Ayer, Edward E. Blodgett, Roland W Boyden, George W. Brown, Louis F. Butler, Earle P. Charlton, Walton L. Crocker, Carl P Dennett, B. H. Bristow Draper, Robert J. Edwards, Wilmot R. Evans, W. Cameron Forbes, F. Abbot Goodhue, Levi H. Greenwood, Frank J. Hale, Frank B. Hopewell, Matt. B. Jones, Herbert W Mason, Frederic C. McDuffie, Everett Morss, Andrew G. Pierce, Jr., Andrew W. Preston, C. G. Rice, Clifford K. Simonds, Nathaniel Stevens, Paul M. Warburg, Albert B. Wells, Sidney W. Winslow, Jr.
London Agents : Lloyds Bank Ltd. (17 Cornhill, E.C.3), Bank of Liverpool and Martins, Ltd., Westminster Bank Ltd. (Lothbury), London Joint City and Midland Bank, Ltd., Barclays Bank, Ltd., National Provincial and Union Bank of England, Ltd.

International Banking Corporation.

[This bank is owned by The National City Bank of New York, but it carries on business as a separate entity.]

Capital and Surplus $10,000,000
Undivided Profits $5,500,000

Head Office 60 Wall Street, New York.
London Office : 36 Bishopsgate, E.C.2.
Manager : W. M. Anderson.
Directors : Charles E. Mitchell (Chairman), James H. Carter, Joseph T Cosby, John A. Garver, Joseph P. Grace, H. T S. Green, Arthur Kavanagh, William A. Simonson, Beekman Winthrop.
President and General Manager : H. T. S. Green.
Vice-President and Treasurer : Lawrence M. Jay.
Local Branches in Panamá : Panamá City, Colón.
Eight Branches in Dominican Republics.
Dividends : 1917, 1918, 1919, 6 per cent.; 1920, 18 per cent.; 1921, 24 per cent.; 1922, 22 per cent.
[See Index to Advertisers.]

Irving Bank—Columbia Trust Company.

Established 1851.

Capital and surplus $28,000,000

Head Office : Woolworth Buildings, New York City.
London Representative : J H. Needham, Pinners' Hall, 54½ Old Broad Street, E.C.2.
Mexican Representative : Joseph W Rowe, Mexico City.
Representative in Porto Rico : Charles W. Fowler, San Juan.
Representative in Cuba : Edmund Enright, Havana.
London Agents : Barclay's Bank, Ltd.; London Joint City and Midland Bank, Ltd.; London County Westminster and Parr's Bank, Ltd.; Cox & Co., National Provincial and Union Bank of England, Ltd.

BANKING FACILITIES.

National City Bank of New York.

[This bank owns the International Banking Corporation (q.v.), which carries on business as a separate entity.]

Established 1812.

Capital, Surplus and Undivided Profits $91,526,528

Head Office: 55 Wall Street, New York.

Directors: Eric P. Swenson (Chairman), Guy Cary, Cleveland H. Dodge, Philip A. S. Franklin, John A. Garver, Joseph P Grace, Cyrus H. McCormick, Gerrish H. Milliken, Charles E. Mitchell, James E. O'Neill, James H. Post, W C. Procter, Percy R. Pyne, Percy A. Rockfeller, Robert W. Stewart, James A. Stillman, Horace S. Wilkinson, Beckman Winthrop.

Executive Management: C. E. Mitchell, William A. Simonson, G. E. Gregory.

London Branches: 36 Bishopsgate, E.C.2.
Trafalgar House, 11 Waterloo Place, S.W.1.
Local Branches.—Argentina: Buenos Aires, Rosario.
Brazil: Rio de Janeiro, Santos, São Paulo, Pernambuco.
Chile: Santiago, Valparaiso.
Colombia: Barranquilla, Bogotá, Medellín.
Cuba: Bayamo, Ciabarien, Camagüey, Cardenas, Ciego de Avila, Cienfuegos, Guantanamo, Havana, Manzanillo, Matanzas, Neuvitas, Pinar del Rio, Placetas del Norte, Remedios, Sagua la Grande, Sancti Spiritus, Santa Clara, Santiago, Unión de Reyes, Yaguajay
Peru: Lima.
Uruguay: Montevideo.
Venezuela Caracas.
Belgium: Antwerp, Brussels.
France: Paris.
Italy: Genoa.
United States: New York.

INTERNATIONAL BANKS,

Head Offices in Canada.

Bank of Montreal.
Toronto.

London Office 47 Threadneedle Street, E.C.2.
Branch: Mexico City
Manager: H. Weldon.

The Bank of Nova Scotia.
Established 1832.

Capital   . $10,000,000

Head Office: Halifax, N.S.
General Manager's and Executive Offices: Toronto.
General Manager: J A. McLeod.
Local Branches—Cuba: Havana (3 branches).
London Correspondents: London Joint City and Midland Bank, Ltd.; Bank of England.
Dividends: 16 per cent.
London Branch: 55 Old Broad Street, E.C.2.

BANKING FACILITIES.

The Canadian Bank of Commerce.
(With which is incorporated The Bank of British Columbia.)
Incorporated 1867.

Capital paid up	$15,000,000
Reserve Fund	$15,000,000

Head Office : Toronto.
London Office   2 Lombard Street, E.C.3.
Local Branches—Brazil : Caixa Postal 2103, Rio de Janeiro.
Cuba : Havana.
Mexico : Avenida San Francisco, 50 Mexico City.
Barbados : Bridgetown.
Jamaica : Kingston.
Trinidad : Port of Spain, San Fernando.

The Royal Bank of Canada.
Incorporated 1869.

Capital authorized	$25,000,000
Capital paid up	$20,400,000

Head Office : Montreal.
London Office   Bank Buildings, Princes Street, E.C.2.

Directors : Sir Herbert S. Holt (President), E. L. Pease, (Vice-President), Jas. Redmond, G. R. Crowe, D. K. Elliott, Hon. W H. Thorne, Hugh Paton, A. J Brown, K.C., W. J Sheppard, C. S. Wilcox, A. E. Dyment, C. E. Neill, Sir Mortimer B. Davis, G. H. Duggan, C. C. Blackadar, John T Ross, R. MacD. Paterson, W H. McWilliams, Capt. Wm. Robinson, A. McTavish Campbell, Robert Adair, William A. Black, C. B. McNaught.

London Manager   T R. Whitley

Dividends : 12 per cent. per annum, payable 3 per cent. quarterly

Local Branches—Argentina   Buenos Aires.
Brazil   Rio de Janeiro, Santos, São Paulo.
Uruguay : Montevideo.
British Guiana : Georgetown, New Amsterdam, Rose Hall.
British Honduras : Belize.
Colombia : Barranquilla.
Costa Rica : San José.
Venezuela   Caracas, Ciudad, Bolivar
Cuba : Antilla, Artemisa, Banes, Bayamo, Cabaiguan, Caibarien, Camaguey, Camajuani, Cardenas, Ciego de Avila, Cienfuegos, Colón, Cruces, Cueto, Cumanayagua, Encrucijada, Florida, Guanajay, Guantanamo, Guines, Havana, Holguin, Jatibonico, Jobabo, Jovellanos, La Esmeralda, Majagua, Manzanillo, Marianao, Matanzas, Miranda, Moron, Nuevitas, Palma Soriano, Pinar del Rio, Placetas del Norte, Puerto Padre, Ranchuelo, Rodas, Saguala Grande, Sancti Spiritus, Santa Clara, Santiago de Cuba, Trinidad, Victoria de las Tunas, Zulueta.

INTERNATIONAL BANKS.

Head Offices, Paris.

Banque Argentine et Française.
Established 1909.

Capital authorized and paid up   Frs. 20,000,000
Head Office   85 Boulevard Haussmann, Paris.

Directors . Charles Oudart (President), G. Jarre (Vice-President), J. Bazin, A. Blanchard, Georges Calvet, G. Fourvel-Rigolleau, Alfred Maupas, E. Verdon.

Manager : M. A. F Bouleix.
Branch   Buenos Aires.

BANKING FACILITIES.

Banque Française et Italienne pour l'Amérique du Sud.

Established 1910, and absorbed the Banco Commericale Italo-Braziliano, in 1917 acquired the Banco Zuizo-Sud-Americano.

Capital authorized	..	.. Frs. 50,000,000
Reserves	.. .	. Frs. 39,000,000

Head Office   12 Rue Halévy, Paris.

Directors : S. Dervillé (President), Louis Dapples (Vice-President), A. Autrand, Ferdinando Bocca, J Chevalier, S. Crespi, R. Delauncy Belleville, L. Della-Torre, H. Fenoglio, H. Finaly, Léon Fould, Paul Gauthier, Jacques Kulp, J. Masurel-Wattine, B. Nogara, E. Oudot, C. Parea, Henri Poirier, G. Puglisi, Cte. H. San Martino di Valperga-Maglione, G. Toeplitz, G. Zuccoli.

Local Branches—Argentina : Branches—Buenos Aires, Rosario de Santa Fé (Telegrams : " Francital ").

Brazil : Branches—São Paulo, Rio de Janeiro, Santos, Curityba, Porto Alegre, Pernambuco, Rio Grande.   Agencies—Araraquara, Barretos, Bebedouro Ourinhos, Botucatú, Caxias, Espirito Santo do Pinhal, Jahú, Mocóca, Paranagua, Ponta Grossa, Rebeirão Preto, São Carlos, São José do Rio Pardo, São Manoel (Telegrams— " Sudameris ").

Chile : Branch—Valparaiso (Telegrams : " Francital ").

Correspondents : Colombia :—Banco Frances e Italiano de Colombia, Bogotá.

Peru : Banco Italiano Lima, Callao, Chincha Alta, Mollendo, Arequipa.

London Agents · Banca Commerciale Italiana; London Joint City and Midland Bank, Ltd., Société Générale de Paris (53 Old Broad Street, E.C.2).

Dividends : 1910–1913, 8 per cent. per annum; 1914, 6 per cent.; 1915–1916, 8 per cent. per annum, 1917–1918, 9 per cent. per annum; 1919, 12 per cent., 1920–1922, 13 per cent. per annum.

Banque Française pour le Brésil.

Capital	.	Frs. 20,000,000

Head Office   1 Boulevard des Capucines, Paris.

Directors : Julian Rouland (President), L. Prangey (Vice-President), André Altermann, A. Manoel Alves Lima, Baron d'Anthouard, Raoul de Chaunac-Lanzac, Count de Legge, Ch. A. Monteiro de Barros, G. Reinhart.

Local Branches : Rio de Janeiro, São Paulo, Santos.

Correspondents—Argentina   Supervielle & Cie., Buenos Aires, Uruguay Supervielle & Cie., Montevideo.

INTERNATIONAL BANKS.

Head Offices in Germany.

Banco Alemán Transatlantico.

(See Deutsche Ueberseeische Bank.)

Brasilianische Bank für Deutschland.

Established 1887

Capital paid up	.	. M.25,000,000
Reserve Funds	.	. M.15,500,000

Head Office   Hamburg.

Managers : G. H. Kaemmerer, E. von Oesterreich.

Local Branches : Bahia, Porto Alegre, Rio de Janeiro, Santos, São Paulo.

Dividends : Nine years to 1912–1913, 10 per cent. per annum; 1913–1914, 6 per cent.; 1914–1915, 1915–1916, 1916–1917, 8 per cent., 1917–1918, 1918–1919, nil; 1919–1920, 15 per cent.; 1920–1921, 25 per cent.; 1921–1922, 40 per cent.

Deutsche-Südamerikanische Bank A.G.
Established 1906.

Capital M.20,000,000

Head Office : 46 Markgrafenstrasse, Berlin, W.56.

Branch Office : Hamburg, A. Fricke.

Directors : W. Tang, K. Schmitt, A. Hübbe, R. Neveling.

Local Branches—Argentina : Buenos Aires.

Brazil : Rio de Janeiro.

Chile : Valparaiso, Santiago.

Mexico : Mexico City.

Dividends : 1900–1913, 5 per cent. per annum; 1914, 8 per cent. No dividends were declared between 1914 and 1918; 1919, 8 per cent.; 1920, 10 per cent.; 1921, 20 per cent.; 1922, 300 per cent.

Deutsche Ueberseeische Bank (Banco Alemán Transatlantico—Banco Allemão Trans-atlantico).
Established in Berlin, 1893.

Capital paid up M.30,000,000

Local Branches—Under the title Banco Alemán Transatlantico—Argentina : Bahia Blanca, Buenos Aires, Córdoba, Mendosa, Rosario de Santa Fé.

Bolivia : La Paz, Oruro.

Chile : Antofagasta, Concepción, Iquique, Santiago, Temuco, Valsivia, Valparaiso.

Peru : Arequipa, Callao, Lima.

Spain : Barcelona, Madrid.

Uruguay : Montevideo.

Under the title Banco Allemão Transatlantico—

Brazil : Curityba, Rio de Janeiro, Santos, São Paulo.

Dividends : For 8 years to 1913, 9 per cent. per annum; four years to 1918, 6 per cent. per annum.; 1919–20, 30 per cent. per annum; 1921, 40 per cent. per annum; 1922, 600 per cent. per annum.

INTERNATIONAL BANKS.

Head Office, Lisbon.

Banco Nacional Ultramarino.
Established 1864.

The State Bank of the Portuguese Colonies.

Capital authorized	Esc. 48,000,000
Capital paid up .. .	Esc. 24,000,000
Reserves	Esc. 30,200,000

Head Office : Lisbon.

London Office : 9 Bishopsgate, E.C.2.

Directors : João Henrique Ulrich (Chairman), Bernardo Homero Machado, Conde de Caria, Henrique José Monteiro de Mendonça, Arthur Porto de Mello e Faro, Conde de Monte Real, José de Cunha Rolla Pereira, Julio Schmidt.

Delegate of the Board : E. F. Davies, O.B.E.

London Manager : J. P. Scottie.

Brazilian Branches.—Bahia, Campos, Manáos, Pará, Parahyba, Pernambuco, Rio de Janeiro, Santos, São Paulo.

Dividends : 1919, 20 per cent.

INTERNATIONAL BANKS.

Head Office, Antwerp.

Banque Italo-Belge.
Established 1911

Capital fully paid .	Frs. 50,000,000
Reserve funds .	Frs. 24,373,739

Head Office : 48 Place de Meir, Antwerp.

London Agency : 50 Old Broad Street, E.C.2.

Directors : Emile Francqui (Chairman), Comm. F H. Balzarotti (Vice-Chairman), Arthur Brys, Fernand Carlier, Georges Deprez, Chevalier de Wouters d'Oplinter, Léon Elsen, Emm. Janssen, Alberto Lodolo, Carlo Orsi, Hector Carlier (Managing Director).

Local Branches—Argentine : Buenos Aires.
Brazil : São Paulo, Rio de Janeiro, Santos, Campinas.
Chile : Valparaiso.
Uruguay : Montevideo.

INTERNATIONAL BANKS.

Head Office, Amsterdam.

Hollandsche Bank voor Zuid-Amerika (Banco Holandés de la America del Sud, Banco Hollandez da América do Sul) (Amsterdam).
Established 1914.

Capital paid up	Fl. 17,580,000

Head Office : Amsterdam (Heerengracht 4).

Managers A van Egmond, J P Hörchner, Jr.

Directors Dr. J P van Tienhoven (Chairman), Victor Bracht, Julius C. Bunge, H. P Cool, Gustave Dunant, Dr. C. J van Dusseldorp, G. H. Hintzen, Dr. A. G. Kröller, W. M. Schaurlleer, C. J den Tex Bondt, W. Westerman.

Local Branches—Argentina : Buenos Aires.
Brazil : Rio de Janeiro, Santos, São Paulo.
Chile : Santiago, Valparaiso.

London Agents : London Joint City and Midland Bank, Ltd., Equitable Trust Co. of New York; Banca Commerciale Italiana.

Dividends For 1914-1915, nil; each of the three years to 1917-1918, 8 per cent.; 1919, 9 per cent., 1920, 10 per cent.; 1921-1922, nil.

INTERNATIONAL BANKS.

Head Office, Rome.

Banca Nazionale de Credito.
Established 1922.

Capital fully paid up .	Lit. 250,000,000

Head Office Rome.

Affiliated Banks : Banque Italio-Francaise de Crédit, Paris, Marseilles and Tunis; Italian Discount and Trust Company, New York, Banca Dalmata di Sconto, Zara and Sebenico; Banca Coloniale de Credito, Asmara.

London Agents : Barclays Bank, Ltd., Westminster Bank, Ltd.

INTERNATIONAL BANKS.

Head Offices, Japan.

The Bank of Taiwan, Limited.
Registered in Japan, 1899.

Capital . . .. Yen 60,000,000

Head Office : Taipeh, Formosa, Japan.
London Office : 25 Old Broad Street, E.C.2.
President : K. Nakagawa; Vice-President : S. Mori.
London Manager : N. Takagi.
Correspondents—Argentina : Buenos Aires, Rosario.
Brazil : Bahia, Rio de Janeiro, São Paulo, etc.
Uruguay : Montevideo.

The Yokohama Specie Bank, Limited (Yokohama Shokin Ginko).

Capital subscribed and paid up . . Yen 100,000,000
Reserve Fund .. .. . Yen 69,000,000

Head Office : Yokohama.
Directors : Kenji Kodama (President), Reitaro Ichinomiya (Vice-President), Nagatane Soma, Yuki Yamakawa, Masunosuke Odagiri, Baron Koyata Iwasaki, Konojo Tatsumi, Shimakichi Suzuki, Fukusaburo Watanabe, Iwao Matsukata, Kaisaku Morimura, Kimpei Taksuchi, Taro Hozumi, Kunizo Mogami, Naozo Igarashi.
Local Branches—Argentina : Buenos Aires.
Brazil : Rio de Janeiro.

BANKS WITH HEAD OFFICES IN SOUTH AMERICA.

Banco Agricola Comercial.
Office : San Salvador (Salvador).

Banco Agricola Hipotecario.
Established 1894.

Capital authorized $12,000,000
Capital subscribed and paid up .. $5,000,000

Head Office : Guatemala City
Directors : Salvador Falla, Juan Valenzuela y Micheo, Daniel Rodriguez.
Manager : A. R. Prentice.
London Agents : Lazard Brothers & Co., Ltd.

Banco de Alagôas.
Established 1915,
as successor to the Banco do Estado de Alagôas.

Capital authorized . 2,000 contos.
Capital subscribed 1,200 contos.

Head Office : Maceió (Brazil).
London Agents : The London Merchant Bank, Ltd., 38 Lombard Street, E.C.3.
Directors : Francisco de Amorim Leão (Managing), Francisco de Assis Roiz de Vasconcellos, F. Polito.
Dividend June 1923, 8 per cent.

Banco Alemán Antioqueño.
Head Office : Medellín (Colombia).

BANKING FACILITIES.

Banco Americano de Guatemala.
Head Office : Guatemala City.

Banco Anglo-Costarricense.
Established 1863.

Capital . .. 1,200,000 colones.

Head Office : San José (Costa Rica).

Directors : Francisco Amerling, Frank N. Cox, Jaime G. Rennett, Nicolas Chabarria, Francesco Jimenez Núñez. Rafael Alvarado C. (Substitute), Panfilo J. Valverde (Substitute).

Manager : Manuel A. Quiros.

London Agents : Frederick Huth & Co.

Dividends : 1921–1922, 12 per cent., 1922–1923, 12½ per cent.

Banco Argentino Uruguay.
Established 1918.

Capital . $2,700,000

Head Office : 138 Reconquista 146, Buenos Aires.

Directors : Federico G. Leloir (President), Aurelio del Cerro (Vice-President), Jorge Lavalle Cobo (Secretary), José Maria Paz Anchorena (Assistant Secretary), Rómulo Ayerza, Pedro Bercetche, Ricardo F Bosch, José A. Dodero, Carlos Maria Morales, Guillermo A. Udaondo.

Manager Pedro C. Cichero.

Banco Atlantida.
Established 1913.

Capital fully paid up . $500,000 U.S. currency.

Head Office : La Ceiba (Honduras).

Local Branches : Tegucigalpa, San Pedro Sula, Puerto Cortes, Tela.

Directors : C. d'Antoni, J Ruis Rivera, E. P Dutu, F. J Lloveras (Manager), John Miceli, George Abadie, Felix P Vaccaro, S. d'Antoni, Juan R. Lopez.

London Correspondents Guaranty Trust Company of New York.

Banco de Bogotá.
Established 1871.

Capital $600,000
Reserve .. $450,000

Head Office : Bogotá (Colombia).

London Agents : London City and Midland Bank, Ltd., Fredk. Huth & Co., National Provincial and Union Bank of England, Ltd. (Princes Street, E.C.2).

Banco de Bolivár.
Head Office : Cartagena (Colombia).

Banco do Brasil.

Capital 100,000 contos.
Reserve Fund . 70,000 contos.

Head Office : Rio de Janeiro.

Local Branches : Manáos, Pará, Maranhão, Pernahyba, Fortaleza, Natal, Parahyba, Receife, Maceió, Aracajú, Bahia, Ilhéos, Victoria, Campos, São Paulo, Santos, Uberaba, Curityba, Florianopolis, Porto Alegre, Corumbá, etc.

London Agents : N. M. Rothschild and Sons; London County Westminster and Parr's Bank, Ltd.

Dividends : 1921–1922, 20 per cent.; 1922–1923, 20 per cent.

BANKING FACILITIES.

Banco Caracas.
Established 1890.

Capital authorized	Bs. 6,000,000
Capital paid up	Bs. 4,500,000

Head Office   Caracas (Venezuela).

Directors : Carlos Vicente Echeverria, Auguste Guinand, Manuel Badaracco, Dr. Julio C. Velutini, Dr. M. F Nuñez.

Manager : Francisco Hernáiz.

London Agents : Westminster Bank, Ltd.

Dividends : Four half-years to June 30, 1923, 15½ per cent., per annum.

Banco de Cartagena.
Head Office : Cartagena (Colombia).

Banco de Chile.
Established 1894.

Head Office : Santiago.

London Office : 94 Gracechurch Street, E.C.2.

Directors : Leonidas Vial (President). Santiago: Augusto Villanueva (President), Napoleon Peró (Vice-President), Carlos Balmaceda, Ramón Bascuñan Varas, Carlos Besa, Pedro Correa Ovalle, Luis Dávila Larrain, Nicanor Marambio, Juan Antonio Orrego.   Valparaiso: Guillermo E. Purcell (President), Jorge C. Kenrick (Vice-President), Carlos Alvarez Condarco, Cirilo H. C. Armstrong, S. Guillermo Cóndon, Jorge H. Jones, Hernán Prieto Vial.

Managers : Santiago, Pedro A. Torres, Valparaiso, Luis Beachemin.

Branches : Forty-five in Chile.

Banco de Chile y Argentina.

Established, 1900, as Banco de Punta Arenas; name changed in 1919.

Capital	$4,600,000

Head Office : Punta Arenas.

Local Branches—Chile : Valparaiso, Castro.

Argentina : Buenos Aires, Rio Gallegos, Santa Cruz, San Julian.

London Agents : Barclays Bank, Ltd.

Banco de Colombia.
Established 1875.

Capital	$1,200,000

Head Office : Bogotá (Colombia).

Manager : Ernesto Michelsen.

London Agents : National Provincial and Union Bank of England, Ltd. (Princes Street, E.C.2); Comptoir d'Escompte de Paris; Crédit Lyonnais.

Banco Comercial.
Established 1857

Capital authorized	$4,000,000
Capital paid up	$2,000,000
Reserve Fund	$1,680,000

Head Office : Casilla de Correo 34, Montevideo (Uruguay).

Directors : José Saavedra (President), Dr. Alejandro Gallinal (Vice-President), Nicolas Peirano, Felix Ortiz de Taranco, Dr. José Irureta Goyena, Dr. José Pardo Santáyana, Pedro Aramendia.

Manager : Arturo Davie.

London Agents : Messrs. Baring Bros. & Co., Ltd.,; London Joint City and Midland Bank, Ltd.

Banco Comercial y Agricola.
Established 1894.

Capital paid up	5,000,000 sucres.

Head Office : Guayaquil (Ecuador).

Banco Comercial del Azul.
Established 1889.

Capital authorized	$10,000,000 (Legal Money).
Capital subscribed	$5,000,000 ,,
Capital paid up	$2,485,850 ,,
Capital reserve	$2,035,625.34 ,,

Head Office   Azul, Argentina.

Branch Offices   Bartolomé Mitre 499, Buenos Aires; Coronel Pringles, Cachar Coronel Dorrego, Cachari.

Directors : Juan Francisco Arechavala (President), Angel L. Sojo (Vice-President), Casto Sáenz Valiente (Secretary), Gregorio Aráoz Alfaro, Juan Francisco Boubée, Alfredo Fortabat, Alejandro Leloir, José Heriberto Martínez, Agustín Vidal.

General Manager and Manager at Buenos Aires   Eduardo C. Gowland.

Manager at Azul : Nicolás Christmann.

London Agents : London County Westminster and Parr's Bank, Ltd.; Comptoir National d'Escompte de Paris.

Banco Comercial de Barranquilla.
Established 1914.

Capital	$500,000

Head Office : Barranquila (Colombia).

Directors   Carlos Daniel Roca (President), Peregrino Puccini (Vice-President), M. J Alzamora, Dr. Alberto R. Osorio, Clodomiro Salas B.

Manager : Dr. José Fuenmayor R.

Dividends   Three half-years to December 1918, 14 per cent., 1919, 15 per cent.; from June 1920 to June 1923, 12 per cent. annually

Banco Commercial do Estado de São Paulo.
Established 1912.

Capital subscribed	30,000 contos.
Capital paid up	18,000 contos.
Reserve Fund	12,000 contos.

Head Office : Rua 15 de Novembro 38, São Paulo.

Directors : Dr. Erasmo Teixeira de Assumpção (President), T B. Muir (Vice-President), Dr. Constantino Gonçalves Fraga (Secretary).

Managing Director : José Maria Whitaker.

Acting Manager : Dr. L. T. Assumpção.

London Agents : Lloyds Bank, Ltd. (20 King William Street); Bank of Scotland.

Agencies : Rio de Janeiro, Santos, Araraquara, Avaré Baurú, Bebedouro, Botucatú, Bragança, Campinas, Catanduva, Franca, Itapetininga, Itapolis, Itú, Mogy-Mirim, Monte Alto, Olympia, Pennapolis, Piracicaba, Pirajuhy, Rio Preto, Santa Adelia, Santa Cruz do Rio Pardo, São Carlos, São João da Bôa Vista, São Manoel, São Simão, Taquaritinga, Taubaté, Tieté.

The Bank has correspondents in practically all the towns in the State of São Paulo and in all the principal towns of the States of the Republic.

Dividends : 1914, 5 per cent.; 1915, 7 per cent.; 1916 and 1917, 8 per cent.; 1918, 10 per cent.; 1919, 11 per cent., 1920 and 1921, 12 per cent.; 1922, 12 per cent.; half year to June, 1923, 6 per cent. (actual).

Banco Commercial Franco-Brasileiro.
Established 1913.

Capital	10,000 contos.

Head Office : Praça Senador Florencio 347, Porto Alegre (Brazil).

Branch Office : São Paulo.

Directors : Coronel Manoel Py, Manoel Alvaro Soares, Armando A. B. da Silva.

Banco Comercial Italiano.
Established 1898.

Capital $10,000,000
Head Office   Bartolomé Mitre 460–468, Buenos Aires.
Directors   José E. Piñero (President), Lorenzo Fontana, Ernesto Cartelhun, Alfredo J Vasena, Francisco Badino, Aquilino C. Colombo, Blas Ferrando.
Secretary : Vicente Casullo.
London Agents : Barclays Bank, Ltd.

Banco Commercial do Maranhão.
Established 1869.

Capital .. . . 2,000 contos.
Head Office . Maranhão (Brazil).
Directors : Manoel Mathias das Neves, Antonio Alves Fontes Martins, José Ignacio Ferreira Pinto, Domingos Ribeiro da Cruz, Joaquim Pereira de Carvalho, Feliciano Moreira de Souza.

Banco Commercial do Pará.
Established 1869.

Capital paid up . 3,000 contos.
Head Office   Pará (Brazil).
London Agents : Lloyds Bank, Ltd. (17 Cornhill, E.C.3), National Provincial and Union Bank of England, Ltd. (2 Princes Street, E.C.2).
Dividends   8 per cent. per annum.

Banco del Comercio.
Established 1919.

Capital paid up . $1,000,000
Reserves $500,000
Head Office : Mercaderes 36, Havana (Cuba).
Branch Office : Avenida de Italia, 67, Havana.
Directors : Bernardo Solis (President), José Gomez Mena (Vice-President), Francisco J Seiglie (Vice-President), Laureano F López (Vice-President), Antonio S. de Buslamonte (Secretary), L. Manuel Santeiro, José R. Villalón, Roberto W Atkins, Juan F. Arguelles, José Alvaré, Aquilino Entrialgo, Elie L. E. Ponvert, Henry A. Rubino, Alfonso Gómez Mena.
London Correspondents   London Joint City and Midland Bank, Ltd.

Banco do Commercio.

Capital . . 7,000 contos.
Head Office : Rio de Janeiro.
President : Conde de Avellar.
London Agents : London Joint City and Midland Bank, Ltd.
Dividends   Year to June 30, 1922, 8 per cent., Year to June 30, 1923, 8 per cent.

Banco do Commercio e Industria de São Paulo.
Established 1890.

Capital paid up . 10,000 contos.
Head Office : São Paulo (Brazil).
Branches : Campinas, Ribeirão Preto, Santos.
London Agents : London Joint City and Midland Bank, Ltd.
Dividends : for the two half-years of 1920, 20 per cent.

BANKING FACILITIES.

Banco de Costa Rica.

Capital paid up	2,000,000 colones.
Reserves	1,400,000 colones.

Head Office : San José (Costa Rica).

Directors : Daniel Núñez (President), Oscar F Rohrmoser (Vice-President), Roberto Jiménez S., Alberto Ortuño, Eladio Prado, Manuel Montejo H., Guillermo Niehaus.

Secretary : Adolfo Cañas.

London Agents : A. Rüffer & Sons, London County Westminster and Parr's Bank, Ltd.

Dividends (1923) : January, 6 per cent.; July, 6 per cent.

Banco de Credito.
Founded 1908.

Capital authorized	$3,000,000
Capital paid up	$2,500,000

Head Office : Montevideo (Uruguay).

Directors   Dr. Antonio J Rius (President), Dr. Jacinto Casaravilla (Vice-President), Dr. Antonio Harán (Secretary), Dr. Vicente Ponce de León, Francisco Rocco, Jorge West, Juan C. Blanco Sienra.

Manager : Dolcey Puig.

London Agents : Kleinwort, Sons, & Co., Glyn, Mills, Currie & Co.

Banco de Credito Hipotecario.
Established 1871.

Capital and Reserves	1,575,000 sucres.

Head Office : Pichincha 201, Guayaquil.

Directors : Francisco Urvina (President), Pedro Miller (Vice-President), Guillermo Higgins C., Manuel Tama, Fed. A. Corenizo C., Juan X. Agiurreo.

Manager : Carlos Marcos.

Banco de Descuento.
Established 1920.

Capital	6,000,000 sucres.

Head Office : Guayaquil (Ecuador).

Manager : C. J Arosemena.

Banco del Ecuador.
Established 1868.

Capital paid up	3,000,000 sucres.

Head Office : Guayaquil (Ecuador).

Directors : L. Guzmán (President), Juan Illingworth (Vice-President), Pedro Miller y Gutierrez (Secretary), Antonio Madinyá, José Rodriguez Bonin, B. Vignolo.

Managers : E. Game, P Arosemena.

London Agents : London Joint City and Midland Bank, Ltd.

Banco de A. Edwards & Cia.
Established 1852.

Capital subscribed	$25,000,000
Capital paid up	$10,000,000

Head Office : Valparaiso.

Branch Office : Santiago.

Directors : Carlos van Buren (President), Carlos R. Edwards (Vice-President), Agustin Edwards, Andrés Geddes, Tomás C. Hobbins, Raúl Edwards, Alberto Hurtado C., Arturo Lyon Peña, Howard Nation.

London Agents : Anglo-South American Bank, Ltd.; Glyn, Mills, Currie & Co.

Banco Escandinavo Argentino, S.A.
Established 1920.

Capital authorized . . .	.	$10,000,000
Capital subscribed and paid up	. .	$3,500,000

Head Office : Calle Sarmiento, 354, Buenos Aires.

Directors : Pedro Storm (President), Dr. Adolfo Labougle, hijo (Vice-President), Johs Bergström, Waldemar Kallevig, W Braimer Jones.

Banco Escandinavo-Brazileiro S.A.
Capital subscribed and paid up . . Kr. 5,000,000

Head Office : Rua da Alfandega 32, Rio de Janeiro.

Banco de España y America.
Established 1912.

Capital authorized . $5,000,000

Head Office : Cangallo, 336, Buenos Aires.

Directors : Juan L. Bisso (President), Dr. Luis C. Soavedra (Vice-President), Pablo Rachou, Alfredo Bradley, Dr. Enrique Garcia Campoamar, Rafael Garcia, Alberto de la Barrera.

Manager : Faustino F. Villabrille.

Dividends : To June 30, 1920, 8 per cent.

Banco Español de Chile.
Established, 1900, as the Banco Español Italiano; name changed in 1907.

Capital paid up .	$60,000,000 (Legal Money)
Reserves .. .	$30,000,000

Head Office : Valparaiso.

Local Branches : Forty in Chile.

Directors : Francisco de Caso (President), Ramón Puelma Besa (Vice-President), Manuel Fernández Garcia, Elisea Gutiérrez, Juan B. Ugarte, Juan Zardoya, Manuel Gonzáleza, José Osuna.

General Manager : Manuel Castro Valdivia. Santiago Branch, Luis A. Larraguibel.

London Agents : London Joint City and Midland Bank, Ltd.; London County Westminster and Parr's Bank, Ltd. (Lothbury, E.C.); Kleinwort, Sons, & Co.

Banco Español del Rio de la Plata.
Established 1886.

Capital .. .. $100,000,000 national money (£8,730,158).

Head Office : 200 Reconquista, Buenos Aires.

London Office : 7 Fenchurch Street, G.P.O., Box 553.

Manager : Alexander Burns.

Branches at Paris, Genoa, Hamburg, Madrid, Barcelona, Bilbao, San Sebastian Seville, Valencia, Vigo, and Coruña.

Directors : Pedro Fernandez (President), Fernando Garcia (Vice-President), Celedonia V. Pereda (Secretary), José Bayona, Manuel B. Goñi, Pedro Ma. Moreno, Joreg A. Santamarina, Baldomero Villamil, Miguel Montserrat.

Manager : Joaquin Herrandis.

Local Branches—Argentina : Adolfo Alsina, Bahia Blanca, Balcarce, Bartolomé Mitre, Córdoba, Dolores, La Plata, Lincoln, Mar del Plata, Mendoza, Mercedes (B. Aires), Nueve de Julio, Pehuajó, Pergamino, Rafaela, Rivadavia, Rosario, Salta, San Juan, San Nicolás, San Pedro (B. Aires), Santa Fé, Santiago del Estero, Tres Arroyos, Tucumán; City of Buenos Aires—ten branches.

Brazil : Rio de Janeiro.

Uruguay : Montevideo.

Banco Frances del Rio de la Plata.
Established 1886.

Capital authorized	Gold $20,000,000
Capital subscribed and paid up	Gold $14,000,000
Reserves	Gold $1,400,000

Head Office : Reconquista 157, Buenos Aires.

Branches : Bahia Blanca, Chivilcoy, Rosario.

Directors   G. Fourvel-Rigolleau (President), F. Delor (Vice-President), H. Becquerel, A. Chovet, G. Jarre, Ch. Oudart, J. P Passicot, C. Dupont, E. Maupas.

Manager   R. Tobler.

London Agents : London Joint City and Midland Bank, Ltd., Crédit Lyonnais, Kleinwort, Sons, & Co., Comptoir National d'Escompte de Paris.

Banco de Galicia y Buenos Aires.
Established 1905.

Capital .. .	$30,000,000 (National Money).

Head Office   Cangallo 445, Buenos Aires.

Directors : Vicente Sanchez (President), Ireno Cucullu, Sebastian Urquijo (Vice-Presidents), Manuel Escasany, José Bidart, Antonio Villcomil, Benito Ros.

Manager : L. Pomiró.

London Agents : London Joint City and Midland Bank, Ltd.

Banco de Guanajuato.

Capital ..	$3,000,000

Head Office : Apartado 25 Guanajuato (Mexico).

Manager : Marcel Barre de Saint-Lew.

Branches : Irapuato, Guadalajara, Zamora.

London Agents   Comptoir National d'Escompte de Paris.

Banco de Guatemala.
Established 1895.

Capital	.. $10,000,000
Capital subscribed and paid up .	. $2,500,000
Reserve Fund	$15,000,000
Contingency Fund	$8,643,500.21

Head Office : Guatemala City

Directors : Adolfo Stahl, Antonio Batres Jauregui, Antonio Carrera Wyld.

Manager : Luis Gatica Arévalo.

Ten Agencies in Guatemala.

London Agents : London Joint City and Midland Bank, Ltd.; London County Westminster and Parr's Bank, Ltd.; Seligman Bros.

Dividends : Each of the five half-years to June 1922, $400 per share. Dividend, June 1923, $450 per share.

Banque de la Guyane.
Founded 1849.

Capital .	Frs. 600,000

Head Office : Cayenne (French Guiana).

Director : E. Rollet.

Branch Office : St. Laurent du Maroni.

London Agents : Comptoir National d'Escompte de Paris.

BANKING FACILITIES.

Banco Hipotecario de Colombia.
Established 1910.

Capital	$800,000
Reserves	$805,500

Head Office : Bogotá (Colombia)

London Agents   National Provincial and Union Bank of England, Ltd. (Princes Street, E.C.2), Anglo-South American Bank, Ltd.

Dividends : To June 1923, 32 per cent.

Banco Hipotecario del Uruguay.

Office   Montevideo (Uruguay).

Directors : Román Freire (President), Dr. Rodolf Meezzera (Vice-President), Solano A. Riestra, Luis Puig, Dr. Juan B. Bado, Dr Antonio M. Rodríguez, E. Garzón.

Secretary : Dr. Enrique Rodríguez Castro.

Manager   Cornelio Guerra.

Banco de Honduras.
Established 1889.

Capital authorized	$1,000,000

Head Office   Tegucigalpa (Honduras).

Branch Office : San Pedro Sula.

Directors   Santos Soto (President), Lic. don Presentación Quesada (Vice-President), Trinidad E. Mendoza, José Maria Agurcia, Leandro Valladares (Secretary), Ignacio Agurcia, Geo. Abodie.

Manager   E. B. Ramos.

London Agents   Lazard Brothers & Co., Ltd.

Banco Industrial.

Head Office ·   Cartagena (Colombia).

Banco Internacional de Costa Rica.

Head Office   San José (Costa Rica).

Established as a Government bank of issue in October 1914 and authorized to issue up to 4,000,000 colones in notes to bearer (guaranted by Government 6 per cent. bonds, and by the unissued balance of the Costa Rica gold refunding bonds of 1911). One-half of this issue to be lent to the Executive Government at 6 per cent. interest, the rate of interest on loans to the agricultural community restricted to 10 per cent. per annum.

Banco Internacional de Guatemala.
Established 1877.

Capital authorized	$3,000,000
Capital subscribed and paid up	$2,000,000

Head Office   Guatemala City.

Directors : Guillermo Aguirre, José Gouband, Carlo Salazar

Manager : Guillermo Dorion.

Agencies   Cobán, Escuintla, Quezaltenango, Retalhuleu.

London Agents : Frederick Huth & Co., Bank of Liverpool and Martins, Ltd.; Baring Brothers & Co., Ltd.; Anglo-South American Bank, Ltd.

Banco Internacional Hipotecario de Mexico.

Office   Mexico City.

BANKING FACILITIES.

Banco Internacional del Peru.
Established 1897.

Capital paid up £P.100,000

Head Office : Lima (Peru).

Directors   Pedro de Osma (President), Benjamin Roca (Vice-President), Luis Albizuri, P. L. Batchelor, Jorge Fort, Antonio Graña, H. S. Hunter, Oscar Ramos Cabiesas, A. Solf y Muro, Claudio Velarde.

Manager : Aristides Porras.

London Agents : London Joint City and Midland Bank, Ltd.

Dividends : For two half-years to June 1914, 8 per cent. per annum; to December 1914, nil; three half-years to June 1917, 5 per cent., two half-years to June 1918, 6 per cent.; two half-years to June 1919, 8 per cent.; two half-years to June 1920, 8 per cent.; two half-years to June 1921, 8 per cent.; two half-years to June 1922, 8 per cent.; two half-years to June 1923, 8 per cent.

Banco de Italia y Rio de La Plata.

Head Office : Buenos Aires.

Directors : Santiago Pinasco (President), Dr. Ernesto Aguirre (Vice-President), Francisco Jannello, José Devoto, Bartolomé Solari, Luis Lamas, Juan Balbi.

Manager   Antonio C. Alemanni.

London Agents : Comptoir National d'Escompte de Paris, Hambro's Bank.

Local Branches : Rosario, Bahia Blanca, Paraná, Concordia, Gualeguaychú, Gualeguay, La Paz, Resistencia, Ensenada, La Plata, etc.

Branches in Uruguay : Victoria, Trenal.

Branch in Italy : Genoa.

Banco Italiano.
Established 1889.

Capital paid up £P.400,000
Reserve Funds . £P.401,585.0.26

Head Office : Lima (Peru).

General Manager : Gino Salocchi.

Manager   Luis Morelli.

Local Branches   Arequipa, Callao, Chincha Alta, Mollendo, and Trujillo.

Directors   Luis Sanguineti (President), Juan Fco. Raffo (Vice-President), Guido Colombo, Luis Lertora, Federico J Milne, Luis Nicolini, Andrés Noziglia, R. Thorne, Ludovico Toeplitz.

Affiliated Bank in London : Banca Commerciale Italiana.

Banco Italiano.

Capital paid up $10,000,000
Reserve Fund $1,400,000
Contingency Fund $646,731.88

Head Office : Valparaiso.

Local Branches : Santiago and Almendral.

London Agents : London Joint City and Midland Bank, Ltd.

Banco de Jalisco.
Established 1898.

Capital .. . $6,000,000

Head Office : Apartado 298 Guadalajara (Mexico).

Manager : H. Bantning.

London Agents : Comptoir National d'Escompte de Paris.

Banco de Londres y Mexico.
Established 1883.

Capital	$21,500,000

Head Office : Avenida 16 de Septiembre y Calle Bolivar, Mexico City.

Banco López.
Established 1919.

Capital subscribed . . .	$4,000,000
Capital paid up	$1,600,000
Reserves	$300,698

Head Office : Bogotá (Colombia).

President : Pedro A. López; Vice-President : Jorge Holguin; General Manager ; E. López Pumanejo.

Local Branches : Barranquilla, Bucaramanga, Cali, Girardot, Manizales.

Affiliated Banks : Banco Social del Tolima, Ibagué; Banco del Huila, Neiva; Banco Repúblicano, Medellín.

London Agents : Lazard Bros. & Co., Ltd.; Anglo-South American Bank, Ltd.; London Joint City and Midland Bank, Ltd.; Barclays Bank, Ltd.

Banco de Maracaibo.
Head Office · Maracaibo (Venezuela).

Banco Mercantil.
Established 1905.

Capital paid up .. .	Bs.12,500,000 Legal Money
Reserves	Bs. 3,235,000 Legal Money

Head Office : Oruro.

Branches : La Paz, Cochabamba, Potosí, Sucre, Tarija, Tupiza.

Chile : Antofagasta.

Managing Director : Luis Winter.

Sub-Managing Director : John Mutch.

London Agents London Joint City and Midland Bank, Ltd.; Anglo-South American Bank, Ltd.; Barclays Bank, Ltd.; Comptoir National d'Escompte de Paris.

Banco Mercantil Americano de Caracas.
(Affiliated with the Bank of Central and South America, Inc., New York.)
Established 1917

Capital authorized .. .	Bs. 10,400,000
Capital paid up	. Bs. 2,600,000

Head Office : Caracas (Venezuela).

Local Branches : La Guaira, Valencia, Maracaibo.

London Correspondents : Guaranty Trust Company of New York; Brown, Shipley & Co.

Banco Mercantil Americano del Peru.
(Affiliated with the Bank of Central and South America, Inc., New York.)
Established 1916.

Capital authorized ..	£P.1,000,000.0.00
Capital paid up	£P 210,000.0.00
Reserve Fund ..	. £P.20,000.0.00

Head Office : Lima (Peru).

Directors : Arthur M. Anderson, James Brown, W Palen Conway, Walter E. Frew, R. F. Loree, H. F. McCreery, Gates W McGarrah, John McHugh, H. Esk Moller, M. A. Oudin, W. C. Potter, J. Luis Schaefer, S. Stern, E. R. Stettinius, Albert Strauss.

Acting Managing Director · F C. Harding.

Local Branches Lima, Arequipa, Chiclayo, Trujillo Piura.

London Correspondents : Guaranty Trust Company of New York, Brown, Shipley, & Co.; Seligman Brothers.

BANKING FACILITIES.

Banco Mercantil de Costa Rica.
(Affiliated with the Bank of Central and South America, Inc., New York.)

Capital paid up	$1.500,000
Reserves ..	$563,000

Head Office : San José (Costa Rica)

London Correspondents   Guaranty Trust Company of New York, Brown, Shipley & Co.; Seligman Brothers.

Banco Mercantil del Paraguay.
Established 1891.

Capital paid up $25,000,000 (legal money).

Head Office : Asunción (Paraguay)

Local Branches : Concepción, Encarnación, Paraguarí, Villa del Pilar, Villa Rica.

London Agents   Knowles & Foster, 48 Moorgate Street, E.C.2.

Administrative Council : Juan B. Gaona (President), José G. Gomez (Vice-President), Atanasio Scura, José Brun, Humberto Casaccia, Federico Krauch, J. J. Manzoni, Juan José Bilba, A. Pecci.

Directors   R. B. Croskey, J A. Vuyk, J B Bidondo.

In moratorium till 1926.

Banco Minero.

Head Office   Chihuahua (Mexico).

Banco de la Mutualidad.
Established 1914.

Capital authorized .	$1,000,000 gold.
Capital paid up (January 1, 1921) ..	$858,400 gold.
Reserves . ..	$123,935 gold.

Head Office : Bucaramanga (Colombia)

Managing Director : V M. Ogliastri.

Dividend : 15 per cent. per annum.

Banco de la Nación Argentina.

Head Office : Buenos Aires.

Banco de la Nación Boliviana.
Established 1911.

The only Bolivian bank of issue.

Capital authorized . .	£4,000,000
Capital paid up ..	1,760,000
Reserve Fund .	331,600

Head Office : La Paz.

Branches : Cochabamba, Oruro, Potosí, Riberalta, Santa Cruz, Sucre, Tarija, Trinidad, Uyuni.

London Agents : Anglo-South American Bank, Ltd.

Banco Nacional.

Capital . . . $40,000,000

Head Office : Santiago.

Local Branches : Valparaiso, Melipilla (Chile).

Directors : Ventura Blanco Viel (President), Guillermo Barros Jara (Vice-President), Luis Barros Borgoño, Pedro Garcia de la H., Carlos Peña Otargui, Arturo Prat C., Alfredo Riesco, Roberto Sanchez G. de la H., Maximo Valdes F., Nicolas Vicuña, Guillermo Wilms.

General Manager : Abel Gomez.

London Agents   Westminster Bank, Ltd.

BANKING FACILITIES.

Banco Nacional Braziliero.
Established 1893.

Capital paid up . .. . 2,000 contos.

Head Office Rio de Janeiro.

London Agents London Joint City and Midland Bank, Ltd.

Dividends : 1915, 7 per cent.

Banco Nacional de Bolivia.
Established 1871

Capital paid up . Bs.11,200,000

Head Office Sucre.

Directors : Antonio J Frias (President), Germán Zelada (Vice-President), Felix de Argandona, Enrique Rosenbluth, Antonio Costas, Enrique Urquidi (Managing Director).

Branches Cochabamba, La Paz, Oruro, Potosí, Tarija, Tupiza, Uyuni.

London Agents London Joint City and Midland Bank, Ltd., Kleinwort, Sons & Co., Frederick Huth & Co., Grace Brothers & Co., Ltd.

Banco Nacional do Commercio.
Established 1895.

Capital subscribed . . Rs. 25,000,000$000
Capital paid up Rs. 12,500,000$000

Head Office : Porto Alegre (Brazil).

Directors : Pedro Benjamin de Oliveira, Carlos Frederico Gomes, and Abilio Chaves de Souza.

Local Branches : Rio Grande, Pelotas, Livramento, Bagé, Uruguayana, Florianopolis, Joinville, Curityba, Corumbá, and 57 other branches in the States of Rio Grande do Sul, Santa Catharina, Paraná, and Matto Grosso.

London Agents : London Joint City and Midland Bank Ltd., Kleinwort, Sons, & Co., J. Henry Schröder & Co., The British Bank of South America, Ltd., etc.

Dividends 1922, 12 per cent.

Banco Nacional de Mexico.
Established 1884.

Capital paid up $32,000,000
Reserves . $20,572,655

Head Office : Mexico City

Directors : José A. Signoret (President), Eusebio Gonzalez (Vice-President), Mauricio Armand-Delille, Léon Barbaroux, Florencio Burgunder, Graciano Guichard, Luis Elguero, Agustin Legorreta, Miguel S. Macedo, Gabriel Mancera, R. Padilla y Salcido, A. L. Suerpérez, Vicente Vértiz.

General Manager : Agustin Legorreta.

Local Branches in the principal towns of Mexico.

Banco Nacional de Panamá.
Established 1904.

Capital paid up Bs.750,000

Head Office : Panamá City

Directors Próspero Pinel (President), Emiliano Ponce, Octavio A. Vallarino Arturo Delvalle, Tomás Gabriel Duque.

BANKING FACILITIES.

Banco Occidental.

Capital $5,000,000

Head Office : San Salvador (Salvador).
Local Branches   Santa Ana, San Miguel, Sonsonate, Santiago de María, Ahuachapán.
Directors . Benjamin Bloom (President), David Bloom, Mauricio Meardi, Federico Mejía (General Manager), Samuel Quirós.
London Agents : Guaranty Trust Co., of New York; Anglo-South American Bank, Ltd.; Lazard Brothers & Co.

Banco Occidental de Mexico.

Office : Mazatlan (Mexico).

Banco de Occidente.

Head Office : Quezaltenango (Guatemala).

Banco Oriental de Mexico.

Office : Puebla (Mexico).

Banco Osorno y la Unión.

Capital authorized and paid up $17,689,025
Reserves $2,853,445

Head Office : Osorno (Chile).
Directors : Hugo Schilling (President), Ricardo Siegle (Vice-President), Sandalio Vásquez C., Conrado Hubach, A. Julio Buschmann, Jerman Hutt, Arturo Montecino R.
Manager   Ernesto Hott S.

Banco do Pará.
Established 1883.

Capital paid up . . . . 4,000 contos.

Office : Pará (Brazil).
Directors : Antonio Faciola (President), Menasses Bensimonã, João Teixeira dos Santos.
London Agents : Westminster Bank, Ltd. (Bartholomew Lane, E.C.2).

Banco Pelotense.
Established 1906.

Capital authorized . . . .. 30,000 contos.
Capital paid up .. . . 15,000 contos.

Head Office : Pelotas (Brazil).
Seventy-seven Branches and Agencies in Brazil.
Directors : Alberto R. Rosa, Plotino Amaro Duarte, Dr. José J de Albuquerque Barros.
Dividends : 1920, 12 per cent.; 1921, 12 per cent.; 1922, 12 per cent.; 1923, 12 per cent., and 4 per cent. bonus.

BANKING FACILITIES.

Banco del Peru y Londres.
Established 1897

Capital subscribed and paid up	..	£P.500,000
Reserve	..	£P.300,000

Head Office   Lima (Peru).

Local Branches : Arequipa, Callao, Chiclayo, Chincha, Alta, Cuzco, Huacho, Huancayo, Ica, Mollendo, Pacasmayo Piura, Trujillo.

Directors : Pedro D. Gallagher (President), Alberto Ayulo (Vice-President), Santiago Acuna, Daniel C. Babbitt, Henry F Hammond, Francisco Mendoza y Barreda, John A. Reed, John W. Stokes, André Tarrade.

Paris Committee : Jacques Kulp (President), Paul Briere, Maurice l'Epine.

Managing Director : Pablo La Rosa.

Manager : S. Paul Windmer.

London Agents : The Anglo-South American Bank, Ltd.

Dividends : 1922, 10 per cent.

Banco del Pichincha.
Quito (Ecuador).

Capital	..	700,000 sucres.

Banco Popular Argentino.
Established 1887.

Capital paid up	$10,514,880 (National Money).

Head Office : Calle Bartolomé Mitre 370, Buenos Aires.

Directors : Juan Carballido (President), A. Elias (Vice-President), Horacio J. Ferrai (Secretary), A. E. Aliverti, A. C. Gandolfo, R. Lescano, A. M. Lynch, J. F. Molinari, A. Maraspin, E. N Viola, R. Otamendi, M. Pereyra Iraola, Luis Valiente Noailles.

Manager : Justo P. Sáenz.

London Agents : London Joint City and Midland Bank, Ltd.

Dividends : 1920–1921, 10 per cent.; 1921–1922, 10 per cent.; 1922–1923, 9 per cent.

Banco Popular del Peru.
Established 1899.

Capital paid up	..	£P.150,000
Reserve Fund and Surplus	..	£P.76,417

Head Office : Lima (Peru).

Manager : Garcia y Lastras.

London Agents : London Joint City and Midland Bank, Ltd.; Barclays Bank, Ltd., Comptoir Nacional d'Escompte de Paris.

Banco Portugues do Brasil.
Established 1918.

Capital subscribed	..	50,000 contos.
Reserve	..	4,824 contos.

Head Office : Rio de Janeiro.

Directors : Visconde de Moraes (President), Alberto Guedes, Bernardo Pinto da Fonseca, Zeferino de Oliveira.

Local Branches : São Paulo, Santos.

BANKING FACILITIES.

Banco de la Provincia de Buenos Aires.
Established 1853.

Capital authorized .	$75,000,000 (National Money).
Capital paid up .	$62,000,000 ,, ,,

Head Office · La Plata.

Sixty-four Branches in Argentina.

Directors   Nicolas Casarino (President), Francesco Mendes Goncalves (Vice-President), Galo Florente (Vice-President), Bartolomé Ginocchio, Pedro Lacau, Carlos Lockwood, Prudencio Monzón, Juan R. Moss, José Raggio, Luis Urrutia, Guillermo Valdes.

Manager   Virginio Maffiei.

London Agents   Barclays Bank, Ltd., Anglo-South American Bank, Ltd., London Joint City and Midland Bank, Ltd., Comptoir National d'Escompte de Paris, Westminster Bank, Ltd. (Bartholomew Lane, E.C.).

Banco da Provincia do Rio Grande do Sul.
Established 1858.

Capital subscribed	..	40,000 contos.
Capital paid up	..	20,000 contos.

Head Office   Porto Alegre (Brazil).

Local Branches : Alegrete, Bagé, Caxias, Cruz Alta, Cachoeira, D. Pedrito, Jagurão, Lageado, Livramento, Passo Fundo, Pelotas, Rio Grande, Rio de Janeiro, Santa Maria, São Gabriel, Taquara, Uruguayana, Novo Hamburgo, São Leopoldo e Montenegro.

General Managers . A. Mostardeio Filho, Dr. Felisberto B. F.Azevdo, Dr. Victor A. Bastean.

London Agents : London Joint City and Midland Bank, Ltd.; Crédit Lyonnais; London and River Plate Bank, Ltd.

Banco do Receife.
Established 1900.

Capital subscribed	.	2,000 contos.
Capital paid up ..	.	1,000 contos.

Head Office : Pernambuco (Brazil).

Manager : M. G. S. Pinto.

Banco de la República.
Established 1908.

Capital	.. ..	6,000,000 gold pesos.
Reserves	.. .	1,824,275.80 gold pesos.

Head Office : Asunción, Paraguay

Local Branch : Encarnación.

President · Quinto Censi.

Manager : Edmundo Tombeur.

Sub-Manager : George H. Pearson.

Directors : Dr. G. Cardús Huerta, Basilio de los Rios, Pedro J Jorba, Francisco Calmejane, Emilio Aceval.

London Agents   Comptoir National d'Escompte de Paris.

BANKING FACILITIES.

Banco de la República Oriental del Uruguay.
Established 1896.

Capital authorized	. . .	$25,000,000
Capital paid up . .	.	$21,228,174.27

Head Office : Calle Solio, Esquina Piedras, Montevideo (Uruguay).

Directors : Dr. Claudio Williman (President), Dr. Eduardo Acevedo (Vice-President), Juan Domingo Lanza, Benjamin S. Viana, Dr. Asdrubal E. Delgado, Dr. Juan Blengio Rocca, Diego Pons.

Manager : O. Morato.

Forty-two branches in Uruguay.

London Agents : London Joint City and Midland Bank, Ltd.

Banco Republicano.

Capital	.	$1,000,000

Head Office   Medellín (Colombia)

Manager : Luis M. Mejía Alvarez.

Banco Salvadoreño.
Established 1885.

Capital subscribed and paid up	Colones	4,000,000
Reserve Fund .	ditto	400,000

Head Office : San Salvador (Salvador).

Agencies : Santa Tecla, San Miguel, Sonsonate, Zacatecoluca, Ahuachapán, Cojutepeque, Santa Ana, Santiago de María.

Directors : Angel Guirola, Miguel Dueñas, J Antonio Rivera, Carlos Alberto Guirola, Francisco Martinez Suarez.

Manager   R. Schleusz.

Banco de Santa Ana.

Capital paid up	.	Colones	85,000
Reserve Fund ..		ditto	65,000

Office   Santa Ana (Salvador).

Manager   P Geoffrey.

Banco de Sonora.
Established 1898.

Capital .	..	$1,500,000
Reserves .		$1,300,000

Head Office : Hermosillo (Mexico).

Branches   Guaymas, Culiacan, Chihuahua.

Directors : Adolfo Bley, Max Müller, L. A. Martinez, Alfredo May, V Aguilar.

Manager : L. Brauer.

Banco de Sucre.

Capital	$2,000,000

Head Office   Medellín (Colombia).

Banco de Tabasco.
Established 1900.

Capital	. ..	$1,000,000 (Mexican)

Head Office : Apartado 18, Villahermosa (Mexico).

Manager   A. Galindo.

London Agents : Comptoir National d'Escompte de Paris.

BANKING FACILITIES.

Banco Territorial.
Established 1886.

Capital . . . . . 700,000 sucres.

Head Office : Guayaquil (Ecuador).
Directors Francisco Garcia Aviles, José Rodriguez Bonin, Jorge Montero Vela,
Dr. Julio, A. Burbano S.
Manager : Julio Burbano Aguirre.
Dividends : 1919, 14 per cent., 1920, 14 per cent., 1921, 16 per cent.: 1922,
16 per cent.

Banco Unión.

Head Office : Cartagena (Colombia).

Banco de Venezuela.
Established 1890.

Capital authorized .	Bs. 24,000,000
Capital paid up	Bs. 18,000,000
Reserves .	Bs. 5,400,030.04

Head Office : Caracas (Venezuela).
Directors : Vicente Lecuna (President), Germán Jiménez, H. Pérez Dupuy.
Alejandro Lara, P Hermoso Fellería, F A. Guzman Alfaro.
Secretary : Ramiro Rendiles.
London Agents : Kleinwort, Sons, and Co.

Banco Yugoslavo de Chile.
(Jugoslovenska Banka i Chile.)
Established 1917

Capital authorized	$20,000,000
Capital paid up . .	$10,000,000
Reserve Funds .	$576,842

Head Office : Valparaiso.
Directors : Pascual Baburizza (Chairman), Eugenio Escobal Cerda (Vice-Chair-
man), Alberto Browne, Miguel Abovich, Vicente Orlandi.
General Manager : Juan Gartner.
Local Branches and Agencies Antofagasta, Punta Arenas, Natales, Porvenir
London Agents London Joint City and Midland Bank, Ltd.

Bank für Chile und Deutschland.
(Banco de Chile y Alemania.)
Established 1895.

Capital paid up . .. . M. 10,000,000

Managers G. H. Kaemmerer, E. von Oesterreich.
Branches in Chile : Concepción, Santiago, Temuco, Valdivia, Valparaiso.
Dividends Each of the five years to 1912, 6 per cent., 1913, 4 per cent., 1914
and 1915, nil, 1916, 6 per cent., 1917–1919, nil; 1920, 8 per cent., 1921, 10 per cent.,
1922, 50 per cent.

Bunge & Born, Limitada.
Sociedad Anonima Comercial Financiera e Industrial.
Successors of Ernesto A. Bunge & J Born.
Established 1884.

Capital .. ' $20,000,000

Head Office : Buenos Aires.
Directors : Edward Bunge (Chairman), Georges Oster, Alfrido Hirsch, Sigismundo
Jacobi.

BANKING FACILITIES.

Compañia de Crédito Agricola e Industrial.
Quito (Ecuador).

Capital . 1,000,000 sucres,

Compañia de Préstamos y Construcciones.
Quito (Ecuador)

Capital .. 1,000,000 sucres.

Gomez Mena (Pedro) & Hijo.
Established 1885

Head Office   Obispo & Aguiar, Havana (Cuba).
Partners : Pedro Gomez Mena, Manuel Gomez Waddington.
Managers : M. Seiglie, A. Casas.
London Agents   Kleinwort, Sons & Co.

Hollandsche Bank voor West-Indie.
(Banco Holandés de las Indias Occidentales.)
Established in 1919 by the Nederlandsche Handel-Maatschappij, Amsterdam,
and the Rotterdamsche Bankvereeniging, Rotterdam.

Capital authorized . . Fl. 5,000,000
Capital subscribed and paid up . Fl. 1,000,000

Head Office : Heerengracht 252, Amsterdam.
Venezuelan Branch : Boulevard del Capetolio, Caracas.
London Bankers : National Provincial and Union Bank of England, Ltd.

Koppel (Alexander) & Co.
Firm established as Koppel & Schrader, 1865, under present title, 1883.
Head Office : Bogotá (Colombia).
Partners : Francis A. Koppel, Sam. B. Koppel, Alexander Koppel.
London Agents : National Provincial and Union Bank of England, Ltd. (2 Princes
Street, E.C.2); London & River Plate Bank Ltd.; Goschen & Cunliffe.

Moreira, Gomes & Cia.
Established 1852.

Capital . 1,100 contos.

Head Office : Pará (Brazil).
London Agents (since 1912)   National Provincial and Union Bank of England,
Ltd. (Princes Street, E.C.2). A private company

Nuevo Banco Italiano.
Established 1887

Head Office : Reconquista and Plaza Mayo, Buenos Aires.

Capital subscribed	$10,000,000 (National Money).	
Capital paid up .. .	$5,500,000	,, ,,
Surplus .	$8,200,000	,, ,,
Deposits	$120,000,000	,, ,,

Branch Offices : Rosario de Santa Fé, Santa Fé, San Fernando (Argentine Rep.).
Directors   Luis Maffioretti (President), Juan Oscamou (Vice-President), H. Taddeo,
Dr A. Berisso, Dr Juan Bruschi, E. S. Landó.
Managers : P Gindice, L. J Rissotto.
London Agents   Kleinwort, Sons, & Co., London Joint City and Midland Bank,
Ltd., Banca Commerciale Italiana.

BANKING FACILITIES.

La Previsora.
Guayaquil (Ecuador).

Capital   ...   .   300,000 sucres.

Sociedad General de Credito.
Established 1920.

Capital   .   1,000,000 sucres.

Head Office   Guayaquil (Ecuador)
President   Juan Marcos
Managers : Carlos A. Leon, J X. Marcos.

Souza (A. F de) & Cia.

Head Office   Pará (Brazil).
London Agents : Lloyds Bank, Ltd.   17 Cornhill, E.C.3)

Supervielle & Cie.
Established 1887

Offices   Buenos Aires   150 Calle San Martin, Montevideo   429 Calle 25 de Mayo

Tornquist (Ernesto) & Cia., Limitada.
Established 1830.

Capital	$12,000,000 Argentine Gold.
Reserves ..	$2,937,988.98 Argentine Gold.

Head Office : Bartolomé Mitre 531-537, Buenos Aires.
Directors : Carlos Alfredo Tornquist, Miles A. Pasman, Dr. Eduardo A. Tornquist, Ernesto Pasman.
Managers : The Directors are all Managing Directors.
Dividends : Ordinary Shares 8 per cent., Preference Shares, 6 per cent.

INSTITUTIONS

BRITISH INSTITUTIONS IN LATIN-AMERICA.

The Missions to Seamen.

11 Buckingham Street, Strand, London, W.C.2

This Society is doing important work for seamen in the South American ports. It provides Chaplains and Seamen's Institutes at Rio de Janeiro, Santos, Rosario, Buenos Aires, and Bahia Blanca on the east coast, and at Callao and Valparaiso on the west. At the last-named port a site has been secured and funds are being raised to build and equip a new institute. At the institute at Buenos Aires it is hoped soon to add a chapel. British ships at Antofagasta, Iquique and Taltal are scarcely numerous enough to justify the opening of a Seamen's Institute; chaplains visit the ships.

The income of the Society in 1922, with the help of legacies, just covered the expenditure.

South American Missionary Society.

20 John Street, Bedford Row, London, W.C.1.

Established 1844 for the purpose of sending missionaries among the aborigines. It founded the diocese of the Falkland Isles, since subdivided, assisted in the foundation of many chaplaincies and gave grants in aid to others, and has established schools and orphanages for the children of British subjects. In all mission centres the Society has industrial teachers. The Society's agent in Buenos Aires is the Rev William Case Morris. The work extends to Venezuela and Spanish Honduras. The Anglican Bishop of Argentina and the Bishop of the Falkland Isles supervise the work of the Society in South America. Secretary, Rev Alan Ewbank.

Anglican Bishop in Argentina The Right Rev E. F Every, D.D., 1902, 25 de Mayo 282, Buenos Aires.

Address in England : 18 Montague Street, Portman Square, London, W

CHAPLAINS.

Rev Canon H. T Morrey Jones, M.A., St. Paul's Rectory, 19 Gl. Conto de Magalhaes, São Paulo, Brazil (Hon.).

Rev. J Washington Jones and Mrs. Jones, 1921, Chubut, Argentina.

Rev H. T Hutchings and Mrs. Hutchings, 1920, Colegio Inglés, Sarratea, F.C.C.A., Argentina.

Rev H. P and Mrs. Griffiths, 1923, Los Cocos, F.C.A. del N., Córdoba, Argentina.

MISSIONS.

At Makthlawaiya, the "Garden Settlement," an island in the swamp, about 100 miles inland, west of the river Paraguay.

Rev. R. A. Bevis, M.A. (Chaplain), and Mrs. Bevis, 1913; Mr P H. H. Logan, 1920.

Address   Mision Inglésa, Casilla 98, Concepción, Paraguay

IN THE ARGENTINE CHACO.

The New Mission, initiated by Mr W Barbrooke Grubb, was opened in 1911 for Indians from the Argentine and Bolivian Chacos, who work in the sugar plantations. Messrs. Leach Bros. offered special facilities at San Pedro, and a station has been opened on the Rio Bermejo, called Algarrobal.

Address : Mision Chaqueña, c/d Srs. Leach Hermanos Embarcacion, F.C.C.N., Argentina.

WESTERN DIOCESE.

The Bishop of the Falkland Islands, Casella, 1259, Valparaiso The Right Rev N S. de Jersey, 1919.

CHAPLAINCIES.

Rev. Canon P J. R. and Mrs. Walker, 1884, Chaplain, Casilla 1305, Santiago, Chile.

Rev. J. R. Tyerman, A.K.C., and Mrs. Tyerman (Hon.), 1882, Casilla 75, Temuco, Chile.

MISSIONS.

THE ARAUCANIAN MISSION IN SOUTHERN CHILE.

Head station of Temuco, the King Edward Memorial Church of the Holy Trinity, the Casa Bishop Stirling, the Anglo-Chilean College, the Printing Office, and a site for the Mapuche Hostel.

Rev. W. and Mrs. Wilson, 1895, Secretary of Mission, Señor Jerado Salas.

Address   Mision Araucana, Casilla 400, Temuco, Chile.

THE ALFRED ROBERTS MEMORIAL HOSPITAL.

Address : Mision Araucana, Casilla 400, Temuco, Chile.

ANGLO-CHILEAN COLLEGE.

Mr. A. W Bevis, Wh. Sch., M.I.M.E., 1909, Director of Girls' and Boys' Schools.

Address · Colegio Inglés, Casilla 462, Temuco, Chile.

CHOLCHOL.

Church, Boarding Schools for Mapuche Boys and Girls, and a Day School Dispensary and six rural Day Schools.

Address   Mision Araucana, Cholchol, Chile.

BRITISH INSTITUTIONS IN LATIN-AMERICA.

MAQUEHUE.
(On the River Quepe.)

Agricultural and Industrial School, Church of the Redeemer.
Address · Mision Araucana, Casilla 400, Temuco, Chile.

SPANISH HONDURAS.

Jurisdiction of the Bishop of British Honduras.

LA CEIRA AND OUT-STATIONS.

Rev. G. R. Newton, 1922.

VENEZUELA.

Jurisdiction of Bishop of Trinidad.

BREED SOCIETIES IN THE UNITED KINGDOM.

Here follows a list of the chief Societies devoted to the breeding of the pedigree stock which plays so important a part in South American agriculture :—

NATIONAL CATTLE BREEDERS' ASSOCIATION OF GREAT BRITAIN. *Secretary*: W W. Chapman, Room 4, Mowbray House, Norfolk Street, Strand, London, W.C.2. *Telegrams*: "Sheepcote, Estrand, London." A.B.C. 5th edition. *Telephone*: Central 5479.

NATIONAL SHEEP BREEDERS' ASSOCIATION OF GREAT BRITAIN. *Secretary*: W W. Chapman, Room 4, Mowbray House, Norfolk Street, Strand, London, W.C.2 *Telegrams*: "Sheepcote, Estrand, London." A.B.C. 5th edition. *Telephone*: Central 5479.

Horses and Ponies :—

SOCIETY	SECRETARY
Arab Horse Society	The Rev D. B. Montefiore, 15 Wyndham Street, Brighton.
Cleveland Bay Horse Society of Great Britain and Ireland.	J Fairfax Blakeborough, M.C., Grove House, Norton, Stockton-on-Tees.
Clydesdale Horse Society of the United Kingdom.	A. MacNeilage, 93 Hope Street, Glasgow
Dales Pony Improvement Society	W Patterson, 5 Cattle Market, Hexham-on-Tyne.
Fell Pony Society	F W Garnett, C.B.E., Dalegarth, Windermere.
Hackney Horse Society	Robert F Ling, 12 Hanover Square, London, W.1.
Hunters Improvement Society	A. B. Charlton, 12 Hanover Square, London, W.1.
New Forest Ponies Association	Thos. Stovold, Harrow Farm, Bransgore, Christchurch, Hampshire.
British Percheron Horse Society	A. W Hewitt, Imperial House, 27 Cavendish Square, London, W.1.
National Pony Society	F H. Badge, 12 Hanover Square, London, W.1.
Shetland Pony Stud Book Society.	R. W Walker, 3 Golden Square, Aberdeen.
Shire Horse Society . .	A. B. Charlton, 12 Hanover Square, London, W.1.
Suffolk Horse Society	Fred Smith, Woodbridge, Suffolk.
Welsh Pony and Cob Society	John R. Bache, The Cedars, Knighton, Radnorshire.
Yorkshire Coach Horse Society	Frederick Walker, 3 Blake Street, York.

Cattle :—

Aberdeen-Angus Cattle Society	James R. Barclay, 137 Union Street, Aberdeen.
English Aberdeen-Angus Cattle Association.	G. G. Macdonald, Estate Office, Apethorpe, Peterborough.
Ayrshire Cattle Herd Book Society.	Hugh Bone, 58 Alloway Street, Ayr.
Blue Albion Cattle Society .	W J Clark, Alport, Bakewell, Derbyshire.
British Friesian Cattle Society	George Hobson, 4 Southampton Row, London, W.C.1.
Dairy Shorthorn Association	H. J Tilly, 16 Bedford Square, London, W.C.1.
Devon Cattle Breeders' Society	John Risdon, Wiveliscombe, Somerset.
Galloway Cattle Society	F N M. Gourlay, Milnton, Tynron, Thornhill, Dumfriesshire.
English Guernsey Cattle Society	Robt. F Ling, 12 Hanover Square, London, W.1.
Royal Agricultural and Horticultural Society of Guernsey	H. Carré, States Arcade, Guernsey.

BREED SOCIETIES IN THE UNITED KINGDOM.

Society	Secretary
Hereford Herd Book Society	W G. C. Britten, 3 Offa Street, Hereford.
Highland Cattle Society of Scotland.	Duncan MacGregor, Clydesdale Bank, Ltd., Oban.
English Jersey Cattle Society	Messrs. T W Hammond and L. J Craufurd, 19 Bloomsbury Square, London, W.C.1.
Royal Jersey Agricultural and Horticultural Society	H. G. Shepard, 3 Mulcaster Street, St. Helier, Jersey
English Kerry and Dexter Cattle Society.	Messrs. Hammond and Craufurd, 19 Bloomsbury Square, London, W.C.1.
Lincolnshire Red Shorthorn Association.	Robert Lamming, St. Benedict's Square, Lincoln.
Longhorn Cattle Breeders' Association.	R. S. Walters, Bingley Hall, Birmingham.
Gloucestershire Cattle Society	G. E. Lloyd-Baker, Hardwicke Court, Gloucester.
Park Cattle Society .	Sir Claud Alexander, Bt., Faygate Wood, Sussex.
Red Poll Cattle Society of Great Britain and Ireland.	C. H. Clarke, 24 Warrington Road, Ipswich Suffolk.
Shorthorn Society of Great Britain and Ireland.	V H. Seymour, 12 Hanover Square, London, W.1.
South Devon Herd Book Society	W Napier Smith, 6 Princess Square, Plymouth.
Sussex Herd Book Society .	A. G. Holland, 12 Hanover Square, London, W.1.
Welsh Black Cattle Society	Parker Mackenzie, F.A.I., Messrs. John Pritchard & Co., Auctioneers, Bangor, N Wales.

Sheep :—

Blackface Sheep Breeders' Association.	John P Mitchell (Solicitor), Comrie, Scotland.
Society of Border Leicester Sheep Breeders.	Miss Rose J E. Grant, 11 St. Ronan's Terrace, Edinburgh.
Cheviot Sheep Society .	John Robson, Newton, Bellingham, Northumberland.
Cotswold Sheep Society	James W. Tayler, Cold Aston, Bourton-on-the-Water, Gloucestershire.
Dartmoor Sheep Breeders' and Flock Book Association.	S. Arthur Yeo, 3 West Street, Okehampton.
Derbyshire Gritstone Sheep Breeders' Society	William J Clark, Alport, Bakewell, Derbyshire.
Dorset Horn Sheep Breeders' Association.	Thomas H. Ensor, Cornhill, Dorchester
Devon Longwooled Sheep Breeders' Society	A. E. Gerrard, Wiveliscombe, Somerset.
Exmoor Horn Sheep Breeders' Society	D. J Tapp, Highercombe, Dulverton, Somerset.
Hampshire Down Sheep Breeders' Association.	W. J Wooff, 49 Canal, Salisbury.
Herdwick Sheep Breeders' Association.	W. Wilson, Stonycroft, Keswick, Cumberland.
Lincoln Longwool Sheep Breeders' Association.	Robert Lamming, St. Benedict's Square, Lincoln.
Kent or Romney Marsh Sheep Breeders' Association.	W A. Ball, 12 Hanover Square, London, W.1.
Kerry Hill (Wales) Sheep Breeders' Association and Flock Book Society	Messrs. Morris, Marshall and Poole, Newtown, Montgomeryshire.
Leicester Sheep Breeders' Association.	W A. Brown, Elms Villa, Driffield, Yorkshire.
Oxford Down Sheep Breeders' Association.	Howard Sammons, 19 George Street, Oxford.
Roscommon Sheep Breeders' Association.	W Shaw Acheson, Rushill, Hillstreet, Drumsna, County Roscommon, Ireland.
Ryeland Sheep Breeders' Association.	W H. Woodcock, St. Cuthbert's, Whitecross Road, Hereford.
Shropshire Sheep Breeders' Association.	Messrs. Alfred Mansell & Co., College Hill, Shrewsbury.

SOCIETY	SECRETARY
South Devon Flock Book Association.	J Todd, 30 High Street, Totnes.
Southdown Sheep Society	Walter Stride, 63 East Street, Chichester.
Suffolk Sheep Society	Miss E. M. Prentice, 25 Marlborough Road, Ipswich.
Welsh Mountain Sheep Flock Book Society.	W G. Roberts, Wern Home Farm, Portmadoc.
Wensleydale Longwool Sheep Breeders' Association.	G. G. Robinson, Underley Farm, Kirkby Lonsdale.

Pigs :—

British Berkshire Pig Society	Edgar Humfrey, Shippon, Abingdon, Berkshire.
Cumberland Pig Breeders' Association.	George M. Bell, Lonsdale Street, Carlisle.
Essex Pig Society . .	A. F White, 17 Duke Street, Chelmsford.
Old Glamorgan Pig Society .	E. and H. David, Bryn, Pendaylan, Cowbridge,Glam.
Gloucester Old Spots Pig Society (Incorporated).	Eldred G. F Walker, Registered Office, Chew Stoke, Bristol.
Large Black Pig Society .	B. J Roche, 12 Hanover Square, London, W.1.
Large White Pig Ulster Society	Kenneth MacRae, Balmoral, Belfast.
National Pig Breeders' Association.	Alec Hobson, 92 Gower Street, London, W.C.1.
Lincolnshire Curly Coated Pig Breeders' Association.	C. Clarke, Holmleigh, Dorrington, Lincoln.
National Pig Breeders' Association.	Alec Hobson, 92 Gower Street, London, W.C.1.
Wessex Saddleback Pig Society	J M. McCarthy, 32 Market Place, Salisbury

Goats :—

British Goat Society	Thos. W Palmer, 5 Fenchurch Street, London, E.C.3.

THE PAN-AMERICAN UNION.

The Pan-American Union is an international organization, with headquarters in Washington, D.C., and is maintained by the following American republics Argentina, Bolivia, Brazil, Chile, Colombia, Costa Rica, Cuba, Dominican Republic, Ecuador, Guatemala, Haiti, Honduras, Mexico, Nicaragua, Panamá, Paraguay, Peru, Salvador, United States, Uruguay, and Venezuela.

Its purpose is the development of closer cultural, commercial, and financial relations between the Republics of the American Continent and to promote friendly intercourse, peace, and closer understanding. It is supported by annual contributions from all the countries, in amounts based upon population. Its affairs are administered by a Director General and Assistant Director, elected by and responsible to a Governing Board, composed of the Secretary of State of the United States and the diplomatic representatives in Washington of the other American governments. The executive officers are assisted by a staff of statisticians, commercial specialists, editors, translators, compilers, librarians, clerks, and stenographers.

PAST AND PRESENT

The building of the Pan-American Union stands in a 5-acre space facing the President's Park. The structure and grounds represent an investment of $1,100,000, of which the American republics contributed $250,000 and Mr Andrew Carnegie $850,000. The building is largely marble. The corner-stone was laid May 11, 1908, and the building dedicated and occupied April 26, 1910.

Formerly known as the International Bureau of the American Republics, the Union was established in 1890 in accordance with resolutions passed at the First Pan-American Conference, Washington, presided over by Mr Blaine, then United States Secretary of State. It was continued by resolutions of the Second Conference at Mexico in 1901, the Third at Rio de Janeiro in 1906, the Fourth at Buenos Aires, in 1910, and the Fifth at Santiago, Chile, in 1923. The Directors who have administered the affairs of the Union are :—

William E. Curtis (1890–1893) executive officer of the First Pan-American Conference, Chief of the Latin American Department of the Chicago Exposition and correspondent of the Chicago Record-Herald. Clinton Furbish (1893–1897), Joseph P Smith (1897–1898), and Frederic Emory (1898–1899) eminent publicists. W W Rockhill (1899–1905) Ambassador to Turkey, Ambassador to Russia, Minister to Greece and China, and Assistant Secretary of State. Williams C. Fox (1905–1907), Consul in Brunswick, Germany, and Minister to Ecuador. John Barrett (1907–1920) United States minister to Siam, Argentina, Panamá, and Colombia.

The present Director General is L. S. Rowe, professor of Political Science, University of Pennsylvania, member of commission to compile and revise laws of Porto Rico, delegate to Third and Fifth Pan-American Conferences, chairman of U.S. delegation to First Pan-American Scientific Conference at Santiago, Chile, member of U.S. Panamá joint claims commission, Assistant Secretary of the Treasury and Chief of the Division of Latin American Affairs of the State Department.

The Assistant Director, Francisco J Yánes, a Venezuelan, has held responsible posts in the foreign service of that country. He represented the Union at the Fourth Pan-American Conference in Buenos Aires and has travelled widely in Latin America.

The Union is in touch with government officials, commercial organizations, manufacturers, merchants, exporters and importers, and shipping interests, in both North and South America. It maintains touch also with editors, professors, students, scientists, and travellers.

PAN-AMERICAN PUBLICATIONS.

The Union publishes Monthly Bulletins, in English, in Spanish, and in Portuguese, and these are separate and distinct publications. The Bulletins are intended to present a record of the conditions, general progress, commerce, laws, enterprises, and development of each republic. The Union publishes handbooks, pamphlets, special reports, and maps, many of them free, while others are distributed at a low charge.

The Columbus Memorial Library of the Union includes 50,000 volumes of official records, history, travel, narrative, description, and statistics, relating to all the American republics. The Union is the custodian of the archives of the International American Conferences, held at intervals of five or six years. It has charge of the correspondence relating thereto, the preparation of programmes, and the convening of new Conferences.

LATIN-AMERICAN PUBLICATIONS IN LONDON.

" South American Handbook " and "Anuario Ibero Americano."—
Published annually, price 7s. 6d., by South American Publications,
Ltd., Atlantic House, Moorgate, E.C.2. Of interest to commercial
travellers, business men, tourists, and sportsmen.

"Board of Trade Journal" and "Commercial Gazette."—Published
weekly, price 6d., post free 7d., by His Majesty's Stationery Office.
Trade information concerning the Latin-American Republics.
(Annual subscription, 30s. post free.)

"Brazil News."—Issued monthly gratis by the Brazilian Consulate-General, Liverpool. Of interest to traders, including commercial
statistics.

"British and Latin-American Trade Gazette."—Organ of the
British and Latin-American Chamber of Commerce. Monthly, price
1s. Address . 13 Bell Yard, Strand, W.C.2. Editions in English,
Spanish, and Portuguese. Official organ of the British and Latin-
American Chamber of Commerce.

"Chilean Review "—Social, Economic and Commercial Survey
of the Republic of Chile. First number, August 1921. Edited by
Vicente Ocheverria, c/o the Chilean Consulate, London. 1s. net.

"Colombian Trade Review "—Official organ of the Colombian
Government Bureau of Information and Trade Propaganda.
Monthly

"Magazine of the South American Missionary Society "—20 John
Street, London, W.C.1

"Pan-American Magazine and New World Review "—Monthly
London Office 50 Great Russell Street, W.C.

"Review of the River Plate."—Published every Friday in Buenos
Aires. London Office 296 Regent Street, London, W.1

"South American Journal and Brazil and River Plate Mail."—
Established 1863. Price 9d. Address : 309–312 Dashwood
House, E.C.2.

"Anglo-South American Guide—Guia Anglo-Sudamericana."—
Published monthly at 1s. Published in English and Spanish. The
South American Press, 101 Fleet Street, E.C.4.

Diplomatic and Consular Reports dealing with the Latin-American
Republics, issued from time to time by the Department of Overseas
Trade, are published by His Majesty's Stationery Office,
Kingsway, W.C.2.

Several banks issue reports on trade in South America for private
circulation among their clients; among them are the Anglo-South
American Bank, Ltd., the British Bank of South America, Ltd.,
London and Brazilian Bank, Ltd., and London and River Plate
Bank, Ltd.

THE DEPARTMENT OF OVERSEAS TRADE.

35 Old Queen Street, London, S.W.1, and 73 Basinghall Street, London, E.C.2.

Telegrams. " Advantage, Parl, London."
Code · A.B.C., 6th Edition.

Telephones   Victoria, 9040, London Wall, 4713.

Parliamentary Secretary   Lieut.-Colonel A. Buckley, D.S.O, M.P

Parliamentary Private Secretary   Lord Apsley, D.S.O., M.C., M.P

Comptroller-General   Sir W H. Clark, K.C.S.I., C.M.G

Directors · R. W Matthew, C.M.G., S. P P Waterlow, C.B.E., Lt.-Col. H. W G. Cole, C.S.I., O.B.E., W. J. Glenny, O.B.E.

Assistant Directors   J A. P Edgcumbe, C.B.E., G. I. H. Lloyd, L. A. Paish, O.B.E., N S. Reyntiens, C. Taylor, P C. Rice, M.B.E., R.E., R. C. Brensley Richards, O.B.E., R. J Craigie (American Section)

COMMERCIAL COUNSELLORS, SECRETARIES, ETC., IN LATIN AMERICA.
ARGENTINA.

H. O. Chalkley, C.B.E., Commercial Secretary, H.B.M. Legation, Buenos Aires. (" Commintell, Buenos Aires.")

BRAZIL.

E. Hambloch, Commercial Secretary, H.B.M. Embassy, Rio de Janeiro. (" Commintell, Rio de Janeiro.")

The Department of Overseas Trade is a centre at which information on all subjects of commercial interest is collected and classified, replies are given to inquiries by traders on the following subjects Foreign and Colonial Contracts open to Tender, and other openings for British Trade   Existing and probable Future Demand for specific lines of British Goods, Extent and nature of competition and the best methods of combating it, Usual methods of business, terms of credit, payment, etc., Agency conditions, Foreign and Colonial Tariff and Customs Regulations, Commercial Statistics, Regulations concerning Commercial Travellers, Certificates of Origin, etc., Registration of Trade Marks, Consular Invoices, Sources of Supply, Prices, etc., of Trade Products, Shipping and Transport, etc.   The Department supplies lists of names of likely importers of British goods or of firms or individuals considered suitable to act as representatives or agents of British firms.

The Department has an extensive Overseas Intelligence system, which comprises the Commercial Diplomatic and Consular Services in Foreign countries, and Trade Commissioners and Imperial Trade Correspondents in the Empire.

The Department organizes Fairs and Exhibitions with the object of attracting important overseas buyers, and bringing them into touch with the British producer   The best known of these Fairs is The British Industries Fair.

When making application for information inquiries should clearly specify :—

(1) the countries concerning which information is required;

(2) the precise kind of goods; and

(3) the particular points in regard to which the information is sought.

GERMAN TRADE WITH CENTRAL AND SOUTH AMERICA.

EXPORTS.

Metric Tons.

	1913.	1921.	1922.
CENTRAL AMERICA :			
Mexico	130,340	16,146	29,381
Guatemala	5,026	2,269	3,974
Salvador	3,988	122	609
Honduras	1,385	382	694
Nicaragua	1,963	119	638
Costa Rica	7,570	684	3,382
Panamá	7,105	2,525	1,781
Cuba	72,447	9,967	11,424
SOUTH AMERICA :			
Argentina	597,364	129,628	341,639
Bolivia	18,093	1,139	3,918
Brazil	470,546	106,662	216,158
Chile	369,921	23,403	62,691
Colombia	29,255	4,646	6,872
Ecuador	6,820	2,285	16,685
Paraguay	3,256	315	518
Peru	28,502	10,380	16,736
Uruguay	69,953	10,323	18,340
Venezuela	18,115	4,856	6,668

IMPORTS.

Metric Tons.

	1913.	1921.	1922.
CENTRAL AMERICA :			
Mexico	47,952	69,240	63,995
Guatemala	22,674	10,261	7,640
Salvador	3,346	652	1,742
Honduras	1,010	529	311
Nicaragua	1,738	532	401
Costa Rica	10,737	1,627	787
Panamá	715	157	310
Cuba	14,342	4,480	16,722
SOUTH AMERICA :			
Argentina	2,146,641	1,374,660	884,830
Bolivia	18,194	5,580	6,174
Brazil	227,512	194,529	111,911
Chile	820,014	15,067	55,534
Colombia	26,211	5,279	2,305
Ecuador	17,377	15,105	9,807
Paraguay	4,234	1,599	1,113
Peru	39,484	866	10,542
Uruguay	27,697	10,330	6,971
Venezuela	17,244	8,335	8,288

LATIN-AMERICAN
DIPLOMATS

LATIN-AMERICAN DIPLOMATS.

ARGENTINA.

H.E. Señor Don José Evaristo Uriburu.
Envoy Extraordinary and Minister Plenipotentiary.

Born February 13, 1880, the son of an ex-President of the Republic, Sr Uriburu, from an early age, took an active part in the politics of the country, and on various occasions was a candidate for the position of National Deputy   Interested all his life in historical research, he has published several interesting works.   He was a member and "vocal" of the Managing Committee of the American Historical and Bibliographical Congress to commemorate the centenary of the Declaration of Argentine Independence, and is a member of the American Academy of History.

In September 1916 he was appointed Municipal Commissioner of the capital. In 1919 he became Director of the National Argentine Bank for the statutory period. On May 12, 1921, he was appointed Envoy Extraordinary and Minister Plenipotentiary to the Court of St. James's.

Carlos Miguens.
Secretary.

Born Buenos Aires, September 12, 1893, he pursued studies in the Faculties of Philosophy and Letters and of Law and Social Science, graduating as diplomat in 1917   Whilst Honorary Attaché to the Foreign Ministry, he was appointed Secretary of Legation, May 29, 1918, and at the beginning of 1920 he was sent as Chargé d'Affaires *ad interim* to Paraguay   He was appointed to London January 1921.

Carlos M. Dominguez.
Financial Secretary.

Youngest son of the late Don Luis L. Dominguez, Argentine statesman, historian, and diplomatist.   Born and educated in Buenos Aires.   Since 1900, Private Secretary to the Argentine Ministers in London and Financial Attaché.   Associated with the Argentine Legation for over twenty years. *London Club* · St. James's.

PAULINO LLAMBI CAMPBELL.
Counsellor.

Born Buenos Aires, July 26, 1876, entered Argentine Diplomatic Service 1901, as First Secretary in Brussels (1901–1904), Berlin (1904–1909), Rome (1909–1911), Brussels (1911–1915), Rio-Janeiro (1915), Counsellor of Legation at The Hague (1916–1921); appointed Counsellor of Legation at London in 1921. Acted as Chargé d'Affaires in Belgium, Germany, Italy, Brazil, Netherlands, and Great Britain. *Distinctions* · Commander of the Royal Orders of the Crown of Belgium, of the Crown of Italy, of Isabel la Católica of Spain, etc., etc. *Clubs :* Travellers', Argentine, Ranelagh.

JORGE GAMES.
Naval Attaché.

Born 35 years ago in Buenos Aires, the son of Dr. Julian Games and Mrs. Manuela Hernandez de Games. Educated in Buenos Aires in the Naval Academy, and at present a Commander in the Argentine Navy Was Naval Assessor to the Argentine Delegation at the Pan-American Congress, April 1923. Has published books on Ballistics and Gunnery; technical articles in the " Boletin del Centro Naval " and " Revista de Publicaciones Navales " ; translated into Spanish the books of Admiral Jellicoe.

BOLIVIA.

H.E. SEÑOR DON ALBERTO GUTIERREZ.
Envoy Extraordinary and Minister Plenipotentiary o, Bolivia in London.

Was born 1863 in Sucre and there educated. Successively he has been Secretary in Washington, and Minister in Santiago, Rio-Janeiro, Bogotá, Quito, Caracas, London. Of literary tastes, he has published some fifteen volumes upon literature and history

H MAMERTO URRIOLAGOITIA.
First Secretary

First Secretary of Legation, and Chargé d'Affaires of the Bolivian Legation in London, was born December 5, 1894, at Sucre, and is the son of Señor Mamerto Urriolagoitia and Corina Harriague. He was educated at Sucre and Paris, and is a Doctor of Political and Social Sciences. Señor Urriolagoitia was Delegate for the Bolivian University to the Latin-American Congress of Students in 1914. He wrote formerly for " La Mañana" of Sucre, still writes articles for the Press, and is a member of various sporting clubs in Bolivia and in London.

BRAZIL.

H.E. Senhor Don Domicio da Gama.

Ambassador of Brazil.

Born October 23, 1862, in Rio de Janeiro. Married, 1912, in New York, Elizabeth Bell Bates. *Diplomatic career*   Secretary in the United States of America (1893), Switzerland, London, Belgium, Paris, Minister in Colombia (1905), Peru (1907), Argentina (1908), Ambassador on Special Mission in Chile (1910), Ambassador in the United States of America from 1911 to 1918; Minister of Foreign Affairs from November 15, 1918, to July 26, 1919; Ambassador in England since November 12, 1919.

Was a journalist in Paris, and has written short stories and essays. Is a member of the Brazilian Academy, and was its President in 1919. Is a Delegate for the United States of America in the International Permanent Commission created by the treaty of September 15, 1914, between Great Britain and that country, and holds the same position for Guatemala on the Commission created by the treaty of September 30, 1913, between that country and the United States of America.

CHILE.

H.E. Señor Don Agustin Edwards.

Envoy Extraordinary and Minister Plenipotentiary

Grand Cross of Isabel la Católica (Spain), Grand Cross of the Crown of Italy, Grand Cross of the Golden Harvest of China, Envoy Extraordinary and Minister Plenipotentiary of Chile to the Court of St. James's; First Delegate of Chile to the League of Nations. Born Santiago, June 16, 1878, married Olga Budge of Santiago, one son. Educated at St. Ignatius, Santiago. Member of House of Representatives, 1899–1910, Vice-President of the same, 1902, Prime Minister, Minister for Foreign Affairs, Envoy Extraordinary and Minister Plenipotentiary to Spain, Italy, Switzerland, and Great Britain, Special Envoy at marriage of King of Spain, 1906, and at the coronation of King George V. *Publications*   Spain (Voyages, 2 vols.); Report of the Geneva International Conference (1 vol.); Notes on Sweden, founded four of the daily papers and five of the magazines now published in Chile. *Recreations ·* Golf, motoring. *Address ·* 22 Grosvenor Square, W.1. *Clubs ·* Travellers', St. James's, Ranelagh, Royal Automobile, Athenæum, Bath; Sandy Lodge Golf.

Santiago de Ossa.

First Secretary

Born December 22, 1889, and educated in Santiago de Chile. His diplomatic career includes appointments as . 1917, Ministerio de Relaciones Exteriores (Chilian Foreign Office); 1918, Second

Secretary to the Legation in Japan; 1921, promoted to First Secretary in January, 1921, Chargé d'Affaires at Tokio; September 1922, Specially attached to the Foreign Office in Chile, Specially attached to the Legation in London. Sport, motoring, and shooting are his recreations.

MANUEL SALINAS.
First Secretary

Chilean Chargé d'Affaires in London. Born March 3, 1885, Santiago de Chile, son of Manuel Salinas and Teresa Fuenzalida de Salinas. Educated at Santiago de Chile. Commander of the Golden Harvest of China. *Diplomatic career* Secretary to the Chilean Legation at Vienna and to the Chilean Embassy at Washington. *Amusements :* Sport in general. *Club* St. James's.

LUIS WADDINGTON
Financial Adviser

Financial Adviser to the Chilean Legation in London Born 1859, Valparaiso. Educated at Valparaiso, married Isabel Cood. *Diplomatic career* Chargé d'Affaires in Belgium. *Club* Royal Wimbledon Golf Club. *Address* 34 Pont Street, S.W.1.

ALEJANDRO ALVAREZ.
Juridical Adviser.

Juridical Adviser to the Chilean Legation in London. Born Santiago de Chile. Educated at Chilean University, Santiago. Chilean Delegate at several International Conferences.

JORGE SILVA.
First Secretary

Lieutenant of Cavalry, First Secretary to the Chilean Legation in London. Born 1896, Calera, Chile. Educated at Santiago de Chile. *Diplomatic career :* Chilean Foreign Office, Master of Ceremonies, also Chief of Code Department, Secretary of the Special Embassies to Buenos Aires in 1915 and 1918. *Amusements* Riding, tennis. *Club* Bath Club.

JUAN NEGRETE.
Military Attaché.

Major in the Chilean Army, Military Attaché to the Chilean Legation in London. Born 1879, Curicó, Chile. Educated at Military School, Santiago de Chile. *Amusements* Sport in general.

JULIO F. A. BITTENCOURT
Air Attaché.

Attaché to the Chilean Legation in London. Born April 7, 1866, Valparaiso; married March 2, 1893, Isabel Squire. Educated at Valparaiso. Knight of the Crown of Italy *Club* · St. James's.

SANTIAGO MONK.
Attaché.

Attaché to the Chilean Legation in London. Born Limache, Valparaiso. Educated at Valparaiso. *Club* . Devonshire.

EDGARDO VON SCHOREDERS.
Naval Attaché.

Commander and Baron. Born December 10, 1883, in Valparaiso, son of the late Baron Icodoro von Schoreders, and educated at the Naval Academy, Valparaiso, he married in 1909 Maria Larrain, youngest daughter of the late Marquis de Casa Larrain; author of the text-book upon torpedoes used in the Torpedo School, he was First Instructor of Torpedo Officers, Captain of the first Chilean submarine, and First Commander of the Chilean Naval Aviation.

AGUSTIN R. EDWARDS.
Attaché.

Attaché to the Chilean Legation in London. Born 1899, Valparaiso. Educated at Eton and Magdalen, Oxford. *Amusements* Sports in general. *Club* . Bath Club.

COLOMBIA.

H.E. SEÑOR DON LUIS CUERVO MARQUEZ.
Envoy Extraordinary and Minister Plenipotentiary

Colombian Minister to Great Britain, was born and educated at Bogotá, and was several times President of the House of Representatives and of the Senate of Colombia. A past President of the Constituent Assembly of Colombia, he was Chargé d'Affaires in Washington in 1900, and Diplomatic Agent at Venezuela in 1904 A man of science and medicine, he was a Professor at the School of Medicine, and several times President of the Colombian Academy of Medicine and Surgery His publications include works on Yellow Fever and the Medical Geography of Colombia. A Commander of the Legion of Honour (France), he is also Comandador de la Real Orden de Carlos III de España, and a member of various scientific societies.

José Medina.
Commercial Attaché.

Born at Medellín, Colombia, May 17, 1892, and educated there and in the University of Liverpool. He married, 1916, Adeline Gertrude Dale, has served as Consul at Liverpool and Director of the Colombian Government Bureau of Information, London. By profession an electrical engineer and ex-member of Municipal Council, he has contributed many articles to newspapers in Spanish and English, and is Editor of the "Colombian Trade Review"

Dr. Alfonso Delgado.
Secretary.

Born at Popayán, Colombia, and took the degree of Doctor of Law at the National University, Bogotá, becoming Secretary of the Law Department of that University. Held high judicial office in his own country, and has been Consul of Colombia at New Orleans, Chancellor of the Colombian Consulate-General in London; Secretary of the Colombian Legation, Washington. Has published poetry and articles. *Address* · 10 Warwick Gardens, Kensington, London, W.14.

CUBA.

General Carlos Garcia-Vélez, K.B.E.
Envoy Extraordinary and Minister Plenipotentiary.

Cuban Envoy Extraordinary and Minister Plenipotentiary in London, was born, April 29, 1869, at Jiguani, Cuba, son of General Calixto García-Iñiguez and Isabel Vélez. Educated at New York and Madrid. Married in 1903 Amalia Martinez Ibor, of Ibor City, Florida. *Diplomatic career* · Minister Plenipotentiary in Mexico, Washington, Buenos Aires, and London, Cuban representative at the coronation of King George V, member of the Pan-American Congress; member of the Allied War Cabinet, Paris. Has made an exhaustive study of the history and development of the New World, and owns a remarkable collection of early books, documents, pamphlets and pictures relating to the Spanish colonies and their settlement. Editor until 1895 of the "Revista Odontologica," Madrid. Collaborator in History of the Spanish-American War Contributor to English-American Reviews.

General Carlos Garcia-Vélez served with distinction with the Army of the East during the Cuban War He co-operated with the United States troops during the siege of Santiago. During the American occupation he was appointed to the provisional administration and instituted sweeping reforms in the Prison system.

Dr. Rafael Rodriguez-Altunaga.
First Secretary.

Doctor in Law, First Secretary of the Cuban Legation in London. Born, January 16, 1887, at Trinidad, Cuba, son of L. Rodriguez-Bocalán and Elena Altunaga-Urquiola. Educated at the University of Havana. *Diplomatic career :* Chargé d'Affaires in Colombia (1911–1918), First Secretary, Uruguay, and Chargé d'Affaires, London. Contributor to law journals and member of various legal societies. Author of "Mercantile Law," a treatise on international mercantile law, published at Madrid, 1917

Dr. Pedro Rodriguez-Capote.
Chargé d'Affaires.

Doctor in Law, Chargé d'Affaires of the Cuban Legation in London, born, March 28, 1896, at New York, son of Alejandro Rodriguez-Capote and Carmen Fernandez de Castro. Educated at the Universidad Nacional, Havana. *Diplomatic career* formerly Attaché to the Cuban Legation at Washington. *Sports* Horsemanship, tennis, etc. *Clubs .* Havana Yacht Club, Vedado Tennis Club (Havana).

ECUADOR.

H.E. Senor Don Enrique Dorn y de Alsua.
Envoy Extraordinary and Minister Plenipotentiary

Ecuadorean Envoy Extraordinary and Minister Plenipotentiary in London and at Paris. Born, October 4, 1862, at Guayaquil. Educated at Paris. *Diplomatic career :* Attaché and Secretary at Paris, London, and Madrid.

Pedro Victor Miller.
Consul-General.

Consul-General for Ecuador in London. Born, March 6, 1882, at Guayaquil, son of Pedro Miller and Matilde Octavia Gutiérrez. Educated at the University of Guayaquil. Married, June 23, 1910, to Mercedes Patricia Wright, daughter of Eduardo Wright and Mariá Teresa de Aguirre. *Other Occupations :* Town Clerk of the Corporation of Guayaquil and a Member of the same several times, Deputy to the Congress, Member of the Chamber of Commerce of Guayaquil, President of the Board of Directors of the Banco de Crédito Hipotecario and the Guayaquil Fire Assurance Company; Secretary of the Banco del Ecuador, Member of the Directory of the Banco Comercial y Agricola, the Sociedad General de Crédito, etc.

PANAMÁ.

CARLOS R. Z. VALLARINO.
Chargé d'Affaires and Consul.

Panamanian Chargé d'Affaires and Consul in London. *Titles* . Cross of the Benemeranza Pontificiale, Third Order of Simon Bolivár. Born November 5, 1857 Youngest son of Carlos Zachrisson and Manuela Vallarino, of Panamá. Educated privately at Panamá. Married, 1879, Aura, youngest daughter of Ramon Vallarino Brajimo and Manuela Arosemena Quezada. First Consul-General for Panamá in Great Britain, Consul at Southampton, St. Nazaire, and London. *Publications* Reports mostly of an official character *Principal Achievements* For six years Member of the Municipal Council of Panamá, took a prominent part in the political events which culminated in the Proclamation of Panamá as an independent Republic (November 3, 1903)

ENRIQUE STAGG.
Attaché.

Attaché of the Panamanian Legation. Born 1804, Valparaiso, son of General Leonardo Stagg and Amalia Flores. Educated at Ecuador. Married, 1878, Elena Obarrio of Panamá. Has served in the Panamanian Consular Service.

ROBERT JOHN TURNER, J.P., F.R.C.I., C.I.S.
Hon. Attaché.

Hon. Attaché of the Panamanian Legation since 1906, Chairman of Turner, Davidson, Ltd. Born 1864, Midlothian, youngest son of Peter Turner Educated privately at Edinburgh. Married, 1896, Lilian Adeline, second daughter of J Lyon, J.P *Diplomatic career* First Consul in London for Panamá. *Publications* Articles on the food question. *Principal Achievements* Associated with the Prime Minister of Australia in the formation of the Commonwealth Government line of steamers.

PARAGUAY.

CAPTAIN ERNESTO IBÁÑEZ.

Captain of Infantry, and Acting Consul-General in charge of Legation. Born June 16, 1888, Paraguay Educated at the Paraguayan University and Military School. Married, 1918, Louisa Irene Davies (British) The founder of "La Acción," newspaper of Asunción, and has contributed extensively to "Alon," "El Liberal," and other journals.

PERU.

DR. RICARDO RIVERA SCHREIBER.

Chargé d'Affaires.

Doctor in Law, Jurisprudence and Political Science, and Corresponding Member of the Royal Latin Spanish Academy   Born November 11, 1892, at Lima, son of Señor Ricardo Rivera, Member of the Peruvian Parliament.   Educated at Lima, the ancient University of San Marcos.   Married, 1919, Mercedes Urquidi de Tezanos Pinto.   In 1916 appointed Consul in Bolivia, he became Consul-General.   In 1917 was Secretary to the Peruvian Legation, at La Paz.   In 1919 formed part of the Peruvian Delegation to the League of Nations.   In 1920 was appointed Second Secretary to the Peruvian Legation in London.   *Publications*   Author of "El Contrato de Seguro sobre la Vida," Lima, 1916, and "L'Avenir International de l'Amérique Latine," Paris, 1919.   Articles on International Law and Jurisprudence particularly concerning North and South America.   Contributor to "La Révue du Droit International de Paris," "Mercurio Peruano," and "El Comercio de Lima."   *Sports* · Tennis, rowing, and motoring.

Active in promoting good relations between Peru and Great Britain.   Presented on behalf of the Peruvian Government the bust of Sir Clements R. Markham to the Royal Geographical Society of London.   *Clubs :* St. James's and Ranelagh.

GERMAN CISNEROS Y RAYGADA.

Chargé d'Affaires.

Grand Cordon of the Double Dragon of China, Knight Commander of Isabel the Catholic, Knight Commander of St. Gregory, Knight Commander of the Crown of Italy, Chevalier of the Legion of Honour, Officer of the Academy of France, Chargé d'Affaires *en titre* for Peru in Great Britain. Born, October 11, 1872, at Lima, son of Luciano B. Cisneros, statesman, orator, and diplomatist, and Josefa Raygada, daughter of the General of that name.   Educated in France and England, and at the University of Lima. Married, 1901, Noemi de Mattos Topin, daughter of Francisco de Mattos Topin and Maria A. Deschamps. *Diplomatic career*   Entered the Peruvian Foreign Office, 1894, Attaché in Switzerland, 1896; Paris, 1899, Second Secretary, Brazil, 1900, where he was Chargé d'Affaires *ad interim*, 1903, Head of the Consular Section of the Foreign Office, Lima, 1904, Sub-Chief of the Diplomatic Section, 1905, Marshal of the Diplomatic Corps, 1908; Chargé d'Affaires *en titre* in Belgium, 1921, Great Britain, 1921

OSCAR VICTOR SALOMON.

Consul-General.

Consul-General for Peru in London.   Born March 6, 1882, at Huarez.   Educated at Lima and New York.   *Diplomatic career*

Chancellor of Peruvian General Consulate at New York, 1904, serving afterwards at Liverpool, Southampton, and Cardiff. *Publications* . Articles on the resources of Peru. Travelled for six years over the coasts, sierras, and forests of Peru.

URUGUAY.

H.E. SEÑOR DON FEDERICO R. VIDIELLA.
Envoy Extraordinary and Minister Plenipotentiary.

Uruguayan Minister to Great Britain from 1909. Born 1850. Twice Minister of Finance, and responsible during the European War for the opening of credit of twelve millions sterling in favour of Great Britain and France. Been Lord Mayor of Montevideo, Minister in Holland, Sweden, Norway, and Denmark, from 1909 to 1916. Founded the Banco de la República. *Amusements* . Specializes in breeding shorthorn cattle on his estates, and also in the cultivation of vines and olives.

CARLOS DE SANTIAGO.
First Secretary.

First Secretary of the Uruguayan Legation. Born 1875, in Montevideo, where he was educated. In 1910 he came to London as Attaché. 1916, Second Secretary 1918, First Secretary As an artist has received medals from the Madrid and Buenos Aires Exhibitions for paintings.

VENEZUELA.

H.E. DR. DIOGENES ESCALANTE.
Envoy Extraordinary and Minister Plenipotentiary.

Envoy Extraordinary and Minister Plenipotentiary for Venezuela to the Court of St. James's, Second Class of the Bolívar Order. Born October 23, 1879, married Isabel Alamo-Ybarra of Caracas, 1914. Educated at University of Los Andes and University of Geneva, where he took the degree of Barrister in law Consul in Liverpool, 1905–1907, Consul-General in Germany, 1908–1909, Secretary of Mission in Paris, 1909–1910, Member of the House of Representatives, 1912–1914, Delegate to the League of Nations, 1920–1921, founded and edited for several years "El Nuevo Diario," the leading daily paper of Caracas; founded two literary magazines, writer on sociological and economical matters. *Recreations* Mountain climbing and travelling.

PASSPORTS AND *VISAS*

PASSPORTS AND *VISAS*.

Head Office · 1 Queen Anne's Gate Buildings, Dartmouth Street, London, S.W.1.

Branch Passport Office   36 Dale Street, Liverpool.

British subjects travelling to foreign countries must be in possession of valid Passports bearing the *visa* of the Consular Representative of the country or countries to be visited.

The addresses in London to which application for the *visa* should be made are given below, with particulars of any special requirements.

(Note.—These regulations are liable to alteration.   Intending travellers are advised to make direct inquiry to the Foreign Consulates at the time of their proposed journey.)

VISAS.

ARGENTINA.—7 Gower Street, W.C. (charge, $2.60 gold).
  Obtainable also at Liverpool, Cardiff, Newport (Mon.), Southampton, Glasgow, Newcastle, and Belfast.   Personal attendance is necessary, and certificates as to health and industrial fitness are required.

BOLIVIA.—20 Copthall Avenue, E.C.2 (charge, 6s.).
  Personal attendance is necessary, also two letters of reference.   Decree of Government of Bolivia requires persons entering Bolivia to be provided with *visa* of Bolivian Consular Officer in London and at Antofagasta, Arica, Puno, Laquiaca, Corumba, Brasilia, as the case may be, reporting themselves to police on arrival.

BRAZIL.—Coventry House, South Place, E.C.2 (charge, 4 milreis).

CHILE.—2 York Gate, N.W (charge, 8s.).
  Personal attendance is necessary

COLOMBIA.—Sicilian House, Sicilian Avenue, Southampton Row, W.C.1 (charge, $2 Colombian).
  Personal application should be made, if possible.

COSTA RICA.—7 Crosby Square, Bishopsgate, E.C.3 (charge, 4s. 6d.).

CUBA.—No *visa* is necessary

ECUADOR.—23 College Hill, Cannon Street, E.C.4 (charge, 8s.).
  Office hours, 10–1.   Visas also granted at Liverpool and Glasgow.   Vaccination and health certificates required.

GUATEMALA.—11 Queen Victoria Street, E.C.4 (charge, 8s.).

HONDURAS.—4 Lloyds Avenue, E.C.3 (charge, $1).
  Hours 11–3; Saturdays, 11–1.   *Visa* granted in any town where there is a Consul or authorized Consular Agent.

MEXICO.—Bush House, Aldwych, W.C.2 (charge, $4 Mexican for 12 months; transit *visa*, $0·40).   Office hours, 9–3.   Two photographs required.   Double fees charged for *visas* granted after 3 p.m.   Visas may also be granted at Liverpool and Glasgow

NICARAGUA.—65 Bishopsgate Street, E.C.2 (charge, 5s.).
  Visas granted on request.   Hours, 10–5.   Visas are also granted in any town in the United Kingdom where there is a Nicaraguan Consul.

PANAMA.—232 Finsbury Pavement House, E.C.2 (charge, to British subjects, 8s. 6d.).

PARAGUAY.—14 Chiswell House, Finsbury Pavement, E.C.2 (charge, $1).
  Hours, 3–4, except Saturdays, when the office is closed.   *Visas* may also be obtained at Manchester, Liverpool, Birmingham, Bradford, Glasgow, Cardiff, and Southampton.

PERU.—36 and 37 Queen Street, E.C.3 (charge, 8s.).

SALVADOR.—7 and 8 Union Court, E.C.2.

Hours, 2–5, except Saturdays, when office is closed. *Visas* may also be obtained at Liverpool, Birmingham, and Glasgow. British subjects travelling to Salvador are under no obligation to have their passports *visé*, but according to the Salvadorean authorities this formality is advisable.

URUGUAY.—67–68 Chancery Lane, W.C.2 (charge, 5s.).

Passengers travelling first class require *visa* of Uruguayan Consul-General; others must have a "certificate of good conduct and fitness for work," signed by some person of authority. Certificates may be obtained on application at the Consulate-General.

VENEZUELA.—104 High Holborn, W.C.

VALIDITY OF PASSPORTS.

A Passport is valid for two years from date of issue, and can be made available for any countries to which the holder is likely to travel during this period.

It can be renewed for four further periods of two years, provided there is sufficient space for further *visas*, but where the Passport contains no further space for *visas*, application must be made for a new Passport.

ENDORSEMENT AND VISA OF PASSPORTS.

During the validity of a Passport, no further endorsement by the Passport Office is required for further journeys to the countries for which the Passport has already been made available by the British Passport Authorities. The *visa* of the Consular Representative of the country to which the bearer is travelling is required for each journey, except where a continuing *visa* has been obtained.

For journeys to countries other than those already named on the Passport, the endorsement of the Passport Office should be obtained.

British subjects returning to the United Kingdom do not, under British regulations, require any British *visa*, but where such *visa* is required in order to comply with the regulations of a foreign government, it can be given free of charge by any salaried British Consular Officer.

The following **forms** of application are in use, and are obtainable direct from the Passport Office, or from Banks, Shipping Agents, etc., in London or the Provinces :—

Form A.—Application for new Passport by adult (fee, 7s. 6d.).

Form B.—Application for new Passport for child under age of 16 (fee, 7s. 6d.).

Form D.—Renewal of Passport issued after 1 February, 1915 (fee, 2s. for each period of two years)

Endorsement Form (fee, 2s.).

Note.—Not less than two clear days' notice should be given for all applications for the issue, endorsement, or renewal of Passports:

PASSPORTS AND *VISAS*.

Applications for Passports should be made on Form A; the regulations and the marginal notes should be carefully complied with.

The whole of the declaration and marginal particulars must be in the applicant's own handwriting.

Duplicate unmounted photographs must be attached.

The application must be accompanied by a full statement of the circumstances in which the applicant desires to leave the country and be supported by satisfactory evidence as to the object of the proposed journey.

Employees of firms, or persons acting on behalf of firms, must produce certificates from their employers as to the nature of the business on which they are proceeding abroad.

The route, destination, and proposed date of departure must be given.

EXTRACT FROM BRITISH ALIENS ORDER, 1920:—

1.—(1) An alien coming from outside the United Kingdom shall not land in the United Kingdom except with the leave of an Immigration Officer.

(2) Leave shall not be given to a former enemy alien to land in the United Kingdom except by permission of the Secretary of State.

(3) Leave shall not be given to an alien to land in the United Kingdom unless he complies with the following conditions, that is to say :—

(a) He is in a position to support himself and his dependents;

(b) If desirous of entering the service of an employer in the United Kingdom he produces a permit in writing for his engagement issued to the employer by the Minister of Labour;

(c) He is not a lunatic, idiot, or mentally deficient;

(d) He is not the subject of a Medical Certificate given to the Immigration Officer by a Medical Inspector that for medical reasons it is undesirable that the alien should be permitted to land;

(e) He has not been sentenced in a foreign country for any extradition crime within the meaning of the Extradition Acts, 1870 to 1906;

(f) He is not the subject of a deportation order in force under the Principal Act, or any Order in Council thereunder, or of an expulsion order under the Aliens Act, 1905.

(g) He has not been prohibited from landing by the Secretary of State;

(h) He fulfils such other requirements as may be prescribed by any general or special instructions of the Secretary of State;

(4) The Secretary of State or an Immigration Officer, in accordance with general or special instructions of the Secretary of State, may attach such conditions as he may think fit to the grant of permission to an alien to land, and the alien shall comply with the conditions so attached.

3.—(1) An Immigration Officer or a Medical Inspector may inspect any alien seeking to land in the United Kingdom, and any such inspection shall be made as soon as possible after his arrival.

(5) Any alien to whom leave to land has been refused (including a seaman engaged at a port outside the United Kingdom and seeking to land for discharge) shall be removed from the United Kingdom by the master of the ship in which he arrived.

N.B.—The above rules do not apply to transmigrants.

ARGENTINE STATE RAILWAYS.

Projected Extensions.

As they stand to-day the Argentine State Railways are said to be capitalized in the books of the Public Works Department at $850,000,000 Argentine paper   In July 1923 the Minister of Public Works announced the intention of the Government to ask permission to incur a further expenditure of $340,000,000, or, say, £30,000,000 approximately, to cover extensions and sundry other items, such as additional rolling stock and improvements to the existing system.   In 1921 the lines of the State were :—

	Gauge.	Kilometres.
Central Norte Argentino	3 ft. 3 in.	. 4,916
Formosa to Embarcación .. .	,,	.. 298

(In the North and North-Eastern regions of the Republic, Córdoba, Tucumán, Salta, Jujuy, with offshoot to Santa Fé, the most southerly point at which connection is made with deep water at the port of this name on the River Parana.)

	Gauge.	Kilometres.
San Antonio	5 ft. 6 in.	.. 452
Puerto Deseado	,,	. 286
Commodore Rivadavia	,,	. 197

(In the Rio Negro and Chubut Territories, commonly spoken of collectively as Patagonia.   These lines formed part of the extensive system planned in 1908 and never carried to completion for lack of funds.)

To these existing lines, there will be added the following extensions, all of which have been surveyed and some of which have been begun :—

Northern Section, gauge 3 ft. 3 in. :—	Length. Kilometres.	Max. gradient. %
Rosario de Lerma to Chilean Frontier	315	.. 25
Embarcación to Yacuiba . ..	181	.. 6
Antilla to Rosario de la Frontera ..	62	9
Catamarca to Tucuman	128	.. 12
Embarcación to Formosa	403	. 3
Metán to Avia Terai .. .	360	3
San Juan to Jachal . ..	181	16
Milagro to Quines .. .	137	. 4

ARGENTINE STATE RAILWAYS.

Northern Section, gauge 3 ft. 3 in. :—	Length. Kilometres.	Max. gradient. %
San Nicolas to Pergamino	70	3
Entre Rios—Corrientes, gauge 4 ft. 8½ in :—		
Federal to Curuzu-Cuatia	166	4
Patagonian Main System, gauge 5 ft. 6 in. :—		
San Antonio to Lake Nahuel Huapi ..	192	16
Patagones to San Antonio	165	8
Zapalla to Chile, via Lonquimay	160	15
Puerto Deseado to Lake Buenos Aires	195	15
Patagonian Light Railways, 0.75 cm. gauge :—		
Madryn to Colony 16 de Octubre ..	550	—
Huahuel Niyeu to Epuyen ..	250	—
Epuyen, Bolsón, and 16 de Octubre .	180	—
Commodore Rivadavia to Colony Las Heras (connecting branch line) ..	90	—

The northern section is designed to facilitate development in the rich semi-tropical provinces, which at present languish through a diminishing population and an inability to find convenient outlets for their products, on account of their distance from consuming centres.

The line to the Chilean frontier is intended eventually to distribute the produce of Salta and Jujuy through the arid north of Chile, the latter Republic carrying the line on to the Port of Antofagasta.

Formosa–Embarcación is more to the north-east, tapping the Bolivian southlands and the headwaters of the Bermejo river The gauge of these lines corresponds to that of the Central Córdoba system and the French lines in the province of Santa Fé, while the section Federal–Curuzu Cuatia accords with the gauge of the Entre Rios systems , the Patagonian lines are at one with the Great Southern track.

LIVE-STOCK IN ARGENTINE.

Census Report, 1922.

	CATTLE.	SHEEP.	PIGS.
TOTALS—			
Argentine Republic ..	37,064,350	30,671,841	1,436,638
PROVINCIAL TOTALS—			
Buenos Aires	15,507,530	12,902,349	621,544
Santa Fé	4,692,543	580,990	13,399
Entre Rios	2,820,905	2,547,015	62,479
Corrientes	3,793,584	2,180,552	47,454
Córdoba	4,102,894	775,489	211,655
San Luis	897,209	470,095	23,794
Santiago del Estero ..	630,350	595,073	53,015
Tucumán	336,898	70,380	39,817
Mendoza	200,463	139,121	6,032
San Juan	58,191	85,823	4,410
La Rioja	188,064	128,372	9,820
Catamarca	307,861	234,916	12,475
Salta	488,658	151,113	23,349
Jujuy	118,241	412,585	9,030
Chaco	598,667	53,291	12,190
Chubut	96,649	2,925,512	4,823
Formosa	523,881	29,121	3,612
La Pampa	1,330,189	1,658,181	42,899
Los Andes	856	86,569	4
Misiones	115,406	9,470	26,387
Neuquen .: ..	141,307	477,041	3,059
Rio Negro	100,571	2,067,612	4,481
Santa Cruz	6,502	1,273,001	378
Tierra del Fuego ..	6,431	318,170	532

LATIN-AMERICAN CURRENCIES.

In the following table the values of the basic monetary units of the countries of the Pan-American Union are given in United States Gold and in "Pan-americanos." The latter is an imaginary unit recommended by the Inter-American High Commission at a meeting held in Buenos Aires, April 12, 1916. Equivalent to 0·33437 gram of gold ·900 fine.

Country	Standard.	Unit.	Value Pan-americanos.	Value U. S. Gold.
Argentina	Gold	Peso	4.82	$0.965
Bolivia	Gold	Boliviano	1.95	0.389
Brazil	Gold	Milreis	2.73	0.546
Chile	Gold	Peso	1.83	0.365
Colombia	Gold	Peso	4.87	0.973
Costa Rica	Gold	Colón	2.33	0.465
Cuba	Gold	Peso	5.00	1.000
Dominican Republic	Gold	Peso	5.00	1.000
Ecuador	Gold	Sucre	2.43	0.487
Guatemala (1)	Silver	Peso (1)	2.41	0.483
Haiti	Gold	Gourde	1.00	0.200
Honduras	Silver	Peso (2)	2.41	0.483
Mexico	Gold	Peso	2.49	0.498
Nicaragua	Gold	Córdoba	5.00	1.000
Panamá	Gold	Balboa	5.00	1.000
Paraguay (2)	Gold	Peso	4.82	0.965
Peru	Gold	Libra	24.33	4.866
Salvador	Gold	Colón	2.50	0.500
United States	Gold	Dollar	5.00	1.000
Uruguay	Gold	Peso	5.17	1.034
Venezuela	Gold	Bolivar	0.97	0.193

(1) Value as at July 1, 1923.
(2) The theoretical standard is the silver peso, as in Guatemala, but actually the standard is the Argentine gold peso.

BRITISH STATUS OF ARGENTINE-BORN CHILDREN.

A useful statement prepared by the Secretary of the British Society in the Argentine Republic relates the procedure whereby children born of British parents in the Argentine may retain or assure their position under the British Nationality and Status of Aliens Act, 1922.

It is to be noted that the acquisition of British Nationality in no wise affects the privileges or obligations of Argentine Nationality of those born in the Argentine :—

1. The British Nationality and Status of Aliens Act of 1922 defines British-born subjects as follows :—

"Any person born out of His Majesty's Dominions whose father was at the time of that person's birth a British subject"

as long as the birth is :—

"registered at a British Consulate within one year after its occurrence, or, in the case of a person born on or after the 1st January, 1915, who would have been a British subject if born before that date, within twelve months after the 1st August, 1922."

2. For British subjects residing within the provinces of Corrientes, Córdoba, Santa Fé, Entre Rios, applications should be made to H.B.M. Consul at Rosario.

3. For British subjects residing in the towns of Bahia Blanca, La Plata, Puerto Madryn, Rio Gallegos, Comodoro Rivadavia, Mendoza, Tucumán, to the Consular Officers at those ports.

4. For British subjects residing in the Capital of Buenos Aires and other provincial districts not mentioned above, apply to H.B.M. Consulate-General, Buenos Aires.

5. A fee of $4.50 m/n. is charged in each case, and for this purpose the father will require to produce :—

I. In the case of children of the first generation born abroad :—
    (a) His passport or birth certificate.
    (b) Civil registry certificate of the child's birth.

II. In the case of children of the second generation born abroad :—
    (c) His British registration papers.
    (d) His marriage certificate.
    (e) Civil registry certificate of the child's birth.

III. In the case of the third and subsequent generations born abroad :—
    (f) His British Registration papers.
    (g) His declaration of retention of British nationality in his twenty-second year
    (h) His marriage certificate.
    (i) Civil registry of the child's birth.

BRITISH STATUS OF ARGENTINE-BORN CHILDREN

6. In case the parents reside in the Camp or at any place where there is no Consular Office, these documents can be sent, in registered envelope, along with a certificate from any well-known resident in the neighbourhood and the fee of $5.00 m/n., to the Secretary of the British Society, Mr. Norman Macqueen, 349 Calle Lavalle, Buenos Aires, who will undertake the registration and return the documents.

N.B.—All Subjects of the Second and Subsequent Generation Born Abroad after 1st January, 1915 :—

> "Shall cease to be a British subject unless within one year after he attains the age of twenty-one, or within such extended period as may be authorized in special cases by regulations made under this Act, he asserts his British Nationality by a declaration of retention of British Nationality registered in such a manner as may be prescribed by regulations made under this Act."

7 All passports must be taken out at H.B.M. Consulate-General, Buenos Aires, for which a fee of $5.40 m/n. is charged, renewals of passports $1.40 m/n.

LONDON & BRAZILIAN BANK, Limited

ESTABLISHED 1862.

Capital Subscribed, £3,000,000.   Capital Paid Up, £1,500,000
Reserve Fund, £1,500,000.

Head Office :

7 TOKENHOUSE YARD, LONDON, E.C. 2

PARIS
5 Rue Scribe.

MANCHESTER
36 Charlotte Street.

NEW YORK
66 Wall Street.

also Branches in

BRAZIL.—Rio de Janeiro. Manáos. Pará. Maranhão. Ceará. Pernambuco. Bahia. Santos. São Paulo. Curityba. Rio Grande do Sul. Pelotas. Porto Alegre.

RIVER PLATE.—Buenos Aires. Rosario. Montevideo.

PORTUGAL.—Lisbon. Oporto.

Banking Business of every description transacted.

Special facilities offered for the financing of

EXPORTS AND IMPORTS.

Current Accounts opened on usual terms.

Deposits received for fixed periods.

Bills collected and negotiated.

Letters of Credit issued.

Commercial Credits established on all Branches and Agencies.

FOREIGN EXCHANGE Department :—

Cable transfers and drafts bought and sold on Brazil, River Plate, Portugal, U.S.A., and on all the principal European Cities.

A special feature is made of Currency Accounts and Forward Contracts.

DRINK AND ENJOY

LIPTON, Ltd., Tea Planters, Ceylon.

Head Office and Export Dept. :

City Road, London, England.

—*Read it yet?*

ALL ABOARD

BY
W. H. KOEBEL

ILLUSTRATED BY H. M. BATEMAN *AND OTHERS*

"ALL ABOARD"

A MOST amusing account of the modern traveller's "life on the ocean wave." The combination of Mr. Koebel's prose with Mr. Bateman's illustrations is irresistible.

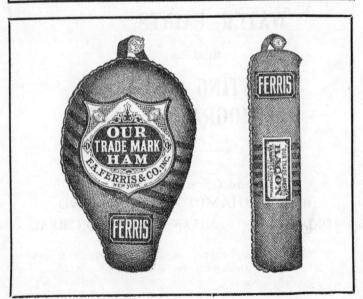